Introduction to British prehistory

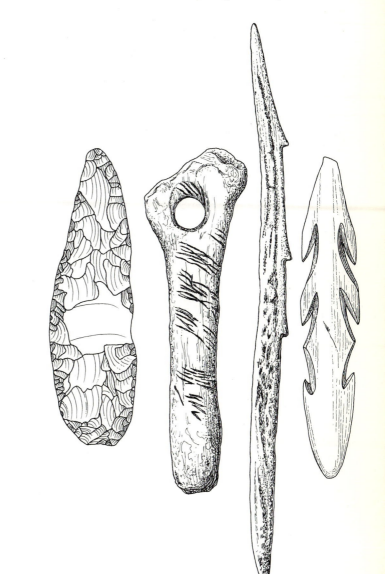

with contributions from T. C. Champion,
J. G. Evans, Mary-Jane Mountain and I. B. M. Ralston
line illustrations by Morna MacGregor

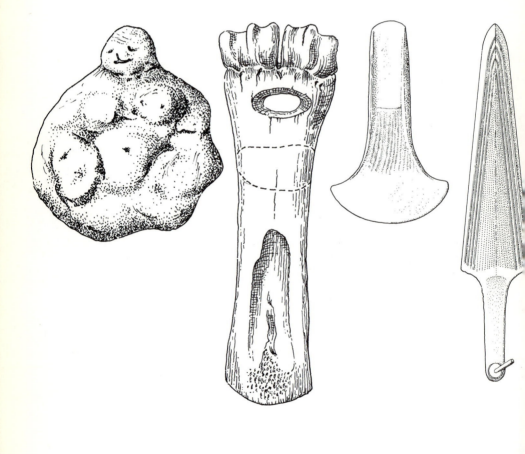

J. V. S. Megaw and D. D. A. Simpson

Introduction to British prehistory

from the arrival of *Homo sapiens* to the Claudian invasion

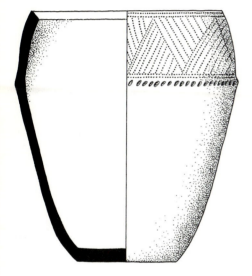

Leicester University Press 1979

First published in 1979 by Leicester University Press

Copyright © Leicester University Press 1979

Designed by Arthur Lockwood
Typeset by CCC, printed and bound in Great Britain by
William Clowes (Beccles) Limited, Beccles and London

British Library Cataloguing in Publication Data
Megaw, John Vincent Stanley
Introduction to British prehistory.
1. Man, Prehistoric—Great Britain
I. Title II. Simpson, Derek Douglas
Alexander
936.1'01   GN805

ISBN 0-7185-1122-0
ISBN 0-7185-1172-7 Pbk

For Ruth and Nancy
(who have also had to live with British prehistory)

Contents

1   The environmental background to British prehistory

The final palaeolithic and mesolithic (10,000–3,700 bc) – the
neolithic (3,700–2,000 bc) – the earlier bronze age (2,000–1,200
bc) – the later bronze age and iron age periods (1,200–1 bc)

2   Exploitation and adaptation in pre-agricultural communities

Homo sapiens sapiens and the beginning of the upper
palaeolithic in Britain – the later upper palaeolithic –
Maglemosian hunters and the earlier mesolithic industries –
the later mesolithic of Britain: Scotland and Ireland – the
latest mesolithic of Britain

3   The first agricultural communities (c. 3,500–2,500 bc)

Introduction – southern and south-eastern Britain: the
Windmill Hill culture – north-east Britain – western Britain
and Ireland

4   The later neolithic (c. 2,500–1,700 bc)

Introduction – passage graves – native late neolithic cultures –
material equipment

5   The early bronze age (c. 2,000–1,300 bc)

Beaker cultures – the Wessex culture – Yorkshire vase food
vessels – Irish bowl food vessels – urns

6   The later bronze age (1,400 bc–500 BC)

Introduction – an outline of the metalworking traditions of the
middle bronze age – foreign connections – the Deverel-
Rimbury complex – settlements in the south-west of England –
settlements and burials in central and northern Britain and
Ireland – the economic basis for the later bronze age – the first
swords – the Wilburton phase – the Ewart Park phase, the
Carp's Tongue complex and post-Wilburton metal technology
– the Dowris phase – Hallstatt C and the end of late bronze
age metallurgy

List of tables

List of illustrations

About the contributors

T. C. Champion M.A., Dip.Archaeol., D.Phil.
Timothy Champion, currently Lecturer in the Department of Archaeology, University of Southamton, trained initially as a classicist and has as his main interest the relations between the classical and 'barbarian' worlds of ancient Europe. He is also concerned in general with the development of early complex societies and the role of technology in society.

J. G. Evans B.Sc., Ph.D., F.S.A.
Senior Lecturer in the Department of Archaeology, University College, Cardiff, John Evans trained in environmental archaeology under Geoffrey Dimbleby at the Institute of Archaeology, University of London. His publications have centred on this field and he has collaborated with Derek Simpson on the excavation of a number of prehistoric sites in Britain.

Morna MacGregor M.A., Ph.D.
Morna MacGregor studied Prehistoric Archaeology and Fine Art at the University of Edinburgh and her doctoral dissertation on the early Celtic art of North Britain was published in 1976. She was formerly Curator of Swindon Museum, while her work as an archaeological illustrator has been widely published.

J. V. S. Megaw M.A., F.S.A.
Vincent Megaw, currently Professor and Head of the Department of Archaeology at the University of Leicester, started his archaeological career in publishing and for ten years was on the staff of the Department of Archaeology at the University of Sydney. A graduate of the University of Edinburgh where he studied under Stuart Piggott and Richard Atkinson, his central concern with pre-Roman Celtic art has led him to travel extensively in Central and Eastern Europe. He also maintains an interest in the archaeology of musical instruments and Australasian prehistory.

Mary-Jane Mountain B.A., Dip.Pre.Archaeol.
Currently Senior Lecturer and Chairman of the Department of Anthropology and Sociology of the University of Papua New Guinea, Mary-Jane Mountain was previously on the staff of the Department of Archaeology of the University of Edinburgh. Her field experience ranges from Cornwall through Poland and Crete to the New Guinea Highlands and her interests centre on hunting and gathering communities, past and present.

I. B. M. Ralston M.A.
Ian Ralston, successively Research Fellow and Lecturer in Archaeology, Department of Geography, University of Aberdeen, is like three of the other contributors to *Introduction to British Prehistory* a graduate of Edinburgh University. He has extensive field experience of later prehistoric sites in north Britain and France and is currently engaged in a long-term field survey project in north-east Scotland. He also has a keen interest in the politics of state and rescue or salvage archaeology.

D. D. A. Simpson M.A., F.S.A.
Derek Simpson, formerly Assistant Curator of the Wiltshire Archaeological and Natural History Society's Museum in Devizes, is Senior Lecturer in Archaeology at the University of Leicester. Also a graduate of Edinburgh University, he has excavated widely in the British Isles from the Outer Hebrides to the South of England and his main field of research and publication is in the earlier prehistory of Europe, particularly the neolithic and earlier bronze age of the British Isles.

Preface

The writing and illustrating of this book came about in an attempt by six individuals concerned largely with the teaching of archaeology to answer a simple practical need. We wished to make available, primarily for first-year university students and those attending extra-mural courses, a straightforward, fully illustrated and referenced guide to the raw material and literature covering the prehistory of the British Isles. The pages that follow attempt to survey the period from the arrival of *Homo sapiens* in the later Pleistocene to the Claudian invasion of southern Britain.

In the five years or so that this book has been in preparation – a confession not a boast – other outlines have of course appeared, notably that edited by Colin Renfrew (1974) based on a week-end conference held in Sheffield in May 1972. Unlike this earlier *British Prehistory* – much consulted by us in preparation of the present volume – we have not consciously aimed at presenting a particularly new view of the past, as that volume did following the recalibration now required of all radiocarbon dates in terms of absolute chronology (see p. 3 below). Rather, like the first volume to appear under the title of *British Prehistory* (Piggott S. 1949), we are concerned here largely with description and not with an individualistic narrative as in the latest work of synthesis to appear (Ashbee 1978).

All of us who have contributed to the present book either as writers or illustrator share some common features of academic upbringing. Despite the fact that our present location ranges from north-east Scotland to Papua New Guinea, there is a general debt to Richard Atkinson and Stuart Piggott whose unique blend of the practical and the theoretical has formed the basis of what some have chosen to isolate as the Edinburgh 'school' of archaeology. If there is indeed such a thing it may be considered to be based on the view that British prehistory is meaningless if isolated from a knowledge, preferably at first hand, of its wider context within Europe as a whole, a view Vere Gordon Childe outstandingly demonstrated during his foundation tenure of the Abercromby Chair of Archaeology and in his own *Prehistoric Communities of the British Isles* (1940). Again despite differing university backgrounds, we were all brought up academically to look upon archaeology as a series of continually altering techniques for reconstructing the past, such techniques being borrowed equally from the sciences and the humanities. Concerning the growing use by archaeologists of the methods and theories of the natural, life and earth sciences, two of us have profited much from the unique facilities for the study of ancient man in his environment offered by the University of London's Institute of Archaeology and a third from working within the framework of a large Department of Geography.

Until recently British archaeologists have not been over-concerned with theoretical concepts and have generally accepted unquestioningly a narrow range of historical possibilities for cultural change (such as invasion). A word may be added here on the current philosophy of archaeology which has been gradually coming into fashion under the somewhat misleading title of the 'new archaeology'. Now largely influenced by those whose theoretical hearts are clearly in North America, a concern for the offering of explanations for certain observed phenomena is being displayed by several archaeologists as an incentive to try out various and often far from new techniques to test general theories (cf. Renfrew 1973a, b). One example is continuing research into the prehistoric ancestors of modern hunter-gatherers and simple farming communities (cf. Megaw 1977). Thus, those of us who have been fortunate enough to work in Australasia have experienced 'archaeology as anthropology' where an old 'model' or theoretical framework, the use of modern ethnographic analogies to explain ancient life-ways, is being used to aid interpretation of the archaeological remains of prehistoric Aboriginals on the coast of New South Wales no less than of the first horticulturalists of Highland Papua New Guinea. Ethnographic parallels – not always any more relevantly applied than in the last century – are also coming into vogue in the discussion of several phases of British prehistory, notably aspects of mesolithic hunter-gatherers (e.g. Clark J. G. D. 1972), but also in much later contexts such as the organization of metalworking in the middle bronze age (e.g. Rowlands 1976b). As one of us has tried to summarize elsewhere (Megaw 1973: 9ff.), the claim that 'new' archaeology is reaching toward a social science is based on the proposition that sociocultural systems form integral wholes. Archaeologists should therefore be able to see their seemingly fragmented studies of ancient technology, economic adaptation and settlement patterns as related subsystems forming parts of a reconstructable whole. This application, both in general and particular, of the principles of modern systems theory cuts right across the views, still widely held in Britain and on the Continent of Europe, of the restricting limitations of archaeological inference allegedly caused by the undoubtedly incomplete nature of the past as recorded by tangible remains. This archaeological statute of limitations was actually being promulgated in the 1950s at just the same period that American scholars were expounding on archaeology as anthropology. In the 1970s in Britain, the latter has become part of a new orthodoxy (cf. Spriggs 1977).

Alongside new approaches within the anthropological model so heavily dependent on North American research, archaeology has also been drawing more heavily on ecological theories and geographical models in recent years. The immediate source of some of this work is to be found in the quantitative and spatial interests which have developed in British university Departments of Geography since the 1960s (cf. Hodder and Orton 1976). Models adopted from this source share certain features and, although their use is often not incontrovertible in archaeological contexts, given the partial character of survival and difficulties in assuring contemporaneity of the data being assessed, such models have contributed to greater archaeological interest in the way sites related to their contemporary environment and landscape and to palaeoecology. The extent of archaeological concern with these techniques is conditioned by the availability of information on the early environment and by our knowledge of the chronological span of a given type of site. Thus their use is at present limited in many areas of Britain to individual site studies: a corollary is the greater interest in areas, such as the Northern Isles, where the survival of large numbers of field monuments – such as burnt mounds, brochs and burial chamber tombs – suggests that analysis will produce useful results (Chapter 7).

If these new theoretical approaches seem confusing and to some not relevant to the newcomer to British archaeology, it is the case that the student of today lives in an age of revolutions in archaeological theory. For this reason, our picture of the past is presented here with as unbiased a use of such theoretical models as possible, using them as aids to heightening the background rather than setting a rigid framework around it.

As if it were not enough that the theoretical concepts of prehistory, the 'why' and the 'what' of the basic processes of archaeological inquiry, should at present be changing, the most widely used scientific method for answering the question 'when' is also under dispute. We refer of course to radiocarbon dating and the 'radiocarbon revolution'.

In this book radiocarbon or C14 dates, and centuries and millennia based on such dates, are expressed, following convention, in years 'bc'. Calendar dates, that is those determined by historical data, tree-ring counting (dendrochronology), or the recalibration of radiocarbon dates, are expressed in years 'BC'. The recalibration of 'raw' radiocarbon dates as received from a laboratory has been found necessary as the result of comparisons between calendrically dated tree-rings – notably of the bristlecone pine (*Pinus longaeva*) of southern California, the oldest living organism in the world – and radiocarbon dates obtained from these growth rings. In all examples earlier than 2,000 years before the present the radiocarbon age determinations have been found to be too young when compared with the dendrochronological dates and in general the older the sample the greater is the discrepancy. It is therefore necessary to correct or recalibrate all radiocarbon dates and a number of recalibration tables have been published. The most widely used is that published by the University of Pennsylvania in its *MASCA Newsletter* (Ralph, Michael and Han 1973; see also Suess and Clark 1976; Warner 1976), although there is as yet no internationally accepted table and Burleigh (1975) has warned archaeologists against presenting dates in recalibrated form until there is a universally accepted standard of conversion. The whole question of recalibration is still under discussion (Watkins 1975; see also Clark R. M. 1975) and some scholars have favoured a conversion table based on Egyptian astronomically calculated dates rather than tree-rings (McKerrel 1975). The arguments centre around an almost Swiftian division between those who support a 'smooth' and those preferring a 'wriggly' calibration curve (Pearson *et al.* 1977; Pilcher and Bailey 1978). We have preferred in this book to cite radiocarbon estimations – unless specifically indicated – as 'uncorrected', or 'bc' or 'ad' dates calculated without further correction by simply subtracting 1950 from the bp ('before present') conventional laboratory citation. Recalibration has important implications for our understanding of past events and in particular in establishing synchronisms between contemporary prehistoric societies (Renfrew 1976: 76ff.). Current interpretations of C14 dates have led to greater precision in establishing a chronological framework, and considerably extend the time-scale in which major cultural and social changes took place; this is particularly true of the neolithic. A further problem in the period of early bronze metallurgy in Europe is the apparent incompatibility of recalibrated radiocarbon dates from this area and cross-dating or historically derived dates for objects from the Aegean and east Mediterranean from contexts long believed to be contemporary with the early bronze age in north-western Europe. This is discussed further in Chapter 5.

The majority of radiocarbon dates quoted in the text are as published in the *Radiocarbon Supplement* of the *American Journal of Science* (1959–60), *Radiocarbon* (annually from 1961) and the Council for British Archaeology's *Archaeological Site Index to Radiocarbon Dates for Great Britain and Ireland* (periodically from 1971); Renfrew's *British Prehistory* (1974), with its emphasis on absolute chronology, includes separate period lists of selected radiocarbon dates. Here a separate Appendix only for later north British prehistory has been added in view of the current lack of adequate consolidated listings (p. 497).

In conclusion, some further words of explanation. We have chosen to be as conservative in political geography as in the presentation of radiocarbon dates. The Scottish, English and Welsh counties are cited as they were prior to local government reorganization in 1974–5. Since, with minor additions, the end point for bibliographical references has been set at December 1976 we trust that this decision will cause a minimum of difficulty. We have also intentionally restricted the number of distribution maps, regarding these as often at the best an indication of partial knowledge. Chapters, though following in general the conventional 'three age' divisions, have been determined more on broadly chronological and cultural grounds than mere typology. All text-books in archaeology – perhaps more than in many other disciplines – are out of date even before they are published; ours is no exception. For example, a marked increase in discoveries, as yet largely unpublished, on the settlement archaeology of the later bronze age will, we are sure, demand drastic revision of the object-biased account of the period given here (Chapter 6; cf. Bowen and Fowler 1978; Bradley 1978); again, new editions are appearing of recent but already standard text-books (e.g. Cunliffe 1974; 2nd edn 1978).[1]

As to authorship, although each of us has assumed particular responsibility for individual sections – J. G. Evans: environmental history; Mary-Jane Mountain: upper palaeolithic and mesolithic; D. D. A. Simpson: neolithic to the beginning of the full bronze age; J. V. S. Megaw: the later bronze age and sections on iron age art; T. C. Champion: the iron age in southern Britain and Ireland; I. B. M. Ralston: the iron age in North Britain – no attempt has been made to avoid some degree of overlap in subject matter between chapters, e.g. the effect of climate on early man, the development of cinerary urns and related forms, the question of Hallstatt C 'invaders' or settlers. Indeed, while we hope that there is no apparent conflict in the individual handling of such topics, it seems to us that such overlaps have some merit in demonstrating the impossibility of devising too hard and fast cultural or chronological divisions in British prehistory.

In addition, it would be improper not to acknowledge here the generous help of various colleagues who have assisted by providing illustrations, commenting on various topics and offering good advice – not alas, always taken. Chief amongst these have been John Campbell, John Coles, David Coombs, Philip Dixon, Kevin Edwards, Alex Gibson, Paul Mellars, Paul Peek and Joan Taylor. Even without the title page, connoisseurs of archaeological drawing will recognize the major contribution to our volume's usefulness made by Morna MacGregor. Thanks are due also to the Department of Archaeology of Glasgow University for generously making their drawing office facilities available over an inordinately long period of time. The index has been prepared by yet another graduate of the Edinburgh school, Elizabeth Fowler. Lastly, or more precisely firstly, we have to thank Jane Pearson, Dorothy Walker, Susan Stephenson and Yvonne Smith and her colleagues at St Mary's, Old Aberdeen, who have managed to translate some truly prehistoric tapes and involuted examples of British handwriting into immaculate typescript.

We have said at the outset that our aim has been to prepare not so much a text-book as an outline guide. Stuart Piggott, writing some 30 years ago an introductory note to his *British Prehistory*, warned his readers of 'the proviso that any interpretation of the sequence of British (and indeed of European) prehistory must be thought of as representing the most likely explanation of a set of facts and observed phenomena *in the present state of our knowledge*' (Piggott S. 1949: 5). If our present attempts to produce such a synthesis can be regarded as containing even some of the most likely explanations then we shall be well pleased and all of us look forward to receiving the corrections and additions which will surely be necessary in any future editions – if our publishers can bear the thought.

J.V.S.M.
D.D.A.S.
Midsummer Day, 1978

Note

1. For those wishing to update their bibliographical knowledge there are two further publications of the CBA: *British Archaeological Abstracts* and the *Archaeological Bibliography for Great Britain and Ireland*, the last issue of the latter available at the time of writing being that for 1974.

1 The environmental background to British prehistory*

The final palaeolithic and mesolithic (10,000–3,700 bc)

The Last Glacial period of the Pleistocene, which lasted from about 70,000 to 8,300 bc, saw Britain as a region of largely treeless land, locked in the grip of a sub-arctic tundra régime. Only in the period from about 25,000 to 8,300 bc were ice-sheets and glaciers present. This was the Full Last Glacial proper (table 1.1). At its height, ice-sheets mantled much of the British Isles (fig. 1.1). The main effects of glaciation were (a) the virtual extinction of life, (b) the deposition of boulder clay either over wide areas or locally as lateral and terminal moraines, and (c) the levelling of the terrain. In mountain areas, corries and U-valleys were formed (Evans J. G. 1975: 55; Gresswell 1958; West 1968: 18).

Outside the immediate area of glaciation (the periglacial zone) various other processes occurred, as a result of the permanently frozen condition of the ground (permafrost) and brief spells of summer melting. These were (a) solifluxion, the downhill sludging of frost-shattered rock debris (including the sarsen rock streams of our chalkland valleys), (b) frost-

Table 1.1 Summary table of main periods, pollen zones and archaeological phases in Britain from 50,000 to 6,000 bp (after Campbell 1977)

Approx. dates bc	Period	Environment and pollen zones	Archaeological phases
8,300–4,000	Postglacial	Boreal to temperate IV–VII	Mesolithic and surviving later upper palaeolithic
13,000–8,300	Late Last Glacial	Sub-arctic to temperate I–III; minor ice readvances	Later upper palaeolithic
25,000–13,000	Full Last Glacial	Maximum ice advances; Arctic to Sub-arctic; evidence of minor ice readvances from c. 25,000; Sub-arctic	None or limited seasonal occupation of earlier upper palaeolithic type
50,000–25,000	Middle Last Glacial	Sub-arctic to temperate	Earlier upper palaeolithic

* For a more detailed account of the topics surveyed here see Evans (1975).

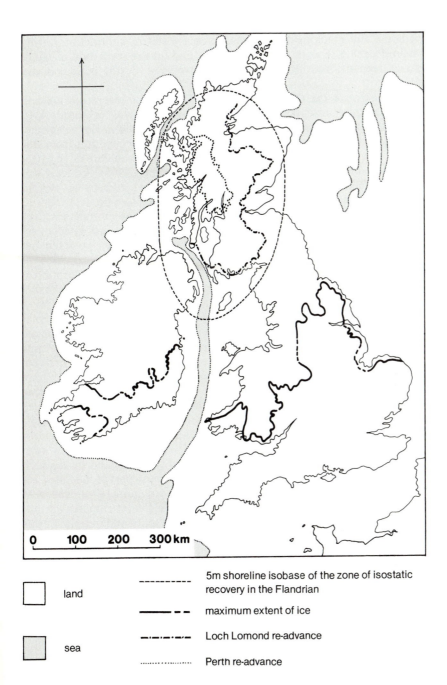

land

sea

5m shoreline isobase of the zone of isostatic recovery in the Flandrian

maximum extent of ice

Loch Lomond re-advance

Perth re-advance

Fig. 1.1 Map of the British Isles showing the coast line and extent of ice-sheets during the last glaciation, the Loch Lomond and Perth re-advance stages, and the 5m shoreline isobase of the zone of postglacial isostatic recovery.

wedging, the cracking of the ground as a result of contraction during severe freezing (Evans J. G. 1972a: 77), and (c) the formation of wind-blown deposits, such as loess (silt) and coversand, during periods of dry climate.

The height of the last glacial was thus a time of severe erosion and wasting of the landscape. Mean annual temperature was less than $-8°C$. Vegetation and animal life were virtually absent, even in the periglacial zone, and there are virtually no records of human occupation from this period with the exception of the anomalous radiocarbon date of $16,510 \pm 340$ bc for the 'Red Lady' of Paviland (Oakley 1968a: 306). Sea level was about 100m below Ordnance Datum and land bridges between Britain and Ireland and England and the Continent existed (see fig. 1.1)

Round about 12,000 bc the climate began to ameliorate and the ice sheets to wane. This is the beginning of the Late Last Glacial. By 10,000 bc there was still a remnant ice sheet in western Scotland but elsewhere only corrie glaciers occurred, in mountain areas such as Snowdonia, the Cairngorms and the Wicklow Mountains. Permafrost conditions no longer obtained, frost-wedging had ceased, and solifluxion was less pronounced, although still a major erosive force.

The countryside abounded in water-filled hollows left in the irregular surface of the boulder clay. Ponds and lakes of various sizes were a much more pronounced feature than they are today. Gradually these became filled in, first with lake sediments, later, as the water shallowed, with reed-swamp deposits, and finally with peat. Because of their waterlogged nature these deposits generally contain pollen, and by extracting and counting the grains of the various plant species at each level we can gain some idea of the vegetational (and climatic) changes which took place as the deposits accumulated. This is known as 'pollen analysis'.

Studies of this kind from various parts of the British Isles have shown that an environment of tundra – mosses, lichens, grasses and shrubs such as dwarf birch and dwarf willow – existed in the early part of the Late Last Glacial (12,000–10,000 bc) (Godwin 1975; Pennington 1974). The next approximately 1,000 years (10,000–8,800 bc) saw greater climatic warmth with stands of birch trees and pine in parts of the south and in Ireland: this is known as the Allerød period after the type-site in Denmark. But ice sheets and corrie glaciers still persisted in the north.

Before the final amelioration of climate to the temperate conditions we enjoy today – the postglacial (or Flandrian) period – there was a return to the colder conditions of pre-Allerød times for about 500 years (8,800–8,300 bc) (table 1.2). These three vegetational/climatic episodes of the Late Last Glacial are known as zones I, II and III. Zones I and III are sometimes known as the Older and Younger Dryas periods after a characteristic plant fossil, *Dryas octopetala*, mountain avens. The evidence of ancient insect faunas suggests a somewhat different model for the temperature changes in the Late Last Glacial, with the period of maximum warmth being in late zone I, zone II seeing a temperature decline (Coope and Brophy 1972). This disparity in the evidence is due to the fact that insects react faster than trees to temperature change.

Table 1.2   Vegetation changes in the Late Last Glacial (after Campbell 1977 and West 1968)

Approx. dates bc	Pollen zone	England	Ireland	Scotland
5,000–3,000	VII Atlantic	Alder, oak, elm, lime	Alder, oak, elm, pine	Alder, oak, elm
7,500–5,000	VI Boreal V	Elm, oak, lime Pine, hazel Hazel, birch, pine	Pine, elm, hazel	Birch, pine and hazel
8,300–7,500	IV Pre-Boreal	Birch and pine	Birch	Birch
9,000–8,300	III	Park tundra	Tundra	Loch Lomond readvance
10,000–9,000	II Allerød	Birch and park tundra	Tundra	Tundra
11,000–10,000	I	Park tundra	Tundra	Perth readvance

Table 1.3   Vegetation changes in Britain from the mesolithic to the iron age

Approx. dates bc and zone names	Pollen zones	Vegetation	Climate
Sub-Atlantic	VIII	Rise of ash, birch, beech and hornbeam Large clearances	Deteriorating
...1,200			
Sub-Boreal	VIIb	Small and large clearances	Stable
...3,200		Elm decline	
Atlantic	VIIa	Mixed oak woodland plus alder	Optimum
...5,300			
Boreal	V and VI	Mixed oak woodland plus pine and hazel	Ameliorating
...7,500			
Pre-Boreal	IV	Birch and pine	Ameliorating

The main animals of the Late Last Glacial were horse, giant Irish deer and reindeer, and carnivores such as wolf, arctic fox and bear. Larger beasts such as mammoth and woolly rhinoceros had become extinct long before this time. As the climate ameliorated, the species of the cold-climate fauna were replaced by more warmth-loving forms. The elk, although occurring in the Late Last Glacial (Hallam *et al.* 1973: 100), became common in early postglacial times as, for example, at Star Carr (Clark J. G. D. 1954: 76) where it was hunted by mesolithic man. Red deer, roe deer, wild boar and giant ox (aurochs), as well as many smaller mammals such as marten, all reflect the encroachment of woodland over the British Isles.

Pollen analysis and the study of plant macro-fossils have given us the details of the way in which the tundra landscape was replaced by forest and the successive stages in its history (Godwin 1975; Mitchell 1976; Pennington 1974). It has also enabled us to establish a basis for the zonation of the postglacial, and, before the advent of radiocarbon determination, a dating scheme (tables 1.2, 1.3). Initially (zone IV), birch woodland predominated but this was rapidly invaded by pine and hazel (zone V). Hardwoods, notably oak and elm, then spread in (zone VI), and later the thermophilous lime appeared (zone VIc) (although not reaching Ireland and Scotland). The introduction of lime marks the beginning of the 'climatic optimum' (or thermal maximum), a warm period in the middle of the postglacial when mean annual temperature was 2°C higher than today. Zone VIIa is marked by a pronounced rise in alder, and climatically is a period of high rainfall.

As the ice sheets melted, the water they had locked up for so long was released, and the level of the sea began to rise. Ireland was cut off at an early stage, although a land bridge with Scotland may have persisted into the early postglacial; the English Channel was flooded and the Straits of Dover breached between 6,000 and 5,000 bc, significantly at the beginning of the Atlantic period whose high rainfall may be attributed to the establishment of full oceanic circulation around Britain. The rising sea drowned river valleys (e.g. the Solent and the Shannon) and in sheltered bays laid down thick deposits of clay. Many of these latter areas gradually evolved to reed swamp and later to fen woodland, thus providing a mosaic of habitats both spatially and temporally. The Somerset Levels (fig. 1.2) and Morecambe Bay are typical, and were favoured by early man as hunting grounds.

In the north of Britain the loss of the great weight of the ice sheets caused the land to rise – a phenomenon known as 'isostatic uplift' – and there was for long a complex interplay between the rising land and the rising level of the sea. Peat beds of early postglacial age lie buried beneath marine clays in various places such as Belfast Lough and the Firth of Forth. Later, as the sea rose faster than the land, beach gravels were laid down. Finally, the land emerged and many of these beaches now lie well above the reach of the sea, some up to 15m O.D.

Man, too, although only at the hunter-gatherer stage, was important in moulding the environment at this early time. In the Late Last Glacial he may have concentrated herds of reindeer and horse to such an extent that their grazing activities prevented, or at least slowed down, the vegetational succession to woodland. Fire was an important factor and there is abundant evidence of widespread conflagrations in Allerød times both in Britain and the Low Countries. We cannot say whether these were man-made, but they may well have been controlled by man for the purposes of corralling game, creating fresh grass, or clearing scrub and woodland (Simmons 1969a: 113).

In mesolithic times there is even greater evidence of fire (Mellars 1976c), and pollen analysis shows that at numerous places (Dartmoor, the Pennines, and the North York Moors) forest recession associated with burning took place where man was present (Dimbleby 1962). In some cases the forest appears to have regenerated to its former condition but in others, particularly in upland situations and in areas of thin sandy soils, the change from woodland to open country was of a more permanent nature.

Clearance of woodland has a damaging effect on the soil in that nutrients, important for maintaining its structure and which were formerly brought up from the subsoil by tree roots, no longer become available (Eyre 1968). This applies particularly to calcium. Thus one expected consequence of forest clearance is soil degradation and erosion, and this indeed has been recorded from sites of mesolithic age (Keef *et al.* 1965: 85). Trees act too as a natural drainage system for the soil. A full-grown oak releases several gallons of water a day from its leaves in the process

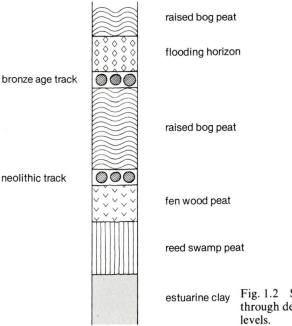

raised bog peat

flooding horizon

bronze age track

raised bog peat

neolithic track

fen wood peat

reed swamp peat

estuarine clay

Fig. 1.2 Schematic section through deposits in the Somerset levels.

known as transpiration. Thus as well as loss of nutrients, deforestation may cause waterlogging and may eventually lead to the formation of peat.

Peat is a deposit made up of organic matter, mainly plants, in which only partial decomposition has taken place. In some cases stems, leaves and seeds are recognizable and can be identified to species. Insect remains are often present. The formation of peat takes place when microbial activity is inhibited, generally through waterlogging and the absence of air. Essentially there are two forms of peat. One, known as topogenous peat, forms as a result of poor drainage conditions and occurs in valleys and other low-lying situations as discussed above. The other, known as ombrogenous peat, forms as a result of high rainfall and mantles whole areas of land irrespective of topography (Godwin 1975: 29). This latter is often known as blanket bog. Topogenous peat, being dependent on ground water, is often rich in nutrients and supports a varied flora. Ombrogenous peat, however, derives all its moisture directly from the atmosphere and is consequently acidic, or sour, supporting an impoverished flora, generally of *Sphagnum* (bog moss), *Eriophorum* (cotton grass) and *Calluna* (heather).

The cause of the onset of ombrogenous peat formation is controversial. One theory suggests that increased precipitation at various times in the past was responsible, and certainly there is evidence for the initiation of this type of peat in many parts of the British Isles at the onset of Atlantic times, when other evidence also suggests an increase in rainfall (see above). A second theory sees the inception of blanket bog formation as a result of deforestation and subsequent soil waterlogging.

We may summarize the main events of the early postglacial as follows: 1. A rise of temperature to 2°C higher than today. 2. A rise of sea level causing severe land loss and the isolation of Britain. 3. Isostatic uplift in the north. 4. A wet period beginning around 5,300 bc and marked by the widespread formation of blanket bog. 5. The spread of various types of woodland. 6. The introduction of a forest fauna.

The neolithic (3,700–2,000 bc)

The neolithic period falls in the later part of the climatic optimum. Mean annual temperature was still higher than that of today, although possibly declining. The amount of rainfall is difficult to assess, although the construction of trackways in the Somerset Levels (see also p. 17 below) throughout the 3rd millennium bc and the continued formation of blanket bog in several upland areas, for example the Wicklow Mountains, suggest a continuation of the conditions established in Atlantic times. In the 2nd millennium several lines of evidence suggest a period of drier climate from about 1,800 to 1,200 bc, and this is further discussed on pp. 17–19 below.

The sea stood at approximately its present level. In low-lying areas the thick deposits of clay laid down in early postglacial times were beginning to support reed swamp and salt-marsh environments as the influence of marine conditions declined. It is not certain to what this change is due. A slight drop in sea level is one possibility but it is likely that local changes such as the silting up of estuaries, the formation of sand bars and storm beaches, and the accumulation of sand dunes were responsible. In the zone of isostatic recovery, the maximum transgression took place in late Atlantic times. At Sutton, a small peninsula just north of Dublin, gravels of the postglacial beach at 4m O.D. (English O.D.: Irish O.D. is about 2·5m lower) interdigitate with a Larnian midden dated to 3,300±110 bc (Mitchell 1976: 131). Further north, in Co. Antrim, the beach gravels attain a height of over 10m O.D. Both the gravels of the raised beach and the clay deposits of low-lying areas were important as areas of early human settlement, probably because they provided variability in the habitat and a certain amount of open country when the majority of Britain was forested.

In some areas around the coast outside the zone of isostatic recovery, land extended beyond its present limits in neolithic times. In the Isles of Scilly chambered tombs and field walls lie submerged. Off the Essex coast at Walton-on-the-Naze, beaker sherds have been recovered from an intertidal land surface (Smith I. F. 1955). Radiocarbon dating of tree stumps in intertidal situations also indicates a 3rd/4th millennium date for some of these. In the Orkneys and Outer Hebrides, the evidence of marine Mollusca in kitchen middens and the presence of deposits of wind-blown sand long since stabilized indicate the former existence of extensive sandy shores where now only rocky coasts prevail (Spencer 1975). At Skara Brae on the west coast of Mainland, Orkney, reed-swamp peat is present in the intertidal zone, suggesting that the neolithic village may have overlooked a freshwater lagoon instead of being directly above the shore as it is today. The flooding of these areas may have been due to local coastal changes – in some cases simply progressive erosion – rather than the result of a secular rise of sea level. The coastal zone must be seen as one of instability, making it attractive to man but at the same time not without its hazards.

The neolithic period in Britain falls within the later part of pollen zone VIIa (zone VII in Ireland) and the first half of VIIb (VIII in Ireland) (table 1.3). The distinction between the two zones is defined mainly by a marked fall in elm pollen – the 'elm decline' – and radiocarbon dates show this to be more or less synchronous over the British Isles, taking place in the few centuries around 3,000 bc (fig. 1.3). The origin of the elm decline was at first thought to be climatic – a fall of temperature marking the end of the climatic optimum. But because other cold-sensitive trees – e.g. lime – do not show a similar decline at this time it is now generally considered that the phenomenon is in some way due to man (Pennington 1974: 63). A much favoured theory is that man was lopping elm branches for cattle fodder, very necessary at a time prior to the establishment of lowland grassland in Britain. Alternatively, elm may have been growing in pure stands on calcareous soils and may thus have been felled selectively (but incidentally) by man in his quest for the best agricultural land (Mitchell 1976: 117). A third possibility is that an insect-borne fungus, akin to that which causes the modern Dutch elm disease, may have been responsible. The introduction of such a disease could well have been brought about by man particularly at a time of widespread movements and new methods of subsistence.

Although the mesolithic period saw periods of forest recession, some of which may have been anthropogenic and a few of which were of a semi-permanent nature, there is no doubt that the main initial impact on the forest came in neolithic times. Neolithic man kept sheep and cattle and cultivated cereals; as far as we know he led a relatively settled life, probably not moving over the great distances of his hunter-gatherer predecessors, and he therefore needed open country. Pollen analysis tells us that in the middle of the postglacial (the Atlantic period) most of Britain up to about 700–875m was forested. Grassland existed only in the montane zone above this level, and in unstable habitat situations such as river flood plains and along the coast. In the latter area, salt spray and wind inhibit tree growth. Areas such as the North York Moors, Salisbury Plain and some of the Scottish islands, such as the Outer Hebrides and Orkney, which we know today as typically open and windswept, were as wooded as the rest of Britain in early Atlantic times.

The impact of neolithic man on the landscape assumed various patterns. In East Anglia, at Hockham Mere (Pennington 1974: fig. 12), the elm decline took place as an isolated phenomenon, there being no other vegetational changes apart from a trace of *Plantago* (plantain) which is characteristically (although not exclusively) associated with man's presence. It is not until later on – we cannot say exactly when – that grasses, heather and other plants of open country spread into the area. Here we are seeing the elm decline as a separate phenomenon from forest clearance. But at Barfield Tarn in the Lake District (another area of early neolithic

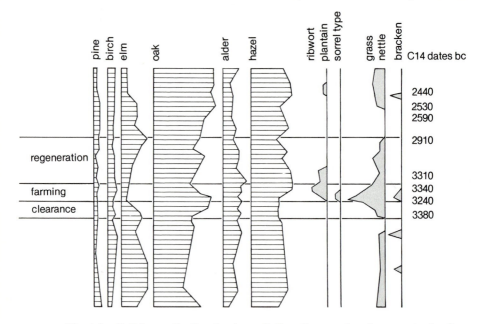

Fig. 1.3 Fallahogy, Co. Londonderry. Pollen diagram showing an episode of temporary clearance and farming in the neolithic (after Smith A. G. 1970b).

colonization) the elm decline *is* associated with the introduction of light-demanding herbs and also of cereals (Pennington 1970: fig. 11). This site shows a phenomenon seen in many other pollen diagrams, namely a slight fall in elm prior to the main decline. In Ireland we find a further difference in that here there is an almost total recovery of elm after its initial marked decline, and only later does it fall off permanently (Smith A. G. 1970b: 83) (fig. 1.3). These differences may all reflect different economic strategies of neolithic man.

With the phenomenon of forest clearance we find equal variation but two broad groups stand out: small, temporary clearances, and larger, permanent clearances. Pollen analysis suggests a general distinction between the area of the Chalk in southern and eastern England as being an area of large clearings, and the rest of the British Isles where only small-scale clearances took place (Turner 1970: 98). But this is a generalization to which there are many exceptions: parts of north-east Ireland, north-west England and some of the Scottish islands, for example, were permanently cleared from the first. There is no evidence of 'slash-and-burn' in neolithic times as defined by Iversen (1941) and J. G. D. Clark (1952: 94). Kevin Edwards has recently shown through detailed pollen analysis and radiocarbon dating that some neolithic clearances in the west of Britain were of several centuries' duration. But he has cautioned that these may not have been single episodes but a succession of small clearances in the area contributing to the pollen catchment.

On the Chalk and in other regions of calcareous soils, pollen is poorly preserved and has been little used in environmental studies. Instead, 'molluscan analysis' can be applied (Evans J. G. 1972b). Chalk soils and sediments are generally rich in the shells of snails, and these can be extracted and identified. There are several species, each having its own habitat requirements, and we can thus obtain some idea about the ancient environment from the composition of the molluscan fauna. A typical example of a snail diagram is that from the buried soil beneath the henge monument of Avebury (fig. 1.4) in which the changes from the open environment of late-glacial times through various types of woodland to the deforestation and subsequent grasslands of the neolithic are all clearly shown.

Buried soils under burial mounds and other kinds of earthwork are an invaluable source of information on ancient environments whether they contain pollen, snails or other indicators (Dimbleby 1977). They may also preserve traces of cultivation. At South Street in north Wiltshire the criss-cross marks of an ard or plough were discovered beneath a neolithic long barrow (Fowler and Evans 1967: 289). Similar marks have been recovered from beneath the blanket peat at Belderg Beg in Co. Mayo where they are within walled fields dated to the neolithic (Caulfield 1974: 3). At both South Street and Belderg Beg the ploughmarks lie at the *base* of a soil and are overlain by hummocks (at South Street) and ridges (at Belderg Beg) suggestive of shallower tillage, probably by spades. Cross-ploughing may thus be an initial process in breaking up the soil and not the regular means of year-by-year cultivation.

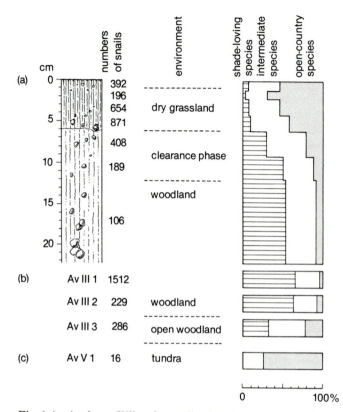

Fig. 1.4   Avebury, Wilts. Generalized land-snail diagram from the buried soil beneath the neolithic henge. a. buried soil; b. tree-root cast; c. periglacial involutions.

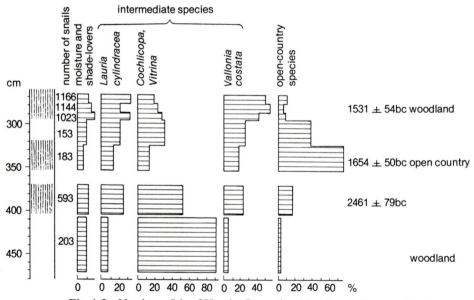

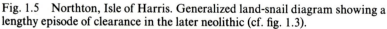

Fig. 1.5   Northton, Isle of Harris. Generalized land-snail diagram showing a lengthy episode of clearance in the later neolithic (cf. fig. 1.3).

Snail analysis can also be used in coastal sand-dune deposits which, particularly on the western coasts of the British Isles, are made up largely of calcareous matter derived from sea shells. At Northton in the Outer Hebrides (fig. 1.5), forest clearance was followed by a long period of open country, longer than in a normal 'small, temporary clearance'. But by beaker times woodland regeneration had taken place. This is a pattern which may have occurred also on the Chalk and other parts of southern England in later neolithic times (Burleigh et al. 1973), and which is recorded, too, in certain pollen diagrams (Seagrief 1959).

It is difficult to define a general picture for the landscape of Britain in neolithic times. Man was emerging as a major force in controlling the environment, particularly in his forest clearance and agricultural activities. But many areas were untouched, notably the very heavy clays of the lowland vales, and areas which were later to degrade into heath and moorland.

The earlier bronze age (2,000–1,200 bc)

The climate of the 2nd millennium bc – from about 2,000 to 1,200 bc – was probably drier than that before or after. Trackways were built in the Somerset Levels sporadically throughout the 3rd millennium to about 2,000 bc but not again until the late bronze age (Coles et al. 1970: fig. 8). Some of the tracks are thought to have been built in response to deteriorating climatic conditions. Thus the stratification in the Levels (see fig. 1.2) shows a layer of ombrogenous *Sphagnum-Eriophorum-Calluna* peat overlying the more eutrophic fenwood peat. This may be a natural succession in the development of the Levels brought about in the first instance by poor surface drainage, but it is just as likely to have been caused by high rainfall. Many of the earlier trackways lie at the base of the *Sphagnum* peat and some within the fen wood stage, and it has been suggested that these reflect a *drying* of the environment as the reed swamp and open water habitat, which would have required boat transport, gave way to more terrestrial conditions. But a later track, the Abbot's Way, is securely within the raised bog, and in any case the building of tracks at all presumably indicates fairly wet conditions whatever the direction of the trends. The evidence of the Somerset Levels is not unequivocal – not least because we do not know the exact function of the trackways or whether their absence in early bronze age times is of climatic significance – but it is highly suggestive.

Within raised bogs throughout western Europe there occur dark layers of very humified peat in which plant remains are often absent. These reflect periods of climatic dryness when the bog surface dried out and oxidation (and indeed soil formation) of the peat took place (Pennington 1974: 78). Overlying these are horizons of fresher peat, formed as the climate once more deteriorated. These are known as recurrence surfaces. Two recurrence surfaces are relevant to this discussion. One falls at about 2,300 bc (i.e. at around the time of the Abbot's Way) and the other at 1,200 bc (Seddon 1967: 173), the latter coinciding with the end of the early bronze age.

In Scottish peat bogs some of the earliest work on vegetational history at the end of the nineteenth century demonstrated a horizon of tree stumps, known as the Upper Forestian, above and below which were *Sphagnum* peat deposits (Godwin 1975: 278). The exact chronological position of this horizon – if indeed it is a single synchronous horizon – is difficult to define. Nevertheless, there is evidence here for a drying of raised bog surfaces in the later part of the postglacial of sufficient duration to allow the development of woodland.

Turning from peat environments we can recall the possible period of woodland regeneration indicated by molluscan analysis in late neolithic times, which is seen to coincide with the earlier of the two recurrence surfaces mentioned above. Subsequently, the environment of the Chalk became open with much grassland, although there is evidence in southern Wessex for the establishment of large areas of field systems in bronze age times which were presumably for cereal cultivation. In the highland zone, too, field systems of reputedly bronze age date – although this is often difficult to substantiate – are to be found well above the present limit of cultivation, and some are now buried beneath blanket bog (Feachem 1973: 332). These are often cited as an indication of more congenial climatic conditions than now obtain although we must not forget the power of agricultural enthusiasm or economic necessity in pushing upwards the limits of cultivation in the face of climatic adversity.

Open country can probably not be created solely by extremes of climatic dryness within the range experienced in postglacial Britain. Other factors, such as the inundation of woodland by sand or by blanket bog, or its destruction by man or his animals, are now held to be the main factors which brought about the development of open landscapes in prehistoric Britain. But once open ground has been created, the total removal of vegetation and the breaking up of the soil either by tillage or overgrazing will create conditions which may lead to soil erosion by wind if the climatic background allows. And this is what we find. At several sites in southern Britain there are horizons of wind-blown silt dating generally to the 2nd millennium. This implies seasonal dryness of a kind which today is only to be found in eastern England, notably Lincolnshire and East Anglia (Cornwall 1953: 137; Evans J. G. 1975: 142).

Vegetational changes in the bronze age were of two kinds. First there are the general trends shown by the forest trees. Elm was at a low level. Ash appears strongly for the first time, and birch increases. The latter two changes are a reflection of the opening up of the forest by man, for ash is a light-demanding tree and birch is an early colonizer of freshly cleared ground. Then there are the detailed changes, and we find that the pattern initiated in neolithic times was extended into the bronze age, or so the pollen record suggests (Turner 1970: 98). The chalklands saw an increase in the amount of open country, and the phenomenon of bronze age astronomy and the siting of round barrow cemeteries on false crests so as to be visible from adjacent groups or from valleys below attests to wide stretches of open country with unbroken views to the horizon. In other parts of the country the pattern of small temporary clearances persisted.

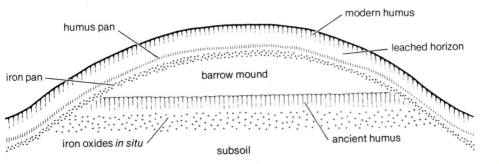

Fig. 1.6   Section through a bronze age barrow showing the ancient brownearth soil and the modern podsol.

It is in the bronze age that we first begin to see the exploitation by farming peoples of areas which are now heath and moorland. Such areas are the North York Moors and the sandy soils of the Weald and Hampshire Basin. It is not known why these areas were not settled by neolithic people since the soils which they supported under hardwood forest were as fertile as those elsewhere (Evans J. G. 1975: 135). This has been shown by the pollen analysis and morphological study of buried soils beneath round barrows (Dimbleby 1962). The bronze age soils are relatively rich in nutrient bases such as calcium and iron, and are known as brownearths. The modern soil in these areas, on the other hand, is strongly leached – iron, calcium and other bases, as well as much organic matter, having been washed down and redeposited as a hard-pan in lower horizons (fig. 1.6). This type of soil is known as a podsol. In the North York Moors pollen analysis of buried soils beneath round barrows shows woodland giving way to small clearings followed by abandonment of the land shortly prior to barrow construction. In some cases the beginnings of podsolization can be seen within the buried soil, and it is considered that this change of soil type is due to man's agricultural activities (Dimbleby 1962).

The formation of an impermeable pan low down in the soil may lead to impeded drainage and subsequently to peat formation. This is an aspect of soil degradation additional to that discussed in the previous section where waterlogging and loss of structure were seen as being a direct result of deforestation. Indeed, at any rate in Ireland, podsols are rare under the blanket peat, and podsolization is not, therefore, a prerequisite of peat formation (Smith A. G. 1970b: 86).

We can summarize the evidence for the earlier bronze age environment of Britain as follows: 1. The climate was warmer and drier than that of today. 2. Peat surfaces dried out and in some cases became forested; wind erosion of soils took place in parts of England. 3. There were three types of land use: small temporary clearances; large-scale clearance or the maintenance of areas already opened up in neolithic times; and the intake of marginal acidic soils. 4. Cultivation extended to greater heights in the highland zone than in iron age times. 5. There was an increase of ash and birch in the woodlands.

The later bronze age and iron age periods (1,200–1 bc)

The period from about 1,200 bc onwards is marked by an increase of rainfall and a decline of temperature. This is known as the Sub-Atlantic period and is approximately equivalent to pollen zone VIII in England, Wales and Scotland (see table 1.3). When originally defined the beginning of the period was put at around 500 bc but radiocarbon dating now indicates an earlier date. The archaeological implications of this are discussed by Piggott (1972: 109). In fact, deterioration probably took place in stages rather than as a continuous process. There is a major recurrence surface at 1,200 bc, recognized for example at Bloak Moss, Ayrshire (Turner 1970: fig. 2), and another at 550 bc. The period as a whole is characterized by renewed peat formation, and in the Somerset Levels there is a second major phase of trackway construction from 900 to 450 bc (Godwin 1966: 11). However, some of these trackways were built in response to flooding by calcareous ground water as indicated by the increase in nutrient-demanding plants, rather than to the renewed growth of ombrogenous peat. Therefore, local environmental, as opposed to climatic, changes cannot be entirely ruled out.

In the pollen record the zone VIIb/VIII transition is ill-defined because man was now an over-riding force in controlling the vegetation, as indeed he may have been since the elm decline. The appearance of beech and hornbeam generally takes place around 500 bc although these trees are absent from Scotland and Ireland until very much later (Pennington 1974: 83). Lime declines, but this, like the earlier fall of elm, may be anthropogenic and is certainly not synchronous over England and Wales (Turner 1962: 328). Birch, pine and ash may show an increase but again this does not take place everywhere. Indeed it becomes unrealistic to zone pollen diagrams in the same way as is done for the earlier postglacial, since each local sequence may differ from the next. A more relevant approach is to consider the vegetational changes in terms of human interference and attempt, by radiocarbon dating or the use of stratified artifacts, to assign the various phases to their correct cultural horizon.

Judith Turner's work is outstanding in this respect (1970: 97). She has shown that in the highland zone, the pattern of small temporary clearances established in neolithic and earlier bronze age times continued on into the later bronze age, until the middle of the 1st millennium bc. Then, at various sites, extensive deforestation took place indicating a considerable increase in the amount of farmland (pasture and/or arable), and Turner points out that this was particularly so where there is evidence of iron age settlement. In other places, and especially in northern Britain, clearance on this large scale did not begin until well into historical times. In Ireland, the early monastic settlements brought about large-scale clearance from around AD 300 (Mitchell 1976).

It was perhaps during the later bronze age that the field systems in upland situations, mentioned in the previous section, were abandoned (Feachem 1973: 332). Abandonment may have been due to their being inundated by bog growth as the climate got wetter, but it may equally have been due to climatic deterioration *per se* – the shorter, cooler and wetter summers providing insufficient time for crops to ripen. The formation of peat may then be seen as a *result* of the abandonment of soils, perhaps over-exploited, not the cause of it. The problem is complex (Limbrey 1975).

On the Chalk, fields laid out in the earlier bronze age were deliberately slighted and traversed by extensive linear earthworks. The implied shift away from cereal farming to stock-raising may also be seen as a function of the deteriorating climate.

The period was one of extensive soil erosion. Chalkland coombes often contain over 2m of chalky loam known as hillwash or ploughwash, material stripped from adjacent slopes as a result of tillage (Evans J. G. 1972b: 311). These deposits often contain iron age and Roman potsherds and they usually overlie richly humic buried soils. Molluscan analysis of these deposits, for example from Pitstone Hill in Buckinghamshire (Evans and Valentine 1974), has shown that their accumulation did not begin with the first impact of man on the forest. Hillwashing was not coincident with clearance and cultivation. The reasons for this are not fully understood. It is possible that progressive tillage and over-cropping gradually caused soil deterioration, at which point erosion would have begun. Alternatively, new, more vigorous methods of tillage in iron age times may have superseded those of the later bronze age. Or climatic deterioration, and in particular the increase in precipitation, may have accelerated erosion.

The formation of 'Celtic' field lynchets is one more aspect of hillwashing as caused by agriculture (Fowler and Evans 1967: 296).

The products of soil erosion also find their way into rivers where they may be deposited as flood loam. Many so-called flood loams may indeed be little more than hillwash reworked to a greater or lesser extent by river action (Mitchell 1976: 150). There has been little examination of superficial flood loams but some at least date from Roman times or later. At Llancarfan in south Wales, for example, there is an accumulation of about 4m of material in a river valley, and contained artifacts indicate this to be of Roman and medieval date. This has caused the canalization of the river and restricted its movement laterally. Thus in earlier prehistoric times, prior to widespread soil erosion, river courses may have been shallower and more braided, occupying the surface of a broad gravel flood plain. This has important implications when one is considering prehistoric river transport, especially as Atkinson points out (1960a: 112), for such massive objects as the Stonehenge bluestones.

Soil degradation may thus lead to a variety of habitat changes. On the dry sandy soils of southern areas of Britain such as the Weald and the Hampshire Basin podsolization results. Wind erosion has been, and still is, an important agency in stripping the valuable surface humus horizon. In wetter areas, blanket peat has formed. In some cases, the bedrock is important in determining the direction of degradation. Thus in areas such as the Pennines and the Burren of western Ireland where millstone grit and carboniferous limestone are closely juxtaposed one can see clearly the thick growth of blanket peat on the former and the bare eroded surface of the latter totally free of soil. It is not clear to what this difference is due but it would seem to have a geological basis. On the Chalk, erosion has taken place resulting in the accumulation of soil in valley bottoms, but nowhere has this process been as severe as on the carboniferous limestone. Overgrazing, particularly by sheep, has resulted in the loss of vegetation and the stripping of the soil surface in mountain districts.

It was from the beginning of the 1st millennium bc onwards that the division of the British Isles into highland and lowland zones (Fox C. F. 1932) really became applicable. A topographical division, with the mountainous areas of the highland zone more hazardous for cultivation and communication, always existed of course. But as we have seen, the more congenial climatic conditions up to 1,200 bc tended to minimize the effects of topography, enabling cultivation of much higher ground than was generally possible after this time. Once deterioration set in, the various processes of soil degradation outlined above began, and they were more severe in the highland zone.

Thus the main characteristics of the later bronze age and iron age periods are: 1. The deterioration of climate. 2. The widespread formation of blanket bog. 3. The creation of large-scale clearances in iron age times in areas which in the bronze age had seen only small temporary clearances. 4. Widespread soil erosion and an increase in the heterogeneity of the landscape.

2 Exploitation and adaptation in pre-agricultural communities

Homo sapiens sapiens and the beginning of the upper palaeolithic in Britain

Homo sapiens sapiens first seems to have made his appearance in Europe about 40,000 years ago. This has meant that for most of his existence he has been concerned with the vagaries of the Pleistocene climate and that some of his early occupation and camping sites, stone tools and domestic refuse have been swept away by later readvances of the ice sheets and glacial outwash deposits. In areas where our immediate ancestors hunted wild animals, collected and gathered plant foods and the products of sea or stream, there may be now several metres of water, and the land links by which men travelled from one place to another are now island chains or the sea bed.

No earlier types of men seem to have used or constructed water transport, so _Homo sapiens sapiens_ was the first man potentially capable of exploring and populating the whole world (Brothwell 1977). The American continent and the Australo–New Guinean land mass (Sahul-land – Allen, Golson and Jones 1977) were probably occupied for the first time during the late Pleistocene,[1] opening their natural environmental resources to the devastating influence of Man the Hunter, with millions of years of accumulated evolutionary experience behind him. Technological progress, though it may seem incredibly slow in retrospect, began to speed up in the late Pleistocene, so that the material changes visible to the archaeologist were progressing in thousands, rather than millions of years. It is these changes, also largely covered in a recent survey (Mellars 1974), which form the subject of the present chapter.

In Europe, the upper palaeolithic industries are thought to have evolved from middle palaeolithic groups, under the influence of new ideas and inventions, such as the marked increase in bone artifacts, the proliferation of the punched blade technique and the production of burins or engraving tools, probably marking considerable advances in the working of organic materials such as wood and bone. The caves in south-western France continued to be occupied by _Homo sapiens sapiens_ after the demise of _Homo sapiens neanderthalensis_ and the classic European sequence of upper palaeolithic industries was first named after the sequence of finds from these caves and rock-shelters, from about 40,000 to about 10,000 years ago, during the climatic fluctuations of the Last Glaciation.

The British Isles were, for the whole of this period, merely a peripheral north-western area of the European landmass, periodically visited by the hunting and collecting parties who were the nomads of Europe. It is not possible in the majority of archaeological sites in the British Isles at this period of time to see a well-defined, easily identifiable set of industrial levels that can be equated with the industries of south-western France. Many of the arctic hunting grounds of the late Pleistocene now lie under the North Sea, the Channel or the Bristol Channel. But during periods when temperatures rose and vegetation thickened, many hunting and gathering parties must have visited, or even lived the whole of their lifespan in the regions that were later to become known as the British Isles. Unfortunately the archaeological evidence, in the first place not very prolific, has suffered from poor excavation and commercial exploitation, as well as a certain lack of interest on the part of research workers in what might appear at first sight to be rather thin, poor material, and a self-conscious overshadowing by the upper palaeolithic of south-west France.

When Dorothy Garrod wrote *The Upper Palaeolithic Age in Britain* in 1926, she tried to classify the archaeological material from the then known sites and collections in terms of the south-west French sequence and used the names British Aurignacian, Gravettian, Proto-Solutrean, Solutrean and Magdalenian, with the use of one local name, the Creswellian. Since then, over more than 50 years, the attitudes of prehistorians concerned with hunting and gathering communities have been expanded considerably by new environmental techniques, much improved dating methods, a more reasonable approach to typological and classificatory problems, together with well-documented ethnographic data from surviving hunting and collecting groups. The most recent and thorough appraisal of the upper palaeolithic material from Britain is by John Campbell (1971, published 1977), in which he makes extensive use of granulometric, faunal and pollen analysis, and radiocarbon dating techniques to extract further information from the Pleistocene deposits. The number of recorded sites has increased since 1926 but not with the dramatic rise that can be seen in relation to sites belonging to the later phases of man's development in the British Isles (fig. 2.1).

Extant physical remains of late Pleistocene *Homo sapiens sapiens* are extremely scarce in Britain. The best known site is still that of the burial of a young man, aged about 25 years and about 1·7m in height, in Paviland Cave on the south coast of the Gower Peninsula in south Wales. It was excavated in 1823 by William Buckland, later to be Dean of Westminster, as well as the first Reader in Geology at the University of Oxford (Buckland 1823). He assumed that the body, which was sprinkled with red ochre, was that of a female 'Ancient Briton', buried at the time south Wales was invaded by the Romans, and the burial was from then on known as 'The Red Lady of Paviland'. Buckland refused to believe that the body could be contemporary with the bones of 'antediluvian' animals. William Sollas, in his further excavations of 1912 (Sollas 1913), came to the more scientific and reasonable conclusion that the male skeleton was certainly in deliberate association with the skull of a mammoth, and that the man was buried with a number of mammoth ivory rods, an ivory bracelet and some shells of *Nerita littoralis*. The site was very prolific in finds, including stone, bone and ivory, but unfortunately it has never been

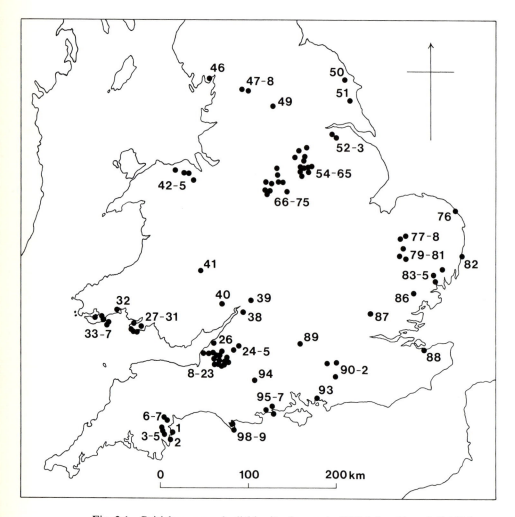

Fig. 2.1   British upper paleolithic sites known in 1971 (after Campbell 1971).

1	Bench Fissure (EUP)
2	Kent's Cavern (EUP; LUP)
3	Tornewton Cave (?EUP; LUP)
4	Three Holes Cave (?LUP)
5	Tor Court Shelter (?LUP)
6	Cow Cave (?EUP)
7	Tramp's Shelter (?LUP)
8	Uphill Cave (EUP)
9	Hutton Cave (?LUP)
10	Banwell Cave (?LUP)
11	Picken's Hole (?EUP)
12	Callow Hill (?LUP)
13	Rowberrow Cave (?LUP)
14	Aveline's Hole (LUP)
15	Flint Jack's Cave (LUP)
16	Gough's Cave (LUP)
17	Great Oone's Hole (?LUP)
18	Soldier's Hole (EUP; LUP)
19	Sun Hole (LUP)
20	Badger Hole (EUP; ?LUP)
21	Bridged Pot Shelter (?LUP)
22	Hyena Den (EUP)
23	Primrose Shelter (?LUP)
24	Herriot's Bridge (?LUP)
25	Chew Park Farm (?LUP)
26	Walton Cave (?EUP)
27	Deborah's Hole (?EUP)
28	Paviland Cave (EUP; LUP)
29	Long Hole (EUP)
30	Nottle Tor (EUP)
31	Cathole (LUP)
32	Coygan Cave (?EUP)
33	Priory Farm Cave (LUP)
34	Hoyle's Mouth (LUP)
35	Little Hoyle (?EUP; LUP)
36	Nana's Cave (LUP)
37	Ogof-yr-Ychen (?EUP; LUP)
38	Eastington (?EUP)
39	Forty Acres (EUP)
40	King Arthur's Cave (EUP; LUP)
41	Arrow Court (?LUP)
42	Plas-yn-Cefn Cave (LUP)
43	Lynx Cave (?LUP)
44	Cae Gwyn Cave (EUP)
45	Ffynnon Beuno Cave (EUP)
46	Kirkhead Cave (?LUP)
47	Kinsey Cave (?LUP)
48	Victoria Cave (?LUP)
49	Washburn Foot (?LUP)
50	Flixton 2 (?LUP)
51	Brigham Hill (?LUP)
52	Sheffield's Hill (?LUP)
53	Risby Warren (?LUP)
54	Edlington Wood (?LUP)
55	Hooton Roberts (?LUP)
56	Bole Hill (?LUP)
57	Dead Man's Cave (LUP)
58	Lob Wells Shelter (?LUP)

59	Ash Tree Cave (?EUP)
60	Pin Hole (EUP; LUP)
61	Robin Hood's Cave (EUP; LUP)
62	Mother Grundy's Parlour (LUP)
63	Langwith Cave (LUP)
64	Church Hole (LUP)
65	Yew Tree Cave (?LUP)
66	Ravenscliffe Cave (?EUP)
67	Old Woman's House Cave (?LUP)
68	Dowel Cave (LUP)
69	Fox Hole (LUP)
70	One Ash Shelter (LUP)
71	Churchdale Shelter (LUP)
72	Harborough Cave (?LUP)
73	Ossum's Cave (LUP)
74	Elder Bush Cave (LUP)
75	Thor's Fissure (LUP)
76	North Gap (?EUP)
77	Methwold (?LUP)
78	Cranwich (LUP)
79	Wangford Warren (?LUP)
80	Mildenhall (?LUP)
81	London Bottom (LUP)
82	Southwold (?EUP)
83	Charsfield (?EUP)
84	Barham (?EUP)
85	Branford Road (EUP)
86	White Colne (EUP)
87	Rikof's Pit (?EUP)
88	Oare (LUP)
89	Crown Acres (LUP)
90	Peper Harow (?EUP)
91	Weydon Pit (?LUP)
92	Bunch Lane (?LUP)
93	Long Island (LUP)
94	Fir Hill (?EUP)
95	Cameron Road (?EUP)
96	Rush Corner (LUP)
97	Hengistbury Head (LUP)
98	Verne Ditch (?LUP)
99	Portland Bill (?LUP)

EUP = Earlier upper palaeolithic
LUP = Later upper palaeolithic

possible to relate them to their stratigraphical sequence, so that they can only be studied as a typological assemblage.

In 1968 a team from the British Museum, led by Dr K. P. Oakley, published a date for 'The Red Lady of Paviland' obtained from the surviving human bone, of $16,510 \pm 340$ bc (Oakley 1968a). This implies that there was human activity possibly only 6km from the edge of the south Welsh ice sheet during the Full Last Glacial period (see table 1.1). This would certainly be in the permafrost zone, so that probably only occasional summer visits to the cave area would be feasible. Other hunting camps of this period would probably have existed on what is now the floor of the Bristol Channel (fig. 2.2).

There were two major periods when hunters and gatherers could fully exploit the faunal and floral resources of the country. It was during the intervening period, about 20,000 to about 15,000 years ago, when most of

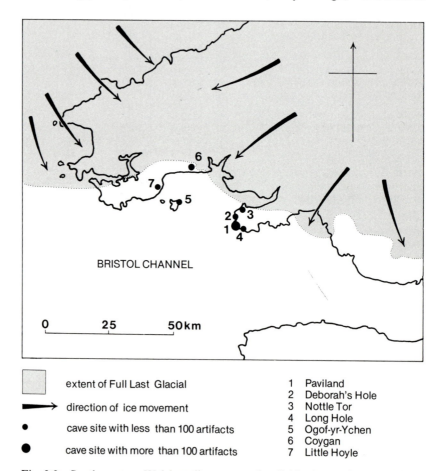

BRISTOL CHANNEL

0	25	50km

▭	extent of Full Last Glacial	1	Paviland
		2	Deborah's Hole
➤	direction of ice movement	3	Nottle Tor
		4	Long Hole
•	cave site with less than 100 artifacts	5	Ogof-yr-Ychen
		6	Coygan
●	cave site with more than 100 artifacts	7	Little Hoyle

Fig. 2.2   South-western Welsh earlier upper palaeolithic sites and suggested Full Last Glacial ice limit (after Campbell 1971).

the country was covered by snow and ice and only occasional foraging parties could visit the southern areas of England and Wales in the height of summer, that the body of the young man was placed in Paviland Cave.[2]

The period before this readvance of glacial conditions has been called the British Middle Last Glacial, when much of north England, the whole of Scotland and probably Ireland too were uninhabitable, but there were also considerable areas marked by plentiful herb and tundra. Here there were arctic fauna such as reindeer, lemming and mammoth and, further south, numerous animals such as horse provided food for hunting parties. Probably during this time Paviland Cave was a base camp for parties travelling to the Bristol Channel sites and further north to the reindeer grazing areas (see fig. 2.8a).

The stone artifacts from Paviland consist of a high proportion of scrapers, most of which are rather thick and heavy. Some of these are nosed and carinated types; there are also a number of burins, including the burin busqué.[3] Other types present include leaf-shaped points and retouched flakes (fig. 2.3). All these tool types occur in the deposits of another well-known cave near Torquay, occupied during the Middle Last Glacial. This is Kent's Cavern, one of the best stratigraphical sites for the whole of the upper palaeolithic period in Britain. Excavations were begun here by a Catholic priest, Father J. McEnery, in 1824. He took careful note of the position of, and the association between, man-made stone artifacts, bones of extinct animals and human bones, but he was unable to publish his results as the theological leaders of the time could not accept an argument that suggested any direct association between man, and animals described as antediluvian in age. The date of the Creation was then firmly believed to be 4,004 bc, as presented by Archbishop James Ussher (AD 1581–1656). However, clear evidence, such as that seen by Father McEnery, was accumulating rapidly and after the publication of *On the Origin of Species* in 1859 and the paper by Sir John Prestwich to the Royal Society in London 'On the occurrence of flint implements associated with the remains of animals of extinct species' in the same year, it became more fashionable to pursue the investigation of early man and his culture.

William Pengelly carried out further excavations in Kent's Cavern between 1865 and 1883 and entered the results in painstaking detail in his daily journal, later to be published in the British Association Reports from 1865 to 1880 (Campbell and Sampson 1971). A date of $26,210 \pm 435$ bc was recently obtained from the tibia of a woolly rhinoceros found by Pengelly in the Great Chamber, associated with a unifacial leaf-shaped point, several nosed scrapers and a saw-edged point. Many leaf-shaped points were found within the Great Chamber, often associated with animal teeth and bone, which might, as Campbell (1977) suggests, indicate an area in which special functions in connection with butchering the carcasses and joints that were brought in from the successful hunting parties were carried out. There are large amounts of hyena bones (*Crocuta crocuta*) that might suggest, along with bones of predators like cave lion, wolf, and arctic bear, that the cave was not used exclusively by Man. But the early upper palaeolithic men living in the cave certainly hunted large numbers of horse (*Equus* cf. *germanicas* or *przewalski*), woolly rhinoceros (*Coelodonta antiquitatis*), deer (*Cervus* or *Rangifer*), and some Giant Irish Elk (*Megaloceros giganteus*) and bison (*Bison priscus*). Pollen analysis shows a fairly open environment round the cave with a high proportion of grasses and herbs, a few willow and juniper bushes and occasional pine, oak and lime trees. The stone and bone artifacts of the earlier upper palaeolithic group at Kent's Cavern include the same heavy scrapers as from Paviland, including again the nosed and carinated types, leaf-shaped points (some of which have been described by some workers as plano-convex shaped spearheads), notched blades (saws), retouched flakes and blades, and some burins and a few bone pins (fig. 2.4, 2.12).

Other sites from which archaeological evidence of the earlier upper palaeolithic phase has been recorded are shown in fig. 2.5. As can be seen, the majority of sites are caves but this does not necessarily present an accurate distribution of the sites actually used at the time, as open sites are far more difficult to find and the evidence must often have been removed

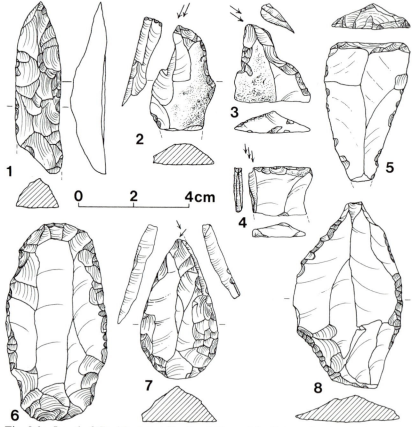

Fig. 2.3   Level of 'Red Lady' at Paviland Cave: 1 leaf-shaped point; 2–4 burins; 5–6 scrapers; 7 burin and scraper; 8 retouched leaf-shaped flake (after Campbell 1971).

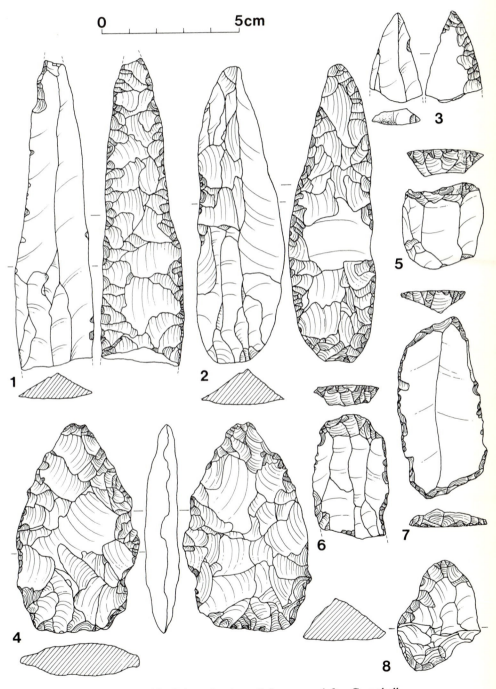

Fig. 2.4 Kent's Cavern: 1–4 leaf-shaped points; 5–8 scrapers (after Campbell 1971).

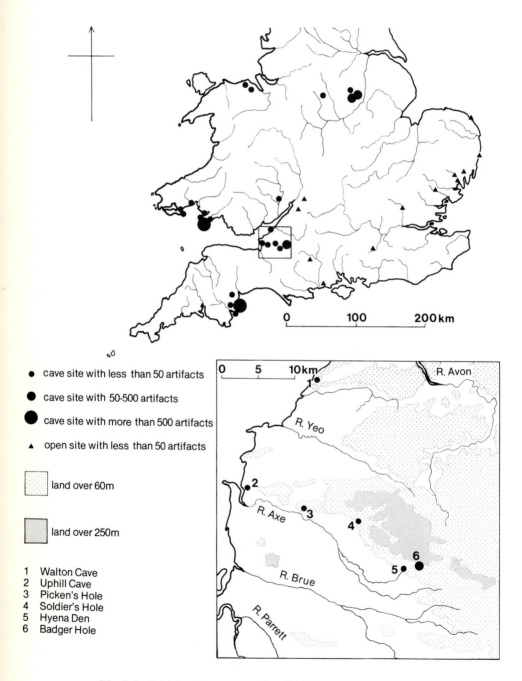

Fig. 2.5   British earlier upper palaeolithic find distribution; *insert* Mendip region sites (after Campbell 1971).

by later activities. Some of the caves must have been base camps, occupied for a considerable period of time, maybe weeks, maybe months or even years, from which hunting parties would set out into different terrains for shorter periods, to take advantage of the seasonal visits of migrating animals such as deer. Not only the large animals that were well adapted to the cold conditions, but also smaller more readily available mammals were caught; for example, the early levels of Cathole in south Wales contained the bones of many shrews (*Sorex* sp.), as well as arctic or varying lemming (*Dicrostonyx torquatus*). Kent's Cavern and Badger Hole, Somerset, were possibly base camps at this time. The inset in fig. 2.5 shows the distribution of other sites around Badger Hole, which contained fewer artifacts and probably represent camping sites of limited use during hunting and gathering expeditions to various outlying environments.

There is no definite cave painting or engraving in Britain but there are examples of bone or ivory fragments which seem to have deliberate designs scratched on them, associated with artifacts of the earlier upper palaeolithic type. One example of this is the ivory point with a bevelled base from Pin Hole Cave, Derbyshire, which has a fish design on it; another example of art is the engraving of the horse found in Robin Hood's Cave, Creswell Crags, although this is more likely to have been contemporary with later upper palaeolithic artifacts (fig. 2.12:8).

There are not yet very many radiocarbon dates for this period of occupation in the British Isles (see fig. 2.6). Those from Kent's Cavern and Robin Hood's Cave, Derbyshire, show that the occupation extended back at least to about 28,000 years ago. Most of the next series of dates cluster around 18,000 years ago, about the last period of time it would have been possible for men to have visited southern Britain before the main phase of the Last Glacial came to its maximum severity, and these remains probably represent seasonal summer visits to south and north Wales, Derbyshire and Somerset. The pollen spectrum from the cave known as Mother Grundy's Parlour, Derbyshire, shows the changing vegetation from an almost treeless state (probably during the Full Last Glacial), with minor fluctuations during the Late Last Glacial and then a dramatic rise in trees and shrubs and a corresponding decline in grass and herb pollen during the last years of pollen zone III and through the whole of pollen zones IV and V (fig. 2.7). Birch, juniper and willow are amongst the earliest shrubs and trees to recolonize an area after a glacial period, followed later by larger forest trees such as elm, oak, and lime. This period of time saw groups of later upper palaeolithic people using Mother Grundy's Parlour, followed during pollen zone VI by groups that have been designated mesolithic in the postglacial periods. (See also tables 1.1, 1.2, 1.3, for information referred to throughout this chapter.)

The later upper palaeolithic

As has been described in the opening chapter, during pollen zone II (the so-called Allerød interstadial) areas of trees and shrubs appeared in place of the barren wastes of tundra with small windblown shrubs that had existed for so long previously (fig. 2.8b). The highland areas would still

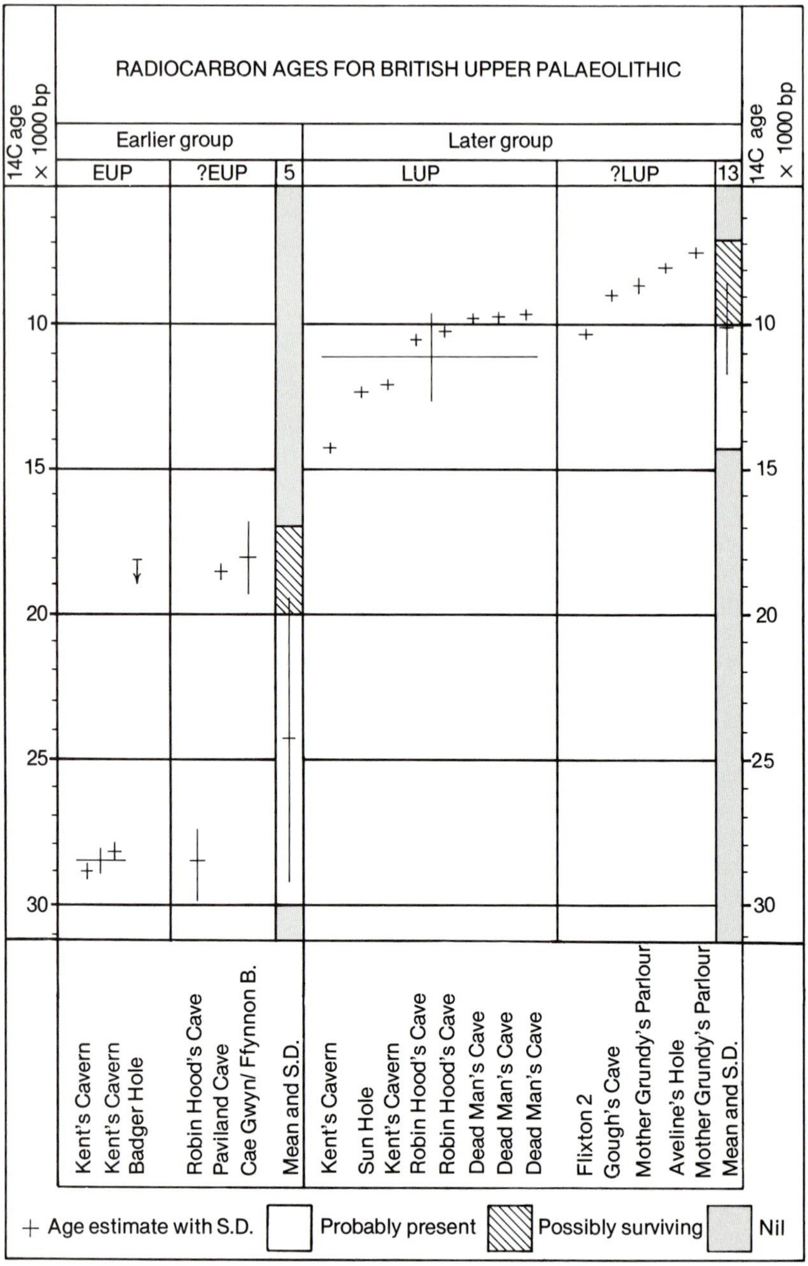

Fig. 2.6   Radiocarbon ages for British upper palaeolithic (after Campbell 1971).

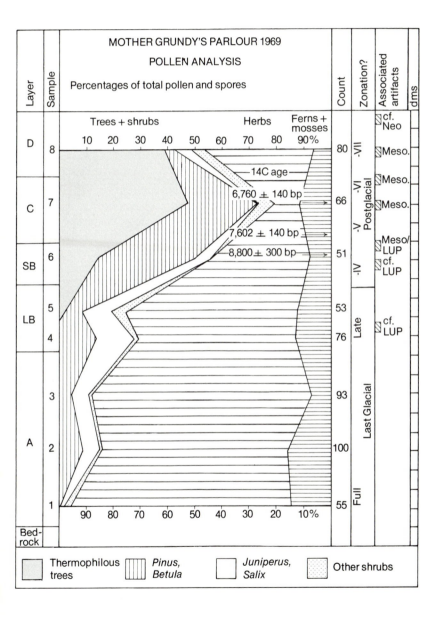

Fig. 2.7 Mother Grundy's Parlour, 1969: pollen analysis (after Campbell 1971).

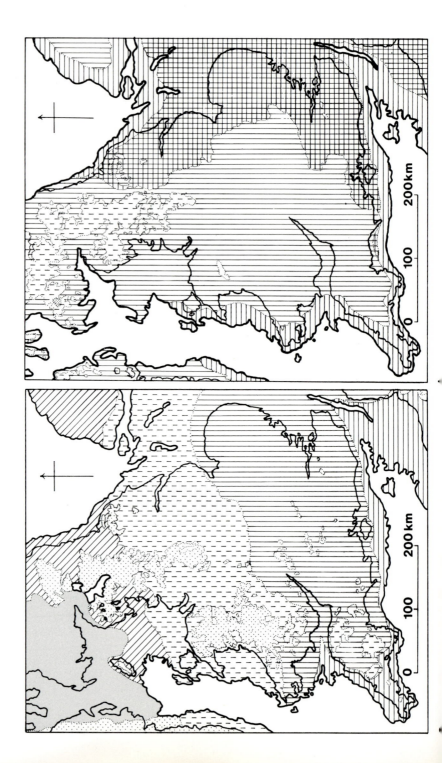

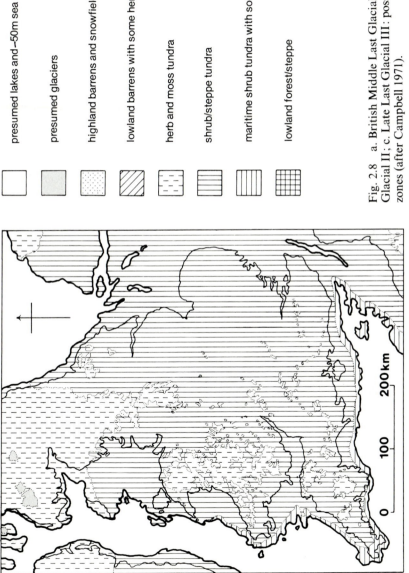

presumed lakes and –50m sea

presumed glaciers

highland barrens and snowfields

lowland barrens with some herbs and mosses

herb and moss tundra

shrub/steppe tundra

maritime shrub tundra with some trees

lowland forest/steppe

Fig. 2.8   a. British Middle Last Glacial; b. Late Last Glacial II; c. Late Last Glacial III: possible vegetation zones (after Campbell 1971).

0   100   200km

c

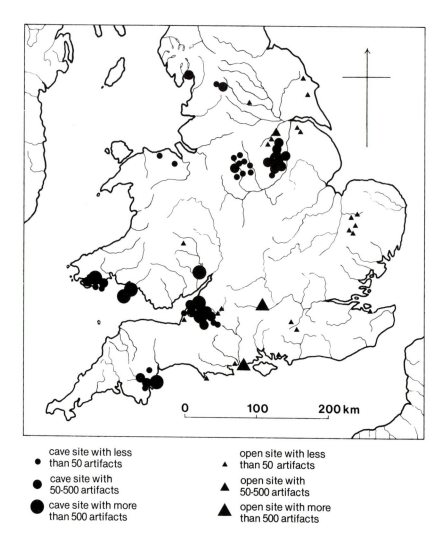

cave site with less
than 50 artifacts

cave site with
50-500 artifacts

cave site with more
than 500 artifacts

open site with less
than 50 artifacts

open site with
50-500 artifacts

open site with more
than 500 artifacts

Fig. 2.9   British later upper palaeolithic find distribution (after Campbell 1971).

have been bare of trees, but in the lower areas, coastal zones and especially the Great Plain that stretched over what is now coastal east England and the North Sea into Denmark and the Low Countries, there were regions of thick forest steppe, probably mainly pine and birch, in which animals such as the Giant Irish Elk and other deer would be excellent game to follow. Both the reindeer and the elk appear in Ireland at this time but there is, as yet, no trace of man. During the colder climate of zone III and the Loch Lomond readvance (see fig. 1.1) the trees would have declined again and shrub tundra re-established itself in many parts of the country, with snowfields on the higher grounds; but after about 8,000 bc gradually the birch and pine returned, the snow and ice retreated and have never returned to the same extent (fig. 2.8c).

The distribution of the archaeological sites of the later upper palaeolithic phase (fig. 2.9) shows a distinct division into two regional areas: northern Britain, especially the eastern and southern foothills of the Pennines; and the south-west of Britain, with concentrations around Kent's Cavern, Devon, and the Cheddar Gorge area of Somerset and in south Wales; there are also scattered open-air sites in southern and eastern Britain. The northern sites may have been used as the summer seasonal sites,[4] or the two areas may have represented varying migration routes from Europe to the British hunting grounds. Campbell (1971; 1977) does not find a valid regional variation in his analysis of the stone artifacts from the two zones, contrary to previous opinions.

The scope of the artifacts in general seems very different from that of the earlier upper palaeolithic assemblage and can be grouped together most conveniently as the later upper palaeolithic of Britain. Kent's Cavern continued as a major site and was in all probability the base camp for the exploitation of many of the good hunting areas now under the Channel, as well as for the higher areas of Dartmoor and the surrounding river valleys. The main element in the stone assemblage is the backed blade. This tool appears in many forms, two of which have been given special significance and have been called the Cheddarian and the Creswellian points (figs. 2.10. 2.11). The Creswellian point is a sub-triangular, obliquely blunted blade with backing down one side and sometimes round the blade end; the Cheddarian point is basically trapezoidal in shape with retouch on the two oblique ends and backing all or part of the way down one side. In the past there have been suggestions (Bohmers 1956; 1963) that these constitute the basis for a regional sub-division of the late British upper palaeolithic into two groups. Campbell (1971; 1977) did not find a statistical basis for this assumption; both points in fact occur in both regions and not to the exclusion of each other in any significant way. Other artifact types that are common at this time are convex or straight backed blades, penknives and shouldered points and, rarely, tanged points (fig. 2.10). There is also a range of rather graceful burins and blade-end scrapers, but not of the solid, heavy varieties that characterized the earlier upper palaeolithic of Britain. The leaf-shaped points have disappeared but bone artifacts are more common than before, as is shown by the presence of needles and four harpoons (fig. 2.12). As with the earlier upper palaeolithic assemblage

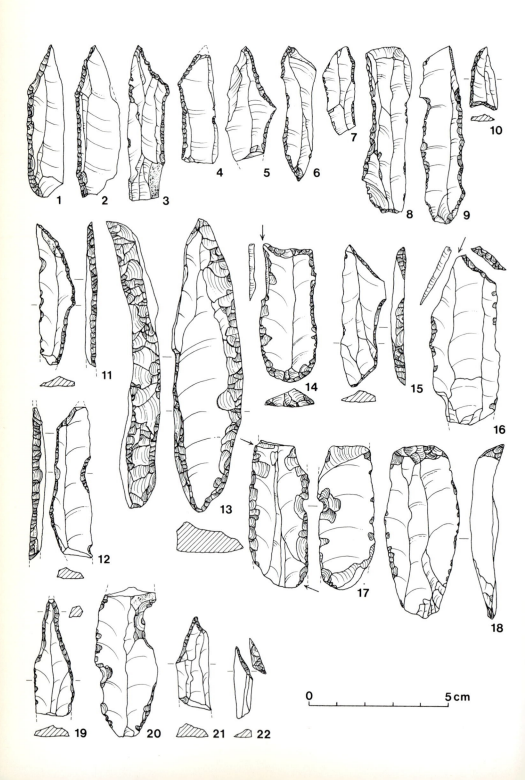

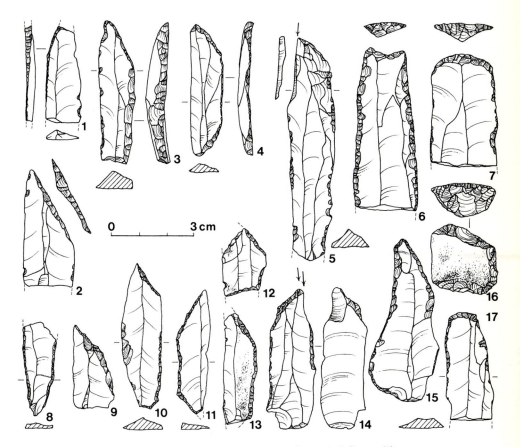

Fig. 2.10   Later upper palaeolithic flint types. Anston Cave: 1–5 Creswellian points; 6–7 partially backed pieces; 8–9 straight backed blades. Langwith Cave: 10 convex backed tool; 11 shouldered backed tool; 12 truncated backed tool; 13 backed tool; 14 multiple backed tool; Gough's Cave: 15 backed blade of truncated shouldered point type; 16 burin; 17 double-ended burin; 18 convex end scraper on blade; 19 borer; 20 notched truncated blade; 21 awl; 22 backed blade (after Campbell 1971; *Antiquity* XLIII 1969).

Fig. 2.11   Later upper palaeolithic flint types. Kent's Cavern: 1 Creswellian point; 2 obliquely blunted point; 3 Creswellian point; 4 Cheddarian point; 5 burin; 6–7 end scrapers on blades; Mother Grundy's Parlour: 8 truncated backed blade; 9 backed blade; 10 Creswellian point; 11 Cheddarian point; 12 truncated shouldered point; 13 shouldered point; 14 burin; 15 awl; 16–17 scrapers (after Campbell 1971).

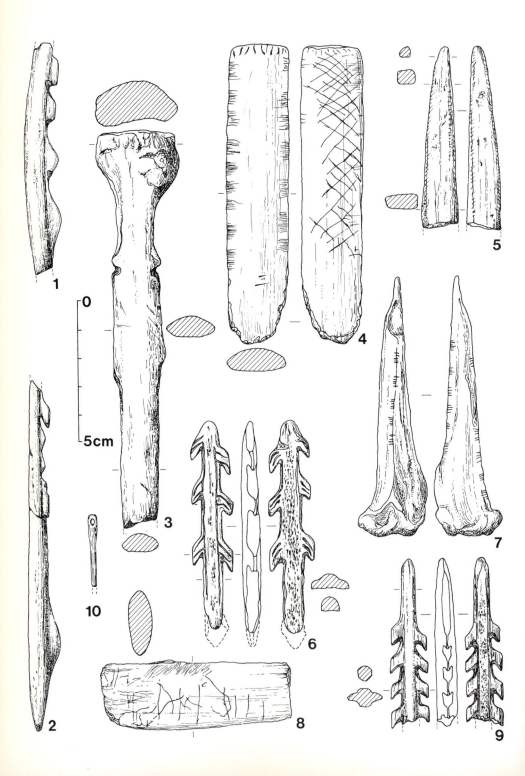

parallels can be made with the continental European Late Glacial material, but it is again difficult to locate exact areas of origin for the British groups. The Ahrensburgian and Federmesser groups from north-western Europe provide a range of parallels (Rust 1956; Schwabedissen 1954), but the tool kit of any one hunting group may vary considerably through the year in response to specific circumstances or tasks being undertaken in particular regions.

In Kent's Cavern the majority of tools from the Black Band in the Vestibule are of the later upper palaeolithic type and there is a radiocarbon date of 13,325 ± 120 bc obtained from a bear bone associated with backed blades and a uniserial bone harpoon (fig. 2.12). Large amounts of horse bone indicate that horses were still the major prey of the hunters inhabiting Kent's Cavern, as well as the Giant Irish Elk and cave bear (*Ursus arctos*). Other contemporary sites show the importance of reindeer (*Rangifer tarandus*), woolly rhinoceros and occasional mammoth, although this is not nearly as common as in earlier phases. There is a general increase in the numbers of smaller mammal bones and teeth, representing shrews, bats, weasels and voles, field mice and varied hare. Bird bones also increase in numbers, especially grouse and ptarmigan, grey-lag goose and whooper swan. Campbell (1971; 1977) suggests that some of the smaller bird bones, such as thrush or magpies, may represent the prey of the larger predatory birds such as owls. There is evidence that some of the bone has been utilized by man for tools or split for the extraction of marrow. Generally the later upper palaeolithic hunters seem to have concentrated less on the larger animals that had been common during the colder periods and to have learnt to increase their ability to snare and catch the smaller forest animals, rodents and birds. Probably due to their fragility, fish bones are rare.

The Mendip area in the later upper palaeolithic period shows the increase in activity in the area since the Full Last Glacial, with two possible base camps at Gough's Cave and Aveline's Hole and over 10 smaller surrounding camp sites. Gough's Cave has produced more than 7,000 artifacts whereas Aveline's Hole had only about 400, but both have good bone finds; the only two British *baton-de-commandements* come from Gough's Cave (fig. 2.13).[5] In south Wales Paviland Cave continued in use and Cathole, just over 10km away on a steep-sided valley slope, may have been a base camp from which to exploit the higher areas of ground of what is now the Gower Peninsula. In the north of England there is an important series of cave sites in the Creswell Caves of Derbyshire. Many of these sites such as Robin Hood's Cave, Mother Grundy's Parlour and Pin Hole contain deposits that show occupation levels continuing through the later

Fig. 2.12   Bone types. 1–2 Kent's Cavern: harpoons, uniserial (associated finds are dated to 13,325 bc); 3 Paviland Cave: bone spatula; 4 Gough's Cave: decorated or tallied bone rib; 5 Soldier's Hole: bone point; 6 Aveline's Hole: biserial harpoon with engravings; 7 Gough's Cave: decorated or tallied bone point; 8 Robin Hood's Cave: rib fragment with engraving of horse's head; 9 Kent's Cavern: biserial harpoon; 10 Kent's Cavern: needle (after Campbell 1971).

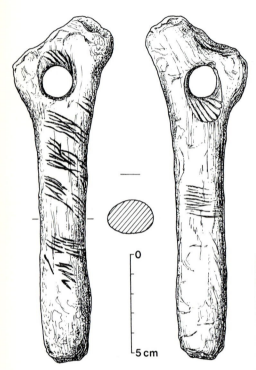

Fig. 2.13   Bone from Gough's Cave
(after Campbell 1971).

Fig. 2.14.   Pin Hole Cave, Derbys.
(photograph: Trevor Ford).

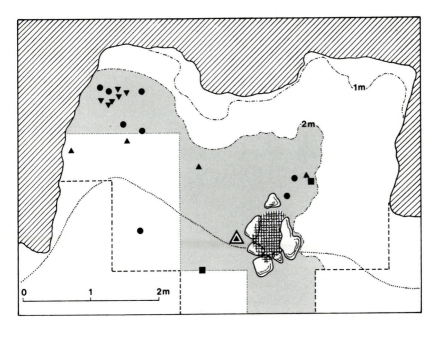

rock wall	● flint artifact
boulder	▲ bone of large mammal
hearth	🔺 humerus of *equus*, 14C age 10,590 ± 90 years bc
bedrock contour	▼ tooth of large mammal
overhang drip-line	■ antler fragment
unexcavated	mammal bone and teeth fragments

Fig. 2.15   Robin's Hood's Cave: plan showing distribution of finds (after Campbell 1971).

upper palaeolithic into the mesolithic phase (figs. 2.14, 2.15). Campbell (1971; 1977) has devised an artifactual sequence for these changes, involving an initial phase with a high percentage of Creswellian points,[6] then adding some shouldered points. In the third phase he sees the decline of the Creswellian points and increase in shouldered points and finally the return of the Creswellian points together with penknife points as the beginnings of the mesolithic industries occur. It is to this last phase that he assigns most of the material from Mother Grundy's Parlour, therefore making it atypical of the complete sequence of the area and unsuitable as a type-site, as Professor Bohmers tried to suggest.

As well as these cave sites there is an increasing number of important open-air sites of the later upper palaeolithic period. These are much more difficult to locate than cave sites and usually only survive in the poorer or more badly drained soils, which have escaped intensive agricultural practices or dense occupation. They are usually reported through surface collections of stone artifacts. They are a very important side of the later upper palaeolithic occupation pattern in the British Isles, as they represent a wider exploitation of surrounding environments than is represented from the cave sites alone; probably in many cases they were seasonal camps, possibly, but not always, summer camps for the specific hunting of some particular animal or the exploitation of some other local natural resource, such as plant material or a source of good flaking stone.

Although there are indications that later upper palaeolithic settlements may exist at a number of open-air localities in southern and eastern England, our knowledge of these sites is extremely limited.[7] In southern England, Hengistbury Head, Hampshire, is the most extensive and thoroughly explored open-air site from the later upper palaeolithic, although it does also contain material from the succeeding mesolithic phase (Mace 1959). Shouldered points, backed blades, fairly large heavy burins and scrapers come from levels containing evidence of fire but no structures or organic material (fig. 2.16). Higher levels and other areas of the site seem to have been occupied later by mesolithic hunters and gatherers. More of these interesting open-air sites, where it might be possible to tie in the stratigraphy of soil and pollen profiles with the typologically changing artifacts, would help to clarify the situation further.

Maglemosian hunters and the earlier mesolithic industries

The division between upper palaeolithic and mesolithic is, like most of the artificial boundaries that subsequent study has imposed on human history, one of controversy and difficulty. These generally wide embracing terms span thousands, or at least hundreds, of years of human development over a wide area covering many different geographical conditions. They are useful only in a broad classificatory fashion, becoming impossible to define in precise terms when narrowed down to a particular condition or boundary. Recently there have been several studies which aim to examine especially the social and subsistence status of mesolithic communities (cf. Clarke D. L. 1976; Jacobi R. M. 1976). Certainly there are strong typological differences between the stone tools from the later upper palaeolithic and mesolithic stages of the pre-agricultural hunters and gatherers of the British Isles. There tends to be a general decrease in the overall size of the backed blades, eventually resulting in the production of microlithic tools and the consequent waste product, the microburin (although not all microliths need to be made in this fashion). Scrapers also tend to decrease in size and often become round in shape, but there is a remarkable increase in the types and varieties of bone and antler artifacts and, where it is preserved, in the use of other organic materials such as shell, bark and fibre. There is also the introduction of apparently new types of artifact, for example the tranchet flaked axe,[8] and later on the polished stone axe. But the whole is a continuous process of adaptation to changing environmental conditions. Recognizable groups of mesolithic artifacts began to appear about 10,000 years ago, thus overlapping with dated sites at the end of the later upper palaeolithic series. Although it has recently been stated (Jacobi R. M. 1973: 245; cf. also Jacobi R. M. 1976) that 'no convincing typological connections can be demonstrated between our local upper palaeolithic ... and any part of our mesolithic', it is evident that some form of continuity and overlap in time does exist, as shown by the range of radiocarbon dates, in the use of the same sites in certain areas, in the progressive decrease in the size of stone tools, and the continuity shown in the use of some technological processes such as that of the groove and splinter method of working antler (fig. 2.19b).

An example of the paradox caused by attempting to define too rigidly the boundaries of broad general archaeological groups occurs at High Furlong, Lancashire, where in 1970 a uniserial barbed bone point, paralleling mesolithic barbed points in shape and size, was found in association with the skeleton of an elk in detritus mud dated to pollen zone II, the Allerød oscillation. However, extensive pollen analysis from the site shows that deposits from zone I to zone IV are present and there must be at least a possibility that the body of the elk gradually sank, by bulk and weight, into an earlier mud level than that forming at the time of its death. However, two radiocarbon dates give results of $9,715 \pm 140$ and $10,250 \pm 160$ bc. The skeleton seems to belong to the species of recent European elk (*Alces alces*), and seems to have been complete before excavation took place. There is good evidence to suggest that the animal was badly injured by hunters but escaped from them, only to drown, possibly in trying to swim the lake or cross the ice, leaving the skeleton eventually to be preserved intact in lake sediments. The animal seems to have been between three and a half and six years old at death and to have been about to shed its antlers, which are normally shed in the period from December to February. The signs of injuries include lesions (Stuart 1976), probably caused both by barbed bone points and flint-tipped weapons, projected with considerable force as the arrows or spearheads penetrated skin, flesh and muscle. At least one of the wounds seems to have been made from close range, almost under the foot of the animal, penetrating upwards as if the hunter was aiming to lame it (fig. 2.17). A uniserial barbed point made of bone, of the type usually dated to the Boreal or Pre-boreal zones, was found near the body. Injuries thought to have been caused by flint-

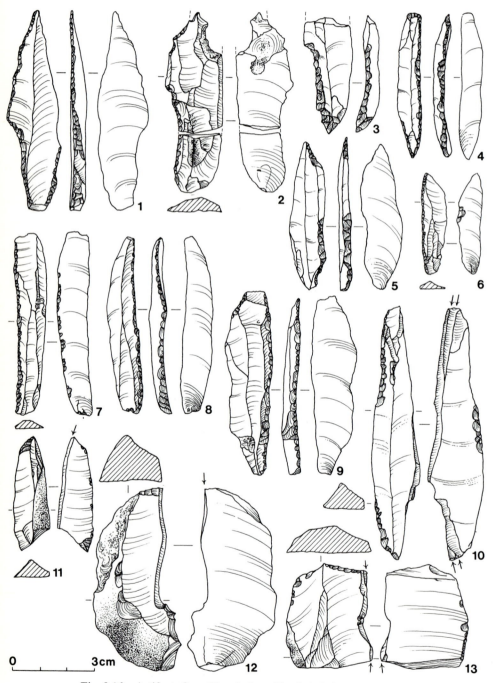

Fig. 2.16   Artifacts from Hengistbury Head. 1–3 shouldered points; 4–9 backed blades; 10–15 burins; 16–20 scrapers; 21–4 cores (after Mace 1959).

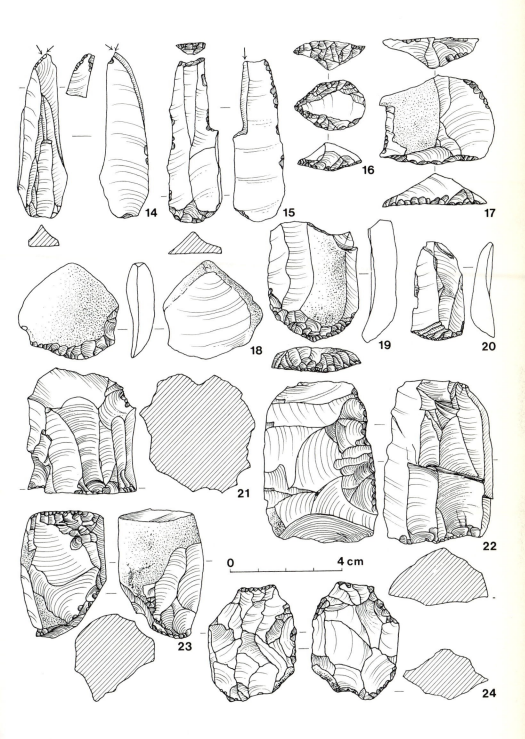

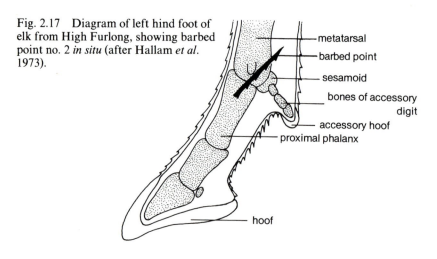

Fig. 2.17   Diagram of left hind foot of elk from High Furlong, showing barbed point no. 2 *in situ* (after Hallam *et al.* 1973).

tipped missiles were found mainly in the thorax area, presumably an attempt to kill the animal outright. It is stated that there are probably axe wounds on the fore foot and the ninth rib (Hallam *et al.* 1973: 119). Some of the lesions were probably caused at least three weeks before the death of the animal, suggesting that a second group of hunters caught up with the already sick elk and caused fatal injuries fairly easily. However it escaped once more but the carcase may have become wedged under the ice, away from natural scavengers, and later sunk to the bottom of the lake. This type of chance discovery provides fascinating information with which to check previous archaeological classification and can, as in this case, provide possible evidence to suggest that certain types of artifact (here the flake stone axe) came into use long before the dated examples that have been found so far. It gives scope for an almost complete reconstruction of an actual incident that occurred in prehistory.

The barbed points that were found at High Furlong were of a similar shape and size to many from the well-known early mesolithic site of Star Carr, Yorkshire. However, the barbed points from that site were mainly of antler (only two were of bone). This is an example of the continuity of style and technique but here using variant materials, changing through from the end of the Late Last Glacial into the postglacial times. As the glacial conditions of the end of the Last Glaciation wore off, sea levels gradually rose, and so in many places did the land, with the isostatic release from the weight of the ice. Once again the vegetation went through the stages of responding to the increased annual temperatures after the slight setbacks caused by the Loch Lomond readvance. As has already been observed, the birch trees were in their turn replaced by the pine and then slowly by hazel, elm, oak and lime. As the vegetation altered so did the contingent fauna, and forest animals took the place of the fauna that had been living in the still cold birch scrub of pollen zone III. During the early phases of the mesolithic period Britain was still linked by the marshy North Sea Plain to north-western Europe, and the hills of the Pennines, with the Welsh mountains and the uplands of the South-western Peninsula to the south and the Border hills and mountains of Scotland to the north, formed the western edge to this vast, flat, wet region, rich in food resources such as fish (both from sea and river), waterfowl and other birds, edible plants and small mammals, and the forest deer and aurochs of the higher, drier, forested regions between the river valleys. Certainly all these regions would have been extensively utilized by the growing populations of hunters and gatherers moving around northern Europe and visiting the British Isles in their nomadic travels, making use of various environments from seasonal camps.

Ireland was only joined to the rest of Britain at periods of high glacial activity by ice sheets, and even at the time when the sea level fell 100m below the present level Ireland was only joined to Britain by a narrow isthmus in the north of the country. The range of fauna and flora has differed in the two countries since the immediate postglacial period, when the Irish Sea reached its present level.[9] No well-documented archaeological finds have been recorded before the postglacial period, although it would have been possible for upper palaeolithic hunters to have visited southern Ireland at times during the last glaciation; but so far mesolithic industries are the earliest record of Man in Ireland.

Star Carr (fig. 2.18), although not the earliest site to be occupied by recognizably mesolithic hunters, is by far the best example of an early mesolithic camp site, containing a remarkable range of evidence and giving excellent possibilities for the reconstruction of the life and environment of the time. The open camp site was situated at the west end of the Vale of Pickering on a muddy gravel slope rising out of the lake, that is now a thick peat area. The occupants constructed a platform of hewn birch timber and brushwood, onto which were thrown stones, wads of clay, moss and occupation debris such as red deer antlers, to provide a reasonably stable living area in the reed swamp at the edge of the water (fig. 2.19a). No remaining signs of any superstructure were found, but it is thought that the platform must have supported huts made of bundled reeds or some form of tent, possibly covered in animal skins. The area of the occupied site was estimated by the density of organic waste material, such as animal bone and vegetable remains, as well as from the amount of artificial material found within each 0·835m^2 (yd^2). This showed that the most dense concentration was over 70 worked flints per 0·835m^2, tailing down to under 18, giving an area of approximately 200m^2 showing signs of intense habitation. Probably no more than three or four families could have camped in this area, giving a maximum of 25 persons to the site at any one time. The immediate environment was one of wet, marshy plains with many birch trees growing in the surrounding forests. Pine was also fairly common in the area and willow closer to the open water and reeds. The hunters must have cleared the site of birch trees before establishing an open clearing, in which plants such as *Polygonum*, *Chenopodium* and *Urtica* grew. In the immediate vicinity there was the opportunity to fish and to hunt the smaller birds and animals that lived round the water's edge. But undoubtedly the main importance of the camp was the seasonal

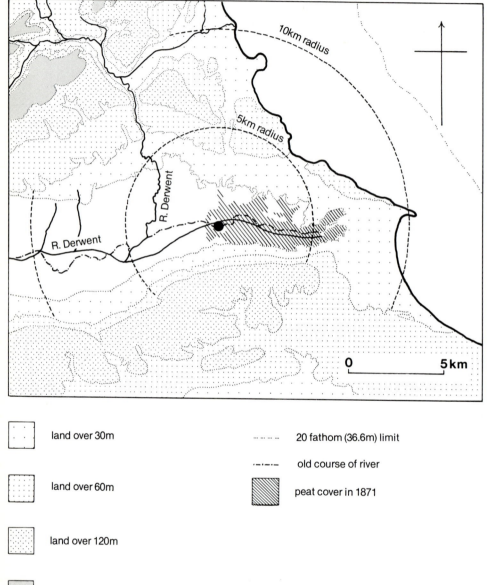

land over 30m

land over 60m

land over 120m

land over 180m

20 fathom (36.6m) limit

old course of river

peat cover in 1871

Fig. 2.18   Star Carr, situated in the Vale of Pickering between the North Yorkshire Moors and the Yorkshire Wolds. The circles enclose zones within one hour's and two hours' walk of the site; the likely site territory is contained within those circles. At the time of the occupation of Star Carr, which was situated on its northern margin, the lake might have occupied about half of the area covered by peat in 1871 (after Clark J. G. D. 1972).

hunting of the deer in the forest, especially the red deer; roe deer and elk were of lesser importance. Further afield the site can be seen as a possible base camp for the exploitation of more distant environmental resources, such as the hill hunting grounds, or the sea shore (fig. 2.18). The site itself, on a previous course of the river Derwent, now lies some 30m below sea level, but land over 60m high can easily be reached within one or two hours' walk from Star Carr. The sea shore at the time of occupation (mid-8th millennium bc in the pollen zone IV Pre-boreal) was probably about where the 20 fathom (36·6m) depth line is today, and would have been about 15km from the site. This was probably the source of the amber found at the site. Most of the materials from Star Carr come from within easy range, such as the pebbles from the local glacial drift, and flint from chalk and stream pebbles. Only small pieces of iron pyrites (worn possibly through firelighting use) probably originated well outside the normal territory of the hunters from the site. Perhaps these were obtained by trading or exchange with neighbouring communities and had passed through many individual hands in a similar fashion to the stone axes, shells or bird of paradise feathers that are found so far from their place of origin in Papua New Guinea communities (cf. Hughes I. 1977: esp. 177ff.).

Star Carr compares with a number of other low-level, waterside sites such as Skipsea, Broxbourne, Thatcham and the Leman and Ower Banks. But there are other early postglacial sites, in the upland areas over 300m above sea level such as the Yorkshire Moors, in which due to their occupation density, certain similarities in flint types and the restricted scale of their finds, have been interpreted by J. G. D. Clark (1972) as the temporary summer camps of the hunters whose winter base camps are in the swampy and forested valleys below. This concept of seasonal variation must be considered of great importance to all upper palaeolithic and mesolithic societies in the British Isles. Most well-documented, ethnographically recorded hunting-gathering societies are highly seasonal in behaviour in response to environmental change. There are exceptional communities that can exploit a well-developed food source (usually fish or shell fish) that provides basic sustenance all year round, allowing a camp to remain in one place for a considerable length of time. These sites probably also existed in the early postglacial period but the average mesolithic camp site shifted with varying seasonal resources especially in response to the movements of migratory animals and birds (Mellars 1976b). The seasonal movements of the red deer herds must have been of vital importance to the placing of camp sites. Star Carr itself was probably occupied – perhaps sporadically – for several years in the winter and spring seasons. Such information can be inferred from the stage of growth of the antlers from the site and knowledge of the period of the year when such development normally takes place. During the winter the red deer tend to remain within a limited territory and to be separated into groups (yards) containing either adult males or the females with their young. Warcock Hill, Lancashire, where there are occasional patches of charcoal and a scatter of worked flints of the 'broad bladed' type[10] with strong

a

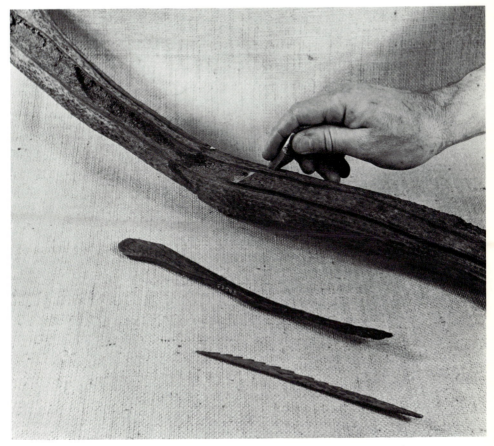

b

Fig. 2.19   a. Star Carr, margin of brushwood platform with sharpened end of
large birch tree to left of 3′ (0·91 m) scale (photograph Walkers Studios Ltd,
Scarborough). b. Star Carr: groove and splinter technique (photograph:
A. Pacitto; courtesy S. E. Thomas).

affinities to the Star Carr assemblage, may well represent the summer encampments of hunters following the summer movements of the deer over much wider areas in the uplands and hill country. Clark has speculated on the possibility of researching the annual territories of several mesolithic groups in the British Isles (Clark J. G. D. 1972: 36). However, the sea, that has encroached about 37m on the land since early postglacial times, must have covered many of the sites.

Star Carr provides information on a wide variety of activities that were being carried out, probably throughout the whole land area available to these early postglacial communities. The importance of hunting is reflected in the analysis of the animal remains. Red deer remains dominate, mainly present in antlers, 83 (of the total of 102) of which had been used for the removal of splinters, used in the production of barbed points for hunting. Most of the bones and antlers come from adult stags, emphasizing the culling activity of the hunters on the male yards in their territory in the winter season, whilst rarely hunting the hinds and immature animals.[11] Elk and roe deer remains are also fairly prominent, and other forest animals include the beaver (*Castor fiber*), wild pig (*Sus scrofa*), aurochs (*Bos primigenius*), fox (*Vulpes vulpes*), wolf (*Canis lupes*), pine marten (*Martes martes*), hedgehog (*Erinaceus europeus*), hare (*Lepus capensis*), and badger (*Meles meles*). Domestic dog (*Canis familiaris*) was already present and shows that domestication had already taken place some generations previously. Some bird species present include common crane, white stork, grebes and divers, lapwing and duck. Both the birds and the smaller forest animals might have been hunted with blunt wooden

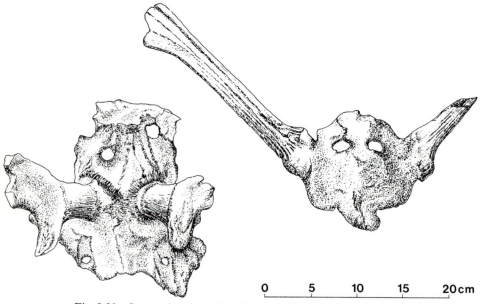

0   5   10   15   20cm

Fig. 2.20   Stag antlers from Star Carr, possibly used as masks (after Clark J. G.D. 1972).

arrows aiming to stun the animal but not to damage the pelt, of a type found in early postglacial contexts in Scandinavia but not recovered from Star Carr. The barbed point seems to have been the main harpoon head, perhaps used in pairs, and the groove and splinter technique by which they were manufactured from the antler (fig. 2.19b) is part of a tradition going back to the early upper palaeolithic Aurignacian industries of south-western France and was particularly strong in the late upper palaeolithic groups of north-west Europe that preceded the mesolithic groups there (Clark and Thompson 1953). Elk antler was used more rarely at Star Carr but there is a series of mattock heads and some elk bone was worked into bodkins, perhaps used for fastening-pins. Possible smoothers for skin working were made from *bos* bone.

The stone artifacts from Star Carr are also largely concerned with hunting and the preparation of animal products. The exception to this is, of course, the axe, primarily used to cut the timbers from the site before the settlement could be founded and then for the manufacture of any necessary wooden artifacts such as arrowshafts, handles, means of transport (boats, skis etc.), but unfortunately the number of wooden artifacts preserved on the site is small. The majority of stone tools are either burins, scrapers or microliths, most being made from local drift flint nodules (fig. 2.21). As well as the finished and broken products there is clear evidence of actual flint working on the site, with large quantities of primary flakes (some showing signs of utilization), cores and core-rejuvenation flakes. Axes and adzes are few in number and small in size, so that for effective use they would need to be mounted in a sleeve of antler, bone or wood, although all of them may have been very much larger when they were first manufactured. The sharply angled bases of the hewn birch timbers at the base of the platform on the site proves the efficiency of these early wood-cutting tools. The microliths belong predominantly to the class of obliquely blunted points up to 4cm in length. To be effective weapons these small points must have been set into a wooden or bone shaft as tips or barbs. There are also triangular-shaped microliths and some elongated trapezes, of which one had resin adhering to it, probably made from birchbark rendered down to a glue. At least some of these microliths were made by notching a small blade that had been retouched to the desired shape and snapping off the unwanted ends or microburins, 15 of which were recovered from the site. The large number of burins, predominantly of the angle type, were most probably used in the removal of the splinters of antler, by the groove and splinter technique mentioned above. Frequently the cores were turned to further practical use after they were too small to produce more blades or flakes, by being made into small scrapers.

Some of the most interesting finds from Star Carr were a series of stag frontlets, with part of the antlers still attached (fig. 2.20). The interiors of the skulls had been hollowed as if to lighten the weight of bone, and it was suggested that the frontlets had been used as masks, either during hunting or ceremonial occasions. A similarly hollowed frontlet of red deer, probably dating from the early postglacial period, was found at the

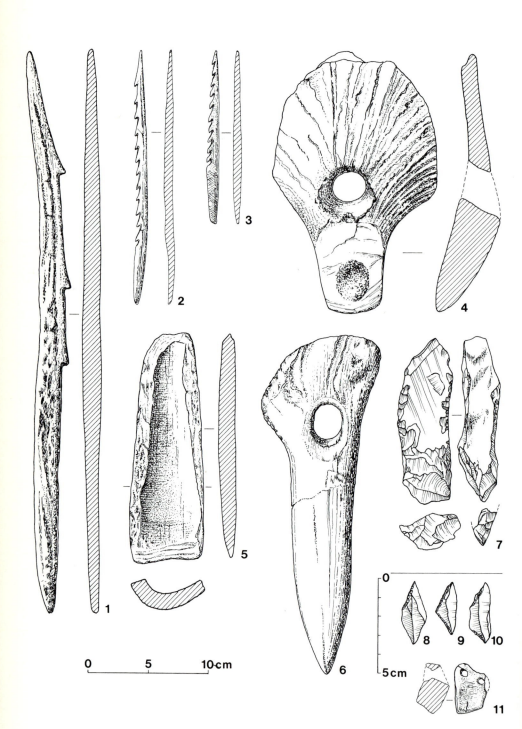

0   5   10 cm

Fig. 2.21 Antler, stone and amber artifacts from Star Carr. 1 barbed point from upper level; 2, 3 barbed points from lower level; 4, 6 perforated mattock heads made respectively from a shed elk antler and from an antler with attached bone from a slain elk; 5 tool made from a portion of aurochs femur with flaked side and polished edge, used probably for leather-working; 7 flint axe; 8–10 microlithic arrowtips; 11 perforated amber bead (after Clark J. G. D. 1972).

Fig. 2.22 Britain in relation to the continent of Europe when sea level was 20 fathoms (36·6m) lower than today (after Clark J. G. D. 1972).

 1 Star Carr
 2 Skipsea
 3 Broxbourne
 4 Leman and Ower
 5 Klosterlund
 6 Duvensee
 7 Hohen Viecheln
 8 Mullerup
 9 Vig
10 Holmegaard
11 Svaerdborg
12 Ageröd
13 Låmmasmägi Kunda

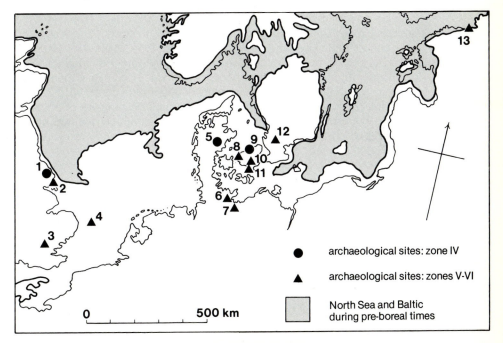

German mesolithic site of Biesdorf (Reinbacher 1956) and another fragment from Hohen Viecheln (Schuldt 1961). The material from this site belongs to the cultural group known as the Maglemosian (fig. 2.19), and it is to the same group that Star Carr and a wide range of other sites in the British Isles, Scandinavia and north-west Europe belong in general terms (Clark J. G. D. 1975: esp. 100ff.). Star Carr is a fairly early example (with radiocarbon dates of $7,607 \pm 210$ and $7,538 \pm 350$ bc), but there are earlier occupation dates from Thatcham, Berkshire ($8,415 \pm 170$ bc).

Thatcham is also an area where Maglemosian hunters established a series of camps at the edge of a lake and exploited the surrounding forests as well as the lake and the immediate vicinity. There are a number of other sites from which the typical Maglemosian assemblage of artifacts has been recovered, but usually with little other evidence of environment, settlement or the more interesting aspects of these early postglacial hunters and gatherers. The distribution of sites of this period in Britain is shown in fig. 2.23. Most of the sites shown are in river valleys or low-lying areas, with a scatter of peripheral sites on the uplands to the west.[12] One of the sites marked is that of Deepcar, Yorkshire (Radley and Mellars 1964), which is situated at the end of a small spur between the rivers Don and Porter, again probably overlooking a lake. Here a settlement pattern was exposed consisting of areas of hearths and concentrations of artifacts inside a roughly circular hollow area, edged on one side by a line of quartzite blocks, lined by another row of rounded gritstones (fig. 2.24). The total area was not available for excavation but it appeared to represent a hut structure, possibly supporting a superstructure of skins and timbers, with areas of the interior levelled up by local sandstone flags. Similar circular arrangements of stones from sites in Schleswig Holstein were interpreted by Rust as the stones that were used to stretch and weigh the guys from simple skin and timber tents (Rust 1956: Abb. 41). The flint types recovered from Deepcar appear to fit within the Maglemosian tradition, although there is an absence of all small geometric microliths, only one rather dubious axe and no bone or antler tools at all (fig. 2.25). As such this restricted assemblage suits the immediate category of a 'broad bladed' Pennine industry dominated by simple obliquely blunted points and scrapers. In south-western Britain there are other industries such as those from Dozmare Pool and Middlezoy (Wainwright G. J. 1960) where although the full range of the Maglemosian assemblage is not present the artifacts can all be fitted within the typological range.

The later mesolithic of Britain: Scotland and Ireland

It seems clear that the 'narrow bladed' Pennine industry developed later in time; in fact there seems to have been a general increase in the variety of types and techniques used by the mesolithic hunters and gatherers around the beginning of the 7th millenium,[13] sufficient to make R. M. Jacobi (1973; 1976) state that, in his opinion, there were probably only two valid sub-groups in the British mesolithic assemblages: those of the earlier mesolithic and those of the later mesolithic, characterized by these new narrow microlithic forms, although the earlier types already

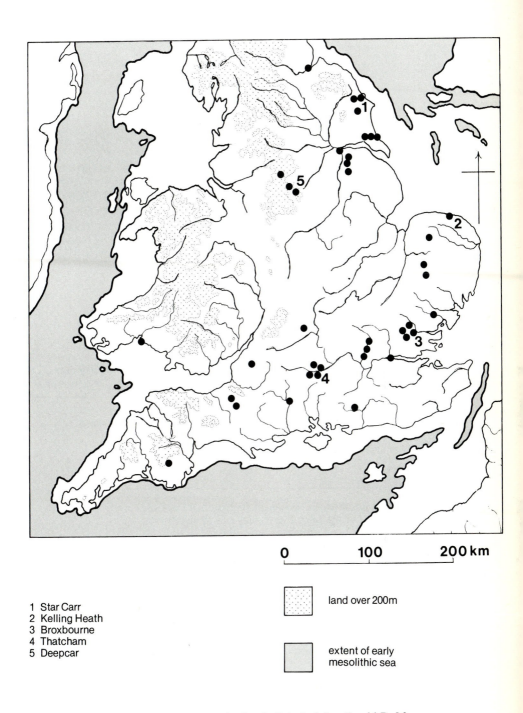

0   100   200 km

1 Star Carr
2 Kelling Heath
3 Broxbourne
4 Thatcham
5 Deepcar

land over 200m

extent of early
mesolithic sea

Fig. 2.23.   Distribution of early mesolithic sites in Britain (after Jacobi R. M. 1973).

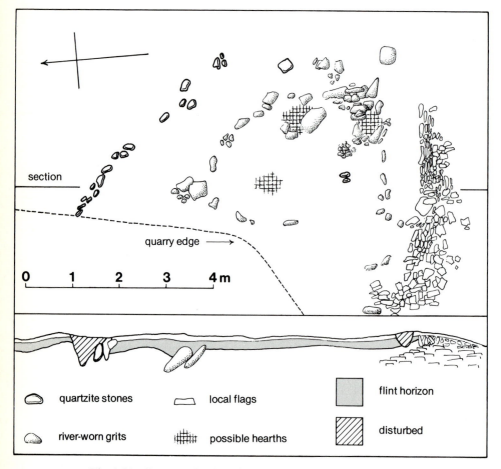

Fig. 2.24   Deepcar, Yorks.: the distribution of local and foreign stone on the northern half of the site (after Radley and Mellars 1964).

Fig. 2.25   Artifacts from Deepcar. 1–5 obliquely blunted points; 6–9 fragmentary pieces; 10 truncated blade fragment; 11–12 scrapers; 13 burin; 14 core; possibly well-worked tranchet core axe (after Radley and Mellars 1964).

established were not discarded. The new types include scalene triangles, narrow microliths, rhomboids and crescents. Sites containing this range of finds, for example the site from Shippea Hill, Cambridgeshire (Clark J. G. D. 1955) have previously been labelled 'of Sauveterrian affinities' because they contain some Sauveterrian types. Jacobi, however, suggests that the affinities may as well lie with the microlithic industries of Belgium and Holland in the 7th and 6th millennia bc as with the true French Sauveterrian industries, and that it is certainly not possible to identify any of the British later mesolithic industries very closely to one particular continental background.

In 1955 J. G. D. Clark published a series of sites under the cultural label of 'of Sauveterrian affinities'. The major site was Peacock's Farm, Shippea Hill, Cambridgeshire. Here geometric microliths were associated with pollen dating from zone VIc, immediately previous to the great rise in alder pollen that occurred at the beginning of the Atlantic period, zone VII (table 1.2). The landscape would still have been dominated by pine with stands of elm, lime and oak. The microliths, made on narrow blades, included obliquely blunted points and geometric forms, such as scalene triangles and crescents, types battered down the whole of one side and sometimes also across the base. Some microburins were found, a few convex scrapers and five angle burins, but no axes (fig. 2.26). It has become increasingly clear that most continental cultural labels are of very limited value in the study of the hunting-gathering communities of the British Isles and tend to confuse the relationships instead of clarifying

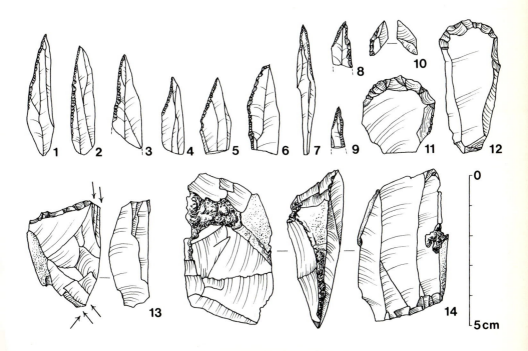

them. This is not to deny that there are strong links between British and continental communities, but interpretation through a model of adaptation to environmental conditions and exploitation of the available raw materials within a territory or zone does seem to make more archaeological sense than trying to superimpose strict continental parallels on to the British stone artifacts (Mellars 1976a; compare Kosłowski 1976).

One factor of importance at this time was the formation of the British Isles, splitting away from their continental link. Obviously the rising sea levels decreased the available land surface and must have increased the need to exploit zones further inland and to increase also the efficiency of the exploitive techniques already in use. Certainly the number and density of mesolithic sites in the British Isles increases from the mid-7th millennium bc onwards, but this cannot be interpreted as a straight rise in population numbers (cf. Brothwell 1972: esp. 79f.). Vast areas of previously swampy ground and forested hunting localities were replaced by open sea or marshy sea shore. The final forming of the Channel has been dated to about 6,500 bc. Continuing coastal erosion, especially along the south coast, has removed further traces of sea shore mesolithic communities existing since that time. Material from Blashenwell, Dorset (Rankine 1961), and Westward Ho!, Devon, shows considerable use of shore resources as well as continued hunting of inland fauna. The kitchen midden at Westward Ho! shows the food waste and environmental

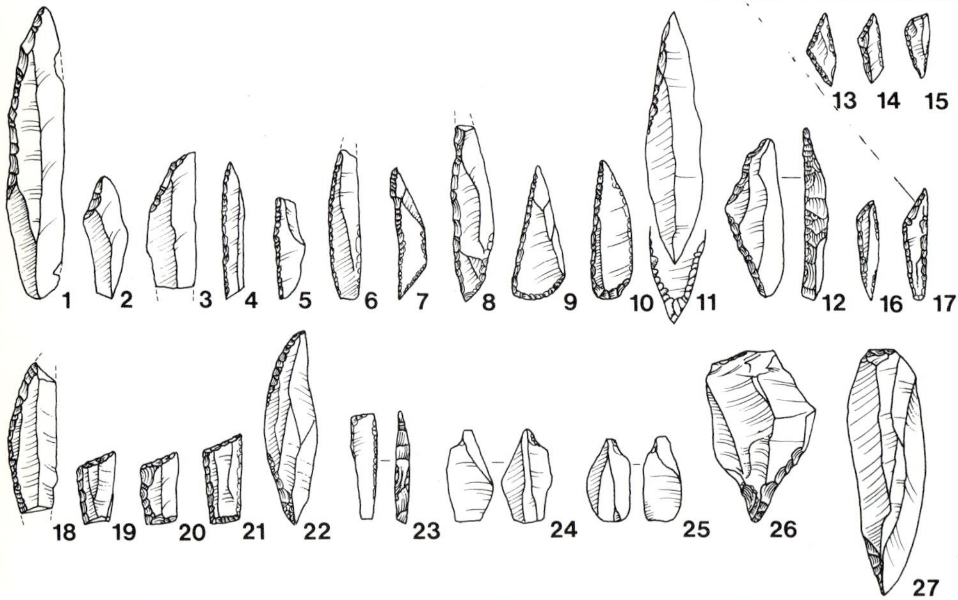

Fig. 2.26   Artifacts from Shippea Hill, Cambs. 1-3 obliquely blunted points; 4–6 types with battered backs; 7–11 types with basal retouch; 12 isosceles triangle; 13–17 scalene triangles; 18 crescent; 19–21 trapezoids; 22–3 trapezes; 24–5 microburins; 26 awl; 27 retouched flake; 28 double-ended angle burin; 29 angle burin; 30 convex scraper; 31 burin; 32 core scraper; 33 core; 34 core rejuvenation or trimming flake (after Clark J. G. D. 1955).

conditions at a period of time probably immediately prior to the radiocarbon date obtained from peat over the top (4,635 ± 130 bc). The site was then at sea level and was covered by peat soon after the accumulation. The molluscs include oyster (*Ostrea edulis*), mussel (*Mytilus edulis*), limpet (*Patella* sp.), winkle (*Littorina littorea*) and *Purpurea lapillus* and *Scrobicularia plana*. Many of these species inhabit the intertidal zones. Animal bone includes red or fallow deer, wild pig, rodents and hedgehog. The pollen in the midden was dominated by oak, hazel and ivy, which seems to indicate dry fenwood conditions. Many other coastal groups existed round the shores of the British Isles during the later part of the mesolithic occupation. There are examples from Cornwall, Wales, Scotland (Coles 1963a) and Ireland. The Oronsay midden sites contain good evidence (Mellars and Payne 1971) for the exploitation of the sea shore (crab, limpet, periwinkle, dog whelk, oyster and lobster), as well as shallow water fishing, carried on maybe with spear or nets, judging by the bones of saithe with some wrasse and ling. These sites are associated with the long-established Obanian artifacts (Clark J. G. D. 1955-6), which include long parallel-sided stone tools probably used for the removal of limpets and other shells from the rocks, hammerstones, and some scrapers and burins and a series of rather small bone and antler harpoons (fig. 2.27). Radiocarbon dates from the middens put their use in the 4th millennium bc (Mellars 1974: 91-92).

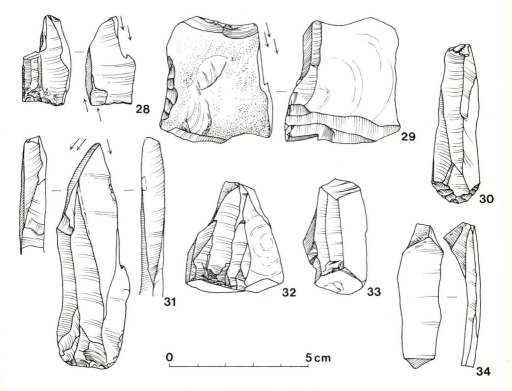

0   5 cm

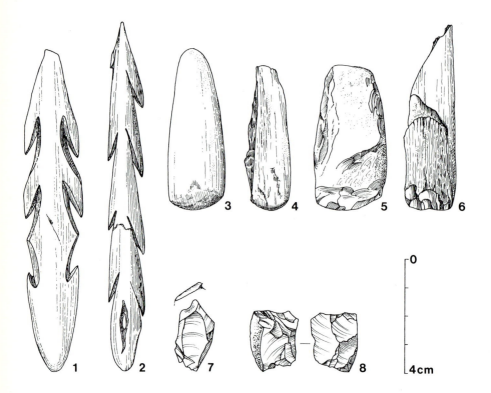

Fig. 2.27   Stone and bone artifacts from the Obanian middens, Scotland (after Clark J. G. D. 1932a).

Fig. 2.28   Morton on Tay: plan of occupation II at T47 *et al.*, with sleeping-place marked by oblong of stake-holes, with other stake-holes set apart, hearth and scatter of artifacts within and to the east of the shelter. Date: 4,840 bc ± 150 bc (with occupation III). Microlithic and other stone tool types from Morton are shown beneath the plan: 1–4 curved retouch; 5–13 various triangles; 14–18 end scrapers (grey flint: 2, 6, 15, 17; brown flint: 8, 16; chert: 4, 7, 10, 11, 13, 18; chalcedony: 9, 12; mudstone: 3, 14; carnelian: 5) (after Coles 1971a).

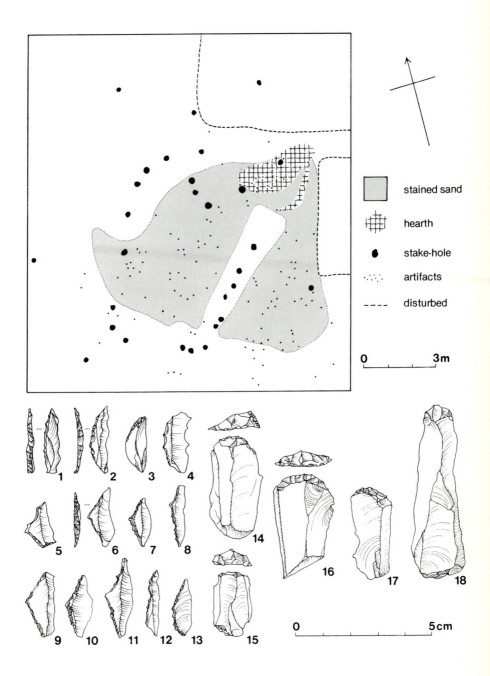

Further to the south and east in Scotland several coastal sites have been found where beach flint was used to manufacture a range of microliths (both obliquely blunted and geometric forms), as well as awls, burins and scrapers. Morton on Tay, just south of Dundee, Fife, supplies excellent evidence of early mesolithic adaptation to the postglacial environment of east coast Scotland (Coles 1971a). The earliest dates indicate that the site, on a promontory, was in use fairly soon after the beginning of the major Scottish postglacial marine transgression, which is estimated to have occurred between about 6–4,000 bc. By the end of occupation ($4,197 \pm 90$ and $4,432 \pm 120$ bc) the site was probably an island cut off from the mainland by about 1km of water, and probably surrounded by much salt water marsh. Very high densities of worked stones were found but these had been disturbed by erosion and ploughing. The first settlement seems to have occurred about 6,000 bc and the last about 4,200 bc. Due to the factors above it was not possible to separate discrete groups of artifacts and therefore the finds probably represent the material culture and debris left after visits to the site by hunting and collecting parties over 1,000 years. A wide variety of activities and occupations can be traced including flint working, possible skin and wood working, shell collecting, food preparation and cooking. There are a number of individual sites which probably represent small seasonal temporary camping sites, leaving hearths, stake-holes, manuports (material brought to the site by man but not deliberately shaped), stained and discoloured soils and artifacts (fig. 2.28). There is no evidence of sustained, intensive occupation but the material seems to be the 'accumulation of sporadic, temporary and interrupted occupations of parts of the promontory by very small numbers of people, considered not to be more than ten persons at any one time' (Coles 1971a: 293).

The raw material for the artifacts derives from the coastal flints of east Fife, the chalcedony and other minerals come from the Lower Old Red Sandstone lavas outcropping south of the Firth of Tay, and other rocks such as quartzite, schist and silicified limestone could have been collected from the glacial gravels of the locality. All these sources of raw material must have lain within the territory of the hunting gathering groups making use of Morton. There are many cores, primary flakes and bashed lumps in the collections. Of the total of flaked stones (about 13,500) over 1,000 show secondary working and a further 1,500 show signs of utilization, which is a surprisingly high proportion compared to other mesolithic sites in Britain. The size and shape of the tool types present reflect the variety of the raw material, but there were a number of round, thumbnail-shaped scrapers, short double-ended flake scrapers, large utilized flakes, irregular burins, a range of microliths including obliquely blunted, triangular and curved, and a few microburins. Coles has not assigned the assemblage to any one cultural group as previously defined, due to the length of the occupation that has obviously caused changing material to be incorporated into the finds. Evidence for specific activities, such as butchery, comes from sheltered Site B, where a long shell midden yielded large quantities of shell and bone refuse and some stone artifacts. Separate floors or accumulations were noticed in the midden build-up, so that a late visit to the site has resulted in bones from red deer, codfish, halibut, guillemot, cormorant and thrush associated with some bone tools, bashed lumps of stone, and primary flakes and flaked stone tools. Shell remains, sometimes directly associated with hearths, have included a wide variety of limpets, periwinkles, cockles, pelican's foot, necklace shell, dog whelk, common mussel, venus shell, Baltic tellin, trough shell and common otter shell. This wide variety of shell reflects varying seasonal conditions along the nearby beaches and river mouths. All can still be found in the locality on rocky and sandy shores, some preferring brackish water or offshore gravel. These migratory bands of hunters and collectors were, however, not only exploiting the sea resources at Morton. Bones of red deer, cattle and wild pig must have come from successful hunts in the open woodland inland from the site, hedgehog and vole from more covered surroundings. The kills seem to have been made in the locality as the carcasses appear to have been butchered on the site. Sea bird remains not unnaturally dominate, while fish include cod (available in inshore waters in late winter and early spring), salmon and sturgeon. The latter could have been caught in the river mouths by spearing or trapping. Boats would certainly have been necessary for the cod fishing and probably were in general use. A dugout canoe (dated to the mid-7th millennium) found beneath the Carse clays at Friarton, Perthshire, in 1880 was probably of the type known and used by the people camping at Morton (Geikie 1880).

Plant remains included a variety of grasses, such as knotgrass, fat hen and chickweed, all weeds from waste land that were used in later prehistoric contexts as food (for example in the stomach contents of the iron age corpse from Tollund, Denmark). Population estimates are complex (cf. Brothwell 1972) but Coles has calculated that from the areas used, the quantity of food refuse present and the length of time involved, possibly a party of 12 persons could have camped on the site for an average of 13 days a year. In total this site presents a picture of the wide exploitation of a territory covering various environmental niches by a small hunting gathering group at all seasons of the year.[14]

Until recently it was thought that the earliest occupation of Ireland belonged to a relatively late stage of the mesolithic, but recent excavations carried out by Peter Woodman at the site of Mount Sandel in the valley of the river Bann have brought to light a series of occupations dated by radiocarbon to between 7,000 and 6,500 bc (Woodman 1973–4, esp. 15; 1977; in press).[15] The mesolithic population of Mount Sandel built a succession of substantial hut-like structures on a promontory overlooking the flood-plain of the river, evidently revisited over a period of several hundred years. The large number of hazel-nut shells suggests autumn occupation while pits associated with these structures may have been used for the storage of food supplies over the winter months; they yielded a large number of fragmentary bones, largely fish and pig and including hare, bird and a little red deer. Indeed the Irish mesolithic seems to have been dominated by a riverine and coastal fishing economy. Typologically, the Mount Sandel industry appears to bear a close resemblance to the later

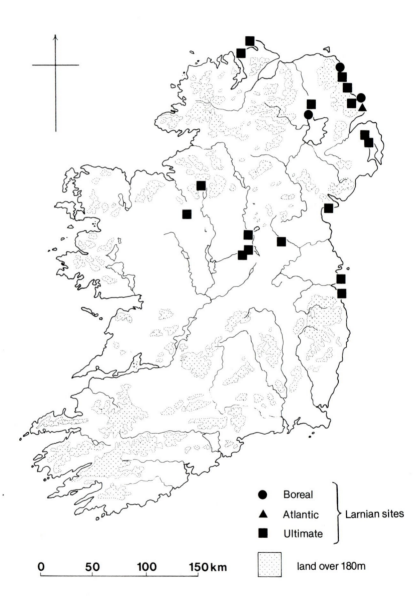

Fig. 2.29   Distribution of Larnian sites in Ireland (after Mitchell, *Ulster Journal of Archaeology 33*, 1970).

mesolithic 'narrow blade' industries of England, characterized by abundant small 'geometric' shapes of microliths manufactured on neat, regular blades. The very early dating assigned to the industry (which includes flake and core axes) provides further confirmation that this distinctive technological pattern was well established over large areas of Britain by the early part of the 7th millennium bc. The later stages of the Irish mesolithic are represented by the industries to which the term 'Larnian' has generally been applied (Mitchell 1971), the classic heavy industries as found on the sand banks of Newferry, Co. Antrim (figs. 2.29, 2.30); radiocarbon dates now extend back to the mid-6th millennium bc. At Toome Bay, Co. Londonderry, one nosed scraper, one triangular point, pieces of worked wood and charcoal were contained in Boreal peat, giving a date of 5,730 bc (no standard deviation published). Mitchell has suggested that one possible explanation of some of the Irish mesolithic tool types, previously thought to have been independently flaked after removal from the parent core, is in fact that to the mesolithic knapper they have been 'no more than debitage produced in large quantities' (Mitchell 1971: 280). The majority of Irish mesolithic material comes from rather later in time, about 3,500 bc, which is in fact probably contemporary with the arrival and influence of the earliest farmers. One possible explanation for the apparent gap in the sequence may be due to the increasing rise in sea level, causing the Irish Channel to widen and become far more hazardous, possibly even becoming an almost total barrier for mesolithic water transport (on the limitations of early water transport amongst hunter-gatherers compare Jones R. M. 1976: esp. 260f.). The boats of the first agriculturalists from the Continent were sufficiently strong to withstand the rigours of both the Channel and the Irish Channel and perhaps these first farmers traded with the remaining mesolithic communities, at sites such as Dalkey Island or Ballynagilly, where the first forest clearance seems to have occurred about 3,200 bc.[16]

The latest mesolithic of Britain

The mesolithic communities of southern Britain continue into the 5th and possibly the 4th millennium bc. Along the south coast a series of mesolithic artifacts made out of Portland chert (first used by the later upper palaeolithic hunters on Hengistbury Head) are dated at Blashenwell, Isle of Purbeck, to 4,500 ± 150 bc (Palmer S. 1970), and the flaked, pointed 'Portland Picks' have now been dated at Culver Well, Dorset, to 5,200 ± 135 bc, and so are definitely of mesolithic manufacture. This level – in a midden – also contained limpet and winkle shells, charcoal, burnt stones, some geometric microliths (including scalene triangles and sub-triangular forms) and seven tranchet axe trimming flakes (Palmer S. 1976).

In the northerly parts of Britain characteristic mesolithic assemblages may have continued into use as late as the 3rd millennium bc, presumably indicating a chronological overlap between the latest mesolithic and earliest agricultural communities in these areas. At the site of Lussa River on Jura, for example, a characteristic mesolithic industry dominated by small triangular and rod-like forms has been dated by two radiocarbon determinations of $2,670 \pm 140$ and $2,250 \pm 100$ bc (Mercer J. 1971). It remains to be seen how far discoveries in other parts of Britain bear out the pattern of a substantial mesolithic–neolithic overlap implied by these datings.

In southern England (both eastern and central) a new class of microliths appears with the extended range of narrow geometric types; these are the asymetrical, hollow-based points, often known as the Horsham point. At Farnham, Surrey (Clark and Rankine 1939), these microliths were associated with shelters that had been sunk slightly in the ground and presumably covered with a light superstructure of timber and skins. At Oakhanger, Hampshire, Horsham points, although present, are very rare and the majority of the microliths are obliquely blunted points and other types occurring in the earlier mesolithic sites. However, the radiocarbon dates from halzelnut shells in the main occupation level (phase III) – in which geometric microliths are absent – at 4,350 and $4,430 \pm 120$ bc (Rankine and Dimbleby 1960) are two of the latest dates for mesolithic occupation in the British Isles, outside the Irish dates already mentioned[17] (fig. 2.31). Similar in date is one of several sites at Wawcott in the Kennet Valley, site III (Froom 1976: $4,170 \pm 134$ bc). The stone industry has affinities with such sites as Farnham and Iping Common, Sussex (Keef *et al.* 1965), and is considered by the excavator to show a progression from 'Maglemosian' to Horsham industries. At Wawcott XXIII, a site marked mainly by scalene triangles, there is an overlapping date of 3910 ± 113 bc. Dimbleby suggests that in the last phase of mesolithic occupation at Oakhanger there is increasing destruction of the forest cover and as at some other sites such as Iping Common, mesolithic communities all over the British Isles were beginning to show the massive potential powers of destruction, alteration and manipulation by which they could influence their natural environment. Undoubtedly, hunting and gathering communities can cause immense changes, through tree clearance, of the particular forms of plant or animal resource (Mellars 1976c). The fairly abrupt introduction to the British Isles of domesticated plants (wheat, barley etc.) and animals (such as sheep and goats) may have produced a quickening effect on the changes to the existing environment within the British Isles (Smith A. G. 1970b), but man had been exerting a positive force, for good or bad, on the effective face of the countryside ever since he had existed there.[18]

Notes

1. This may be only a temporary state of knowledge as there are intriguing possibilities from the Keilor terraces near Melbourne, Victoria, that earlier forms of men (up to 50,000 years ago) may have been present in Australia,

Fig. 2.30   1–9 flint objects including tranchet axeheads of Movius's Late Larnian type from Cushenden, Larne, Glenarm, Island Magee; 10–12 and 26–31 objects of flint and wood from Toome Bay, Co. Antrim, and Sutton, Co. Dublin; 13–25 flints of Movius's Early Larnian type from Cushenden, Rough Island and Island Magee.

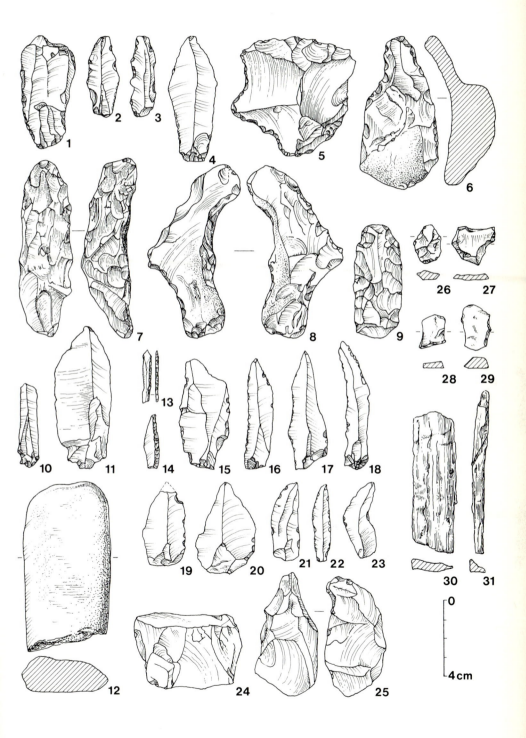

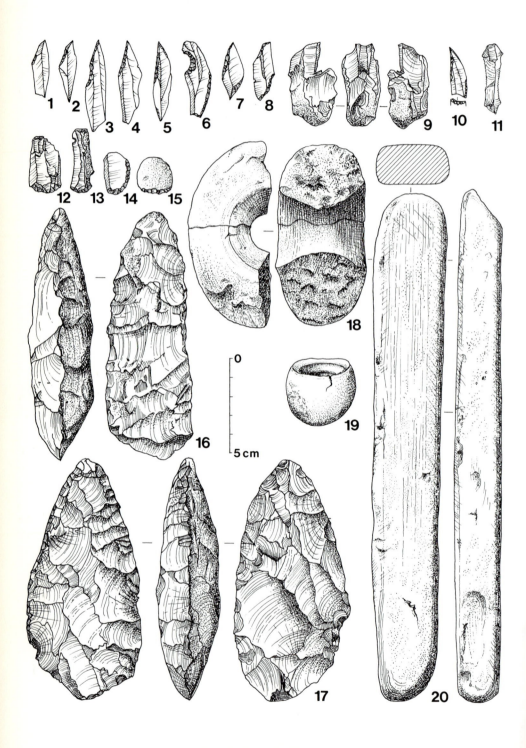

implying much earlier sea crossings (cf. Mulvaney 1975: 128ff.; Bowler 1976: 59ff.); even earlier dates are announced from Western Australia.

2. B. S. Johns has pointed out that there is at least the possibility of error from unknown contamination in the 'Red Lady of Paviland' date. However, opinions generally seem to accept that it is within the bounds of possibility that Paviland and other neighbouring caves were in fact in use for short visits, even at the period of intense glacial activity about 16,500 bc (Bowen D. Q. 1970 and Johns 1971; see also Molleson 1976).

3. For a clear explanation with simple illustrations of the stone tool types found in the upper palaeolithic industries see Bordaz 1970. There are also useful illustrations in the plates at the end of Oakley 1968b.

4. Campbell suggests that there may be a seasonal movement between the south-western sites and those in the north along the lines of the suggested seasonal shift between the central German Magdalenian sites and those further north belonging to the contemporary Hamburgian groups (see also Clarke D. V. 1976). Recent work on Jura has revealed a late Pleistocene industry of tanged points dated to 11,000 bc.

5. These artifacts were most probably used as arrow-shaft straighteners.

6. There are now radiocarbon dates going back to nearly 8,000 bc for bone and antler associated with Creswellian points, straight backed blades and burins of the typical later upper palaeolithic types from Anston Cave, Yorkshire. This has been published as a Creswellian site by Mellars (1969).

7. For example, Campbell in fact does not think that such sites as Brigham Hill, Yorkshire represent later upper palaeolithic material at all, but classes it together with Star Carr as early mesolithic. Manby (1966a) published the site as belonging to the Creswellian industry.

8. A tranchet edge is defined by J. G. D. Clark (1932a: xxii) 'as applying to tools of which the cutting edge is formed by the intersection of two or more flake surfaces. In the case of a core tool the edge is obtained by a special blow struck transversely at one corner of the extremity'.

9. There are certain plants that do not appear in postglacial Ireland and these include *Tibia cordata, Fagus sylvatica* and *Carpinus betula*.

10. Buckley in the 1920s referred to the 'broad and narrow bladed' industries of the Pennine mesolithic assemblages (Buckley 1921; 1924). These groups have been used by Radley and Mellars (1964) in their discussion on the affinities of the Deepcar and other Pennine mesolithic assemblages. The broad bladed group has a restricted range of microliths without geometric forms, whereas the later narrow bladed tradition sites can occur in which there are no obliquely blunted points present at all.

11. Mellars (1976c) has recently drawn attention to the possible deliberate use of fire by mesolithic man to increase and control animal stock, a method employed by the now extinct Tasmanian Aboriginals. Other aspects of deliberate 'harvesting' of animals are to be seen at Star Carr with the selective culling of male red deer, while at Oakhanger and other sites in southern Britain and Switzerland there is evidence for the deliberate harvesting of ivy as winter fodder (Simmons and Dimbleby 1974). Such pre-neolithic indications

Fig. 2.31 Artifacts from Oakhanger. 1–5 obliquely blunted points; 6 notched backed blade; 7–8 rhomboid points; 9 burin; 10 Horsham point; 11 saw; 12–15 flake scrapers; 16–17 trachet axes; 18 sarsen stone macehead with hour-glass perforation; 19–20 carstone cup and pebble rubber (after Rankine and Dimbleby 1960).

of 'farming' activities have clear parallels in the final palaeolithic and mesolithic of the Near East (cf. Legge 1977).

12. Jacobi explains the break in distribution between Cambridge and Lincoln as due to late infilling of the Wash and Fen areas, possibly covering sites of the earlier mesolithic period.

13. On the Hebridean island of Jura an industry of trapezes and scalene triangles is dated to around 6,000 bc.

14. Although the climatic and therefore the ecological conditions are obviously totally different, there are some interesting broad environmental parallels to be made with the recent work by Drs Betty Meehan and Rhys Jones amongst the Aboriginal hunters and gatherers on the coast of Arnhem Land, Northern Territory, Australia (Meehan 1977 and Jones R. M. 1978).

15. A further study which will fill out the hitherto brief reviews of the mesolithic in Ireland is in production (Woodman, in press).

16. Possibly the farmers were providing an outlet for the products of the local hunting and gathering populations, allowing for a marked increase in the number of sites of the Ultimate Larnians. 'Here for a short time, before being absorbed into the neolithic way of life, they flourished as specialised fishermen, catching and smoking fish in large quantities' (Mitchell 1971: 282). Study of evidence for early hunter-gatherers and farming communities outside north-western Europe, however, shows how much the two types of economy may overlap (cf. Megaw 1977).

17. In the view of Jacobi the large number of convex scrapers on this site, as against the smaller numbers of microliths, saws and axes, might present an argument here for the continued retention of the early mesolithic assemblages for a very specialized function in later periods. For example the Oakhanger site may have been used as an autumn skin preparation site. There may also be the possibility that the radiocarbon dates were too young, due to recent humus that could have been absorbed into the samples (Jacobi R. M. 1973: 238).

18. The whole body of knowledge about the upper palaeolithic and mesolithic industries of the British Isles is expanding at the time of writing with the publication of several theses concerned with the analysis of the material. This means perhaps even more than for later periods of British prehistory that many of the well-established ideas still in wide use stand a good chance of being superseded by more up-to-date work in the next few years.

3 The first agricultural communities (c. 3,500–2,500 bc)

Introduction

Radiocarbon dates now suggest that the earliest agricultural communities crossed from the continental landmass to settle in the British Isles in the middle of the 4th millennium bc. Of necessity they brought with them the seed corn and the flocks and herds which were to establish the first neolithic agrarian and agricultural economy in this country. Though the ancestry and origins of the wild forms of both plants and animals which form the composition of this agricultural economy lie ultimately in the Near East and in western Asia (Bender 1975) one may safely assume that those communities who first settled with these techniques in the British Isles came from the shores of the continental European landmass immediately bordering the English Channel and the North Sea. In view, too, of the vulnerability of the standing and growing crops and also of the dependence on winter fodder for stock it would appear most unlikely that such cross-Channel movements by primitive agriculturalists would have taken place other than in the three months of August, September and October after the harvest and before the necessity to gather in fodder for the animals during the winter months. We may further postulate that the movements into Britain of these first farmers were in the form of small communities rather than large-scale settlements by large numbers of individuals. Case (1969a) has argued convincingly that the mode of transport used by these primitive farmers was probably the skin boat whose existence is well attested by the Norwegian rock carvings of the Scandinavian stone age; he suggests a type of boat similar to that of the Eskimo umiak, which also survives in north-western Europe in a distant related form in the curragh of the west coast of Ireland. For such skin boats a maximum length of about 9m appears to apply and it would have been capable of carrying some three tons of cargo, crew, passengers and stores. Case suggests that with a crew of eight and one steersman such a skin boat would carry 3–4 cattle, or 15 pigs, or 25 sheep or goats. Although such skin boats are extremely sea-worthy vessels, by their very nature they are open boats which would make seed corn extremely vulnerable to soaking; also animals – cattle, sheep, pigs and goats – could only be carried in a thrown position, under which circumstances it would be extremely difficult to feed and water them. In view of these limitations it appears most likely that the early voyages by agriculturalists to the British Isles involved comparatively short journeys, thus reducing the dangers to the corn and also limiting the period, of necessity extremely short, in which animals could be carried in a tied position and without food or water. One would think that given these conditions, the south and south-east parts of the British Isles, that area immediately adjacent to the Continent, would be the first to be settled. On the other hand, current radiocarbon dates suggest that a very wide area both in Britain and in Ireland was settled at approximately the same time, that is to say the middle of the 4th millennium bc.

Apart from the botanical and molluscan evidence for the interference in the environment by these first agriculturalists, the earliest indications of settlement by neolithic communities are those of the monuments which they erected. The majority of such sites are either ceremonial or funerary in character and it would appear most unlikely that the grandiose structures to be discussed below represent the products of the earliest agriculturalists to settle in this country. One must assume an initial period after the settlement of the British Isles in which all efforts were concentrated on the production of food and the increase in numbers both of herds and crops, when there would be little time available to devote to the construction either of major funerary monuments, ceremonial sites or even, perhaps, of substantial settlements. One may therefore reasonably assume that these earliest neolithic monuments for which there are radiocarbon dates do not in fact reflect the structures erected by the first, second, or even perhaps the third generation of agriculturalists to settle in this country. One must accept a period of adjustment and settlement before such times when communities could meet and collectively erect such outstanding structures as the megalithic tombs of the north and the west, the causewayed enclosures of southern and eastern Britain or, indeed, those great ceremonial ways or cursūs again found in the south and east of the British Isles.

In spite of the increasing evidence that both the highland and lowland zones of Britain were settled in the middle of the 4th millennium bc almost simultaneously, at least as far as radiocarbon dates indicate, it is still true that the most comprehensive picture one has for these early agricultural communities is that from southern and south-eastern Britain. This is, in part, an historical accident in that in this area there has been intensive archaeological research, both in field work and excavation, extending over some two centuries. In the lowland zone of Britain, roughly south and east of a line from the Wash to the Bristol Channel, the material remains of these early agriculturalists has been termed the Windmill Hill culture after a hilltop site near Avebury in Wiltshire where it was first recognized (fig. 3.2). The settlement pattern in this southern and south-eastern area shows a marked preference for chalk lands, suggesting that something more was sought than freedom from heavily wooded areas; in fact evidence is now increasing to suggest that the chalk lands supported a thick oak forest in the same way as the heavier clay soils of central England (Evans J. G. 1971b). It would therefore appear that the main attraction in these areas was the soil itself, light and readily cultivable by the implements at the disposal of these first agriculturalists.

Southern and south-eastern Britain: the Windmill Hill culture

The recognizable field monuments of the Windmill Hill culture fall into six major groups: causewayed enclosures, houses, flint mines, long barrows, long mortuary enclosures and possibly cursūs.

Causewayed enclosures   There are some 40 known examples of causewayed enclosures, 23 of which have been proved by excavation and the remainder located either by field work or by aerial photography (Smith I. F. 1971; Wilson 1975; Palmer R. 1976). The sites themselves are distributed as far west as Hembury in Devon and eastwards to Orsett in Essex, and the majority are still confined to the area south of the Thames Valley. The enclosures are frequently situated on hilltops although aerial reconnaissance has located a number of low-lying sites on river terraces (Selkirk 1977b). In plan the enclosures consist of roughly oval areas enclosed by from one to four concentric ditches with internal banks broken by numerous unexcavated causeways at frequent but irregular intervals.

The enclosures at Maiden Castle in Dorset and Knap Hill (Connah 1965) in Wiltshire have the banks and ditches following the contours of the hill (fig. 3.1: 5–6). In all other hilltop sites the banks and ditches run across the contours suggesting that the plans of the sites were laid out regardless of the local topography, the object being to produce an oval or circular enclosure rather than – as in the later hillforts – a defensive structure built to follow the lines of the hill. The tendency, too, for the ditches to run down the slopes suggests that the sites were placed to face in a particular direction. There appears, too, to be no correlation between size and complexity of plan: the largest and one of the most complex, Windmill Hill, has three lines of banks and ditches, and one of the smallest sites enclosing only three acres at Rybury in Wiltshire has four lines of banks and ditches. The enclosures vary from 365m, the maximum diameter at Windmill Hill, to 164·5m at Knap Hill (fig. 3.1: 2 and 5).

The ditches of the enclosures are normally flat-bottomed with almost vertical sides; presumably when dug these were in fact vertical. There is a tendency in sites of two or more concentric ditches for these to increase in depth from the innermost enclosure outwards. The interrupted construction of the ditches suggests gangs of labourers digging out individual sections rather than deliberate provision of numerous entrances. In many cases there are corresponding gaps in the banks opposite undug areas between the lengths of ditches but these may not be original. Cattle and sheep would tend to walk across the causeways and erode the banks, and one must bear in mind that the majority of the causewayed enclosures are in areas of downland which have been grazed by animals for some five millennia.

Only at Whitehawk in Sussex (Curwen 1934a; 1936) has a timber gate structure been recognized associated with one of the gaps in the bank. At this same site there appears too to have been posts set in the bank, possibly as a revetment, and similar structures may have existed at Hembury in Devon which were later thrown into the ditch and burnt (Smith I. F. 1971). At only two of the enclosures were any traces of timber-built

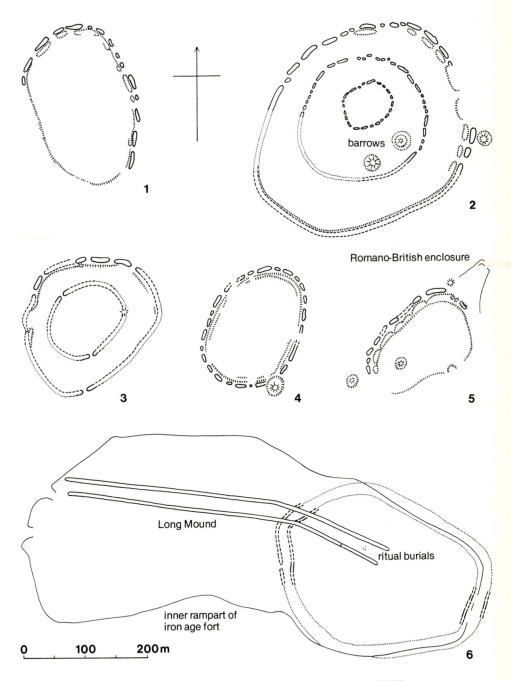

Fig. 3.1   Plans of causewayed enclosures. 1 Barkhale, Sussex; 2 Windmill Hill,
Wilts.; 3 Robin Hood's Ball, Wilts.; 4 Whitesheet, Wilts.; 5 Knap Hill, Wilts.; 6
Maiden Castle, Dorset (after Piggott S. 1954 and Crittall 1973).

structures found within the earthworks. At Hembury immediately within the post setting interpreted as a gateway was an oval or sub-rectangular hut 8·5m by 3·6m, defined by post-holes. At Windmill Hill excavations revealed a setting of posts which appeared to represent one end of a rectangular hut. The timber building here, however, appears to pre-date the earthworks and similar pre-enclosure occupation has been recovered from Robin Hood's Ball in Wiltshire (Thomas N. de L.' E. W. 1964). Other enclosures revealed in their interiors occasional pits containing rubbish and occupation material, but one must bear in mind the generally limited nature of excavations within the enclosures. A notable exception is the site at Staines in Middlesex where the whole of the area enclosed by a ditch contained a mass of pits, post-holes, gullies and hearths (Robertson-Mackay 1962). In no case was it possible to reconstruct or recognize possible house plans.

Although, therefore, there is little in the interior of the majority of the enclosures in the way of structures or traces of occupation, the ditches themselves in many cases produced large quantities of food remains, potsherds and flint and bone tools. Among the animal remains from the ditches there is an overwhelming preponderance of bones of cattle followed in quantity by pig, sheep or goat, dog and a comparatively small proportion of red and roe deer (Piggott S. 1954: 28). Amongst the cattle bones there is a high percentage of the remains of young animals implying perhaps the necessity to reduce the size of herds at the approach of winter owing to inadequate supplies of fodder to support large numbers of animals throughout the winter months. Many of the bones also show traces of knife cuts at points convenient for the removal of sinews from their attachments and other cuts associated with the removal of flesh and skin. On this evidence Piggott (1954) has suggested that the causewayed enclosures represented cattle kraals to which the herds belonging to a number of neighbouring small groups were brought in the autumn for the purposes of identification, barter and slaughter. Judging by the tools found in the ditches, skinning and dressing was also practised at this time. The size of the camps, Piggott suggested, implied some form of corporate activity in their construction and the conditions of agriculture prevailing at the time would certainly not have afforded the food necessary for a large permanent community living within these earthworks.

More recent work, however, particularly at Windmill Hill (Smith I. F. 1965), suggests that this interpretation is only partially correct and that although the camps almost certainly were occupied only seasonally in late autumn, they served as more than mere cattle kraals. This re-interpretation is based on the nature of the material and the manner of its occurrence in the ditches. In addition to the disarticulated remains of animals, many showing the bones being split to extract the marrow, there also are a number of burials of complete animals whose skeletons show none of the normal traces of dismemberment or knife cuts associated with skinning.

Fig. 3.2   Windmill Hill causewayed enclosure (photograph: Cambridge University Committee for Aerial Photography: Crown Copyright).

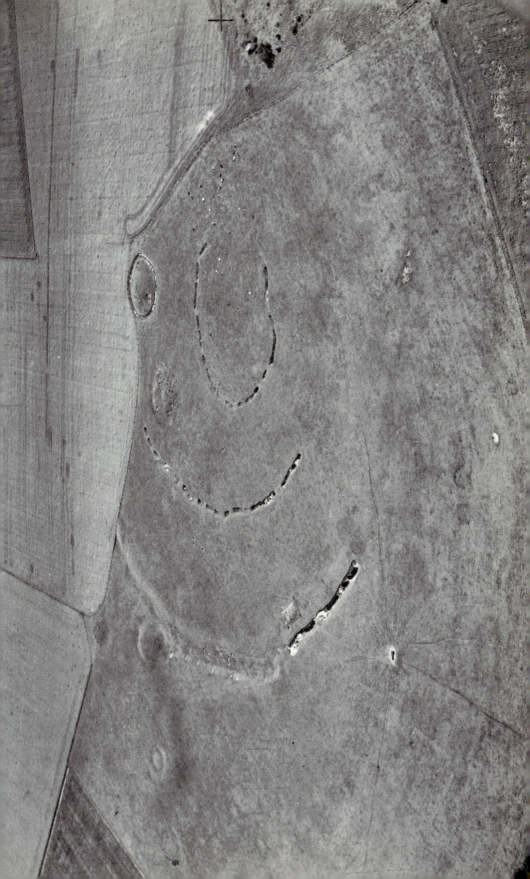

There is also the unusual nature of the bone deposits in the ditches themselves. These in some cases occur in layers more than 30cm thick extending for 6–9m horizontally along the length of the ditch. Immediately after these large deposits of animal bones were placed in the ditch they appear to have been covered by chalk rubble obtained by pushing a portion of the bank back into the ditch. This phenomenon is observable at a number of sites and notably at Windmill Hill, Hembury, Whitesheet, Staines, The Trundle and Whitehawk (fig. 3.3). None of the bones show any traces of having been gnawed by rodents or dogs, for whose presence there is ample evidence, for example at Windmill Hill. Both these features are distinctly odd. As one knows from the evidence of other neolithic sites both in Britain and the Continent early agricultural communities were not particularly given to hygiene and tidiness and normally lived in the midst of a squalid mass of occupation debris and food remains. The careful burial of large quantities of animal bones and of whole animals therefore suggests some form of ritual practice, in the case of whole animals an offering and in the case of food remains the aftermath perhaps of a ritual feast, or even a funerary function as implied by the human skull deposits in the ditches at Hambledon, Dorset (Selkirk 1975). Furthermore the occurrence in the ditches of the enclosures of pottery containing grits obtainable only many miles from the site – noticeably the gabbro wares of material obtained from the Lizard Head in Cornwall (Peacock 1969a) or tempered with oolite from the Bath–Frome region – and also the occurrence of axes of igneous rock from axe factories in both Cornwall and the Lake District all imply the coming together of peoples from a wide area to barter and also, judging by the animal bone evidence, to perform certain religious or magical ceremonies. The camps or enclosures would therefore be comparable to medieval fairs serving as religious, economic and social centres. Under such conditions the banks and ditches of the camp may be regarded simply as delimiting the area of the fair or meeting place and certainly even in early neolithic times the ditches of many of the enclosures would have been almost completely silted up, either naturally or artificially, and the banks greatly reduced by having much of the material thrown back into the ditches to cover the layers of animal bones. At this stage they could have formed only a symbolic barrier around the area of the enclosure itself.

However, one should perhaps be wary of interpreting the function of all causewayed enclosures as uniform, particularly in view of the considerable variation both in form and size of these earthworks and the varying situations in which they occur. At Knap Hill in Wiltshire, for example (Connah 1965), a univallate enclosure, the excavator suggested that the site may have been defensive and drew attention to the fact that the ditch enclosed part of the hill slope to reduce the area of dead ground. The second neolithic structure at Crickley Hill, Gloucestershire, with a broad and deep ditch and a stone revetted internal bank erected over the earlier and infilled causewayed ditch, is even more indicative of defence (Dixon 1972). Similarly, the low-lying situation of sites such as Abingdon and Staines and other sites in south-eastern Britain might again imply a slightly differing function for these monuments. The site at Hembury, too, must be set apart from the other causewayed enclosures since the interrupted bank and ditch in this case cuts off a promontory and is not a concentric earthwork as in normal causewayed enclosures.

Houses   Few houses of the Windmill Hill culture have been recorded, the best-known settlement being that at Haldon in Devon, 17 miles from the Hembury causewayed enclosure (Clark J. G. D. 1938). The site lies at a height of 244m above sea level on a subsoil of clay with flints. In spite of the unfavourable conditions it was possible to identify the foundations of a rectangular house with wall footings of stone in which were set the sockets for wooden uprights. Two posts along the axis suggest a gabled roof with an entrance at one corner of the building. There is a hearth delimited by a flanking wall in one corner of the hut. Within the structure were two occupation levels separated by a layer of sterile sand suggesting perhaps intermittent occupation of the building. In the vicinity of the

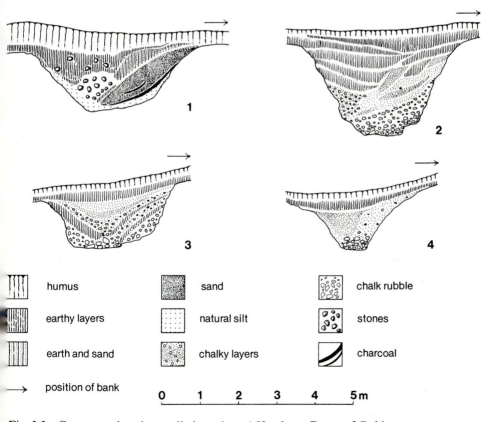

	humus		sand		chalk rubble
	earthy layers		natural silt		stones
	earth and sand		chalky layers		charcoal
→	position of bank				

0   1   2   3   4   5 m

Fig. 3.3   Causewayed enclosure ditch sections. 1 Hembury, Devon; 2 Robin Hood's Ball, Wilts.; 3 Windmill Hill, Wilts.; 4 Whitesheet, Wilts. (after Smith I. F. 1966 and 1971).

house were hearths and traces of occupation but no further buildings could be recognized.

At Clegyr Boia near St David's Head in Pembrokeshire was a settlement similar to that at Haldon. The main feature was a rectangular house built into an angle of the outcropping rock with two rows of four post-holes and stone footings on one of the long sides. Similar rectangular houses have been recorded at Fengate, Peterborough (Pryor 1974), and Llandegai, north Wales (Houlder 1968). This rarity of house structures presents a problem. That these agriculturalists were capable of building substantial monuments is well attested both in the funerary and ritual sites mentioned above and to be discussed below.

The few surviving house plans would suggest small social units based upon an isolated farmstead. An exception, so far unique at this period in the British Isles, is the hilltop site at Carn Brea, Cornwall. Here the eastern summit was defended by a substantial stone wall within which were a series of hut platforms. Associated with what appears to be a defensive structure were large quantities of early neolithic pottery. The discovery of several hundred leaf-shaped arrowheads, many broken, suggests that the site had indeed been subject to attack (Selkirk 1974a).

Why then are their domestic structures so few and far between? A number of theories have been volunteered to explain the absence or near absence of such settlement sites. A common explanation is that an agricultural community based on shifting cultivation would have little need or indeed little time to construct large and permanent dwelling sites. Again it has been suggested that archaeologists have been searching in the wrong places – on the tops of the Downs where in general both the barrows and causewayed enclosures lie, rather than in the valley bottoms where now more and more evidence suggests, and common sense would also indicate, that settlements would occur adjacent to water, essential both for man and livestock, and where game would be abundant. If this is so it is not surprising that few domestic sites have been recovered in view of the enormous accumulation of hill wash and other material that would have built up over the last 5,000 years in the valley bottoms over such settlement sites.

Settlement sites have however been inferred from the discovery of pits unassociated with any other structures (Field et al. 1964). These pits, which vary from 90 to 200cm in diameter and from 30 to 120cm in depth, are similar to the occasional pits which have been found inside causewayed enclosures and in such large numbers at the Staines site. The pits themselves, which occur either singly or in clusters, contain a variety of material including sherds, flint and bone tools, carbonized wood and general occupation debris. There is a notable concentration of such pits in the territory of the Windmill Hill culture, that is to say in southern and south-eastern Britain, and they are conspicuous by their absence or scarcity in highland zones of the north and north-west.

Because of the frequent occurrence of burnt material in the filling of such pits they have been interpreted from time to time as representing fire pits and hearths. On the other hand no pit so far excavated shows traces of burning actually on its sides. The burnt material must represent the debris of hearths and fires brought to the pits from some distance and therefore the secondary use of such pits once they had ceased to fulfil their original purpose. Because of their form and distribution I. F. Smith has suggested that such pits could represent disused storage pits almost certainly used for the collection of grain, and in one case, at Hembury, remains of carbonized grain – in this case spelt – were actually found in one of the pits within the enclosure. She further drew attention to the fact that the distribution of these neolithic pits has a very marked similarity to that of iron age grain storage pits, which again show a noticeable concentration in south-eastern Britain. She therefore postulated a contrasting economy in the lowland and highland zones of Britain: in the south and east a dependence on cereal growing and in the north and west, where such pits are extremely rare, an emphasis on stock raising and animal husbandry. It should be remembered however that the sub-soil in many areas of the north and west would be unsuitable for the excavation of such storage pits and neolithic farmers in these highland zones may have been obliged to find some other means of storing their grain above ground which would leave little or no trace in the archaeological record.

Flint mines   That the agricultural economy was sufficiently developed in southern Britain even in the early neolithic is suggested by the existence of at least one possible group of specialized craftsmen who could have only been supported from a surplus of agricultural produce. These are the flint miners.

The necessity for mining flint was dictated by the geology of the upper chalk in which the flint occurs in horizontal seams separated by intervening layers of barren chalk. Furthermore the superior nodules come from the deeper seams and this fact once appreciated led to the development of galleried mines in Norfolk and Sussex. Two main forms of mine occur: the first is an open-cast type consisting of a broad and shallow shaft exploiting the seams buried only a metre or two beneath the chalk, as for example at Harrow Hill in Sussex; the second, deep shafts from which radiate numerous horizontal galleries following the flint seams. The most famous of these mines is Grimes Graves in Norfolk where shafts up to 15m in depth occur (Sieveking *et al.* 1973).

Access to the pits was in some cases by steps cut in the side of the shaft but in the deeper pits there must have been some form of ladder, either a notched tree trunk or a rope. At Cissbury in Sussex the remains of a carbonized pole was found in the fill of a disused mine shaft. Further confirmation of the presence of a ladder came from Grimes Graves where at the bottoms of the shafts and in the galleries were found the skeletons of numerous voles and also antlers which had been gnawed by these rodents. If the latter had fallen into the shafts they would certainly have been killed and in fact they must have run down an existing ladder or pole.

After one mine shaft had been worked out others were dug in the immediate vicinity and the debris from these shafts was thrown into the disused mine. These disused and partially filled up mine shafts also appear to have been utilized by the miners as wind shelters and working areas, judging by the presence of fires and occupation debris in a number of them. The galleries were certainly lit in a number of cases; not only have soot marks been observed on the roofs but charcoal indicating burnt-out torches, and small chalk cups probably serving as fat lamps, have been found.

On all mining sites in the area of the shafts there appear to have been a large number of working places where flint nodules were chipped into implements. By far the most important but not necessarily the most numerous products of the mines were axes which must have been manufactured in enormous quantities. It is as yet not possible to work out with any degree of certainty the geographical limits of areas which were served by an individual mine, although work is proceeding on this subject. The small hoards of flint axes which have been found within the area of the Windmill Hill culture probably represent the exports from such a mining site.

At the base of one of the shafts at Grimes Graves was built up a pedestal of chalk blocks with a small chalk figurine representing an obese and pregnant woman with beside it a chalk phallus (fig. 3.9: 1). In front of this group was a pile of flint arranged in the form of a triangle with a chalk cup in the base of the triangle opposite the figurine. Seven antler picks lay on this flint 'altar'. This remarkable group represents one of the most positive pieces of evidence for primitive religion or magic in neolithic Britain. The figure is presumably that of a mother goddess or earth goddess and as the shrine was erected in a pit particularly poor in flint it may represent an appeal to the earth goddess for a more plentiful supply. Other more stylized and fragmentary figurines and phalli in chalk (fig. 3.9) have been recorded from a number of causewayed camps and there is a unique example in wood from Somerset (Coles 1968).

Apart from these rare cult objects the only other evidence for religious beliefs amongst the neolithic farmers is that of disposal of the dead. A number of casual burials have been found in the ditches of causewayed enclosures and the disused shafts of flint mines. In some cases these are represented by complete skeletons, in others only by fragments, particularly skull fragments, scattered amongst occupation debris and food remains. Cannibalism has been suggested to account for the fragmentary human remains mixed with other debris on domestic sites. A more likely and less dramatic explanation is that they represent the skulls and skeletal material removed from ritual and funerary sites of a type to be discussed below.

Apart from these casual burials and fragmentary human remains from flint mines and causewayed enclosures a number of flat graves have been recorded containing single inhumation burials, in some cases the grave being marked by a post (Piggott S. 1954: 48). At Pangbourne in Berkshire there was a complete inhumed skeleton of a female accompanied by her Abingdon bowl. At Handley Hill in Dorset the skeleton was disarticulated, again accompanied by fragments of pottery, while at Rushmore in Dorset only a pelvis and a flint axe were found in the pit. Similar burials of animals in flat graves, again in some cases marked by posts, have also been recorded. It is uncertain under such circumstances whether the important feature is the post, perhaps a totem pole, or the burial itself, the post serving only as a marker to the position of the flat grave. Such flat graves, however, are rare.

Long barrows and long mortuary enclosures   The most distinctive and characteristic form of burial is that beneath an earthen long barrow (Ashbee 1970) or more rarely oval barrow (Drewett 1975). These consist of great elongated mounds of chalk rubble and earth flanked by quarry ditches. Some 230 long barrows have been recorded within the territory of the Windmill Hill culture. A few examples have been found as far north as northern Norfolk but the major concentrations are in Wessex (fig. 3.4).

In this region the barrows seem to form five major groups. From south to north these are the Dorset-Ridgeway group, the Cranborne Chase group, a group on the western part of Salisbury Plain, a second Salisbury Plain group in the east and finally a north Wiltshire group. These groupings appear to have a significant relationship to the distribution of causewayed enclosures as in each of the regional groups at least one causewayed enclosure appears to occur. In the Dorset group, Maiden Castle; in the Cranborne Chase group, Hambledon Hill; in the east Salisbury Plain group, Whitesheet Hill; in the west Salisbury Plain group, Robin Hood's Ball; and in the north Wiltshire group, the type-site of Windmill Hill itself and also the small camp at Knap Hill (Renfrew 1973c).

The distribution of long barrows shows a marked preference for chalk and the barrows themselves are generally set in upland and prominent situations, though occasional examples have been found in the valley bottoms as at Holdenhurst in Hampshire lying on the gravels of the River Stour. The mounds have a generally east–west orientation, a notable exception being the group on Cranborne Chase, where the variation appears to have been brought about by the siting of the mounds on predominantly north-north-west–south-south-east ridges. The mounds themselves vary in length from less than 30m to examples up to 122m long and there is a small, distinctive group of bank barrows in Dorset, the largest example of which – overlying the causewayed enclosure at Maiden Castle – is almost half a kilometre long. The majority of mounds, however, are between 30 and 60m in length.

Two basic forms have been recognized: one in which the mound itself is parallel-sided and generally of uniform height from end to end; the other type trapezoid in plan and tending to be broader and higher at its eastern end. Many of the mounds also appear to be markedly ridged in cross-section. The flanking quarry ditches generally run parallel with the long axis of the mound although in some cases they may extend round part of the tail or head of the mound with only a narrow entrance gap or causeway remaining. No regional variations in external mound form can be recognized other than a general tendency for small barrows to be numerous in the area of Stonehenge.

The most consistently recurring feature in the mound structure of

Fig. 3.4   The distribution of long barrows and long cairns without apparent stone chambers (after Ashbee 1970, Henshall 1970 and Manby 1970).

land over 100m

land over 400m

0   100   200   300 km

excavated long barrows, composed largely of chalk rubble and earth derived from the ditch, is the existence in a number of examples of a primary core of turf presumably representing material stripped from the ditch. At Holdenhurst this turf was also piled up to form a revetment or retaining wall around the perimeter of the mound (Piggott S. 1937a).

In two barrows in the north Wiltshire group, at South Street and Beckhampton (fig. 3.5: 2), the mounds themselves were divided up into a series of compartments or bays by means of stakes (Smith and Evans 1968). In each case there was an axial row of stakes and pairs of lateral rows leading off from it. In the case of the South Street site it was possible to see during the excavation that the silts and marls of varied colours which had been dug from the ditch had been placed progressively in the bays. The significance of such an arrangement is uncertain although it may have been an aid in the actual construction of the mound if in fact this had taken place over a considerable period of time, the stakes and presumably linked hurdle work preventing slipping and weathering of the mound during the intervals in its construction.

The burials were generally placed beneath the broader and higher eastern end. The number of individuals recorded buried beneath long barrows varies considerably. At South Street and Beckhampton in the north Wiltshire group no corpses at all were recovered in spite of the ideal chalk conditions for the preservation of skeletal material. Both sites must therefore be considered as cenotaphs. In a number of other cases single burials have been recorded. The normal form of burial is that of multiple interment generally by inhumation, the largest number being over 50 recorded beneath the Fussell's Lodge barrow in the west Salisbury Plain group (Ashbee 1966a) (fig. 3.5: 1), although the average number appears to be six (Atkinson 1968). The corpses were generally placed on the old land surface or more rarely in pits. A noticeable feature of many of the burials is their markedly disarticulated condition and also the incomplete nature of the surviving skeletal material. In some cases articulated and fragmentary skeletons are found in a single deposit and there may be a considerable variation in the degree of erosion and weathering to which individual bones have been subjected. The disarticulated condition of so many of the skeletons in the long barrows implies that the corpses had been exposed for a sufficient period before burial for the flesh to decay and in the unlikely event of 20 or 30 individuals in a community dying at one time one can only conclude that the dead were stored in some way until their numbers had accumulated sufficiently to warrant the construction of a long barrow.

The remains of such mortuary houses or long mortuary enclosures have been recognized in a number of modern long barrow excavations. Such mortuary enclosures also exist as freestanding monuments not covered by a long barrow and it is now clear that in a number of cases the construction of the long barrow itself represents the final process in a long and in some cases quite complicated sequence of events reflected in the structures found dug in the subsoil beneath the barrow itself. Modern excavation techniques can recover the plan and forms of such structures but little or nothing of the motives which prompted their construction or the actual function of many of the structures themselves. The earliest excavated example of a long mortuary enclosure was that beneath the Wor Barrow in Dorset, excavated by General Pitt-Rivers (1898) although not identified by him as such at the time. It consisted of a rectangular bedding trench in which were set small posts forming a palisaded enclosure which narrowed to a porch at the south-eastern end. A very much larger and more complex mortuary enclosure occurred beneath the Fussell's Lodge long barrow in Wiltshire (Ashbee 1966a). Here a wedge-shaped palisade trench 42m long contained vertical timbers set 45–60cm apart and ranging from about 30cm in diameter at the narrower western end and the long sides of the enclosure to almost 91cm in diameter at the east (fig. 3.5: 1). Immediately outside the entrance were four very large posts marking what was perhaps a porched entrance. The numerous fragmentary inhumation burials lay immediately inside this porched entrance covered by a low cairn of flints. The burials themselves overlay three large axial pits which the excavator suggested had contained posts forming supports for a roofed mortuary structure. Many of the bones were badly broken in the deposit and were fragmentary and mixed with earth. The excavator suggested that some of the fractures were the result of the collapse of the mortuary house and that the bones had been exposed or more probably buried elsewhere and dug up to be interred in the timber mortuary house.

This interpretation of the features of the eastern end of the Fussell's Lodge long barrow was influenced in part by the discoveries beneath a small oval long barrow at Wayland's Smithy in Berkshire (Atkinson 1965). The small primary long barrow here lay buried beneath the very much larger wedge-shaped mound associated with a transepted megalithic tomb (fig. 3.11: 4). The nine partially articulated inhumation burials beneath this primary mound lay within a rectangular timber and stone enclosure. At either end of the enclosure were two massive pits within which the decayed remains of large D-shaped timbers could be detected. These appeared to represent a single split tree trunk, their function being to support a ridge pole of a tent-like wooden structure. Sarsen slabs had been placed against the lateral roof timbers and from the angle of such slabs it appeared the ridge pole was about 137cm above the floor of the enclosure. However, the great size of the two terminal timber uprights suggests that these may have projected a considerable distance above the level of the ridge pole itself and indeed may have extended above the mound. The partially articulated condition of the skeletons makes it unlikely that the corpses had been buried elsewhere and disinterred for inclusion in the mortuary structure. The excavator suggested that the corpses may have been exposed to the air, under which conditions they would be liable to attack by birds and scavengers. The converging settings of posts in front of the mortuary house at Wayland's Smithy itself may have supported just such a platform and whatever its function this external post structure pre-dated the enclosure.

The existence of pitch-roofed mortuary houses has been claimed beneath other long barrows but the majority of such sites were excavated

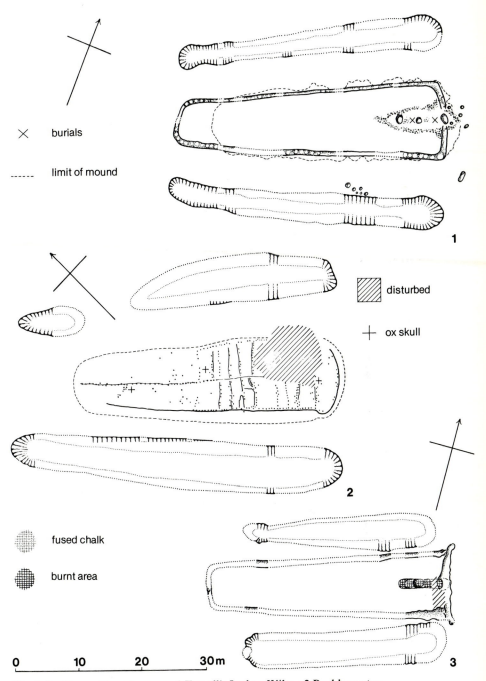

×   burials

-----   limit of mound

▨   disturbed

+   ox skull

▦   fused chalk

▦   burnt area

Fig. 3.5   Plans of long barrows. 1 Fussell's Lodge, Wilts.; 2 Beckhampton Road, Wilts.; 3 Willerby Wold, E. Yorks. (after Ashbee 1966a, Smith and Evans 1968 and Manby 1963).

in the eighteenth and nineteenth centuries, and the scanty account of such excavations makes positive interpretation extremely difficult (Simpson D. D. A. 1968b). The most complicated of all the pre-barrow structures were those recovered beneath the long barrow at Nutbane in Hampshire (Morgan 1959). The earliest of the pre-barrow structures, all of which were concentrated in the area later to be covered by the broader and higher eastern end of the mound, was a small mortuary enclosure defined by ditches within which were placed three disarticulated inhumation burials. Immediately to the east of this deposit was a small rectangular timber building defined by post-holes. This forecourt building was subsequently demolished and replaced by a larger rectangular timber structure. Leading from this and partially enclosing it was a bedding trench in which were set timber uprights forming a free-standing colonnade; possibly contemporary with this phase was the insertion of the fourth and, in this case, final articulated inhumation in the mortuary enclosure which itself was surrounded by a light hurdle-work fence. The final act was the setting on fire of these timber structures and while the timbers were still burning work was begun on the excavation of the flanking quarry ditches, the chalk material being heaped onto the still burning and smouldering timber building.

Long mortuary enclosures as free-standing structures not covered by later long barrows occur in Wiltshire and Oxfordshire. The Wiltshire example on Normanton Down is an oblong enclosure with rounded ends orientated east-south-east–west-north-west (Vatcher 1961). The ditches were dug in the irregular causewayed technique of the causewayed enclosures and immediately within the entrance at the eastern end were two bedding trenches for posts, each bedding trench containing three posts supported at their bases by horizontal timbers. No skeletal material was associated with this site, the corpses presumably having been removed for interment elsewhere beneath a long mound.

The other free-standing enclosures are those at Dorchester, in Oxfordshire (Atkinson 1951). The excavated example, 64m long and 5m wide, was bounded by a V-sectioned ditch some 1·5m wide with an internal bank. No finds other than a fragment of human mandible were recovered. Two other similar enclosures occur in the same area. All are associated with the final class of field monument – the cursus.

Cursūs A cursus is an extremely long rectangular earthwork defined by a pair of banks and ditches, the bank lying within the ditch. The longest known cursus is the Dorset Cursus, over 8km long (Atkinson 1955), and other substantial examples occur near Stonehenge, some 2·7km long and at Dorchester in Oxfordshire over 1·2km long. The Dorset Cursus has a long barrow placed at right-angles to its axis and a further long barrow incorporated in the line of the bank and ditch. At Stonehenge one end of the cursus is formed by a long barrow set at right angles to its longitudinal axis, while at Dorchester in Oxfordshire three long mortuary enclosures are again in intimate association with the cursus. The implication is that like the long barrow and long mortuary enclosure the cursus is associated with some ritual in connection with the dead and may in fact delimit ceremonial ways along which the dead were carried to their place of final interment.

One final aspect of the funerary monuments of the Windmill Hill culture concerns the number of individuals buried beneath the long barrows and the implications in relation to the total population and also possibly to the social structure involved. Atkinson (1968) records 229 surviving long barrows and assumes because of their size that it is unlikely that many have been completely obliterated. He therefore suggests an original total of some 250 sites. Of these, 35 have records of burials beneath them and have yielded a total of 254 corpses. If one excludes the human material from Fussell's Lodge, which included a high percentage of infant remains, then the average number of individuals buried beneath the excavated long barrows is six. In the 250 postulated long barrows, therefore, the total number of corpses would be in the range of 1,500 to 3,000. These figures would suggest that during the period of the Windmill Hill culture no more than two or three individuals were buried in a barrow per year. If one assumes a death rate of 40 per 1,000 per year this number of deaths would take place annually in a population of 40 to 75 people. As Atkinson points out, however, this would assume a static population which would be unlikely. He argues for an exponential increase of the long barrow population of England during this millennium which would give a figure in its last century of between 70 and 140 individuals and correspondingly less in the preceding centuries. What may be inferred from these figures is that in fact those buried beneath earthen long barrows represent only a percentage of the total neolithic population of southern Britain.

At first sight it would in fact appear that even the long barrows themselves and their construction would be beyond the means of a single family unit. On the other hand the excavator of Fussell's Lodge in Wiltshire, a site which is of above average size for Wessex long barrows, calculated that it required some 5,000 man-hours for its construction or work for six men for a period of four months (Ashbee 1966a). On the other hand, the construction of causewayed enclosures and, above all, cursus monuments, would require the corporate effort of large numbers of people far beyond the capacities of even a large family group and, in fact, the material from the former group of monuments does suggest the coming together of peoples from a widely dispersed area.

If, then, only a small percentage of the neolithic population was entitled to burial beneath these large and imposing long barrows, it may be safely assumed that such individuals were in fact the privileged element in contemporary society. The absence of elaborate grave goods in association with the human material from the long barrows may not preclude such an interpretation, bearing in mind possible social prejudice in connection with the deposition of elaborate grave goods with the dead and also the technological limitations of the period in that many display items or parade objects may have been rendered in an organic material, and may therefore not have survived. Given, therefore, the possibility of a stratified society on the basis of the limited number of individuals buried beneath long barrows one might see in the Wessex region the groupings of long barrows into five major regional units as reflecting a social or tribal entity each controlled by a ruling aristocracy buried beneath the long barrows themselves; the focal point in each region would be the causewayed enclosure where group efforts would be co-ordinated for social, religious and economic functions. One may see here the beginning of Renfrew's (1973c) socio-political units of chiefdoms, better illustrated archaeologically in the later neolithic and above all in the first half of the 2nd millennium bc.

Material equipment   Turning now to the material equipment of these early agriculturalists in southern and south-eastern Britain it should be emphasized that the majority of such finds come from causewayed enclosures, and specifically from the ditches. With a few notable exceptions such as Fussell's Lodge the long barrows have yielded few grave goods accompanying the inhumation burials while long mortuary enclosures and cursūs are virtually devoid of any finds.

Because of their durability the most consistently recurring finds in such sites are sherds of pottery. The vessels are round-bottomed bowls, well-made, dark-faced wares with smooth and often burnished surfaces; what used in fact to be considered part of the general family of Western neolithic pottery (Piggott S. 1954). In those contexts which are demonstrably early in terms of stratigraphy or radiocarbon dates the wares frequently appear to be plain with simple or at the most slightly rolled-over rims (fig. 3.6). Two basic forms are represented: one group is characterized by deep bag-shaped vessels of coarse ware with a rather leathery texture, perhaps indicating the original organic prototypes of the form, with a pair of plain or perforated lugs (fig. 3.6: 3–4). The second group, finer wares with generally thinner wall sections, are characterized by comparatively shallow bowls with an S-shaped profile or with a shoulder which may be in the form of a very marked carination (fig. 3.6: 2). In southern Britain such vessels are found in stratigraphically early contexts such as the pre-enclosure phase of settlement at Windmill Hill, but are most characteristic of the south-western province, being well represented at the promontory enclosure of Hembury in Devon and the hilltop settlement site at Carn Brea near Redruth in Cornwall. Following on this initial plain ware tradition there follows a period when both increasing elaboration of rim forms and the application of decoration to the surface of the vessels before firing becomes characteristic. These later and largely insular pottery forms fall roughly into a number of regional variants within the Windmill Hill culture province proper. These later decorated pottery forms are more difficult to parallel directly on the Continent and presumably represent the establishment of local traditions after the initial impact phase of neolithic settlement.

Within the territory of the Windmill Hill culture a series of pottery styles are recognizable (fig. 3.7). Although each has in general a regional concentration there is in fact considerable geographical overlap. In the

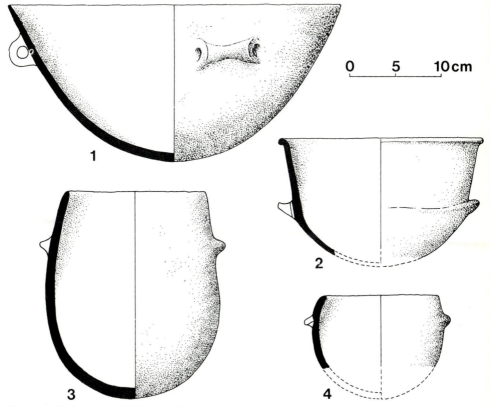

Fig. 3.6 Plain early/middle neolithic pottery. 1 Hembury, Devon; 2 Carn Brea, Cornwall; 3 Chelms Comb, Sussex; 4 Norton Bavant, Wilts. (after Piggott S. 1954).

extreme south-west what has been termed as Hembury ware, after the type-site of the promontory enclosure, maintains the characteristic of complete lack of ornament on the vessels as in the earliest pottery forms. Highly individualistic in this regional group is the application of a horizontal and tubular handle with the ends expanded like the mouths of a trumpet – the so-called trumpet lug (fig. 3.6: 1). Although the major concentration of such forms is in the extreme south-west of Britain examples are found as far east as Whitehawk in Sussex.

The second sub-group of pottery forms takes its name from Windmill Hill itself, with a concentration of finds in north Dorset and Wiltshire. In general the forms are smooth-profiled baggy bowls with simple rims, although small cups are also common. Decoration tends to be confined to the area immediately below the rim and consists of vertical, incised striations or rows of pin-pricks.

In the Upper Thames Valley and named after the causewayed enclosure of Abingdon in Berkshire there is a series of vessels with elaborately thickened and rolled-over rims, the area between the rim and carination

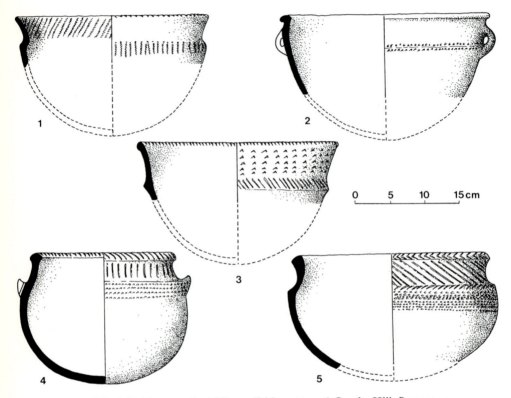

Fig. 3.7 Decorated middle neolithic pottery. 1 Combe Hill, Sussex;
2 Abingdon, Berks.; 3 Haylands House, I.O.W.; 4 Ipswich, Suffolk (after
Piggott S. 1954).

being decorated with an incision or stamped impressions (fig. 3.7: 2). The
carinated vessels which are characteristic of this series frequently have
lugs developed into elaborate strap handles and like the other regional
forms of pottery the predominant material used in tempering the vessels
is pounded shell rather than flint grit. It is possible that Abingdon ware
represents the early use of ornament on neolithic pottery as a bowl of this
group was found beneath the Fussell's Lodge long barrow which has a
radiocarbon date in the late 4th millennium bc.

In south-eastern Britain the dominant form is a wide-mouthed carinated
bowl lavishly ornamented both on the rim, neck and shoulder (fig. 3.7: 3).
North of the Thames, in East Anglia and named after the site of
Mildenhall in Suffolk, is a further series of vessels with elaborately
thickened rims frequently rolled over with abundant incised ornament or
punctuations both on the rim, between the rim and shoulder and extending
some distance below the carination (fig. 3.7: 5).

It must again be emphasized that although these individual forms are
characteristic or are most numerous in the geographical region mentioned
earlier there is considerable geographical overlap; this is not surprising in

view of the evidence from the causewayed enclosures of groups coming together from a wide area. The only other ceramic form which is common to a number of these regions is a pottery spoon.

As the main weight of settlement in southern and south-eastern Britain appears to be on the chalk it is not surprising that the principal stone tools are manufactured from flint. Most important amongst these tools must have been the flint axe, either chipped or chipped and polished (fig. 3.8: 9). All such axes are manufactured from flint cores and are thin-butted, normally with oval sections. Although chipped and polished flint axes are the most numerous forms from sites of the Windmill Hill culture in southern Britain, axes of igneous rock in particular from sources in Cornwall and the Lake District are also found, and these and their significance will be discussed below (fig. 3.8: 10). Flaked leaf-shaped points (fig. 3.8: 8) were used to tip arrow-shafts and two contemporary longbows of yew were recovered from the peat deposits of the Somerset Levels at Meare Heath (Clark J. G. D. 1963). Both bows are over 1·5m in length and resemble the longbows of medieval England. Larger flint projectile points probably served as javelin or spear-heads.

In addition to these specialized flint forms there is a wide variety of scrapers which occur in great quantities in the ditches of causewayed enclosures. Most are large, heavy and frequently horse-shoe shaped (fig. 3.8: 7). Such tools, presumably, were used in the preparation of animal skins in the removal of fatty tissue. Knives produced from flakes are another common tool type in the ditches of causewayed enclosures and presumably, again, were used in the skinning and preparation of hides. As well as recognizable work-tools there are large numbers of flakes and blades without retouch or blunted only on their backs. Amongst the bone and antler tools the most frequent types are picks made from the antlers of red or, more rarely, roe deer. Such tools occur frequently in the ditches of causewayed enclosures and long barrows and in the galleries and shafts of flint mines and presumably were used in their excavation. The antlers themselves are both shed and cut from animals killed in the chase. A complementary excavation tool for such work was a shovel made from the shoulder blade generally of an ox or less frequently of red deer or pig. At Harrow Hill in Sussex one of the shoulder blades of an ox had been hollowed out at its articular end to accommodate a handle either of antler bone or wood, although in most cases there is no trace of reworking or fashioning of the scapulae. The material dug from the ditches of causewayed camps and long barrows and from the shafts of flint mines would presumably have been carried away in baskets although no traces of these containers survive.

The other very characteristic antler artifact from the Windmill Hill province is a comb made from a section of shaft of red deer antler with the cut end grooved into a ring of teeth, the working being by the burin technique (fig. 3.8: 1). The teeth themselves are carefully pointed and in most surviving examples they show some degree of polish and wear. Such combs are found throughout the territory of the Windmill Hill culture with the exception of the extreme south-west where the generally acid

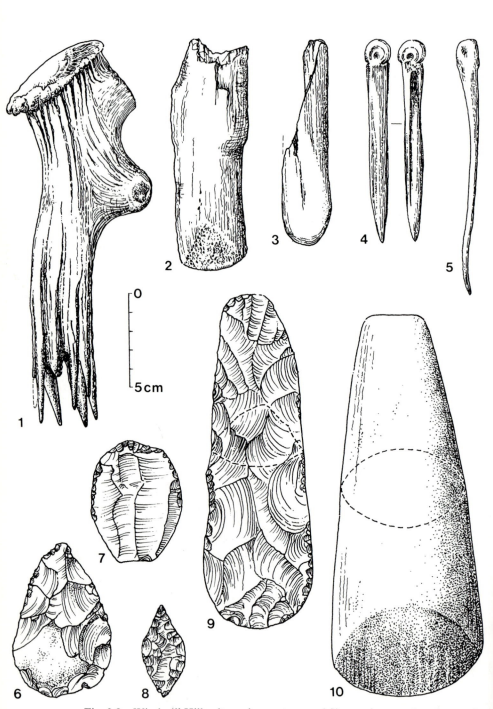

Fig. 3.8   Windmill Hill culture: bone, stone and flint equipment. 1 antler comb; 2 bone 'chisel'; 3 bone polisher; 4–5 bone points; 6–7 flint scrapers; 8 leaf-shaped flint arrowhead; 9 flint axe; 10 polished stone axe (after Piggott S. 1954).

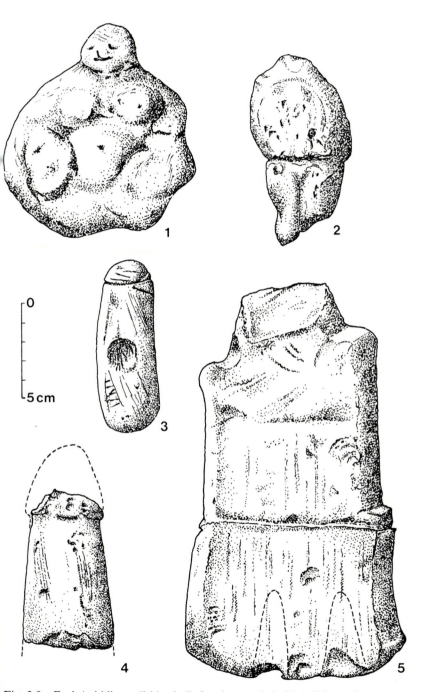

Fig. 3.9 Early/middle neolithic chalk figurines and phalli. 1 Grimes Graves, Norfolk; 2–3 Windmill Hill, Wilts.; 4 Thickthorn, Dorset; 5 Maiden Castle, Dorset (after Piggott S. 1954).

soils are detrimental to the survival of bone or antler material. Like the flint scrapers these antler combs are probably to be associated with the preparation of animal skins; almost identical forms are used by the Eskimos for the removal of loose hair from the animal skins. Again probably used for the dressing and preparation of the animal skins and leatherworking is a series of bone points and skewers and also bone chisels serving like the flint scrapers for the removal of fatty tissues (fig. 3.8: 2, 4–5).

In a stone-using agricultural community one may safely assume that a great variety of objects both utilitarian and decorative were manufactured in wood. In general, wooden objects survive only as carbonized and

Fig. 3.10   Plan of ard marks beneath South Street long barrow, Wilts. (after Evans J. G. 1971b).

fragmentary remains as in the case of the post-holes of domestic or funerary sites. An indication, however, of the skill and sophistication of wood-working is provided by the finds from the timber trackways in the Somerset Levels, both in terms of the construction of the main members of the trackways themselves, and also in the rare wooden objects associated with them (Coles *et al.* 1973).

Economy   A final aspect of these early agriculturalists in southern and south-eastern Britain is that of their economy. The material from the causewayed enclosures indicates that stock-raising, with a predominance of cattle, was an important element in their economy. Evidence of cereal production is afforded by the occurrence of grain impressions on pottery and by the carbonized remains of cereals from storage pits. Such finds indicate a mixed crop of wheat and barley (Helbaek 1952). The grain itself was ground and prepared by means of rubbers and dish-shaped or 'saucer' querns of sandstone. A number of knives and sickles of flint also have the characteristic silica gloss associated with the cutting of plant stems and may be considered as reaping equipment.

Of the size and nature of the fields in which such crops were grown we know as yet very little, but that they were, in some cases at any rate, cultivated by traction plough is indicated by the discovery of criss-cross plough marks beneath the long barrow at South Street in north Wiltshire (fig. 3.10) (Smith and Evans 1968). From the rather later continental evidence in the form of rock carvings and models both in clay and in bronze it may safely be assumed that the plough itself was in fact drawn by a pair of oxen (Fowler 1971). Such evidence of ploughing in the form of grooves cut by the ard in the chalk sub-soil would only survive where the cultivated area had been covered by subsequent earthworks as at South Street. In view of the fact that some 60cm of the chalk sub-soil has been removed by weathering and passed into solution in the last 5,000 years such physical limitations suggest that one will never know the extent and area of the fields of these first agriculturalists in southern Britain, unlike the surviving palimpsest of 'Celtic' field systems of the latter half of the 2nd and 1st millennium bc. The evidence from sub-barrow soils, for example in Wiltshire, does suggest variations of intensity of land use, perhaps related to altitude (Whittle 1977: 22).

North-east Britain

In the area to the north-east of the Windmill Hill culture province, in Lincolnshire, north-eastern England and eastern Scotland, the evidence for early agricultural settlement is scarcer and also more limited in its nature. In part, this may be a consequence of a lesser amount of field work and excavation, and also of local geological conditions. But the causewayed enclosure, which could hardly fail to be detected, is conspicuously absent, and the lack of the evidence which these monuments provide in the south of Britain is responsible to some considerable extent for the rather limited picture which one has of agricultural communities in this northern and north-eastern area. Apart from occasional presumed grain storage pits similar to those in the south there is an almost total absence of settlement sites. The surviving monuments are funerary or ritual in character, again presenting a very one-sided picture of the society in this area.

Long barrows   The characteristic burial monument in the south, the long barrow, is well represented although more sparsely distributed in the north-eastern province (Ashbee 1970). The only major concentrations are on the chalk of Lincolnshire and the East Riding of Yorkshire, though scattered examples occur as far north-east as Caithness (fig. 3.4). In the latter region, however, the mounds are composed of stones rather than earth or rubble. It is only in Yorkshire that extensive excavation both in the nineteenth and in the present century have taken place on these sites. In Lincolnshire only the Giants' Hills long barrow at Skendleby (Phillips 1936), and in eastern Scotland the site at Dalladies in Kincardineshire (Piggott S. 1971–2), have been excavated by modern methods. In this north-eastern region there are a little under 100 long barrows, the majority conforming to the trapezoid form dominant in southern Britain. A few rare mounds with parallel sides such as that at Fortingall in Perthshire are however known (Henshall 1972: 478).

In Yorkshire, and it is only in this region that generalizations can be made, the long barrows may be divided into two categories on the basis of the burial rite (Manby 1970). The mound at Kilham, first excavated by Greenwell in the nineteenth century and recently re-excavated, covered multiple inhumation burials like the long barrows of southern Britain (Manby 1976). The monument at Hanging Grimston also probably originally covered inhumed remains. To the south, the Giants' Hills long barrow in Lincolnshire also covered disarticulated inhumation burials and the same rite probably applied at Dalladies. Cremation long barrows make up the majority of known long barrow sites in eastern Yorkshire. Two, the sites at East Heslerton and Willerby Wold, have been excavated extensively in recent times. The East Heslerton site is unusual amongst Yorkshire long barrows in having survived the depredations of nineteenth-century antiquaries (Vatcher 1965). It is also by far the longest mound in the area, some 124m from east to west and 9m wide at the broader eastern end. The total denudation of the mound and the heavy ploughing of the chalk sub-soil had left only the floors of the various pits, ditches and bedding trenches preserved. The bedding trenches were of a discontinuous nature and appear to represent a mortuary enclosure similar to those in southern Britain and known in other north-eastern long barrows. The excavator considered the varying widths of the enclosure to represent successive eastern extensions of the mound to accommodate new burials, although it has also been associated with dilapidation and repair.

The other published modern excavation of a cremation long barrow at Willerby Wold (fig. 3.5: 3) represents the re-excavation of a site originally dug in the nineteenth century (Manby 1963). Like East Heslerton the Willerby Wold monument is sited in an imposing position on the northern scarp of the Wolds immediately above a deep dry valley. The recent excavations have shown that the mound itself covered the bedding trench of a trapezoid mortuary enclosure 35m long with a concave façade at the eastern end. The stratigraphy suggests that the façade had been erected before the mortuary enclosure. From the centre of this façade running axially in a westerly direction into the mound itself ran the deposit of cremated bone which was composed of a ridge of stacked flint and chalk blocks intermixed with timber and flanked by low turf walls to the north and south. The heat from the firing of the crematorium had been sufficient to fuse the chalk rubble and shatter the flint. The chalk rubble in the axial pit in the façade and the second pit to the west was similarly affected. The bones themselves were in a remarkably disarticulated condition, again suggesting a considerable period of exposure before cremation. This feature of a so-called crematorium trench had been noted by nineteenth-century excavators in other long and round barrows in east Yorkshire. Canon Greenwell believed that the mode of construction of such crematoria was in fact to leave an open trench after the construction of the mound in which corpses were placed and on top of which was piled combustible material, the whole mass then being set on fire, the heat being so intense in some cases as to convert the limestone, in the case of a limestone core, to lime or to fuse the chalk rubble. He drew attention to the fact that those corpses or fragments of human material lying towards the perimeter of the mound were more completely burnt than those towards the centre, as the result of the incomplete oxygenation of the deposit towards the centre. The evidence from Nutbane in Hampshire and from Willerby Wold itself and other recent excavations would suggest that the state of the cremated material is more likely to be explained in terms of the burning of some form of wooden structure in which the corpses were stored. The burning of the southern British monument beneath the long barrow at Nutbane is unusual, whereas in Yorkshire the burning of the timber structures at the eastern end appears to have been standard practice, resulting in the perhaps accidental cremation of the fragmentary and disarticulated human remains within the wooden enclosure.

In eastern and in north-eastern Britain, as in the south, recent excavations have suggested that the erection of a long and generally trapezoid mound covering disarticulated inhumation or cremation burials in fact represented only the final stage in a complex series of pre-mound structures. Comparable in complexity to the Nutbane site is that at Kilham on the Yorkshire Wolds (Manby 1976). The earliest features on the site appear to be two narrow vertically-sided flat-bottomed ditches at the western end of the later mound. These ditches may have flanked a long and narrow primary mound similar to that at Lambourne in Berkshire. The second stage involved the construction of a trapezoid timber enclosure represented by a bedding trench broken by three entrance gaps. Within this enclosure were two structures: first, placed centrally in the enclosure was a square setting of four posts very close to the enclosure bedding trench of the first phase. At the eastern end of the mound but not quite axial to the enclosure were the remains of what may have been a timber mortuary house. This had been disturbed by an earlier nineteenth-century excavation but probably consisted of a timber-walled passage partially revetted by an earthen bank, perhaps with a flat timber roof. This structure covered a burial pavement of earth and chalk slabs on which rested some five disarticulated and three undisturbed inhumation burials. The eastern end of the mortuary house opened on to an entrance into the mortuary enclosure itself. Beyond the enclosure was an avenue of free-standing posts, the northern branch of which continued into the enclosure. The dual nature of the monument with a western mound and an eastern mortuary enclosure is reflected in the flanking quarry ditches, four in number. The deeper western ditches provided the majority of the rubble for the complete filling of this portion of the mortuary enclosure. At this time the eastern portion containing the mortuary house was open and remained so during the deposition of the burials. The enclosure at this point was destroyed by fire and the area covered with rubble quarried from the eastern ditches.

From the few excavated examples of eastern and north-eastern long barrows it does appear that the eastern end of the mortuary enclosure was provided with a concave façade in contrast to the straight or entranced façade of the enclosures of southern Britain. The majority of such pre-mound timber and earth structures in the eastern and north-eastern province, as in the south, appeared to have the covering mound set axially to them and this may have given the impression that the pre-mound structures and the digging of the quarry ditches and the construction of the covering mound represent a comparatively short period of activity on the site and a continuous one. On the other hand, at Dalladies the pre-mound mortuary structures were offset and not on the long-axis of the covering mound (Piggott 1971–2). Although such pre-mound timber structures are most frequently encountered beneath the earthen mounds of southern and eastern Britain it is now quite clear that in the north and west several of the stone cairns covering megalithic chambers have a timber rather than a stone monument as their primary structure. These will be discussed below.

Round barrows   The second important category of burial monument in the north-eastern area is that of a round rather than a long or trapezoid mound. All but two of such sites were excavated in the nineteenth century and the information associated with them is therefore limited. Mortimer's Huggate and Warter Wold Barrow 254, and Greenwell's Barrow VI in the parish of Heslerton, covered concave façade bedding trenches similar to those beneath long barrows, in both cases associated with early neolithic pottery. An example of a so-called crematorium trench was found beneath a round barrow at Willy Howe, again excavated in the nineteenth century. On Calais Wold in the East Riding a large round mound covered a central pit containing cremations mixed with disturbed unburnt bones, and to the north-east a slab pavement on which lay ten crouched inhumations, associated with neolithic artifacts.

The only neolithic round mound in Yorkshire excavated by modern methods is that at Ayton Moor in the North Riding of Yorkshire overlooking the Vale of Pickering, first dug in the nineteenth century and re-excavated in the early 1960s. Beneath the mound composed of small limestone slabs was a rectangular mortuary enclosure 3m long adjacent to which was a setting of timber uprights running from the perimeter of the mound to its centre, which appeared to have formed the uprights of a roofed structure, covered by the later mound. Within this timber mortuary house were two corpses, at least one of which had been deposited in an articulated condition. The mortuary house, as in the case of a number of those beneath the long mounds, had been set on fire after the mound had been erected over it and the intense heat converted the limestone adjacent to it and above it to lime. The outer of the two corpses lay in a crouched position and had been almost totally cremated *in situ* whereas that towards the centre of the mound showed only partial firing, a feature noted by Greenwell in the burials beneath a number of long barrows. The grave goods associated with these burials again were early neolithic.

Similar multiple cremations were found beneath the round barrows at Copt Hill in Durham and Ford in Northumberland, and these probably provide a link with the other major concentration of presumed neolithic and early neolithic round barrows in east central Scotland. The greatest concentration of these sites is in the Tay Valley but examples occur as far south as Perth and east to Kincardine. All have a markedly lowland distribution, below the 152m contour, and the majority occur on the alluvial gravels of the valley floors. The mounds themselves vary from 12 to 40m in diameter and from 1 to 9m in height. Many support stands of trees, and although a number show disturbance with central depressions suggesting they have been opened the only recorded excavation is that at Pitnacree in central Perthshire (Coles and Simpson 1965). This consisted of a turf mound, without a surrounding quarry ditch, which covered a horseshoe-shaped stone bank. Within the stone bank was a rectangular enclosure of stone reminiscent of the mortuary enclosures of the long barrows of east Yorkshire and southern Britain. On the old land surface and beneath the structure were scattered cremation burials associated with early neolithic pottery (fig. 3. 15: 2). The primary structures, which appeared to be unrelated to the later stone and turf monument, were two massive ramped pits which contained D-shaped timbers set 2m apart, very similar to the primary posts at Wayland's Smithy in Berkshire though in this case apparently free-standing structures and not supporting any form of roofed building.

Domestic sites and the economy   The only other ceremonial monuments in this north-eastern area are rare examples of cursūs such as those at Rudston in the East Riding of Yorkshire or at Huntingtower in Perthshire. Domestic sites are equally scarce. In Yorkshire the occurrence of neolithic pottery and occupation debris beneath later single-grave round barrows suggests that these later monuments were in some cases erected over earlier neolithic domestic sites and does not necessarily imply cultural or chronological continuity between the early phase of neolithic settlement and the appearance of single grave cultures at the beginning of the 2nd millennium bc. The choice of these areas occupied by earlier neolithic settlements for the erection of barrows covering single grave burials is presumably because such settlements were established in areas of forest clearance so that the later builders of funerary monuments would only have to clear secondary scrub before the erection of the barrows. In Yorkshire itself the only undoubted settlement site is Beacon Hill, Flamborough, East Riding, and here only a few hearths and hollows were recorded together with pottery of the early and middle neolithic (Moor J. W. 1963).

In the chalk and limestone areas of Lincolnshire and Yorkshire the scarcity of settlement sites, as in southern Britain, may be due to the fact that such settlements did not in fact lie on the tops of the Wolds but in the valley bottoms, and therefore are now covered by many feet of sediment and hill-wash (see Chapter 1). Some support for this view is provided by the molluscan evidence from the Giants' Hills long barrow at Skendleby in Lincolnshire (Phillips 1936). The large axial pit to the east of the burial deposit here contained sherds, charcoal and occupation debris and also a molluscan fauna in which shade-loving species were predominant. This was in contrast with the land-snails from the ditch and the barrow mound itself which suggested an open scrub or heathland environment. The excavator very reasonably suggested therefore that the occupation debris with this incorporation of shade-loving and damp-loving mollusca represented occupation material brought from the wooded valley-bottom site to the top of the Wolds where the long barrow was constructed. Further to the north-east occasional pits such as those at Easterton of Roseisle, Moray, attest to domestic sites (Walker 1968). The rarity of domestic sites makes it difficult to make any positive statements regarding the economy though storage pits do suggest grain growing, in spite of the almost total absence of querns and rubbers from the eastern and north-eastern area.

The study of soil profiles beneath the Willerby Wold long barrow has shown that the surface vegetation was a close-cropped grass suggesting stock-breeding as the dominant element in the economy. In burial deposits the remains of what might be funeral feasts show bones of ox and pig, the latter in surprisingly large proportions compared with the evidence from southern Britain at the same period. At Hanging Grimston the discovery of a concentration of pig bones seemingly ritually deposited has led to the idea of a pig cult which might support the theory of a pastoral economy. The remarkably thick fossil soil beneath the round barrow at Pitnacree in Perthshire and the apparently disturbed nature of the material in this soil has suggested that the area may have been ploughed before the erection of the mound. The use of turf for the construction of the Dalladies long mound demonstrates the existence of open grassland in the vicinity of the site.

Material equipment: pottery   The pottery from this north-eastern province falls into three major groups. All are round-based vessels, undecorated, the surface treatment being restricted to finger-tip vertical fluting on a number of examples. The majority of the vessels are of hard, dark wares, pitted with holes resulting from the weathering out of chalk or limestone tempering. This first group accounts for some 60 per cent of the pottery; the vessels normally have sinuous S-shaped profiles with a thickened and everted rim and are known as Heslerton ware.

A sub-group within the Heslerton series termed Towthorpe ware is represented by a vessel from the settlement site of Beacon Hill, from a number of the inhumation round barrows and probably from the cremation site at Pitnacree. This group includes the rare examples of lugged vessels and all show beaded rather than thickened and everted rims.

The other well-defined group is of a finer-grained, hard paste of varying colour from red to black on a single sherd. The form of this latter group is distinctive, having a sharp carinated profile with an everted rim. Such vessels are termed Grimston ware.

Material equipment: stone axes   Amongst stone and flint tools those which appear to be most significant, and certainly have been studied in the greatest detail, are the axes of igneous rock. Such products are, of course, also found in early neolithic contexts in southern Britain, but as the sources of these axes are basically northern and north-western in the highland zone it would seem most appropriate to consider them here. The axes themselves are ground and polished, or more rarely flaked, in some cases representing the re-flaking of an earlier polished axe. The majority are of oval section with a rounded or pointed tapering butt. Petrological thin-sectioning of a large number of these axes and a comparison with geological samples has located the sources of many of the axes either specifically to individual outcrops or within restricted geographical regions. These sources have been divided into specific geological groups (Evans *et al.* 1972). Of course, not all the recognized sources for the production of tools were in operation during the early or even the middle neolithic phase, and there is still a lamentable dearth of radiocarbon dates associated either with the factory sites themselves or with their products in sealed archaeological horizons. The working areas where igneous rock was exploited for the manufacture of ground stone tools have been termed axe factories, perhaps an unfortunate term since little is known about the nature of the organization involved either in the initial exploitation of the raw material or its final finishing, distribution and trade. In all cases where a specific factory site can be identified on the ground only preliminary working in the form of the roughing out of the final shape of the axe appears to have taken place. In the majority of such axe factory sites scree material appears to have been utilized for the initial production of tools. An important exception is the site of Mynydd Rhiw in Caernarvonshire, where only a small seam of suitable igneous rock was visible on the surface (Houlder 1961). In this case the seam itself was followed below ground to a depth of over 3m.

Radiocarbon dates and associations in conjunction with the number and distribution of the products of individual factories suggest that the principal sources in the early and middle neolithic were a series of factory sites in Cornwall, some of which cannot yet be precisely located though, perhaps significantly, a number are adjacent to the important settlement site of Carn Brea. In the north-west the major production centres were those at Graig Llwyd in north Wales and Great Langdale in Westmorland. Across the Irish Sea contemporary early factory sites were being worked at Tievebulliagh and Rathlin Island, Co. Antrim (Jope 1952). In every case the distribution pattern of the products of the factories shows a concentration in the vicinity of the outcrops themselves, but all these major centres appear to have provided a considerable number of axe types for the early and middle neolithic settlements of southern and south-eastern Britain. In addition to these major centres of axe production there were minor factories as at Nuneaton in Warwickshire, possibly in the Charnwood Forest region of north-west Leicestershire (Shotton 1959) and at Killin in the Tay Valley in Perthshire (Ritchie P. R. 1968).

At Mynydd Rhiw the considerable proportion of knives and edged tools in addition to axes suggested to the excavator that there the working of the outcrop represented largely local exploitation rather than large-scale manufacture for the dissemination of axes over a wide geographical area. It is possible, of course, in the case of these so-called minor factories, that further thin-sectioning of axes in museums coupled with additional field work and the preparation of new distribution maps will show that these too were of more than limited regional significance.

An enduring problem in connection with the products of such factory sites is where the final grinding and the finishing processes took place. Still the only really convincing site where such was accomplished is that at Ehenside Tarn in Cumberland (Piggott S. 1954: 295). This lakeside settlement was uncovered when the tarn was drained in the nineteenth century. Along the ancient shore was a series of hearths associated with early and later neolithic pottery. The considerable quantity of organic material included a few rare wooden objects from neolithic contexts in the British Isles, but the most significant finds were a series of axes, many of great size, in various stages of completion, from simple rough-outs to partially ground and completed specimens, all from the factory site of Great Langdale. Associated with these axes were grinders and rubbers of sandstone used in the finishing processes. Other possible finishing sites may exist at Dyserth Castle and Gwaunysgor in Flintshire and at Merthyr Mawr Warren in Glamorgan (Houlder 1961). At the two former sites axes and rough-outs or chips from polished axes occurred. The re-flaking and shaping of the damaged and broken axes at such sites is highly suggestive of part of the business of trading.

There are two final aspects of the problem of the axe trade which must be considered: who was responsible for the working of the outcrops; and what is the significance of the axes themselves and their distribution pattern. In 1954 the available evidence suggested that the igneous rock outcrops were not exploited until a fairly late phase of the neolithic in this country. Stuart Piggott (1954: 287) associated such workings with the resurgence of native and mesolithic elements in the British Isles mingling with the introduced agricultural communities. He argued plausibly that the very considerable distances which separated the outcrops of igneous rocks from the centres of neolithic settlement in the south and east where many of the axes were found involved a considerable understanding of the natural routeways to the north and west and such would be more familiar to hunters and gatherers used to wandering over a considerable area of territory. The recognition since then of the primacy of the working of a number of these axe factory sites has cast some doubt on this original interpretation. On the other hand the excavator of the Mynydd Rhiw site drew attention to the mesolithic character of a number of the implements (Houlder 1961); a mesolithic contribution at an early stage of agricultural settlement in the British Isles would appear more plausible in view of the absence of evidence suggesting the survival of such indigenous hunting and fishing groups for any considerable period after the initial impact phase of neolithic settlement.

What is the significance of the axe trade? It is possible to locate the sources of many of the ground and polished stone implements found either as stray finds or on domestic or ritual sites of the early and middle neolithic. The preparation of distribution maps can also indicate the routes whereby such products have found their way to settlements in southern and eastern Britain. Recent studies would indicate redistribution centres far from the rock sources (Selkirk 1977a). The superiority of a ground axe of igneous rock over a flint one is beyond dispute in terms of durability and resistance to fracture. Like the flint axe it is generally considered a primary element in the process of forest clearance by primitive agriculturalists. Such clearance could, however, have been more effectively and economically accomplished by burning followed by subsequent grazing by animals to prevent regeneration. The axes would therefore be more likely to be used in woodworking than in the clearance of forests.

Ethnographic sources tell us, moreover, that the axe in modern primitive contexts, and perhaps also in the neolithic of western Europe, was not only a tool but also an object of prestige and social and religious significance (Clark J. G. D. 1965; Hughes I. 1977). If axes of igneous rock were indeed trade products, what was given in return by those communities who received them? Perhaps some form of organic, and therefore perishable, substance which would leave no trace in the archaeological record was traded. It is equally conceivable that the exchange of axes between neighbouring or even distant communities reflected social contact at least in terms of the objects themselves, even though there may have been underlying economic motives.

Flaked and polished flint axes are also found in north Britain. As might be expected, the major concentration is on the chalk of Lincolnshire and the East Riding of Yorkshire, but finds occur further north-east with a markedly coastal and riverine distribution. This can be clearly seen in the distribution of such finds in east central Scotland, where axes of igneous rock have a generally inland and riverine distribution while the flint forms are markedly coastal. Such northern finds presumably represent exports from the flint-bearing regions to the south, though it is remarkable that as yet no flint mines have been found either in Yorkshire or in Lincolnshire, and yet the size and quality of many of the axes in the north-east precludes the use of flint pebbles from the glacially derived deposits or coastal sources. The other diagnostic early neolithic flint type, the leaf-shaped arrow-head, is also widely distributed, generally in the form of stray finds as far north as Morayshire (Atkinson 1962). Other artifacts of flint, particularly scrapers and also waste chips, often form part of the occupation debris enclosed in the eastern end of the long mounds and scattered on the old land surface beneath barrows; as in the south, little work has been done on the categorizing of such material either in terms of form or of association. The scraper forms in the north-east are generally small blade types with a number of saws.

Bone artifacts are poorly represented. These include a bone pin from Willerby Wold and an antler comb similar to those in the Windmill Hill province from a pit underneath a round barrow at Garton Slack in the East Riding of Yorkshire. Recent excavations at Kilham produced the handle of an antler pick bearing two incised rings, and such implements can be expected in association with the ditches of large earthworks. Further north the generally acid soil conditions have been detrimental to the preservation of bone, antler and other organic materials.

Western Britain and Ireland

In the west and north of Britain contemporary early neolithic settlement is evidenced either by cereal pollens and forest clearance, by pollen diagrams from peat and lake sediments, or by collective stonebuilt megalithic or chambered tombs. These represent the only major monuments of the early neolithic in this western and north-western area and provide an even more one-sided picture of settlement than that of southern and eastern Britain. Radiocarbon dates now suggest that collective tombs were being constructed in various regions of the highland zone of the British Isles over a period of at least a millennium and as yet only four groups can be demonstrably associated with the earliest neolithic agriculturalists in western and north-western Britain. These are the Cotswold–Severn tombs of south-western Britain, the portal dolmens of central and northern Wales, the Clyde tombs of western and south-western Scotland and the court cairns in Northern Ireland.

Cotswold–Severn tombs The 180 or so tombs in the Cotswold–Severn group consist of a scattered group of monuments in coastal south Wales, a small concentration in the Black Mountains in Brecknockshire, further isolated monuments in Somerset, a small group in north Wiltshire and the major concentration in the Cotswolds in Gloucestershire (Corcoran 1969). In terms of tomb structure three basic types appear to be represented; simple terminal chambers, transepted terminal chambers and lateral chambers (fig. 3.11). All three forms are generally covered by a wedge-shaped long mound or cairn, in Wales and in the Cotswolds stone-built of small stone slabs presumably gathered over a wide area; in north Wiltshire the construction is similar to that of the earthen long barrows whose distribution area they share. Like the barrows they are provided with

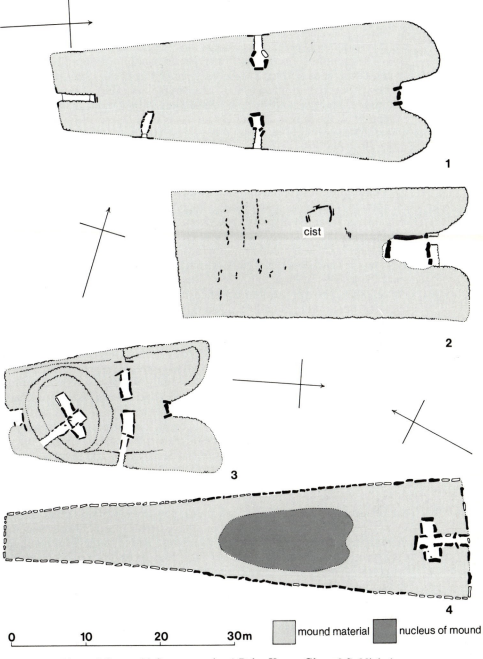

Fig. 3.11   Plans of Cotswold–Severn tombs. 1 Belas Knap, Glos.; 2 St Nicholas, Glam.; 3 Ty Isaf, Breck.; 4 Wayland's Smithy, Berks. (after Corcoran 1969 and 1972).

flanking quarry ditches from which the rubble of the chalk mound was obtained, in some cases with a primary spine of sarsen boulders (Piggott S. 1962b). As with the earthen long barrows, the mounds covering the chambers of Cotswold–Severn tombs have a generally east–west orientation. The mounds covering all three types are again broader and higher at their eastern ends and tend to be cusp-shaped or in-curving towards the entrance passage in the case of the simple terminal and transepted terminal chambers, and even in those sites with lateral chambers. An exception is the phase II monument at Wayland's Smithy, Berkshire, where the eastern end is a simple flat face (Atkinson 1965) (fig. 3.12). At some sites there is evidence of pre-mound activity in the form of the burning-off of scrub prior to the construction of the monument. In all three categories of tomb the mound either covered, or in some cases was revetted by, a carefully constructed dry-stone wall of small stone slabs, although at Wayland's Smithy II and probably the West Kennet mound in north Wiltshire a more massive sarsen kerb was employed.

Internally the mound itself was in some cases divided by means of axial and lateral lines of dry-stone walling forming a series of compartments, as at Randwick in Gloucestershire and Ascott-under-Wychwood in Oxfordshire (Selkirk 1971). The tombs with simple terminal chambers consist of rectangular box-like structures of orthostatic construction with the capstone or stones resting directly on these uprights (fig. 3.11: 2). Wedge-shaped mounds of such chambers were set at the broader eastern end and generally were approached by a cusp-shaped forecourt. One Brecknockshire site at Pentre Ifan had the simple rectangular stone chamber enclosed by a small circular cairn. The tombs with terminal transepted chambers are again generally set beneath long, usually wedge-shaped, mounds, access to the chambers being from the broader and eastern end approached again by a cuspidal forecourt. The tomb proper consists of a passage from which lead off pairs of side chambers, rather in the manner of the transepts in a Christian church. The number of transepts varies from one as at Wayland's Smithy (fig. 3.11: 4) to three at Stoney Littleton in Somerset.

The chambers themselves are again of generally orthostatic construction but in a number of cases the interstices between the uprights are filled with fine dry-stone walling as at West Kennet (Piggott S. 1962b). At this site the orthostats were of sarsen sandstone presumably obtained from the Downs in the area adjacent to the site, whereas the oolitic limestone forming the slabs of the filling has its nearest source in the Chippenham area some 12 miles from the site. At West Kennet and in a number of the other transepted tombs some corbelling had been used to reduce the area to be roofed by capstones. There is some evidence from a number of the transepted tombs to suggest that the covering wedge-shaped mound, as with earthen long barrows, represents one of the final acts in the erection of a series of pre-long mound structures (Corcoran 1972).

At Notgrove in Gloucestershire, to the west of the transepted chamber itself was a small closed polygonal chamber set within its own small circular cairn with a well-built revetment wall. This was later incorporated beneath the wedge-shaped mound covering the transepted tomb. One of the finest examples of multi-period construction is of course Wayland's Smithy: the primary monument was an earthen long barrow covering a timber mortuary house later covered by the wedge-shaped mound erected to incorporate the megalithic tomb (fig. 3.11: 4).

The final group of lateral chambered tombs also consists of simple rectangular chambers of orthostatic construction, although in this case access to the chamber is by means of a frequently long passage leading from the sides of the covering wedge-shaped mound (fig. 3.11: 1). The importance of the form of the covering mound regardless of the arrangement of the chambers beneath it is reflected in the provision of a false or blind entrance at the inner end of the cusp-shaped forecourt at the broader and higher eastern end. The blind entrance is defined by a pair of uprights and a lintel slab built into the solid mass of the cairn material. Access to the passages of such laterally chambered mounds at Rodmarton, Gloucestershire, and in one of the tombs beneath the mound at Belas Knap, was by means of a port-hole-like entrance consisting either of a circular hole worked in a blocking slab or the working of a semi-circular or lunate opening in a juxtaposed pair of slabs. In this group again there is some evidence of multi-period construction. At Belas Knap (fig. 3.11: 1) the three lateral chambers and simple terminal chamber at the south-south-western end were all enclosed within small round cairns though the excavation was too imprecise to determine the relationship between these and the wedge-shaped covering mound – although the unusual orientation of the wedge-shaped mound in this case may have been necessitated by the pre-existence of the four chambers with their own individual round cairns. Again the southern end of the tomb was set at an angle to the long axis of the mound, perhaps implying a pre-existing structure. More conclusive evidence of multi-period construction is provided by Ty Isaf, Brecknockshire (fig. 3.11: 3). The basic structure here was a transepted tomb covered by a round mound forming part of a larger wedge-shaped structure with two lateral chambers and a blind entrance on the north. The primary structures are considered to be two lateral chambers covered by the wedge-shaped cairn and a forecourt delimited by the inner line of dry-stone walling. At a later stage the transepted tomb with its covering mound was inserted into the wedge-shaped cairn. To do this part of the long cairn was removed but the western revetment was left unbroken. At this stage an outer wall was added to the composite structure, involving the lengthening of the passages in the lateral chambers.

In addition to these basic tomb types there are a number of long mounds in the north Cotswold region with blind entrances which never appear to have covered any form of megalithic structure. Like the earthen long barrows of the adjacent areas of southern Britain the Cotswold–Severn tombs were designed to accommodate collective burials by inhumation, though in some cases the bones exhibit traces of charring; it has been suggested this is a result of ritual fires being lit in the chambers. The total number of corpses interred varies from three to 48. In general, as with the earthen long barrows, the skeletal material is in a remarkably disarticulated condition, though in the collective stone-built tombs the disarray is more likely to be the result of the insertion of fresh corpses into the existing tomb chamber.

The most detailed evidence for the primary contents of such a Cotswold–Severn tomb is that provided by the excavation at West Kennet in Wiltshire. This, the largest tomb in the Cotswold–Severn group, was first excavated in the nineteenth century when the terminal chamber was discovered, but the two pairs of central chambers were excavated in the 1950s (Piggott 1962b). These chambers produced a total of 46 inhumation burials, the majority of which were disarticulated although there was some evidence to suggest the stacking of long bones and skulls in groups at the sides of the chambers. The grouping of bones has been noted in other Cotswold–Severn tombs and in addition the peculiar habit of inserting finger bones into the interstices of the dry-stone walling of the chambers. Another feature of the skeletal material from West Kennet was the absence of a considerable number of long bones and skulls amongst the total bulk of skeletal material. One can only infer that such portions

Fig. 3.12   Façade of chambered tomb at Wayland's Smithy, Berks. (photograph: H. A. W. Burl).

of the skeleton were in fact deliberately removed from the chambers during the process of the deposition of later interments in the tomb; the appearance of fragmentary human remains in the adjacent causewayed enclosure at Windmill Hill might be accounted for in this way. Such objects may have been removed for cult or magical purposes and these finds in the ditches do not in fact provide evidence for cannibalism as has been suggested in the past.

After the final burial had been deposited in the tomb chamber the corpses were left either uncovered or protected with only a light film of soil. A notable exception again is the West Kennet tomb, and the evidence here also suggests veneration of the tomb itself over a very considerable period of time from the middle to the late neolithic, a span of something in the region of a thousand years. At this site after the final corpse had been deposited in the chamber the whole of the tomb, both the chambers and passage, was deliberately filled with chalk rubble containing a mixture of sherds, animal bones, flints and other artifacts all apparently inserted during a single operation. The excavator suggested that such material represented offerings made over a period of many centuries, in some adjacent shrine or depository ultimately to be consigned to the tomb in its final blocking.

Such longevity of use raises problems in assessing the total number of individuals buried in the tomb. It is possible of course that the tombs themselves were cleared of their deposits from time to time, if in fact many were in use over this immense period, and evidence for such clearing out of the tombs and their contents is provided from elsewhere in Europe. On the other hand, an examination of the skeletal material from the tomb at Lanhill in Wiltshire suggested that the nine individuals were members of an individual family group and the same has been suggested for West Kennet. If these are in fact the collective tombs of family groups then in view of the life-span of the tombs themselves they could not have contained all members of a single dynasty nor could they have been erected by an enlarged family group, as the building of megalithic tombs involves very much more labour than that of the erection of an earthen long barrow. For example, the capstone at Tinkinswood in Glamorgan, weighing over 50 tons, would have involved the labour of at least 200 individuals in its removal and erection on the site (Atkinson 1961: 61). The marked disparity of the percentages of male and female corpses in such tombs further suggests that only certain individuals were entitled to interment in these monuments. One may therefore infer even more conclusively than in the case of the earthen long barrows that only certain privileged members of the community were deposited in these tombs.

The small finds from the Cotswold–Severn tombs are more numerous than those from the adjacent earthen long barrows but equally restricted in character. Where it is possible to isolate pottery in apparent primary contexts, as at West Kennet, it is related to Abingdon ware in the Windmill Hill series, having elaborate club-sectioned or rolled-over rims. In the case of the megalithic tombs, however, a wide variety of later pottery forms are also encountered; in most cases in a secondary context

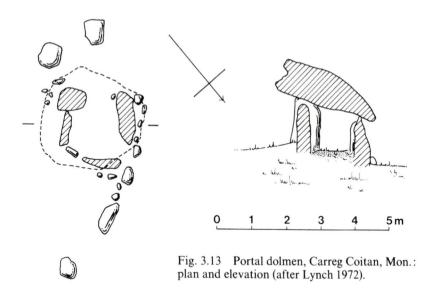

Fig. 3.13   Portal dolmen, Carreg Coitan, Mon.:
plan and elevation (after Lynch 1972).

either in the subsequent filling of the tomb or associated with the final blocking of the forecourt area.

A further ceramic link with the Windmill Hill culture is provided by the occurrence of pottery spoons in a number of the tombs. Two Gloucestershire tombs produced flattened oval beads of shale which again are paralleled in the causewayed enclosures at Hembury, Maiden Castle and Windmill Hill. If the raw material for such beads does in fact come from Kimmeridge in Dorset then it is one of the few pieces of evidence from the tombs themselves for trade over any distance, in view of the total absence of conclusive evidence of the occurrence of axes of igneous rock in any of the chambers.

The only other consistently recurring artifact is a bone scoop or chisel, generally made from the split long-bone of an ox. Such a tool, probably associated with skin dressing or leatherworking, is again represented on sites of the Windmill Hill culture although not so frequently as in the tombs of the Cotswold–Severn group.

Portal dolmens   In north Wales the presumably early group of megalithic tombs has as its most characteristic form a structure known as a portal dolmen. The burial chamber proper is rectangular in plan and composed of four upright slabs supporting a capstone which frequently slopes towards the rear of the chamber. The frontal pair of slabs project beyond the chamber itself forming a porch-like entrance forecourt (fig. 3.13). The entrance to the chamber is often blocked by a slab which may reach right up to the capstone. Although such forms of monument are numerous in Wales the majority are extremely ruinous and in many cases all traces of the covering cairn have been removed.

The only example of this category of monument which has been excavated by modern scientific methods is that at Dyffryn Ardudwy in Merionethshire (Powell 1973). The first structure here was a portal dolmen enclosed within its own small oval cairn (fig. 3.14: 3); the approach to the entrance of the dolmen itself was marked by a low façade of laid rather than upright stones, B-shaped in plan. At a later date this round cairn with its portal dolmen was covered by a very much larger rectangular cairn with, to the east of the original structure, a second dolmen-type burial chamber, again with possible traces of an incurved façaded forecourt. The pottery from the chambers consisted of carinated bowls with simple or rolled-over rims very similar to those from the settlement site at Clegyr Boia and a whole series of plain, carinated neolithic bowls from south-western Britain.

Similar monuments are also found in Cornwall, and also on the other side of the Irish Sea. In both these regions, however, they are considered late (Herity and Eogan 1977: 85).

Northwards again in south-western and western Scotland and in Northern Ireland it was for long considered that the megalithic structures of these areas represented a common architectural tradition and cultural community. More recent work however has tended to stress the dissimilarities rather than the likenesses between the monuments in the two areas.

Clyde tombs   In west and south-west Scotland the tombs are now generally termed Clyde cairns. They are represented by over 80 monuments distributed from Argyll to Galloway with a few rare examples extending eastwards to Perthshire. Childe long ago drew attention to the coastal distribution of such sites which he associated rightly with a preference for the gravel areas of raised beaches which would support a light and readily cultivable soil attractive to settlement by primitive agriculturalists. There is some evidence at least in the typology of the tombs to suggest that it was the lowland areas which were first settled by megalith builders in south-western and western Scotland and only at a later date the less hospitable upland region (Scott J. G. 1970), simple and 'early' forms occurring at lower altitudes than the more elaborate monuments.

Both chambers and cairn plans in this Clyde area show considerable variety of form. The chambers themselves are rectangular in plan, frequently with the side slabs overlapping and producing a telescopic effect. A capstone generally rests directly on the orthostats with only a minimum of corbelling. The entrance to the chamber proper may either be undifferentiated, or defined by a pair of flanking portal stones, or approached by an elaborate crescentic façade of large upright slabs. The chambers themselves are frequently divided up by means of a series of transverse septal slabs which reach to no more than half the total height of the chamber. The floors of the chambers are in some cases cobbled or paved. The mounds covering these chambers show a considerable variety in plan from round to oval or rectangular or wedge-shaped though the latter form is the most frequent but not necessarily the earliest. The composition of the mound is almost invariably stone.

Recent excavations and the reappraisal of earlier excavated sites suggest that in this region, as in the area of the Cotswold–Severn group, the tombs themselves are in some cases of multi-period construction. This is perhaps best illustrated in the two sites of Mid Gleniron I and II (Corcoran 1970). Site I consisted of two simple rectangular orthostatic chambers originally enclosed in small circular cairns set one behind the other (fig. 3.14). The two monuments were later incorporated beneath a wedge-shaped mound with a crescentic façade at the eastern end; presumably contemporary with this addition was the construction of a lateral chamber set midway between the two earlier monuments. At Mid Gleniron II, again the first phase consisted of a simple orthostatic chamber beneath its own small round cairn; this was covered by a later wedge-shaped mound associated with a further rectangular stone-built chamber approached by a slightly curved façade. At Mid Gleniron II, the orientation of the entrance of the earlier monument beneath the round cairn and that of the later structure beneath the wedge-shaped mound showed a change in axis of 90 degrees, whereas in Mid Gleniron I the initial axis of the earlier pair of monuments was retained.

Similar continuity of axis in tomb plan may be seen at the site of Cairnholy I in Kirkcudbright (Piggott and Powell 1948–9). In its final form the chamber consisted of two compartments divided by septal slabs although the rear, and by inference earlier, structure was in fact a simple stone box; access to this rear chamber from the outer one would have been impossible in view of the height of the septal slab. The second and outer compartment consists of a pair of very much taller orthostats giving the site at this stage the appearance of a portal dolmen. Possibly later still in the sequence is the addition of two further orthostats to the original portal stones, forming a second outer chamber leading out to an elaborate crescentic forecourt revetted with large upright slabs. A somewhat similar sequence can be postulated for the adjacent site of Cairnholy II and in other monuments in the Clyde region (Scott J. G. 1969: 192).

At Lochhill in Kirkcudbright the primary monument was a timber or timber and stone structure (Masters 1973). The first phase consisted of three axial pits, the two terminal ones supporting D-shaped timbers, the central one a pair of posts, and this feature fronted on to a slightly crescentic timber façade reminiscent of the façades beneath the earthen long barrows in north-eastern England and similar, too, to the monument at Dalladies (Piggott S. 1971–2). The three pits supporting timbers were set within a rectangular area revetted with granite boulders. Within this structure were the remains of an oak plank floor. Lying partially on this floor and partially in the stone filling of the mortuary structure were several deposits of cremated bone, probably representing the remains of a single individual. This timber structure was burnt down before the erection of a later cairn. The cairn itself was of typical wedge-shaped plan with a slightly crescentic stone façade at the north-eastern end. This gave access to an orthostatic chamber which itself may be of two building phases. The four innermost orthostats of the chamber may have stood independently in front of the timber façade and were later incorporated as part of the enlarged chamber beneath the wedge-shaped cairn. The cairn, too, suggests two structural phases indicated by a double revetment wall

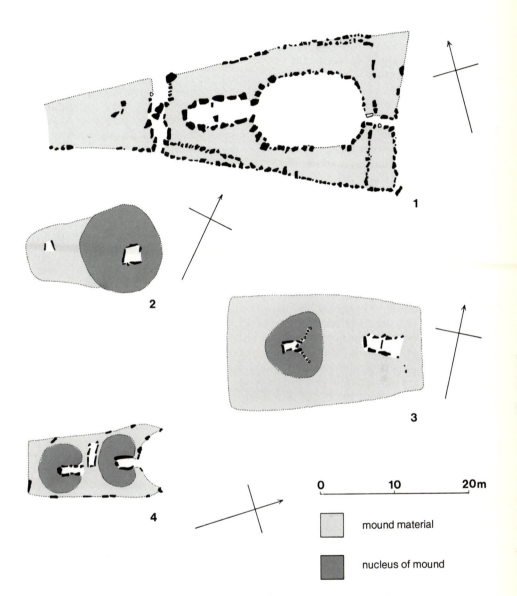

Fig. 3.14   Chambered tombs of multi-period construction. 1 Creevykeel, Sligo;
2 Pen-y-Wyrlod, Breck.; 3 Dyffryn Ardudwy, Merioneth; 4 Mid Gleniron I,
Wigtowns. (after Corcoran 1972).

on the north-west side. The inner wall may represent the original plan for a mound intended to cover only the mortuary structures. Later this was enlarged to form the wedge-shaped mound covering the orthostatic chamber.

The pottery from the Clyde tombs includes a percentage of plain round-based wares, consisting of bowls characterized by heavy expanded rims with almost vertical necks (fig. 3.15:6); and a second group of smooth-profiled bowls with lugs at or immediately below a simple rim. Another group of wares characteristic of the Clyde series of tombs are the so-called Beacharra bowls (fig. 3.15:3). These again are round-based vessels with a very sharp carination from which rises an almost vertical neck leading to an elaborate rim with an inturned collar. The vessels are profusely decorated by means of channelling, incision and at least in one case impressions made with a piece of whipped cord.

Later neolithic and single grave pottery has also been recorded from Clyde tombs though in no case are these demonstrably contemporary with the construction or primary use of the tomb. Other grave goods in the tombs are comparatively rare. They consist of piercing arrow-heads of leaf-shaped form in flint or chert and flint knives of plano-convex form, the working generally being confined to the convex surface, in some cases leaving a portion of the original cortex. Axes of igneous rock are rare and only one has been found in an unequivocal position associated with tombs of this group. Most interesting in terms of possible trading and exploitation of foreign-derived material is the discovery of implements or flakes of pitchstone in over a dozen of the tombs. The most likely source for such material is the Isle of Arran (Ritchie P. R. 1968: 121).

Both inhumed and cremated remains have been recovered from the chambers although inhumations are the more numerous, with a maximum of over 40 individuals from a single chamber. It must be borne in mind that the generally acid soil conditions in the areas where Clyde tombs were constructed would have been more detrimental to the survival of inhumed corpses than of burnt remains. The inhumations themselves are generally in a disarticulated condition, in some cases with the grouping of the long bones and skulls in specific parts of the chambers, as was noted in some tombs in the Cotswold–Severn region. One cannot argue for the primacy of one or other of the burial rites, because some tombs produced both rites in contemporary positions in the chambers, and in other cases inhumations were earlier than cremations and vice-versa. The disarticulated nature of many of the inhumation burials and the frequently varied chronological range of the finds in the chambers themselves, and the occurrence of fragmentary deposits of bones and broken pottery in the forecourt areas outside the chambers, give the impression – apparent in other chamber tomb groups – that the chambers themselves were cleared out periodically both of corpses and associated grave goods, and that even where the tomb appears to have an intact primary deposit this may in fact not be contemporary with the actual erection of the monument. Such a feature of course raises problems in connection with the dating of the tombs themselves, and dates either in the form of relative dating from associations or of charcoal from the chambers cannot be assumed to date the construction of the monuments themselves.

Court cairns On the other side of the North Channel in the northern area of Ireland there is a superficially similar group of megalithic tombs, the Carlingford element of Piggott's original Clyde–Carlingford culture which are now more conveniently grouped together under the heading of 'Court cairns' (De Valera 1960). These are distributed across the northern part of Ireland from Strangford Lough in the east to Mayo in the west. The greatest concentrations are in the latter county and Sligo and Leitrim. It is in this region, too, that the most elaborate forms of monument occur. The chambers themselves are again of orthostatic construction, in some cases divided into a series of compartments by means of projecting jamb-stones linked with septal slabs, frequently opening onto an elaborate crescentic forecourt. In some cases in the west this is almost completely closed, forming the so-called 'lobster claw' plan (fig. 3.14:1). The covering mounds, generally of stone, are normally wedge-shaped in plan as in the Clyde tombs and the Cotswold–Severn group.

The human remains from the chambers are almost invariably represented by fragments of cremated bone, representing no more than one or two individuals, and only a small percentage of the total skeletal material even of this number. These token cremation deposits frequently lie on a pavement of stone slabs and cobbling and form part of a matrix of earth containing carbonized material, sherds of pottery and fragments of animal remains (Case 1969b). In almost every case such material appears to represent a single-stage deposition and not the successive interment of burials over a considerable period of time. Because of the unusual nature of the contents of these megalithic structures Case has gone so far as to suggest that they are not primarily sepulchral in function and that the earth matrix with its fragments of burnt bone, sherds and debris represents scraped-up occupation material from settlement sites and that such monuments should be regarded as shrines rather than tombs. The frequently elaborate façades and forecourt areas, some of which have produced evidence for considerable ritual activity, would then be the scene for continuing ceremonial practices over a considerable period of time. Later perhaps in function than these megalithic shrines are a series of open sites, in some cases defined by an enclosure ditch in which there are numerous pits and a spread of settlement debris containing sherds of pottery and fragments of bones, material very similar to that from the court cairn chambers (Case 1969b).

As in the Clyde and Cotswold–Severn tombs multi-period construction is apparent in a number of the Irish court cairns. At Barns Lower, Co. Tyrone, a wedge-shaped mound covered five and possibly six chambers (Corcoran 1972: 37). The cairn itself had been considerably disturbed, making it difficult to recognize any structural sequence. The primary structure, however, may have been the inner two segments of a four-segmented chamber opening to the south-west. This inner pair of segments

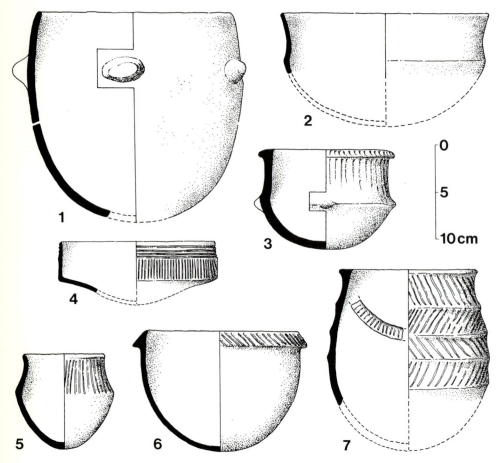

Fig. 3.15   Scottish early and middle neolithic pottery. 1 Pitcaple, Aberdeens.; 2 Pitnacree, Perths.; 3 Achnacree, Argylls.; 4 Northton, Harris; 5 Unival, North Uist; 6 Rudh an Dunain, Skye; 7 Northton, Harris (after McInnes 1969).

of orthostatic construction was built of very much larger stones, and the partially ruined outer pair of much smaller orthostats with panels of dry-stone walling. Subsequently further chambers would have been added behind and to the north-east of this structure, the whole being finally covered by a long trapezoid cairn.

Similarly at Annaghmore, Co. Armagh, a three-segmented chamber opening on to a deeply recurved forecourt covered by a comparatively short wedge-shaped cairn had the later addition behind the primary chamber of two opposed oval chambers covered by additional mound material and entered laterally (Corcoran 1972: 37).

Multi-period construction with the primary monument of timber is also represented at Doey's Cairn, Co. Antrim (Evans E. E. 1938). Here a cremation trench in the Yorkshire manner covered three axial pits possibly designed to contain timbers. Subsequently built on top of this structure was a segmented chamber covered by a wedge-shaped cairn. Such a sequence is strongly reminiscent of the timber and later megalithic monument at Lochhill in Kirkcudbright and the position of this site in relation to the Irish monument and those in Yorkshire may be significant.

As in the other areas where megalithic tombs are the principal evidence for early neolithic settlement the evidence for domestic sites and house structures is extremely scanty. At Ballyglass in Co. Mayo (O'Nuallain 1972) a rectangular house 12m long and defined in part by bedding trenches, in part by individual post-holes, was partially overlain by the chamber and cairn of a court cairn. Similar rectangular house plans have been recovered from Ballynagilly, Co. Tyrone, and from Lough Gur, Co. Limerick (ApSimon 1976b; ÓRíordáin 1954). At Ballynagilly the botanical evidence suggests the existence of fields and cultivation activities in the vicinity of the site and this has subsequently been confirmed archaeologically by the recognition that a number of field systems and enclosures defined by dry-stone walls, many discovered during peat cutting, belong to the neolithic period (Herity 1971). At Millin Bay in Co. Down such a field wall was shown to antedate the construction of a late neolithic cairn (Collins and Waterman 1955). As in other areas of primary neolithic settlement in the British Isles, the pottery includes a high percentage of smooth profiled bowls and carinated vessels with rims varying from simple rounded forms to elaborate club-shaped, thickened examples. Associated with these plain wares are lesser quantities of vessels termed Ballyalton bowls by Case (1961). These are shouldered vessels but with the diameter of the rim less than that of the shoulder and decorated with linear grooves and twisted cord impressions. The only important non-ceramic associations are leaf- or lozenge-shaped flint arrow-heads, horseshoe-shaped scrapers and ground stone axes from the axe factory at Tievebulliagh, Co. Antrim.

Chronology and origins   The evidence of radiocarbon dating suggests that all the material so far discussed, though in some cases having certain regional peculiarities, presents a broadly contemporary cultural spectrum. There is certainly no evidence for the primacy of settlement in southern or south-eastern Britain; indeed, the earliest radiocarbon dates obtained so far from a neolithic site are those from Ballynagilly, Co. Tyrone, with a date of 3,795 ± 90 bc. In southern Britain the earliest dates are those from the long barrow at Lambourn, Berkshire, of 3,415 ± 180 bc, the ditch from the settlement of Hembury in Devon of 3,330 ± 150 bc, and the flint mines at Findon in Sussex of 3,390 ± 150 bc. These and other early radiocarbon dates link the three principal categories of monument which define the Windmill Hill culture, and this association is confirmed by the material remains from these sites. Ironically the type-site itself, the causewayed enclosure at Windmill Hill, has yielded a date from the primary ditch silt of 2,580 ± 150 bc although there is evidence for pre-enclosure neolithic activity in terms of a date of 2,690 ± 150 bc, from charcoal from the pre-bank occupation. Early settlement in East Anglia is attested at the site of Broomheath, Norfolk, with the earliest date from a pit of 2,629 ± 65 bc.

To the north-east there is the early date of 3,010 ± 150 bc for the long barrow at Willerby Wold, East Riding of Yorkshire, and for Kilham in the same county of 2,880 ± 125 bc (Manby 1976). North-eastwards, the long barrow of Dalladies, Kincardineshire, has a date of 3,240 ± 105 bc. In the north-west the originally anomalous date of 3,014 ± 300 bc for the axe-finishing site of the products of the Langdale axe factory at Ehenside Tarn in Cumberland would now fit quite happily into the pattern, as do the dates of 3,160 ± 110 bc and 3,120 ± 105 bc for the Clyde tombs of Monamore in Arran and Lochhill, Dumfriesshire.

It must be emphasized that these radiocarbon dates come very largely from impressive and labour-consuming funerary and ceremonial sites which are unlikely to be the earliest products of the primary neolithic settlers in the British Isles. Be that as it may, the evidence of radiocarbon dating does suggest the very rapid spread of early agriculturalists throughout the British Isles: the problem is to determine, first, the inter-relationship of the groups within these islands and, secondly, their ultimate source on the Continent.

To consider first of all the internal evidence, the pattern appears to be that of largely self-sufficient agricultural communities living for most of the year in comparatively isolated family groups, and externally dependent only in terms of either flint or igneous rock for the production of axes. Larger and periodic social groupings are, however, suggested by the existence of the causewayed enclosures on the chalk of southern Britain and, serving the same function as a social focus, possibly the long barrows and megalithic chambered tombs in the north and the west, and the ceremonial sites of the Goodlands type in Ireland (Fleming 1972; 1973).

Amongst the funerary monuments themselves there is also the clearly unifying feature of the trapezoid mound, either of earth in southern and eastern Britain, or of stone in the north and west, covering chambers either of wood or stone. Accepting the conditions outlined at the beginning of this chapter for the introduction of a farming economy in the British Isles, it follows that the appearance of agriculturalists with their flocks and herds and seed corn as an introduced phenomenon from the continental land-mass of Europe must also have been associated with the introduction of other aspects of material culture, most recently from those areas of Europe immediately adjacent to the British Isles. Radiocarbon dates now indicate that north-western and western Europe had been settled by agriculturalists by the second half of the 4th millennium bc, and the problem is to determine which area or areas were the homeland of the earliest farming communities in the British Isles.

It was for long accepted that the early neolithic cultures in the British Isles as best expressed in southern Britain in the material equipment of the Windmill Hill culture belonged to the general family of western neolithic cultures represented by the Chassey culture in France, the Cortaillod culture in Switzerland, the Almeria culture in the Iberian peninsula and the Michelsberg culture of Belgium, southern Germany and northern Switzerland. The Danubian or Linearbandkeramik cultures of central Europe extending as far north-west as the Low Countries, and the

Trichterbecker, TRB or funnel beaker cultures of southern Scandinavia on the other hand were considered as entirely continental phenomena contributing nothing to the material culture of the earliest agriculturalists in the British Isles.

A reassessment of the continental relationships of the earliest British neolithic cultures by Piggott (1955; 1961) was stimulated by Vogt's study (1953) of the origins of the Michelsberg culture, the latter long considered to stand in a cousinly relationship to that of Windmill Hill in that they shared similarities both in pottery styles, stone and bone equipment, and in the construction of hill-top enclosures and flint mines. In this milieu the unchambered earthen long barrows in Brittany appeared to provide suitable continental parallels for the British monuments (Piggott S. 1937b). Vogt, however, suggested that the Michelsberg culture was in fact simply a southern extension of the TRB culture of southern Scandinavia. From a British standpoint this opens up once more the problem of the continental relationships of the early neolithic material in these islands. If, in fact, Michelsberg belonged to the northern sphere of early neolithic cultures then a similar origin could be suggested for many of the phenomena found in the British Isles. Current opinion does, in fact, suggest a dual origin for the earliest neolithic groups in the British Isles as was expressed some years ago in Piggott's paper, 'Windmill Hill, East or West?' (1955). What might still be considered truly western is material from south-western Britain represented by pottery in the Hembury style with wide-mouthed carinated vessels, in some cases with trumpet lugs, and by promontory enclosures at the type-site itself, which have their closest parallels in Brittany in the regional variant of the Chassey culture. Long barrows on the other hand are conspicuously absent in south-western Britain and the Breton examples suggested in the 1930s as being ancestral to the British material are now considered by French archaeologists to be north-western European phenomena. Admittedly on the basis, as yet, of only a single radiocarbon date the introduction of this form of monument must be comparatively late in the neolithic of the Breton peninsula. In northern Europe in the TRB culture many of the aspects of the early neolithic in the British Isles are equally well represented, and now radiocarbon dates indicate contemporaneity, so this culture zone could have been one of the prime influences and sources of the early neolithic in the British Isles. What is considered the most convincing evidence in favour of a TRB element in the British early neolithic is provided by a recent series of long barrow excavations in Britain, and with the recognition first at Wayland's Smithy that these mounds contain at their broader and generally eastern end a rectangular wooden mortuary house with a gabled roof covering the area in which lay multiple inhumation burials.

A further feature now shown by excavation to be frequent and recurrent is the enclosing of the funerary area by an elongated rectangular or trapezoid structure either of wooden posts or a turf revetment or a ditch. In the area forward of the mortuary house, timber forecourt features and structures have been found, sometimes ritually burnt as at Nutbane in

Hampshire (Morgan 1959). Once recognized, the presence of such a mortuary house may be inferred from earlier excavations (Ashbee 1966a). At Fussell's Lodge, if there is such a mortuary house then this is found in conjunction with a trapezoid enclosure. In view of the date of 3,230 ±150 bc at this site both must be features of the early neolithic.

Related to the long barrows are the long mortuary enclosures, in some cases representing a primary stage in the funerary ritual. The Normanton Down mortuary enclosure contains what is now interpreted as bedding trenches for a gabled roof structure. Parallels for the paved and roofed mortuary house in Britain have recently been established in northern Europe. At Konens Høj in Denmark (Daniel 1967) such a structure, admittedly not beneath a mound but having a paved floor, gabled roof with end posts and sides held by stones comparable, in the view of the excavator, to Wayland's Smithy, contained a single burial with a TRB C vessel. This produced a radiocarbon date of 2,900 ±100 bc. The Salten grave in Jutland with a comparable ornament of copper may also have been covered by a gabled timber roof.

Flint mines are also an aspect of the Belgian Michelsberg culture and in Poland the TRB area flint mines are associated with TRB C pottery. Amongst the small finds, leaf-shaped flint arrow-heads, generally considered as a western neolithic type and the predominant form in the Windmill Hill culture, are found in Poland in TRB C contexts and Polish archaeologists interpret these in terms of western contacts, possibly with Britain. Perhaps the most characteristic organic tool of the Windmill Hill culture, the antler comb, also has parallels in the Belgian flint mines of Spiennes and a stray find comes from Kiel in the territory of the TRB culture.

The pottery presents the most difficult problem of all. Atkinson (1962) has stressed the presence in eastern and northern Britain of an open-shouldered bowl tradition with a broadly everted neck. In the 1930s archaeologists looked to the Michelsberg culture for parallels but there seemed to be chronological difficulties in that the Michelsberg culture was thought to be too late to be ancestral to the British early neolithic and the idea was put aside in favour of an origin for the whole in the western Chassey and allied cultures. Now radiocarbon dates indicate mid-4th millennium beginnings for the Michelsberg. If one accepts the TRB element in pottery as well, then the British shouldered bowls in southern and eastern parts of the country and comparable pottery in Ireland would be variants of the round-based shallow form of TRB B pottery. The vertically striated Whitehawk ware would then be equivalent to TRB C. In his study of the TRB culture in Denmark Becker (1948) looked to western contacts to explain the round-based characteristics of his B group so that the eastern-derived pottery in Britain, if such it is, may have an original western ancestry but transmitted to this country from northern Europe with other components of the TRB culture. Dutch archaeologists now believe that a group of Michelsberg peoples did, in fact, cross to Britain from Belgium and influenced the Windmill Hill culture and they regard the Michelsberg as part of TRB.

It should, however, be emphasized that all the features mentioned above as having possible TRB links – pottery, enclosures, long barrows and timber mortuary houses – are not the whole TRB culture but only aspects of it picked out of the cultural whole. This again raises the problem of the movement of agriculturalists over a considerable distance to virgin territory. Should we expect to find their ancestral material culture perfectly duplicated in the area in which they settled? In particular, in view of what has been suggested above as far as the primary phases of occupation are concerned, would they be more concerned with land-taking rather than with construction of ceremonial and funerary monuments or the perfect reproduction of other aspects of their material culture from the homelands from which they came? It is perhaps more surprising that one can find so many precise parallels on the Continent for the material equipment and monuments of the early settlers in the British Isles. The pattern at the moment appears to be a dual one in that the western or south-western material in Britain is of Breton origin whereas that in central, southern and eastern Britain, ultimately transmitted to western Scotland and Ireland, has a northern origin.

The megalithic tombs themselves were long considered to be one of the clearest aspects of the diffusion of an idea expressed in terms of grandiose funerary monuments throughout the Atlantic coast of Europe. The evidence from recent excavations in Britain demonstrates that in many cases what appear to be superficially elaborate structures had comparatively simple beginnings in terms of a single chambered box-like structure. This makes the continental derivations or origins of such monuments very much more difficult to determine, particularly in view of the apparent existence of wooden prototypes beneath earthen funerary structures. The apparent continental analogies of the developed and presumably late monuments of the Cotswold–Severn, Clyde and court cairn series may in fact represent parallel evolutionary architectural forms and it is no longer necessary to invoke a primary source on the European landmass for such monuments.

4 The later neolithic (c. 2,500–1,700 bc)

Introduction

The evidence from the second half of the 3rd millennium bc suggests further insular development of regional forms and styles, in material equipment and monuments, among the inhabitants of the British Isles. The one possible exception where continental sources might again be invoked for the introduction of new ideas is the appearance and construction of megalithic passage graves, in which there is a marked distinction between the height and width of the entrance passage and burial chamber.

Passage graves

The Boyne tombs The most impressive of these groups are the Boyne tombs of Ireland, distributed in a series of four great cemeteries from east to west: Newgrange in the bend of the Boyne, Loughcrew, Carrowkeel and Carrowmore in Sligo (ÓRíordáin and Daniel 1964; Herity 1974). These cemeteries are in fact dispersed groups of megalithic tombs scattered over an area of several square miles. This tendency for grouping of tombs and their prominent and hilltop situations contrasts, however, with other chambered tombs so far discussed.

The chambers are normally covered by round cairns, the chambers themselves falling into two major groups: firstly, comparatively small circular burial chambers generally covered by cairns 15m or less in diameter; and secondly, the great tombs such as Newgrange itself, where the chamber is of roughly cruciform plan, the covering mounds being as much as 76m in diameter and 15m high (fig. 4.1: 3). In both groups the passage is of orthostatic construction and the chamber roofed by corbelling. The cairns are generally revetted with a kerb of upright slabs although the entrance itself is unelaborate, unlike the Clyde, court cairns and Cotswold–Severn groups, suggesting perhaps little funerary or ritual activity in the vicinity of the entrance itself – although at Bryn Celli Ddu in Anglesey (Hemp 1930; Lynch 1970: 58) there was a pit containing the crouched skeleton of an ox immediately outside the entrance passage. Information concerning the structure of Boyne tombs has been considerably enhanced in recent years by the excavations of two of the most spectacular members of this series, the great tombs at Newgrange (O'Kelly C. 1967) and Knowth (Eogan 1973) in the bend of the Boyne, the latter still in process of excavation. At Newgrange the mound was surrounded by a free-standing circle of upright stones and the layout of this circle in relation to the mound suggests that the former was either earlier or contemporary with the passage grave itself. Excavation of this site has demonstrated that the mound, although superficially of stone construction, in fact consists of alternate layers of turf and stones, probably with the final capping in the form of quartz pebbles derived from the river valley beneath the site. Immediately above the entrance passage was a box-like construction, perhaps an offering place as suggested by the excavator (O'Kelly M. J. 1973). A possible astronomical function for this roof is indicated by the fact that it would admit light to the central chamber at the winter solstice, even when the entrance to the tomb was sealed (Patrick 1974). The upper, that is the invisible, sides of the capstones of the passage had a series of grooves cut on their surfaces, the possible object being to drain off rain water percolating through the cairn in order to keep the passage and chamber dry. The passage, 19m long, gave access to a corbelled chamber 6m high off which led three subsidiary chambers forming the typical cruciform plan of the larger Irish passage graves. Within each chamber was a stone basin designed to contain cremation burials.

The other great passage grave currently being excavated at Knowth presents even more remarkable evidence for its construction. The principal monument at Knowth itself has now been shown to be the largest tomb of a minor cemetery within the main Boyne cemetery, for around the great mound were grouped a series of lesser cairns covering simple passage graves; however, at least one of the smaller tombs is probably earlier than the major monument as the kerb of the latter respects the position of the small passage grave. As at Newgrange, the principal mound at Knowth was of complex construction, consisting of alternating layers of turf, shale and water-worn stones derived from the valley of the Boyne itself. Two chambers have so far been located beneath the principal mound, one of cruciform construction, typical of the chambers beneath the larger monuments, and the second a simple round chamber.

Although it has not yet been demonstrated by excavation, it would appear that Knowth presents one of the few cases of multi-period construction in an Irish passage grave. The simple circular burial chamber beneath the mound is approached by a long orthostatic passage which has a dog-leg bend. One could see this change in alignment of the passage in terms of the enlargement of the original cairn covering a small simple circular burial chamber at a time when the more complex cruciform passage was added, involving the lengthening of the passage approach to the original chamber on a slightly different alignment associated with the enlargment of the mound itself. The only other Boyne tombs where multi-period construction appears to be attested are at Fourknocks 2 (Hartnett 1971), where the primary structure was a cremation trench in the Yorkshire manner later covered by a cairn associated with a passage grave; and at Bryn Celli Ddu in Anglesey (Lynch 1970: 58), where a Boyne passage grave appears to have been constructed on top of a pre-existing henge monument.

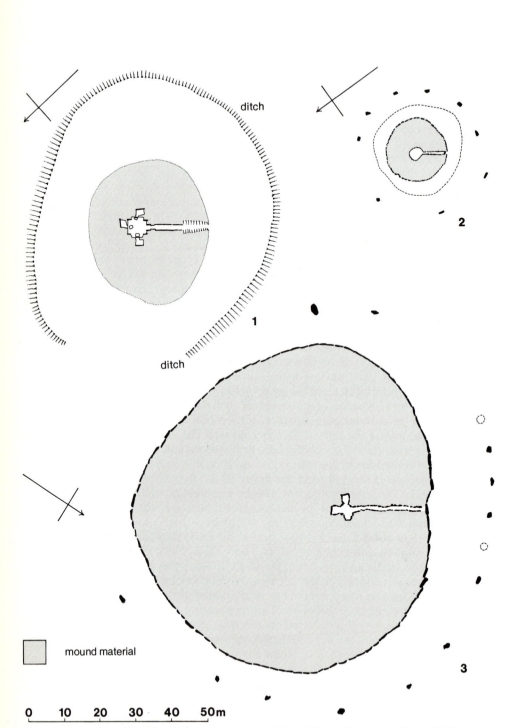

Fig. 4.1   Plans of passage graves. 1 Maes Howe, Orkney; 2 Clava, N.E. Inverness.; 3 Newgrange, Co. Meath (after Henshall 1963 and Herity and Eogan 1977).

One of the most remarkable aspects of the Boyne passage graves is the mural art which occurs on the stones of the kerb, passage and chamber, and in one case at Knowth on the external and interior surfaces of a stone basin. The art itself is produced either by incision or more normally by pounding or pecking the surface of the stone (Shee 1973). At Fourknocks 1 (Hartnett 1971: 226) and Newgrange (ÓRíordáin and Daniel 1964: 58) it has been claimed that a metal chisel had been used to execute some of the motifs but experiments have shown that similar results could be achieved with a flint tool. It is possible that the original layout of the decoration was produced by painting the surface of the stone and subsequently pecking in the roughed-out designs, in view of the fact that in a number of cases the actual lines of ornament tend to expand towards the base of the design as would be normal in a brush stroke. The motifs themselves consist very largely of non-representational, curvilinear or geometric patterns, normally scattered haphazardly over the surface of any single stone and not forming any type of organized design. Some of the curvilinear designs have been interpreted as stylized representations of eyes or a human face and these have been compared, rather unconvincingly, with the face- or face-and-figure motif carved on the walls of some French collective tombs and executed on bone phalanges and slate plaques in Iberia (Fleming 1969).

Within the fairly wide range of motifs it is noticeable that a number of monuments display a preference for a particular design. For example at Newgrange the lozenge and zig-zag were found on the greatest number of surfaces (fig. 4.2) whereas at Knowth the circle motif is the dominant one. The significance of these designs is of course a matter for mere speculation. Their occurrence on funerary monuments would suggest that they have some religious significance. Some of this art was certainly executed on the stones before their incorporation into a monument, as in many cases the designs are invisible in the positions in which they have been erected. Equally clearly, other decorated stones had the work executed *in situ* and it was intended to be visible to a visitor to the site; it may be significant that many of the finest and most elaborate designs belong to this latter category.

In considering the function of the art one of the most interesting and enigmatic stones is that which blocks the entrance to the western chamber at Knowth. A feature of many of the kerbstones at Knowth is the ordered arrangement of the decoration in contrast to that in the majority of other decorated passage graves, and in this entrance stone the motif which covers the whole of the outer face of the stone consists of a series of concentric rectangles bisected by a vertical groove. At the back of the chamber of this western passage grave is a stone identically decorated and one can only think of the kerb stone as forming some kind of marker indicating the presence of the entrance to the passage itself.

The majority of the excavated passage graves have shown signs of disturbance or earlier robbing but it is clear that the normal burial rite is that of cremation. Cremation must have taken place some distance from the site and the bones deposited in stone basins, where they exist, or on flat slabs placed on the floor of the chamber. The grave goods themselves, invariably unburnt, are found mixed with these bone deposits. The characteristic pottery, Carrowkeel ware, consists of small smooth-profiled bowls of coarse texture and thick-walled, the external surfaces decorated most frequently in a stab-and-drag technique using a sharp pointed tool. The commonest design is that of one or two horizontal lines produced in this technique immediately below the rim followed by a series of roughly vertical bands of ornament beneath it. Other consistently recurring grave goods are a series of very large pins of bone and antler, frequently with elaborate poppy- or mushroom-shaped heads. It is possible that such pins were used to secure some form of organic container in which the cremated human remains were placed. Finally there are a series of barrel-shaped beads produced from a variety of stones, and a series of pendants, the commonest form being pestle-shaped and perhaps copying maceheads of similar form.

West Scottish passage graves   The remaining groups of passage graves are found in Scotland. In the south-west there is a small group of 12 tombs named after the site of Bargrennan, Kirkcudbright (Henshall 1972). These are small passage graves of both orthostatic and dry-stone walled construction, in some cases having little distinction between the entrance

Fig. 4.2   Decorated kerb stone, Newgrange, Co. Meath (photograph: D. D. A. Simpson).

passage and chamber proper. The chambers are generally covered by round cairns. Little is known of the contents of these chambers. At Bargrennan scattered cremations were found in the chamber and passage. From the passage came sherds of coarse cordoned or shell-impressed wares, which have their nearest parallels in late neolithic coastal settlements in the same area.

Northwards again in the islands of the Inner and Outer Hebrides and the adjacent areas of the west Scottish mainland is a further group of passage graves, the Hebridean group, which has its principal concentration in the southern islands of the Outer Hebrides and in particular, North Uist. The chambers in tombs of this group are comparatively large in relation to the size of the complete mound and are oval or circular in plan, generally of orthostatic construction with a little corbelling below the roof. Four of the tombs in the group are covered by square cairns and six by long. Such monuments provide evidence of multi-period construction, the primary cairn being the circular one with additional mound material subsequently added to it. In some cases further cairn material may also be added to a circular monument without changing its superficial shape.

Finally, at Callanish, Lewis, a small passage grave appears to have been inserted into a pre-existing stone circle with related avenues and alignments (see below). Few of the tombs have been excavated but the little evidence which survives suggests both inhumation and cremation rites were practised. The grave goods include Beacharra pottery similar to that from Clyde tombs and also, from Unival in North Uist (Scott W. L. 1947–8), multiple carinated vessels decorated with incised herringbone ornament characteristic of the local Hebridean late neolithic.

North Scottish passage graves The western coast of Scotland from Skye to Cape Wrath presents an uninviting landscape for primitive agricultural-ists, but in Caithness and down the east coast of the Cromarty Firth the relatively flat coastal strip was settled, and a similar lowland environment in the Orkney Islands was exploited by passage grave builders. The morphology of these north Scottish passage graves is extremely compli-cated. Two major tomb types may be distinguished; firstly the so-called 'stalled cairns' in which pairs of slabs set on edge project into the passage or chamber dividing it up into a series of bays and also reducing the span of the area to be roofed by corbelling or capstones. The type-site is that of Camster, Caithness. Excavation here suggests that the primary structures were small stalled passage graves contained within their own circular cairns, the whole group later being covered by a long wedge-shaped mound. The long mounds of Yarrows type as recognized by Piggott also probably represent the later addition of cairn material to originally small roughly circular structures. In the cairns of Camster and Yarrows type the long mound appears to be unrelated to the ground area of the chambers which it was designed to cover. In other monuments on the other hand the elongated mound had a functional purpose in that one development appears to be the multiplication of the bays culminating in a monument like Midhowe in Orkney with a long cairn covering a very long chamber with 28 bays, entered by a short passage at one end of the cairn. Here the length of the cairn is functional, being designed to cover the greatly elongated burial chamber. A further development at two sites of Camster type is that of a double-decker tomb with two chambers, the capstones of one forming the roof of the other, each chamber approached by a passage from opposite sides of the cairn. All these abnormalities appear to be purely local developments and not the result of outside contact, although the covering of some of the simple passage graves with greatly elongated wedge-shaped mounds echoes a similar practice in the Clyde tombs, court cairns and Cotswold–Severn group.

The second major series of tombs in the north Scottish group is named after the remarkable monument of Maes Howe in Orkney (fig. 4.1: 1 and fig. 4.3). The basic chamber plan is of cruciform design reminiscent of some of the great tombs of the Boyne series of Ireland but as in the Camster group developments include multiplicity of secondary chambers. In the monument on the Holm of Papa Westray in Orkney the number of these chambers has been so increased that a long rather than the more normal circular mound was required to cover the chamber structure. Maes Howe itself is the most accomplished and sophisticated chambered tomb in the British Isles. As at Knowth and Newgrange the mound is of complex construction consisting of alternating layers of earth, peat and stone

Fig. 4.3   Maes Howe, Orkney (photograph: Cambridge University Committee for Aerial Photography: Crown Copyright).

forming a mound 45m in diameter and 7m high. The mound stands within an oval area 76m by 60m surrounded by a ditch 13m wide and 1·8m deep. Again this may be comparable to the enclosing of the Newgrange monument by a free-standing stone circle. The platform on which the monument lies was artificially levelled by filling in depressions with clay, again a unique feature.

The burial chamber is approached by an entrance passage 11m long partly formed of side and roofing slabs over 5·5m in length (fig. 4.4). Immediately inside the entrance passage is a recess designed to contain a single massive blocking stone. The passage gives access to a chamber, 4·5m square, the sides vertical for the first 1·5m and then corbelled for the remaining 3m. Careful oblique splitting and dressing of the stones used in the corbelling has enabled a gentle curve to be produced. In each corner of the chamber the vaulting is supported by buttresses. Three cells opening at waist level in the main chamber produce the cruciform plan. Originally each of these cells was blocked by a single slab; these are now lying on the floor of the chamber, and when in position it would have been extremely difficult to detect the presence of these secondary chambers. The tomb itself was broken into through the corbelled roof by the Vikings some time in the 1150s and they left records of their depredation on the walls of the chamber. The runic inscriptions refer to the discovery of treasure at Maes Howe and this can only mean that metal grave goods were included amongst the objects which accompanied the dead in this tomb, although of course nothing survives either of the original burials or of the objects which accompanied them.

Although in its quality and architectural refinements Maes Howe is unique in the British Isles, standing in relation to other megalithic tombs in the way that Stonehenge does to stone circles, there is a series of monuments in Orkney which has the same high standard of dry-stone walling and a tendency to build high chimney-like vaults. A number of the tombs in this series have pecked representations of eye-brow and circular motifs, reminiscent of the art of the Boyne tombs of Ireland. Both inhumation and cremation rites are attested from the tombs in this group and a consistent feature is the considerable quantity of animal remains also found in the chambers; in addition to the bones of domestic food animals, other animal bones – principally ox and pig and wild game, notably red deer, and in two cases the skulls of seven and 24 dogs respectively – were recovered from chambers. Grave goods include plain and carinated baggy bowls, a series of shallow vessels with a very marked shoulder or carination termed Unstan ware, which is also represented in the Outer Hebrides (fig. 3.15:4), and mace heads and knobbed and spiked stone objects of unknown function which have parallels in the remarkable village sites of Rinyo and Skara Brae (see below p. 143). The only other possibly contemporary monument which requires mention in Orkney is the so-called Dwarfie Stane (fig. 4.5). This is a sandstone mass on the island of Hoy, 8·5m long and 4·2m wide, in which is cut a short passage leading to an oval chamber 2·7m by 1·5m. Originally this passage was blocked by a massive stone which now lies outside the entrance. Nothing

Fig. 4.4 Maes Howe, Orkney: passage and chamber (photograph: J. V. S. Megaw).

Fig. 4.5 Dwarfie Stane, Hoy, Orkney (photograph: J. V. S. Megaw).

is known of the contents of this rock-cut tomb which is unique in the British Isles.

Northwards again, in Shetland there is a further series of megalithic tombs represented by over 70 sites. The chambers themselves are covered by heel-shaped cairns with a slightly crescentic forecourt giving access to small chambers either rectangular or trefoil-shaped in plan.

A unique feature in Shetland, however, is that the domestic sites of the chambered tomb builders have also survived and been recognized (Calder 1955–6). Over 60 such house sites have been recorded in Shetland (fig. 4.7:4). Probably not all of them are contemporary with the heel-shaped cairns, but the evidence of distribution of these two categories of monument, their similarities in construction and plan and the finds from both groups of monument indicate that some at least of the houses were almost certainly constructed by the builders of the megalithic tombs, although such a house type has a long life in Shetland, surviving for example in the late bronze age levels of the settlement of Jarlshof (Hamilton 1956: 18). Even more significant is that some of these houses are associated with enclosures and field systems defined by dry-stone dykes. Some of these enclosures probably served as animal pounds, and in spite of the generally acid soil conditions sufficient animal remains have survived to suggest both sheep and oxen among the domestic stock. Cereal growing, however, is also attested by the discovery of large quantities of barley at the site of Stanydale (Calder 1949–50) and by the considerable number of querns from these house sites and by stone plough-shares.

Similar in general plan and construction to the houses and the tombs but set apart both by size and its internal fittings, Stanydale was interpreted by its excavator as a temple. It is certainly not a normal house and may, in fact, have been either a religious structure or a public building. The site is oval in plan with a shallow crescentic forecourt and set axially within it were two large post-holes containing carbonized lumps of timbers 25·5cm in diameter. The wood has been identified as spruce, a tree which is not native to Scotland; the most likely source of this timber is in fact driftwood derived from North America. Some 762 linear metres of timbers would have been necessary to support the roof, suggesting in the generally treeless environment of Shetland that large quantities of driftwood were readily available. It is possible, of course, that the Stanydale site was an open enclosure and that the two timbers represented free-standing structures of totemic form.

The Clava cairns The last major group of passage graves are the Clava tombs, concentrated in the north-eastern end of the Great Glen (Henshall 1963: 12). The 50 or so sites are distributed in three principal regions: the southern one part of the Central Highland massif; the second the coastal area between the mountains and the shores of the Moray Firth; the third in the lands to the west of the Great Glen. The distribution suggests a move up the Great Glen to north-eastern Scotland. The sites themselves, unlike many of the passage grave groups, have a generally low-lying and riverine situation, most lying on gravels. A few upland sites do exist but these tend to be adjacent to areas of good farmland. At least one group, that of Clava itself, forms a small cemetery with some eight sites scattered over more than a square kilometre. Many of the monuments have been very badly damaged and the further ones have almost certainly been removed as the result of later cultivation.

Two categories of monument exist: simple passage graves and ring cairns. The passage graves are covered by circular cairns between 9m and 17m in diameter invariably revetted by a massive stone kerb (fig. 4.1: 2). The entrance passage itself always faces between south and west, a most unusual orientation amongst British chambered tomb groups. The stones of the kerb are graduated in height though not always systematically; the largest stones tend to occur on either side of the entrance and the smallest at the diametrically opposite side of the circle. The stones are generally set in stone holes, and additional cairn material frequently occurs outside the kerb and appears to have been deliberately placed to provide extra revetment material. At two sites, flat platforms of stones extend beyond the kerb. The lintelled passage gives access to a circular, corbelled burial chamber between 3m and 4m in diameter. The cairns are invariably surrounded by a free-standing circle of stones, graded in height like the kerb stones, the taller stones of the circle flanking the entrance passage to the tomb proper (fig. 4.6). The ring cairns, which in plan resemble large

Fig. 4.6   Clava, N.E. Inverness: passage grave and stone circle (photograph: D. D. A. Simpson).

stone doughnuts, are revetted both internally and externally, again with kerbstones with a central open court which produces no evidence of originally having been roofed. Ring cairns tend to be larger than passage graves, varying between 12·8m and 26·8m in diameter with central areas 4·8m to 10·3m in diameter. As in the passage graves, the external kerbstones of the ring cairns are graded in height with the larger stones on the south-west. The further feature they share with the passage graves is that some at least are surrounded by free-standing circles of stones, again graded in height, the larger stones being on the south-west.

The distribution of passage graves and ring cairns is very similar and they appear to represent two distinct but contemporary tomb types. Little is known either of the burial rites or grave goods which accompany the burials in either category of site. In the passage grave of Corriemony (Piggott S. 1954–6) a single crouched inhumation burial lay on the floor of the chamber but at two other passage grave sites cremation was recorded. A number of the stones in the kerb, passage and chamber bear pecked cup marks, in no case set in prominent positions. Cup marks also exist on boulders and natural rock surfaces in the vicinity of the tombs and it may be that in some cases previously decorated boulders were accidentally incorporated in the fabric of the monuments, although it would appear likely that the builders of the Clava tombs and those who executed cup marks on natural surfaces were one and the same group.

Grave goods are virtually non-existent and, indeed, the only object which has any claim to contemporaneity with the use of tombs is part of a burnt bone pin from the passage at Corriemony. All the passage grave groups discussed above might reasonably be considered as representing primary, if comparatively late, neolithic settlement in the areas where they are found and similarly the designs of the tombs themselves might imply sea-going excursions by peoples from the European land mass producing this architectural tradition in the British Isles.

Native late neolithic cultures

Houses and settlements The remaining artifacts and structures which characterize the later neolithic of the British Isles must, however, be viewed entirely as insular developments owing nothing to continental influence. The recognition of these later native neolithic groups in Britain relies largely on a number of distinctive pottery traditions and artifacts and a distinctive form of ceremonial monument. Little is known of domestic sites and, in particular, of house structures; those structures which may be interpreted as buildings are almost entirely confined to the highland zone of Britain. At Mount Pleasant in Glamorgan a stone and post structure was discovered beneath a later early bronze age cairn (fig. 4.7: 1). The house, for such it must be, was rectangular in plan 5·7m long and 3·3m wide, defined by stone footings and post-holes suggesting a pitched roofed building. A very similar rectangular house, again defined by stone footings and posts, at Ronaldsway on the Isle of Man, was of approximately the same size (fig. 4.7: 2). In this case, however, unlike Mount Pleasant, the house has a central hearth. The building itself was

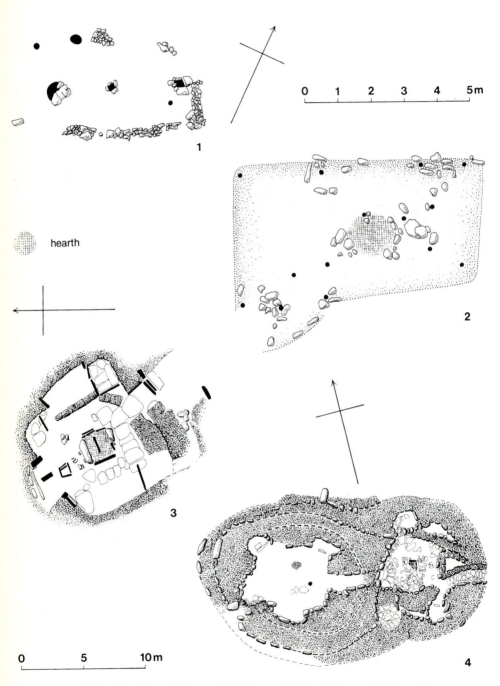

Fig. 4.7   Plans of late neolithic houses. 1 Mount Pleasant, Glam.; 2 Ronaldsway, I.O.M.; 3 Rinyo, Orkney; 4 Benie House, Shetland (after McInnes 1971).

partially subterranean and perhaps wattle lined and the considerable quantity of occupation debris from the house floor suggested prolonged occupation (Bruce and Megaw 1947). In both cases the buildings appear to be isolated homesteads, whereas the best known and most remarkable of the late neolithic settlement sites at Skara Brae (Childe 1931; Clarke D. V. 1976) and Rinyo (Childe 1938–9) (fig. 4.7: 3) in Orkney represent an agglomeration of houses forming what one might consider a village. In both settlements the excellent state of preservation and details of the internal fittings of the houses are due to the use of stone rather than timber for their construction. Some timber was certainly available in the Orkney Islands at this time but the Orkney flag which fractures readily into rectangular slabs presents ideal building material for dry-stone wall construction. The better preserved site at Skara Brae consisted of a series of rectangular houses between 4·5m and 6m with rounded corners, linked one to another by means of dry-stone walled passages (fig. 4.8). The whole settlement was semi-subterranean, being partially buried beneath a great midden representing the debris of the occupants of the houses themselves.

With one exception, the houses presented a uniform pattern in their internal fittings. At the centre of each house was a rectangular stone hearth and to the right and left of the lintelled entrance passage were two stone beds, the one on the right invariably being larger than that on the left, possibly implying that the man occupied the right-hand bed and the woman the left. The beds themselves would presumably have been lined with straw, heather or peat. Facing the entrance was a two-tiered dresser and around the walls were a series of compartments and chambers (fig. 4.9). Similar stone box-like structures were sunk into the floors of the houses and in a number of cases these were caulked and lined with clay to make them waterproof, presumably to enable fish and shell-fish to be kept alive until they were required for food.

The roofing of the houses presents a considerable problem. The dry-stone built walls rise vertically for some 1·5m and then are gently corbelled, but the amount of collapsed material found inside any given building was not enough to suggest that the entire roof structure was completed by this technique. The discovery of a number of whale jawbones in one of the houses suggested to the excavator that these may have provided rafters for the support of sod or peat roofs. It is equally likely now in view of the palaeo-botanical evidence that timber could have served a similar purpose although no trace survives.

Beneath the walls of one of the houses were found the crouched inhumation burials of two aged women. Such might be interpreted as a foundation sacrifice, although in a primitive society whose members would have a comparatively short life expectancy elderly members of the community would be respected and venerated as they are in modern primitive societies and it is more likely that these interments should be interpreted in terms of ancestor worship and the wisdom and power of the aged.

Until the recent series of excavations at Skara Brae (Clarke D. V. 1976) there was no evidence of cereal production, in contrast to the contemporary

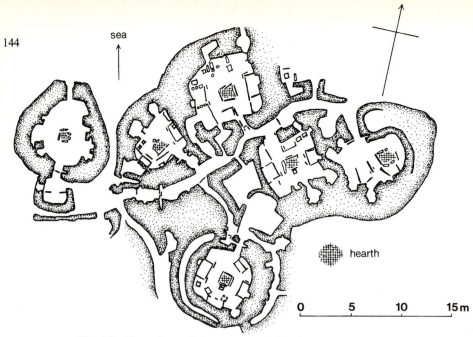

sea

hearth

0   5   10   15 m

Fig. 4.8   Skara Brae, Orkney: general plan (after Childe 1931).

Fig. 4.9   Skara Brae, House VII (photograph: D. D. A. Simpson).

evidence in the south. Amongst the bones of domesticated animals sheep were as numerically important as cattle. The importance of sheep in the Orkneys at this time has generally been considered to indicate a relatively open and treeless environment, as these animals do not flourish in forested conditions, unlike cattle and pigs. The sea also provided a ready food supply, not only in terms of sea mammals but also shell-fish which formed a high percentage of the contents of the midden in which the site was partially buried.

The finds from the house floors included a series of basins of stone and the hollowed-out vertebrae of whales associated with mauls and pounders. These were originally considered to be for pounding and grinding up fish bones for the production of meal but the recent palaeo-botanical evidence suggests that they may also serve as querns for grinding cereals. The wealth of surviving structural and particularly internal detail regarding the fitments of the houses at Skara Brae raises the problem of whether the structures in stone in this settlement and at Rinyo represent a straightforward translation into more durable material of features normally rendered in wood in the south, or whether the peculiar characteristics of the Orkney flag stimulated the builders to the production of refinements in house interiors unrepresented elsewhere.

A site as yet unique in this period is that at Meldon Bridge, Peeblesshire (Burgess 1976d). Here a promontory of some 8ha was defended by a massive timber wall with posts up to 0·6m in diameter, running between a river and a tributary stream. Within the defended area were pits, some containing late neolithic impressed wares, and at least one circular timber setting 9m in diameter with a central post. The excavator compared this structure to the post circles at Marden and Durrington Walls.

In the lowland zone of Britain the evidence for domestic sites is provided almost entirely by pits and scatters of occupation debris and hearths (McInnes 1971). All the pits occur on light, readily cultivated soils and are best interpreted as grain storage pits similar to those associated with early neolithic material. However, none of these late neolithic pits contain carbonized grain nor were grain impressions found on any of the sherds of pottery from them, although daub and the impression of withies have been noted in a number of cases. These storage pits, if such they are, are not normally associated with any structures although at Honington in Suffolk adjacent to the pits were a series of oval dark patches which the excavator suggested were the floors of tents or light huts (fig. 4.10: 1). The greatest concentration of flints and sherds occurred in these discoloured areas. At Playden in Sussex at the centre of a ditched enclosure 19·8m in diameter was a series of sleeper trenches and post-holes of a building 5·4m in diameter (fig. 4.10: 2). This structure had been set on fire, the timbers being dumped in the outer ditch and the central area later covered with white sand and becoming a flint knapping area—a feature which suggests that this site may have had a ceremonial or ritual function, rather than representing the remainder of a domestic structure.

The sub-rectangular ditched enclosures at Sonning in Berkshire and Fengate, Peterborough (fig. 4.11), should also perhaps be interpreted as

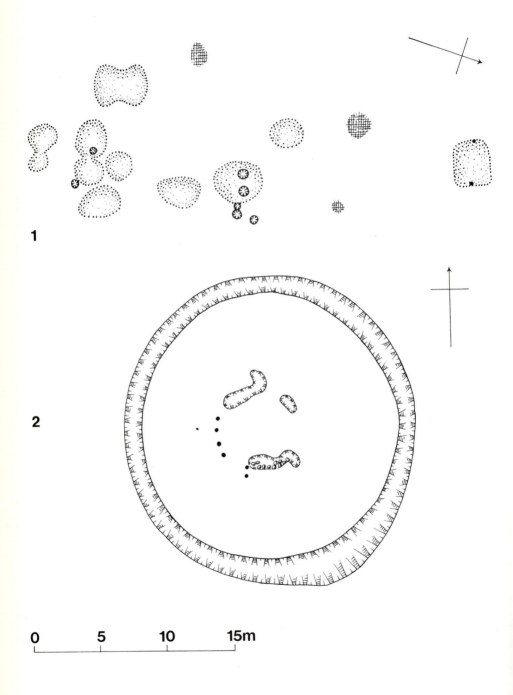

Fig. 4.10   Late neolithic settlement and enclosure. 1 Honington, Suffolk; 2 Playden, Sussex (after McInnes 1971).

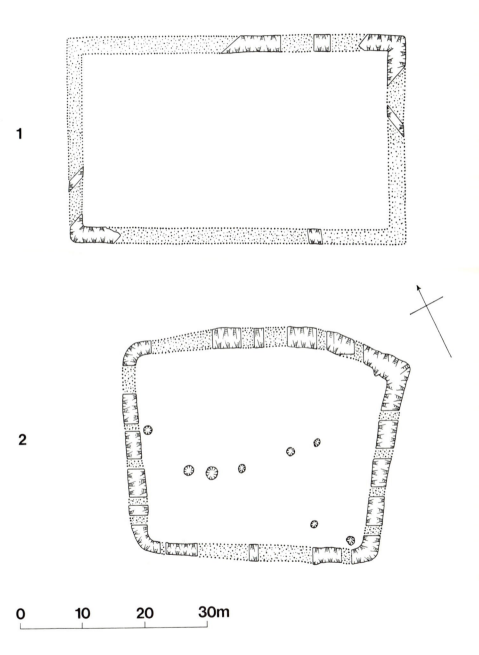

Fig. 4.11   Late neolithic enclosures. 1 Fengate, Peterborough; 2 Sonning, Berks. (after McInnes 1971).

ceremonial sites, particularly in view of the absence of occupation debris associated with the monuments. Similar, although smaller, square-ditched enclosures are known from Dorchester, Oxfordshire (Atkinson *et al.* 1949), and Windmill Hill, Wiltshire (Smith I. F. 1965). The rarity of late neolithic structures might be due to the nature of the buildings themselves. Single post-holes have been noted associated with general scatters of occupation debris and these might be the only surviving evidence for a light circular hut or tent similar to the Indian tepee with a central pole and footings either of stone blocks or sods.

At Lyles Hill, Co. Antrim, the excavator postulated the existence of a sod house where there were no post-holes. The site consisted of a hearth 1·2m in diameter with charcoal and occupation debris covering an area of 4·5m by 2·4m. Similarly, buildings of cruck construction need only rest on stone footings and do not require to be sunk into post-holes. Certainly extensive areas of grassland must have existed by the end of the 3rd millennium bc as attested by the use of turf in the construction of earthen long barrows and passage graves and also perhaps represented skeuo-morphically in the post and panel construction of many chambered tombs.

The nature of the economy itself (see below) suggests that some late neolithic groups practised a partially transhumant existence and under such conditions substantial and permanent house structures would probably not be necessary. That they were capable of constructing large timber buildings is attested by the existence of such structures in some cases within the only major category of monument erected during this period, the henge, and some of these may in fact have been domestic structures.

Henges A henge may be defined as a circular area enclosed by a bank and a ditch, the bank normally lying outside the ditch and broken by one or more entrances. Over 80 monuments of this class have been recognized; they are generally found in low-lying situations, often in close proximity to water. The sites are widely distributed throughout the British Isles from Cornwall to the Orkney Islands but five areas show noticeable concentrations (fig. 4.12). These are in the vicinity of the Salisbury Avon, in the Mendips (this group is unusual in standing on high ground), the Thames, in the area of Ripon in Yorkshire, in the valley of the bend of the Boyne in Ireland and in the region of the Moray Firth in Inverness-shire.

Henge monuments may be divided into two major categories: Class I henges with a single entrance; Class II with two or more. They vary in diameter from small monuments such as that at Fargo Plantation in Wiltshire, 10·6m in diameter, to the great ceremonial sites such as Avebury or Durrington in Wiltshire with diameters in excess of 305m. In general, too, Class I henges tend to be smaller than Class II, Class I having an average diameter of 73m and Class II henges having an average of 140m (Burl 1969). Class I henges also tend to be more strictly circular in plan in comparison with Class II. This may reflect the generally greater size of Class II henges and the difficulty of manipulating, presumably, a piece of twine or gut in laying out the circles in the first place over such a

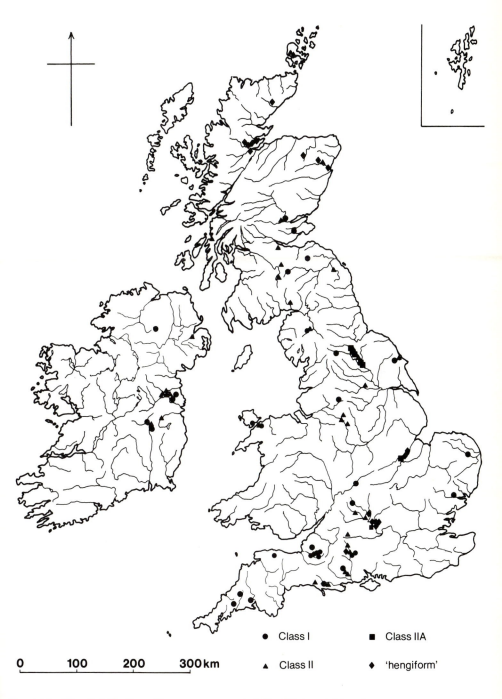

Class I

Class IIA

Class II

'hengiform'

0   100   200   300 km

Fig. 4.12   The distribution of henge monuments (after Wainwright and
Longworth 1971).

large radius, while further irregularities may be the result of provision of two or more entrances. No specific orientations can be discerned in Class I henges when considered on a country-wide basis, but regional groups do appear to favour some specific points of the compass; for example in the Mendips either a northerly or southerly orientation for the entrance, and in Wales a westerly one. Class II henges, on the other hand, have a generally north-west–south-east orientation. Doubts have recently been expressed as to whether the very small henges such as those at Fargo and the Dorchester series should in fact be grouped together with the larger monuments over 30m in diameter (Burl 1969). Such small enclosures may simply be burial places surrounded by a ditch and, in fact, none of the Dorchester henges had true entrances.

The internal and external structures associated with henges are extremely varied and in some cases no such features have been discovered after excavation. The external structures consist of outlying stones in four cases; and internally, pairs of portal stones flanking the entrance, timber structures in eight sites, pits in seven and burials either by inhumation or cremation. Both burials and central structures are more frequently associated with Class II monuments. Outlying stones, particularly the Heel Stone, which lies about 30m from the entrance of Stonehenge I, have been considered to have astronomical significance (Thom 1967; 1971; 1975) and the same has been suggested for site 4 at Hanborough, Oxfordshire, where a post-hole about 4·8m outside the entrance in conjunction with a stake-hole in the centre of the site was thought by the excavators to have a possible alignment for celestial observation. It could equally be argued that the function of such outliers, as in the case of stone circles with similar features, was directional, to locate the actual site itself. This is particularly true of Stonehenge. The Heel Stone at Stonehenge has long been considered as having significance in terms of midsummer sunrise observations. It must be borne in mind, however, that this stone was probably the only substantial above-ground feature of the site in the first phase, which consisted of the earthwork itself, the ring of 36 Aubrey holes immediately inside the area defined by the bank and ditch, and the cremation cemetery extending over the ring of the pits, the bank and the floor of the ditch (figs. 4.13, 4.14). In this first phase in the long and complex history of the earthwork, the only visible structures other than the Heel Stone and the two portal stones immediately inside the entrance would be the timber uprights in the area of the entrance, possibly associated with astronomical observations (Hoyle 1977). It is, of course, possible that the central area of the Phase I monument accommodated some form of timber setting but all traces of this have been obliterated by subsequent building. Under such circumstances, therefore, and presupposing the considerable area of forest clearance and open grassland in the vicinity of the site at this period, the Heel Stone projecting 4·8m above the ground would be the only indication of the existence of the site and would have provided a guide and a marker for those attending the ceremonies taking place within it.

It is only in its second building phase that Stonehenge produces clear

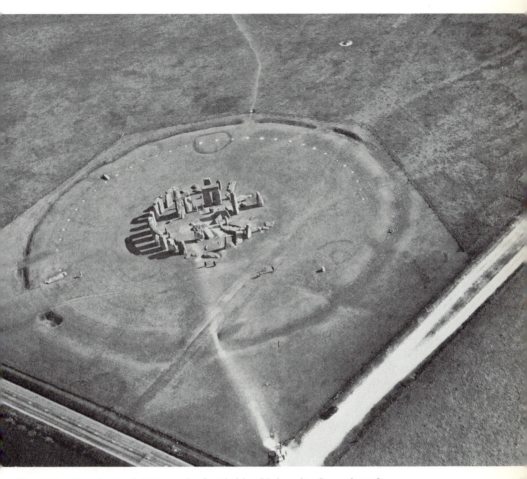

Fig. 4.13 Stonehenge (photograph: Cambridge University Committee for Aerial Photography: Crown Copyright).

evidence of a substantial stone structure within the area defined by the earlier Class I henge (Atkinson 1960a). This involved the erection of the 82 undressed bluestones in a double circle at the centre of the site – although the work was probably never completed. In 1923 the source of the three principal rock types represented by the bluestones was identified as lying in the Prescelly Mountains in Pembrokeshire. Recent suggestions that these could have been carried to the Wessex region through glacial action (Kellaway 1971) have met with little support. The route whereby the bluestones were transported to Stonehenge must remain problematic, although a sea route along the south coast of Wales to the Severn and thence by the sheltered waters of the Bristol Avon to its confluence with the Frome followed by a short porterage to the Wylye and its confluence with the Salisbury Avon and thence to Amesbury appears most likely. The final part of the route is probably marked by the Avenue, a pair of banks and ditches some 22·5m apart which follows a gently undulating path across the downs from near Amesbury to Stonehenge. The association of bluestone fragments with sherds of beaker pottery in the secondary ditch silt at Stonehenge and a radiocarbon date of 1,620 ± 100 bc from the base of an unfinished stone hole in the double bluestone circle indicates that the makers of this pottery were responsible for this second building phase. What prompted this prodigious undertaking cannot be determined but it clearly has important social and political implications for the archaeology of the period. The culmination of this feat of engineering and architecture was Stonehenge III, involving the transport of the sarsens, some weighing up to 50 tons, from the Marlborough Downs some 20 miles to the north, their dressing and erection in a circle of 30 uprights linked by mortice and tenon joints to a continuous ring of lintels and enclosing a horse-shoe-shaped setting of five trilithons. This, and the two subsequent phases involving the re-incorporation of the bluestones in the plan of the monument, belong to the early bronze age.

In the Wessex area there are four other sites which, like Stonehenge, must be considered as monuments set apart from the general run of henges, if not for their architectural refinements at least for their very great size. These are the sites of Avebury and Marden in north Wiltshire, Durrington Walls on the southern edge of Salisbury Plain and Mount Pleasant near Dorchester in Dorset (fig. 4.17). A fifth may be the site of Wauluds Bank, Leagrave, in Bedfordshire.

The four Wessex henges are all of Class II and vary between 365m and 518m in diameter. The best known of these large Wessex henges is Avebury, the only example with four entrances (Smith I. F. 1965). Here the bank encloses an area just under 365m in diameter within which there was originally an outer circle of 100 undressed sarsens enclosing two smaller stone circles (figs. 4.15, 4.16). At the centre of the northern circle was a so-called cove, a box-like structure with three uprights, and within the southern circle was a linear feature of standing stones. From the south-eastern entrance of Avebury there ran an avenue of paired stones for a distance of approximately 400m to a second ceremonial site, the so-called Sanctuary on Overton Hill. Like the Avebury stones themselves the uprights in the avenue consisted of undressed sarsen slabs, but care appears to have been taken in the choice of shape. Two basic forms are represented, a tall pillar-like stone and a broad, flat stone. These are juxtaposed along the length of the avenue, only the north-western end of which still survives as a visible feature. The contrasting forms of these two stone types has suggested to some archaeologists that they may represent male and female symbols, the pillar-like stone being the male and the broad and squat stone the female, and therefore the monument is to be associated with some form of fertility rites. A further avenue, running from the western entrance of the henge, was recorded by the eighteenth-century antiquary William Stukeley. Only one stone of this setting and the surviving stone of a second cove are still visible.

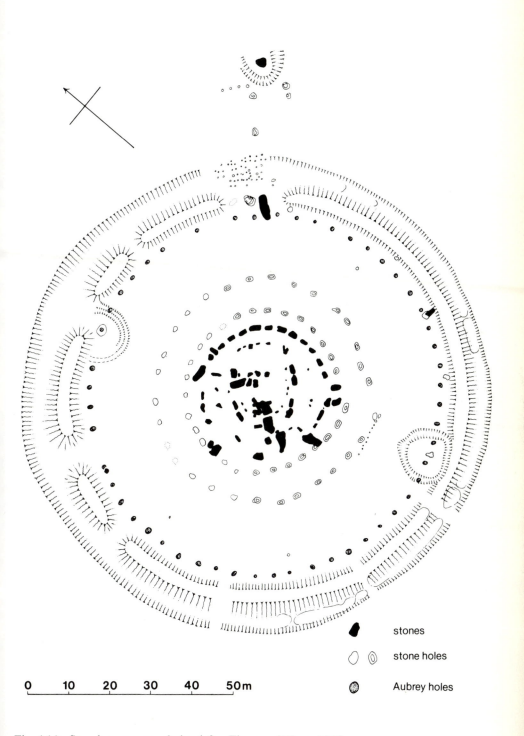

stones

stone holes

Aubrey holes

0   10   20   30   40   50m

Fig. 4.14 Stonehenge; general plan (after Thom and Thom 1974).

Fig. 4.15   Avebury (photograph: Cambridge University Committee for Aerial Photography: Crown Copyright).

Fig. 4.16   Avebury, southern circle (photograph: D. D. A. Simpson).

The second monument, on Overton Hill, was a complex stone and timber structure (Cunnington 1931). The first three phases represent successively larger, circular timber buildings or settings of wooden uprights, and the final phase a double circle of standing stones which was linked to the avenue and ultimately to the Avebury henge (Piggott S. 1940; Wainwright and Longworth 1971: 361).

Few small finds were associated with the Avebury henge and the paucity of material suggested to at least one of the excavators that the site may have been deliberately kept clean. At the base of two of the stones of the avenue were found inhumation burials accompanied by beaker pottery and at the base of a third stone a vessel related to Rinyo-Clacton pottery or grooved ware (see below, p. 170).

Only small areas of Marden, Durrington and Mount Pleasant have been excavated but the unifying feature of all three sites is that in those areas which have been examined the ground plans of circular timber structures, possibly roofed, have been uncovered. At Marden (Wainwright G. J. 1971) the timber building was found immediately inside one of the entrance causeways and a similar structure occupied the same position at Durrington, while a second smaller concentric post-hole structure lay some 150m to the north-east (fig. 4.17: 1, 4). Although only a small area of the interior of Durrington has so far been examined by excavation, geophysical surveys carried out over the entire inner area of the site would suggest the presence of further timber structures in the area defined by the bank and ditch (fig. 4.18). Another interesting feature at Durrington is the association with the monument of large quantities of occupation debris, a feature which is not on the whole characteristic of henges.

Finally, at Mount Pleasant the concentric timber structure lay within a small single entrance henge which itself was enclosed by the major bank and ditch of the Class II monument (fig. 4.17: 3). An added complexity at this site is the bedding trench of a substantial timber palisade, inside the henge ditch and running approximately concentric to it, but without gaps in the palisade corresponding to the entrance causeway; it is therefore likely to belong to a separate structural phase.

The dating of henges may in part be determined by the cultural associations and in part by a growing number of radiocarbon dates from organic material associated with them. Atkinson (1951) associated Class I generally with native late neolithic pottery, in particular Rinyo-Clacton, and Class II with beaker wares; this division is still generally true today. Radiocarbon dating gives mid-3rd millennium dates at the sites of Arminghall in Norfolk, Barford, Warwickshire and Llandegai in Caernarvonshire, and dates at the end of the 3rd millennium bc for the Wessex henges of Stonehenge, Avebury, Woodhenge, Durrington, Marden and Mount Pleasant. The present dating evidence would therefore suggest that the earliest henges lie outside the Wessex area.

Henges generally occupy low-lying and indefensible situations. The normal absence of occupation debris and the association of burials, pits or settings of standing stones in their interiors suggest that these are either religious or ritual structures, and the specific orientations of the Class II

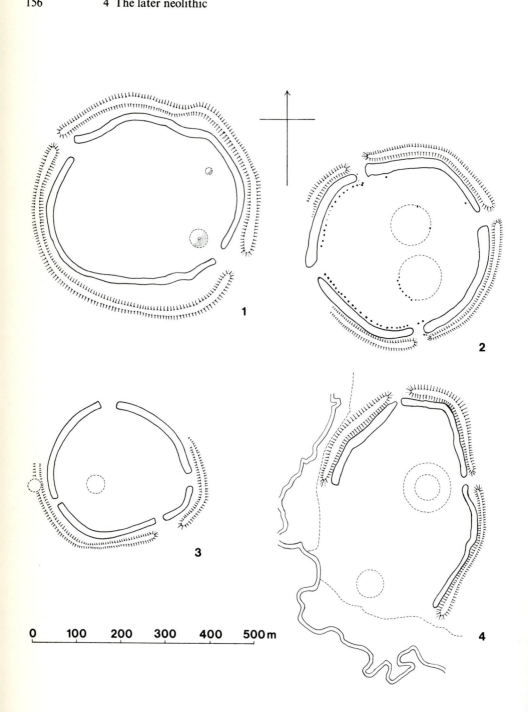

Fig. 4.17   Plans of henge monuments. 1 Durrington Walls, Wilts.; 2 Avebury, Wilts.; 3 Mount Pleasant, Dorset; 4 Marden, Wilts. (after Wainwright and Longworth 1971).

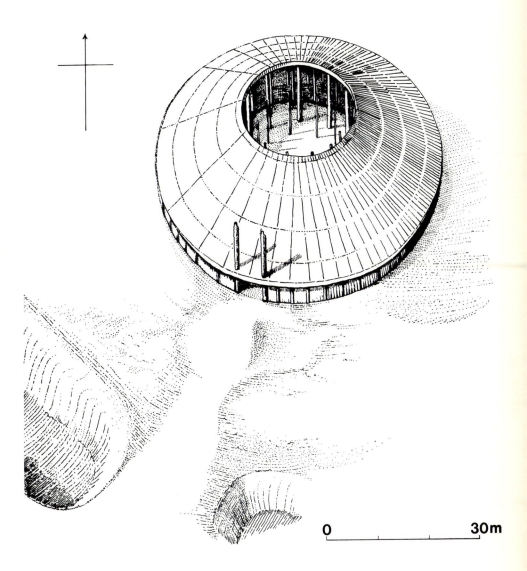

Fig. 4.18   Durrington Walls, Wilts.: reconstruction of southern timber structure
(after Wainwright and Longworth 1971).

monuments and of certain regional groups of Class I henges link them with some form of solar deity or with astronomical observations, although not necessarily requiring any detailed mathematical knowledge in their layout. A further clue to the function and origins of the henges is provided by the association with these monuments of axes in contexts which, on the whole, can only be regarded as ceremonial or ritual (Houlder 1976). At Llandegai an axe from the Graig Llwyd factory was buried blade downwards beneath the toe of the bank in the entrance to the Class I henge (Houlder 1968). At Stonehenge and Woodhenge (fig. 4.19) axes of chalk, clearly non-functional, were recovered, and from the main ditch at Mount Pleasant came a bronze axe in mint condition; finally, there are the carvings of axes on the sarsen uprights of the Phase III monument at Stonehenge.

Whatever the function of the henges, either ceremonial or religious, it is clear that this is a purely insular phenomenon: no parallels exist on the Continent for such structures. In seeking an indigenous origin for the henges certain clear parallels are evident between these and the earlier causewayed enclosures, both in the nature of their construction – for example the interrupted ditches at Stonehenge I and Mount Pleasant – and in their apparently overlapping functions. In the Wessex area, too, the causewayed enclosures and henges are juxtaposed, the latter apparently taking over both chronologically and functionally some at least of the elements of the earlier monuments (Renfrew 1973c). In Dorset the causewayed enclosure at Maiden Castle was replaced by the henge at Mount Pleasant, and in Wiltshire there is the same relationship between

Fig. 4.19   Chalk axes, Woodhenge, Wilts.; length of larger axe 9·7cm (photograph A. Pacitto: courtesy S. E. Thomas).

the causewayed enclosure at Robin Hood's Ball and the henge at Durrington, the causewayed enclosure at Knap Hill and the site of the henge at Marden, and finally, of course, the type-site at Windmill Hill replaced by the henge at Avebury. This is perhaps, however, to over-simplify the problem, for the causewayed enclosures whose functions, or some of them, appear to be taken over by henges are in every case superseded by very large henges which form a distinctive category in the Wessex area. Chronologically the earliest henges appear to lie in the area to the north of that in which the earlier causewayed enclosures were constructed and it would appear that henges were, in fact, developed initially outside the area *sensu stricto* of the Windmill Hill culture itself, and one must assume that the causewayed enclosures continued to function after some of the northern henges were built. It is only at a late date in the neolithic of southern Britain, when the construction and use of causewayed camps was abandoned, that the major henges in this area appear perhaps half a millennium after the earliest henges in the Midlands and in the north of England. To derive all the henges from earlier causewayed enclosures is perhaps an oversimplification in view of the varying nature of the structures found inside henge monuments themselves.

In the north it would be fair to say that many of the henges appear to be constructed to function in direct relationship to the axe trade but, of course, a trade in axes was only one aspect of the function of causewayed enclosures in the south. From the archaeological evidence and from their distribution pattern, the major henges of southern Britain do, in fact, appear to take over as focal centres from the earlier causewayed enclosures. The same may not apply to some of the northern henges or to the small structures such as those represented at Dorchester which are primarily funerary in character.

Stone circles Closely related to the problem of the origins and function of henges is that of the stone circles which, in some cases, are found inside these earthworks (fig. 4.20). The 900 or so stone circles in the British Isles appear to involve two basic traditions: a southern tradition associated with what Burl (1976a) has called 'ceremonial stone circles', whose functions in many ways are similar to those of henges, and where associated burials are secondary in importance to the main purpose of the monument; and the tradition found in Scotland and Ireland in which the circles appear to be primarily funerary in intent (fig. 4.21). Both these traditions appear to have quite separate origins, beginning in the middle and second half of the 3rd millennium bc, but representing a long and enduring pattern which survives for over a millennium: towards the end of the period of stone circles construction the two traditions appear to amalgamate to some extent. It has been suggested that timber circles, such as those at Woodhenge and Bleasdale or Arminghall, may represent prototypes for the construction of the stone circles in the highland zone of Britain where suitable building material was available, and indeed many more timber circles exist in the lowland zone than in the north. In some cases it can be demonstrated that an earlier timber monument as at Croft

Moraig in Perthshire (Piggott and Simpson 1971), preceded a stone setting, although this is not generally the case, and of the 70 or so stone circles excavated since the 1930s only four have revealed timber structures. The circles are concentrated in Aberdeenshire, Ulster, Cumbria, the Peak District, Cornwall, Dartmoor and Wiltshire; just over 20 per cent of this total concentration has been excavated although the majority of the excavations took place in the nineteenth century or earlier. Finds have been meagre, in particular at the ceremonial circles of southern Britain.

To consider, first, the ceremonial circles of the south it would appear that they bear certain resemblances to sites in the henge tradition. It could be argued that the stone circles are, in fact, translations of the earthen bank and ditch of the henge, the change being dictated largely by geological considerations. Atkinson (1951), however, drew attention to the dichotomy in the distribution of the stone circles and henges, the former having a marked western concentration while the latter tend to occur in the east. On the other hand there are certain areas in which the two categories overlap: one of these is Cumbria. There one has the henges of Mayburgh and King Arthur's Round Table and 11 great stone circles with diameters averaging 43·8m. Of the 11, there are five sites – Swinside, the Carles Castlerigg (fig. 4.22), Elva Plain, Long Meg and her Daughters and possibly Brats Hill, all in Cumberland – which share certain similarities with the henges. Firstly, their diameters are considerably greater than the average diameter of stone circles in the British Isles and although not quite half that of the average diameters of Class II henge monuments the lesser size is offset by the greater amount of effort involved in their construction; the moving and manipulation of large stones

Fig. 4.20   Henge and stone circle, Ring of Brodgar, Orkney (photograph: D. D. A. Simpson).

involves considerably more man-hours than the digging of a bank and ditch of comparable diameter. To erect a stone circle 36·5m in diameter and to construct a bank and ditch 73m in diameter probably involved the same number of man-hours. The characteristic features of these suggested early stone circles in Cumbria consist of the use of a large number of closely contiguous stones, many of them over 1m in height; the provision of banks surrounding the circle; the clear demarcation of an entrance either by a gap in the stone setting itself or by the provision of portal stones; and the occurrence of outliers at the Carles and Swinside – all characteristics which link the monuments with henges. Another possibly contemporary early circle lies across the Irish Sea at Ballynoe in Co. Down, again sharing many of these features. Another probably significant link between the henges and these early stone circles in Cumbria is the relationship of the circles themselves to a series of postulated routes and trackways for the transportation and distribution of stone axes from their sources. Each of the circles lies close to such routeways and at least two polishing sites at Portinscale, Keswick, and Kell Bank, Gosforth, lie within a mile of one of the great stone circles, while a roughout for a stone axe was found within the Carles circle and a polished stone axe came from the circle at Grey Croft. It would appear, therefore, that as with the henges, these postulated early circles in Cumbria can be associated with the stone axe trade and possibly with the axe as a cult or ceremonial object (Burl 1976a: 81).

These early stone circles in Cumbria are stationed approximately eight or ten miles apart and it might be suggested that they serve as rallying points for a social or tribal area of these dimensions. In this they contrast

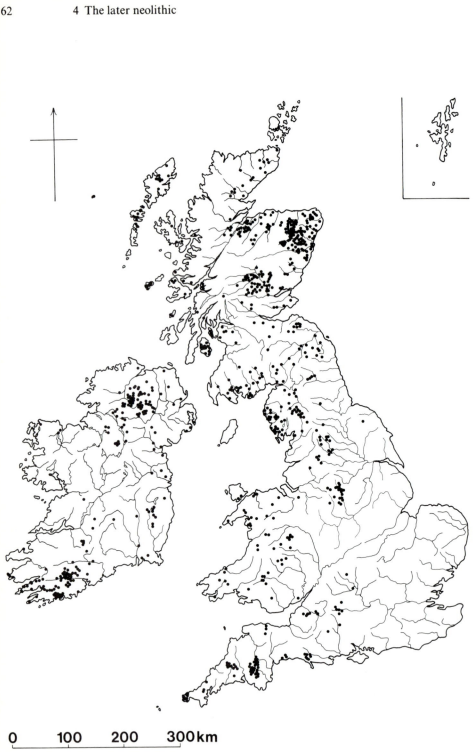

0   100   200   300km

Fig. 4.21   The distribution of stone circles (after Burl 1976a).

with the later ceremonial stone circles which frequently cluster together in pairs or small groups. Apart from the smaller size of the later circles there is a tendency also towards formalizing the structure itself, 12 stones being a common number – with its implications of numeracy on the part of the builders (Burl 1976b). Other developments include the provision of avenues of paired standing stones approaching the site, centre stones, and a general tendency for the circles themselves to be oval or elliptical in plan. These subsequent developments, beginning in the early 2nd millennium bc, took place not only in Cumbria but also in Cornwall and Dumfriesshire, again areas either connected with or peripheral to the trade in stone axes, and by the middle of the 2nd millennium such ceremonial circles were also being constructed in north Wessex, in Ireland and possibly also in Brittany, in the double circle at Er Lannic. The final developments in ceremonial stone circle construction also showed an increase in the use of such circles for burial although this is not to imply that this was their primary function and in some areas, at least, the adoption of this practice may be the result of contact with the builders of the primarily funerary stone circles of northern Britain.

This second tradition, largely in Scotland and Ireland, accounts for about half the total number of known stone circles in the British Isles. The primary area for the development of the sepulchral tradition appears to be Aberdeenshire. Concentrated in this county but spreading to the regions both to the north and south is a category of monument known as a recumbent stone circle (Burl 1969–70). This consists essentially of a circle of free-standing stones graded in height, the taller stones being concentrated in the south-western area and with the two tallest stones flanking a prostrate block or recumbent stone which gives its name to this

Fig. 4.22   Stone circle, Castlerigg, Cumb. (photograph: D. D. A. Simpson).

group of circles (fig. 4.23). Within the circles of stone there is generally a ring cairn covering cremation burials. There are just under 100 circles which belong to this class in north-eastern Scotland. The monuments are frequently set in a prominent position, not on the summit of a hill but on a slight mound or terrace which breaks the gradient of the hillside, and in one or two cases it does appear that the sites where the circles are constructed were artificially levelled. The earliest of the recumbent stone circles, both in terms of their associated finds and architectural features, have an average diameter of between 18m and 24m. The pillar stones flanking the recumbent are over 2m high, and the recumbent itself may be over 4m in length. The largest such stone is at Old Keig where the recumbent is over 4·8m long and weighs about 48 tons (Childe 1933–4). Occasionally the stones of the circle and in particular the flanking pillar stones appear to be dressed, to fit more snugly against the recumbent stone. It has been suggested, too, that the bases of a number of the stones of a circle were tooled into a rough tooth-shaped or beak-shaped form to enable them to be erected more easily. On the other hand this may have been simply a choice of suitably shaped stones rather than deliberate working. The ring cairns themselves are not conspicuous features and the largest is probably no more than 1m in height, while frequently the cairn is represented more by a platform of stones than an elevated structure. The burials generally occur within the central area defined by the inner kerb of the cairn. The recumbent stone is in some cases linked to the ring cairn by a low cairn platform or by projecting parallel stone slabs. Cup marks occur on a number of the stones and in particular show a noticeable concentration on the recumbent stone and its flanking pillars; in at least one case such carvings must have been executed before the erection of the circle itself.

The burials within the central area of the ring cairns are normally found in pits, in some cases stone lined, although at Loanhead of Daviot for example the ten pits within the central area of the ring cairn contained no cremated bone, and the human remains in this case occupied a compacted layer about 5cm thick, which covered the entire central area. The generally accepted origin for the recumbent stone circles of Aberdeenshire is in the ring cairns and passage graves of the Clava series of Inverness, the shared features being the south-western orientation, the grading, stones increasing in height towards the south-west, the fact that in all three monuments the graded stone circle surrounds either a ring cairn, or a passage grave, and cup marks on the stones of all three classes of site. In the area to the south, and derivative from the recumbent stone circle tradition, are a whole series of circles in Perthshire, most frequently represented by settings of four, six or eight stones (fig. 4.24). Their links with the recumbent stone circle tradition are demonstrated by the grading in height of the stones, again with the taller stones on the south-west, their hill-slope situation and the occurrence of cup marks – the latter, particularly with the four stone settings or four posters, confined to the south-eastern stone (Burl 1971).

Excavated sites which have produced material remains again demonstrate the continuity of the funerary tradition. In some cases the cremated

Fig. 4.23   Loanhead of Daviot, Aberdeens.: recumbent stone and flankers
(photograph: J. V. S. Megaw).

Fig. 4.24   Fortingall, Perth: two 8-stone circles under excavation (photograph:
D. D. A. Simpson).

human remains are contained in collared urns of the middle of the 2nd millennium bc. With such sites we have moved almost a millennium from the beginnings of the ceremonial and funerary stone circle traditions and from the henges with which the ceremonial sites are closely linked. We must now return again to the mid-3rd millennium bc to consider the pottery and other artifacts which characterize the indigenous native societies. As in so much of British prehistory there is a heavy reliance on one of the most enduring artifact types representing human activity, namely pottery.

Material equipment

Peterborough and impressed wares In the native late neolithic there are basically two pottery traditions, those of Peterborough and Rinyo-Clacton or grooved ware, the former existing as a recognizable category only in the southern part of Britain. The Peterborough styles also appear to be simply a pottery tradition rather than one aspect of a distinctive late neolithic culture, whereas the further associations of stone and bone equipment and monuments with Rinyo-Clacton grooved ware do suggest the ceramic element in a recognizable archaeological culture.

Pottery of the Peterborough tradition may be divided into three distinctive styles, Ebbsfleet, Mortlake and Fengate (Piggott S. 1962a), and initially these three styles appear to represent a chronological sequence although latterly all styles were contemporary. It should also be emphasized that this stylistic classification, supported by radiocarbon dates and stratigraphy, applies only to the southern part of Britain, as far north as Yorkshire. Even in this area distinctive regional styles already emerge and this is so even more strongly further to the north and west, as will presently be seen. Vessels in the Ebbsfleet tradition are necked bowls, round-based, in some cases with comparatively slack S-shaped profile, in others with a sharp carination (fig. 3.7: 1). The ware itself is generally of fine quality, thin-walled and well fired with simple rims. Decoration is restrained and

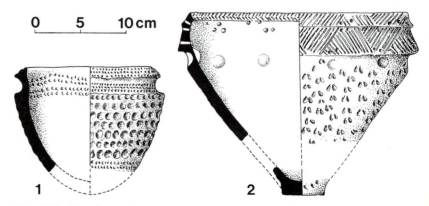

Fig. 4.25   Peterborough ware, West Kennet, Wilts. 1 Mortlake style; 2 Fengate style (after Piggott S. 1962b).

normally confined to the upper part of the vessel, in particular the neck and the area at or immediately beneath the carination. The most frequent technique is an incised lattice pattern although, more rarely, twisted or whipped cord impressions are used to produce the ornament. Pits, too, frequently occur on the neck, the technique being to impress the finger-tip onto the unfired clay. The round-based bowl form continued in the Mortlake style, but in this series the vessels are thick-walled, poorly fired with large lumps of grit tempering (fig. 4.25: 1). Rim forms, too, become increasingly elaborate with a tendency for an internal bevel which becomes a platform for decoration. The decoration itself is most frequently executed by impressions made with a piece of whipped or twisted cord or by impressing the articular end of a small bird or mammal bone into the clay. The commonest design executed by these techniques is that of a herringbone pattern, and the decoration itself now frequently covers the entire outer surface of the vessel extending into the rim bevel. In the final series, Fengate ware, the tradition for poorly fired and thick-walled vessels continues but now the profiles are completely different (fig. 4.25: 2). The developed rim forms as first seen in Mortlake ware show increasing elaboration in the form of an invariable internal rim bevel, and the outer profile of the rim is now developed into a collar or overhanging rim. The lower part of the body is sub-conical, falling to a narrow flat base. The earlier decorative techniques continue in the Fengate series but there is now an increasing use of finger-pinching or rustication, particularly on the lower part of the body of the vessel, and also the application of incised or grooved lines generally on the collar, to produce hatched, triangular and chevron patterns.

The majority of Peterborough pottery comes from what can be generally described as domestic sites, either in the form of surface scatters of sherds associated with flint material and other occupational debris or pits of the type discussed in Chapter 3 and generally considered to be grain storage pits, although grain impressions have been found on only two sherds of Peterborough pottery (Field *et al.* 1964). A great deal of this Peterborough pottery has been found in rivers or in pits on their banks. These occurrences and the frequent use of bird bones to decorate the pottery suggest the importance of hunting birds and in particular water fowl in the economy of the makers of this pottery style. At the end of the 3rd millennium bc extensive areas of forest must have been cleared to produce grasslands on the downs of Wessex and the Wolds of the East Riding of Yorkshire, providing a suitable habitat for the grazing of water-fowl, and in particular geese, and it may be significant that it is in these areas that one finds a marked concentration of Peterborough pottery (McInnes 1971). The hunting of red deer is also indicated by the occurrence of bones and antlers in a number of sites.

Peterborough pottery has also been found in the ditches of causewayed enclosures; generally the sherds themselves occur in the secondary filling of the ditch, although at Combe Hill and Whitehawk Ebbsfleet ware was associated with the primary silt and at the latter site it was in fact the only pottery represented in this primary context. Some 12 cave and rock shelter sites have also yielded sherds of Peterborough pottery and the majority of these must again be considered as domestic. The two exceptions are Gop Cave in Flintshire and Church Dale Cave in Derbyshire where Peterborough pottery was associated with multiple inhumation burials, some contained within massive stone cists erected inside the caves. Peterborough pottery is also associated with seven earthen long barrows; in five the sherds occurred in the secondary silt of the barrow ditches and in only one, at Hinton Abner, was Ebbsfleet ware found in the primary silt although in no case was pottery associated with the actual burials beneath the mound. Similar secondary contexts for this pottery occur in nine chambered tombs, the material coming, however, from the secondary filling of the chambers, the forecourt blocking, or pits in the forecourt area itself or in the mound. Pottery has also come from some two dozen round barrows, the majority of the finds being incorporated either in the body of the mound or in the ditch silting, and again in no case was the pottery associated with any burials found in the barrows. The simplest explanation for the occurrence of sherds whether in the ditch, the mound or on the old land surface beneath it is that these sherds belong to earlier occupation on a site later adopted, presumably because of clearance of forest and scrub, for the construction of a round mound. The flint and stone associations with Peterborough pottery from these varied categories of site again reinforce the concept that this is a pottery tradition rather than a distinctive archaeological culture. The associations include polished flint axes, grain rubbers, two doubtful associations of polished stone axes, a leaf-shaped arrowhead and various categories of non-diagnostic artifacts. There are, therefore, no distinctive types, either of field monuments or small finds, associated with Peterborough pottery and most of the associations can, in fact, be linked with the Windmill Hill culture complex. As I. F. Smith (1974) has demonstrated, it is from this pottery tradition of Windmill Hill that the Peterborough styles develop.

The implications of Peterborough pottery in socio-cultural terms, however, are still far from clear. The pottery itself can be shown to represent development from and continuation of traditions arising out of the regional forms of Windmill Hill pottery of southern Britain, and that pottery is associated, generally in a secondary context, with two of the principal categories of monument which characterize that culture, namely causewayed enclosures and earthen long barrows. Yet there is no indication that the makers of the later forms of Peterborough pottery were responsible for the continued construction of these monuments, although an enduring interest is implied by the occurrence of the wares in secondary contexts on a number of sites. To explain the absence of characteristic categories of monument associated with Peterborough pottery is difficult: one can only fall back on the archaeological evidence, in particular that of animal remains, to suggest that a change in the economy from one based on mixed farming, cereal production and stock raising, to a largely pastoral economy encouraged the development of a nomadic society whose way of life discouraged or made unnecessary the erection of large ceremonial or funerary sites, or even substantial and enduring domestic structures.

If the evidence for continuing native neolithic traditions in the south is unsatisfactory then the picture in the north and the west is even more so. Although the three principal forms of Ebbsfleet, Mortlake and Fengate wares are recognizable in Yorkshire there appears to be a further and purely regional element in the later neolithic pottery tradition in this area, and this is even more true of regions further north. The distinctive character of some of the Yorkshire material has led Manby (1975) to suggest there a Rudston style equivalent to the Mortlake wares of southern Britain. In Scotland sherds of what would in the south be called Mortlake and Fengate wares have been found, for example at Hedderwick, East Lothian, and Cairnholy in Galloway, but such discoveries are rare. As in the southern Peterborough tradition there is in Scotland a series of late neolithic pottery forms united by their fabric which is coarse, with the use of large grits, reddish in colour and tending to be poorly fired. Similarly, the use of whipped cord, bird bone and stick impressions and fingertip rustication can all be paralleled in the southern British Peterborough tradition. Whereas in the south distinctive and initially chronologically separate styles can be recognized, in the north both the arrangement of the decoration and the forms of the vessels on which this is executed make such a refined classification impossible, and the term 'impressed ware' has been suggested to describe this native late neolithic pottery tradition (McInnes 1969).

Although the repertoire of decorative techniques and forms is limited, their frequency and occurrence varies very considerably from one site to another, making any broad classification at the moment impossible. For example, at the settlement site of Grandtully in Perthshire, the principal forms are simple rounded bowls with expanded and flattened rims and collared vessels, the dominant decorative techniques being twisted cord impressions on the former and fingertip impressions and rustication on the latter; while at Glenluce in Wigtownshire the main forms are deep straight-sided vessels with flattened or everted rims and the decoration is predominantly bird bone and whipped cord impressions (McInnes 1969). In the Western Isles on the other hand there are deep multiple-carinated vessels decorated with incised herringbone patterns (fig. 3.15: 7), and shallow bowls with a developed collar decorated with grooved vertical and horizontal lines; the latter form is the so-called Unstan ware, named after the megalithic tomb in Orkney, though almost certainly the tradition developed in north-western Scotland (fig. 3.15: 4). Although these extremely localized forms of late neolithic pottery in Scotland do share certain characteristics with the formal Peterborough groups to the south, their relationship is probably more a cousinly one rather than representing a direct movement of people or introduction of ideas from the south. Parallels for the shapes and for some of the decorative techniques found on these Scottish impressed wares exist amongst the earlier neolithic pottery of the area, in particular Beacharra ware from the megalithic tombs in the west. A similar ancestry may be invoked for the deep bag-shaped vessels with thickened collared rims decorated with incised ornament belonging to the Ronaldsway culture of the Isle of Man and best represented at the house site of Ronaldsway itself. Such pottery was also associated with a cemetery consisting of ten deposits of cremated human bone, one contained in a vessel of Ronaldsway type. Westwards in Ireland this impressed ware tradition is reflected in round-based bowls with developed, thickened or overhanging rims decorated with twisted and whipped cord impressions in the Sandhills style (Case 1961).

A unifying feature amongst all these late neolithic pottery traditions is the general deterioration of fabric in comparison with earlier pottery styles, the increasing elaboration of vessel form, particularly the rim, and the use of impressed decoration. With a few rare exceptions, the scarcity of grain impressions and the predominance of cattle amongst the bones of domestic species from sites, and the general distribution and conditions under which such varied impressed wares are found, all imply a largely transhumant agricultural society still dependent – as were earlier neolithic communities – on the same basic raw materials both organic and inorganic, probably forming smaller social units than the earlier communities, and not given to such large corporate ventures as the construction of causewayed enclosures, long barrows and megalithic tombs.

Although the similarity of certain British impressed ware forms to similar pottery traditions on the Continent and in particular in Scandinavia, have long been recognized (Piggott S. 1954; Case 1963), it is no longer necessary to view the appearance of such pottery in the British Isles as representing fresh incursions of peoples from across the North Sea, or indeed to explain the emergence of such traditions as the acculturation of indigenous mesolithic hunting and fishing peoples as a result of contact with earlier farming communities. Apart from the total absence of mesolithic forms of bone, flint or stone associated with the impressed ware pottery style, there is no evidence to suggest the survival of purely hunting and fishing communities in the British Isles into the middle of the 3rd millennium bc when such impressed wares styles were beginning to appear.

The Rinyo-Clacton tradition   While the impressed wares in the British Isles exhibit many regional forms both in profile and decoration, the second major pottery tradition of the late neolithic, the Rinyo-Clacton or grooved ware pottery, represents a remarkable homogeneity both in form and decoration from the extreme north to the extreme south of Britain, although virtually unrepresented across the Irish Sea (Wainwright and Longworth 1971). The earlier term of 'grooved ware pottery style' was replaced by 'Rinyo-Clacton pottery' or 'Rinyo-Clacton culture' by Piggott to emphasize what he believed to be the unity of the material culture over the very wide area of Britain where this pottery is found, using the two type-sites of Rinyo in Orkney and Clacton-on-Sea in Essex. Since then there has been a tendency to return once more to the term 'grooved ware', giving it the same weight in archaeological terms as the Peterborough tradition in late neolithic pottery, rather than considering it as one aspect of a whole range of material equipment and monuments which characterize a distinctive archaeological culture. It is proposed here to return again to Piggott's original designation of Rinyo-Clacton culture both because the term grooved ware is too explicit to define all the decorative forms of the pottery itself and also because it is possible to demonstrate associations between the Rinyo-Clacton pottery and other types of artifact and archaeological site.

In the pottery four basic sub-styles can be recognized, all apparently contemporary; common to all is the general form of the vessel, which has a slab-sided, bucket-shaped profile with a flat base, thick-walled and very poorly fired. Vessels in the Clacton style have grooved decoration arranged either in multiple chevron or incised lozenge or triangular patterns; in the latter two cases the ornament is frequently infilled by punching, the only applied or plastic decoration occurring on the internal rim bevel (fig. 4.26: 1). Pots of the Woodlands style are decorated with applied ornament arranged in either horizontal or converging bands, in the latter case frequently with blobs of clay or knots applied at the point of junction. These applied cordons frequently have slashed or notched decoration executed on them (fig. 4.26: 2). In the Durrington or Woodhenge style the

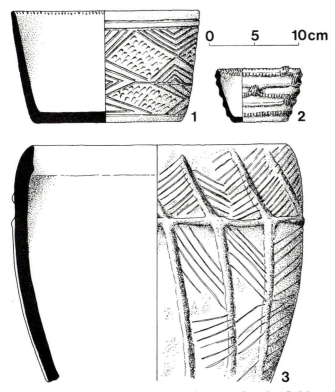

Fig. 4.26   Rinyo-Clacton or grooved ware. 1 Creeting St Mary, Suffolk; 2 Woodlands, Wilts.; 3 Durrington Walls, Wilts. (after Piggott S. 1954, Stone 1949 and Wainwright and Longworth 1971).

body of the vessel is frequently divided up into a series of vertical panels by means of vertical incised lines or applied plastic strips, the panels being filled with grooved chevron ornament (fig. 4.26: 3). A further motif first recognized at Durrington Walls itself as an element in this style is grooved spirals or concentric circles. The final style, the Rinyo or Skara Brae style, has an overwhelming preponderance of plastic ornament in the form of applied cordons, pellets and roundels. All four styles are represented at Skara Brae, suggesting a broad contemporaneity.

Of the 116 sites listed by Wainwright and Longworth (1971) as having produced Rinyo-Clacton pottery over half would be considered as domestic. A considerable number of so-called stray finds might also be brought together under this heading. The majority of such domestic occurrences are from storage pits of one form or another, although their interpretation as grain storage pits is less likely as no single sherd of Rinyo-Clacton pottery, or any pit from which such pottery has come, has produced either carbonized grain or grain impressions, although cereals have recently been recognized at Skara Brae. Most important among the domestic associations are the complexes of stone-built houses at Rinyo and Skara Brae in Orkney; in addition two cave sites in the south-west at Torbryan in Devon and Cockleswood in Somerset have produced sherds of Rinyo-Clacton pottery in what appear to be domestic contexts; lastly, there are sherds from the flint mines of Church Hill near Findon in Sussex.

More important perhaps than these associations in terms of recognizing a distinct Rinyo-Clacton culture is the occurrence of sherds at six henge monuments and three other ceremonial sites. The henges are those at Maumbury Rings in Dorset, Avebury, Durrington Walls, Marden, Stonehenge I and Woodhenge in Wiltshire. The association of this pottery with three of the great henges in Wessex – Avebury, Durrington Walls and Marden – is significant and certainly at Durrington Walls, Marden and Woodhenge the overwhelming preponderance of Rinyo-Clacton pottery makes it quite clear that its makers were responsible for the construction of these monuments. Rinyo-Clacton pottery also came from Dorchester Site I, a continuous oval ring ditch surrounding a pennanular ring of 13 pits, and a single sherd of the pottery was recorded as coming from one of the stone-holes of the West Kennet Avenue. Sherds have also been found in the upper ditch-fill of three causewayed enclosures at the same level as beaker pottery (see Chapter 3). There are similar secondary associations for five chambered tombs, although Rinyo-Clacton pottery has seldom been recorded in direct association with any form of burial, either by inhumation or cremation. Although the pottery was clearly used in some cases at ceremonies associated with henge monuments it occurs in funerary contexts in only two cases, at Eddisbury, Cheshire (Wainright G. J. 1971: 201) and Winhill, Derbyshire (Bateman 1861: 254).

It is the other associations, organic and inorganic, with Rinyo-Clacton pottery which give credibility to the concept of the pottery itself reflecting a distinctive material culture. Amongst the inorganic associations, the most numerous (but of little help in establishing cultural relationships) are flint scrapers, the commonest form being an end flake type. More distinctive are transverse or cutting arrowheads of flint (fig. 4.27: 5) and so-called plano-convex flint knives, with the upper convex surface carefully retouched and pressure-flaked. Saws or serrated flakes are associated at 12 sites with Rinyo-Clacton pottery and there is a single find of a polished discoidal knife with pottery from Lawford in Essex. Amongst the stone equipment the most important are axes or fragments of axes, being products of Cornish axe-factories and those at Graig Llwyd and Great Langdale – a not surprising link in view of the associations of henge monuments both with the stone axe trade and the cult of the axe, and the fact that in a number of major henges grooved ware figures predominantly. The other important stone form is the macehead, four of which have been recorded with grooved ware, and these belong to the two major types described by Roe (1968), the ovoid and pestle-shaped forms (fig. 4.27: 2). A great variety of specialized stone tools have come from the northern sites of Rinyo and Skara Brae. Many of these have no precise parallels in contemporary assemblages in the British Isles and as Piggott (1954) and Gjessing (1953) have pointed out, some at least appear to indicate circumpolar traditions as do some of the artifacts from contemporary sites in Shetland (fig. 4.28: 11–12). Finally may be mentioned the chalk axes from Woodhenge (fig. 4.19) and Stonehenge, presumably ritual in function, and two unique carved plaques from King Barrow Wood near Stonehenge which will be discussed below.

Amongst the bone and ivory associations there are simple pins and awls but more important are skewer pins of cylindrical section with domed or

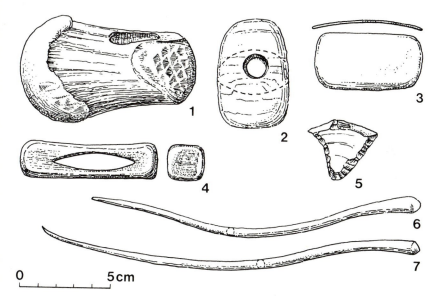

0   5 cm

Fig. 4.27   Late neolithic equipment. 1 antler macehead; 2 stone macehead; 3 polished flint knife; 4 jet belt fastener; 5 petit tranchet derivative arrowhead; 6–7 bone 'skewer pins' (after Piggott S. 1954).

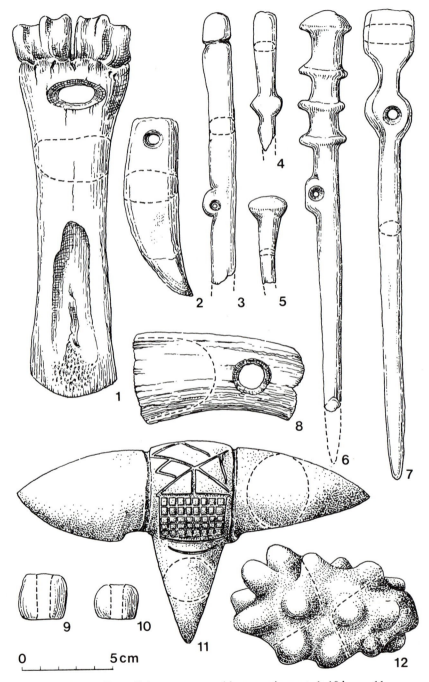

Fig. 4.28   Skara Brae, Orkney: stone and bone equipment. 1–10 bone; 11–12 stone (after Piggott S. 1954).

slightly cylindrical heads (fig. 4.27: 6–7), and pins provided with lateral bulbs on the shanks which are perforated. From Skara Brae there also come a further series of very large pins up to 24cm long with spatulate heads which find their parallels in the pins from the Boyne passage graves in Ireland (fig. 4.28: 4–7). Many of these objects associated with Rinyo-Clacton pottery, and in particular the flint and bone forms, comprise elements in what Piggott in 1954 tentatively recognized as the Dorchester culture – a culture without a distinctive pottery style but characterized by a series of flint, stone and bone artifacts, cremation cemeteries such as those at Dorchester-on-Thames in Oxfordshire, certain ritual monuments of henge type, and in a number of cases cremation burials beneath very large round mounds, particularly in Yorkshire and the Pennines. The best known of these barrow sites is that of Howe Hill, Duggleby, in the East Riding of Yorkshire. The barrow itself was 38m in diameter and 6m high; a large central pit grave contained an inhumation with a vessel which has since been lost. Adjacent to this large pit grave was a shallow grave containing two inhumation burials, one accompanied by transverse arrow-heads and a bone skewer pin, the other by a polished flint knife (fig. 4.27: 3). In the body of the mound itself were 50 cremation burials, some again accompanied by skewer pins, one with a pin with perforated bulb on its shank, and by transverse arrow-heads. The enormous barrow, Willy Howe, also in the East Riding of Yorkshire, 7·3m high and 39·6m in diameter, also probably belongs to the category as did the great mound which originally stood inside the henge monument at Marden in Wiltshire and the so-called Conker barrow that stands on the bank on the west side of the henge at Mount Pleasant in Dorset.

It is possible, too, that the largest of all the round mounds in Britain and indeed in western Europe, Silbury Hill, Wiltshire, may also be included in this group. Its proximity to the Avebury-West Kennet Avenue-Sanctuary complex and the recent radiocarbon dates from Silbury itself support this assertion. In spite of a number of attempts at tunnelling into the mound both vertically and horizontally, no burials have yet been recovered from it, although the most recent excavations have demonstrated that the structure itself is complex in form. The primary monument consisted of a mound of turf and gravel 36·5m in diameter, revetted with timber uprights. Subsequently this was covered by a barrow of chalk rubble obtained from an encircling quarry ditch. Before there was any appreciable weathering in the ditch of this Phase II monument the structure was once again added to but this time on a grandiose scale to produce the final monument which can be seen today. This involved the digging of a further enormous quarry ditch to provide material for the greatly enlarged mound which buried the earlier mound and its quarry ditch. It was composed of chalk blocks which were arranged in a series of steps, presumably to prevent any slipping or weathering of the mound material back into the ditch. Subsequently each of these steps was filled in with further chalk rubble to produce the smooth profile which one sees today. The monument, however, was never completed and the topmost step is still visible both from the ground and from the air (Vatcher and Vatcher 1976). It is possible, therefore, through the flint and bone associations to extend the range of material equipment which one can link with Rinyo-Clacton pottery and to see Piggott's Dorchester culture as another aspect of the general Rinyo-Clacton complex including henges, distinctive stone and flint types, cremation cemeteries and, in some cases, gigantic round mounds. The associations, too, suggest that this same grouping might encompass Roe's so-called Macehead complex, many of the associations of which again find parallels both in the Dorchester material and in associations with Rinyo-Clacton pottery.

Though all the material equipment and monuments of the Rinyo-Clacton culture, including the pottery, appear to be purely insular developments one other element remains to be considered. That is the apparent link with the art, material equipment and perhaps even the monuments themselves of the Boyne passage graves of Ireland. The similarity in certain pin forms associated with Rinyo-Clacton pottery and with the Irish passage graves has already been mentioned. More striking perhaps are elements of the passage grave art which appear associated with late neolithic material in Britain. Most striking is the double-spiral

Fig. 4.29   Carved chalk cylinders from Folkton, Yorks.; diameter of largest cylinder 14cm. (photograph A. Pacitto: courtesy S. E. Thomas).

lozenge design executed on one of the sherds at Skara Brae (Piggott S. 1954) which finds precise parallels in a motif pecked on the surface of one of the kerb stones at Newgrange (fig. 4.2). Further links with the Boyne art style may be provided by the use of the spiral pattern on Rinyo-Clacton ware from Durrington and from Malford and Ipswich in Suffolk (Wainwright and Longworth 1971: 70–1). The three small chalk cylinders or drums which accompanied an inhumation burial beneath a round barrow at Folkton in the East Riding of Yorkshire (fig. 4.29) have incised curvilinear and geometric designs which again find their closest parallels in Boyne art (Greenwell 1890). Two small incised chalk plaques from King Barrow Wood near Stonehenge are decorated with a lozenge-chevron pattern and an opposed Greek key design respectively (Vatcher 1969); these motifs also occur scratched on the walls and roofs of the houses at Skara Brae and again these designs find parallels in the art of the Boyne tombs. Boyne art motifs also occur pecked on natural rock surfaces in the highland zone of Britain and in some cases boulders bearing these designs have been incorporated into the fabric of stone cist graves containing pottery and artifacts of the middle 2nd millennium bc. In many cases, however, the unsuitable shape and size of these stones and the fact, too, that in some cases only part of the original design has been preserved on the stone, portions having been broken off to incorporate it into the cist, suggest the re-use of earlier decorated stones and does not imply that the Boyne art motifs on these decorated cists are necessarily contemporary with the contents of the grave (Simpson and Thawley 1973). Amongst small artifacts may be mentioned an antler hammer or macehead from Garboldisham in Suffolk decorated with a spiral pattern (Edwardson 1965), and carved stone balls with spiral ornament from Towie, Aberdeenshire, Elgin, Morayshire, and Glasterlaw in Angus (Atkinson 1962: 28).

While, therefore, it is possible to demonstrate some link between late neolithic cultures in Britain and the art of the Boyne passage graves in Ireland, the processes whereby these cultural elements were transmitted from west to east is uncertain though it is most likely to have been accomplished by the movement of small objects of mobiliary art such as those described above or even some form of personal decoration, either on garments or even tattoo marks on the skin itself.

The somewhat shadowy groups represented by the Peterborough and impressed ware traditions and by the pottery and equipment at sites of the Rinyo-Clacton culture represent only elements in the complex of societies which occupied Britain in the late neolithic. From the beginning of the 2nd millennium bc, side by side with the groups described above there is a final and better-defined element, that represented by the intrusive pottery traditions and equipment, including the earliest metal objects, introduced by the manufacturers of beaker pottery.

5 The early bronze age (c. 2,000–1,300 bc)

Beaker cultures

The last major incursion of peoples from the Continent to settle in the British Isles for over a millennium took place in the early centuries of the 2nd millennium bc. The culture, or cultures, of these immigrants is named after the characteristic drinking cup or beaker that they placed in graves with their dead. Their arrival has often been considered as a watershed in British prehistory, marking a major social and economic change and probably, too, associated with a distinctive physical type (Brothwell 1960; Brothwell and Krzanowski 1974). It is certainly true that a major change in burial rites took place, from the collective inhumation or cremation characteristic of the indigenous neolithic cultures to that of generally crouched single inhumation burials either in flat graves or in pits beneath round barrows; although as we shall see below this is something of a generalization (Petersen 1972). In economic terms a most important innovation is the introduction of metal ornaments, tools and weapons and the techniques of metalworking (Butler and van der Waals 1966). On the other hand the makers of beaker pottery settled in Britain in an area which already had a considerable indigenous neolithic population and the disparate groups described in the previous chapter continued to exist either side by side with, or as elements in, a mixed society which included the makers of beaker pottery. In spite of the warlike nature of some of the grave goods associated with beakers there is no evidence for the establishment of a beaker autocracy over the indigenous population during these formative centuries and the material from sites such as henges suggests a considerable intermingling of various groups of natives and newcomers. It is this amalgam of aboriginal and innovating traditions which forms the basis for societies in the early bronze age in the middle of the 2nd millennium bc.

Beaker pottery   The distinctive pottery which gives its name to the beaker cultures was first subjected to detailed study by Abercromby in 1912. In his great work *A Study of the Bronze Age Pottery of Great Britain and Ireland* he listed and illustrated a corpus of all the known beaker pottery from the British Isles, and from a study of form and decoration divided it into three major and what he considered chronological groups, A, B and C. Until the 1950s Abercromby's classification, with further refinements of alphabetical subdivision, remained the basis for beaker classification. In 1963 Piggott (1963a) sought to replace the alphabetical classification of

Abercromby with a descriptive classification based on the form of the vessel itself. He followed Abercromby in having a basically tripartite division, but now British beakers were divided into long-necked, bell and short-necked beakers, a variant of Abercromby's initial A, B, C classification. These regroupings, however, were still based on Abercromby's original corpus and it was only in 1970 with the publication of D. L. Clarke's *Beaker Pottery of Great Britain and Ireland* that a new and very much more comprehensive corpus of known beaker material became available and with it a more elaborate classification of the pottery. Clarke suggested the existence of seven major intrusive groups of beaker-making peoples crossing the North Sea to settle in Britain. Developing out of these intrusive groups, and representing in Clarke's view two distinctive social complexes, were two major native traditions, a northern and a southern, each capable of further typological and chronological subdivision.

The earliest of these waves of beaker settlers is marked by the appearance of all-over corded (AOC) beakers. The vessels in this series have a bell-shaped body, in some cases with a slightly carinated profile, with the outer surface either totally or partially covered with impressions made with a fine two-strand twisted cord. There is a higher percentage of dark brown and reddish vessels in this series than in any of the other British beaker groups. There are marked concentrations of AOC beakers in the Upper Thames area, the lands round the Wash and Humber and in eastern Scotland. AOC beakers from domestic sites (see below) are associated with large undecorated beaker forms and vessels ornamented with paired finger-nail rusticated decoration. The associations in graves of beakers of this type include barbed and tanged arrow-heads, a gold ear-ring of basket-shaped form from Kirkhaugh in Northumberland and a second possible ear-ring fragment in bronze from Salen, on the island of Mull; otherwise there are no metal associations with vessels of this group.

The European bell beaker group (E) are also vessels of bell-shaped form, but in some cases slightly carinated, and they may be provided with a cordon or collar at the rim. The decoration is executed by means of impressions made with a blunt-toothed comb and consists either of horizontal lines of such impressions arranged in an all-over, repeating pattern or, more commonly, horizontal bands of lattice, zig-zag, triangular or lozenge motifs bordered by horizontal lines, again of comb impressions, separated one from another by undecorated zones forming a repeating pattern. Over 105 sites have produced vessels of this type, the majority in Wessex and East Anglia with an eastern distribution northwards through Yorkshire into eastern Scotland. The associations in graves include barbed and tanged arrow-heads, small copper awls with square section and a gold ear-ring from Radley in Berkshire.

The third group, the Wessex-middle Rhine beakers (W/MR), have a dense concentration on the Wessex chalk in the area previously occupied by makers of European bell beakers. In form there is a move away from the low flaring rim and bell silhouette to a taller, slim outline with rim diameter equal to or less than the belly and the waist set high on the vessel (fig. 5.1:1). A number of the vessels have a distinctly biconical body and

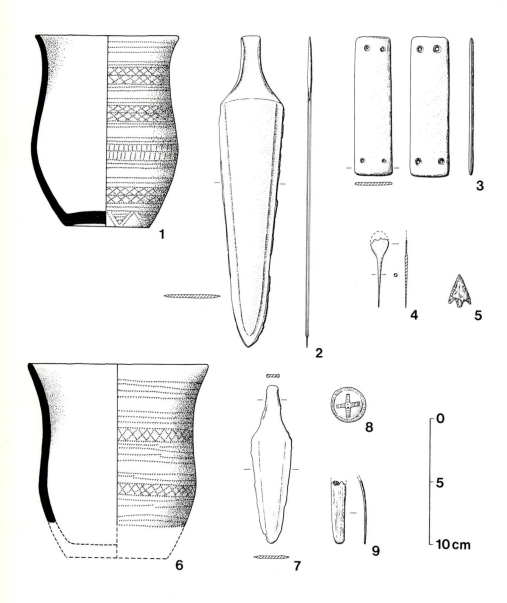

Fig. 5.1   Beaker grave groups. 1–5 Roundway, Wilts.; 6–9 Mere, Wilts. (after Annable and Simpson 1964).

rather straight short neck. The ware itself is of a very high quality and frequently the vessels are bright red in colour with a finish like sealing wax. Decoration is again normally executed by comb impressions, the combs being longer than those in the European bell beaker series. Zoned ornament is the norm, the motifs being lattice, ladder and chequer patterns and also metope and panel motifs; very frequently this horizontal ornament breaks down towards the base, which is decorated with a series of filled pendant triangles. The associations in graves consist of tanged and, in one case, riveted copper daggers, awls and tubular beads of copper, a racquet pin from Roundway in Wiltshire and decorated gold discs from Mere, also in Wiltshire (fig. 5.1). The stone associations include barbed and tanged arrow-heads, archers' wrist-guards or bracers of rectangular form with two or four perforations, and a single flint dagger presumably copying the metal forms from West Overton, Wiltshire.

The graves in this Wessex-middle Rhine group are very much richer than those of the earlier beaker groups and, in particular, there is a small series of very rich male graves in the group which appear to represent an aristocracy. The graves of Dorchester in Oxfordshire, and Winterslow, Mere and Roundway in Wiltshire, account for about 60 per cent of all the significant associations. Eighty per cent of all Wessex-middle Rhine beakers are found within an 80km radius of Stonehenge and it is possible that the members of this group were responsible for erection of the bluestone structure, Phase II, at this site. The concentration of finds in the area round about Stonehenge (fig. 5.12), which appears to provide a focal point, suggests that this Wessex-middle Rhine beaker group played an important contributory part not only in the development of the political importance of Wessex at the beginning of the early bronze age, as expressed in the Phase III structure at Stonehenge, but also in the emergence of the early bronze age 'Wessex culture' in this same area.

The north British-middle Rhine group (N/MR) is, according to Clarke, contemporary with the Wessex-middle Rhine group and has a complementary distribution, the finds occurring north of the Thames and in eastern England and Scotland. North British-middle Rhine beakers are, in profile, similar to Wessex-middle Rhine forms and are distinguished by predominant motifs of broad herringbone-filled zones and simple pendant fringes. Associations in graves include barbed and tanged arrow-heads and a dagger of flint, a gold disc from Farleigh Wick in Wiltshire and a bone belt-ring or ring pendant from Stanton Harcourt in Oxfordshire. The north British-north Rhine group (N/NR) is concentrated in eastern Yorkshire, Northumberland and around the shores of the Moray Firth. The vessels in this series have squat, globular profiles with smoothly recurved necks and waists set just below the rim. The belly diameter is generally greater than that of the rim and many have a protruding foot. In decoration the most consistent feature of the group is the multiple lined or grooved neck. Decoration on the belly is normally executed by grooving or incision, frequently zoned. No metalwork is associated with the pottery of this type in graves and apart from undiagnostic flint and bone forms the only significant associations are conical jet or shale buttons with 'V' perforations. An unusual feature in graves of this group is the occurrence on six sites of cremation rather than inhumation burials.

The sixth of Clarke's intrusive beaker groups, the 'barbed wire' group, is confined to southern England and Wales. The vessels themselves are frequently globular in profile and decorated with impressions made with a thread-wound stamp. The decoration is generally arranged in broad zones consisting of hatched or lattice-filled bands. Amongst the associations there is an absence of metalwork and in the flint equipment the only significant grouping is that of barbed and tanged arrow-heads.

The final intrusive group, the primary north British-Dutch beaker group (N1/D), is considered to provide the foundations for the subsequent indigenous development in northern Britain of the developed, late and final phases of the north British beaker series (N2–4). The vessels are generally smaller in size than preceding groups and have a distinct neck separated from the ovoid body by a marked waist which occurs usually within the upper third of the vessel. A distinguishing feature in the fabric, too, is the absence of crushed pot grit in the tempering, unlike vessels in the other intrusive groups described above. The decoration is generally executed by means of comb impressions and the dominant form is that of three bands of ornament on rim, belly and foot.

An innovation in design is the use of fringe motifs to emphasize the border in narrow lattice, ladder and ermine patterns. A few examples of these beakers occur in Wessex and East Anglia but the major concentrations are in Yorkshire, Northumberland and eastern Scotland, all finds being within 25 miles of the sea. Associations in graves are poor and are limited to flint scrapers.

There is also one further insular group which occupies a region intermediate between the two major areas of northern and southern traditions with concentrations in Norfolk and Suffolk. This is the East Anglian group (E. ANG.); the vessels are small with an ovoid or globular body and a sinuous profile with waist and base diameters approximately equal. A protruding foot is also very common. Decoration is very simple and consists of horizontal lines in all-over style. These forms are closely linked by shape and decorative motifs to the barbed wire, north British and north Rhine groups, and the series of vessels appears to represent the local, long-lasting admixture of these intrusive beaker groups and an indigenous and local neolithic population manufacturing Mildenhall ware.

The developed north British beaker group (N2) evolves out of the N1/D group and consists of vessels with a very considerable range of shapes, though generally having a ovoid body with long or a short neck. The major concentrations of the form are in eastern coastal Scotland, the Borders and the Yorkshire Wolds; it is the latter area which has produced the most richly furnished graves, suggesting perhaps the centre of commercial power trading metal and possibly bracers across the North Sea. The major associations include tanged daggers with a single rivet in the tang, perforated jet buttons and waisted bracers with four perforations. Decoration on the neck generally consists of a series of zones with larger panels of ornament on the body and there is a growing use of incision.

N3 beakers are found in the same areas as those of the N2 tradition but there is a considerable expansion westwards in Scotland using the Great Glen route, suggesting trade and metalworking; this is probably the period of the Migdale-Marnoch metalworking tradition (Coles 1968–9) (fig. 5.7). Associations include rectangular two-holed bracers, pulley-rings (probably belt fasteners) and, again, single-riveted tanged daggers.

In the final northern group (N4) two principal forms are represented – one in which the waist is abandoned in favour of smooth curves with a broad flat base the same diameter as the waist, and the other in which the waist is highly emphasized and the neck exaggerated with the belly greater in diameter than that of the rim. The commonest decorative technique is that of incision, and motifs are spread in two broad zones on the neck and body of the vessel. No metal is associated with the vessels of this group, in striking contrast to contemporary cultures, and the only significant associations are waisted four-holed bracers and flat rectangular two-holed forms. N4 beakers are confined entirely to Scotland, largely to the eastern coastal areas.

In the southern tradition, primary southern beakers (S1) have an angular profile with a well-defined waist, the neck generally funnel-shaped with straight or convex external walls, belly and rim diameter being equal. These features are shared with the developed northern beaker groups. The decoration is predominantly filled neck and zoned belly and many of the motifs, generally executed by means of comb impressions, appear to be derived from the Wessex-middle Rhine tradition.

A growing development first seen in S1 beakers and peculiar to the southern British tradition is that of reserved or floating patterns. There are no metal associations other than bronze awls but the considerable variety of grave goods include a flint dagger, jet or shale pulley-rings, jet and amber buttons, and flint or stone axes including in one case a perforated stone battle axe (fig. 5.2: 2). Vessels of this type are found in southern and south-eastern Britain from Yorkshire to Wessex. In developed southern beakers (S2) the long-necked form becomes dominant with the waist situated about half-way up the body of the vessel, and purely southern beaker patterns are now dominant, the most frequent motifs being hexagon, floating lozenge and panel forms. The vessels are found in the same areas as S1 beakers but there is also a western extension into Wales, the Borders and the north of Ireland. The numerous associations include three-riveted bronze daggers, bronze arm-rings, sheet bronze basket ear-rings, flint daggers (fig. 5.2: 11), and barbed and tanged arrow-heads with neatly squared-off barb and tang – the so-called Breton type. Other consistent associations are V-bored buttons and pulley-rings of jet or shale, and slate whetstones (fig. 5.2: 3, 4, 6–7). Some of these associations (Breton arrow-heads, whetstones and riveted daggers) suggest contemporaneity with the first phase of the Wessex culture and it may be significant that these Wessex I types found with S2 beakers are found outside the central Wessex area. The makers of S2 beakers appear to have had a definite interest in stone circles and henges, especially those containing free-standing uprights, in that burials are frequently sited adjacent to

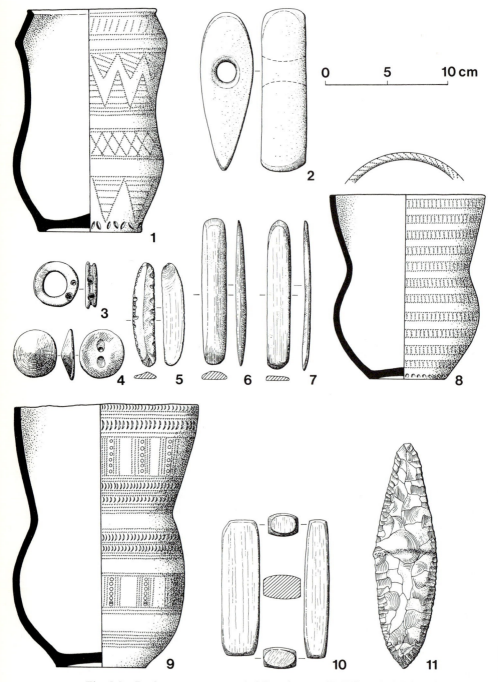

Fig. 5.2   Beaker grave groups. 1–2 Durrington 67, Wilts.; 3–8 Winterbourne Stoke G54, Wilts.; 9–11 Amesbury G54, Wilts. (after Crittall 1973).

these two categories of monument, although there is no evidence to suggest
that the makers of this group of beakers were responsible for their
construction.

Late southern beakers (S3) have a long neck which is now cylindrical
and there is an increasing slackness in the profiles. All S3 beakers have
filled neck and filled body decoration, the patterns as before, but now the
floating lozenge is the most popular motif followed by the filled hexagon.
The distribution pattern is as before but the importance of the Fen area
recurs during the life of S3 beakers, possibly, as Clarke suggested, because
the makers of beaker pottery were ousted from Wessex at this time.
Associations are similar to those of the S2 group.

In the final southern beaker group (S4) the waist neck element is
abandoned to produce a slab-sided vessel. The filled hexagon motif is now
the commonest and is frequently executed by incision. S4 beakers are
widely distributed from East Anglia to north-eastern Scotland. Associations include three-rivet daggers of bronze, bronze awls, and disc beads of
shale. There is a complete absence of archer's equipment. In addition to
the normal beaker forms handled mugs decorated with southern British
motifs also occur throughout the series (fig. 5.3).

Fig. 5.3   Beaker mugs, Cambs.; height of beaker on left 20·5cm (photograph
A. Pacitto: courtesy S. E. Thomas).

Clarke's beaker classification as summarized above has been generally accepted and his groupings are referred to in current literature in Britain. On the other hand, serious criticisms of the classification have been raised by Dutch archaeologists (Lanting and van der Waals 1972). These criticisms are concerned both with the methodology, the means whereby Clarke arrived at his groupings, and also the purely archaeological evidence in terms of comparisons of pottery forms in Britain and on the Continent, with associations, and with the evidence of dating. Clarke argues that the shape of the beaker is, in part, functional whereas decorative motifs and style, that is the manner in which the individual motifs are arranged on the surface of the vessel, are largely non-functional and therefore more likely to indicate a human tradition. For this reason greater weight was given to the motifs and style in his original analysis. It could, however, be argued that variability in shape within certain limitations may be as much the result of taste and tradition as decoration on the vessel. Their second methodological criticism concerns the concept of graded importance, of weighted value. In his first attempts to group and classify British beaker pottery Clarke used the technique of matrix analysis (Clarke D. L. 1962), a technique in which traits which are considered to be diagnostic are correlated, one with another, each trait being considered of equal importance. The result of this sorting process produced five clusters of traits which Clarke interpreted as representing human groups. In fact the results were sufficiently imprecise to make it necessary to emphasize or weight certain traits at the expense of others and to supplement this classification with the evidence of association, burial rites and stratigraphy. The extent, however, to which the principle of graded importance was applied to this material is not explained nor the means whereby the other archaeological evidence was integrated into the ultimate classification. A further problem is that of distribution. In examining the distribution maps of Clarke's seven intrusive beaker groups, doubts arise as to the reality of these divisions. A surprising number of beakers from one and the same area represent different intrusive traditions while in other cases vessels thought to represent a particular intrusive group are widely scattered throughout the British Isles. In preparing these distributions Clarke was using motifs rather than pots. A beaker is not a northern beaker because it is necessarily found in the north of Britain but because that is the area where the motifs on it are most frequently found. Certain anomalies arise out of this system, for example the occurrence of a considerable number of northern beakers in Wessex or the association in a single grave, as at Glen Forsa, Mull, of both a northern and a southern beaker. Study of beaker distributions in Britain shows a number of areas which appear to be focal, forming distinctive centres of beaker settlement, notably north-east Scotland, south-east Scotland and north-eastern England, Yorkshire, East Anglia and Wessex; Dutch archaeologists suggest that a more realistic picture of the development of beaker societies in the British Isles could be achieved by a study of pottery and associations in these focal areas. Such a study emphasizes local development in ceramic evolution and makes it unnecessary to invoke numerous movements of distinctive beaker groups across the North Sea to the British Isles, since developments in these focal areas are seen as the result more of continuing contact with other regions in the British Isles and with the Continent than major population movements. This concept is strengthened because the Dutch were able to demonstrate the lack of both chronological and geographical evidence to support a continental origin for north British-middle Rhine and north British-north Rhine groups, and similarly the absence of precise parallels on the Continent for Wessex-middle Rhine and primary north British-Dutch beakers. The isolation, too, of the barbed wire group as representing a distinctive beaker human group is questioned in that the only truly diagnostic character of such vessels is the use of a cord-wound stamp. Many of the motifs executed in this technique would, if they had been produced by comb impressions, have caused the vessels carrying such ornament to be included in one or other of Clarke's intrusive beaker groups and, indeed, the actual barbed wire technique they suggest might be a British innovation, later introduced to the adjacent coastal areas of the Continent.

The Dutch go on to suggest an alternative developmental scheme for British beakers based on a study of vessels in four of their suggested focal areas – these being Wessex, East Anglia, Yorkshire, and north-eastern England/south-eastern Scotland. Other authors have applied their classification elsewhere in Britain (e.g. Ritchie and Shepherd 1973; ApSimon 1976: 48). The scheme they propose is best documented in the Wessex area where it is represented by seven successive steps; for the other areas they have studied a similar sequence appears to exist. As with Clarke's scheme theirs is a typological one supported by a number of important associations which appear to corroborate the typological development.

In their Wessex focal region the first step is marked by all-over corded beakers which are typologically considered early, on the basis of their profile and interior rim decoration. Within this first step they would also include the only four maritime beakers from the British Isles, a form which Clarke grouped together with his European bell beaker series but whose distinctive characteristics were pointed out initially by Piggott (1963a). Their second step is marked by the beginnings of regional development with beakers whose profiles and decoration still owe much to the vessels of the first phase, although now the profile is more angular with the belly carination set low down on the body of the vessel and the decoration simple repeating horizontal zones bordered by lines of comb impressions. All-over corded beakers continue in this step and this form is also imitated in vessels decorated with repeating horizontal lines of comb impressions. In step three the vessels are more slender in their proportions and the decorative motifs very much more varied. The small number of vessels which characterize step four show a growing accentuation of the neck area produced either by a flaring of the neck profile or by contrasting decoration or both. Decoration on the neck normally consists of a solid band of horizontal ornament with zoned motifs occurring on the belly but with a diminished use of horizontal lines to border these panels of decoration. In step five the neck is further accentuated with a sharp flaring rim and the neck area itself has grown proportionally in relation to the total height of the vessel. Decorative motifs are now more complex, repetitive designs disappear and there is an increasing emphasis on vertical decoration bridging the horizontal zones. In step six the distinction between neck and body begins to fade and the neck itself is frequently more cylindrical in profile with an increasing emphasis on the globularity of the lower part of the body. Ornament is now spread in two or three broad bands over the surface of the vessel. In step seven the distinction between neck and body is lost and the vessels have a rather slab-sided appearance while the decoration is frequently an all-over design rather than the zoning system of the earlier stages.

This proposed sequence is borne out to a considerable extent by associations. Step one is marked by an absence of any significant objects buried with the beakers; step two has gold discs, basket-shaped ear-rings, and narrow tanged copper daggers. Steps three and four have broad-tanged copper daggers and in four appears the first broad-tanged dagger with a true rivet hole. Bracers also occur with beakers of steps two and three. Jet buttons and pulley-rings are restricted to steps five and six, and in steps six and seven tangless riveted daggers appear for the first time, as do perforated shaft-hole battle-axes.

In all burials of these various steps the orientation where known is north–south, males being buried with their heads towards the north and females with their heads to the south, in both cases facing east.

For the three other focal areas which the Dutch have considered for study a similar developmental sequence appears to exist, although individual steps are not so clearly represented as in Wessex. They conclude therefore that the earliest step is marked by the appearance of all-over corded beakers representing an innovating group from the Continent. Of the four focal regions studied, only in Wessex are all-over corded beakers immediately succeeded by vessels decorated with zoned ornament produced by comb impressions. The further north one moves from Wessex the later is the adoption of comb ornament.

In general the chronological and typological development suggested by the Dutch is similar to Clarke's scheme, the major differences being that they place Clarke's East Anglian group earlier than his northern or southern British beaker traditions, and his northern group earlier than the southern, while his S1 to S3 sequence is hardly recognizable in the Dutch scheme; but it is in the interpretation of the evidence that the fundamental difference lies. Instead of seven immigrant beaker groups coming from across the North Sea the Dutch would see one major influence, that of the makers of all-over corded beakers, followed by regional developments and sustained contacts both between regions and with the Continent. The continental links are most clearly demonstrable in Wessex and in fact the whole beaker development as outlined by Lanting and van der Waals for Wessex is closely paralleled by contemporary events across the North Sea in the Rhineland (van der Waals and Glasbergen 1955; Lanting, Mook and van der Waals 1973). Eventually other areas of Britain caught up with

Wessex and with continental developments.

An alternative view of the development of beaker societies in Britain has most recently been put forward by Case (1977). He would consider the beaker culture under three phases. The early phase he associated with cord-impressed beakers introduced not, as suggested by Clarke and Lanting and van der Waals, as a result of immigration, but through contact, in terms of trade and exchange, between British communities and the makers of corded ware pottery on the Continent. The middle phase sees an actual population movement from the Continent associated with a distinct physical type, the introduction of metalworking and a recognizable 'beaker culture'. The late phase, entirely insular in character and persisting after the beaker culture had disappeared on the Continent, represents a development and continuum from the middle phase with some innovations in metal and stone types.

Beaker burials   The material evidence for the makers of beaker pottery comes almost entirely from funerary contexts and such evidence inevitably presents a very one-sided picture of their society. As previously noted, one of the major innovations introduced by these groups into Britain is that of a change in burial rite from collective inhumation or cremation to individual or single grave burials. The normal, though not invariable, rite was that of inhumation, frequently covered by a round barrow (Ashbee 1960). In southern Britain the grave is normally a pit excavated in the subsoil and of roughly oval plan. Such round barrows are comparatively small and in some cases as at Crichel Down, Dorset, or Roundway, Wiltshire, both over 1·6m in depth, the 'barrow' may represent material originally dug out to provide the grave which could not be returned to it. In other cases, however, where a surrounding quarry ditch exists it is clear that a deliberately built mound was intended. In the Peak District of Derbyshire and the chalk wolds in the East Riding of Yorkshire pit graves are again the rule, although in the latter area the covering mounds were in many cases of great size (Mortimer 1905).

In the north of England and in Scotland the crouched inhumation was normally contained in a stone-lined grave or cist; the majority of these appear to be flat graves although in a number of cases the burials are again covered by a round cairn. It is possible, of course, that in the highland zone many more cist burials containing beakers were originally covered by cairns, subsequently robbed to provide building material. In the south, too, low mounds may have been completely obliterated by later ploughing and so-called flat cemeteries of beaker burials as at Cassington in Oxfordshire may originally have been covered by such low mounds. A number of beaker barrows covered circular settings of stake- or post-holes serving either as a revetment for the mound itself or representing a pre-barrow structure (Ashbee 1957). In other cases circular or penannular stone banks lay on the old ground surface buried beneath the mound.

At West Overton G6B in north Wiltshire, for example, the turf and earth mound covered an annular stone bank composed of burnt flint nodules and lumps of sarsen which had also been subjected to varying

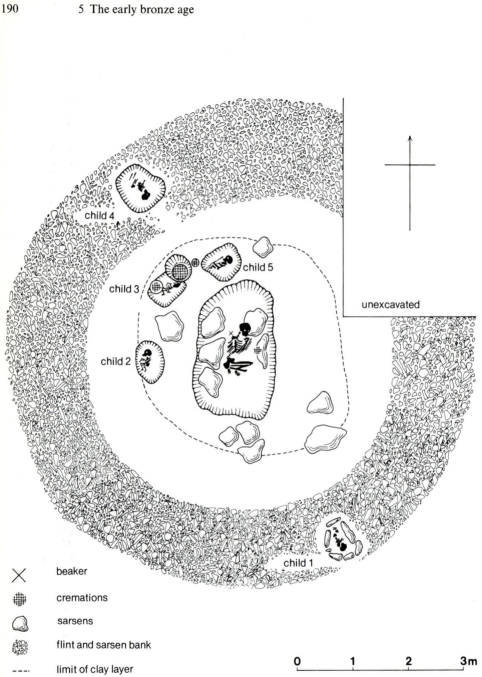

child 4

child 3

child 5

child 2

unexcavated

child 1

✕   beaker

⊞   cremations

⬠   sarsens

▓   flint and sarsen bank

----   limit of clay layer

0   1   2   3m

Fig. 5.4   Plan of beaker barrow, West Overton G6b, Wilts. (after Smith and Simpson 1966).

degrees of heat (Smith and Simpson 1966). Beneath the bank itself were two crouched inhumations of children, one in a pit grave, the other in a stone cist. Set centrally within the area enclosed by the stone bank was a large oval pit containing a crouched male inhumation accompanied by a beaker and other grave goods (fig. 5.4). A cremation also lay in the same grave. To the north and west of the central grave were three further pits containing the crouched inhumed remains of children and two cremations in collared urns. All these graves had been sealed by a layer of grey clay and the deposition of this layer must represent the final act before the erection of the mound.

At West Overton and other beaker barrows, although one may still speak of single grave burials it is clear that in many cases a number of burials were placed in their own pit graves in an area which was subsequently to be sealed by the covering barrow. In Yorkshire, in particular, it is also noticeable that many of the very large pit graves beneath the barrows contain successive interments, each accompanied by beaker or later bronze age pottery (Petersen 1972). In such sites, it would be reasonable to presume that the grave pit itself had remained open for a considerable period of time, for the successive deposition of corpses and the existence of timber or, in some cases, stone settings beneath such mounds probably served to delimit and mark the position of the grave for future interments.

Apart from such single grave burials beaker pottery has also been found, normally in a secondary context, in association with a number of megalithic tombs, notably those of the Cotswold–Severn and Clyde series. One group in Ireland, the so-called 'wedge-shaped' gallery graves, appear to be almost exclusively associated with beaker material and may represent the adoption of the megalithic building tradition by the makers of this pottery (De Valera and Ó Nualláin 1961). Again, a purely insular development was the adoption of the henge, normally of the Class II form, by the makers of beaker pottery from the indigenous neolithic population.

Although many hundreds of beaker burials have been recorded from the British Isles, when we turn to other aspects of this society the evidence is extremely slender, in particular where domestic sites are concerned (Simpson D. D. A. 1971).

Beaker domestic sites   Numerous finds of occupation material associated with sherds of beaker pottery have been discovered in sand-dune areas in the British Isles, notably in East Anglia, Lincolnshire and in western coastal areas of England and Scotland. No house structures are normally associated with such settlement debris, however. In part this might be accounted for by inadequate excavation as the majority of such sites have been exposed by the purely natural processes of erosion and weathering. On the other hand at Ballynagilly in Co. Tyrone, where an extensive area of the low hill of glacial gravel and sand rising some 15m above the peat bog which surround it was stripped, no recognizable house plans were recovered although the excavator postulated three possible house sites marked by a conspicuous concentration of finds. Various suggestions have been made to account for this scarcity of house plans. In the chalk and limestone areas it may be that subsequent weathering of the natural subsoil has reduced all traces other than those of major and deep post-hole structures, and some support for this view is provided by the discovery of settlement sites including post structures beneath later round barrows. An economic argument is that beaker societies were basically pastoral and nomadic, not requiring any permanent or substantial domestic structures, but this is in part belied by other economic evidence both from the pottery and from certain recognizable house forms.

Ten sites in the British Isles have produced evidence of structures which might be interpreted as domestic (Simpson D. D. A. 1971). At Lough Gur in Co. Limerick the majority of the houses are associated with middle neolithic and native pottery. At site D, on the other hand, where the bulk of the finds were beaker, were two oval houses 6·7m in diameter defined by post-holes (fig 5.5: 1). In the second Irish site, Downpatrick, Co. Down, were two houses, the smaller 3·9m in diameter defined by individual post-holes, and the second 9·7m in diameter defined by posts and gulleys, bedding trenches for the insertion of close-set timbers (fig. 5.5: 2). At the latter site although there were numerous sherds of cordoned vessels there was also some undoubted beaker pottery. In neither case was there any evidence for the economic activities of the occupants of these buildings.

At Beacon Hill, Flamborough, East Riding of Yorkshire, level 3 contained sherds of beaker pottery and the truncated ground plan of an oval structure defined by posts and stone packing (fig. 5.5: 4). A hearth lay outside the building. At Swarkeston in Derbyshire were two post structures, partially covered by a later early bronze age round barrow. The first consisted of a funnel-shaped setting of stake-holes which was traced for some 12m, being 76cm wide at its narrowest point. Adjacent to this was a structure 3·6m square with a small annexe defined by more substantial post-holes. The majority of the beaker pottery was found outside this latter structure, which appeared to have been kept clean, and this the excavator interpreted as the ground plan of a small building. Less certainly domestic in character is a site at Woodhead in Cumberland where a bank of stone 7·9m in diameter and 76cm high enclosed a pit 2m deep containing a jet button and a pulley ring (fig. 5.6: 4). Adjacent to this pit were two post-holes which the excavator suggested were for a stepped post supporting a tent-like roof. It is equally possible, however, that this structure was funerary in function. The internal pit would have been of a size suitable for containing either a crouched or even an extended inhumation burial, all traces of which would have been destroyed in the acid soil conditions, leaving only the jet button and the pulley ring as possible grave goods. Parallels for such a monument can be cited from Burnt Common in Devon and Chatton Sandyford in Northumberland (Jobey 1968a), in both cases clearly funerary in function.

In the coastal sand dunes of Gwithian, Cornwall, were found two superimposed beaker houses. The earlier was a circular structure 4·5m in diameter defined by individual post-holes with a central post, offset from which was a hearth (Megaw 1976a). The later building was 7·6m in

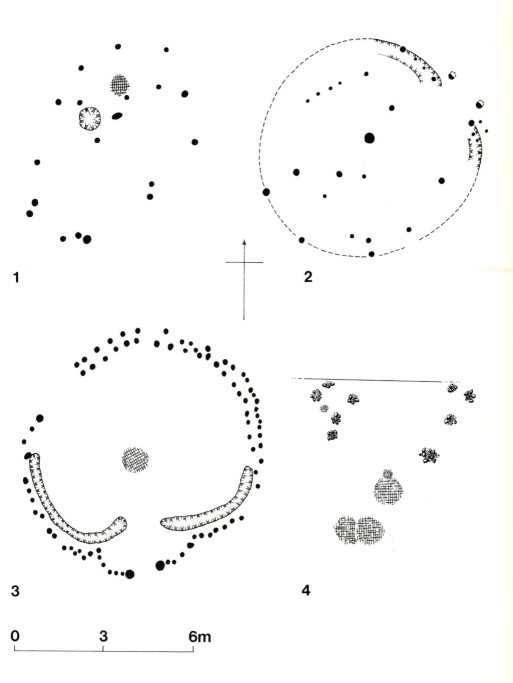

Fig. 5.5   Plans of beaker houses. 1 Lough Gur, Co. Limerick; 2 Downpatrick,
Co. Down; 3 Gwithian, Cornwall; 4 Flamborough, Yorks. (after Simpson
D. D. A. 1971).

diameter, defined in part by posts, in part by gulleys for close-set timbers (fig. 5.5: 3). Both houses had been set within palisaded enclosures and remanent magnetic dating of the hearths in the two houses suggested an interval of no more than 50 years between them. Additional paired posts have been interpreted as corn-drying racks and further evidence for economic activities is provided by fragments of saddle querns used as packing material in the gulleys. Herding is also indicated by quantities of mammalian remains and a partial dependence on the sea by numerous finds of shell-fish from the midden layers associated with these two structures. Like the other beaker house sites so far considered the pottery from Gwithian, although it included beaker forms, also had coarser wares decorated with crudely executed chevron designs and plaited cord made, it has been suggested, by indigenous neolithic groups in imitation of beakers. A number of these vessels have cordons.

The beaker settlement site at Northton on the Isle of Harris, in the Outer Hebrides, existed in a similar environmental setting (Simpson D. D. A. 1976). In the lower of the two beaker occupation levels were found the remains of two oval stone structures, the better preserved being 8·5m long and 4·2m wide; both were orientated north-east–south-west fig. 5.6: 3). The walls were of dry-stone construction and survived to a height of about 91cm while tumbled material within the enclosure added no more than 91cm to the total height of the structure. The extremely crude construction suggests that it was never intended as a free-standing building but rather as a revetment wall to a pit dug in the sand dunes. Within the dry-stone walled structure was a series of stake-holes too insubstantial to have supported any major roofing structure spanning the area defined by the dry-stone walling. It appears likely that both 'buildings' were intended merely to prevent the sand weathering back into the excavated pit; within this area, sheltered from the wind, would have been erected a light tent-like structure. Among large quantities of mammalian remains the dominant species were sheep, suggesting a comparatively open environment, followed by cattle, while hunting is indicated by the bones and antlers of red deer. The sea was a further source of food as indicated by large quantities of marine shells, in particular limpets, fragments of crabs and sea urchins, and the bones of sea mammals. No trace of milling equipment was found on the site, nor did any of the many thousands of sherds of beaker pottery from either horizon contain grain impressions, although both cereals and evidence of ploughing were recovered from the beaker settlement at Rosinish on the neighbouring island of Benbecula (Shepherd 1976).

A very much more extensive beaker domestic complex has been partially excavated at Belle Tout in Sussex. Here there were originally two rectangular enclosures which have been largely destroyed by coastal erosion (Bradley 1970). Within the surviving enclosure were five timber built structures, three circular, one rectangular and one trapezoid (fig. 5.6: 1–2). Further timber-built trapezoid houses tentatively ascribed to the beaker cultures have been excavated at Willington in Nottinghamshire where there was a considerable mixture of later iron age sherds.

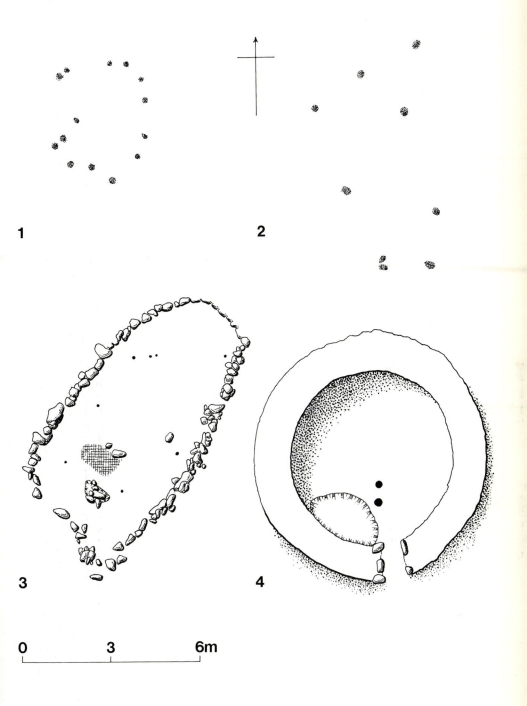

Fig. 5.6   Plans of beaker houses. 1–2 Belle Tout, Sussex; 3 Northton, Harris; 4 Woodhead, Cumb. (after Simpson D. D. A. 1971).

The above account of the houses in Britain suggests considerable variety in form but this may be in part a reflection of differing local geological and other environmental conditions. Apart from the Phase I house at Gwithian none appear to have had central post-holes. Those at Swarkeston, Belle Tout, Lough Gur and House II at Gwithian probably had domed roofs formed by bending over stakes or withies; tent-like roofs are likely for Northton and Woodhead. A recurring feature is a pit or pits adjacent to the hearth, recalling the stone versions from the villages of Rinyo and Skara Brae. With the exception of Belle Tout, the houses exist as single structures or at most in pairs suggesting a comparatively small social unit, probably that of a single family.

The finds from these houses allow no broad generalizations regarding the economy of the makers of beaker pottery; indeed, a number of the sites have produced no economic evidence at all. The Northton settlers appear to have subsisted entirely by pastoralism and hunting and gathering, supporting the contention that beaker groups were semi-nomadic. On the other hand, at Gwithian a sedentary existence is implied by grain rubbers and corn-drying racks. Further evidence for cereal production is provided by the putative grain storage pits containing sherds of beaker pottery (Field *et al.* 1964), by the later beaker ploughing at South Street in north Wiltshire (Fowler and Evans 1967), and by grain impressions on a number of beakers in the British Isles. The latter evidence suggests that barley had supplanted wheat as the principal cereal crop (Helbaek 1952), although this view has recently been challenged (Dennell 1976). That flax was grown is indicated by a large number of seed impressions on a beaker from Handley Down, Dorset; whether the seed was used as a cereal or for the manufacture of textiles is, of course, uncertain, although it may be significant that the earliest example of fabric from prehistoric Britain comes from a barrow at Kellythorpe in the East Riding of Yorkshire where a crouched inhumation burial appears to have been covered with a woven shroud. The use of moss or sedge matting as material for shrouds later in the bronze age might indicate a deficiency of wool, at least in some areas of southern Britain (Henshall 1950), and it is tempting to think that the garment in which the corpse from the Kellythorpe barrow was wrapped may in fact have been linen.

The zoological evidence is at present insufficient to make any generalizations concerning the preference for or dominance of one particular species of domesticated animal, and the predominance of any one species almost certainly varied from area to area depending on local environmental conditions and perhaps to some extent on deliberate choice on the part of beaker groups for a particular livelihood. One may contrast, for example, the evidence from Northton where sheep was the dominant domestic species but where hunting is represented by a large number of bones and antlers of red deer, with the animal remains from the settlement on the periphery of the great passage grave at Newgrange in the bend of the Boyne where cattle were the dominant domestic species with only small numbers of sheep, goat and pig, and wild forms represented by the remains of only a single red deer. Of particular interest from the latter site are a number of horse bones, probably of domesticated animals (Van Wijngaarden-Bakker 1974).

Material equipment   As we have seen, the evidence for beaker societies comes almost entirely from their graves and it is from these funerary contexts that the other objects characteristic of the beaker cultures come, although only a very small percentage of graves are furnished with material other than a beaker. Most significant amongst these associations are the earliest metal objects from archaeological contexts in the British Isles. The first and most characteristic of these is a series of copper knives or daggers with triangular blades and either a simple tang or a tang with rivet holes for the attachment of the organic, presumably wood or bone, hilt plates (Hardaker 1974; Gerloff 1975: 27). Analysis of the metals used in the manufacture of the knives from Dorchester in Oxfordshire and Roundway in Wiltshire have shown these to be of central European ores; but a similar tanged knife from Winterslow in Wiltshire was of Irish copper, suggesting a very rapid expansion and exploitation of the Irish copper deposits (Case 1966). A very much larger number of artifacts of smelted copper from Ireland suggest that it was the principal centre of metallurgy in the British Isles at this period, and the copper deposits at Mount Gabriel, Co. Cork, may have begun to be mined at this time (Jackson J. S. 1968; Deady and Doran 1972).

Tanged and riveted knives similar to those from English beaker graves are known from Ireland and a link with a further early metal type is provided by a hoard in Knocknague in Co. Galway where a tanged knife was found in association with three flat copper axes and three double pointed awls, types found in association with beaker burials in the rest of Britain (Harbison 1968; 1969b). The three axes are thick-butted type A, typologically the earliest group of metal axes in the British Isles (Britton 1963), and generally considered to be related to the so-called trapeze-shaped flat axe which has a wide distribution in western Europe, although the Irish and the rare examples of such type A axes in Scotland cannot be precisely paralleled in the continental forms (Coles 1968–9). All these broad-butted flat axes have proved to be of copper. No moulds for this type of axe have so far been recovered but presumably only a mould of the simplest kind would have been required, either a hollow in the sand or in a piece of fired clay. Although no moulds survive, rough castings for such axes are known from Tonderghie, Wigtownshire, and from near Perth (Coles 1968–9). Such pieces would be finally finished by grinding, forging and hammering. The thick-butted axes fall into two major types, those with straight sides from butt to blade and those in which the sides are slightly concave, the latter being considered later and probably influenced by more developed forms of axe, not introduced into the British Isles until c. 1,800 bc (Case 1966). Carvings of such axes occur on cists in the Kilmartin valley, Argyll (Simpson and Thawley 1973).

Although the earliest copper objects have been found in graves of the beaker culture it has been suggested from time to time that such objects were not in fact manufactured by beaker groups but were imported into

Britain from Ireland, as the products of metal-smiths who had already established this new technology before the arrival of the makers of beakers in the British Isles. Such Irish metalworkers have generally been associated with the appearance of passage graves of the Boyne series in Ireland (Childe 1940: 113). On the other hand no metal object has ever been recovered from a primary context in an Irish passage grave, nor are passage graves found in Munster in south-west Ireland, where the principal concentration of type A axes with straight sides centres. The weight of evidence would still favour the makers of beaker pottery as the earliest metallurgists in the British Isles (Case 1966).

The maintenance of continental contacts reflected in parallelisms in

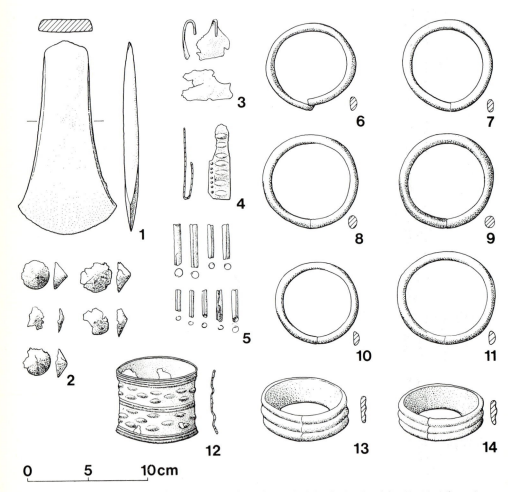

Fig. 5.7   Metalwork from a hoard at Migdale, Sutherland (1–11, 13–14), and a grave at Melfort, Argyll (12) (after Coles 1968–9).

form and decoration on beakers on both sides of the North Sea ensures that this early copper-using phase of metallurgy in the British Isles was swiftly superseded c. 1,800 bc by a new and very much wider range of objects, produced now in the alloy of copper and tin. The principal area of stimulus for these new ideas and forms appears to be Saxo-Thuringia. This second metalworking phase is termed in Scotland the Migdale-Marnoch tradition, after a hoard of axes from Migdale in Sutherland (fig. 5.7) and a stone mould for the casting of such axes from Marnoch in Banffshire (Britton 1963), and in Ireland the Impact phase (Case 1966), emphasizing both the innovatory character of this new tradition and also its importance and longevity in the metalworking traditions of the early bronze age.

Most important amongst the new forms was the thin-butted or type B axe, which represents an improvement in technology in that such axes could be mounted on a lighter and more manageable haft split for the insertion of the butt of the axe. In this series are the earliest examples of Irish decorated axes, and various sub-types within the general series have been recognized (Megaw and Hardy 1938). The axes were cast in open stone moulds, generally of sandstone (fig. 6.2: 1). In Scotland there is a marked concentration of these moulds in the north-east in the same area as bronzes of this tradition, although curiously the majority of the known copper resources in Scotland lie in the south-west. Similarly in Ireland the majority of finds are in the north although the mining centres remain southern. Again it is the hoards which provide a link between metal objects found in graves and a wider range of products either as stray finds or grouped together in such hoards (Harbison 1968; 1969a; 1969b). The hoards are generally considered to be the stock-in-trade of the metal merchants or, in the case of smaller groupings, as belonging to a single individual and representing his own personal objects. It is curious, however, that many hoards – particularly of axes – appear to be deliberately broken; the possibility therefore arises that such groupings of metal buried in the ground were not, in fact, deposited for safety during periods of unrest but represent an actual offering or votive deposit (Coles 1968–9: 33). No thin-butted axe has ever been found in a grave with a beaker, but that these products were contemporary with and part of the same metalworking tradition as objects found as grave furniture with such vessels is indicated by associations such as that in the hoard at Auchnacree, Angus, which in addition to thin-butted axes included two flat bronze daggers with multiple rivets for attachment to the hilt (Coles 1968–9: 65).

Such riveted daggers are well known from beaker graves in Britain and Piggott (1963a) has suggested five major groups in this series which appear to represent a typological and chronological development. The earliest are small riveted triangular knives and daggers with the lower edge of the hilt plate cut to an omega form, as in the grave group from Dorchester-on-Thames in Oxfordshire. Such forms have counterparts in the middle Rhine region and analysis of the Dorchester pieces suggests that it is in fact an import from this area. The second group consists of larger triangular daggers, again normally with an omega-shaped hilt outline but with insular variants in which the hilt edge is either a broad 'U' shape or a 'W' outline. The third series represents the development of a purely insular form with a tongue-shaped blade with a rounded tip, a considerable increase in the size of the blade itself, and the provision of large rivets. The later forms of riveted daggers without beaker associations represent developments in the full early bronze age and will be discussed later (Gerloff 1975).

At Birr, Co. Offaly, a hoard of type A and B axes also included a halberd (Case 1966: 154), and near Edenkilly, Morayshire, a cist which may have contained an inhumation produced a halberd and two thin-butted flat axes in the Migdale-Marnoch tradition, indicating that this type too belongs to the period of beaker metallurgy in the British Isles (Coles 1968–9:40). The halberd forms in the British Isles have a triangular blade, in some cases asymmetrical, with a markedly thickened midrib, the blade itself being attached to the handle to which it was mounted at right-angles in the same plane by means of three or more rivets, frequently of considerable size. Where the mounting has left a mark across the blade, this is always straight and runs at right-angles or slightly obliquely to the long axis of the blade. In the British Isles such halberds have an almost exclusively highland zone distribution and are more numerous in Ireland than anywhere else in western Europe. This Irish concentration originally gave rise to the theory that this type of weapon was developed in Ireland and exported to the Continent (ÓRíordáin 1937). On the other hand metal analysis of halberds of 'Irish type' from the Continent have shown these to be of European ores although, ironically, the metal-shafted halberd in the Dieskau hoard characteristic of central Europe appeared on analysis to be manufactured from Irish ores (Butler and van der Waals 1964). It has been pointed out, too that the development of this type of weapon is most likely to have taken place in an area where the battle-axe was the traditional weapon, since the halberd is simply a dagger blade mounted in the same way as a stone battle-axe; the most likely area for this development would be north-central Europe, though the most recent study of Irish halberds is less certain as to their precise area of continental origin (Harbison 1969a).

Further bronze types associated with this industry include plain and ribbed penannular rings, again probably of Saxo-Thuringian origin, and tubular beads and basket-shaped ear-rings represented in bronze in the Migdale hoard (fig. 5.7). Such basket-shaped ear-rings are also represented in gold at Orbliston, Morayshire (fig. 5.8), at Kirkhaugh, Northumberland, in association with an all-over corded beaker, and at Eynsham, Oxfordshire, with a beaker which both in Clarke's and Lanting and van der Waals' typology would be considered early. These finds suggest that the working of gold in the British Isles was contemporary with the first working and production of indigenous copper objects. In addition to the gold basket-shaped ear-rings, equally early – or earlier – must be the small discs of sheet gold bearing a punched cruciform pattern such as that from Mere in Wiltshire, again associated with an early form of beaker and represented more numerously in Ireland, unfortunately without any archaeological context or association (fig. 5.9). The basket-shaped ear-ring from Orbliston provides a tenuous link with the great series of collars or lunulae of sheet gold which represent both in their numbers and in their weight of bullion the most important series of gold objects of the first half of the 2nd millennium bc (Taylor 1970a). The ear-ring appears to have been recovered from a cist beneath a cairn which was later demolished for ballast for the construction of a railway, and from this ballast came the sheet gold crescentic lunula. The only other significant association of such neck ornaments is that from Harlyn Bay in Cornwall where a pair of lunulae were found in association with a flat axe (since lost). Like halberds, lunulae when recovered in any archaeological context whatsoever tend to be associated one with another without any other distinguishing artifacts, nor do they come from graves. A number have been recovered buried beneath prominent landmarks such as large standing stones and the rarity with which these objects are associated with graves has suggested that they were not considered as individual property but belonged to a larger social unit such as a family or a clan.

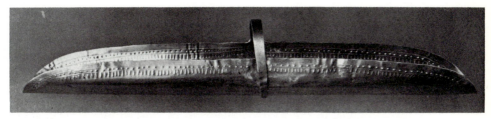

Fig. 5.8   Gold basket ear-ring, Orbliston, Moray.; length 10·3cm (photograph: J. J. Taylor).

Fig. 5.9   Gold discs, Ballina, Co. Mayo; diameter of larger disc 8cm (photograph: J. J. Taylor).

Stylistically and in terms of distribution the lunulae may be divided into three major groups (Taylor 1970a). The most sophisticated is the classical group whose technique of manufacture and quality of decoration set them apart from other lunulae. Although containing more gold in terms of weight than the other two groups, ornaments in this series are very much thinner and the collars broader, while the close similarity in design in a number of pieces in this series suggests the work of a single master craftsman. A characteristic feature in the decoration of the horns in this series is the symmetrical arrangement of the decoration, the pattern on one horn reflected in the form of a mirror image on the opposing terminal. The majority – all but five – of the lunulae in this classic series come from Ireland where there is a marked concentration in the north.

The second group, the unaccomplished lunulae, are inferior both in decoration and in the narrow form of the collar itself, which contains less gold. This group is probably contemporary with the classical series although in at least one case a lunula decorated in the classical style from Ballinagroun, Co. Kerry, had the design almost obliterated to be replaced with decoration in the unaccomplished style. All examples in this series are confined to Ireland.

The third series, the provincial group, is very thick and sparsely decorated and with one exception all examples lie outside Ireland. The products of individual craftsmen are readily recognized in this series. The lunulae from Harlyn Bay, Cornwall, St Potan and Kerivoa, Côtes-du-Nord, appear to be the products of a single goldsmith, and in view of the delicate nature of the finished product it is likely that the goldsmith carried ingot blanks such as the Arlon ring and the rod with broad lunula-like terminals in the Kerivoa hoard, to be worked into lunulae at the source of his market for an individual purchaser. The complex geometric designs in the horns of such lunulae have long been considered as skeuomorphic representations of the complex borings in amber spacer-plate necklaces associated with the early bronze age Wessex culture of southern Britain. These were imitated in jet in the north and west where the complex borings were reproduced in the form of engravings on the simply bored spacers of jet necklaces. These in turn provided the model for the incised motifs on lunulae, therefore giving a comparatively late date for these gold ornaments (Craw 1928–9). Taylor (1970a), however, has argued convincingly for a reversal of this sequence and has emphasized the close similarity in motif between the designs on the lunulae horns and the decoration on beakers, in particular those of Clarke's northern and southern British indigenous series which would be replaced by Lanting and van der Waals in the 'developed' stages of their typology of British beakers. These arguments and the somewhat tenuous associations in graves and hoards would suggest that at least the first phase in the production of lunulae should be associated with beaker metallurgy in the advanced stage of the impact phase, when ideas and techniques were entering the British Isles from northern Europe and particularly Saxo-Thuringia. The distribution of hoards and stray finds suggests that the route was that across the North Sea through Scotland to Ireland, the main centre of metalworking in the British Isles at this period.

Amongst the stone and flint types from beaker graves the most important associations are those with archery (Clarke J. G. D. 1963). The normal arrowhead type was a barbed and tanged form, the majority small, fairly roughly flaked, and having tangs projecting beyond the pair of barbs (fig. 5.1: 5). There is also a smaller group of greater size carefully flaked and having the barbs and tang neatly squared off and of the same length: this latter appears to have late associations with beakers in Britain and persists into the developed phase of the early bronze age.

Complementary to the arrowheads are archers' wrist-guards or bracers designed to protect the wrist from recoil from the bowstring when the arrow is released. Three principal forms are represented from British beaker graves: firstly, a rather slender type with rounded ends, with a single perforation at each end and a flat cross-section; secondly, a rectangular type, with one, or normally two (or even three) perforations at each end, again of roughly flat rectangular cross-section (fig. 5.1: 3); thirdly, waisted in profile with a pair of perforations at each end and concavo-convex in cross-section. The bracer itself appears to have been secured, in some cases with rivets, to some form of organic lining, probably leather; in the grave group at Kellythorpe, Yorkshire, the rivets had been capped with gold.

Metal daggers were also copied in finely flaked flint form (fig. 5.2: 11). It has been suggested that such flint daggers were made primarily for funerary purposes, the metal prototypes being considered too precious to be placed in a grave. On the other hand, the working on some flint daggers from funerary contexts suggests that in fact they were functional. In a number it is noticeable that the blade area itself has been carefully pressure-flaked whereas the hilt end has been left deliberately rough, and in some cases the junction between handle and blade is marked by one or more notches to facilitate the attachment of the organic binding or mounts to the haft. The majority of such daggers are found in east and south-eastern Britain, perhaps partly a reflection of the availability of suitable flint in this area; equally important may be its distance from the main metalworking centres in the north and west.

The last major stone type associated with beakers, and in a number of cases found in graves with flint daggers, is the stone battle-axe (Roe 1966). Two principal forms are represented: the Woodhenge group has a rounded butt and either flat or slightly convex profile (fig. 5.2: 2), the shaft-hole perforation occurring towards the butt end of the weapon; the Calais Wold group has a rounded butt, but is waisted, concave in profile and in some cases the shaft-hole perforation is set centrally. Axes of both groups which have been petrologically examined appear to have been manufactured largely from Cornish rocks, although material from the Lake District was also utilized. In addition, and most significant, the axes of spotted dolerite from the Prescelly Mountains used the same material as that in the bluestone circle of the beaker phase at Stonehenge. It cannot of course be demonstrated if it was the utilization of this stone for the manufacture of battle-axes which first prompted beaker groups in the Wessex area to exploit it for the erection of the bluestone circles at Stonehenge, or if the prestige and sanctity associated with the monument encouraged the use of Prescelly stone for the production of axes.

As to objects of foreign stone, mention should be made of fragments of Niedermendig lava, from the Eifel region in the Rhineland, from the Sanctuary on Overton Hill, the area of the Avebury Avenue, and from Stonehenge. In Germany this material was used by beaker groups for the manufacture of querns and the Wiltshire fragments may represent the remains of such equipment imported or introduced into Britain by immigrant beaker societies.

The final series of stone artifacts are the so-called 'sponge-finger stones' so-named because of their close resemblance to biscuits of this type (Smith and Simpson 1966). The characteristic of this group are, in addition to their elongated form with gently rounded ends, a plano-convex cross-section and a surface which has been carefully ground and polished (fig. 5.2: 6–7). The raw material used in the manufacture of such artifacts is invariably soft, easily worked rock, in most cases slate. In a number of examples there is a very slight flat bevel on the lower plain surface at one or both ends. Such wear suggests that the tools were used in a back and forth rubbing motion, the convex face being kept uppermost.

The objects in the central grave at West Overton G6B provide a link between the stone sponge fingers and spatulae of antler or bone. These spatulae, made from slivers of bone or antler, show traces of abrasion or polishing at one, or more rarely both, ends (fig. 5.1: 9). These objects and their function have variously been described as pottery working tools, net rules or mesh rules, and perhaps most convincingly as part either of an archer's equipment or components in a leatherworking assemblage (Smith and Simpson 1966). Spatulae are invariably associated with male graves and, as D. L. Clarke (1970: 203) has pointed out, frequently have archery associations; he compares the beaker tools with the Eskimo sets of spatulate bone spanners used for twisting bow-strings, tensioning sinew bow backing and preparing feather flights. On the other hand the group at West Overton G6B lacked any other items of archery equipment while the other tools, the sponge fingers, bronze awl and strike-a-light, could all be associated with leatherworking. The spatula from Amesbury G51 again came from a group lacking archery equipment but including once more the double pointed awl and two charred wooden objects which the excavator interpreted as a leatherworker's board and beater (Smith and Simpson 1966: 135). Finally a considerable number of both bone and antler spatulae were recovered from the two beaker occupation horizons at Northton in the Isle of Harris, which same levels produced numerous bone points and large quantities of animal remains, notably sheep and deer (Simpson D. D. A. 1976). There was once more a total absence of archery equipment. In view of this evidence it would perhaps be more reasonable to interpret the spatulae as tools used for the softening and burnishing of leather, and indeed where leather goods are still made by hand today almost identical bone equipment is employed.

Also from Northton came three small combs with finely cut teeth, manufactured from the rib bones of mammals, with pointed butts and in one case a central perforation (Simpson D. D. A. 1976). Such implements were almost certainly used in the decoration of beaker pottery, though ironically none of the many hundreds of comb-ornamented sherds from the settlement site were decorated with any of the three combs recovered. A similar potter's comb comes from the beaker levels at Gwithian in Cornwall (Megaw 1976a: 61; Simpson D. D. A. 1976: 230, fig. 12.6).

Finally amongst the bone equipment may be mentioned the unique horn ladle found inside a beaker at Broomend in Aberdeenshire (Clarke D. L. 1970: fig. 543). Both the shape and fabric of beakers make them ideal drinking vessels and in fact they were named drinking cups by nineteenth-century antiquaries, while several handled versions of beakers bear a striking resemblance to the modern beer mug; it is tempting to think that such vessels would have been placed in graves with the dead, filled with some alcoholic brew. Burgess (1976d) has indeed suggested that the ubiquity of beakers in Europe might be associated with the spread of a cult, an element of which was the drinking of alcohol from such vessels.

The last major group of materials associated with beaker burials are objects of shale or jet. These consist of necklaces of simple disc beads, conical buttons with complex V-bored perforations on the plane surface (fig. 5.2: 4), and so-called pulley-rings. The earliest forms of pulley-ring appear to be simple rings either of bone or jet which have continental parallels (Clarke D. L. 1970: 299). The more developed form of pulley-ring was provided with three perforations for its attachment to the belt and is decorated with radial striations, perhaps a skeuomorphic represen-tation of the original binding of the simpler form of ring (fig. 5.2: 3). These jet objects may give some clue as to the form of clothing worn by beaker groups and certainly suggest that the dead were, in at least some cases, buried with fitted garments rather than a simple shroud. The buttons and pulley-rings along with the daggers, battle axes and archery and leatherworking equipment appear to be exclusively male associations. The position of the belt-ring at the waist and of the V-bored button at the neck of the skeleton imply that males may have worn some form of kilt-like lower garment fastened with a belt or a sash and over this a cloak fastened with a button at the neck, forms of garment which are familiar from the later Danish bronze age coffin burials (Glob 1974). The only objects consistently associated with female burials are necklaces of jet beads, bronze awls and basket ear-rings, although these metal forms are not exclusively associated with women. On the Danish analogy, it is likely that the women wore a short skirt covered by a jerkin without any fastenings.

A marked discrepancy both in number and variety of grave goods as between male and female burials might imply a diminished role for women within beaker societies. This is in interesting contrast to the richly furnished female graves of the early bronze age Wessex culture of southern Britain, which overlaps and succeeds that of the beaker societies in that area (see below, p. 207).

As well as showing a sexual division as grave goods, the objects associated with beakers described above also appear to fall into a series of distinct chronological groups. The earliest, associated with all-over corded beakers and those of European form, consist of basket-shaped ear-rings, copper awls, tanged copper daggers and barbed and tanged arrow-heads. From the eighteenth century bc the considerable range of bronze types which characterized the Migdale-Marnoch bronze industries in Scotland and the contemporary impact phase of Irish metallurgy is paralleled by an increasing variety of grave goods, noticeably more extensive use of tanged and riveted tanged daggers, the first wrist-guards, belt-rings, bone and antler spatulae and flint daggers copying the metal forms. Lastly in the series of developing associations one has the various forms of bronze riveted dagger, again copied in flint, metal bracelets and V-perforated buttons and belt-rings of jet, once more associated with an archery complex, although some of the late forms of arrow-head are of the developed squared-off barbed and tanged type.

Whether the appearance of the makers of beaker pottery in the British Isles is seen as representing a series of cross-Channel movements, as suggested by Clarke, or an initial settlement but with maintained contact with the continental homeland as posited by Lanting and van der Waals, there is general agreement that the area of the Continent to which one should look for the origins of our British beaker groups is the middle and lower Rhine and adjacent portions of the North Sea coast. Piggott (1963a) and Savory (1955) suggested a possible Breton and western Atlantic element among the beaker material from Britain, although represented by a relatively small number of vessels. Such Breton links, however, do find an echo in Clarke's contention that the Wessex-middle Rhine beakers in Britain and a contemporary group of beakers in Brittany share a common source in the middle Rhine region and such may be important for the later, demonstrable, contacts between the two areas in the early bronze age. As regards the continental origins of the European bell beaker cultures, two principal areas have been suggested: Iberia, and north-western and west-central Europe, although the prospect of a dual origin has recently been reiterated by Harrison (1974; 1977). The earlier Iberian theory would see beaker pottery and the characteristic archery equipment as developing both in central and in coastal Iberia, possibly from earlier neolithic impressed ware cultures, although the form of the beaker itself cannot be paralleled amongst such vessels and a basketry model has to be invoked. From Iberia the makers of the coastal or maritime groups of bell beakers divisible into an eastern and western element (Savory 1968: 174) would have spread, in the case of the western group, northwards along the Atlantic coasts of Europe to Brittany and ultimately to the Paris Basin, whilst the eastern maritime group moved eastwards along the western Mediterranean corridor, up the Rhône valley and across the Alpine passes to central Europe; this movement is frequently claimed to be associated with the dissemination of a knowledge of metalworking, and to account for the movements of beaker groups as representing prospectors in search of metal ores, notably copper and gold.

In the north-eastern movement the bell beaker groups, it was considered, came into contact with another series of cultures expanding westwards, the battle-axe/corded ware cultures, and the region where this contact took place is the Rhineland. Intermingling between these initially distinct cultural groups in the Rhineland produced a series of hybrid cultures. The mixing of the two traditions is reflected most clearly in the pottery, which appears to owe something both to the corded ware/battle-axe culture traditions and to those of the west European bell beakers, notably in the appearance of vessels of bell beaker profile but decorated all over with horizontal lines of twisted cord impressions. However, such all-over corded beakers are also found in western and south-western Europe and to explain their appearance in western areas Sangmeister (1963) devised the reflux theory. This suggested a return by these hybrid corded ware/bell beaker groups westwards and south-westwards to the original homeland areas of the Iberian bell beaker cultures; however, radiocarbon dates from the middle and lower Rhine for all-over corded beakers show them, in fact, to have been earlier than European bell beakers (Lanting, Mook and van der Waals 1973). In view of these chronological implications Clarke (1970: 47) put the all-over corded beakers at the beginning of his bell beaker development in Europe but still suggested a south-western origin for these cultures, in this case in the lands bordering the Gulf of Lyons. There, forms of early bell beakers are found, and the motifs for the beakers can be paralleled in the local Chassey and impressed ware cultures, but again not shape: once more, a basketry model had to be invoked. He suggested that the date for this development in the Lyons area was not earlier than the middle of the 3rd millennium bc.

Recent studies of the Dutch regional form of corded ware, the protruding foot beaker, the all-over corded beakers and bell beakers, are based largely on carbon-14 chronology but also take into account ceramic technology, associations and grave form and suggest a unilinear development from protruding foot beaker through all-over corded beaker to bell beaker and therefore a tentative origin for the European bell beaker cultures in the lower and middle Rhine regions (Lanting, Mook and van der Waals 1973).

The Wessex culture

By the beginning of the sixteenth century bc the practice of placing beakers in graves with the dead had ceased in the Wessex area, although surviving elsewhere, notably in the north, during that century. Similarly the Migdale-Marnoch tradition and related industries of Ireland were to endure after the period of Clarke's insular forms of beaker ware and to be associated with new pottery types. There developed in southern Britain new metallurgical traditions contemporary with the Migdale-Marnoch technologies of the highland zone, the former representing a further stimulus from continental sources, and sources which are post-beaker in date. These new metal types and their associated material are so distinctive and appear to represent such a break with the earlier beaker material as to suggest a new culture – the 'Wessex culture' as defined by Piggott in 1938. Information about this culture is derived almost exclusively from round barrows, the majority of them excavated in the eighteenth and nineteenth centuries. From a study of the grave goods from these barrows Piggott isolated just under 100 graves which contained objects sufficiently exotic, as compared with those of the preceding period, and with sufficient uniformity in their recurring associations, as to characterize the burials of this culture. The only exception to the purely funerary evidence for the Wessex culture is provided by the third building phase of the sarsen and re-used bluestone structures at Stonehenge and also by a possible cattle enclosure at Rams Hill, Berkshire (Piggott and Piggott 1940; Bradley and Ellison 1975).

The Wessex culture barrows tend to cluster together in cemeteries either linear in form, one barrow arranged behind another, or nuclear, with the cemetery expanding from a primary or 'founder's' barrow (Grinsell 1953) (fig. 5.10; fig. 5.12). In these barrow cemeteries it is in some cases possible to demonstrate by horizontal stratigraphy a chronological development from a primary burial and mound, in some cases a beaker one not associated with Wessex culture material, and the subsequent erection of

Fig. 5.10   Round barrow cemetery, Oakley Down, Dorset. Barrow types include disc (foreground), bell and bowl barrows (photograph: Cambridge University Committee for Aerial Photography: Crown Copyright).

further mounds to form the cemetery or, in the case of the nuclear cemetery, a primary barrow forming the core structure and later mounds being grouped about it. The barrows themselves may include those of a simple bowl form, a round mound surrounded by its ditch, characteristic of beaker groups. New and exotic groups are the bell barrow, with a large mound set on a platform which separates it from its surrounding quarry ditch, which frequently has an external bank; the disc barrow, a similarly bermed structure but with the mound itself a comparatively small structure occupying a small area of the total enclosure defined by the ditch and external bank; and finally the saucer barrow, again a very low mound but in this case the mound material covering the whole area enclosed by the ditch and external bank (fig. 5.11). The recognition of individual categories of barrow is, of course, in many cases extremely difficult when the mounds have been levelled by later cultivation. It may be that the mound form itself is related to the sex of the dead beneath it in that the bell barrows generally cover male burials and disc barrows are the graves of females (Grinsell 1974), although such equations are generally based on the character of the grave goods rather than on anatomical evidence.

The structure of the barrows frequently includes a primary turf stack covering the central burial, and in some cases pre-mound timber settings of posts or stakes (Christie 1967). The burials generally lie in a pit grave or more rarely on the old land surface. The pit itself may be lined with timbers or sarsens and, in some cases, with inhumation burials placed in a wooden coffin, either plank-built or made from a hollowed-out tree trunk; there are also references in earlier reports to cremations being contained in small wooden boxes (Ashbee 1960: 86). From a study of the dagger types from the graves ApSimon (1954) proposed a two-period classification for the culture. Atkinson (1960b) was able to demonstrate that further associations with ApSimon's dagger forms also suggested two chronological periods, and most recently Gerloff (1975) has divided the daggers of Wessex I into three sub-groups. In general the graves of Wessex I contain inhumation burials and are notable for the inclusion in a number of cases of gold objects amongst the grave goods while having a comparative rarity of ceramic associations. To Wessex I belong some of the most richly furnished graves and among them are examples which might be considered as princely or chieftain's burials (Annable and Simpson 1964). Notable amongst these is the grave group from Bush Barrow in the Wilsford Barrow cemetery near Stonehenge (fig. 5.13).

This burial was that of an inhumed male and unusual both in that the body lay in an extended position on its back, and that it was placed on the old land surface rather than in a pit grave. The body was originally accompanied by three daggers, only two of which survive, and these represent the largest examples of such weapons recorded in a Wessex culture grave. The larger dagger, which is of bronze, belongs to Gerloff's Armorico-British B type having a blade of triangular outline and a markedly thickened midrib (fig. 5.13: 2). The blade itself was secured to its organic haft by means of six tiny rivets arranged on each side of a small projected tongue or languette which presumably fitted into the hilt, which

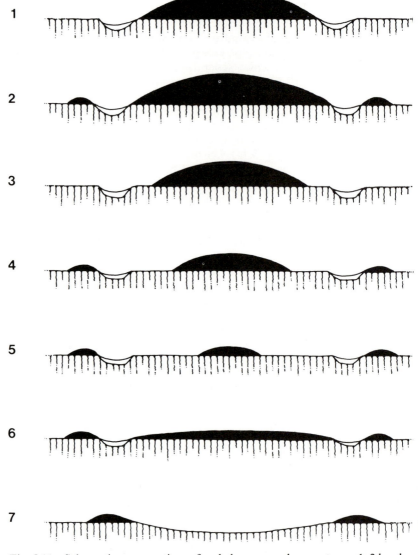

Fig. 5.11   Schematic cross-sections of early bronze age barrow types. 1–2 bowl; 3–4 bell; 5 disc; 6 saucer; 7 pond (after Ashbee 1960).

Fig. 5.12   Map of the Stonehenge region (after Piggott S. 1951).

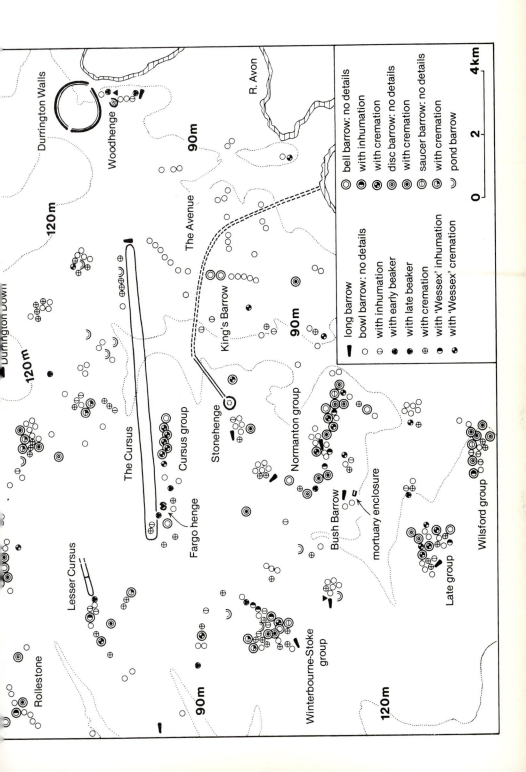

had an omega-shaped base. The smaller dagger, of Gerloff's Armorico-British A type, again had a triangular-shaped blade but was flat in cross-section and was provided with six rivets and a projecting languette (fig. 5.13:1). Analysis indicated that this smaller dagger was of copper. In both cases traces of the wood and leather scabbards in which the daggers were contained survived as corroded impressions on the blades. The most remarkable feature of the copper dagger was the decoration on its pommel which was composed of thousands of tiny lengths of gold wire, no more than 2mm in length, arranged in a chevron pattern. Similar decoration was applied to the pommel of the dagger from Hammeldon in Devon (Gerloff 1975: pl. 18, 194). So detailed is the work as to suggest that some form of lens, probably of rock crystal, would be required for the insertion of the gold wire. The only other copper or bronze object was an axe with tapering butt expanded to a crescentic cutting edge with low flanges, probably cast (fig. 5.13:3). Cloth impressions are visible on one face of this tool.

Behind the head was a series of bronze or copper rivets which have frequently been interpreted as the inorganic components of a wooden shield, but the rivets are too small to have secured anything thicker than leather and a helmet is perhaps more likely (fig. 5.13:6). On the chest lay a lozenge-shaped plate of sheet gold perforated at each end of the long axis and decorated with a delicately traced geometric design (fig. 5.13:11). The other major sheet gold piece was a belt hook with the hook and plate being manufactured separately and then the hook, itself, hammered over the plate (fig. 5.13:9). Perforations again occur at each corner of the plate. The same delicate incision is used to produce the ornament on this piece although here the technique is even more accomplished in that the grooved lines executed freehand carefully echo the concave and convex outline of the plate itself. The third gold object was a small lozenge decorated in the same technique (fig. 5.13:10). The thinness of the sheet gold and the provision of perforations in the two larger pieces suggest that in fact they were mounted onto some organic substance, presumably wood or leather which has not survived. Beside the right arm was a macehead made from a fossil stromatoporoid, egg-shaped and smoothly polished over the whole of its surface (fig. 5.13:4). The source of this material is near Teignmouth in Devon. This macehead appears to have had a simple wooden handle although in earlier reconstructions it was ornamented with the pair of dentated bone mounts and dentated ferrules which in all probability form part of a separate wand or staff (fig. 5.13:5).

Three further male burials may, on the basis of their rich grave goods, be included in this category of princely burials of the first phase of the Wessex culture. The objects from the Clandon Barrow, Dorset, included a macehead or sceptre of polished shale or jet inlaid with gold studs (Stone 1958: pl. 43), a rectangular gold breastplate, again with geometric ornament (fig. 5.14), and an amber cup. Barrow 7, Ridgeway, in Dorset, covered a grave with a dagger of Gerloff's Armorico-British A type, and a flanged axe similar to that from Bush Barrow and, again, bearing cloth impressions. The dagger was provided with a sheet gold pommel which

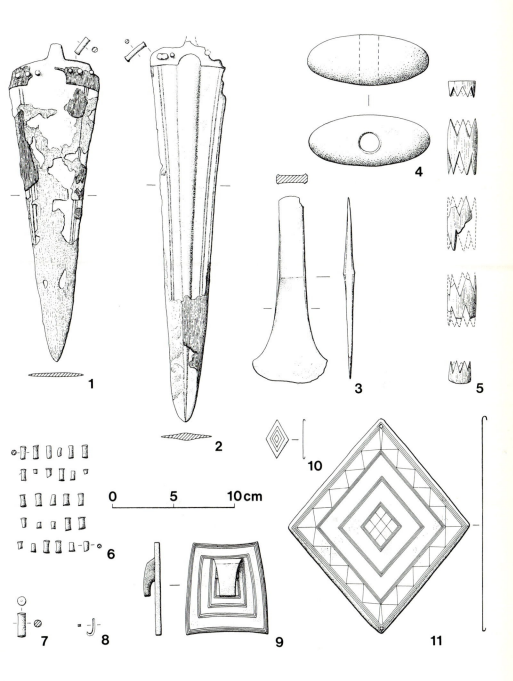

Fig. 5.13   Grave group, Bush Barrow, Wilts. (after Annable and Simpson 1964).

had been attached to its haft by minute gold pins reminiscent of the gold
wire ornament on the Bush Barrow and Hammeldon daggers (Taylor
1970b). And finally, outside the main area of the culture, at Little
Cressingham in Norfolk, a male inhumation was accompanied by a
dagger of Armorico-British A type, a sheet gold pommel mount, a
rectangular sheet gold breastplate again with geometric ornament, but of
rather crude execution, and a series of amber beads and pendants (Piggott
S. 1938: 93).

Women appear to have been accorded equally rich burial and this
might imply some change in their status as compared with females in the
preceding beaker phase. However, it should be emphasized that the
recognition of female graves in the Wessex culture is based very largely on
the character of the grave goods themselves rather than on anthropological
examination of the human remains, which has been carried out in very
few cases. At Manton, near Marlborough, a female inhumation was
accompanied by a rich series of goods which included a gold-bound amber
pendant, a miniature copy of a halberd with gold shaft and bronze blade,
a gold-bound shale biconical bead and a small knife dagger with an amber
pommel. Also included in the group were two diminutive pottery vessels
to which general category Colt Hoare gave the term 'incense cups' because
of the frequent perforations in the body of the vessel. One of the vessels
from Manton is decorated on its outer surface with numerous round pellets
of clay and these so-called grape cups appear to be characteristic of the
first phase of the Wessex culture, being associated in particular with
female graves and representing one of the few groups of pottery
associations of Wessex I. A grave group from Wilsford G8 also included

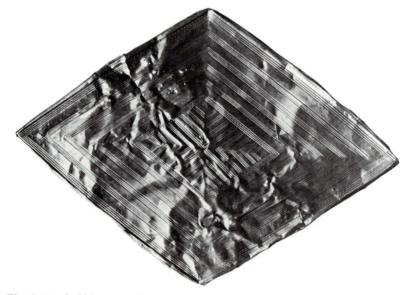

Fig. 5.14   Gold lozenge, Clandon, Dorset; length 15·5cm (photograph:
J. J. Taylor).

an incense cup, halberd pendant (in this case with the shank of amber bound with gold and with a metal blade), and gold-bound amber discs (fig. 5.15): additional to this repertoire were pendants of amber, a large V-perforated conical shale button sheathed in gold, and a bronze pendant or ear-ring covered with sheet gold and provided with a V-perforation through the thickest point. Finally, from Upton Lovell G2, the so-called Golden Barrow, came a grape cup and shale button, again covered in sheet gold but with an elaborate cruciform pattern on its base (like the plate from Clandon and probably by the same hand), sheet gold armlet, decorated in the same geometric pattern as the other Wessex I gold pieces, and part of a multi-strand necklace of amber, the beads being of disc form and separated by rectangular spacer plates with complex borings.

The group of male inhumation burials accompanied by daggers of Bush Barrow type but without the accompanying gold objects may be considered as warrior graves. Also included in this category would be graves containing shaft-hole battle-axes of developed type such as those of greenstone from Wilsford G58, Wiltshire (Annable and Simpson 1964: 47), and another example from a barrow on Windmill Hill in Wiltshire which is a product of the Cwym Mawr factory on the Montgomery–Shropshire border. The latter find is interesting in that it was associated with a grape cup, a type normally to be considered as part of the equipment of a female grave. Another interesting ceramic association with a warrior's grave is that from an elm tree-trunk coffin from Winterbourne Stoke G5, Wiltshire. The group consisted of two Class IA daggers and a vessel of smooth red ware with a globular body and sharp shoulder leading to a narrow neck just above whose carination were five upright perforated lugs

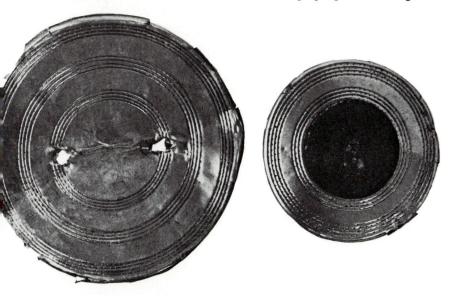

Fig. 5.15   Gold button cover (left; diameter 4·1cm) and gold-bound amber disc (right; diameter 2·8cm), Wilsford G8, Wilts. (photograph: J. J. Taylor).

or handles (Annable and Simpson 1964: 105). The association of the vessel with the other objects has been questioned (e.g. Thomas N. de L'E.W. 1966: 5) but there can be little doubt as to its authenticity or its similarity to contemporary British vessels. A number of these male graves appear to contain objects transitional between Wessex I and Wessex II. At Winterbourne Kame, Dorset, an Armorico-British C dagger with slightly ogival outline was associated with a true ogival dagger typical of Wessex II and in Wilsford G23, Wiltshire, a similar dagger was associated with other equipment characteristic of Wessex II (fig. 5.17: 1). This group also included the perforated leg-bone of a swan which has been interpreted as a bone flute (fig 5.17: 5). The rarity of ceramic associations other than grape cups with Wessex I burials might imply that organic containers were normally used during this period or may simply reflect prejudice on the part of society against the placing of such vessels in graves. That alternative materials were used for cups is, however, indicated by the occurrence of such objects in amber and shale in Wessex contexts. Both the amber and shale cups show great skill in their manufacture and it has been suggested that some may have been turned on a lathe, although the very careful polishing has removed all traces of such work.

Fig. 5.16   Gold cup, Rillaton, Cornwall; height 8·5cm (photograph A. Pacitto: courtesy S. E. Thomas).

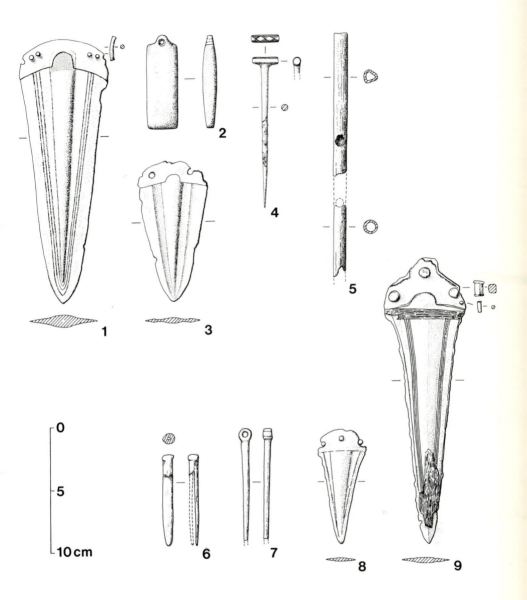

Fig. 5.17 Wessex grave groups. 1–5 Wilsford G23, Wilts.; 6–9 Wilsford G56, Wilts. (after Annable and Simpson 1964).

The second phase of the Wessex culture is traditionally dated c. 1,500 bc. Although some of the objects characteristic of Wessex I are found in graves of the second phase of the culture, notably beads and spacer-plate necklaces of amber and stone battle axes, the later series of graves are characterized by their own distinctive series of objects and are marked by a change in burial rite from inhumation to cremation, the cremated human remains in some instances being placed in a collared urn, a type which is widely distributed in the British Isles outside the Wessex area (see below, p. 237).

The metal types in this Wessex II period also have more widespread distribution in the British Isles and it is likely that the centres of metal manufacture had shifted from the Wessex area proper. In general, graves of Wessex II have a less rich character than those of the earlier period, due in part to the virtual absence of gold objects, a notable exception being the handled cup from Rillaton, Cornwall (fig. 5.16). It is therefore not possible to recognize princely or chieftains' graves in this phase. In the series which may be considered as warriors' graves on the basis of their contents, the most notable item is a dagger with a markedly thickened and frequently lozenge-sectioned midrib, with an ogival outline to the blade which is echoed in parallel grooves running on either side of the midrib, itself frequently decorated with a dotted or pointillé pattern (fig. 5.17: 9). The blade is attached to the hilt by means of three or, more rarely, four, large rivets and the hilt again has an omega-shaped outline to its base. A feature of a number of these Wessex II warriors' graves is the inclusion of a smaller dagger or knife dagger with the larger weapon (fig. 5.17: 3, 8).

Other objects characteristic of these male graves are whetstones, perforated presumably for attachment to the warrior's belt (fig. 5.17: 2), and pairs of bone tweezers (fig. 5.17: 6), the function of which was probably depilatory – it is interesting to note that a quantity of human eye-brow hair was discovered in a grave at Winterslow in Wiltshire (Stoves 1948). A possible change in the fashion of clothing is also indicated by the appearance for the first time, again in male graves, of pins, a type of dress fastening normally associated with woven garments as opposed to the buttons of the Wessex I period which are more appropriate to the wearing of leather clothing (fig. 5.17: 4). The metal pins have elaborate crutch, ring or globe heads; the ring and crutch-headed examples were also copied in bone.

Most important new forms in, presumptively, female graves are beads of faience, a blue vitreous paste. In the Wessex area proper, the commonest form is a segmented type, longitudinally perforated, although ring- or disc- and star-shaped forms also occur (fig. 5.18). Generally only single or small groups have been found deposited in graves, but at Upton Lovell G1, Wiltshire, ten segmented faience beads formed part of a necklace which also included examples in shale and amber.

The grape cups of Wessex I are replaced by a new group of miniature vessels, the so-called Aldbourne cups (fig. 5.19). These vessels generally have a vertical body and a flared neck and are frequently horizontally perforated through the wall; rarely they are provided with lids (Piggott S.

Fig. 5.18 Faience beads. Segmented, Upton Lovell, Wilts.; disc, Ireland; star, Doll Tor, Stanton Moor, Derbys.; maximum diameter of star bead 1·4cm (photographs: R. A. P. Peek).

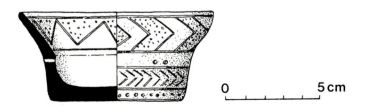

0   5 cm

Fig. 5.19 Aldbourne cup, Durrington 65, Wilts. (after Annable and Simpson 1964).

1938: 74). The geometric chevron and lozenge designs are executed by incision, channelling or, occasionally, cord impressions.

The range of metal objects found in graves of phase II may be further extended by the association of such objects with further metal types in hoards which appear for the first time in the second phase of the culture. The metalworking tradition of this period in southern Britain takes its name from a hoard on Arreton Down on the Isle of Wight (fig. 5.20) (Britton 1963). The contents of this hoard illustrate a considerable range of objects not found in Wessex II graves and the distribution of some of the objects of this tradition are peripheral to the Wessex region. In addition to ogival daggers similar to those found in graves the new types from these hoards, unrepresented in a funerary context, consist of axes, spearheads and various forms of metalworking equipment. All the objects must have been produced in a two-piece mould but as only one example in stone survives from Bodwrdin in Anglesey (Manby 1966b) it must be assumed that clay normally was employed.

The axes were invariably of thin-butted type with an expanded and crescentic cutting edge and provided with prominent flanges (fig. 5.20: 5–7). These tools are frequently decorated with a variety of geometric designs. Spearheads represent a considerable range of form. Typologically the earliest are those with triangular or ogival blades, thickened midrib and grooves following the outline of the blade and provided with a long projecting tang with a single rivet hole set at the end (fig. 5.20: 2). These appear to be a wholly British invention, probably derived from daggers of the same period. The Arreton hoard also included a tanged spearhead with a separate collar (since lost) which appears to be transitional between the tanged form and the true socketed spearhead (fig. 5.20: 3). The latter have triangular or ogival blades and may have a pair of cast loops set close to the mouth of the socket (Burgess and Cowen 1972). Finally from the hoards of Westbury-on-Trym in Gloucestershire and Plymstock in Devon come single examples of chisels or tracers, probably used by the metalsmith in the decoration of axes and for punching out rivet holes in spearheads and daggers (Piggott S. 1938: 88) (fig. 5.20: 4).

The material so far described from the Wessex barrows suggests that it comes from aristocratic or warrior graves. Many more of the round barrows of the Wessex area have produced non-beaker material which is extremely difficult to assign to either phase of the Wessex culture (Annable and Simpson 1964: 27). The graves themselves may contain a simple unaccompanied cremation, or a cremation in a collared urn without artifacts other than simple bone pins, beads of bone, shale and amber and conical V-perforated buttons in the same materials. Many such simply furnished graves are covered by bowl barrows and are therefore not strictly assignable to the Wessex period, but could belong to the pre- or post-Wessex phase. On the other hand, others are covered by bell or disc barrows, forms intimately associated with the Wessex culture, and it is tempting to interpret such material as the burials of the poorer elements in Wessex society, although the labour involved in their construction is as great as that in many of the 'royal' barrows.

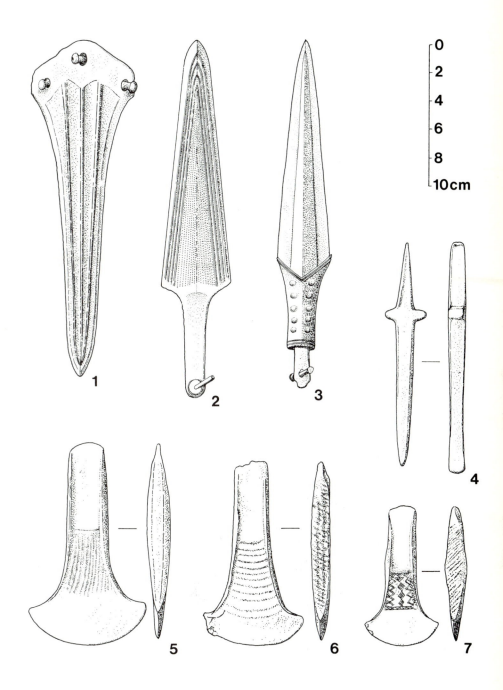

Fig. 5.20 Metalwork in the Arreton tradition. 1–3 Arreton Down, I.O.W.;
4–7 Westbury-on-Trym, Glos. (after Britton 1963).

Since its isolation and recognition by Piggott the Wessex culture has long been considered as an aristocratic, warlike society whose wealth was based on trade and, in particular, on the control of the flow of Irish gold and other ores along the transpeninsular route from south Wales, through Wessex to the Continent, and on the exploitation of the equally important tin ores of Cornwall. The people were further regarded as immigrants who established themselves as overlords over the indigenous late neolithic and beaker populations. In recent years these concepts have come under attack and doubts have been expressed as to the status of the material as actually representative of a distinct archaeological culture. Its continental origins have also been questioned (Clark J. G. D. 1966), as have the widespread commercial contacts implicit amongst much of the material from the graves (Renfrew 1968; Newton and Renfrew 1970). This latter aspect is fundamental to the problem of the dating of the Wessex culture, and as the chronology of the early bronze age cultures elsewhere in the British Isles is firmly tied to the dating of Wessex itself, the dating of the Wessex material becomes critical for the chronology of the whole of the early bronze age in Britain. Certainly the Wessex material fulfils some of the criteria for the definition of an archaeological culture in that it represents a consistently recurring series of monuments and artifacts (although in this case they are all funerary in character) having a limited distribution both in time and space. Admittedly the total number of such assemblages is small but this vacuum may be in part filled by the series of poorly furnished graves. That one is dealing with an aristocratic society or such an element in that society is apparent from the grave evidence, although the importance and the volume of gold in these graves should not be over-exaggerated, for as Taylor has pointed out all the gold from these contexts added together would make but one or at most two Irish lunulae (Coles and Taylor 1971).

The third building phase of Stonehenge itself also suggests some form of centralized political authority to command the necessary resources for its construction and in this phase at Stonehenge one may see the welding together of the original five separate neolithic social or tribal units of Wessex into a single larger territory (Renfrew 1973a). The economic arguments based on metal trade for the rise of this society are more difficult to sustain. In the, admittedly, comparatively small series of early bronze age metal products from southern Britain, Brittany and Holland which have been analysed, Irish ores appear to be unimportant; also, there is a distinct lack of Irish products in Wessex graves, and one of the most notable absences is that of the halberd represented in Wessex merely by a series of miniature pendants. An eastern source rather than a western one is most likely for the models for these ornaments. Irish gold may have been used for the manufacture of the Wessex ornaments but there are very few Wessex culture objects in Ireland (Flanagan 1961) and these appear to be derivative products – the exception is a pair of sandstone moulds for the production of tanged spearheads in the Arreton tradition from Omagh, Co. Tyrone, although it should be remembered that Arreton metalwork was probably not produced in Wessex.

An alternative explanation for the economic growth of Wessex at this period, convincingly argued by Fleming (1971b), is the increasing development of pastoralism; ethnographic parallels indicate that such activities are more likely to give rise to a stratified warrior society than an economy based either on cereal production or mixed farming.

The problems of origin and chronology are best examined within the two phases of the culture. First it is important to emphasize that this is a barrow culture characterized in Wessex I by single graves containing a generally crouched inhumation similar to that of the preceding beaker cultures in the same area. Chronological overlaps between beaker and Wessex material are demonstrated at West Overton G6B (Smith and Simpson 1966) and at Fargo Plantation (Stone 1938), both in Wiltshire, and a number of the Wessex barrow cemeteries appear to have grown up around earlier beaker barrows. The concentration of richly furnished beaker graves of Clarke's Wessex-middle Rhine group in the area later dominated by the Wessex culture provides a basis for, or at least an important element in, the development of the latter culture; continuity in actual artifact types is represented by the continuing use of conical buttons, disc beads, barbed and tanged arrowheads and, in female graves, small knife daggers similar to those from earlier beaker contexts. Not so apparent in Wessex I are contributions from the native late neolithic cultures, but Upton Lovell G2 (a), Wiltshire, covered a grave which contained polished stone axes and rubbers and numerous bone points, which appear to owe something to native late neolithic traditions (Piggott S. 1962b). However, the most characteristic metal type of Wessex I, the six-riveted dagger, has its closest relationship in Brittany in the Armorican early bronze age cultures (Giot *et al.* 1960: 128).

In Armorica the barrows fall into two series, the presumptively earlier containing a wide range of metal objects, many of which are of copper; in the second barrow series metal objects, invariably of bronze, are much less numerous but pottery appears for the first time: the most characteristic vessel is a high-shouldered form normally undecorated but having four broad strap handles attached to the upper part of the vessel linking the shoulder and the rim. Bush Barrow type daggers are closely paralleled amongst weapons from the first barrow series and the same inlaid gold wire technique is used to produce chevron patterns on a number of the pommels and leather sheaths of the weapons (Briard 1970). The more developed Armorico-British C Wessex daggers are best paralleled in weapons from the second barrow series. Further parallels for Wessex I material include axes similar to that from Bush Barrow and arrowheads with neatly squared-off barbs and tangs, although the latter are not precisely similar to British examples, and at variance with the Wessex evidence is the frequent construction of a large closed stone chamber beneath the mound, perhaps a reflection of local geological conditions.

In spite of these differences it is clear that at the beginnings of the early bronze age southern Britain and Brittany presented a single cultural province, one whose cultural roots lie in earlier single grave traditions. This uniformity has variously been explained as a movement of peoples from Brittany to Wessex or *vice versa* (Burgess 1974: 184). A likely alternative is that the shared traits of Brittany and Wessex were derived from a common external source, the Únĕtice culture of north-central Europe (Annable and Simpson 1964: 21). This is a single grave barrow culture developing from earlier beaker corded ware traditions. Prototypes for the western daggers exist in the metal-hilted forms of the Saale-Oder-Elbe type, as components in such great hoards as Dieskau and Neuenhieligen, the six rivets being represented in skeuomorphic form on the lower part of the hilt (Uenze 1938). It is not necessary, of course, to invoke population movements to explain such similarities, but rather the continuing of those links with the great metal centres of west-central Europe first established by the expansion of beaker groups. The higher percentage of copper objects in the Armorican barrow series and also the presence of halberds might suggest the forging of links between this area and central Europe earlier than those of Wessex. The pendants in the form of miniature halberds from Wessex culture contexts appear to have been modelled on the metal-shafted halberds exclusive to central Europe, and north European contacts also appear to be implicit in the use of Baltic amber for the manufacture of spacer-plate necklaces, cups and dagger pommels – although amber of Baltic origin can be picked up on the coast of East Anglia and it may be significant that one of the most elaborate Wessex culture burials outside the main Wessex area is from Little Cressingham in Norfolk (Piggott S. 1938: 93).

Foreign links claimed for material from Wessex I graves are with the Aegean and the east Mediterranean and, in particular, with the Mycenaean civilization of southern Greece whose material remains are so brilliantly illustrated by the finds from the two royal shaft grave circles at Mycenae itself (Marinatos and Hirmer 1960; Mylonas 1957). The Wessex goldwork bears a certain similarity in technique to that of the shaft grave gold but the geometric motifs which decorate it are widespread both in metalwork and pottery throughout central and western Europe, and Taylor's recognition of the hand of a single craftsman in the working of objects from a number of graves in Wessex would suggest that the gold is, in fact, the work of local craftsmen (Coles and Taylor 1971). More convincing are the gold-bound amber discs whose form can be paralleled in a find from Knossos and from other sites in the east Mediterranean where gold is also employed to bind discs of faience and other materials (Piggott S. 1938: 80). The peculiar methods of attaching the strap handle to the body of the Rillaton gold cup by means of diamond-shaped washers is again a trick practised by Mycenaean craftsmen, noticeably in the gold and silver cups from the shaft graves. Similar diamond-shaped washers were used for the handle attachment of another gold cup from Fritzdorf in Germany (Piggott S. 1965: 134, pl. XVII (a)). Neither cup, however, appears to be of Mycenaean manufacture. The corrugated beaker-like shape of the Rillaton cup can, in fact, be precisely paralleled in a handled beaker from Balmuick in Perthshire (Clarke D. L. 1970: 417), while the Fritzdorf metal vessel is a copy of the handled clay forms characteristic of the Únĕtice culture. The native origin of those cups seems confirmed by the recent discovery in a Breton barrow grave with timber coffin dated to 1,400 ± 35 bc of a silver cup very similar to Fritzdorf (Briard 1978). This Breton find – associated with three early class B daggers, a bronze flat axe and 45 arrowheads – has been compared with yet another gold cup (now lost) from Ploumilliau. It is only, therefore, a craftsman's device which links the vessels of precious metal in these disparate areas.

The small penannular pendant from Wilsford in Wiltshire and stray finds from Folkestone and Dover have recently been claimed as Cypriot ear-rings (Branigan 1970). While such may be the case for the two stray finds composed entirely of gold and therefore flexible, the Wilsford example has a copper or bronze core covered in gold with a 'V'-perforation for suspension. Such an object, of course, would be inflexible and it is difficult to see how it could have been clipped on to the ear. More convincing as a reflection of Aegean contacts are the dentated bone mounds from the Bush Barrow staff or wand. Very similar bone pieces have been found in shaft grave 'Iota' of the new grave circle of Mycenae. Equally convincing as evidence for far-flung trade are the amber spacer-plate necklaces with complex borings found in Wessex contexts and also at Kakovatos, Pylos and Mycenae itself (Sandars 1959). The peculiar nature of the complex borings on spacer plates makes it unlikely that these would have been independently invented in two such widely separated areas of Europe, and in view of the rather crude nature of the beads and spacers themselves it would appear more likely that these are north-west European products exported to the Mycenaean world.

Finally Branigan (1970) has drawn attention to the stray finds of a Cypriot dagger from Winterbourne Bassett in Wiltshire and a Cypriot sword from Egton Moor, Yorkshire. These finds have, however, been interpreted as acquisitions by collectors in the eastern Mediterranean which were later discarded. A recent survey of the evidence (Watkins 1976) confirms that there can no longer be any good claim for Cypriot hook-tang weapons being exported to western Europe. It was this similarity in artifacts and the apparent contacts inherent in the forms which appeared to establish a series of synchronisms between the barbarian world of northern and western Europe in the early bronze age and the semi-literate civilizations in the Near East, synchronisms established not only, of course, for the early bronze age in southern Britain but for contemporary societies over a wide area of the central and western European continent, summed up in the late Professor Gordon Childe's classic phrase, 'the irradiation of European barbarism by oriental civilisation' (1939: 10). Crucial to these synchronisms, before the development of radiocarbon dating as an independent means of assessing the chronology of preliterate societies in central and western Europe, were the contacts with the Mycenaean world, in particular the relationships apparent in the material from the two great grave circles of Mycenae. The dating of the shaft graves at Mycenae is based on the occurrence in the tombs of a series of objects of Egyptian manufacture which, in their turn, provide synchronisms with the historic chronology of dynastic Egypt; on the basis of these imports the new grave circle is dated to the period between 1650 and 1550 BC and the circle excavated by Heinrich Schliemann in the nineteenth century to the period 1550–1450 BC (Snodgrass 1975). The Mycenaean contacts therefore provided the lynch-pin for the chronology of the early bronze age in central and western Europe. So precise were the historical dates, admittedly derived at second hand from Mycenae, that for long the newly introduced technique of radiocarbon dating was considered too imprecise to add further detail to the dates arrived at through these synchronisms with the Aegean. Even now, no radiocarbon dates exist for the first phase of the Wessex culture, chiefly because of the absence of suitable materials for such determinations, but for the presumptively contemporary early Únětice and Armorican barrow groups the few dates available in the late 1960s and early 1970s appeared to confirm the Aegean cross-dating in that these dates belonged to the second half of the seventeenth and first half of the sixteenth centuries bc.

It was only when the reliability of radiocarbon determinations came to be checked against the absolute dates obtained by dendrochronology – the counting of the annual growth rings of trees, initially of the sequoias of California and subsequently the bristlecone pine – that discrepancies arose between the basically immutable Mycenaean dates based ultimately on Egyptian historic chronology, and the recalibrated dates obtained from radiocarbon determinations of organic materials. The bristlecone pine tree, the longest-living organism in the world, which has a restricted distribution in the arid and upland regions of southern California, has provided an absolute chronology extending back over some 6,000 years.

Dates produced by counting the growth rings of these trees and samples taken from calendrically dated rings and submitted for C14 determination have consistently yielded dates which are too young (for the period prior to 2,000 bp), the discrepancy tending to increase with antiquity, although there are slight, but for the period of the European early bronze age important, fluctuations. As mentioned in the Preface (p. 3), tables now exist for the conversion of 'raw' C14 dates, that most in use being the MASCA chart (Ralph et al. 1973), but as yet there is no internationally agreed table and warnings have been expressed by physicists to archaeologists recalibrating laboratory-derived dates using one or other of such systems (Burleigh 1975). However, on the basis of the original coarse recalibration curve published by Suess (1965), Renfrew (1968) drew attention to the chronological 'fault line' between the historically based chronology of the Aegean and its long assumed links with the early bronze age cultures of western and central Europe where recalibrated dates appeared to make such links untenable. The application of the C14 technique to archaeological material of the early bronze age in north-western Europe was a late phenomenon for the very reason that the margin of error in such a technique was considered too great to add refinement to those synchronic dates whereby the preliterate societies of barbarian Europe were linked with the historic civilizations of the eastern Mediterranean and ultimately with Egypt. When in fact the first C14 dates were published – for example from the great mortuary house beneath the princely barrow of Helmsdorf in Germany or from the Armorican barrow burial of Kervingar, Finistère, both in the seventeenth century bc – such dates only appeared to confirm the long accepted chronology based on cross-dating with south-eastern Europe. When recalibrated, however, such dates would suggest a beginning for the Únětice and Armorican early bronze age cultures in the nineteenth century BC.

Objections may, however, be raised to these dates in relation to the beginnings of the Wessex culture. Although links are demonstrable between southern Britain, Brittany and central Europe in the early bronze age, there is really no need to suggest that the bronzes from the Wessex graves are necessarily contemporary with related products in the great metalworking centres of Europe, any more than one need believe that the beginning of copperworking in Ireland was contemporaneous with the rise of copper industries in central Europe. Further, the wood samples taken from the mortuary houses of the princely tombs may have come from heart wood of ancient and slow-growing trees, therefore producing dates considerably older than that of the use of the timbers in the construction of the tombs (Giot 1971). Until radiocarbon dates have been obtained for Wessex I material discrepancies between historical and recalibrated radiocarbon dates cannot really be resolved, and even the usefulness of such comparisons has recently been questioned, particularly as there is a series of radiocarbon dates from Aegean sites for this critical period of north–south relations (Snodgrass 1975); like should be compared with like, Aegean C14 dates with north-west European ones and not historical dates from the eastern Mediterranean with C14 dates from north-west Europe.

Coles and Taylor (1971) have argued, partly on the basis of the goldwork, that the Wessex I phase may have been a relatively short one, no more than the life of the master craftsman whose hand is apparent in the gold from Bush Barrow, Upton Lovell, Manton, Clandon and Wilsford G8. The gold evidence need only indicate that the period of deposition of gold in graves was a comparatively short one and need not imply that other grave groups containing objects characteristic of Wessex I but without gold have to be compressed into this short period. The argument, too, of the comparatively unworn condition of the gold pieces, indicating that they were made very shortly before their burial, is not particularly convincing as such finery may only have been worn on ceremonial occasions and could have served several generations of chieftains.

For Wessex II, again, both continental and Aegean links are apparent. The relationships with Brittany are now less clear. Radiocarbon dates for the two barrow series in Brittany fail to separate the groups chronologically (Giot 1971), while the ring-headed pins of Únětice type associated with Wessex II graves (Annable and Simpson 1964: 101) are found in barrows of the Armorican first series. The transitional Armorico-British C daggers (Gerloff 1975: 78), are paralleled, if not precisely, in second series barrows in Brittany. Clear Wessex-central European links are indicated by crutch- and ring-headed pins of the Únětice culture and bulb-headed pins (Annable and Simpson 1964: 112) in the central European Tumulus

Bronze cultures. Continental parallels for the ogival Wessex II daggers are more difficult to find but weapons of the Sögel series (Gerloff 1975: 116) could provide possible prototypes. Aegean links have been argued on the basis of four bronze double axes (Branigan 1970) from the British Isles, all occurring as stray finds but showing remarkable homogeneity both in form and size and which can be paralleled in a small group from the Aegean dated 1450–1400 BC. These have, however, generally been dismissed as modern collectors' pieces (Briggs 1973) and, as has just been noted, equal doubts have been cast on the 'Cypriot sword' from Egton Moor, Yorkshire, and similar weapons from north-western Europe (Watkins 1976).

Most controversial regarding their eastern Mediterranean and Oriental links are faience beads (Stone and Thomas 1956). The British examples consist of segmented, star- and disc-shaped forms although a high percentage of the associations in the Wessex graves are of the segmented variety. Initial studies by Beck and Stone (1935) and Stone and Thomas (1956) involved the examination of beads from central and western Europe including the British Isles, and a comparison between these beads, both morphologically and analytically, and east Mediterranean and Egyptian examples. No clear relationship was demonstrable in their chemical composition but on formal comparisons Stone suggested that the closest parallels to the British beads were Egyptian. The European distribution of such beads indicated two possible routes to Britain: one through central Europe, more or less in the reverse direction to the southward flow of amber, and an alternative route along the Mediterranean corridor and up the Atlantic coasts of Europe. The original analytical data were re-examined statistically by Newton and Renfrew (1970), who suggested that the composition of the British beads set them apart both from continental and Egyptian forms and that the British beads were of local manufacture. This view has been challenged by McKerrell (1972) as the result of the re-analysis of many of the British beads. He drew attention to the high lead content of the bronze used to give the beads their characteristic bluish colour. Lead seldom occurs in British bronze tools or weapons before a late stage in the bronze age, his argument being that the bronze used in the manufacture of the beads should be of the same composition as other contemporary metalwork. Such conditions existed in Egypt where both the faience and the Egyptian bronzes have a high lead content. In a parallel programme by Aspinall and Warren (1973) it was shown that the British beads have a very high tin content while central European beads have a much higher silver and antimony content similar to central European bronzes. Three separate sources of manufacture therefore appear to be indicated by these analyses. They argue that the very high tin content of the British faience, far higher than would be suitable for a bronze tool, indicates that bronze on its own was not used in the preparation of the glaze on the beads and that the tin must have been deliberately added to the compound. Under such circumstances a comparison between the constituents of faience glaze and the composition of contemporary bronzes as an indicator of local or foreign manufacture of the beads was not relevant. What has emerged from these new analytical studies is the considerable variety in the composition of the faience beads even in the British Isles, in spite of the comparatively small number of known examples, particularly of the segmented series. This might imply lack of controlled conditions in their manufacture or equally likely that the British beads do in fact represent imports from an external source, the British material representing only a small percentage of the total output; and such conditions prevailed only in the eastern Mediterranean and in the Near East. Even if the British segmented beads do in fact represent imports from the eastern Mediterranean their comparatively small numbers do not suggest extensive or prolonged trading associations with this area, and all the British segmented beads may represent only one (or a few) trading consignments; it is tempting to see this period of contact as associated with the maximum expansion of Mycenaean trading ventures in the central Mediterranean and particularly in the Lipari Islands (Brea 1957: 126) where the greatest concentration of pottery belongs to the period 1450–1350 BC, precisely that century which produces the closest and best dated Egyptian parallels for the British material (Branigan 1970).

Four dates are now available from funerary contexts for the second phase of the Wessex culture although regrettably none are satisfactory either in terms of their distance from the main centre of the Wessex culture or from contexts from which the samples for radiocarbon determination were selected. The date of 1,239 ± 46 bc from the great Hove barrow in Sussex was obtained from the tree-trunk coffin which contained an amber cup, polished stone battle axe, perforated whetstone and an ogival dagger; a classic group of the second phase of the Wessex culture (Selkirk 1972b). The charcoal from the old land surface beneath a large round barrow at Earls Barton, Northamptonshire, yielded dates of 1,219 ± 51 bc and 1,264 ± 64 bc. Although not directly associated, an ogival dagger was found in the mound 20cm above the old land surface (Selkirk 1972a). At both these sites the samples came from large timbers and the age determinations may be considerably earlier than the utilization of the wood. A date of 1,119 ± 45 bc was obtained from cremated bone associated with an ogival dagger, whetstone, tweezers and a bone pin beneath a bell barrow at Edmonsham, Dorset (Proudfoot E. 1963). At variance with these dates is one of 1,750 ± 180 bc from a plank covering a central cremation pit beneath a round barrow at Butterbump, Lincolnshire. A badly corroded dagger, believed to be of ogival type, lay on the old land surface 1·8m distant and was considered by the excavator to be contemporary with the cremation pit (May 1976: 81). With the exception of the last, recalibration would give dates in the fifteenth and fourteenth centuries BC and leave open the possibility of Aegean and east Mediterranean synchronisms.

The hundred or so graves which have so far been discussed for the Wessex region are clearly numerically unimportant, both in southern Britain itself and certainly in comparison with the total number of presumptively early bronze age burials recorded from elsewhere in the

British Isles. However, until many more radiocarbon dates are available for the Wessex material and from other contexts in the early bronze age in Britain, the chronology of the non-Wessex material must rely very heavily on associations or presumptive links with this small group of aristocratic graves. In Wessex itself as in other regions the evidence for this period is provided almost entirely by funerary associations, the exception being stone circles which continued to be constructed during this period and beyond it in some areas (Burl 1976a).

There appear to have been two traditions in funerary ritual single grave burial, initially by inhumations and cremation, generally in an urn. The single grave tradition is represented in the Wessex material itself, being of ultimate beaker origin in which a single burial, either by inhumation or cremation, is accompanied by a vessel and – more rarely in non-Wessex culture contexts – by other grave goods. This tradition is best expressed in terms of food vessels, a category of early bronze age ceramic which has become a catch-all term for pottery which would otherwise fit uneasily into the other major groups of late neolithic and early bronze age pottery forms. Even within the categories of what are generally accepted as food vessels there is a great range of form and decoration; but basically two major and originally distinct groups may be recognized: the Yorkshire vase food vessel and the Irish bowl food vessel (ApSimon 1959).

Yorkshire vase food vessels

As the name implies, the Yorkshire vase food vessel is a tall pot whose body diameter is less than its total height with a thickened and internally bevelled rim, one or more shoulders or carinations and a subconical body falling to a comparatively narrow base which may be accentuated in the form of a protruding foot (Kitson Clark 1938). A frequent although not universal feature is the provision of stops or lugs, either perforated or unperforated at the point of maximum body diameter and generally linking two ridges or carinations (fig. 5.21 : 7, 8). Decoration may cover the whole of the outer surface of the vessel and the internal rim bevel, or may be confined to the upper part of the pot, stopping at the carination or only slightly below it. By far the commonest decorative motif is that of a herringbone pattern or a variant thereof either in the form of a debased herringbone design or a split design in which the basic herringbone motif is divided up by a series of horizontal lines of ornament. Stopped vessels form a high percentage of this series and the decoration itself is most frequently executed by means of incision or impressions made with a spatulate object, more rarely by impressions made with a piece of twisted or whipped cord. A smaller number of vessels are decorated either all over the outer surface or on the upper part only with horizontal lines of twisted or whipped cord impressions, or rows of impressions made with a piece of wood or the articular end of a small mammalian or bird bone. In these groups stops occur less frequently. A general characteristic of the ornament of nearly all Yorkshire vase food vessels is the simplicity of the decoration and its tendency to occur as an all-over repeating pattern; complex zoned ornament is extremely rare and it may be significant that in the small

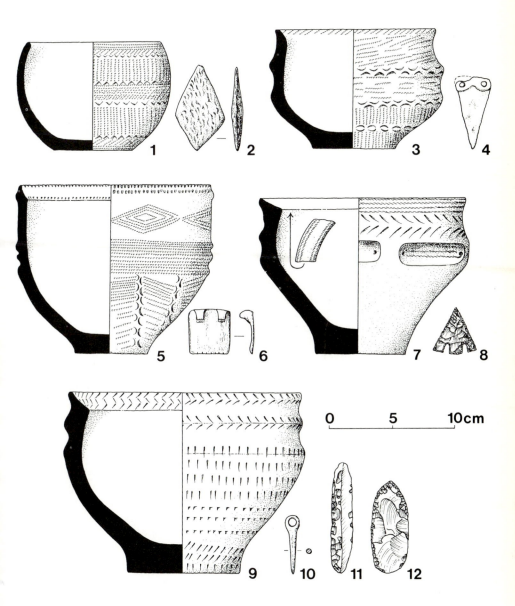

Fig. 5.21 Food vessel grave groups. 1–2 Omagh, Co. Tyrone; 3–4 Corky, Co. Antrim; 5–6 Killicarney, Co. Cavan; 7–8 Rudston LXIII, E. Yorks.; 9–12 Wharram Percy 47, E. Yorks. (after Simpson D. D. A. 1968a).

group of vessels bearing more complex designs the most frequent technique used to produce the decoration is comb impression, extremely rare in all the other decorative groups. A related and contemporary series of vessels is concentrated in southern Britain (fig. 6.8: 1, 2, 4).

The major concentration of vase food vessels is in Yorkshire and in particular on the chalk Wolds of the East Riding, with lesser concentrations on the limestone of the Peak District of Derbyshire and a northward distribution from Yorkshire to north-eastern England and eastern Scotland. In western Britain and Ireland only a few examples are known. In Yorkshire the vessel normally accompanies a crouched or, rarely, extended inhumation in a deep pit grave beneath a large and prominent round barrow (fig. 5.22). Further north this pit grave tradition gives way to cists, particularly in east-central Scotland. In Yorkshire the pit grave itself may be lined with wood or the body may lie on planks or be contained in a plank-built or tree trunk coffin (Elgee 1930: 73). Stratigraphy and associations in the Yorkshire barrows suggest that all the principal decorative forms of vase food vessel are contemporary one with another, and that the provision of perforated or unperforated stops has no chronological significance. The only object which is consistently associated with Yorkshire vases is a plano-convex flint knife of elongated, leaf-shaped form and generally carefully retouched over the whole of the convex surface (Clark J. G. D. 1932b; Simpson D. D. A. 1968a) (fig. 5.21: 12). Such knives are also known from late neolithic flint assemblages, from the chambers of Clyde tombs (Piggott 1954: 175), and they are occasionally associated with urns of one form or another, but numerically the most consistently recurring ceramic type is the food vessel; the knife may be considered as a component in the material equipment of the makers of this pottery. These small knives look rather like female equipment although in fact they are equally distributed between the sexes in graves. Such flint knives might be compared with the small metal riveted knives found in presumptively female graves in Wessex culture contexts and represent the products of a more materially impoverished society in northern England. These small bronze knives have in fact been found occasionally associated with vase food vessels although they have little chronological value, as the forms first appear on the Continent in Reinecke A1 contexts and have a very long life.

Other possible chronological equations with Wessex would be spacer-plate necklaces of jet, contemporary with the amber forms of Wessex and derived, as suggested above, like them from the gold lunulae first produced in the period of beaker technology. Other grave goods suggesting contemporaneity with Wessex would be a large bronze D-sectioned ring from Ratho, Midlothian, bone cylinder beads with a lozenge pattern from Folkton Barrow LXXI, East Riding of Yorkshire, and a polished bone pin with expanded, perforated head from Wharram Percy Barrow 47 (fig. 5.21: 10) which looks like a copy of the metal forms from Wessex culture contexts (Simpson D. D. A. 1968a). The broad contemporaneity of Yorkshire vase food vessels with the Wessex culture is also supported by barrow stratigraphy in terms of the relationship between these vessels,

Fig. 5.22   Food vessel cairn, Irton Moor, Yorks. (photograph: D. D. A. Simpson).

beakers and various urn forms. Although food vessels have been found in a contemporary position with both beakers and urns in a number of cases, there is no evidence from any site for a food vessel in a stratigraphically earlier position than a beaker or later than a burial with a collared urn. Although one can no longer accept the old 'chest of drawers' sequence beaker – food vessel – urn, and both associations and barrow stratigraphy suggest a considerable chronological overlap among the three groups, the sequence can in no instance be reversed and this raises considerable problems both about the relationship between the makers of these various pottery forms and also of course the possible significance of the pottery types themselves as an indicator of human groups or societies. Unfortunately few clearly domestic assemblages of Yorkshire vase food vessels have so far been recovered, although in a number of coastal sites fragments of vase food vessels have been found in occupation horizons; but generally these are mixed with other ceramic types as at Risby Warren in Lincolnshire (Riley 1957) or Kilellan Farm, Islay, Argyll (Burgess 1976c), interesting in view of the discrete associations of the pottery forms when these occur in funerary contexts.

The possible insular sources for the origins of Yorkshire vase food vessels are the later styles of Peterborough pottery, beakers and collared urns. The 15 basic decorative motifs listed by Longworth (1961) for primary series collared urns are all paralleled in Yorkshire vase food vessels and what he considered as the earliest forms of collared urn share with Yorkshire vases a predominance of herringbone ornament executed by incision and whipped and twisted cord. On the other hand the cremation rite and the size and shape of the urn are quite unlike those of food vessels and in many areas the distribution of urns and food vessels is complementary. In Derbyshire, for example, the food vessel graves are concentrated on the limestone whereas urn burials are found on the gritstone; in Yorkshire, food vessels come most frequently from the chalk of the East Riding whereas urns are concentrated on the limestone of the North Riding. It would appear more likely that the similarities of decoration in the two pottery forms are the result of a common borrowing from the Peterborough pottery tradition. From this source could be derived herringbone ornament, cord and incised techniques, horizontal lines of cord, interrupted cord line and rows of bird bone·and similar impressions. Horizontal cord, rows of impressions and incised ornament also form part of the repertoire of beaker decoration. The commonest of all designs on Yorkshire vase food vessels, the herringbone pattern, is characteristic of Clarke's north British-middle Rhine group of beakers. Other points in favour of a beaker origin are the shared traditions of inhumation burial beneath a barrow, and the similar distribution of beakers and vase food vessels in northern England and Scotland as opposed to the complementary distribution of collared urns. The biconical form of the vase food vessel with its narrow base, in some cases with a protruding foot, might be compared with Fengate forms or protruding foot beakers but the thickened and internally bevelled rim and above all the stops are alien to native neolithic and beaker pottery.

Kitson Clark (1938) suggested a possible corded ware element in Yorkshire vase food vessels. The small series of footed bowls and vases, and vessels with quatrefoil bases, are the most obvious examples. The stops on vase food vessels might be derived from the rare amphorae associated with protruding foot beakers in the Netherlands (van der Waals and Glasbergen 1955: 12) where herringbone and derived herringbone patterns, either on the upper part or covering the whole of the outer surface of the vessel, are also common. On the other hand, all these features might be more economically explained in terms of purely insular developments; even polypod bowls are known from beaker contexts in Britain (Stone 1958: 66) and could have been introduced by the makers of beaker pottery, later to become a small but distinctive element in the food vessel tradition. Beaker societies appear to have formed the basic element in many bronze age cultures in central and western Europe and in some, corded ware elements are apparent as in the handled or lugged vessels in Poland and Brittany. It is unnecessary to invoke fresh invasions or major population movements to explain these similarities in view of the common beaker substratum in these areas, any more than one must seek to explain vase food vessels in terms of corded ware/battle-axe invasions.

Irish bowl food vessels

Two forms of Irish bowl food vessel are apparent. One is a smooth-profiled bowl provided in some cases with a medial constriction and the other is a ridged or shouldered bowl, the profile broken by one, two, or most commonly three or more carinations or ridges (Herity and Eogan 1977: 133) (fig. 5.21: 1, 3). That the difference in vessel profile in the two forms may be of some significance is suggested to some extent by the differing motifs and techniques used to decorate the two categories. The rim profiles in both forms may be round or slightly bevelled internally with a well-fired fabric tempered with finely pounded grit. In the ridged bowl series the dominant decorative pattern is that of complex, repeating horizontal ornament, most frequently executed by impressions made with a square-toothed comb. False relief ornament is also common and many of the vessels are decorated on their bases with a star-shaped or cruciform design. The commonest design on the smooth profiled bowls is vertical lines or grooves generally arranged in two panels above and below the medial constriction. In this series incision as opposed to comb impressions, is the dominant technique with false relief occurring less frequently. The major concentrations of both types are in north-eastern Ireland with lesser concentrations in the Dublin and Wicklow regions and in the coastal areas of north-eastern and south-western Scotland, where the ridged bowl is the dominant form (Simpson D. D. A. 1965). As with Yorkshire vase food vessels, Irish bowls come largely from funerary contexts although occupation sites are known from coastal sand dune areas (Liversage 1968) and two rectangular structures of post and sod construction on Coney Island, Lough Neagh, are probably houses (Addyman 1965). Both inhumation and cremation were practised, the remains being placed in a pit or more normally a cist; they were in some cases grouped into small cemeteries (Waddell 1970), either flat or covered by mounds referred to as cemetery mounds or multiple cist cairns (Evans and Megaw 1937); the later monuments may reflect an enduring neolithic tradition of collective burial (Savory 1972), and bowl food vessels have also been inserted into the mounds and chambers of earlier megalithic tombs, particularly passage graves. Mutual pottery associations suggest that some at least of the ornamental groups in the Irish bowl series are contemporary. As with the Yorkshire vase food vessels, Irish bowls show considerable chronological overlap with other ceramic types. Contemporaneity with the Wessex culture is also suggested by associations of spacer-plate jet necklaces in a number of cases; by probable segmented faience beads from Lug na Curran, Co. Laois, and in the form of a bone belt hook from Killicarney, Co. Cavan (fig. 5.21: 6), similar to the sheet gold case for such a belt fastener from the Bush Barrow grave (Simpson D. D. A. 1968a). In the absence of more closely datable associations or radiocarbon determinations a sequence can be built up for bowls: at the head are those ornamented with lozenge and chevron patterns; from this stage development could take the form of multiplication of the bands of decoration producing in the end an all-over repeating pattern; or the conjoined lozenges might become separate panels, with at the end of the series vessels in which the panels become attenuated, producing pots decorated with vertical lines of ornament (Simpson 1968a: 208). It is this final form which has been compared with the gold bowls of Montelius III in northern Europe although the similarities are by no means close. The gold vessels, admittedly, have a star pattern on the base but such a feature is widespread in European bronze age pottery and metal vessels. In support of this link it has been suggested that the lenticular bosses on the Melfort bronze armlet, associated with a spacer-plate jet necklace, similar to those from Irish bowl contexts should be compared with the ornament on the Mold peytrel (Powell 1953), in turn related to north European goldwork of Montelius III. This, however, would imply a very long life for the necklace type which the other evidence does not support, nor do any Irish bowl food vessel associations imply a date after 1,400 bc.

Various theories have been put forward about the origins of the Irish bowl series. The earliest, but one which has frequently been re-stated, would derive these vessels from native Irish neolithic pottery and even the rite of single inhumation in a cist may have neolithic antecedents (Kilbride-Jones 1939). Bowl-shaped forms comparable to the Irish food vessels certainly do occur in some groups of late neolithic material, notably Sandhills Ware (Case 1961), but the decorative motifs and techniques are difficult to parallel. The same applies to the suggestion for an origin in Iberia in the Palmella bowls, which relies heavily on the occurrence of star and cruciform patterns on the bases of vessels in the two areas (Scott W. L. 1951). Some decorative features are also shared but the same patterns and motifs occur on beakers and beaker-derived pottery over a wide area of Europe. Beakers with which the bowls are associated in Iberia are unrepresented in Britain. Most convincing is the suggested origin for the series in southern British beakers. ApSimon (1959) emphasized the predominance of square-toothed comb impressions in ornament, and to a lesser extent incision, as features which could best be paralleled on beakers and motifs such as chevrons, panels, lozenges, triangles, frequently reserved, specifically on southern British beaker forms. The main stumbling block, however, is shape. A number of slab-sided vessels in the bowl series, it is suggested, are reminiscent of squashed-down beakers and what appear to be transitional forms between southern British beakers and bowl food vessels are represented in a series of pots from the settlement site of Dalkey Island, Co. Dublin (Liversage 1968). A possible continental source for elements in the form and decoration of Irish bowls suggests itself, however, when one considers the distribution of these vessels and compares it with that of early bronze age metal types. The distribution of bowls in Ireland, with notable concentrations in metalliferous regions, suggests that their makers were concerned with the exploitation of Irish gold and copper deposits and in the dissemination of such characteristic products as lunulae, decorated axes and halberds. Much of the trade in these commodities appears to have bypassed Wessex, travelling by routes further to the north or south-west. It must be significant that Irish bowl food vessels are concentrated along important trade routes; along the western sea route up the south-west coast of Scotland, with a notable concentration in the Kilmartin Valley, Argyll (Campbell, Scott and Piggott 1960–1), where a short porterage would be necessary to avoid the dangerous currents off the Mull of Kintyre; at each end of the Great Glen and one find actually in the centre of the rift; and in eastern Scotland, one of the jumping-off points for continental trade. The continental distribution of north British metalwork indicates a trade route across Westphalia and the Netherlands to central Germany. In Holland a small group of putatively Irish axes is found in the region where late beakers of Veluwe type are concentrated. These beakers, contemporary with Wessex I, are squat, bowl-shaped pots with internally bevelled rim decorated with comb and less frequently incision and with a tendency to produce relief or false relief ornament (van der Waals and Glasbergen 1955). The dominant motifs are panelled and lozenge patterns occurring as a broad zone around the middle of the pot and bordered by repeating horizontal ornament; in some there is also a tendency towards vertical ornament on the lower part of the vessel. All of these features are paralleled on Irish bowls and provide a possible alternative origin for such elements in Ireland. Their introduction into Ireland might be associated with the 'Impact phase' in Irish metallurgy (Case 1966) although again it must be admitted one could argue for parallel but independent development in Ireland and the Low Countries based on a common beaker tradition.

Urns

The other remaining early bronze age ceramic types, whatever their interrelationships and possibly diverse origins, have one feature in common, their function. Although occasionally accompanying inhumation burials, notably those of the collared urn series, or more rarely coming from apparently domestic contexts, their function is generally that of a receptacle for cremated human remains although the contexts in which these occur are again very diverse. Urns of various categories have been found, apparently, in primary contexts beneath round barrows or cairns constructed to cover them, but more frequently where associated with mounds the urns have been inserted as secondary burials into an existing barrow erected by beaker or food vessel groups; and more frequently still they occur either in flat cemeteries or within some form of funerary enclosure defined either by a bank of earth or stones or a free-standing circle of upright monoliths.

The collared or overhanging rim urn, as the name implies, has a developed rim, generally internally bevelled, which may be straight, convex or even slightly concave in profile (Longworth 1961). The vessel is generally carinated with the lower half sub-conical in form and frequently with a protruding foot (fig. 5.23: 2). Decoration is confined to the area above the carination or extending only a short way below it and to the internal rim bevel. Motifs consist of herringbone ornament, horizontal, diagonal or vertical lines or rows of decoration, square and pendant triangle motifs frequently infilled with hatching. This ornament is generally executed by means of impressions of twisted or whipped cord, stick and bird bone impressions and incision. Within the collared urn tradition Longworth distinguished a primary series which he derived largely from Peterborough ware and in particular from vessels in the Fengate style. He distinguished in the primary series eight traits, five formal and three decorative, which represented continuity from the Peterborough pottery tradition and argued that the more traits a vessel had the closer it was to the Peterborough tradition and therefore early. Urns with two or more traits he classed as belonging to the primary series. To support this argument he used the radiocarbon date of 1,540 ± 150 bc from the late neolithic surface in the Outer Ditch at Windmill Hill which yielded a primary series vessel, although subsequent radiocarbon dates suggest that the multiplicity of traits is not necessarily an indicator of an early date for a vessel. He could suggest no single region for the origins of the collared urn tradition and argued that it could have developed in all areas where Peterborough pottery was well represented. Collared urn cremations are in some cases accompanied by pygmy vessels either in the urn itself or placed beside. More rarely such miniature vessels are associated with cordoned or encrusted urns. They may also accompany inhumations (Longworth 1966–7) or unurned cremations or may even contain cremated human remains; in such cases these are generally of infants or young children. The commonest forms are biconical although occasionally they may be miniature versions of Yorkshire vase food vessels (Scott W. L. 1951: 81; fig. 2, 20–2). The walls are generally perforated as in the Wessex incense cups. Some vessels are decorated; the commonest motifs are filled triangle and chevron patterns and oblique lines executed by incision or, more rarely, cord, bird bone or stick impressions. Associations again suggest contemporaneity with the Wessex culture. At Brackmont Mill, Fife (Waterston 1940–1), a miniature vessel was accompanied by an ivory belt hook and bone toggle, the former reminiscent of the gold form from Bush Barrow; and at Loose Howe, Yorkshire, another miniature vessel accompanied a secondary cremation and bronze trefoil-headed pin related to pins from Wessex II contexts (Elgee and Elgee 1949). The origins for such pygmy vessels are to be sought once more amongst native late neolithic pottery. Undecorated miniature vessels appear quite early in native neolithic contexts and in the Ronaldsway culture of the Isle of Man (Bruce and Megaw 1947). Such vessels also form part of the Rinyo-Clacton pottery tradition and an example very similar to early bronze age pygmy vessels comes from a chambered tomb at Unival in North Uist (Scott W. L. 1947–8).

Cordoned urns are generally tall vessels with rim diameter less than that of the body, which is generally in the form of a smooth convex curve broken by one or more horizontal cordons which in some cases is the only decoration (fig. 5.23: 1). Where further ornament occurs the predominant motifs are triangles, in some cases infilled, or lattice patterns executed in twisted or whipped cord impressions or more rarely incision. The only consistently recurring association with cordoned urns in Ireland, Scotland and the north of England are bronze razors which fall into two classes (Butler and Smith 1956; Binchy 1967). Class Ia, razor knives, have a short broad tang with one or two rivet holes. Class Ib, the true razors, have a long narrow tang, in some cases with lattice patterns on the midrib. Where

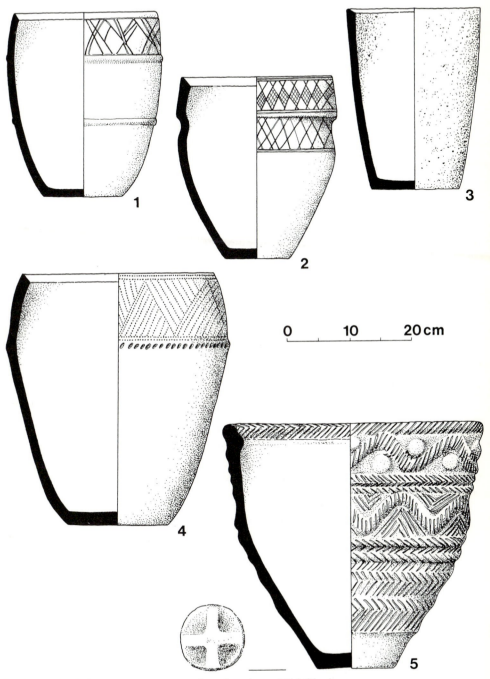

Fig. 5.23   Early bronze age urn types. 1 cordoned urn, Mid Gleniron, Wigtowns.; 2 collared urn, Largs, Ayrs.; 3 bucket urn, Largs, Ayr.; 4 biconical urn, Cherhill, Wilts.; 5 encrusted urn, Upper Meganey, Co. Kildare (after Morrison 1968, Smith I. F. 1961 and Kavanagh 1973).

indentifiable such burials are those of males. It is uncertain why there should be this close link between razors and cordoned urns especially as in a number of cases the urns with razor associations occur in cemeteries where other urn types are also represented. The razor associations would suggest contemporaneity with Wessex as they have been found with faience beads; also, on a mould from Inchnagree, Co. Cork, matrices for a razor occurred on the same mould as matrices for four large ogival daggers of Wessex II form. Other chronologically important associations with cordoned urns include a bone, crutch-headed pin from Balneil, Wigtownshire, and ring-headed pins from Harristown, Co. Waterford. Once more the origin of this ceramic form appears to lie in native late neolithic wares. One suggested origin is in Lough Gur Class II pottery with an origin for the type in Ireland with a spread across the Irish Sea marked by coastal distribution in south-west Scotland. Other possible prototypes exist, however, in undecorated variants of Rinyo-Clacton ware and in at least one case at Eddisbury, Cheshire, a Rinyo-Clacton vessel had been used as an urn (Smith I. F. 1974: 119); while the association of bone skewer pins, again a component in the Rinyo-Clacton culture, with a cordoned urn from Kirkburn, Dumfriesshire, may be significant in considering the origins of this type (Morrison 1968: 90).

In profile, encrusted urns normally present an uninterrupted convex curve from rim to base, or more rarely are carinated with rims thickened and internally bevelled, in some cases in the form of a series of steps (Kavanagh 1973) (fig. 5.23: 5). The most characteristic feature is an applied strip of clay forming a running chevron pattern between the rim and carination, frequently with applied blobs or bosses between the chevrons. Vertical cordons are common on the lower part of the body. Incised ornament may occur either on the applied strips or on the intervening voids and lower part of the body. Applied decoration occurs occasionally too on the inside of the base. Many of these motifs also occur on enlarged food vessels. Encrusted urns normally occur in cemeteries, either in pits or small cists unmarked by any covering mound. In some cases such a mound was constructed over the burials but more frequently an existing mound was utilized, or even a natural glacial feature. In Ireland these vessels have been found in association with food vessels and pygmy cups, but other grave goods are few. The origins of this urn form are uncertain and in fact ApSimon (1969: 39; 1972) rejects the idea of the encrusted urn as a distinctive pottery form and draws attention to the use of plastic ornament on other early bronze age pottery. Others again have suggested a development from food vessel forms in north-east England and eastern Scotland with a subsequent spread of the type to Ireland and south Wales. A movement in the reverse direction has also been argued and even a continental origin in the lower Rhine, at least for the tradition if not the pottery form itself (Kavanagh 1973). Most recently, Waddell (1976) has placed encrusted urns in a general 'vase tradition' of ultimately native neolithic origin contrasting with the beaker-influenced 'bowl tradition'. It is the former which he sees as 'the major pottery and funerary tradition of the developed early bronze age in Ireland'.

Bucket urns are slab-sided vessels of coarse ware, generally undecorated, which have frequently been relegated to the latter part of the bronze age (figs. 5.23: 3; 6.9: 2). Associations with collared urns, as at Ardeer, Ayrshire, and Largs, Ayrshire, and with segmented and star faience beads suggest that these simple forms again belong to the period of the early bronze age (Morrison 1968: 83). The simplicity of the type makes a consideration of its origins difficult although the fabric and the form can be paralleled both in Ireland, in Class II ware, and amongst the so-called flat-rimmed pottery from sites in eastern Scotland which again have their origins in middle and late neolithic ceramic traditions, as demonstrated in the associations in the stone circle at Croftmoraig, Perthshire (Piggott and Simpson 1971).

Biconical urns show a marked concentration in Wessex but with an important outlying group in East Anglia (Smith I. F. 1961). As the name suggests these are bipartite vessels with a single carination which is in some cases masked by an applied horizontal cordon; they have a rim diameter which is less than that of the maximum body diameter (fig. 5.23: 4). The rims are normally everted and have a marked internal bevel which is in general concave in profile. Decoration is confined to the area above the carination and consists of triangles, frequently hatched, chevrons, contrasting panels of vertical and horizontal ornament, executed in twisted cord. Finger printing occurs frequently on the rim, cordon or shoulder and many of the urns have applied lugs or horse-shoe shaped handles, the latter set above the carination (fig. 6.7).

The Ardleigh Group in Essex and Sussex (see p. 261 below) appears to be related to the Wessex biconical series, sharing features such as profile and the frequent use of applied, horse-shoe-shaped handles, although in this group the most characteristic feature is the application of finger-tip ornament (Longworth 1960) (fig. 6.9: 1).

Biconical urns seem to occur most frequently as secondary insertions into existing bell barrows although primary graves have been recorded beneath disc barrows and these appear to be smaller than those covering material associated with the Wessex culture. Associations are few and have limited chronological value. As with cordoned urns, Class Ib razors occur (fig. 6.7: 1) and these, together with associations of segmented faience beads, indicate contemporaneity with the latter part of the Wessex culture. A closely similar series of urns, the Hilversum urns, occurs in the Netherlands and these, together with special barrow types and other foreign phenomena, have been until recently regarded by Dutch archaeologists as introductions by settlers from the British Isles (Glasbergen 1954) – the object being to set up continental trading posts for the distribution of bronzes of British origin or produced by smiths working in an insular tradition, although this view has been questioned (Burgess 1974: 182). In Holland, the Hilversum urns occur on settlement sites associated with late Veluwe beakers which in their turn appear to be contemporary with the Wessex culture. But the question of possible British colonization of the Low Countries is better left to a survey of developments during the later bronze age (p. 282).

6 The later bronze age (1,400 bc–500 BC)*

Introduction: metal typology and technology

In recent years the detailed regional examination of the metal typology of the later bronze age and the gradual increase in our knowledge of both funerary and settlement sites dated relatively securely by radiocarbon have contributed to a revision of previously held views. The period covered by the term 'later bronze age' runs from the end of the Wessex culture of southern England to the first appearance in about the sixth century BC of types associated with the later phases of the continental Hallstatt Iron Age and the subsequent widespread adoption of the new metal, iron, itself. Conventional radiocarbon dating gives this period a 1,000-year time-span, but corrected dates for its start now increase its length by some three centuries at least (fig. 6.1).

Hawkes' *Scheme for the British Bronze Age*, devised in 1960 but never formally published (cf. Coles 1961), adhered to the classic tripartite model of 'Early', 'Middle', and 'Late' phases for the bronze age and to a conventional chronology based largely on cross-dating. Hawkes also used the changes in implement typology and ceramic forms to draw attention to the largely insular nature of many developments in the earlier stages of the period – what Hawkes considered to be the middle bronze age, ranging from c. 1,400 to 900 BC. As previously noted (p. 240), the formerly accepted correlation of the rite of cremations placed in urns with continental late bronze age urnfields (with a starting point c. 1,200 BC more or less fixed by historical dating from the west Mediterranean as well as by C14) is no longer valid. In his pioneering survey of bronze age pottery Abercromby (1912) also looked to the urnfields for the source of the so-called 'Deverel-Rimbury' pottery of southern England. This pottery – divided into 'barrel', 'bucket' and 'globular' urn forms – is now recorded from domestic as well as funerary contexts (fig. 6.9). While once considered as an eighth century BC introduction, it is now generally placed in a 'middle' rather than 'late' context in the bronze age – though there is still some support for the former theory that the Deverel-Rimbury 'culture' continued until the introduction of iron (cf. Cunliffe 1974: 24).[1]

If pottery developments in the later bronze age of the British Isles are

---

* In this chapter the absence of a large body of C14 ('bc') dates has led to the use of 'conventional' or ultimately – though by no means securely fixed – historical ('BC') dates based on Mediterranean chronologies. Towards the end of the period, the absolute chronology of the continental late bronze and early iron ages is of some limited use.

now to be largely regarded as insular, certain features in the development of metal types show, on the contrary, clear continental influence. Especially significant areas are north-western France and the Atlantic seaboard, northern Germany and – more disputably – Scandinavia (Smith M. A. 1959; Butler 1963; Rowlands 1976b). Technological innovations of continental origin do not, however, necessitate resurrecting the earlier vogue amongst archaeologists to ascribe all major changes in British prehistory to 'invasion' or wholesale settlement (Clark J. G. D. 1966: esp. 184; Hawkes 1972: 114–15), although it is still sometimes claimed, with reference to south-east England, that such features as the appearance of the first true swords (fig. 6.24) or hilltop-defended settlements with walls of partial timber construction are due to a more direct influence such as population movement rather than to trade or indirect contact.

In attempting an overall picture of the British Isles during the later bronze age, we are once more largely limited by the accident of the survival of evidence. The developed middle bronze age of southern England, the 'Deverel-Rimbury culture', if by no means a uniform culture in the strict Childe-like sense (Barrett 1976), is represented by settlements, field systems and related enclosures, occasionally with related cemeteries (Holden 1972) (fig. 6.10–11). The former continue the evidence for small-scale arable cultivation in the neolithic and earlier bronze age (p. 103). Both funerary and domestic sites can also be linked not only by pottery but occasionally by metal types. Outside the south of England, the lack of associated grave goods and the continuing vogue for cremation burial which follows on the decline of the Wessex culture and its related groups in the south-west and north of England, and the virtual absence of metal in domestic sites, match an equal lack of pottery in bronze hoards. Indeed, one difficulty in arguing for the continuity of southern Deverel-Rimbury elements through the later bronze age is the fact that at present we know comparatively little of the burials, settlements and associated pottery over much of the British Isles, although recent studies are helping considerably (cf. Burgess 1976a; Challis and Harding 1975).[2] This lack of evidence must be set against the realization that many features heretofore regarded as definitely iron age ('Celtic' fields, round houses and storage pits) occur for the first time in association in this very Deverel-Rimbury 'culture'.

The gradual decline in the custom of putting grave goods other than pottery in barrow burials of the latter part of the early bronze age has been noted in Chapter 5. In the later bronze age this custom declines though does not totally disappear. Unassociated cremation burials are certainly more frequent. These may be secondary insertions in earlier structures, as in the case of the Deverel, Dorset, bowl barrow, first described in splendidly gothic prose by the excavator W. A. Miles in 1826 (cf. Grinsell 1959: 120). Here an early bronze age barrow was re-used for at least 20 cremations in urns. There are other virtually flat, unmarked cremation cemeteries, such as the site of Rimbury, also in Dorset. The latter burial rite really continues the pattern for the often circular, flat cremation cemeteries which occur in the later neolithic henge monuments.

In the absence of a more complete range of radiocarbon dates[3] we must

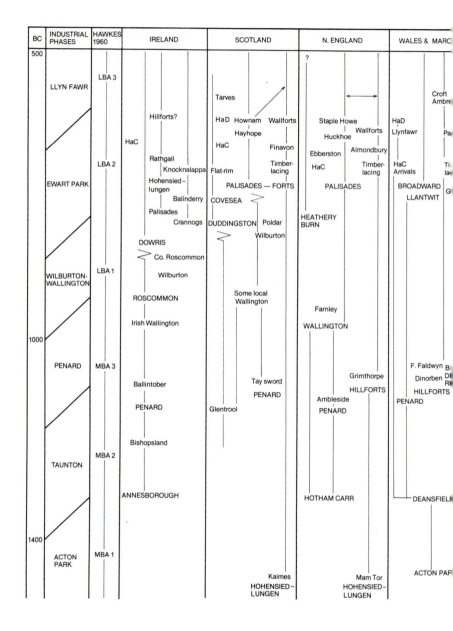

Fig. 6.1   Comparative table: the later bronze age of the British Isles compared with central and western Europe (after Burgess 1968c, Burgess 1976c and Butler 1963).

ESSEX & S.W. ENGLAND	S.E. ENGLAND	FRANCE — Brittany	FRANCE — Picardy Normandy etc.	CENTRAL EUROPE	NORTHERN EUROPE
			?		MONTELIUS VI
Eldon's Seat II ?			Saint Bugan		? later M V
	HaD	HA. II	HA. II	HaD	
	IRON / W. Harling		AMORICAN AXES		
Armorican Axes / Hillforts	Sompting	HA. I	HA. I	HaC	M V
	HaC / Ivinghoe				
Ham Hill	Isleham / Hillforts?				
GURSEY Cadbury / Eldon's Seat I	Wilburton / Plumpton B				
ADWARD Hohensied-lungen	CARP'S TONGUE	CARP'S TONGUE		Ha B3	
	?				
ripheral ...burton (Peripheral Wilburton)				Ha B1-2	later M IV
	Andover			Ha A2	earlier M IV
	WILBURTON	SAINT-BRIEUC-DES-IFFS		Ha A1	
					M III
			Picardy Pins		
...iton PENARD	Appleby	ROSNOËN			
	Eriswell				
	Blackrock / PENARD			— BRONZE D	earlier M III
				TUMULUS C	M II B-C
South Lodge	Plumpton A				
Thorny Down	Itford Hill				
Taunton / DEVEREL-RIMBURY	Barton Bendish	BAUX-s.-CROIX-MONT-s.-AIGNAN		TUMULUS B2	M IIA
RNAMENT ORIZON (Ornament Horizon)	ORNAMENT HORIZON	PORTRIEUX			
	Ardleigh ?				
	Shield palstaves	TRÉBOUL	SHIELD PALSTAVES	TUMULUS B1	LATE M I
NIGHTON	Shearplace I-II				
	TREVISKER	Rams Hill			

turn instead to the increasing number of modern regional studies of the technology and typology of bronze hoards. It is here that Burgess, Coles and Savory have contributed a number of important survey papers which have largely superseded Hawkes' 1960 scheme (cf. Burgess 1968a, b, c; 1974 with fig. 26; 1976b with fig. 4.9; Coles 1959–60; 1963–4; Savory 1965a, b; see also Langmaid 1976). Others have underlined the importance of French influence on British later bronze age industries (cf. Briard 1965; 1973: esp. 145ff.; Rowlands 1976b); and Butler (1963), following pioneering work by M. A. Smith (1959), has recorded the nature of contact across the North Sea (fig. 6.1).

Hawkes' scheme (1960) defined the beginning of his three phases of the middle bronze age as being represented by a single insular bronze culture – a view scarcely supported by more detailed regional studies. In conventional chronology, Hawkes' Middle Bronze I (1,400–1,200 BC) was marked by some slight evidence for stock enclosures and barley growing, development of various early bronze age types including the Wessex biconical urn and, in the south-west, the beginning of the 'Trevisker' series (qv. p. 281) (fig. 6.16). In metalwork, only in the south-east was there to be seen evidence of a new foreign-influenced metallurgy, particularly with the first palstaves, the elongated form of axe with narrow blade and carefully cast stop ridge. Hawkes' subsequent Middle Bronze Age II (to c. 1,000 BC) was the main phase not only of industrial development as marked by the so-called 'ornament horizon' but also of the 'Deverel-Rimbury' settlements belonging mainly to southern Britain. The last stages of middle bronze age technology were considered by Hawkes to be largely transitional, the most important feature being the first appearance of new military equipment with the insular development of true leaf-shaped swords (fig. 6.24) – again in the south-east and again as a result of foreign contact; the circular metal shield of bronze may also have been introduced (Coles 1963b) (fig. 6.42:1).

In the developing technology of later bronze age Britain basic metallurgical differences can be detected. An extensive programme of metallurgical analyses (Brown and Blin-Stoyle 1959a, b; Allen, Britton and Coghlan 1970) has shown that, while in the earlier and middle phases of the period in southern Britain most metalwork was made of ordinary tin-bronze, the following period was marked by the introduction of a new alloy, lead-bronze. This was in use before the late bronze age in Wales (Savory 1976c: 116), in contrast to north-east England where lead alloying was long delayed (Burgess 1968a: esp. App. I). The advantage of adding lead to a tin-bronze is that it facilitates pouring in the casting process, and subsequent working. In the south-east of Britain this innovation, occurring about 1,000 BC at the beginning of the so-called 'Penard phase', is marked by the first mass production of the new swords and related forms.

Clearly, technological innovations did not occur uniformly throughout the British Isles and we await the results of comparable analyses from Scotland and the west of Britain. But it is only from the eighth century BC that we find lead-bronze swords, axes and spears throughout the British Isles as part of what appears to be a different industrial revolution in which regional industries are most clearly defined on the basis of varying local forms of socketed axe.

In the earlier part of the later bronze age two-piece stone moulds were largely used for casting; they have been found mainly in the north of the British Isles and in Ireland (fig. 6.2). Two-piece moulds of stone are known from early bronze age times and remained the main type known in the middle period, but other and more complex innovations – such as the hollow casting required in the production of socketed spears needing cores (Hodges 1964: 69–73) – occurred in the course of the early stages of the middle bronze age (Tylecote 1962: 107ff.; 1976: 31ff.; Herity and Eogan 1977: 139ff. and fig. 64). Although there is Irish evidence for workshops of the period using clay crucibles and moulds, including one for an early basal-looped spear head (Ó Ríordáin 1954: 384ff.), clay moulds elsewhere are scarce. There is, however, an indication that moulds of metal were used to cast early Group I or shield-decorated palstaves, exported to and imitated on the Continent. Bronze moulds, previously thought to be introduced only into the latest bronze industries in Britain (Hodges 1954; 1960), are a common feature of north European technology, commencing in the Montelius II phase (Butler 1963: 65ff.); three bronze moulds for palstaves can be dated to the middle bronze age of southern Britain (Rowlands 1976b: 10 and App. A 2). The standard British mould type must, however, have been of clay, since bronze moulds would themselves have had to be cast, and finds of stone moulds are peculiar to the highland zone regions. Clay moulds were almost certainly in general use in the course of the middle bronze age; indeed, certain types of palstave demand the use of such moulds and the laborious production of either bronze or stone moulds seems incompatible with the large size of some middle bronze age hoards.[4]

An outline of the metalworking traditions of the middle bronze age (fig. 6.1)

Poverty of burial rite does not necessarily indicate economic decline. Recently a number of studies have reviewed the possible nature of social change and the organization of technology and trade in the later bronze age (Rowlands 1971b; 1976b; Coombs 1975a: esp. 75f.). However this may be, the reduction in quantity of grave goods (Burgess 1976a) towards the end of the early bronze age is a general phenomenon throughout the British Isles. In contrast to this, there was a marked expansion in the range of metal types developed within what we must now, conventionally at least, refer to as the later bronze age.[5]

In his review of the main technological developments in the British Isles from the end of the early bronze age to the beginning of the late bronze age, as conventionally marked by the general introduction of leaded bronze in southern Britain, Burgess (1974) offers a succinct summary of this material and, like Hawkes, sees three main phases. The earliest phase, named after the Acton Park, Denbighshire, find (fig. 6.3) has comparatively few hoards and weapons. The phase includes two groups of Burgess' own (1968b) classification of rapiers (fig. 6.4:22), a form found almost exclusively isolated or in hoards (Coombs 1975a: 50) and which developed from early bronze age ogival daggers;[6] some of the early looped spear-heads may be contemporary and none of these weapons are associated with tools (qv. p. 277 below). Hoards in Brittany, north Germany and the Netherlands ('Tréboul': Briard 1965; 'Illsmoor': Butler 1963) include rapiers and so-called Acton Park palstaves which may not be imports so much as products of parallel industries (fig. 6.6). It is clear that north Wales, the Thames and East Anglia were the main centres of industrial activity. Burgess' 'Taunton' phase is to be equated with M. A. Smith's (1959) 'ornament horizon' which appears to be marked by southern England taking over from Wales as an important centre for the development of local tools such as the later series of flanged palstaves. Contact with France and the import of twisted torcs and armlets and smaller ornaments (fig. 6.3:4), as well as tools, produced the stimulus for local forms, notably quoit pins and 'Sussex loops' (fig. 6.3:11). Gold and bronze ribbon torcs produced both in Britain and Ireland were exported back to the Continent, though the dating of these last is not secure (Herity and Eogan 1977: 176). Somerset is considered a centre for developments stemming from importation of the new types.[7]

In southern Britain, instead of flat and cast-flanged axes, both decorated and plain, we find the palstave. Instead of the various types of riveted daggers elongation leads to the appearance of tapering bladed rapiers (so defined when the blades are over 35cm long) (fig. 6.25:1–4); spear-heads with midribs and true sockets replace earlier tanged and related forms. Spear-heads with a peg-hole through their sockets are a late introduction in Britain, though present on the Continent from the development of the basic form (Butler 1963: 102f.). The regional differences in this phase of

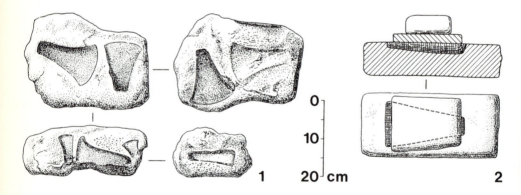

Fig. 6.2   Moulds of the earlier and later bronze age. 1 Ballyglisheen, Co. Carlow: stone open mould for flat axes with (2) schematic drawing of weighted cover on mould; 3 Killymaddy, Co. Antrim: closed (double) stone mould; 4 Gwithian, Cornwall: stone mould for socketed axe; 5 Jarlshof, Shetland: pottery moulds for (a) sunflower pin, (b) gouge, (c) sword, (d) socketed axe, and (e) mould gate; 6 Southall, Middx: bronze mould for socketed axe. (1, 2, 6 after Tylecote 1962; 3 after Herity and Eogan 1977; 4 after Rowlands 1976a; 5 after Hamilton 1956).

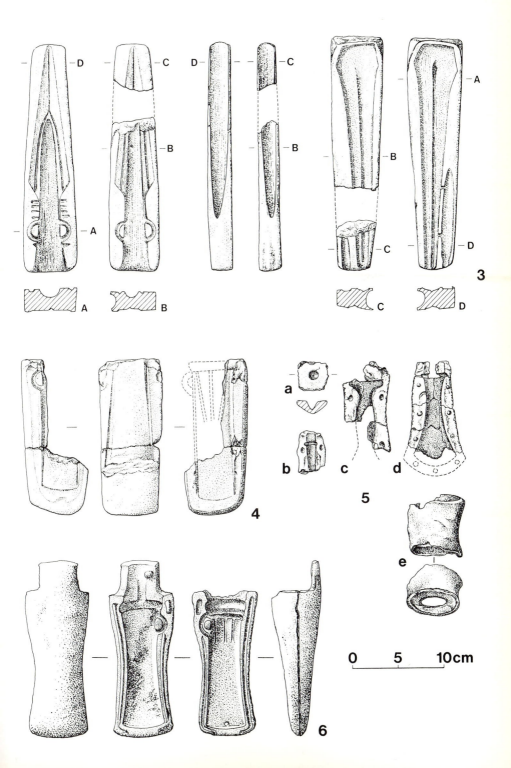

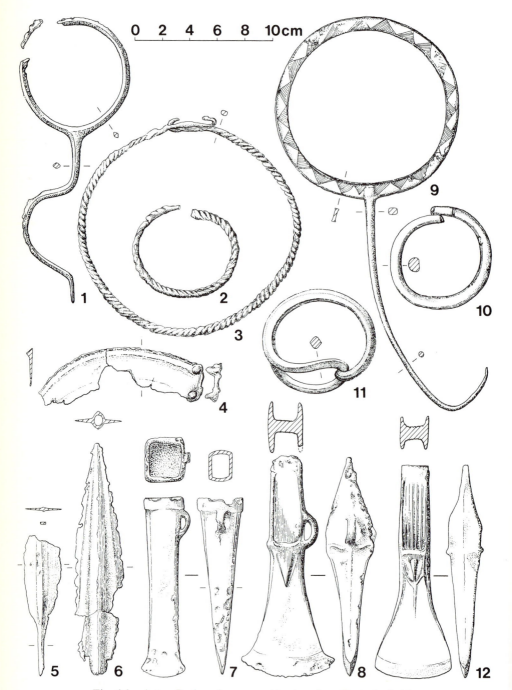

Fig. 6.3   Acton Park and ornament horizon hoards: typical objects.
1–8 Taunton Workhouse, Somerset; 9–10, 12 Barton Bendish, Norfolk;
11 Blackrock, Brighton, Sussex (after *Inv. Arch.* G B.43 and 7).

bronze technology include, amongst other things, a marked divergence between the south-east of England, Wales, and the border country of the Marches, where the palstave was adopted, in contrast to the north and west of England, Scotland (Coles 1963–4) and Ireland (Eogan 1964: 268f.; Herity and Eogan 1977: 159f.), where the flanged axe and later variants continued in use.

Late radiocarbon dates have also emerged which seem to indicate in certain areas what might be regarded as a developed Wessex culture contemporary with the new technology; there is even the occasional occurrence of fine grave goods such as the Mold, Flintshire, sheet-gold cape (Powell 1953).[8] The most important typological developments are to be found in the south of England and these are the ones which must be regarded as contemporary with the evolution of the 'Deverel-Rimbury culture'. A number of variant types of palstave were produced as a development from late Irish flanged axes (Rowlands 1976b: 27ff.) (fig. 6.3: 8, 12). Particularly significant is the so-called 'Acton Park', Group I or North Welsh shield-decorated type, whose concentration in Wales may reflect exploitation of local copper ores. This is one of several British forms to find their way to the Continent (fig. 6.6:1–2), but Rowlands has shown East Anglia to be a centre of shield palstaves with French connections. Shield-decorated and other types of palstave both with low and high flanges were as noted produced in bronze moulds.[9] During Period III of the north European Montelius sequence, connections with Scandinavia and northern Germany have been regarded as being indicated by a range of bronze ornaments, including rings cast in imitation of those made of twisted rods of metal. However, this form is also known in France, as are other ornaments of various types: this has given rise to the concept of the 'ornament horizon' for the appearance of these objects in England (Smith M. A. 1959); Butler (1963: 218–23) preferred the term 'Taunton-Barton Bendish phase' after two of the key southern hoards. There are groups related to the ornament horizon both in Scotland (Coles 1963–4 – 'Glentrool phase') and in Ireland (Eogan 1964 – 'Bishopsland phase') which reflect the furthest northerly and western spread of influence ultimately of central European origin (fig. 6.4).

Besides the classic objects of the ornament horizon, sickles with little cast buttons (fig. 6.3:4), perhaps in imitation of rivets, and a range of tools and pins also occur. Finds of characteristic ornament horizon objects in East Anglia, also an important area for the production of various types of the new socketed spears, suggest that it may have been a region of considerable ceremonial significance.

In the north of England we can note a few unlooped shield-decorated palstaves and rapiers. These are types characteristic of southern English industries, but the dominant form in the north was the flanged axe as in Scotland and Ireland; on the whole in this early stage of the later bronze age the north of England is an area unmarked by technological innovation or experiment (Burgess 1968a).

In Ireland, in the middle bronze age as now defined (Eogan 1964; Herity and Eogan 1977), weapons consisted of spear-heads with kite-shaped blades and loops on their sockets and well-defined midribs – a type which occurs in late bronze age hoards. There were also basal looped spear-heads, and those with loops on their sockets and leaf-shaped blades. Basal-looped spear-heads also occur on continental sites, as for example at Liesbüttel in Schleswig-Holstein which is ascribed to Montelius IIa (Butler 1963: 98ff.). The main forms are axes with haft and wing flanges, and palstaves reflecting western continental European forms, as well as Irish variations of rapiers with trapeze-shaped butts and Class I razors, associated in the south of England with Wessex biconical urns (fig. 6.7:1). Technologically, many of these Irish types show knowledge of advanced casting procedures, and stone moulds from Killymaddy, Co. Antrim (Coghlan and Raftery 1961; Herity and Eogan 1977: 153ff.) show the contemporaneity of early rapiers and socket-looped spears (fig. 6.2:3).

Following this initial period in Ireland the Bishopsland phase sees the continuation of Ireland's position as a centre of goldsmithing – perhaps now as a result of new exploiters of Wicklow gold – with the production of

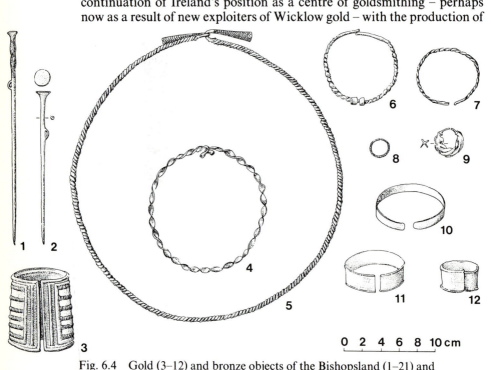

Fig. 6.4   Gold (3–12) and bronze objects of the Bishopsland (1–21) and Glentrool (22–34) phases. Pins: 1 'Ireland'; 2 Corran, Co. Antrim; 3 Derrinboy, Co. Offaly: ribbed bracelet; 4 Lisdroone, Co. Mayo: ribbon torc; 5 Co. Mayo: bar flange-twisted torc; twisted bracelets: 6 Skelly, Co. Tyrone, and 7 St John's, Co. Kildare; earrings: 8 Ireland: bar twisted and 9 Castlereagh, Co. Roscommon: flange-twisted; 10 Vesnoy, Co. Roscommon: penannular bracelet; 'tress-rings': 11 St John's, Co. Kildare, and 12 Derrinboy, Co. Offaly (after Eogan 1964 and Herity and Eogan 1977); 13–21 Bishopsland, Co. Kildare: selection of bronze tools from hoard (after Herity and Eogan 1977); 22–34 Glentrool, Kirkcudbright: amber (30) and bronze hoard (after Coles 1963–4).

types which in the south of England are frequently of bronze rather than the richer metal (fig. 6.4:1–12). Gold bar torcs with recurved terminals (fig. 6.4:5) may be an Irish development of continental bronze torcs (Eogan 1967). Some 90 are known with a distribution not only in Ireland but also in southern Britain and with a scattering in France (fig. 6.5). Other characteristic objects include cast bronze torcs or neck rings, as in the Annesborough, Co. Armagh, find which includes a British low-flanged palstave like those of the south-western ornament horizon. Another of the 11 hoards ascribed to this phase, the eponymous Bishopsland, Co. Kildare, hoard near the Wicklow gold ore source, includes a range of tools such as socketed hammers, punches and a range of chisels and saws (fig. 6.4:13–21). We have already noted just what a large proportion of objects in Irish hoards throughout the later bronze age are not weapons but rather tools or ornaments, in contrast with lowland Britain.

Turning to Scotland, the review by Coles (1963–4) of the earlier phases of what we have been defining here as the middle stage of bronze age

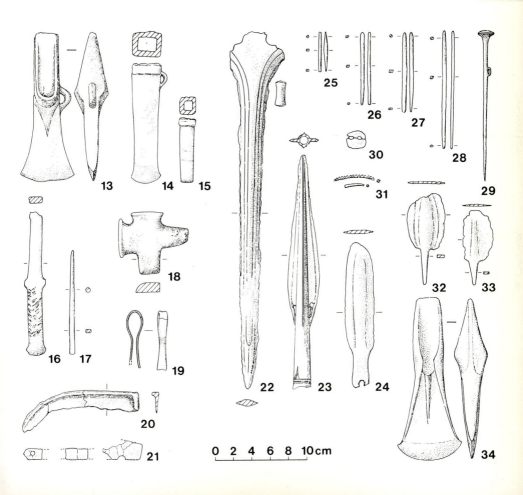

metallurgy shows that the period is marked by types which all recognizably derive from previous early bronze age forms – flanged axes, early socket-looped spears and dirks and daggers with two rivets, the last again perhaps showing some influence from the continental Tumulus bronze age. Following this so-called 'Caverton' phase, the 'Auchterhouse' phase is marked particularly by high-flanged axes and basal-looped spears. These axes are related to those of Butler's 'Illsmoor' phase (cf. p. 255 below) of the Low Countries and northern Germany (Reinecke Tumulus bronze age B2 or around 1,400 BC).

The last phase of the middle bronze age in Scotland is named after a small hoard from Glentrool, Kirkcudbright (fig. 6.4:22–34), which contains a fragment of an imitation twisted bar torc – a clear link with the south British ornament horizon. Some 50 gold ribbon torcs come from Scotland, including at least 36 from Law Farm, Morayshire. This hoard also contained a bronze ribbon torc, a presumed insular invention as found in the Edington Burtle, Somerset, hoard (Coles 1963–4: 124).[10] Other forms linking the far north with the south include early socketed axes, although the tools noticeable in contemporary finds from Ireland and England are largely absent. The north-west of Scotland seems to be a metallurgical blank, on present evidence at least. The ubiquitous basal-looped spear-heads are found, while other forms such as wing-flanged axes appear, as do disc-headed pins, a form found in the Irish Sea region

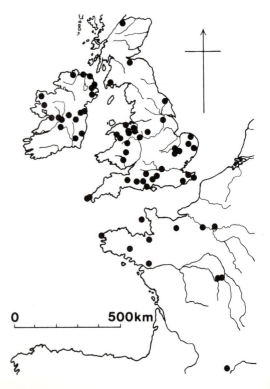

Fig. 6.5   Distribution map of later bronze age Irish gold bar torcs (after Herity and Eogan 1977).

0   500km

though not in southern Britain, and one which, on perhaps too general grounds, has been connected with the technology of northern Europe (Eogan 1964: 302–7).

Foreign connections and the beginning of the British later bronze age

There is no doubt that in the early stages of the bronze industries of later bronze age Britain, there was frequent and diverse contact with contemporary metallurgical centres on the Continent (fig. 6.25). As has been noted further above (p. 251), it is assumed that shield-ornamented 'Acton Park' and related palstaves were being exported from centres in Wales or southern England; the appearance of closely similar types in north-western France (Gaucher and Mohen 1974) would suggest direct and continuing intercourse between metalsmiths on either side of the Channel. Armorican pottery, which has to some recalled south-western urn forms – probably erroneously (Giot *et al.* 1960: 128ff.; cf. ApSimon and Greenfield 1972: 363–4) – is the least significant of indications of a long-continuing and close relationship between northern France and southern England. Early recognition of these links came with discoveries made at Ramsgate in Kent. A somewhat exceptional inhumation burial in a chalk-cut pit was associated with at least two arm rings of so-called Bignan type (fig. 6.15:3–4) decorated in the style of the 'Picardy pins' found in similar circumstances in a bucket urn at Ramsgate (Hawkes 1942), and a ribbed cast-bronze wristlet (fig. 6.15:5–6) of a form characteristic of the ornament horizon. The Bignan armlets are typical west French types (Rowlands 1971a; Burgess 1976a: 98).

With regard to the origin and external connections of middle bronze age metalworking industries, Rowlands' work (1976b; esp. 154ff.) indicates that already, towards the end of the Wessex culture, metalworking was being developed under Irish influence outside the main Wessex region, in the Fens, the lower Thames Valley, the south coast and the south-west of England. Ornament hoards of the south coast-Dorset-Somerset region contrast with the tools and specialized weapons of the Thames Valley and East Anglia. Not only the introduction into south-western Britain of such new types as the high-flanged palstave, but also the analysis of certain hoards such as the small personal hoard with pottery close to Trevisker styles 2–3 (qv. p. 281 below) from a metalsmith's hut at Tredarvah near Penzance, seem to confirm that Irish influence and trade in raw materials such as tin and copper were almost certainly factors (cf. Thomas A. C. 1964; Fox A. 1973: 111ff.; cf. also p. 277 below). The 'ornament horizon' nature of Irish hoards such as that from Annesborough supports the connection (Eogan 1964: 286–8). In Ireland, however, the main early middle bronze age types as just noted – flanged axes, kite-shaped spearheads – are firmly related to the preceding local forms. Beyond Britain it is on the basis of imported axe types, particularly the north German socketed 'Hademarschen' form, that Butler (1963) defined two main phases of trading activity which he termed the 'Illsmoor' and 'Ostenfeld' phases, matched by the introduction into Britain of such continental Tumulus bronze age – or Reinecke B – types as the rapier (Trump 1962;

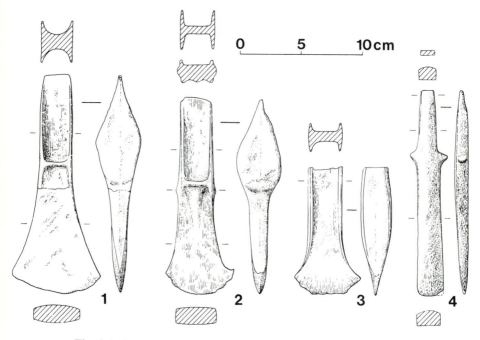

Fig. 6.6   Voorhout, South Holland: objects from bronze hoard (after Butler 1963).

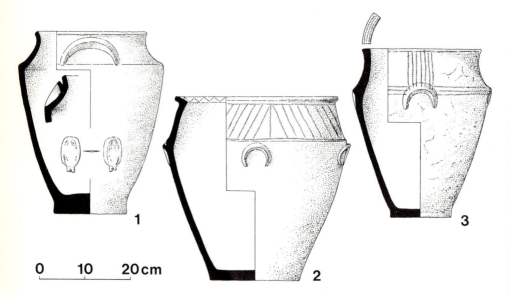

Fig. 6.7   Biconical urns with horse-shoe handles. 1 Amesbury, Wilts., barrow G71 with (inset) bronze razor; 2 Bulford, Wilts., barrow 47; 3 Budel, North Brabant (after Smith 1966 and De Laet and Glasbergen 1959).

1968). Important in this context are the shield pattern or 'Group I' palstaves which occur in Dutch and north German hoards such as the south Holland coastal hoard of Voorhout (Butler 1963: 51; 1969; but see further n. 21 below) (fig. 6.6). Rowlands (1976b: 146) prefers to see this type as East Anglian in view of its greatest concentration in this region and emphasizes the comparison between the pottery of sites such as the Ardleigh, Essex, cemetery (fig. 6.9:1) and Vogelenzang, not far from Voorhout – comparisons which follow on the clear links between Wessex and the Hilversum urns (fig. 6.7) (p. 241 above; cf. Smith I. F. 1961: 117–118). In turn Burgess (1974: 313 n.228) indicates evidence for trading and perhaps the manufacture of his Group I palstave in Ireland by north Welsh smiths.

The Blackrock, Sussex, hoard (Piggott C.M. 1949a; Butler 1963: 217ff.) contains, in addition to three of the locally produced 'Sussex loops' (fig. 6.3:11), clear evidence of north European contact not only in a decorated finger ring but also in a solid-hilted dagger, a Montelius II type which tends to support Burgess' recent claim for an up-dating of the foreign elements in the ornament horizon to this period (Burgess 1976b: 73f.).[11] The same hoard, however, includes a bracelet similar to forms of Montelius IV date which suggests that the find could be late in the ornament horizon (cf. Herity and Eogan 1977: 180).

An indication of the importance of early Urnfield contacts in the middle bronze age can be seen in two decorated pins with conical heads from the Gwithian, Cornwall, Layer 3 farming settlement (see also p. 283). These have close affinities with early Urnfield Reinecke D pins of the so-called 'Mels-Rixheim' group (Rowlands 1976a). From the same level is a fragment of a schistose stone mould for a socketed axe with converging cast rib decoration with traces of lead and tin (fig. 6.2:4). Burgess (1976b) sees this type of axe as a contemporary development from early Urnfield prototypes to the so-called Taunton-Hademarschen axes (fig. 6.3:7; 6.15:10; 6.30:3) of the ornament horizon (Butler 1963: 75–81), and uses the mould as argument for suggesting a commencement of the Penard phase in absolute dating to around the twelfth to eleventh centuries BC.

In the developed phase of the middle bronze age, it used to be considered that there was a European Montelius III background to the ornament horizon which added exotic forms to the native repertoire of palstaves, side- and basal-looped spears and trapezoid-hilted rapiers (Smith M. A. 1959; Butler 1963). As has been noted, this view has been largely replaced by arguments for strong connections with the industries of northern France as defined by Briard (1965; 1973), as shown by a close relationship between palstaves found in hoards on both sides of the Channel (fig. 6.25: 5–6). Arm rings and spiral twisted ornaments – the latter concentrated in England in the south-west – as well as the so-called Rosnoën swords (fig. 6.24:3) of Burgess' Penard phase as found in the Thames Valley, are other aspects of this French connection, though Burgess (1976b: 72–3) does not seem to accept Rowlands' arguments (1976b: 150–2) for broad contemporaneity of the ornament horizon and Penard phase. Certainly north French pins and arm rings found on the south coast seem to have a distribution separate from such types which do ultimately reflect central or north European traditions – the twisted ornaments, knobbed sickles and ribbed rather than incised armlets of Somerset, Dorset and south Wiltshire (fig. 6.15:5–6). A general central and northern source similar to that suggested by Smith for ribbed bracelets, knobbed sickles and certain pin types must apply for early continental Urnfield material found in Britain, such as the rare median winged axes (fig. 6.25:7), a type also associated with the north French Rosnoën hoards. An interaction may be postulated between the local metalworking centres of the Thames Valley and East Anglia and those of northern France, setting the background for the continuing technological exchange across the Channel of the 'Wilburton' and succeeding 'Carp's Tongue' industries of the full late bronze age. By contrast, in the heartland of the earlier Wessex culture the absence of the new middle bronze age forms may in part be explained by survival of early bronze age traditions obsolete elsewhere.

It was, however, regions such as the Thames Valley which became the centres for the new development of weapons like the rapier and leaf-shaped sword. New types like the cast flanged stop-ridge axe introduced from northern France influenced the subsequent development of the palstave in contrast to the socketed axe of north German inspiration. Whether or not the success of the southern and eastern smiths was the reason for even more extensive contact between other regions of Britain and the Continent, the later stages of the bronze age show the importance of the 'Atlantic' industries of the west European seaboard. There are indications of the late survival of middle bronze age metalworking traditions in the early stages of the late bronze age 'Wilburton' complex of south-east England (fig. 6.27), with its standard use of lead-bronze alloying (Burgess 1968c: 9) – anticipated in middle bronze age Wales. New peg-

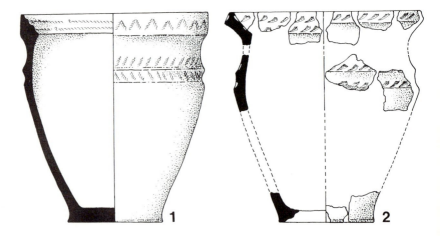

Fig. 6.8   Earl's Farm Down, Amesbury, Wilts.: pottery from successive stages of the use of a round barrow. 1–2, 4 food vessels; 3 miniature ? bucket urn; 5–6, 8 collared urns; 7 globular urn (after Christie 1967).

hole spears, however, appear with socketed axes and leaf swords, as do occasional middle bronze age types such as palstaves in founders' hoards of the Carp's Tongue complex – for instance, the rough-cast example from Shoebury, Essex (Rowlands 1976b: App.J). Indeed, it is more than likely that no strict periodicization so far developed can adequately reflect the complex interrelations and chronological overlapping of the industries of the later bronze age.[12]

In sum, as far as the ornament horizon is concerned, the researches of both Rowlands and J. J. Taylor (1970a; cf. p. 255 above) seem to indicate a continuation from early bronze age times of a connection between northern France and southern Britain. As for gold work, ultimately both Scandinavia and northern France were influenced by technological developments in central Europe but there seems little to support earlier arguments for a direct connection between Scandinavia and the British Isles. If France introduced to Britain the technique of bar-twisted ornaments and composite tools, Britain exported axes, ribbon torcs and perhaps sheet metal.

The Deverel-Rimbury complex and the evidence for settlements and burials in the later bronze age of southern Britain

Having reviewed some aspects of the metal typology of the later bronze age it is necessary now to examine the evidence for other aspects of the material remains of the period.

Like many archaeological cultural terms, 'Deverel-Rimbury' is a handily vague label in need of and gradually receiving closer definition in terms of local regional boundaries. It is doubtful if the use of the word 'culture' – with all its implications of a totality of material features stemming from

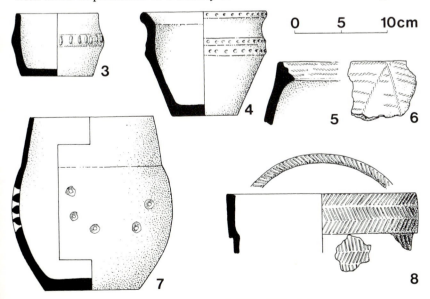

human activity – can now in fact correctly be ascribed to the southern British Deverel-Rimbury group (Barrett 1976; Rowlands 1976b: 215–18). The term 'complex' has been preferred by Barrett to describe the three particular elements which have been isolated: pottery styles, cremation cemeteries – sometimes as secondary insertions in earlier barrows (cf. fig. 6.8; Christie 1967) – and settlements associated with field (and other enclosure) boundaries. Abercromby's original 1912 definition of Deverel-Rimbury urns as an intrusive element from the continental late bronze age Urnfield culture was in the first instance superseded by the realization that some at least of the pottery forms could best be related to the insular development of early bronze age cinerary urns, particularly the Wessex biconical and bucket urns with ultimately neolithic-inspired applied cordons, and that the complex in general could be firmly placed in a middle bronze age context (Smith M. A. 1959: 155–9; Smith I. F. 1961; cf. also Piggott S. 1973: 382–403). The Wessex forms have been considered to have a parallel development in the pre-Urnfield Hilversum and later Drakenstein urns of the southern Low Countries (fig. 6.7) – even if recently some doubts have been raised as to whether the latter necessarily resulted from direct British influences or indeed settlement in the latter part of the Wessex culture.

The firm placing of 'classic' bucket, barrel and globular Deverel-Rimbury urns c. 1,200–1,000 BC resulted from M. A. Smith's identification in 1959 of the continental sources of the southern ornament horizon (fig. 6.9). Deverel-Rimbury associations with such metalwork are few but significant, and include settlement sites as well as burials (see p. 272 below). Recently there has been an attempt to isolate Deverel-Rimbury features in the pottery of definitely late bronze age sites such as Eldon's Seat, Dorset, where shouldered vessels indicate the shape of iron age things to come (Cunliffe and Phillipson 1968; Cunliffe 1974: 24f.). Radiocarbon dates from a Dorset cemetery complex at Simons Ground centre on 600 bc, which certainly suggests survival of some elements of the complex beyond a probable termination of its main features c. 1,000 bc. In contrast, not only biconical urns but late neolithic grooved ware has been seen as having a part to play in the origins of Deverel-Rimbury ceramics; there is even some dating evidence which places barrel urns in an early bronze age context (Barrett 1976: 291f.; Burgess 1974: 216). The globular urns with their more coastal distribution and virtual absence from the extreme south-east have decoration which has been claimed to be connected with south-western Trevisker styles (cf. Rahtz and ApSimon 1962: 319–21) (fig. 6.16). Parallels have also been sought in southern Germany and the western Alpine region as well as southern France. In the now generally agreed continental, and particularly northern French, origin of palstaves, arm rings and pin types in southern England, support can be seen for a return to an earlier view of a continental origin for some elements of Deverel-Rimbury pottery too (fig. 6.9), particularly globular urns but also the barrel urns of Cranborne Chase. Rowlands (1976b: 216–218) suggests coastal settlement in Sussex and Kent with more extensive inland intrusions in Dorset, Hampshire and Wiltshire – the last-named being an area of mixed pottery traditions *par excellence*. Bradley suggests that many of the local variations in Deverel-Rimbury material culture may reflect the existence of single social units (Bradley and Ellison 1975: 112). Contrary to Rowlands' view, however, north French metalwork tends to be concentrated outside the south Dorset area – but there are some indications of early central Urnfields metalwork reaching Britain (see p. 257).

The main areas of the culture were originally considered to be between Bournemouth and Cranborne Chase, with a second area in Dorset south and west of the river Stour and north into Wiltshire. There are, however, important settlements in Sussex (Drewett 1978) with secondary areas running up into Gloucestershire and the Lincolnshire Wolds. Other significant regional groupings have been identified in the Thames Valley, East Anglia and the Midlands (Burgess 1974: 214–15; Barrett 1976). Indeed, evidence for extensive field systems and related farmsteads of bronze age date now extends from Dartmoor to northern Yorkshire.

Excavations at Ardleigh in Essex (cf. Erith and Longworth 1960; Couchman 1975) (fig. 6.9:1) indicate that the pottery shares elements with, and may be derived from, that of south Hampshire while the pottery of the Lower Thames region (Barrett 1973) includes biconical, bucket and some globular forms none of which seem to survive beyond the middle bronze age. The extreme south-west of England has a rather different character but points of contact may again be demonstrated. With regard to the wider aspects of Deverel-Rimbury settlement patterns, the decline of exploitation of the chalk downland in the later neolithic and earlier bronze age is counter-balanced by settlement and exploitation of a wider range of environments; the siting of enclosed settlements such as Rams Hill, Berkshire, on the edge of the chalk (fig. 6.12) may be explained by this extension of land use operating contemporaneously with the main period of the Deverel-Rimbury complex (Bradley and Ellison 1975: esp. 190ff.). Downland valleys, rivers and coastal plains are all areas marked by a concentration of Deverel-Rimbury material.

Apart from the evidence for settlements and their related field systems and enclosures, the main feature which has been used in establishing the regional groups is pottery (Calkin 1962; Rahtz and ApSimon 1962). Thus as far as globular urns in Wessex are concerned the decoration of the early bronze age 'accessory cups' may be significant but the pottery traditions of the south-west also have a part to play. In this context the site of Shearplace Hill in Dorset is an important link between the two regions of the south-west and the south and central area, the more particularly since it appears that Deverel-Rimbury pottery was associated with collared and possibly biconical urn forms (Rahtz and ApSimon 1962: 309f.).

The first of the Deverel-Rimbury settlements to be examined were those of South Lodge, Dorset, with its scanty but important metalwork (fig. 6.25:14) and Marton Down within Cranborne Chase, excavated by Pitt-Rivers (1898) – the former with its attendant barrow cemetery and field system currently being the subject of extensive re-investigation. Like other sites in Wiltshire such as Ogbourne Down and Boscombe Down these are

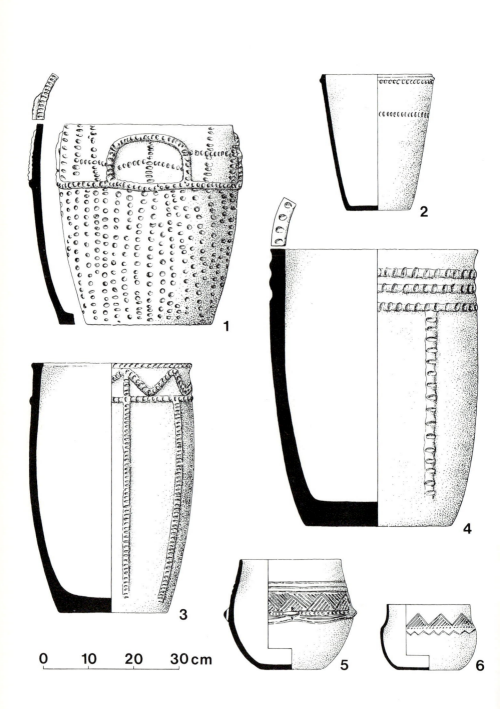

Fig. 6.9   Deverel-Rimbury pottery. 1 Ardleigh, Essex: bucket urn;
2 Bournemouth, Dorset: bucket urn; 3 Bower Chalke, Wilts.: barrel urn;
4 Amesbury, Wilts.: barrel urn; 5–6 Thorny Down, Wilts.: globular urns (after
Erith and Longworth 1960, Calkin 1962 and Piggott S. 1973).

rectilinear enclosures with internal banks and ditches. The ditches have either narrow square bottoms or deep V-shaped profiles – the latter perhaps no more than the silted version of the former – and may have been cut for the placing of post or brushwood fences. The earlier accounts of these enclosures (which measure up to half a hectare in area) record no signs of internal structures, but this must simply reflect the limited nature of the actual excavations. One of the other ten sites excavated within Wiltshire (probably only a mere fraction of the original total), that at Boscome Down East (Stone 1936), is close by a running linear earthwork of a type usually considered as demarcating ranch boundaries for a predominantly stock-raising community. Indeed, since the time of Pitt-Rivers these rectilinear enclosures themselves have been considered as cattle pounds and the general use of the ditches and banks explained in terms of the need to keep animals in – or out – rather than for any more warlike purposes.[13]

Other sites give unambiguous evidence of occupation. At Thorny Down, Wiltshire (Stone 1941), only one side is protected by a ditch, the other three having retaining banks. Complete stripping of the interior area revealed nearly 300 post- and stake-holes interpreted as marking the plans of at least nine circular huts with saddle-querns, related cooking places and other structures.[14] The mass of burnt flint had a probable source in the nearby Easton Down flint mines, whose continuous use from their beaker origins is suggested by the discovery in the immediate surroundings of a middle bronze age urnfield and Deverel-Rimbury pottery (Stone 1933a, b). These burnt flints at Easton Down, so-called 'pot-boilers', may have been used in corn-parching or in the cooking of meat suspended in skins, a feature which has been deduced on the basis of Irish experiments (O'Kelly M.J. 1954; Hodges 1955). In addition to the classic Deverel-Rimbury pottery forms, Thorny Down, South Lodge and a third Wessex site at New Barn Down in Sussex with extensive field system (Curwen 1934b) include finds of small socket-looped spears, the form characteristic of the early stages of native post-Wessex culture metallurgy.

A degree of metalworking must be associated with settlements at Thorny Down and several other sites. These have produced oval razors with marked midribs, a developed form of the simple tanged class I razors (an earlier bronze age type) occasionally found with Wessex biconical urns (Butler and Smith 1956; Butler 1963: 115f.; Coles 1963–4: 120f.) (fig. 6.7: 1),[15] and, once more at Thorny Down, fragmentary cast and ribbed bracelets; here again is evidence for the continental-based 'ornament horizon'. At South Lodge both Class I and II razors are associated with barrel urn sherds, the former from the primary silt of the settlement ditch. A number of ornament horizon hoards have been found in the close vicinity of Wessex/Deverel-Rimbury settlements. At Ebbesbourne Wake on Elcombe Down, Wiltshire, a hoard was found including no less than 16 bracelets linked together with a spiral twisted bronze torc (Piggott S. 1973: 391–2; Rowlands 1976b: 217, 271-2), in the plough soil of an ancient field. In the south-west, buried in a field bank at Towednack, north

Cornwall, was the contents of a goldsmith's workshop, including both finished and unfinished objects. Two twisted torcs with expanded terminals, the so-called 'Tara' form (fig. 6.4:5), one made of several individually twisted strands and several faceted but otherwise unworked curved bars (the first stage in the manufacture of such torc forms), point to this assemblage being that of an itinerant Irish smith perhaps exploiting the south-western trade in return for local tin (Hawkes 1932; Eogan 1967: 144–5).

The unenclosed Chalton, Hampshire, settlement (Cunliffe 1970), dated to 1,243 ± 69 bc, consists of a large circular hut and two smaller huts. There were two pits or possible working areas, as found at Thorny Down, and a number of storage areas. On the floor within the large hut, in addition to a Group III palstave, were an awl or tracer tool and a knife. Also found was a continental Late Urnfield ribbed boss (Rowlands 1976b: 160) which certainly seems too early for the radiocarbon date. Indeed, it might be considered as further evidence for a late extension of middle bronze age traditions.

Of the smaller-scale ditched settlements, that excavated at Shearplace, Dorset (Rahtz and ApSimon 1962), is important because the two circular huts with double rings of posts as at Thorny Down (a form which, however one interprets the roofing, can be seen continuing through to the iron age: fig. 6.14:1; Avery and Close-Brooks 1969) are associated with a radiocarbon date of 1,180 ± 180 bc based on a sample which combines charcoal from the first two phases of the site's occupation. A curious find from Shearplace Hill is a toothed and perforated bone comb, a form associated with weaving and usually considered as a type-fossil of the early iron age;[16] indeed the dating of this settlement seems open to some doubt. The radiocarbon estimation, however, compares with a number of other settlement sites including Chalton.

Much larger sites are known in the south of England than those so far described, particularly in the area of the Sussex Downs where there is a group of nucleated or village-like settlements. Recent work in East Sussex (Drewett 1978) has produced further evidence of farmstead settlements in the neighbourhood of round barrow groups, notably at Black Patch, Alciston, where a group of five round houses has been excavated with attendant storage pits containing a considerable quantity of emmer wheat (*Triticum dicoccum*) and hulled barley (*Hordeum vulgare*). Cattle and sheep were kept and deer hunted for venison. Evidence for spinning comes from clay loom weights found inside one of the huts; more remarkable was the find of a number of bronzes including spiral rings, a razor, daggers, knives and an awl.

One of two sites excavated before the Second World War on Plumpton Plain on the top of the Sussex Downs (Curwen and Holleyman 1935; Hawkes 1935), site A, is a very similar farmstead to Itford Hill – to be described below – with circular houses, compounds and droveways. The site, which also included some metalwork in an otherwise scanty distribution of pottery and domestic rubbish, may be indicative of brief seasonal occupation. There was, however, a range of stone artifacts reminiscent of much earlier traditions – a feature also evident on other Sussex sites. Each enclosure at Plumpton Plain contained at least one circular hut of about 7–8m in diameter, linked to a number of compounds by a sunken trackway 200m long.

The Plumpton Plain banked field systems, like those extending over a considerable area on a number of other sites, belong to the class once thought characteristically iron age and so christened 'Celtic' fields (fig. 6.10). These fields are marked by a number of gentle banks on the downhill of the slope, running parallel to the contours. These 'lynchets' should not be confused with intentional terrace cultivation, but are the product of continuous ploughing leading to soil creep, added to in the process of clearing the arable area of rubble – a very necessary task in view of the simple wooden ard-plough which on Scandinavian parallels we must assume to be all that was available to bronze age farming communities (Glob 1951).[17]

Careful excavation of both the settlement and neighbouring cemetery on Itford Hill, Beddington, Sussex, has revealed a full picture of the occupation of such a site (Burstow and Holleyman 1957; Holden 1972) (fig. 6.11:1). At Itford Hill, dated to $1,000 \pm 35$ bc on the basis of carbonized barley, there were some eight enclosures within a generally rectangular area leading down to the fields where crops were grown and cattle and sheep tended. The Itford settlement seems to have been occupied by about 20 to 30 people, perhaps an extended family group, who dwelt on the site for probably not much more than a generation, to judge from the general lack of signs of rebuilding. The main farmstead comprised not only living quarters but a weaving shed and associated storage areas. One hut which did show signs of rebuilding had in its second phase a 1m-square setting for a primitive upright loom; several baked clay loom weights were found trodden into the floor.

In the rebuilding of this hut two storage pits were included, from one of which some four kilos of carbonized unthreshed barley (*Hordeum tetrastichum* and *Hordeum hexastichum*) were recovered. However, only five grains of emmer wheat were found amongst the barley, though there were present no less than 14 different species of weeds associated with cultivation. It should be noted, however, that a recent re-examination of the all-too-scanty evidence for cereal species identification in prehistoric Britain (Dennell 1976) suggests that, contrary to the pioneering studies of Helbaek (1952), there is no good evidence for a change in popularity from wheat to barley in the later prehistoric periods. Evidence for the growing of broad and club wheat (*Triticum aestivocompactum*) as well as barley comes from the middle bronze age settlement at Abingdon, Berkshire, in the upper Thames Valley (Jones M. 1978). Also in the Itford Hill huts were fragments of stone querns made from greenstone from the South Down greensand ridge. The somewhat earlier Chalton, Hampshire, site (Cunliffe 1970) also gives evidence for cereal cultivation: it has a large storage pit with sufficient grain for no less than 15 people for at least a year.

Although within the Itford Hill settlement, sherds from nearly 100

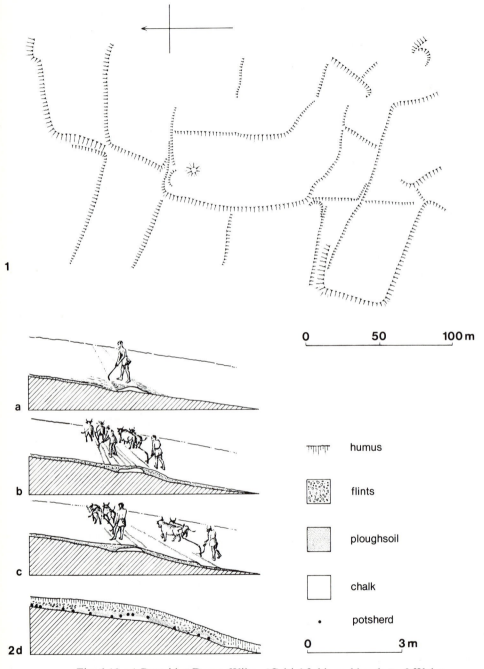

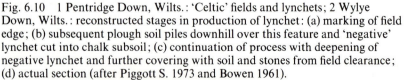

Fig. 6.10   1 Pentridge Down, Wilts.: 'Celtic' fields and lynchets; 2 Wylye Down, Wilts.: reconstructed stages in production of lynchet: (a) marking of field edge; (b) subsequent plough soil piles downhill over this feature and 'negative' lynchet cut into chalk subsoil; (c) continuation of process with deepening of negative lynchet and further covering with soil and stones from field clearance; (d) actual section (after Piggott S. 1973 and Bowen 1961).

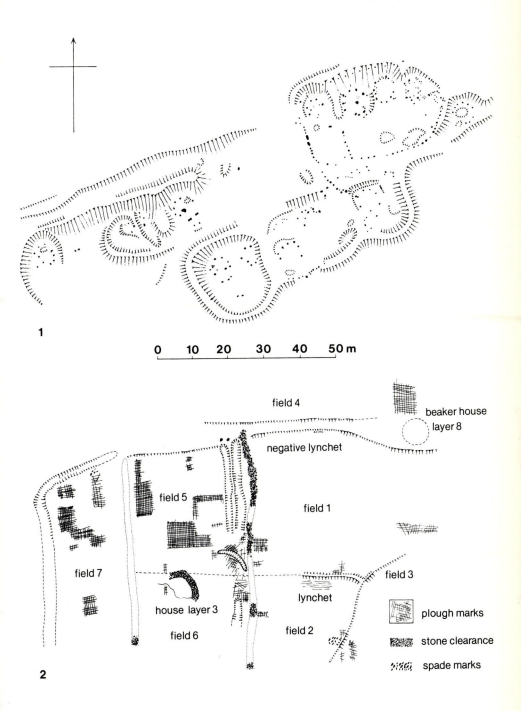

1

0   10   20   30   40   50 m

field 4

beaker house
layer 8

negative lynchet

field 5

field 1

field 7

lynchet

field 3

house layer 3

field 6

field 2

plough marks

stone clearance

spade marks

2

Fig. 6.11   Middle bronze age settlements in southern England. 1 Itford Hill, Sussex; 2 Gwithian, Cornwall (after Burstow and Holleyman 1957 and Megaw 1976a).

different vessels related mainly to the bucket and barrel forms were recovered, the absence of the matching pieces suggests that some at least of the pottery must have been carried outside the habitation areas, perhaps accidentally in the course of mucking out and manuring the fields; this theory is supported by evidence from the contemporary north Cornish farming hamlet at Gwithian (Megaw, Thomas and Wailes 1960–1; Megaw 1976a). The animals represented at Itford Hill seem to be more or less equal numbers of sheep and oxen. The latter are the small breed known as *Bos longifrons*, first identifiable in beaker contexts and probably introduced from the Continent at that time, and considered likely to be the ancestor of modern milk cattle. This species is distinct from the larger, earlier neolithic type, *Bos primigenius*, which is considered to be ancestral to the larger modern meat cattle. Few wild animals have been recovered on sites such as Itford Hill although red deer is not unknown. The presence of horse bones does not necessarily mean that we are dealing with the horse even as a traction animal (see further below). In fact oxen seem to be the predominant species; and on the basis of currently available evidence this is certainly the case at other 'Deverel-Rimbury' sites such as South Lodge (cf. Piggott S. 1973: 400ff.). At Harrow Hill, Sussex, beside an area of flint mining exploited from the neolithic through the bronze age, is a square-ditched enclosure with a palisade set into a shallow bank; although not certain, a later bronze age date is not unlikely. Within a comparatively limited area of this enclosure some 100 cattle skulls were found (Holleyman 1937). Following the analogy of butchering practices evidenced from earlier prehistoric sites in Western Asia, one explanation may be variable dispersal of the carcase in the course of slaughtering for meat (cf. Perkins and Daly 1968).

In Wiltshire an economy comparable to that on the South Downs can be observed. Actual grain, as well as grain impressions – both hulled and naked barley – on characteristic Deverel-Rimbury pottery, add to the general evidence of saddle querns at South Lodge and Thorny Down. Sheep, goat and pig are the main domesticated species and cattle of the *Bos longifrons* type again predominate. The seeming decrease in pig may be associated with the reduction in forest cover and consequent lack of suitable foraging, while the presence of horse-bones, though suggestive of domestication, may rather indicate the use of the horse for meat and perhaps even for milking purposes. Only from such north-eastern sites as the eighth-century BC Heathery Burn, Co. Durham, cave can one be more certain of evidence for horse domestication (Greenwell 1894; Britton 1971) (fig. 6.34) – though domestication does not necessarily mean riding (cf. Powell 1971). Sheep, on the other hand, though obviously an important food source, were also being bred for wool, to judge from the occasional artifactual evidence of loom weights if not the bone 'weaving comb' from Shearplace Hill.

Mention has been made of the archaic aspect of the stone industries of Sussex sites; in Wiltshire flint certainly continues to play an important part and the forms represented are related to types found elsewhere with the earlier biconical urns. Despite the not infrequent evidence for a prosperous metal industry there is little or no sign of actual smithing sites.

The recently published further investigations on Rams Hill, Berkshire, follow those originally carried out by the Piggotts (Piggott and Piggott 1940; Piggott C. M. 1942); they are on a site not far from the Uffington iron age hillfort and have revealed a pre-iron age sequence of defences commencing with a stone-faced rampart, followed by timber revetting and palisade with timber inturned entrance (Bradley and Ellison 1975) (fig. 6.12). Although the pottery shows little or no resemblance to classic Deverel-Rimbury forms, plain jars may be compared with those at the cemetery attached to the settlement on Itford Hill, Sussex, where the style can be seen to be a late regional variant of the Sussex Deverel-Rimbury group dated at the site to $1,000 \pm 35$ bc (Holden 1972). Rams Hill has a wide range of fabrics comparable also with the north-eastern settlement of Staple Howe, Yorkshire (Brewster 1963), and suggests external contacts or intermittent local assemblies.

At the bottom of the inner ditch was a sherd of a Wessex biconical urn,

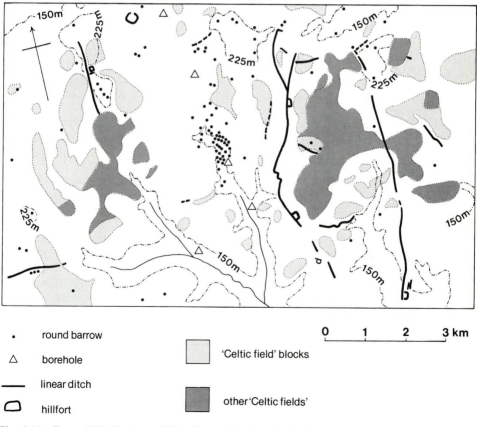

•	round barrow		☐	'Celtic field' blocks
△	borehole			
—	linear ditch		▨	other 'Celtic fields'
◻	hillfort			

0   1   2   3 km

Fig. 6.12   Rams Hill, Berks.: middle phase of land-use (after Bradley and Ellison 1975).

while an early bronze age collared urn was also found in a primary position. Nearby are the 26 Lambourn barrows, one of the best preserved of such groups, which range in date from a neolithic earthen long barrow through to the extensive re-use of a bowl barrow as a later bronze age cremation cemetery.

Radiocarbon dates for the palisade phase range from $1,050 \pm 70$ bc to 740 ± 70 bc while a comparable date of $1,060 \pm 70$ bc was obtained from one of the rebuilding phases of the southernmost of the two entrances to the site. At this latter entrance the remains of dog, sheep or goat, and piglet seem to indicate foundation burials rather than just ordinary domestic refuse. Internally there are signs of a track and shallow pits as well as huts.

Occupation of the Rams Hill enclosure thus seems to have been intermittent – perhaps seasonal on the pattern suggested for neolithic causewayed camps – and the economy largely pastoral with cattle predominating. The site may have controlled the division of pasture in open grassland marked by linear ditch systems cut across by the later iron age fortifications. The main significance of the Rams Hill enclosure is perhaps the evidence it adds to the longevity of insular traditions in timber defensive works.

In this context, and recalling the probability that many sites continued in occupation virtually without interruption into the iron age, attention should be drawn to a South Downs group of linear earthworks, cross-ridge and spur dykes similar to the 'sunken ways' of Itford Hill, as well as to a group of rectangular enclosures mostly on the hilltops which, though probably in many cases of iron age date, suggest continuity back to a much earlier period. This suggestion of the earlier date for the origins of small farmstead enclosures is supported by the association of biconical urns at Shearplace Hill and the presence of early bronze age or even beaker pottery on certain Sussex sites (cf. Holden 1972). To the west we should recall the extensive Wiltshire ditch systems which appear to link the Snail Down early bronze age barrow cemetery with the prominent hillfort of Sidbury Hill. Here a V-bottom ditch with a bank facing towards the cemetery appears to protect the latter from the agricultural activities marked by an extensive 'Celtic' field system. The ditch may be observed to make a bend deliberately to avoid one of the earlier barrows and, if not securely dated, has been shown by excavation to stop short of the iron age hillfort's defences (Thomas and Thomas 1955: 141–2; Annable 1958). As with the extensive linear earthworks system around the iron age fort of Quarley Hill in Hampshire, which again can be shown to be pre-hillfort in its construction, there is much to be said for the theory first propounded by Hawkes (1939a) that these systems are related to later bronze age cattle-ranching activities in the same way as more recent field surveys in the Lambourn Valley suggest the laying out of parallel strips linking water meadows with hill pasture, a land use pattern which in Wessex continued into medieval times (Bradley 1971a; Bradley and Ellison 1975: 171ff.).

At Ivinghoe Beacon, Buckinghamshire, which has a cross-timber reinforced rampart, a group of bronzes possibly associated with some of the circular huts on the site belongs to the late bronze age local 'Bexley Heath' or 'Carp's Tongue' complex of about the eighth century bc (Cotton and Frere 1968; qv. also p. 364). Despite the lack of definite association of such bronzes in a primary context in these early defended sites, it is clear that the distinction culturally between late bronze age and iron age is becoming more and more blurred as a useful cultural marker, while recent and as yet unpublished evidence from the Thames Valley indicates the association of 'Ewart Park' bronzes with a range of local and clearly domestic pottery.

There is of course evidence for smaller-scale individual settlements. At Eldon's Seat on the south Dorset coast a site associated in iron age times with the Kimmeridge shale industry was first occupied in the seventh or sixth century BC by people using pottery of barrel-like forms (Cunliffe and Phillipson 1968). This community of mixed farmers – as is indicated by saddle-querns and the remains of cattle, sheep or goats and pig, as well as evidence for the collecting of limpets from the shore – is to be contrasted with the more complex economic pattern of centralized communities represented most significantly by the earlier middle bronze age occupants of the defended enclosure of Rams Hill.

While considering early hilltop settlements with evidence for timber reinforced ramparts, Crickley Hill near Gloucester must be mentioned, a site to be discussed further in the next chapter (qv. 364; Dixon 1973; 1976; n.d.; Dixon and Borne 1977). The long-house phase – associated with timber interlace – precedes the introduction of round house plans, and radiocarbon dates indicate construction around 500 bc; there is as yet however no associated dateable metalwork. In the south of England there are then several settlement sites to which the term 'later prehistoric' would seem applicable, eschewing the old Three Ages terminology entirely. Three further sites may be mentioned in this context.

Lower down the slope from the Deverel-Rimbury settlement, Site B at Plumpton Plain was demarcated by a single stretch of bank with further round houses and storage pits containing much pottery, including urn forms with hatched triangle decoration which Hawkes claimed as French imports of the Urnfield period (Hawkes 1935: 57), a bronze socketed knife and a winged flanged axe (Curwen and Holleyman 1935). These last two should be referred to a developed stage of later bronze age metallurgy already briefly mentioned, the so-called 'Carp's Tongue complex' of Atlantic affiliations (cf. Savory 1948; Burgess 1968c: 17ff.) (figs. 6.23, 6.31–2). Iron traces on a series of whetstones from Site B may be due to natural staining (O'Connor 1975b), though, as will be noted further, there are indications that the use of iron in Britain may well have preceded the end of what is still formally considered as the late bronze age. At Weston Wood, Surrey (Harding J. M. 1964), a group of circular houses and their related field system with evidence of cross-ploughing is dated to 510 ± 110 bc. A punch, a metal rod of leaded bronze and a number of copper droplets are indications of on-site metalworking; Cunliffe (1974: 34) regards the pottery as marking a stage after the 'ultimate Deverel-Rimbury stage' of Eldon's Seat.

A settlement discovered following a storm in 1938 off the coast of Minnis Bay, Birchington, Kent, is an even more problematic site (Worsfold 1943; Jessup 1970: 130ff.). Though it was claimed as a pile dwelling, a recent reconsideration of the site (Champion T. C. 1977) indicates that all of the timber work and supposed gravel bank is post-prehistoric. There is, however, evidence of a late bronze age farmstead eroded to below sea-level some time after abandonment. Pottery – carinated bowls and jars with finger-tip decoration – and rush-lined storage pits cut into the chalk, with botanical evidence for crop-husbandry, seem contemporary with deposition of a hoard of some 73 bronzes and founders' waste. Sword fragments, ornaments, spear-heads, socketed and winged axes and tools and a cauldron handle fragment all are representative of the Carp's Tongue complex. One may still compare Minnis Bay and the riverside settlement at Old England, Brentford, Middlesex (Wheeler 1929) – also with Carp's Tongue material and a decorated Urnfield razor (Piggott C. M. 1946: fig. 9) – as possible trading centres.

One unique Wiltshire site which introduces the subject of ritual and burial in the earlier stages of the later bronze age of southern England is the Wilsford shaft (Ashbee 1966b; Piggott S. 1975: 345–6). The shaft lies to the south of Stonehenge, itself a ritual site which on radiocarbon evidence must have been in use at the same time as the Deverel-Rimbury farmsteads, in view of the date for phase III bc of $1,240 \pm 105$ bc (Atkinson 1967). In the excavation of the Wilsford shaft, at first thought to be a Wessex culture pond barrow, a pit measuring at least 33m in depth and 2m in diameter was discovered cut into the solid chalk. The sides of this shaft were carefully trimmed, apparently with metal axe blades, and the water-logged nature of nearly half the shaft had allowed the preservation of cereals, straw and pollen as well as wooden stave-built tubs and an apparently lathe-turned bowl – the earliest evidence for the use of the lathe in British prehistory. These wooden finds are dated to $1,380 \pm 90$ bc (Ashbee 1966b) and although, particularly after correction, this seems an early date for Deverel-Rimbury associations, the presence deep in the shaft of unweathered barrel and globular urn fragments seems to confirm its use in this period (cf. Barrett 1976: 291–2). The 'ritual' nature of the shaft, rather than its interpretation simply as a well, rests on evidence for deep pits of later iron age date (q.v. p. 406 below). Similar shafts are known from both Britain and the Continent though for the period under review only a much shallower shaft 8m deep at Swanwick, Hampshire, can be cited. The upper levels of this Swanwick shaft contained loom weights of Deverel-Rimbury form while at the bottom was an upright post with traces of blood or flesh (Fox C. F. 1928; Piggott S. 1963b).

It has already been observed that the burial rite of the Deverel-Rimbury culture and related groups is mainly inurned cremation either as secondary burials in earlier constructed barrows or in flat cemeteries. At Latch Farm near Christchurch, Hampshire, a barrow with a central cinerary urn burial was surrounded by some 90 later cremations (Piggott C. M. 1938). These ranged from up-ended Deverel-Rimbury vessels in shallow pits, to upright urns covered with slabs, unassociated cremations, and those contained within larger vessels but with smaller accessory vessels, perhaps filled originally with offerings for the dead. At Ardleigh in Essex a regional variation of barrel urn with applied decoration (fig. 6.9:1) is found in a series of some 100 burials which were set out in a linear arrangement, but there is also a series of associated ring ditch burials (Erith and Longworth 1960; Couchman 1975); other large-scale flat cemeteries occur in Hampshire. In the west Midlands inurned cremations have also been discovered, that at Ryton-on-Dunsmore, Worcestershire, being dated to 850–750 bc (Burgess 1974: 214–15).

Although some 12 per cent of excavated barrows in Wiltshire are associated with primary Deverel-Rimbury burials, the mounds being somewhat lower in profile than those of the earlier period, it is a curious distributional fact that in northern Wessex we find stock enclosures as we have described and no cremation graves, while in the south the reverse is true; this may, however, be no more than the accident of intensive agriculture in the latter area in the course of recent times, destroying evidence of prehistoric cemeteries.

The development in certain areas of Deverel-Rimbury cemeteries alongside important Wessex barrow cemeteries – for example, the 100 graves of Rimbury itself – even suggests to Barrett (1976: 298) that the early stages of the flat cemeteries with their general lack of associated grave goods (only nine with metal objects out of several thousand known: Burgess 1976a) may include sufficient early bronze age burials to explain the gap between definitely dated graves and the population estimates arrived at by Atkinson (1972).[18] There is, however, a curious lack of correlation between various forms of cremation sites and the settlements of central Wessex which suggests something more than chance. There is, for example, an absence of settlements and burials of the later bronze age in the area of Stonehenge which might suggest a population shift; though there is some slight evidence – including, as noted above, radiocarbon dates from Stonehenge itself – to suggest a continuity from Wessex culture times on the Plain.

Indeed, as with pottery traditions, continuity rather than external introduction is likely to explain the cremation rite of the later bronze age. The concept of the cremation cemetery existing side by side with barrow construction, at least in northern Britain, extends back into later neolithic times and the re-adoption of the rite in the early bronze age of southern England continues beyond the gradual decline of the use of the barrow.

It is also noticeable that in contrast to earlier practices, there is no distinction between the pottery of settlements and burials in the period under review. The penannular ditch around the barrow associated with the Itford Hill settlement (fig. 6. 11:1) had a setting of stakes in it; the central cremation was contained within an urn and a number of other urns and cremations were found around the perimeter of the mound (Holden 1972). The generally worn nature of the barrow pottery and the fact that one sherd of a decorated globular urn matches part of a vessel found in the settlement suggests that far from special funerary ware being produced, the dead had to be content with domestic cast-offs. Another feature of the

Itford Hill barrow is some 40,000 struck flints. There were very few finished artifacts, but with attendant hammer stones and cores, identifiable types within this assemblage appear at first sight to have their closest affinities with late neolithic forms. This should not be regarded as a chronological indicator since, for example, at Martin Down in Cranborne Chase (Pitt-Rivers 1898: 188ff.), nearly 2,000 flints were recovered, and a somewhat similar situation seems to have occurred at the cremation cemetery at Kimpton near Andover where flints were used to construct a platform (Dacre 1968). We may recall that from the Itford Hill settlement only flint – and surprisingly little in contrast to that found in the area of the barrow – was recovered. Absence of metal implements does not of course necessarily mean that they are not being used; on the contrary, owing to the obvious value of any metal objects in the course of prehistory it is more than likely that implements would not only be used for as long as possible but 'recycled' either by being melted down and recast on the spot or used as exchange for finished objects. It has been observed that at the somewhat earlier biconical urn site of Mildenhall Fen, Suffolk (Clark J. G. D. 1936), where a large flint industry has survived together with a range of animal bones, no bronze was recovered even though examination of the cuts on the bones show that these could only have been produced by metal artifacts.

Settlements of the later bronze age in the south-west of England

The south-west of England, particularly the high ground of Dartmoor and Exmoor (cf. Fox A. 1973: 100ff.; Cunliffe 1974: 17ff.), is another important area demonstrating varying dependence on both arable and pastoral subsistence economies. A detailed picture is available for the ecological pattern of the high moorland in the later bronze age (Simmons and Proudfoot 1969). Below a region of blanket bog and the limit of the thick forest was a densely settled area of open grassland interspersed with scrub. On valley slopes there is evidence for pastoralists exploiting areas cleared in the neolithic and subsequently prevented from regeneration by continuous grazing and the general effects of leaching. Both mixed economy and, to the east, mainly arable sites can also be found with enclosed and nucleated settlements. The walls of the enclosures or pounds often have a fine facing of granite boulders with a core of smaller material inside, and a range of huts, both circular and sub-rectangular, is sometimes attached directly to the outer wall: these may have been stock pens rather than areas of settlement. The number of huts varies from five to upwards of 20 or 30 and the area enclosed within the pound may be as much as 10–15 hectares. On Dartmoor these pastoral enclosures are concentrated in the south and western valleys on the south-facing slopes in good relation to water supplies. There are three main types of settlement on the moors; walled enclosures associated with circular huts as at Dean Moor in the Avon valley, open groups of houses and those scattered amongst well-defined field boundaries. Although some of the small enclosures appear to have been walled garden plots, as at Rider's Rings on Dartmoor (fig.

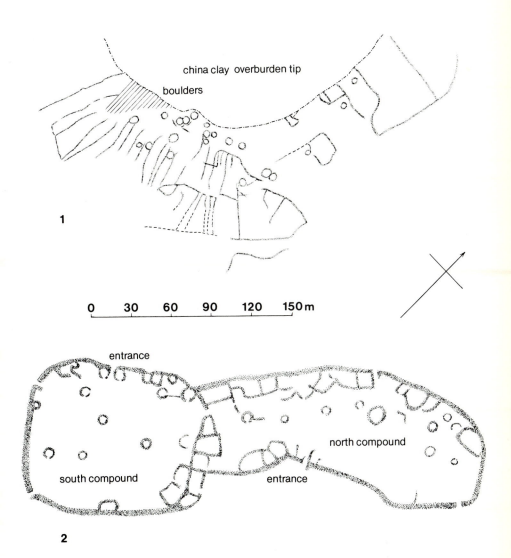

Fig. 6.13 Middle bronze age settlements. 1 Stannon Down, St Breuard, Cornwall: arable fields to south-west, stock enclosures to north-east; 2 Rider's Rings, Dartmoor, Devon: enclosed settlement (after Fox A. 1973 and Mercer 1975).

6.13:2), there is little direct evidence of arable agriculture, despite evidence for saddle querns from Dean Moor. A detailed study of the siting and possible catchment areas of the Dartmoor settlements does suggest, however, the use of an in- and outfield system as practised in recent times in Scotland (Denford 1975).

At Dean Moor the actual form of the huts can be ascertained as the result of excavation (Fox A. 1957) (fig. 6.14:2–3). Conical thatched roofs were supported on a central upright post with an inner ring supporting the weight of the end of the timbers, which were fixed into the low stone footings of the wall; recent full-scale reconstructions of these houses – as well as those further to the west (fig. 6:14:1) – and the fortunate recovery of organic materials have indicated the manner in which the lighter timbers would have been keyed on to the main ones with withies and the whole covered with sods. The interior of the huts at Dean Moor showed that on the lower side of the hut were the kitchen and working areas

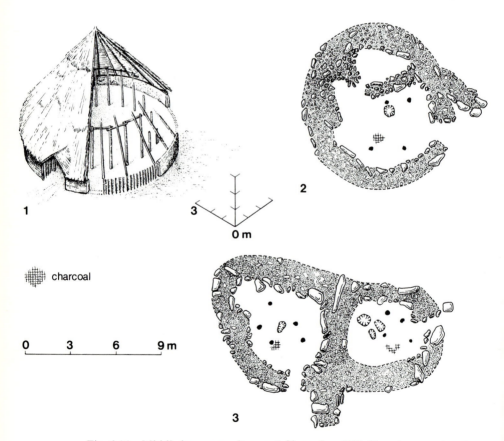

charcoal

0   3   6   9 m

Fig. 6.14   Middle bronze age houses. 1 Shearplace Hill, Dorset: reconstruction of house plan; 2–3 Dean Moor: enclosed settlement (after Avery and Close-Brooks 1969 and Fox A. 1973).

together with the hearth, edged with small stones. The common feature of the enclosed or nucleated settlement, a number of related farmsteads surrounding a central courtyard, was to continue into the subsequent pre-Roman iron age of the south-west. These enclosed sites may possibly be linked with the later bronze age settlements on the western seaboard of Scotland, though the evidence for these is scanty.

Evidence for metalworking is clear, but only from chance deposits of finished and partially finished objects. Although sites on the metalliferous granite of Dartmoor such as Dean Moor were obviously well placed for metalworking, the evidence is at the moment slight. It is possible that the smelting hearths were concentrated largely around the so far undiscovered areas of individual ore mines. A single pebble of cassiterite (tin) and a whetstone come from Hut 7 on Dean Moor and a dump of iron ore which had remained unworked through, presumably, lack of knowledge of smelting and forging processes was found in the core of a wall in Hut 2 on the same site.[19]

Apart from finds such as Dean Moor which, whatever the significance of the broken iron ore, certainly suggest local working, it can be shown from analysis that local metals were in all likelihood being used in the production of typical artifacts of middle bronze age date. The clearest evidence for this is in the form of actual moulds. Mention has already been made of the axe mould from the coastal settlement of Gwithian, Cornwall (p. 257) (fig. 6.2:4), while two sets of twin or bi-valve stone moulds were found at Knighton in alluvial clay in the river gravels of the Teign Valley (Hodges 1960; Rowlands 1976b: 10ff.). These moulds, which had apparently been tied together in pairs, had been carved to take a matrix for casting both rapiers and tapering ribbed strips for making bracelets and rings similar to those in the Edington Burtle, Somerset, ornament horizon hoard (originally contained within a wooden box and previously referred to in connection with its bronze ribbon torc; Rowlands 1976b: 255). The moulds are made of presumably local mica schist.

On the more fertile, better drained, eastern side of Dartmoor we observe larger and more open settlements with associated long fields demarcated by low stone boundaries, and houses which are larger and better constructed than those of the settlements just described (Fox A. 1954). Internal divisions into domestic and working areas can be ascertained. Pottery found on these sites may be matched with that of middle bronze age date as found in the north Cornish settlements of Trevisker and Gwithian (cf. Thomas A.C. 1969: 12–13; and p. 281 below) (fig. 6.11:2). Such western sites are by no means without evidence of continental connections; adjacent to a small farmstead and field system on Horridge Common, Devon, was found a Bohemian palstave of a type contemporary with the so-called ornament horizon (Fox and Britton 1969). Evidence for metalworking does not come only from ores; at Tredarvah near Penzance, as has already been mentioned, a metalworker's hut contained slag and finished bronzes including the large loop-headed quoit pin characteristic of the Somerset ornament horizon hoards, as well as a high flanged palstave, a socketed spear, a tanged knife and pin with side loop and also south-western cord and incised ornament pottery of the Gwithian-Trevisker series (Thomas A.C. 1964; Fox A. 1973: 111ff.; Rowlands 1976b: 8, 276).

The extent of land enclosure prior to climatic and soil deterioration, the gradual abandonment of marginal areas on Dartmoor and a peak in depopulation around 600 BC, are strikingly indicated by the linear stone banks or 'reaves', clearly contemporary with the later bronze age enclosures, which can be seen particularly on the southern edge of Dartmoor (Fleming, Collis and Jones 1973; Fleming 1976; 1978). It seems that, with a more favourable climate in the 2nd millennium BC, land up to c. 450m was densely settled and even utilized for plough, or rather ard, agriculture. These walls, which mostly run along the contours, seem reasonably regarded as marking land use divisions or some form of 'infield' and 'outfield' pattern such as is suggested not only for the Dartmoor settlements but also for the South Downs in the iron age; evidence is increasing for similar land use in a much earlier period. Even if we prefer to see these walls as territorial boundaries delineating separate areas of pasture, the implications for a highly organized form of agriculture are clear (cf. Bradley 1971a; Bradley and Ellison 1975: 199ff.). Unlike the earlier Wessex culture and related groups, we can make few certain pronouncements on the likelihood of a stratified chieftain society based on centralization, control and redistribution of food supplies. One may hazard a guess that the probably mixed rather than predominantly pastoral economy in the south-west would have been likely to have stimulated greater economic efficiency than that postulated for the early bronze age in southern Britain. Equally the evidence may be thought to indicate a rather more loosely knit community of individual clans (cf. Fleming 1971b).

One new piece of evidence which does, however, certainly suggest centralization and local control in part of the south-west, comparable with Wessex sites such as Rams Hill, can be mentioned here. On a low hill at Norton Fitzwarren, just outside Taunton, the site of an iron age hillfort has been shown to overlie an irregular V-cut ditch which runs around the perimeter of the natural hillside. A scatter of characteristic south-western cord-impressed pottery of middle bronze age Gwithian-Trevisker form (fig. 6.16) indicates the early date of this ditch. Associated with another small ditch to the north-west of the site, and contained within a pit, was a hoard of eight decorated ornament horizon cast bronze bracelets with affinities in France (fig. 6.15). The find position of these bracelets – which include the Bignan type – suggests that they had been deposited tied together. They were associated with two native south-western high-flanged palstaves and an early form of socketed bronze axe (Langmaid 1971; 1976: 15).

A different type of settlement can be seen from the examination of two north Cornish coastal settlements. First is Trevisker, St Eval, where the site of a bronze age settlement, occupied subsequently in the iron age after a period of abandonment, lies on the local slate or killas and is dated by radiocarbon to 1,110±95 bc (ApSimon and Greenfield 1972). The site,

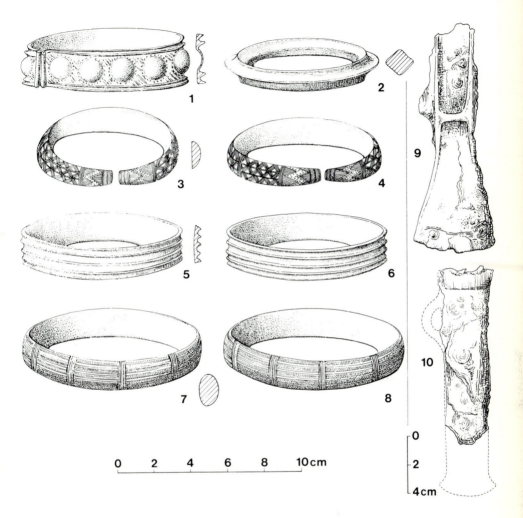

Fig. 6.15   Norton Fitzwarren, Somerset: bronze 'ornament horizon' hoard of bracelets: 1–8 partially restored, 9 palstave and 10 socketed axe (after Langmaid 1971).

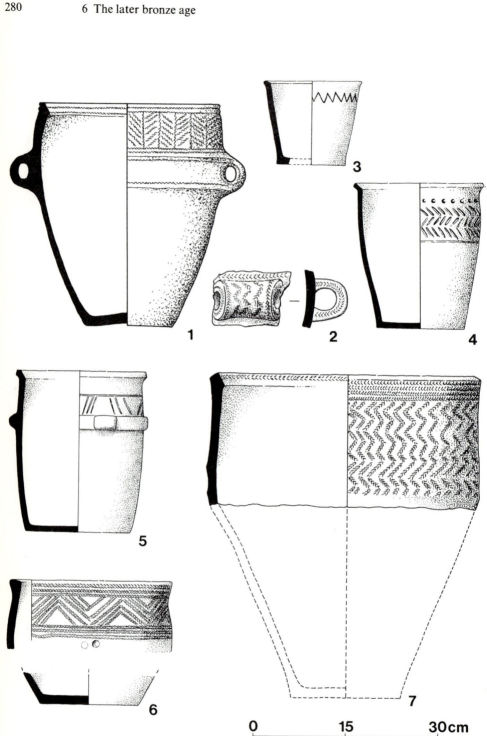

Fig. 6.16   Cornish later bronze age pottery. 1–2, 7 Trevisker Style 1; 6 Style 2; 3–5 Style 4 (1 from Crig-a-mennis, Liskey; 2 Crantock; 3, 4, 6 Trevisker, St Eval; 5 Dartmoor); 7 Hardelot, Pas-de-Calais (after Christie 1960, ApSimon 1957–8, ApSimon and Greenfield 1972 and Mariette 1961).

excavated first in 1956, was that of a small agricultural settlement. It was probably contained within a bank and consisted of at least two circular timber huts about 8m in diameter, one having a floor worn down considerably into the bedrock, perhaps as the result of continuing cleaning or mucking out. The post-hole structures consisted of a double post wall with lintels which probably supported radial rafters and incorporated oak timbers of up to 22cm in diameter; one of the excavated huts had been subsequently rebuilt. The type of timber house represented at Trevisker is similar to that already described at Shearplace Hill and on Dartmoor. Two other structures at Trevisker are less easy to interpret, one possibly being a barn or store whose plan is basically rectangular with no sign of timbered ends, indicating that here the construction may have been of turf. This exceptional plan for later bronze age houses in southern England is not entirely without parallel since somewhat similar plans can be found amongst the few structures which can be associated with a later bronze age date in Ireland at Ballinderry, Co. Offaly (Hencken 1942: 6–29).

Trevisker lies surrounded by various barrow groups and its construction must have been in a period when the area had a light cover of scrub that consisted mainly of rough pasture largely cleared of forest. In addition to evidence for cereal crop growing indicated by rubbing stones and a saddle quern, a hoard of cassiterite pebbles and signs of bronzeworking suggest not only local metalsmithing but actual tin extraction. Trevisker may have been only one of upwards of 50 such settlements with a total population of some 250 linked by, amongst other things, intensive local pottery production exploiting the gabbroic clay of the Lizard peninsula.

The pottery sequence of the bronze age settlement at Trevisker, together with that from Gwithian, establishes a basic system for the later bronze age of the whole of the south-west (fig. 6.16). The decorative style develops from comb ornament to cord impression and then simple incised ornament. At the start of the south-west pottery sequence is the use of often plaited cord impressions particularly on the so-called 'ribbon-handle' urns which seem to have had some influence on the development of the Dorset biconical urns.[20] Vessels related to this general form (but not actually with precisely similar handles) are present in the lower levels – Layer 5 – of bronze age Gwithian and form, a style referred to by Ap Simon as Trevisker Style 1 (fig. 6.16:1–2); these may have horizontal lugs. The use of herringbone and chevron motifs in the impressed decoration of this pottery seems linked to that of the early bronze age collared urn series. Ultimately, as with the collared urns, much of this decoration pattern can be observed amongst beaker pottery motifs and, together with the very nature of the Cornish settlements, argues yet again for a considerable degree of continuity of settlement from the early 2nd millennium BC. Subsequent developments in south-western pottery see the continuation of twisted rather than plaited cord (fig. 6.16:6), but there is a gradual movement towards incised and grooved decoration with occasional finger-tip ornamentation and a cordon applied to the body, which is now as frequently straight as round-sided in profile. These are ApSimon's Trevisker Styles 2 and 3. A final group, Trevisker Style 4, related to pottery from the upper, Layer 3 farmstead at Gwithian shows that cord ornament has died out and the rough zig-zag and chevron designs are now exclusively executed by incision. Square lugs – a feature to be noted on Scillonian pottery – rather than pierced handles, take the place of the earlier more rounded handles (fig. 6.16:3–5). This south-western pottery has, as has been noted, close counterparts amongst the fabrics found in the Dartmoor settlements.

Whatever the ultimate native origins of Trevisker ware and the closely related, if not indeed earlier, Gwithian series, it is clear that there is no need to look for them beyond the British Isles to the central and north European late neolithic corded ware groups (cf. ApSimon 1957–8). On the contrary, not only at the end of the early bronze age does Trevisker Style 1 with its lugged handles and cord decoration have an important part to play in the evolution of Dorset biconical urns (Calkin 1962) – though not the northern biconicals (ApSimon 1972) – but the Shearplace Hill evidence also suggests to ApSimon that Dorset globulars are influenced by the south-western series (Rahtz and ApSimon 1962: 319). The British connections with the Hilversum culture of the Netherlands at the end of the early bronze age and the production of British types by local smiths as suggested by the Voorhout hoard (fig. 6.6) were first indicated by Glasbergen (1954; 1957: 89ff.) and Butler (1963: esp. 211ff.). Although doubt must now be cast on the British manufacture if not inspiration of Voorhout (cf. p. 257), this general view has received considerable support from the discovery of Trevisker Style 1 pottery made of characteristic Cornish gabbroic clay in a settlement at Hardelot in the Pas-de-Calais (Mariette 1961) (fig. 6.16:7); the identification of pottery from Marquise, also in the Pas-de-Calais, as biconical/Hilversum ware (Dunning 1936; Gaucher and Mohen 1974: 42–3) once more suggests contemporary and interconnecting pottery styles on both sides of the Channel[21] (fig. 6.7).

The settlement at Gwithian at the mouth of a river estuary on the north side of St Ives Bay contains evidence also for a small farmstead of middle to late bronze age date (Megaw, Thomas and Wailes 1960–1; Megaw 1976a; Thomas A.C. 1978) (fig. 6.11:2). Two periods of occupation, Layers 3 and 5, are separated by a sterile sand blow. At its greatest extent, about 2ha, the settlement consisted of at least three sub-rectangular houses with stone footings. The Layer 5 homestead, which is associated with some eight fields with lynchets and field banks, remains at present unexcavated. Uphill within a circular ditched enclosure, however, evidence for cross-ploughing or ard cultivation was first noticed in the British Isles (fig. 6.17). This evidence remains the earliest for the south-west (Fowler and Evans 1967; Fowler P.J. 1971; Mercer 1975: 37). A single date from three apparent cremations by the ring ditch in Layer 5 gives a *terminus post quem* for the settlement of $1,120 \pm 130$ bc comparable with Trevisker, St Eval. In turn these two south-western dates match those from the 'Deverel-Rimbury' settlements of Shearplace Hill ($1,180 \pm 180$ bc; Rahtz and ApSimon 1962 – a sample made up from several locations) and Itford Hill ($1,000 \pm 35$ bc; Holden 1972) (fig. 6.11:1). All of these dates, after recalibration, overlap with the conventional chronology for the later

Wessex culture (cf. p. 229). In Layer 3 were found the fragments of three pins, two certainly being early Urnfield imports (Rowlands 1976a; cf. p. 257). The Gwithian fields seem to have been ploughed over several seasons and manuring can be inferred from the abraded sherds – some with impressions of barley – and domestic rubbish found in the plough soil. The awkward uphill angles, the 'headlands', where the simple ard (tipped with stone as indicated by a broken Group XII greenstone fragment in one of the furrows) could not easily be turned, were dug by hand and impressions of a heart-shaped spade similar to the modern Cornish shovel have been found (Thomas A.C. 1970); as well as true lynchets there are linear closure banks and a stone terrace. Grinding querns indicate cereal cropping, and apart from cattle, sheep and pigs, and possibly horse, the marine

Fig. 6.17 Gwithian, Cornwall: middle bronze age cross-ploughing marks at base of Layer 5 plough soil; scale in inches and feet (photograph J. V. S. Megaw).

environment continued to be exploited as it had been in the area from later mesolithic times. As elsewhere in the south-west the associated stone industry shows little change from that of the late neolithic.

The pottery from Gwithian Layer 5 includes both cord-impressed and incised ware and is comparable with elements of Trevisker styles 1–2 (fig. 6.16:1–2, 6). Twisted and plaited cord first appears at Gwithian, however, in a context which is contemporary with and immediately post-beaker (cf. p. 194 above). In Layer 3, decoration is only incised and is to be compared in turn with ApSimon's Trevisker Style 4 (fig. 6.16:3–5), although as with more easterly sites there appear to be localized differences in these domestic wares. Certain features – such as occasional trumpet lugs – indicate that indigenous neolithic as well as early bronze age traits must influence the later ceramic history of the south-west. In this connection one should note the bone comb from Gwithian Layer 5, very similar to those assumed to have been used for decorating beaker pottery.

The presence at Gwithian and Trevisker of houses of basically rectangular rather than round plan indicates that the contrast between the preference on the Continent throughout prehistory for rectangular house plans, and the British tendency towards 'circularity', may to some large degree be illusory – a point which recent iron age excavations emphasize (cf. p. 381; contra, e.g. Thomas A.C. 1959–60). In the Gwithian houses three well-defined hearths set round with beach pebbles have been found as well as a possible corn-drying kiln close by a collection of saddle quern fragments and rubbing stones. The occupation of this upper level on the Gwithian site may have lasted upwards of two centuries; near one of the hearths just described were found the fragments of a steatite or schistose mould for a square-mouthed socketed axe (p. 257 above).

The gradual recognition that field and enclosure systems from Dartmoor to Land's End may be of middle rather than late bronze or iron age date may be extended to the complex of walls and huts now partially or totally below sea level which have been observed on the Isles of Scilly. On Nornour a round house was recently excavated yielding pottery which resembles forms found both at Gwithian and Trevisker and A.C. Thomas (1978) has drawn attention to fields in Scilly still to be detected under modern or medieval agricultural systems, and in particular the lynchets of classic 'Celtic' field pattern on Halangy Down, St Mary's. The pottery associated with the Scillonian entrance graves – which despite the absence of metal clearly continue into the period of the bronze age on the mainland – with its combination of twisted cord and comb-stamping, also has many features similar to that of the early Gwithian-Trevisker series (cf. Ashbee 1974: esp. 286ff.).

A succession from an early to middle bronze age mixed farming settlement similar to that at Gwithian can be found on the granite of Bodmin Moor where rescue excavations at Stannon Moor have shown incised wares following on earlier impressed decoration as in Gwithian Layer 5 (Mercer 1970a; 1975: 38–9; Thomas A.C. 1978). After clearance, a number of narrow parallel plots probably cultivated by spade rather than plough were set out to the south-west of some 20 hut-circles, while to the east and walled off from the village are a number of open stock enclosures which must have provided the basis for the site's economy (fig. 6.13:1). Notwithstanding, permanent arable areas were maintained on the moors, as for example at Horridge Common, Dartmoor, a site similar to Stannon (Fox and Britton 1969). The gradual degenerative effects of clearance and grazing and subsequent peat formation must have contributed to the eventual desertion of such sites. With increasing climatic deterioration to the east on the Somerset Levels around 1,100 bc, wooden trackways were again being constructed (fig. 6.18) (Coles 1972; Coles, Orme, Hibbert and Jones 1975; Coles and Orme 1976), as they were in the Ancholme Valley in Lincolnshire where the construction of the Brigg trackway may be compared to that of Meare (May 1976: 112ff.).

If one compares the siting in Cornwall of hoards, chance finds and settlements for the later bronze age and contrasts this pattern with the distribution of known bronze age barrows it is noticeable that the latter tend to cluster on or near the 80m contour (on or just below the skyline), in contrast to the largely low-lying and predominantly riverine or coastal distribution of the actual farms – an important point to bear in mind when considering the significance of possible related groupings of funerary and domestic monuments (Thomas A.C. 1969).

In the later prehistoric period of the south-west the continuing distribution of presumably more permanent and strategically placed coastal settlements complementary to the enclosures and open fields of Dartmoor has been suggested as indicating the kind of loose-knit society known historically from highland areas of Britain (cf. ApSimon and Greenfield 1972: 366). This pattern is perhaps to be contrasted with the more rigidly divided chieftain-based allocation of land usage suggested for Wessex in at least the early bronze age, if not the late neolithic as well. Certainly extensive deforestation of the lower plateau land of the south-west was a feature of the later bronze age. Subsequent reduction of population and final abandonment of these upland areas must have more or less coincided with the development of the first iron age communities of southern England.

Settlements and burials in central and northern Britain and Ireland

The settlements and cultural history of the area between the Trent and the Tyne has recently been reviewed (Challis and Harding 1975). Lincolnshire has the benefit of a detailed survey which often looks beyond the county's boundaries (May 1976: esp. 95ff.), while several studies have covered the metalwork, marked from the outset of the middle bronze age by a preference for flanged axes in place of palstaves (Burgess 1968a; Davey 1971; 1973).

The theory that in the North of England the collared urn lasted well into Hawkes' Middle Bronze II phase (Hawkes 1960; Longworth 1965: 35ff.) seems unsupported by currently available radiocarbon dates. Flat cremation cemeteries, however, with coarse bucket- and barrel-shaped urns, are known from Yorkshire and Lincolnshire – though the latter are largely undecorated and not close to the southern 'Deverel-Rimbury'

Fig. 6.18   Meare Heath, Som.: Trackway 1, view to north showing walking surface provided by longitudinal planks. C14 dates centre on 3,000 BP (photograph J. M. Coles).

forms.[22] In the west Midlands there are two dates from a ring ditch cemetery at Bromfield, Shropshire, which includes bucket and barrel urns decorated with applied horse-shoes and cordons. The dates are 850 ± 71 bc and 762 ± 75 bc (Stanford 1972); there are, however, dates contemporary with the c. 1,200–1,000 bc range of southern 'Deverel-Rimbury' sites from another Shropshire cremation cemetery at Sharpstones Hill near Shrewsbury, although there is no associated pottery. On Ampleforth Moor, Yorkshire, a series of barrows containing pottery similar to that from the Grimthorpe fort and the Heathery Burn, Co. Durham, cave is dated to the sixth century bc (Wainwright and Longworth 1969). This, however, is a site which can equally be considered within an iron age context (see Chapter 7, p. 406).

After the widespread clearing of the Yorkshire moorlands for arable rather than pastoral use in the early bronze age, indicated by the extensive cairn-fields (cf. Fleming 1971a), actual settlement structures of later bronze age date are less well attested. Against a background of assumed largely shifting agriculture in an area which since historic times has been the subject of intensive land use, this is hardly surprising. It is suggested that the southern round houses may be matched by such northern sites as West Brandon, Co. Durham (Jobey 1962), with its 'early' single post-ring structure; better evidence comes from Bramston in the East Riding of Yorkshire (Varley 1948). Timbers were preserved of a rectangular structure with cobble flooring in what was a fenland setting. Radiocarbon dates centre on 1,000 bc and other houses may remain to be excavated. From further south May (1976: 109ff.) has given an interim account of another site in low-lying marshy conditions. Beside the river Witham near Washingborough, Lincolnshire, apart from wood fragments, some of which are worked, domestic refuse included 50 per cent of cattle bones with the rest of faunal remains including waterfowl, red deer and horse. The horse may well have been ridden in view of the curved antler cheek-piece, an ultimately central European Urnfield type known from other late bronze sites, notably the Heathery Burn cave, Co. Durham (cf. Britnell 1976) (fig. 6.34:20). Pottery from the Washingborough site is said to reflect northern French Late Urnfield forms; a radiocarbon date of 303 ± 70 bc seems certainly on the late side even when recalibrated. Finds in the vicinity of the Brigg trackway in the Ancholme Valley indicate its late bronze age date and include pottery and bronze comparable with material from Heathery Burn (May 1976 113–14). A radiocarbon date from the track near the findspot of a peg-socketed spear-head is 602 ± 120 bc.

Evidence for the extensive farming of marginal land in the Fenland region comes from the long-term re-excavation of the complex of sites in the area around Fengate on the outskirts of Peterborough (Pryor 1976). C14 dates indicate the use of a considerable rectangular field system with boundary ditches established in the later neolithic until c. 1,100–900 bc or the Penard phase as evidenced by the discovery of a middle bronze age spear point low in the filling of one of the ditches. Abandonment of the fields seems to have been due to a combination of climatic deterioration, shortage of grazing land and probable population pressures.

It is, however, the evidence of hilltop settlements from the Welsh Marches through the Midlands and to the north which provides Britain south of the Border with the most significant evidence for later bronze age economy. Challis and Harding (1975: 100ff.; cf. also Harding D. W. 1976a for summaries of many sites noted in the following paragraphs) have summarized the evidence for a number of palisaded structures and other defensive sites dating to the period 1,000–500 bc, which may be compared with the discussion of similar structures of iron age date north of the Border (Ritchie A. 1970; qv. p. 451 below). Several sites have evidence of early palisade defences; Eston Nab, a promontory site above the Tees; Castle Hill, Edisbury; Old Oswestry, Shropshire (Varley 1948); from the Marches, the earliest period of the Breiddin, Montgomeryshire – a site with late bronze age metalwork including pins, a socketed axe and hammer and radiocarbon dates in the ninth century bc; Mam Tor in Derbyshire and Breedon-on-the-Hill, Leicestershire. Most of these are associated with pottery considered to be possibly or probably of late bronze age date. In addition claims have been made for the existence of upwards of 100 palisaded or stockade enclosures in the Tyne/Tees region and, whatever the truth of this may be, the increase both in number and size of such defended sites in the course of the 2nd millennium bc raises questions about the causes of such developments, causes to be examined further in Chapter 7 below; climatic deterioration, population pressures, and increased territorial organization of arable and pastoral land – reflected also in the increasingly warlike nature of the surviving metalwork – are all possibilities (cf. Avery 1976: esp. 54).

In terms of absolute chronology, the earliest dates come first of all from the 6-hectare site of Mam Tor in the bleak Derbyshire Peak District (fig. 6.19). Here at some 500m above sea level a series of hut circles lies within a simple ditch and dump constructed rampart. Although it has not so far been possible to date this fortification, which apparently was without a timber palisade, the site has produced a considerable range of coarse pottery with generally bucket-shaped profiles. Two huts have so far been excavated, revealing double circle post construction; fragments of shale bracelets, whetstones and (as at the Breiddin) a fragment of a characteristic late bronze age socketed axe with cast rib decoration, may be compared with two radiocarbon estimations: $1,180 \pm 132$ and $1,130 \pm 115$ bc. These dates, which certainly are earlier than that which would normally be assigned to this type of socketed axe, are the earliest so far recorded from a hillfort in the British Isles. At Dinorben in Denbighshire, timber-strengthened rampart construction of a hillfort on an inland promontory commenced, according to radiocarbon dates, between the ninth and seventh centuries bc, dating not inconsistent with the hoard of Parc-y-meirch below the crags to the west of Dinorben (Savory 1971b; 1976a, c). Previous late bronze age occupation is dated 945 ± 95 bc and the fortifications were destroyed during this period before subsequent reconstruction. Pottery from hut floors at Dinorben includes some that Savory considers to be of later bronze age date, while a fragment of a crook-headed pin is a form considered to be of Urnfield origin.[23]

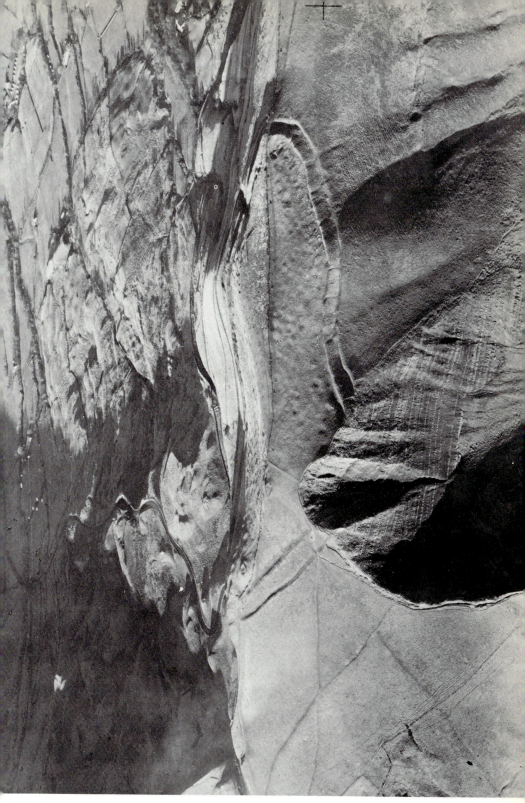

Fig. 6.19   Mam Tor, Derbys.: view of bronze age hillfort from east (photograph
Airviews (M/cr) Ltd Manchester Airport).

Outside the classic southern Deverel-Rimbury area with its dominant rite of cremation there are a number of burials with associated grave goods which indicate the adoption of inhumation for warriors of the Wilburton and subsequent Ewart Park phases. Burgess (1976a) suggests that the earlier of these inhumations could be related to the establishment of the early hillforts – possibly by French immigrants – particularly in the Welsh Marches in the post-ornament horizon Penard phase. The more widespread nature of inhumation burials in the post-Wilburton phase suggests a link with the dissemination of late bronze age types and technology north and west in a period when the sword is a key feature of hoards, particularly in the north of England and Scotland (Coombs 1975b).

Timber-framed ramparts, as found in southern England at Ivinghoe Beacon, are a feature of the 3-hectare site of Grimthorpe on the edge of the Yorkshire Wolds (Stead 1968), where bones from the ditch are dated to 690 ± 130 bc, while near Huddersfield at Castle Hill, Almondbury, Varley (1976) has dated the first univallate phase of a fortified settlement (following a period of open occupation) to 595 ± 180 bc.

A single row of outward-pointing stakes links Castle Hill with another sixth-century bc fort far to the west. At the southern end of the Isle of Man at a level some 500m above the sea is the desolate site of South Barrule, a double-rampart-defended circular enclosure in which can be traced the remains of some 70 huts (Gelling 1970; 1972). A mass of pottery has been recovered from this isolated site; the simple bucket-shaped forms have parallels not so much with the more southern types we have been discussing but rather with the long-lasting bronze age pottery traditions of the Outer Isles of Scotland. A striking feature of this Isle of Man site, the second highest point on the island, is the evidence for an outer barrier of stakes set into the ground slanting upwards, a technique termed *chevaux de frise* which translated into stone is a feature of many iron age sites on the Continent, but which may also be paralleled at the iron age fort of Kaimes in Lowland Scotland (cf. Harbison 1971). Whatever the significance of other fortified sites with scattered bronze age finds,[24] at Barrule, which has a single radiocarbon estimation of 523 ± 84 bc, it seems clear that we must be dealing with an important centre of a local community, and not with foreign settlers introducing new bronze types and new forms of defensive construction techniques. This last, however, is certainly a point to bear in mind in considering the development of hillforts in the British Isles and is a matter discussed in an iron age context in Chapter 7, p. 412.

In the later stages of the bronze age there is a gradual increase of defended hilltop settlements (or *Hohensiedlungen* to use the German term) with their indications for a changing political, if not economic, structure paralleled by a number of defended sites in the highland zone of Britain (Burgess 1974: 219ff.). It is more difficult to claim such sites as clear evidence of continental migration (cf. Hawkes 1972). As we have seen, there is evidence from Yorkshire that the hillforts at Almondbury or Grimthorpe were first constructed in later bronze age times, while on

Castle Hill above Scarborough (Smith R. A. 1928; Rutter 1959) a number
of pits contained bronzes including a tanged chisel, socketed axe and
harness-rings related to those found at the important Heathery Burn, Co.
Durham, cave site (Hawkes and Smith 1957: 149ff.; Britton 1971). Pottery
with slightly convex profiles and bucket-urn-like applied cordons can be
matched both at Heathery Burn (fig. 6.34) and with that from the palisade-
defended settlement of Staple Howe on the north edge of the Yorkshire
Wolds (Brewster 1963) (fig. 6.20), as well as from the region of the Brigg
trackway in Lincolnshire (May 1976: 114; cf. also p. 285. At Staple Howe,
some three circular huts were associated with a rectangular setting of large
post-holes interpreted as the base for a granary. Evidence for weaving on
an upright loom is supplied not only by loom weights but by post settings.
Other isolated four-square post settings suggest storage, and though not
necessarily associated with the early phase of the site's occupation, a small
group of bronzes includes an early Class II razor; there is also a
radiocarbon date of 450 ± 150 bc. – again not necessarily associated with
the earliest phase. This site, with its evidence for subsistence economy
incorporating some hunting, scarcely looks like the settlement of a new
incoming continental element (cf. further pp. 339, 372).

   As for the general distribution and dating of palisaded enclosures
discussed in greater detail in the next chapter, a recent survey (Ritchie A.
1970) has shown that there are at least 60 such sites concentrated in the
Cheviot Hills of southern Scotland, though excavation has shown that
palisades are not unknown south of the Border. Despite the comparative
paucity of finds within palisaded sites, such as have been excavated show
that many must date at least to the earlier part of the 1st millennium bc;

Fig. 6.20   Staple Howe, Yorks.: reconstruction of latest phase of settlement
(after Brewster 1963).

the site of Huckhoe, Northumberland (Jobey 1968b), has an internal setting of four post-holes recalling the 'drying racks' or 'granaries' of Staple Howe (fig. 6.20); there is also a radiocarbon date for the site of 510 ± 40 bc. The date from Staple Howe seems late for its continental Hallstatt C crescentic razor (fig. 6.43:13), as found also in southern Scotland at Traprain Law. The Staple Howe razor comes from a primary position in the first palisade trench and suggests that similar structures south of the border are also of a comparatively early date.

In contrast to all the settlements so far described, there is good evidence for later bronze age occupation in a number of shoreline caves from both east and west Britain. Cave deposits in south Wales include material comparable with that from the southern 'Deverel-Rimbury' complex (Savory 1965a: 97f.), notably pottery found with a rapier and class I razor from Ogof-yr-esgyrn cave, Brecknock (Mason 1968). Most important in this context, however, are the sites of Heathery Burn in Co. Durham (fig. 6.34) and Covesea Cave, Morayshire (Benton 1930–1). The Covesea material includes bronze open or penannular bracelets of a type generally associated with the latest phases of the north German bronze age (cf. Hawkes and Clarke 1963: esp. 235f.). Both Heathery Burn and Covesea contain a clearly locally-made range of pottery with some vessels of a hard gritty texture with angular profile (fig. 6.34: 27–9). This latter 'flat-rimmed' ware was in the past perhaps over-enthusiastically compared with north-western German forms of the eighth century BC (cf. Coles and Taylor 1969–70; Challis and Harding 1975: 35ff.; and p. 319 below). As well as the 'flat-rimmed' ware, the bronzes from Heathery Burn are notable for the presence of harness and wagon fittings (fig. 6.34:10, 14–15), including typical later Urnfield Hallstatt B forms, as also found in Wales in the Parc-y-meirch find below the Dinorben hillfort (fig. 6.43:6–8, 10) (Savory 1976c), as well as in a hoard at Horsehope Knowe, Peeblesshire (Piggott S. 1953b). Whatever the status of 'flat-rimmed' ware, the seventh and sixth centuries BC seem clearly to have been a period of at least indirect continental contact, just as was the ornament horizon half a millennium earlier in the south of Britain.

The native element in the later bronze age of the north of Britain must not be ignored. The most extensive settlement uncovered so far in Scotland is that represented by the earliest stage of the occupation of Jarlshof on Mainland Island in the Shetlands (Hamilton 1956: 18ff.) (fig. 7.59). The location, on Sumburgh Head, is well positioned as the first landfall from the approach north from Orkney; it is well supplied with fresh water and good grazing and shows signs of having been occupied from neolithic times: the pattern of settlement clearly reflects a long tradition (Piggott S. 1966: 7). The site gets its name from a ruined sixteenth-century AD house immortalized by Sir Walter Scott in his novel *The Pirate* and its archaeological importance, as at Skara Brae, was revealed following a storm in the late nineteenth century. The internal divisions within the houses include provision for cattle stalling. The faunal evidence is for the rearing of pig and sheep as well as cattle, although there is also an indication of corn-growing and a number of trough-shaped querns were recovered. Imported steatite bowls were also found and a considerable number of stone implements – a feature not surprising in an area so comparatively remote from the sources of raw minerals for metalworking. The bronzesmith who set up his workshop within one of the houses may have been Irish in origin (cf. Herity and Eogan 1977: 212); amongst the forms which he was producing on the site from clay moulds were socketed axes, late 'Ewart Park' swords (cf. p. 313) – moulds for which were found also on Traprain Law – gouges, and amongst decorative pieces the so-called 'sunflower' pin, a type with a long life formerly considered to be of Irish-Scandinavian origin.[25] More than 200 fragments of clay moulds and pouring gates were found around a pit lined with clean sand, presumably used for casting processes (fig. 6.2:5). A supply of clay was close by and a stone trough was also in the area. The type of pottery present at Jarlshof is of the general 'flat-rimmed' form as observed at Covesea and elsewhere. There is little doubt that such wares belong to a strictly local tradition; similar wares are associated with two other houses of later bronze age date from the Shetlands, one at Skaill, Deerness, and another at Clickhimin, on a peninsula near Lerwick. A first stage in the latter site's history is marked by a farmhouse similar to the houses of Jarlshof (Hamilton 1968b).

Moving to Ireland, most of the evidence is from waterside or true lake settlements. It has been suggested that, in contrast to southern Britain, Ireland did not share the type of settled systematic land exploitation, but little can be said of the economy of the period, though recent field work in the west of Ireland indicates extensive field systems which could well be of bronze age date. Such features as the probable extensive use of wood and even skins, the latter suspended over a firepit following a technique which is certainly recorded in the sixth century AD (O'Kelly M. J. 1954), together with finds of 'flesh-hooks' (Jockenhövel 1974) (fig. 6.45), are amongst many suggestions which have been advanced to add to the scanty evidence for settlement in this period. The presence, however, of the so-called 'crannóg' or artificial island settlement is clear enough. Rarely do these comprise more than a single, usually circular, house and their isolated but protected position is certainly suggestive of a fairly unsettled period.[26]

Of such settlements the earliest is the site of Knockadoon, Lough Gur, where as already noted (p. 125) there are not only neolithic rectangular and circular houses but some sign of a middle bronze age or 'Bishopsland' tradition occupation, as indicated by two-piece clay moulds for socket-looped spear-heads and rapiers (Ó Ríordáin 1954: 384ff.). Two hoards of later bronze age 'Covesea' type (cf. Hawkes and Clarke 1963: esp. 230ff.), gold penannular armlets and a neckring of Bishopsland form have been found in two pits on Downpatrick Hill, Co. Down, later the site of an iron age fort (Proudfoot 1955; 1957; cf. also Raftery B. 1976b; 351ff.). Here is another possible candidate for a later bronze age *Hohensiedlung*. Eogan (Herity and Eogan 1977: 187ff.) identifies some six settlements of later bronze age date, contemporary probably with the 'Ewart Park' phase in Britain. Chief amongst these are the settlements of Ballinderry Crannóg no. 2, Co. Offaly, and Knocknalappa, Co. Clare. At the first site (subsequently occupied in the Early Christian period: Hencken 1942) a short phase of occupation interrupted by flooding is marked by superimposed layers of brushwood, and at least two separate groups of structures. Cattle bones predominated amongst the faunal remains but sheep, pigs and goats were also present. There was some evidence for corn-growing and also for fowling and red deer hunting – as at Staple Howe – though strangely no sign of fishing activities; pottery was of the general 'flat-rimmed' category. At Knocknalappa there was not only flat-rimmed ware but also a sunflower-headed pin and a late form of leaf-shaped 'Ewart Park' sword (Raftery J. 1942) (fig. 6.37:2; 6.43:3). Again amongst the bones cattle predominated, with some sheep or goat and scanty evidence for hunting and fowling. At both Ballinderry and Knocknalappa cheek-pieces of bone are, as at Heathery Burn, indicative of the introduction of the horse, probably for riding as well as traction (cf. Britnell 1976). Another site – so far largely unpublished – whose swampy find conditions allowed a fair degree of preservation is Rathtinaun Crannóg in Lough Gara, Co. Sligo (Raftery B. 1972: 2–3). A foundation of brushwood and peat was retained by wooden piles; a number of hearths lined with clay were also found but no definite house plans. Finds from the lowest levels include a gold penannular ring and 'flat-rimmed' ware. Near the settlement, but not unfortunately in stratigraphic association with it, a hoard of metal objects including a number of amber beads and two polished boar tusks contained ornament types of the late 'Dowris' industry (Eogan 1964). The late bronze age levels of the crannóg site are radiocarbon dated to around 200 bc; this might seem to support the survival in Ireland of late bronze age metalworking traditions into a period of iron technology. Following a period of abandonment, occupation material includes a bifid razor, a swan's neck pin and a forged axe, all of iron. The Lough Gara dates certainly appear to create problems but as will be discussed further in Chapter 7 there is a growing tendency to support arguments for an early – and independent – introduction of primitive iron technology in the late phases of the Irish late bronze age 'Dowris' tradition (figs. 6.37; 6.40), perhaps by the sixth century bc (cf. Champion T. C. 1971; Scott B. G. 1974a, b.).

At the hillforts of Navan, Co. Armagh (=Emain Macha: Waterman 1970), and Rathgall, Co. Wicklow (Raftery B. 1976a), there are also indications of late bronze age occupation. From Navan comes a series of radiocarbon dates, the earliest being 650 ± 50 bc; an early destruction layer is dated 465 ± 50 bc and there is a fragment of a bronze-socketed sickle – another 'Dowris' type (fig. 6.40:12–13). Both sites have evidence again for ironworking. Immediately outside the V-shaped ditch there were the remains of an impressive timber structure and, in the vicinity of an area of cobbling and a hearth, more than 400 clay mould fragments for late bronze age swords, spear-heads, socketed axes and gouges or chisels, all clear evidence of late bronze age metalworking; the remains of a bowl furnace were found in the silt of the fort's ditched defences, such furnaces being characteristic of the earliest phases of iron smelting. Rathgall also seems to have the only good evidence for a late bronze age cremation burial in Ireland; a bronze bar toggle is one of a small group of Irish finds, including another example from Navan, which appear to be Montelius V imports of the eighth/seventh century BC (Raftery B. 1975).

Coastal cave sites occur in Ireland, with evidence of later bronze age occupation, as in the north and south-west parts of England and Wales. Typical of these is a cave at Whitechurch, Co. Waterford (Coffey 1912). Overall, such evidence as there is for the economy of later bronze age Ireland suggests that corn-growing was not uncommon: there are saddle-querns from such sites as Ballinderry, Knocknalappa and Rathgall. Stock raising, of cattle in particular and to a lesser degree sheep or goats and pigs, seems to have been more important than in the west of Britain, with the exception of Rathgall. There are no burials which can be securely dated, since it is clearly impossible in the absence of radiocarbon estimates to date simple cremations to a particular period of the bronze age – or indeed later periods – in the absence of associated grave goods (cf. Flanagan 1976).

As a footnote to this section, some comments should be added on water transport in the later bronze age, clearly demanded by such evidence as the Jarlshof 'Irish' smith (Hamilton 1956: 26ff.) and a hoard containing Irish late bronze age gold from Morvah, Cornwall (Hawkes and Clarke 1963: 231ff.). The archaeological evidence for boats in the later bronze age is not as positive as the clearly maritime connections required by the metalwork of the period. There are, however, some significant indications from the east of England. The mouth of the Humber and north Lincolnshire have produced remains of more than half-a-dozen vessels of which the three from North Ferriby have been most extensively studied (Wright 1976; Greenhill 1976: esp. 111–12) (fig. 6.21). Together with the Brigg boat, excavated in 1974 (McGrail 1975), such vessels indicate construction of both dug-outs and oak-plank boats some 15m long and capable of carrying up to four tonnes. The Ferriby boats are radiocarbon dated to around 1,350 bc; that from Brigg in the Ancholme Valley to c. 650 bc (McGrail and Switsur 1975; May 1976: 116ff.) and the Humber evidence is sufficient to suggest to the excavator the presence of a veritable prehistoric boat-yard. From Ireland are two dug-outs from Lough Eskragh, Co. Tyrone – hardly ocean-going vessels though (Collins and Seaby 1960). The Roos Carr, Yorkshire, wooden model, also from the Humber estuary, may also in view of the warriors' round shields be of bronze age date (fig. 6.42:2) (Piggott and Daniel 1951: pl. 30; cf. Megaw 1970: no. 284), as also the gold-inlaid ?shale bowl from Caergwrle, Flintshire – not far from the find-spot of the Mold gold cape (Powell 1953). The inlaid decoration has been interpreted as representing round shields and oars, or possibly stitching in the manner of the flush plank construction of the North Ferriby boats (Corcoran 1961; Savory 1976b: 16); Hawkes (1971) suggests that the bowl may copy Phoenician boats[27] (fig. 6.22). Finally, a hoard of some 90 bronzes found at Dover Harbour in a cleft of the wave platform includes fragments of Rosnoën swords, median winged axes and other finds all indicative of an origin in northern or eastern France at the beginning of the British late bronze age (Coombs 1975b; Stevens, Philp

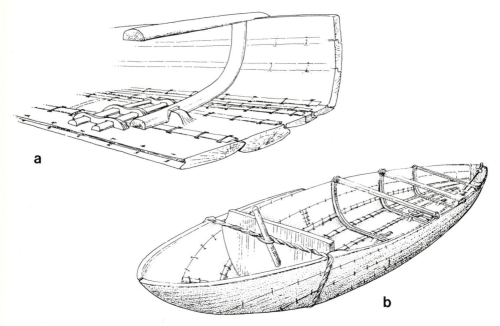

Fig. 6.21   North Ferriby, Lincs.: reconstruction of boat with (a) detail of suggested method of fitting frames (after Wright E. V. and C. W. 1947 and 1976).

Fig. 6.22   1–2 Caergwrle, Flints.: ?shale bowl in form of ship with gold leaf inlay; length 18·2 cm, width 11·1 cm (photograph National Museum of Wales).

and Williams 1976). Even more recently, the discovery of a further three French swords near Moor Sands, Salcombe, Devon, also strongly suggests a wreck site. These two finds seem most likely to represent part of the cargo from the boats whose cross-Channel voyaging established the French connection in the industries of the British ornament horizon.[28]

The economic basis for the later bronze age technology of the British Isles

As observed at the beginning of this chapter, much the greatest body of evidence for the later bronze age is in the form of hoards, usually found in isolated contexts.

The classification of bronze age hoards goes back to Sir John Evans (1881), who developed a tripartite division into 'personal', 'merchant's' and 'founder's' hoards. To these three classes has been added the concept of the 'craftsman's' hoard, distinguished from the largely scrap content of the founder's hoards by the concentration on specialized tools (Hodges 1957; Eogan 1964: 310ff.). McArdle in an unpublished thesis (1969) has also added a tinker's or specialist trader's class and Coles (1959–60) and Butler (1963) refer to votive hoards. However, there are difficulties in supporting such classifications. Coles (1959–60: 37ff.) has pointed out that Hodges' view of a weapon-using class controlling bronze production as opposed to a more even distribution of wealth in Ireland is vitiated by the largely unprovenanced nature of much Irish material. Coombs (1972) in his study of late bronze age metalwork has indicated some of the arguments against Childe's (1958) view of the role in prehistory of the itinerant smith. Rowlands' discussion of the ethnographic evidence for largely localized control of smiths' activities is backed up by a detailed examination of the middle bronze age hoards of southern England which shows that distributions tend to be 'highly localised with little evidence of specimens being traded over long distances' (Rowlands 1971b; 1976b: esp. 99ff.). The same would appear to be true of the later phases of the bronze age. There is certainly some evidence of traders' or merchants' hoards contemporary with the period of Hallstatt C introductions into Britain, with, notably, the large-faceted 'Sompting' class of axe (fig. 6.30: 5) (Burgess 1969). Whether, as Coombs suggests, such hoards reflect troubled times forcing the largely sedentary smiths to move with their products is more debatable.[29] Evidence of repairing and other tinkering activities is certainly present in several hoards. For example, in the 'Wilburton tradition' Isleham, Cambridgeshire, hoard (Britton 1960; Burgess 1968c: esp. 37), one of the waggon fittings has been repaired with a small amount of additional metal. Strange though it may seem, the considerable range of tools present in many hoards rarely if ever show any signs of repair. In contrast, vessels of sheet metal, both flat-based buckets and cauldrons (cf. p. 328 below), frequently show signs of being repaired by the addition of new sheet metal (cf. Hawkes and Smith 1957; Herity and Eogan 1977: 202ff.) – indeed in a true tinkering tradition.

The majority of the small-sized hoards of Scotland and Ireland are limited to one or two types and certainly swords are more frequently included in hoards in Scotland than elsewhere in the British Isles. Axes are most often to be found in Scottish and Irish hoards and the latter frequently include tools and personal ornaments, but swords are absent (figs. 6.37; 6.40). Equally the rare occurrence of scrap and indications of specialist hoards contrasts with the much more extensive evidence for hoards in southern Britain with, in the south-east, the preponderance of socketed axe production in the late bronze age (fig. 6.30).

In the south of England the majority of hoards appear to be founder's hoards (fig. 6.23), notably the enormous Isleham hoard with its 6,500 pieces; scrap metal as well as finished objects may have been collected from other centres. The predominance of weapons in the later hoards and their largely uniform – and sometimes clearly ritual – nature suggest a close relationship between the smith and a ruling warrior caste, supported by the presence of not only weapons but horse gear, cauldrons and related objects (Coombs 1975b: esp. 68ff.; Bradley and Ellison 1975: 113). The frequency of spears in southern hoards as opposed to the swords of north Britain may reflect differences in fighting techniques. The Broadward hoards centred on the Thames Valley itself are considered to have included votive deposits by a spear-bearing warrior class (Burgess, Coombs and Davies 1972) (figs. 6.26c; 6.33). The growth of military activity evidenced by the metal typology of the later bronze age hoards is matched by the evolution of defended settlements. Population increase and climatic decline (Piggott S. 1972) coincide with an apparent increase in pastoralism,

Fig. 6.23   Minster, Kent: bronze founder's hoard including Carp's Tongue complex types; length of hog back knife on right 8cm (photograph A. Pacitto: courtesy S. E. Thomas).

as marked by the extensive ditch systems of the southern Downlands, and raiding and the resultant need to defend one's herds, a key feature of many pastoral communities (Bradley 1971a).

That much abused term 'ritual' must also apply to certain hoards (cf. Coombs 1975a; 70) notably, the bronze horns (Coles 1963b; Megaw 1968: 346ff.) (fig. 6.39) and metal shields of the late bronze age – the latter shown by experiment to have been for parade rather than defence (Coles 1962; 1975) (fig. 6.42:1) (see further p. 331 below). From the beginning of the middle bronze age there is the concentration of otherwise unassociated hoards of rapiers in the Cambridgeshire Fens (Trump 1968). From eastern Britain also comes the Appleby, Lincolnshire, hoard; this dates from perhaps the beginning of the late bronze age in view of its combination of rapier and early sword types with a ribbed socketed axe and pegged spearhead (cf. p. 313 below). The objects, some of which seem to have been deliberately broken in antiquity, were carefully laid out, suggesting a votive deposit.

In Ireland, where hoards are much less numerous than in Britain south of the Border, the absence of burials which can be assigned to the later bronze age and the location of many hoards in peat bogs has indicated to Eogan (1964: 311ff.) that they may represent 'graveless grave goods'. Other concentrations of objects such as those in the area of the Lower Shannon and many finds in the Thames have also suggested ritual deposition, as well-evidenced throughout prehistory on the Continent as well as in the British Isles (cf. Torbrügge 1972; Wegner 1976). Other finds which are less easy to interpret include, from Ireland, the Dowris, Co. Offaly, 'hoard' (figs. 6.37:5, 6.39:1, 6.40:4, 11) which, not least for its size, may indicate deposition over a lengthy period (cf. Coles 1971b) as with later iron age finds, again probably of a ritual nature, notably the Llyn Cerrig Bach, Anglesey, deposit (cf. Fox C. F. 1946). In this context T. C. Champion (1971: 18–19) has pointed out the problems of dating hoards on the basis of exotic imports; clearly such finds can only give a general *terminus post quem* with all the imponderables of time-lag due to heirlooms and so forth (cf. Hawkes and Smith 1957: 188).

The first swords, the Penard phase, and the transition to full late bronze age

Following the 'ornament horizon' period and at a time when objects of the Taunton phase were still current, the first continental Urnfield elements of Reinecke D/Hallstatt A introduced a new element in British metal technology; a similar source is often claimed as influential in the appearance of hillforts (cf. p. 290). Burgess' Penard phase (fig. 6.25), beginning conventionally in the twelfth or eleventh century BC (see p. 257 above), the period which Hawkes referred to in 1960 as Middle Bronze Age III, is a particularly important phase in the development of the bronze industry. It sees not only the introduction of many continental metal types but also considerable experimentation on the part of British smiths and the introduction of new and improved forms, some of which were inspired by the Continent but others of which, such as the Group IV notched-butt rapiers, were indigenous developments (fig. 6.25:1, 4).

One type which may be studied in some detail as a key to developments in this transitional period is the sword with true leaf-shaped profile (fig. 6.24). Burgess mentions the continental early late bronze age 'Rixheim' swords together with rod-tanged or 'Monza' swords – a type common in northern Italy and Switzerland (Peroni 1970) – as amongst Urnfield imports to Britain (Burgess 1968c: 34; 1974: 205)[30]; Rowlands (1976b: 75f.) lists three rod-tanged swords from Britain but accepts no certain finds of the true Rixheim form. The significance of this continental form is that most authorities look to the Rixheim sword to provide the antecedent for the hilts of the early British so-called 'Lambeth' and 'Chelsea' types, in whose development Burgess sees a strong local rapier element. The hilt form of these swords, however, is evidently not derived from British rapiers, since all true rapiers have only two rivet holes or notches, and all these sword forms have four. In favour of the Rixheim argument one can point out that Lambeth swords are obviously related to north-west French Rosnoën swords (fig. 6.24:3) (Briard 1965: esp. 151ff.), which are also regarded as being developed from Rixheim swords; it is quite possible that all the British examples are imports from France. Two finds may be cited to indicate the close overlapping of these types. The Eriswell, Suffolk, sword which was formerly thought to be a Rixheim type is now judged to be a rod-tanged type (Briscoe and Furness 1955) and its cross-section is the same as that of the Lambeth swords. The Appleby hoard from Lincolnshire (Davey and Knowles 1972; May 1976: 95ff.) contains two examples of the Rosnoën sword which are virtually identical to those found in France. They are in association with Group IV rapiers, a solid-hilted lozenge-bladed sword, a basal-looped spear-head and a peg-socketed spear-head. This satisfactorily draws all these types together, and links the hoard with those from the Penard, Glamorgan, type-site (Crawford and Wheeler 1920–1) and from Ambleside, now lost (Fell and Coles 1965), the latter with a transitional palstave and a pointed spear ferrule, another feature of the Penard phase.

Unlike the Lambeth sword, the so-called Chelsea sword has a leaf-shaped blade. It also has a hilt rib like many of the Lambeth and Rosnoën examples. It does not seem to occur in hoards and it is very rare in France. It is perhaps a British development born of leaf-shaped and Lambeth swords. The related Irish Class I or Ballintober sword (Eogan 1965) has a notch or 'ricasso' which breaks the line of the blade, and, though again rare, is also known from France (fig. 6. 24:5). From the distribution of Ballintober swords and other objects there seems to have been a close connection between Ireland and the Thames Valley via south Wales. The distribution of Lambeth, Chelsea and Ballintober swords is riverine in France and Britain and all the known analysed examples are of non-leaded bronze.

The traditional view is that British leaf-shaped sword forms resulted from the introduction of the continental flange-hilted swords of so-called 'Erbenheim' and 'Hemigkofen' type (Cowen 1951; Rowlands 1976b: 80 f.). None of the swords so far discussed has a flanged hilt, a feature which begins with these Urnfield importations, one of which occurs in the

Rosnoën hoard. The short, heavily proportioned Hemigkofen sword developed in central Europe and probably spread to the west late in Hallstatt A, where it appears to be the earliest common type of leaf-shaped sword, clearly influencing the production of the Western group of Ballintober swords. Of the British examples, all are in the south-east and six of these in the Thames Valley; this association with water is also attested in western France. In the main Urnfield homeland of central and western Europe, however, association with water is very rare and the majority of the swords are found in graves. This association of water in the west and graves in the east is also apparent with the early iron age Hallstatt C swords (Cowen 1967).[31]

The somewhat earlier Erbenheim sword is a rather more elegant form with a long leaf-shaped blade and normally no ricasso or thumb grip; when the ricasso is present it represents a second stage of development. Usually there is a large number of rivet holes and they sometimes run into each other in the same manner as on the Hemigkofen sword. At the end of the grip there is a pommel tang – a flat spade-like projection which is a distinctive feature of the sword (fig. 6.24:1). There are only three known examples of this sword in Britain.

With regard to the so-called British U- and V-shouldered forms, to use the typology first devised by Parker Brewis (1922–3), there are in the British record a number of swords which are typologically later than the Erbenheim and Hemigkofen swords but which are not found in 'Wilburton' contexts or any other type of hoard. Once more they are concentrated in the Thames Valley and it is assumed that they must be local developments made before the beginning of the Wilburton phase; seven such swords come from Ireland (Eogan 1965) and one as far north as the Tay (Coles 1959–60: 22). Two swords which have been analysed, from the Thames at Wandsworth, contain lead. These may be typologically the earliest swords of lead-bronze in the country.

The British U and V types are also known in Europe where they are judged to be imports (Cowen 1952; Butler 1963: 119ff.). The dateable associations abroad are really little better than they are in this country but a fragment from a hoard in Brittany, if valid, would date it to the equivalent of our Wilburton phase (Briard 1965). Only a handful of the objects of the late bronze age which have been analysed so far have such a high tin content as these swords (Brown and Blin-Stoyle 1959a).

Turning to objects other than swords, it is in the Penard phase that a new form of sickle, the cylinder- or ring-socketed sickle, appears (Fox C. F. 1939) (fig. 6.25:11). This seems to be an indigenous invention with continental parallels and is perhaps to be seen as an example of the increasing technical competence of the local smiths. Leaf-shaped peg-hole spear-heads make a reappearance for the first time since the Arreton Down phase of the Wessex culture (cf. p. 301). Also new are the so-called 'transitional' palstaves (fig. 6.25:6) and a type of basal-looped spear-head with grooves flanking the rounded midrib of a form different from those of the Arreton phase. The outline of the blades tends to be roughly triangular.

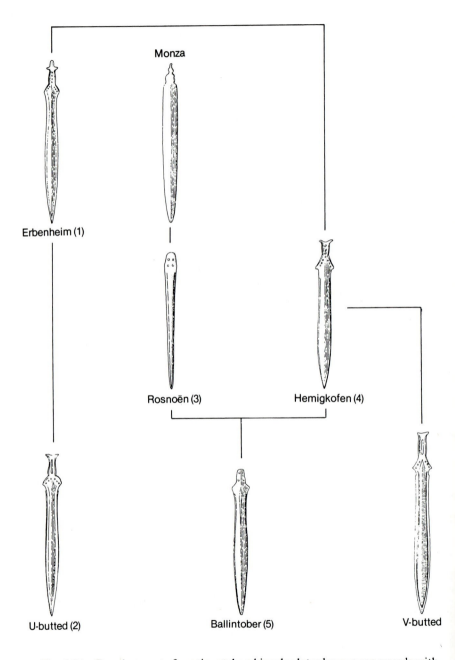

Fig. 6.24   Development of continental and insular later bronze age swords with (opposite) some examples: 1 ?Abbeville, Marne; 2 River Thames at Hammersmith; 3a River Thames at Lambeth; 3b River Seine at Rouen; 4 River Thames at Hammersmith; 5a Pont de Pirmil, Nantes; 5b Ballintober, Co. Mayo (after Eogan 1965 and Burgess 1968c).

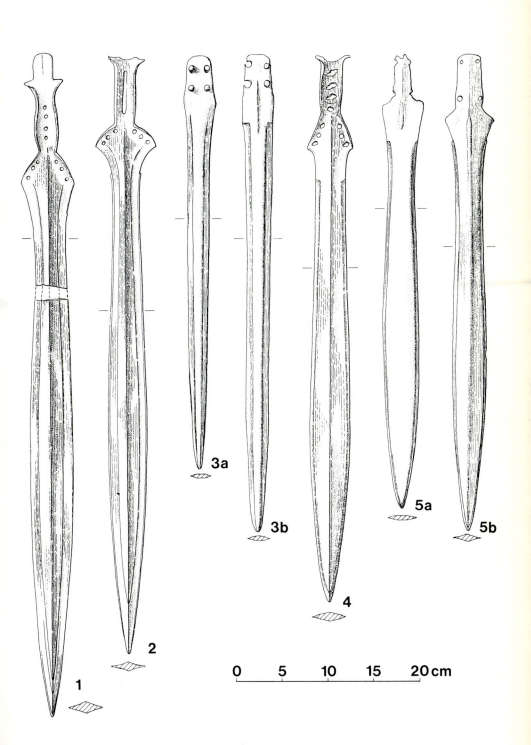

1

2

3a

3b

4

5a

5b

0   5   10   15   20 cm

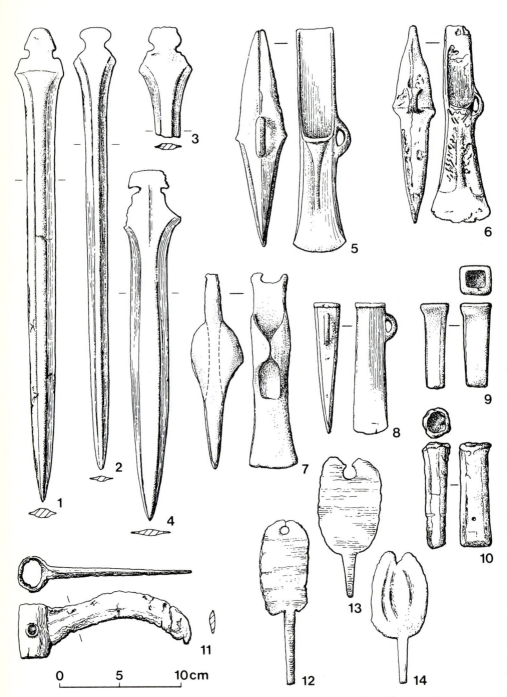

Fig. 6.25   Continental and insular examples of Penard and Rosnoën bronzes:
1, 6, 11: Downham Market, Norfolk; 2 River Loire at Nantes; 3 Noireau,
Calvados; 4 Cutts, Co. Derry; 5 Kergoustance, Finistère; 7 Sketty, Glam.;
8 Penard, Glam.; 9, 12 Rosnoën, Finistère; 10 ? Burgesses' Meadow, Oxford;
13 River Thames at Richmond; 14 South Lodge Camp, Dorset (after Burgess
1968c).

In Scotland and Ireland during the Penard phase there seems to have been little development beyond the occasional introduction of the new weapon types just discussed. Eogan (Herity and Eogan 1977: 180ff.) suggests continuation of the Bishopsland industries into the period of the Penard 'Urnfield' innovations and points to the 'flesh-hook' in the Bishopsland hoard itself (cf. p. 253; Jockenhövel 1974). Ireland also has examples of cylinder-socketed sickles. Scotland also continued its Irish-influenced 'Glentrool' industries and south-west Scotland seems to have retained the use of palstaves and rapiers well into the succeeding phase of Burgess' scheme which marks the beginning of what, since Hawkes (1960), has been recognized as the commencement of the late bronze age proper.

The Wilburton phase

To begin with a technical note, Wilburton material contains such a high proportion of lead, 7 per cent or more, that the reason for the addition must be questioned (Brown and Blin-Stoyle 1959a: 193ff.). The addition of lead makes casting easier, but above about 2 per cent of lead a bronze-edged tool will be softer than one that does not contain any lead at all. The explanation most often advanced is that by adding lead the smith conserved his more valuable raw materials, namely copper and tin. One of the characteristic features of the Wilburton industry, however, is the large number of thin-walled hollow cast forms, and a generous addition of lead would have facilitated their manufacture.

The Wilburton industry (fig. 6.27) (cf. Savory 1958: 28ff; Burgess 1968c: 9ff.), commencing in the tenth century BC, as suggested by Butler's (1963: 69ff.) correlation with Montelius IV or Hallstatt B1, is now no longer regarded as being representative of the country as a whole. It has a restricted distribution in the south-east of England and even there it is a very distinctive industry (fig. 6.26a). Wilburton hoards are for the most part composed of scrap material, that is, they are founders' hoards but they have a very strong martial element (Coombs 1975a: 61ff.). The sword and the peg-socketed spear predominate (fig. 6.27:7–8) and in two key hoards there is a discernible 'horsey' element (cf. Hawkes and Smith 1957: 153ff.). At Wilburton, Cambridgeshire, itself there are horse bits, and the great Isleham hoard also in Cambridgeshire (Britton 1960) contains vehicle fittings as well as two other prestige features, cauldron and 'flesh-hook' fragments (the former having normally been thought to date not before 750 BC: Hawkes and Smith 1957: 131; cf. p. 293). The Wilburton industry is confined in its first phase to Cambridgeshire, Lincolnshire, Hampshire and the middle Thames; in its later manifestation as represented by Isleham it also occurs in Nottinghamshire, Kent, Suffolk and Norfolk. There is no material from Devon and Cornwall and little south of the Thames. It shows strong family relationships with the St Brieuc-des-Iffs industry of north-west France (Briard 1965: 175ff.) but there are differences; for example, there are far more spears in the British hoards than there are in France and the axes differ. The developed or so-called 'late' palstaves occur in both industries (fig. 6.27:11). The indented socketed axe (fig. 6.27:10) is characteristic of Wilburton though it does

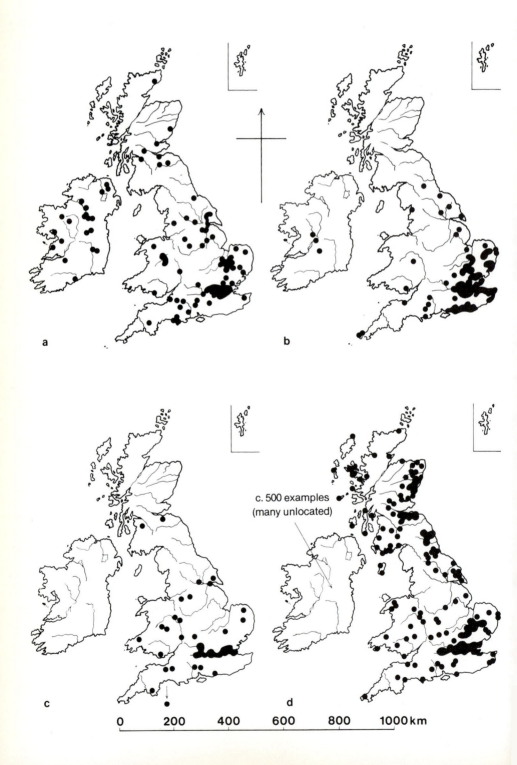

c. 500 examples
(many unlocated)

a

b

c

d

0   200   400   600   800   1000 km

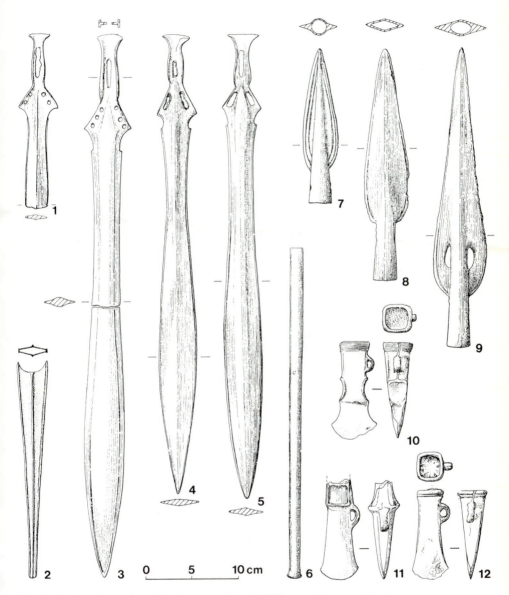

Fig. 6.27   Continental and insular examples of 'Wilburton' bronzes. 1 St Anne
de Campbon Brivet, Loire Atlantique; 2 River Thames at Sion Reach;
3 Carnstroan, Co. Antrim; 4 River Thames at Battersea; 5 Kerguerou,
Finistère; 6, 8, 9, 11 Guilsfield, Montgomerys.; 7 Walthamstow, Essex; 10, 12
Wilburton, Cambs. (after Eogan 1964 and Burgess 1968c).

Left Fig. 6.26 Generalized distribution maps of later bronze age types. a.
Wilburton complex; b. Carp's Tongue complex; c. Broadward complex; d.
Ewart Park and related swords (after Burgess, Coombs and Davies 1972).

occur occasionally in France; its real counterpart in the French industry is the median axe or the early form of the end-winged axe which is not known in this country until later.

The leaf-shaped sword is the main type and appears to be derived from the earlier forms of the Penard phase (fig. 6.27:1–5). Its low-flanged shoulders are not clearly or consistently either U- or V-shaped; its most distinctive features are a terminal that is generally straight with pointed ends, and a slotted tang with two or four holes or again slots in the shoulders. Cambridgeshire and Hampshire have the most hoards with swords in them and the middle Thames has the greatest number of single finds of swords. Other key Wilburton hoards of the earlier group came from near Andover in Hampshire (the date is indicated by the sword form and lack of exotic spears) and Nettleham in Lincolnshire which contains a basal-looped spear-head with very low lead content (Davey 1973: 96f.; May 1976: 104f.). Some of the later hoards of this phase, marked by such forms as developed sword types and socketed tools (fig. 6.27:12), are Blackmoor in Hampshire and the important Guilsfield, Montgomeryshire, find (Savory 1965b) (fig. 6.27:6, 8, 9, 11). Ingots are rare in Wilburton hoards despite the fact that they are mostly made up of scrap; Coombs (1972; 1975a: 70) suggests that many hoards such as Wilburton itself and that from Broadward, Shropshire (Burgess, Coombs and Davies 1972; cf. p. 317), may represent scrap collected after battle. As for other objects, the Wilburton industry shares with its French counterpart long tongue-shaped chapes (fig. 6.27:2), associated with the swords, tubular ferrules (fig. 6.27:6) and pegged spear-heads (fig. 6.27:7–8), but it has in addition a series of sectioned hollow lozenge spear-heads, stepped-blade hollow spear-heads, and spear-heads with lunate openings (fig. 6.27:9) (Burgess, Coombs and Davies 1972: 213f.). It does not normally have gouges and chisels or indeed any tools other than axes as a normal component; hammers, sickles and mould fragments are restricted to the Isleham hoard. The Wilburton phase is, then, mainly concerned with martial bronzes and may represent the emergence of an equestrian aristocracy.

Contemporary with Wilburton, in the northern part of England is what has been defined as the 'Wallington' phase or tradition (Burgess 1968a) (fig. 6.28). The Wallington metal types, which are present also in Ireland, are defined as being 'transitional' forms of palstaves, square socketed axes with mouth mouldings but slightly less slender than the Wilburton varieties, and socketed axes with flat collars; these socketed axe forms must have been developed under southern influence. In general, however, northern metalwork follows the traditions of the previous phase. Thus Burgess' type III and IV dirks and rapiers occur in Wallington contexts, as do basal-looped spears; protected loop spears are a local development out of earlier forms. The 'transitional' palstave is the dominant axe form; this, though developed in southern England, appears to have been adopted also in the north. True palstaves are rare in the north before the Wallington phase. The socketed axes in Wallington hoards show obvious Irish affinities with rope moulding and flat collar. The hoards containing Wallington material are found mainly in Northumberland and Yorkshire and there is very little continental influence or even imports apparent in the region – one median axe of central Urnfield type at Hull, and a socketed axe of possible north German Montelius IV type. It is also noticeable that in this period the northern part of the country is virtually swordless and that all of the Wallington material that has been analysed has been found to be cast from tin-bronze, leading only being introduced in the following phase (Burgess 1968a: 28f.).

In Wales there is only sporadic Wilburton and Wallington material, most of the former being concentrated in the single and late – judging by the socketed axe and gouge types – Guilsfield hoard (Savory 1965b; Davies 1967). One assumes that after the activity of the Acton Park and Penard phases there was no general adoption of new traditions until about the eighth century BC, though there is evidence of an early (perhaps independent) introduction of lead alloying (cf. p. 312).[32] The Wilburton sword seems to have been adopted in Scotland in what Coles (1959–60: 24ff.) terms his 'Poldar' phase, although only that from the Berwickshire type-site has all the features of the typical southern slotted-tang form. Tongue chapes and spear ferrules – and some perhaps used as whip or goad terminals (Piggott S. 1953b: 179) – have a very long life in Scotland; while the Crosbie, Berwickshire, hoard – the only hoard well-attested in

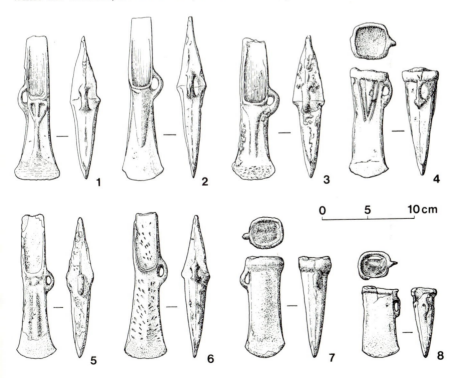

Fig. 6.28 North of England axe types: 1–4 Carr Moorside, Yorks.; 5–8 Wallington, Northumberland (after Burgess 1968a).

this phase – includes with its local Wilburton sword and chape a middle bronze age kite-shaped spear blade indicating, as in Ireland and Wales, the long survival of earlier 'Glentrool' types. As at Isleham and, from an earlier context, Bishopsland, there is a single find of a flesh-hook whose date however must remain uncertain (p. 338 below; cf. Jockenhövel 1974); the 'horsey' element of later Wilburton hoards is absent in Scotland and is rare in Ireland and Wales. Another class of objects whose date may fall within the Poldar phase are the sheet bronze shields, most common being the Yetholm type with ribs alternating with bosses (Coles 1962) (fig. 6.42:1).

In Ireland, as in Wales and Scotland, there is little or no indication of major new developments contemporary with the Wilburton hoards. Eogan's (1964: 288ff.) 'Roscommon phase' has only the one eponymous authenticated hoard which, on the evidence of its bag-shaped socketed axes and flat plate scrap as found in the Guilsfield and Isleham hoards, must date to the eighth century BC. Certainly a small number of Wilburton swords, Eogan's (1965) Classes 2 and 3, occur as do a few tongue chapes and tubular ferrules, possibly to be related to isolated trading or as the result of a late movement north and west. Otherwise, however, group IV or 'Lisburn' (Trump 1962) rapiers, protected loop spear-heads and local 'transitional' palstaves suggest again the continuance of middle bronze age metalworking traditions, though it is rather confusing of Burgess (1968c: 37f.) to refer this to the Wallington tradition with its implication of English dominance of local industries.

Problems of the nature and dating of 'foreign' elements in the Wilburton phase still remain. For example, with regard to the Welby hoard in Leicestershire (Powell 1950; cf. p. 319) (fig. 6.29:1–10), it has been pointed out that the original dating was based on the assumption that the various central European parallels for the Welby cruciform handle attachments (fig. 6.29:9–10) were of seventh century BC date – the absolute dating being arrived at by correlation with the fixed chronology of Italy. The relevant material on the Continent has however now been assigned to Hallstatt B1 (tenth century BC) and in particular the comparable Scandinavian material has been redated to Montelius IV or also Hallstatt B1 (Thrane 1965). If the Isleham hoard – which like so many hoards may have been deposited over a period of time – can also be updated at least in part, the disc sliders it shares with Welby (fig. 6.29:8) no longer present a problem. The Welby bronze bowl with its omphalos or dimpled base and ribbed profile, is in fact a unique form (fig. 6.29:6), though it has been regarded as a copy both of late Urnfield rilled pottery and of iron age furrowed bowls (cf. p. 398). Coombs (1972) points out that socketed axes in the Welby hoard (fig. 6.29:2) link it with the Great Freeman Street hoard in Nottinghamshire, and this is either late Wilburton or immediately post-Wilburton in date; it is also linked with the Newark hoard which contains 'phalerae' or possible harness discs as at Heathery Burn (fig. 6.34:14–15) and, again, Isleham. Discs of this type have been shown to indicate Hallstatt B1 influence (O'Connor 1975a) and may even indicate long-range connections with the Swiss late bronze age for which the rare

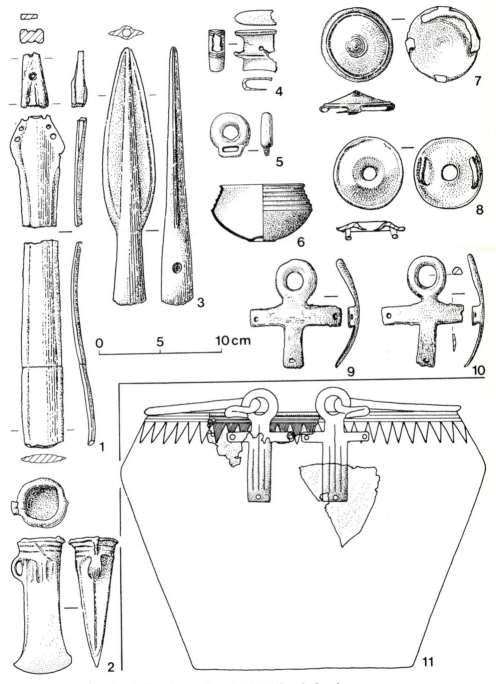

Fig. 6.29 1–10 Welby, Leics.: bronze hoard; 11 Adabrock, Lewis;
reconstructed bronze bowl (after *Inv. Arch.* G B. 24 and Coles 1959–60).

examples of antennae-hilted swords in Britain lend further support (cf. May 1976: 105; Coombs 1974). All of this might suggest that Welby is an early indication of the new exotic late Urnfield elements noticeable in Britain from the tenth century BC on.

The Ewart Park phase, the Carp's Tongue complex and post-Wilburton metal technology

The last of Burgess' main phases of later bronze age technology, which corresponds with Hawkes' (1960) Late Bronze Age 1 and 2 commencing in the eighth century BC, is marked by an industrial revolution in terms of volume and variety of production. Lead alloying is now general in local groups which are insular in character but, as Burgess (1968c: 17ff., 209) points out, reflect a wide range of exotic influences from as far afield as the Mediterranean. Notwithstanding the continuing tradition of votive deposition (cf. p. 299; Torbrügge 1972), the increase in the number of hoards, particularly those of late Irish gold (cf. Hawkes and Clarke 1963: 240) (figs. 6.37, 6.38), may reflect not only the stresses on an increasing population during a period of continuing climatic deterioration (cf. p. 298 above; Piggott S. 1972) but unsettled political conditions stemming from central and western Europe. This is the period of the rise of the Hallstatt C iron age and is reflected in Ireland and the south-east of Britain by the corresponding concentration of Hallstatt C-derived material – though largely found as stray objects – and hoards (fig. 6.43). The Wilburton tradition, replaced in the south-east by the Carp's Tongue complex with its strong northern French and Atlantic component (Savory 1948) (fig. 6.26b, 6.31–2), may have brought lead-bronze alloying and the new 'Ewart Park' sword to the west and north (fig. 6.26d); certainly both were ubiquitous by the end of the eighth century BC (cf. Burgess, Coombs and Davies 1972: esp. 226). Native hoards in the new phase consist either entirely of axes and scrap or of axes with tools, spears and the new swords.

The so-called Ewart Park sword was first defined by Cowen in 1933 on the basis of a Northumberland find and is a development of the Wilburton sword (fig. 6.43:3). The main diagnostic features of the hilt are the two or three rivet holes – only very rarely slots – for fixing the hilt plates and the lozenge shape produced by the slope of the shoulders and the line in the typically straight ricasso. Though the peg-socketed spear and a range of tools are, with the new sword, a common feature, spears suffer a decline in popularity in the post-Wilburton phase with the exception of the Broadward complex (cf. p. 317; Burgess, Coombs and Davies 1972) (fig. 6.33).

The socketed axe continues in a wide variety of forms marked by specialized hoards of immediate post-Wilburton date and, with the spear, is one of the best indicators of regional differences (cf. Burgess 1968c: 19ff.) (fig. 6.30); for example a faceted form of ultimately European origin seems to have its main English concentration in East Anglia and into Lincolnshire, though the only mould for this type comes from Somerset (Hodges 1960); a British faceted axe is known in a Montelius V hoard at Gurki in Poland (Butler 1963: 87). There is a bag-shaped variety too in

East Anglia and north Lincolnshire which possibly has associations with the Scottish and Irish material of the late Adabrock and Dowris phases (fig. 6.30:5–6).[33] The ribbed or 'Yorkshire' variety of axe (Fox C.F. 1933: 158), again, is almost entirely an eastern type (fig. 6.30:1). A few early axes in the south-east have a Carp's Tongue connection and these axe hoards in turn show links with the 'transitional Wilburton', Blackmoor, Hampshire, hoard with its Ewart Park and developed Wilburton swords.

Associated with the Carp's Tongue complex are wing-decorated axes (fig. 6.32:4), a bronze two-piece mould for which has been found at Worthing, Sussex (Green M.J. 1973). Wing-decorated axes are never found in large numbers in the hoards and they are often associated with true winged axes; both forms, though, occur on the Continent and in particular along the Atlantic seaboard (fig. 6.31:4). The winged axe itself is generally considered as ultimately a North Alpine introduction. Scotland and north Wales seem to have had no local axe industries, though in the Bristol Channel area a variant 'South Welsh' socketed axe (fig. 6.30:3) was, like the Ewart Park sword and the so-called 'Enfield' type of spear, exported to France. South Welsh axes form part of what has been termed the 'Llantwit-Stogursey' industry (cf. Savory 1965b: 186f.; Burgess, Coombs and Davies 1972; McNeil 1973), Stogursey itself linking elements of Broadward, Carp's Tongue and northern 'Heathery Burn' traditions.

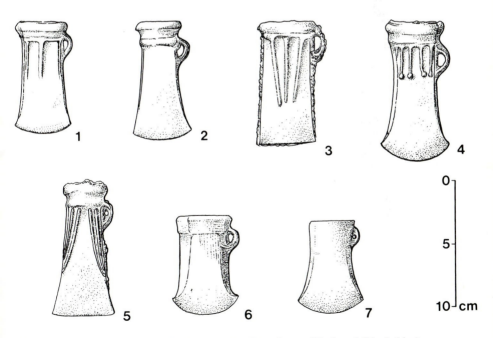

Fig. 6.30 Late bronze age socketed axes. 1–2 Everthorpe, Yorks.: 1 'Yorkshire' type; 2 Northern type; 3 Llantwit Major, Glamorgan: South Welsh type; 4 Frettenham, Norfolk: massive pellet-decorated axe; 5 Watton, Norfolk: faceted axe; 6–7 Norfolk: 'Irish' bag-shaped form (after Langmaid 1976).

The 'Carp's Tongue' or 'Bexley Heath' complex, with its particularly strong French contacts (Savory 1948; Briard 1965: 199ff.; Burgess 1968c: 17ff.), is found in the south-east of England, with a marked concentration in the Thames Valley and on the coast (fig. 6.26b). The origin of the Carp's Tongue complex is not certain but it is probably centred on north-west France where in Brittany alone there are over 50 hoards which have Carp's Tongue swords. As in Britain, such hoards consist mostly of scrap (fig. 6.23), while the Atlantic bronze age in general is marked by large hoards, some of which are contemporary with the first local use of iron. Alpine Europe, Italy and Crete have all been suggested as areas of origin

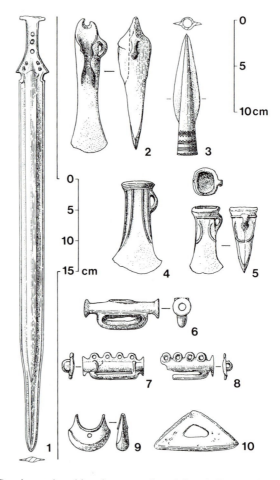

Fig. 6.31   Continental and insular examples of Carp's Tongue bronzes: 1 River Thames; 2 River Thames at Brentford; 3 Chingford Reservoir, Essex; 4 Menez Testa, Finistère; 5 River Thames at Old England; 6 Watford, Herts.; 7 Prairie de Mauves, Nantes; 8 River Thames at Sion Reach; 9 Levington, Suffolk; 10 Eaton, Norwich (after Burgess 1968c).

for the complex and in particular its characteristic sword type (figs. 6.31:1, 6.32:1). It is probable, however, that the Carp's Tongue sword, with its T-shaped terminal, slotted or riveted tang and squarish ricasso of late Urnfield Erbenheim inspiration (Cowen 1956), and its bag-shaped chape (fig. 6.31:9, 6.32:9), developed in the north from the St Nazaire type of sword which occurs in the St Brieuc-des-Iffs hoards of Brittany – and, in fragments, at Isleham.[34] Geographically, there are no real overlaps of Carp's Tongue and Wilburton industries in Britain, and it must be emphasized that the distribution of the complex is indeed quite restricted. It is confined to the Cambridgeshire, Essex and Suffolk area and the lower Thames Valley and is often found with the late native Ewart Park sword (fig. 6.32). The Carp's Tongue sword itself does not occur south of the Thames save on the south coast and in east Kent, and is only known in complete form in three cases. Neither the theory that the Carp's Tongue material represents evidence of an invasion from the area of the Rhône (Evans E. E. 1930), nor Savory's original minimal view that the material was imported into Britain as scrap (Savory 1948: 162) seems supportable. Some of the so-called 'bric-à-brac' – not so common in Britain as in France – such as slides and 'bugle-shaped' objects (fig. 6.31:6–8; 6.32:14) (Jockenhövel 1972) may, like the wing-decorated and pellet-ornamented axes (fig. 6.30:4), be of local origin; certainly other types such as socketed knives and bifid razors first appear in the Wilburton phase (Coombs 1972). Hog's back knives (fig. 6.31:10, 6.32:22) and ribbed bracelets are also part of a common technological area which extends from south-east England to Spain and the Somme Basin; true winged axes (fig. 6.31:2, 6.32:2) and vase-headed pins show the influence of more easterly continental metalworking traditions.

The distribution of the varying forms of the Carp's Tongue sword complex as a whole shows how markedly western, and indeed Atlantic, a phenomenon it is, the sword itself as just noted having originated in north-western France. It should also be observed that, as in earlier phases, the importation of continental forms into Britain is balanced by the appearance in France of native British types – Ewart Park swords, later forms of socketed axes and socketed sickles as well as British cauldron forms. Indeed, more insular types can be found on the Continent than definite imports in the British Isles.

In Wales outside the area of the Welsh Marches, neither the Wilburton nor to an even greater degree the Carp's Tongue complex are well represented; for the former the Guilsfield, Montgomeryshire, hoard is an exception (fig. 6.27:6, 8, 9, 11). In place of the continental-influenced industries of the south and east, it seems that local crafts-centres based on the exploitation of the copper ores of north-west Wales continued middle bronze age traditions, including that of lead alloying, which in Wales seems to have been established at a significantly early date (Savory 1976c: 116; Burgess 1976b: 75). But, as Savory has indicated, there are signs of contact between the Loire-Gironde estuary region of the Atlantic sea-board and Welsh coastal areas as far north as Anglesey.

Another element in the Welsh later bronze age is the striking

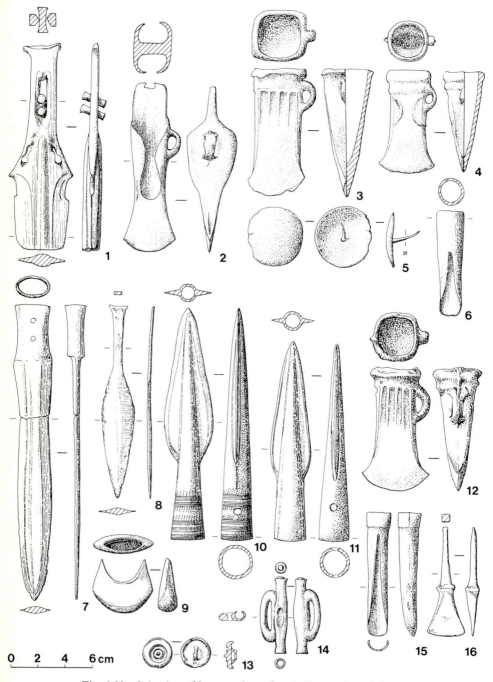

Fig. 6.32   Selection of bronzes from Carp's Tongue hoards in eastern England.
1–6 Addington, Surrey; 7–16 Reach Fen, Cambs.; 17–23 Meldreth, Cambs.
(after *Inv. Arch.* G B.54, 17, 13).

concentration of defended hilltop settlements in the Welsh Marches (cf. also p. 288); several of these, notably Dinorben, the Breiddin and Fridd Faldwyn (cf. Harding D.W. 1976a) were clearly established in the late bronze age, like the contemporary site of Grimthorpe in Yorkshire (Stead 1968). This seems to continue the pattern of continental contact in the eighth–seventh centuries BC. Important here is the Parc-y-meirch find made in 1868 below the Dinorben, Denbighshire, hillfort (Gardner and Savory 1964; Savory 1971a; Savory 1976c: 117–20) (fig. 6.43:6–8, 10). The objects in the find – possibly a burial rather than a hoard – all appear to be harness mounts including objects with affinities with the southern Baltic or, more significantly, the later Urnfields of central France; there is a link here with the Carp's Tongue complex of southern Britain, particularly in the so-called 'bugle-shaped' objects.

The so-called Broadward complex as defined by Burgess and others is a notably insular development (Burgess, Coombs and Davies 1972; Coombs 1975a) (figs. 6.26c, 6.33). It does not occur in Ireland or on the Continent and – like Wilburton – is essentially martial in character. It must owe a considerable debt to the Wilburton tradition, since ferrules and chapes occur and leaded bronze is ubiquitous. Save for late palstaves there are no tools to speak of. It is distributed along the Thames Valley with a few outliers in Berkshire and Hampshire, and then occurs in the Devon and Somerset area but not further west. It goes through south Wales and the Marches into Cheshire and Yorkshire. Significantly, it does not occur in the main Wilburton concentration of East Anglia save as occasional scrap fragments in hoards of that area. There is no horse gear and though there are a few Ewart Park swords it is essentially a spear complex.

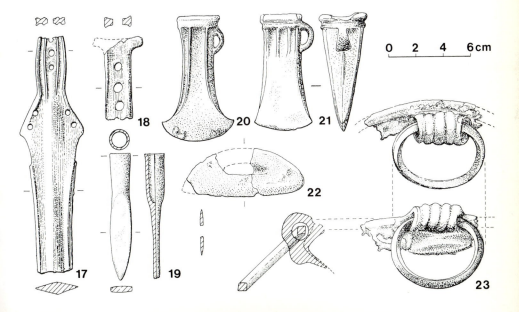

The characteristic spear type, apart from the hollow-bladed forms again to be seen in Wilburton, is the barbed form (fig. 6.33:5–7). This is a puzzle piece as to function since it is of such a size and the barbs are so placed that these weapons seem designed for display rather than for use. Some of the spears in the Broadward complex have triangular decoration rare in the British Isles. Most of the complete examples of the main barbed spear type are single finds, the large majority of them from rivers and in particular the Thames. Of the rest, most are in the east or south-east in hoards where the barbed spears occur only as intrusive scrap. As to its relative date, there are no distinctive fragments of Broadward material in the transitional Wilburton hoards but three of these hoards do have spear types which are most probably ancestral to the barbed form.

All in all the evidence suggests that the Broadward complex developed in the Thames Valley out of Wilburton and is immediately post-Wilburton in date. The Wilburton complex is replaced by the later Ewart Park and Carp's Tongue industries, the emphasis in the south and east being no longer martial, and there is a movement of smiths to the north and west seeking new markets for Wilburton styles and possibly introducing their bronzes to areas outside the south-east as they go.

In the north of England, Burgess (1968c: 19ff.; Burgess, Coombs and Davies 1972: 234) has referred to a 'Heathery Burn' tradition though in reality it is marked by little else than further variations of the regional socketed axe industries already mentioned (p. 312), notably the three-ribbed 'Yorkshire' type (Fox C.F. 1933: 158) (fig. 6.30, 1) and related

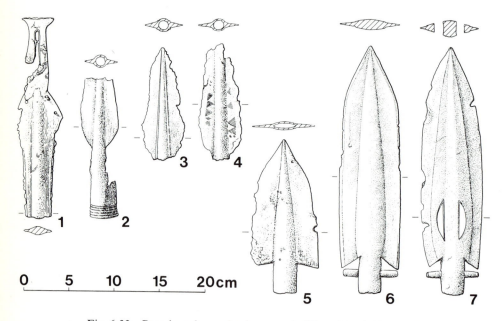

Fig. 6.33   Broadward complex bronzes. 1–5 Broadward, Herefords.; 6,7 Broadness, Kent (after Burgess, Coombs and Davies 1972).

forms. Apart from axes and a few tools, Ewart Park swords and pegged spears – and also a few of the special Broadward type – occur in the region. The type-site however is unique both for the area and for Britain. In a cave situated in the carboniferous limestone of Co. Durham not far from Stanhope, quarrying in the last century brought to light a whole range of finds distributed along the 150m or so of its length and generally sealed under a thin skin of stalagmite (Greenwell 1894; Britton 1971; cf. also p. 292) (fig. 6.34). Broken animal bones, traces of fires and at least one entire human skeleton indicate that here was an occupation site. On-site smithing is indicated by tongs (fig. 6.34:13), a casting jet, a fragment of a copper or bronze ingot and one half of a bronze bivalve mould (fig. 6.34:9) for the casting of socketed axes of the 'Yorkshire' type (also a feature of the site). There are other common native types such as at least one Ewart Park sword (fig. 6.34:1), peg-socketed spears (fig. 6.34:4), a small range of tools and a Class II razor (fig. 6.34:11), as well as a bucket of riveted sheet bronze with cast fittings. Pottery of the so-called 'flat-rimmed' class (fig. 6.34:27–9) and penannular bronze 'Covesea' bracelets (fig. 6.34:26) may be compared with material from other north British sites (cf. Hawkes and Smith 1957; esp. 148ff.). Indications of contacts further afield, however, are given by bronze axle mountings (fig. 6.34:10) and bronze discs of various types (fig. 6.34:14–15) – probable harness fittings to be compared, as has already been noted, elsewhere in Britain in such hoards as Welby (Powell 1950) (fig. 6.29:7–8) and Parc-y-meirch (Savory 1976c; cf. p. 317), but with a background in the later Urnfields of central Europe (O'Connor 1975a). Cheek-pieces of antler (fig. 6.34:20), a less sophisticated form of the method of harnessing indicated by the bronze mounts found in the Wilburton and Isleham hoards, also have parallels in central Europe and especially in Switzerland (Britnell 1976).[35] Together with the evidence for carpentry tools (fig. 6.34:5–6) necessary for constructing vehicles, Heathery Burn offers the best evidence for the appearance in Britain in the eighth and seventh centuries BC of horse-driving equipment, an essential feature of the emergent Hallstatt iron age society though one which has its roots in the previous phases of the continental Urnfields (cf. Powell 1971).

Turning to Scotland once more, Coles' (1959–60) 'Duddingston', 'Covesea' and 'Ballimore' phases come within the Ewart Park phase as defined by Burgess. The Ballimore material, named after an Argyll scrap hoard, represents not so much a phase as a number of late regional centres concerned largely with the production of socketed axes. The Ewart Park sword is not at all well represented in the Borders but it is comparatively plentiful in the west (cf. Coles and Livens 1958), though in general there is not much late bronze age material found along the north-west coast and on the Islands.[36] Possibly the swords represent a coastal movement of warriors similar to that which has been suggested for later Hallstatt C material. Local versions of Ewart Park swords – the Minch type – develop only later in north-west Scotland. There are moulds for Ewart Park swords at Traprain Law and Jarlshof on Shetland (fig. 6.2:5c) (cf. p. 292). Local variants of south-eastern types of axes occur in the Duddingston Loch

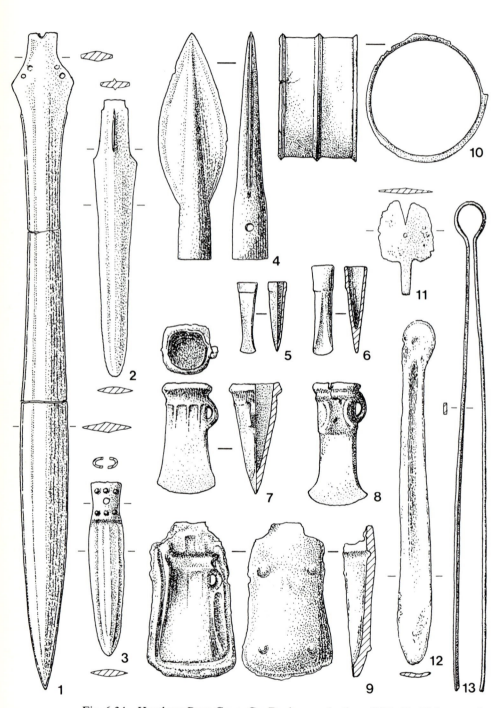

Fig. 6.34 Heathery Burn Cave, Co. Durham: selection of (12, 19, 20) bone and antler, (16, 17, 27–9) pottery, and (remainder) bronze objects (after Hawkes and Smith 1957 and *Inv. Arch.* G B.55).

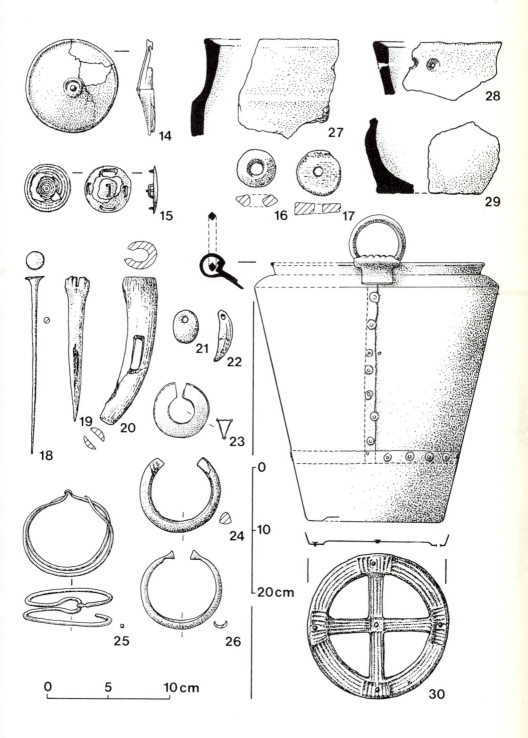

hoard and the earliest faceted socketed and bag-shaped axes are also found (fig. 6.30:6–7). The bag-shaped examples are probably of Irish influence, although in this period the role played by Ireland is less important than local production. The faceted socketed axe distribution covers east, central and south-east Scotland.

In Scotland, buckets and cauldrons may belong to the Duddingston phase. Such ribbon pellet axes – a Carp's Tongue form (fig. 6.30:4) – as occur in Scotland are presumed to belong also to the Duddingston phase. Coles believes that Duddingston material continued to the end of the late bronze age but that other regional industries apparently developed, for example Covesea. This latter group falls within this general period and is defined by bronze penannular bracelets and necklets with rings, notably as found in the Braes of Gight, Aberdeenshire, hoard, all of which were formerly considered to have close links with northern European Montelius V material (cf. Coles 1959–60: 4ff.; Hawkes and Clarke 1963: esp. 235ff.), but the 'flat-rimmed' pottery forms already discussed are now best seen as locally developed. The Covesea group is severely restricted and does not seem to have much effect on the other areas of Scotland. An interesting old find is a hoard found placed under a cairn at Glentanar, Aberdeenshire (Pearce 1970–1) (fig. 6.35). In this hoard were a number of socketed axes,

Fig. 6.35   Glentanar, Aberdeens.: late bronze age hoard. Height of cast bronze cups 7·2cm (photograph National Museum of Antiquities of Scotland).

Right Fig. 6.36   Distribution map of Irish gold and bronze 'dress-fasteners' and related bracelets (after Hawkes and Clarke 1963).

six penannular armlets and a number of fragmentary armlets, as well as a pair of cast bronze ribbed and handled bowls, each of which had been cast from the same two-piece mould. The axes from Glentanar are forms well known in the east of England in the later bronze age and include variants as found at Horsehope Knowe; the armlets are of the 'Covesea' form as found at Heathery Burn with its 'horsey' gear. The other rings in the Glentanar hoard recall this 'horsey' element which in general is lacking in other Scottish hoards (but cf. Piggott S. 1953b) but is present also in the Wilburton phase Welby hoard with its ribbed bronze bowl (Powell 1950; p. 310 above) (fig. 6.29:6). In general the Glentanar bowls, like Welby, may be said to recall continental early Hallstatt sheet bronze working but, as with other features of the British later bronze age, it seems rash to claim these general points of similarity as proof of the arrival in northern Scotland of settlers from the Continent (fig. 7.55).

One important feature of the Ewart Park phase in Scotland is the appearance not only of Irish axe forms but also of Irish gold-work: gold bracelets and local styles in bronze, with evenly expanded terminals, as discussed by Proudfoot (1955) in connection with the Castle Hill, Downpatrick find, and the related 'dress-fasteners' (fig. 6.37:10–11) and bracelets with cup-shaped terminals (fig. 6.37:12–13), occur in consider-

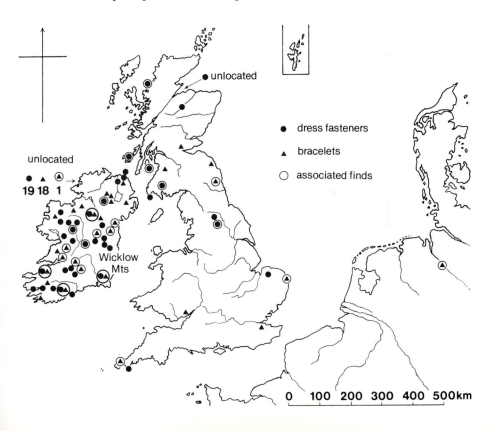

able numbers. The three dozen gold bracelets of the former type found on Islay may reasonably be considered as an Irish trader's hoard, while the cup-terminalled gold ring from Gahlstorf in Lower Saxony has been regarded as an import received through north British intermediaries (Hawkes and Clarke 1963: 209ff.) (fig. 6.36).

The Dowris phase, buckets, cauldrons and sheet metalworking

The final period of Irish bronze technology has been named by Eogan (1964: 293ff.) the 'Dowris' phase, after the Co. Offaly find for which, as has already been noted, the term 'hoard' gives perhaps too much of an impression of contemporaneity (cf. Coles 1971b). The view has been advanced that in this phase, commencing around the eighth century BC, Ireland received considerable stimulus from northern rather than Atlantic Europe – although actual imported prototypes are extremely rare (cf. Herity and Eogan 1977: 212ff.). It is also in this phase that it is considered possible for the first time to define Irish regional groupings (Eogan 1974a), notably amongst the spectacular sheet gold metalwork (fig. 6.37). For example, the so-called 'sleeve fasteners' (fig. 6.37:9) (Eogan 1972), certain pin types (Eogan 1974b), bracelets and 'A' class cauldrons (see p. 328 below) have a more north and easterly distribution, suggestive at least in part of British influence. Other products of highly skilled smiths in the Shannon valley and gold-work such as the massive gorgets (Eogan 1931) (fig. 6.38) and lock-rings (fig. 6.37:6–7) (too late in date for previously-held views of Nordic influence), seem to be concentrated in north Munster, an area not marked by natural ore deposits but one nonetheless of extremely large and rich hoards.

Eogan considers southern Britain and the west Baltic to play the most important roles in the Dowris phase, in addition to a continuing native industry. There may have been some direct contact with the 'Atlantic province' of western France; in the case of some gold-work, V-notched shields (fig. 6.42:3–4) (as represented elsewhere in Europe only by carvings in southern Spain) and cauldrons, it has been argued – though again not convincingly (cf. p. 331) – that there was a link with the Mediterranean. Though not well represented in Ireland, 'horsey' gear does include phalerae (O'Connor 1975a) and rattle-pendants, those from Lissanode, Co, Westmeath, possibly having been originally found with bronze cheek-pieces (Rynne 1972) (fig. 6.43:9). As we have seen (cf. p. 319), such material is currently referred to Urnfield sources in central Europe, or contemporary objects in the Baltic region. Disc-headed and related pins (Eogan 1974b) (fig. 6.37:1–3) have also been claimed to indicate contemporary and direct contact, reflecting a north European need for metals at a time when central European sources were denied them – though the absence of indisputable north-European objects in Ireland must again be noted. The Irish end-blow and side-blow horns (fig. 6.39), much more restricted musically than their counterparts, the Danish *lurer* of Montelius IV/V date (Coles 1963b; 1967; Megaw 1968), reflect current Irish casting skills. Together with the bronze rattles or 'crotals' of the Dowris find (fig. 6.37:5) they may possibly be part of a common north

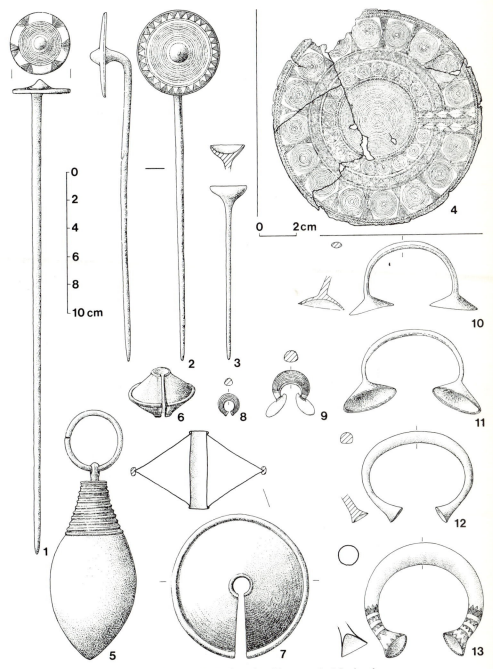

Fig. 6.37   Irish Dowris phase bronze (1–3, 5) and gold types: 1, 3 Ireland;
2 Boolybrien, Co. Clare; 4, 11 Latton, Co. Cavan; 5 Dowris, Co. Offaly; 6 nr
Limerick; 7 Gorteenreagh, Co. Clare; 8, 9 Belfast, Co. Antrim; 10, 12 Kilmoyly,
Co. Kerry; 13 Brahalish, Co. Cork (after Eogan 1964 and Herity and Eogan
1977).

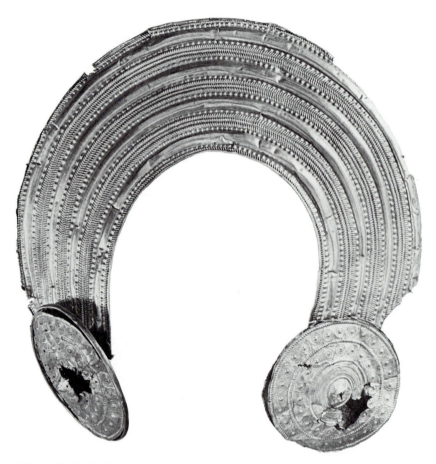

Fig. 6.38   Ireland: later bronze age gold gorgets. 1 Borrisnoe, Co. Tipperary;
diameter of terminal discs c. 10cm (photograph National Museum of Ireland);
2 Shannongrove, Co. Limerick; diameter of terminal discs c. 9·7cm (photograph
Victoria and Albert Museum, Crown Copyright reserved).

1

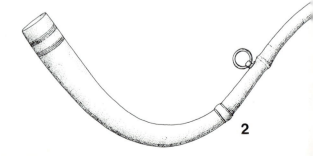

2

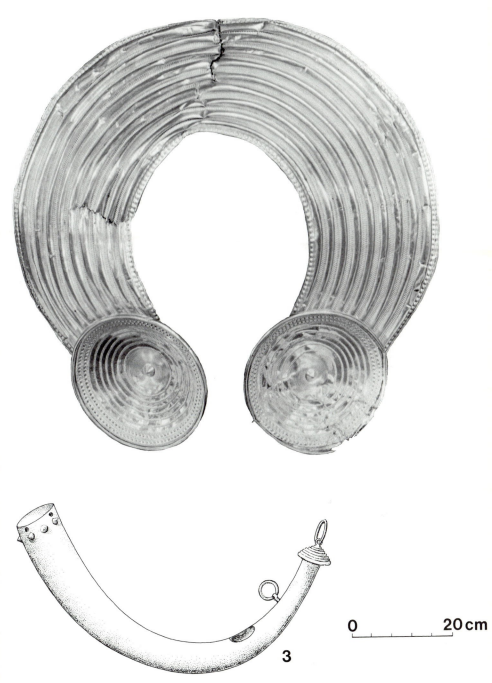

Fig. 6.39   Irish cast bronze end- (1–2) and side-blow horns. 1 Dowris, Co. Offaly; 2 Drumbest, Co. Antrim; 3 Dunmanway, Co. Cork (after Coles 1963b).

European bull-cult (cf. Coles 1965), but are again hardly likely to be the result of direct Baltic contact.[37] In short, the case for a Nordic element in the Irish late bronze age is at best non-proven.

As for less exotic objects, the Dowris phase includes swords which are a Ewart Park equivalent (fig. 6.43:4), short chapes which may have developed out of Wilburton and are comparable to some in the Broadward complex and also bag-shaped chapes of Carp's Tongue affinity. There are also plain leaf-shaped spears with peg-holes, and lunate and developed basal-looped spears. Socketed axes, both octagonal and hexagonal, faced with a circular mouth, recall certain north British forms (p. 312) (fig. 6.30: 6–7) and there are also oval axes with oval mouths which have a true bag-shape with a very wide cutting edge; this type really dominates the Irish series. All these seem to be developed out of similar earlier forms and may be ultimately of northern German origin. In addition, associated with Dowris hoards, there are ribbed and rectangular section forms which may have some relationship with the Yorkshire axes. Class II razors also occur, as do a range of other tools (fig. 6.40).

All the Dowris knives have two edges; there are socketed and tanged varieties. The Thorndon type of socketed knife with curved blade which is absent in southern England occurs in France and in north Germany and it may have developed in the Carp's Tongue industry (fig. 6.40:1–2). The tanged form of knife is present in two varieties (fig. 6.40:3–4), a plain tang and one with a longitudinal rib comparable to that seen on the knife – now lost – from the Great Freeman Street hoard in Nottingham, which contains other Carp's Tongue objects (Clark and Godwin 1940: 60ff.). Both of these types are regarded as native and they may begin at the same time as the Wilburton phase. Socketed sickles also occur in Dowris contexts (fig. 6.40:13). With the possible exception of some of the peculiar bag-shaped axe forms, most of the Dowris tool material is the same as that found elsewhere in contemporary British contexts.

The bucket of sheet bronze from the Dowris find is related to that from the Heathery Burn site but the latter's cast wheel-shaped base plate is an insular development of the continental 'Kurd' bucket (von Merhart 1952: 29ff.) (fig. 6.34:30). The basic difference between Irish-British and continental buckets and cauldrons is the former's use of cast rather than riveted and folded-over fittings (fig. 6.32:23) (Hawkes and Smith 1957). The traditional view of sheet-bronze buckets and cauldrons in the British Isles has been that they are confined to the Ewart Park phase. Actual 'Kurd' buckets as found in the Whigsborough or Dowris hoards and at Nannau in Merioneth (fig. 6.41), have been dated to sometime in the eighth century with production of Irish-British buckets commencing 700 BC or just after. Irish-British buckets occur not only in Ireland and the north of Britain but also in the south, with fragments from the Bagmoor, Lincolnshire, hoard (Davey 1973: 94ff.; May 1976: 105ff.) and the South Cadbury hillfort (Alcock 1972b).

With regard to cauldrons as again found at Dowris, the old classification of Leeds (1930) commenced with an A form with corrugated neck and a spheroid or conoid body; this type is also subdivided. The B cauldron has

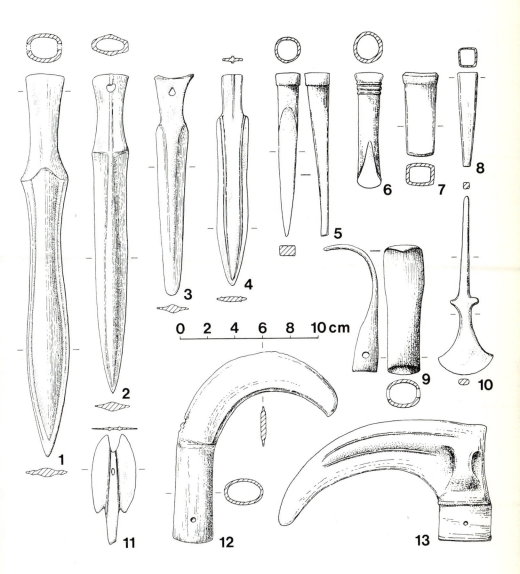

Fig. 6.40   Irish bronze tools of the Dowris phase. 1 Ireland; 2 Kilmore, Co. Galway; 3 Co. Antrim; 4,11 Dowris, Co. Offaly; 5 Rees, Co. Tipperary; 6 Bootown, Co. Antrim; 7 Trillick, Co. Tyrone; 8 Ballinderry, Co. Offaly; 9, 10 Knockmaon, Co. Waterford; 12 Athlone, Co. Westmeath; 13 Bolltiaghadine, Co. Clare (after Eogan 1964).

no corrugated neck, is spheroid to sub-conoid in profile and is divided into a B1 type which has a staple with internal flanges and a B2 form which has a continuous staple. Instead of being cast direct onto the rim this was cast separately and joined to the rim by various means. The class A cauldron occurs in British contexts from East Anglia at Isleham, Cambridgeshire, and Feltwell, Norfolk, the latter being a Ewart Park Carp's Tongue complex hoard, the former being usually considered as late Wilburton. B1 and B2 cauldrons have been regarded as showing contacts with Hallstatt C or early iron age influences as represented by the Llyn Fawr, Merioneth, hoard (fig. 6.44) (cf. Savory 1976c) and those at Sompting, Sussex (Curwen 1948); however both types again occur in purely native contexts such as the Dowris hoard (cf. Eogan 1964: 344) and the Minnis Bay Carp's Tongue hoard (Worsfold 1943). Hawkes and Smith favour Kurd buckets being brought to Britain in the second half of the eighth century and cauldrons being introduced round about 700 BC. They argue in fact for an origin of the A cauldrons in the Greek *dinos* of the 'Orientalizing' period, the B form being distributed via the Atlantic Carp's Tongue area. There are in fact several points that can be made about the above arguments (cf. Coombs 1972). Firstly it should be remarked that the buckets in British hoards, though apparently having late associations, are all found in much-used condition or as scrap material; of the Irish 'Kurd' buckets two have local staples which may suggest that possibly the difference in date

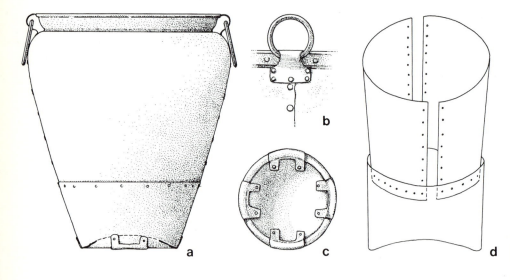

Fig. 6.41   Nannau, Merioneth: bronze bucket with (b) elevation of handle; (c) plan of base, and (d) exploded construction diagram (after Hawkes and Smith 1957 and Tylecote 1962).

between Kurd buckets and 'A' cauldrons is not very great. With regard to cauldrons, the majority come from Ireland (as do 'flesh-hooks': Jocken-hövel 1974) (fig. 6.45). The distribution of B cauldrons outside Britain, one in France and two in Spain, does not seem to support the argument for a Greek prototype which is in any case beaten out of a single sheet of metal while the British ones are riveted from a number of sheets like the buckets; their handles, as with the Irish-British buckets, are cast on, while the Greek ones are riveted.

If we consider the origins of insular sheet metalworking, the first beaten bronze metalwork seems to be from the Eriswell, Suffolk, hoard (Briscoe and Furness 1955; Trump 1968: 219ff.), and although the association of this beaten bronze with a rod-tanged sword and rapier is open to question it seems probable that it dates from the Penard phase. Socketed hammers – hammers being essential for sheet metalworking – also date from the Penard phase and from a little earlier, since many occur in the Taunton phase or ornament horizon. The use of the rivet on sheet metal is also attested in Danish contexts for this period (Thrane 1965). All this then suggests that the necessary expertise was available for local cauldron and bucket production at a much earlier date than hitherto considered.

Further argument contrary to Hawkes' and Smith's view of a Mediterranean origin for sheet metalworking in Britain is supplied by recent views of the origin for the British circular bronze shields (fig. 6.42:1), the majority of which come from rivers and bogs and none of which have been found in association with other material.[38] Coles (1962), following Hencken (1950), regarded the shields as stemming from east Mediterranean material of ninth–eighth century BC date. Recent central European evidence suggests (cf. Patay 1968) a commencement at least two centuries earlier in the Urnfield period – Reinecke D/Hallstatt A2–B1. Gräslund's (1967) emphasis on the development of the U- and V-notched shields from leather prototypes which have survived in Ireland (fig. 6.42:4) adds to the view that far from the shield having been developed first in the East, the concept was a west and north European one. However that may be, sheet metalworking must have commenced in Britain well before the introduction of the Ewart Park industries.

Hallstatt C and the end of late bronze age metallurgy

Since the question of continental iron age contacts with the British Isles will be further reviewed in the next chapter, only a few points need be made here.

The appearance of Hallstatt C material in Britain, conventionally set in the mid-seventh century BC, is primarily connected with the appearance of new sword forms (fig. 6.43). On the Continent there are two types of Hallstatt C bronze swords, the so-called Mindelheim and Gündlingen types. The two are contemporaneous, though the Mindelheim form – which is related to contempory iron forms – need not concern us here since no examples are known in Britain. The Gündlingen type, by far the more numerous, has a pommel tang, broad and shallow butt, and long elegant

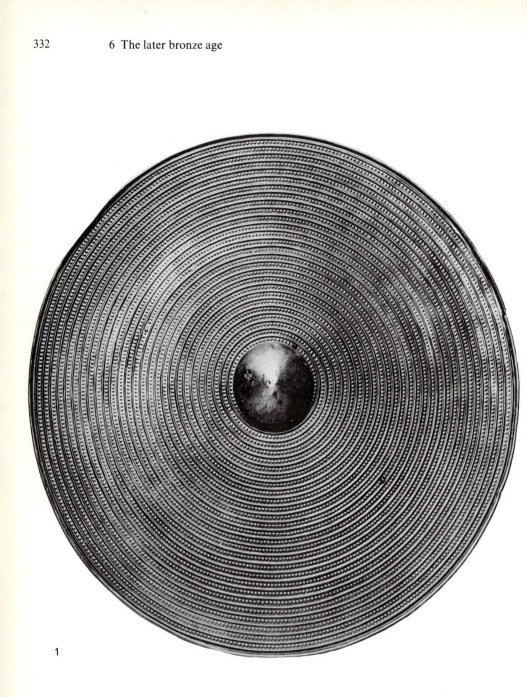

1

Fig. 6.42   1 Moel Siabod, Caerns.; bronze shield of Yetholm type; diameter 64·8cm (photograph courtesy Trustees of the British Museum); 2 Roos Carr, Holderness, Yorks.: one of five pinewood figures found set into a simple wooden boat model; the surviving eye is a quartzite pebble. Possibly of later bronze age date; height of head 5cm (photograph D. D-A. Simpson: courtesy S. E. Thomas); 3 Cloonlara, Co. Mayo: oak shield mould; diameter 48cm (photograph National Museum of Ireland); 4 Clonbrin, Co. Longford; leather shield; diameter 50cm (photograph National Museum of Ireland).

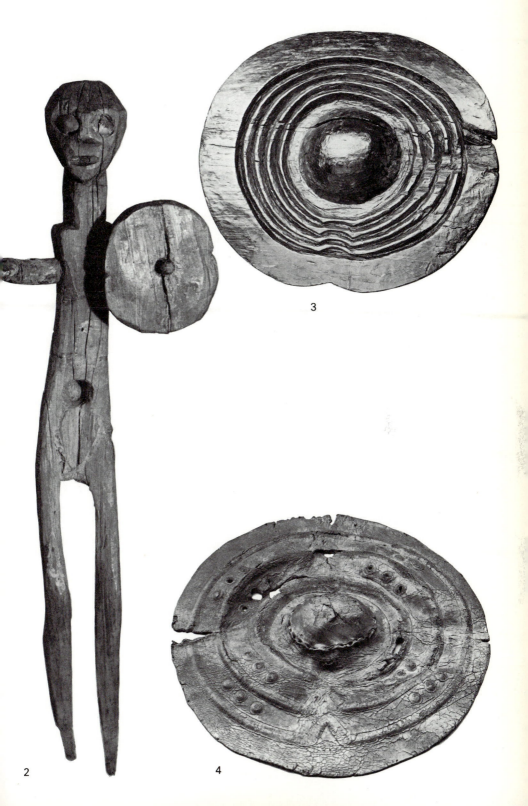

3

2   4

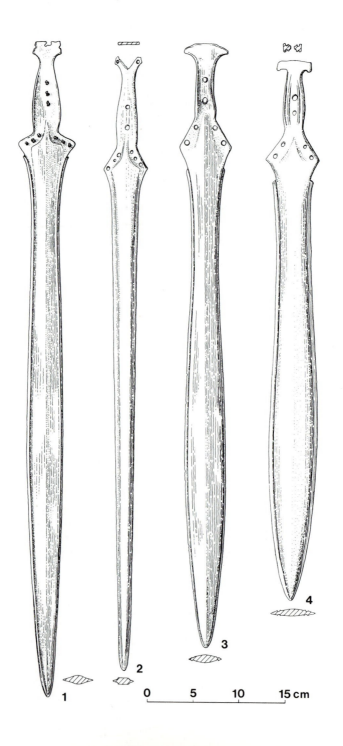

narrow blades. The distribution of this type in Europe is wide, covering central Europe, central and eastern France, the Low Countries and Scandinavia, as well as the British Isles which have nearly a third of the total known examples. These swords are most commonly found in graves in central Europe and of those that are not found in graves about half are from rivers and bogs. There are no grave finds in Britain – if one disallows the rather doubtful example of a sword found with a winged chape at Ebberston in Yorkshire (cf. Hodson 1964: 100) (fig. 6.43:1, 5) – and the percentage of river and bog finds is higher than that on the Continent. All the finds in Britain are of bronze (Cowen 1967), with the exception of the fragmentary iron sword from Llyn Fawr (fig. 6.44).

The distribution of Hallstatt swords, which does not entirely match that of other Hallstatt material in the British Isles, is concentrated in the Thames Valley, with a scatter up the east coast to Scotland. There are also nearly 50 examples from Ireland, significantly different in blade type from those found in the rest of Britain (Eogan 1965: class 5), though they do not appear in the south-east or extreme south-west. Few of these swords were imported: only Cowen's classes a2 and b which show a marked easterly distribution. Most must have been locally produced variants. It is

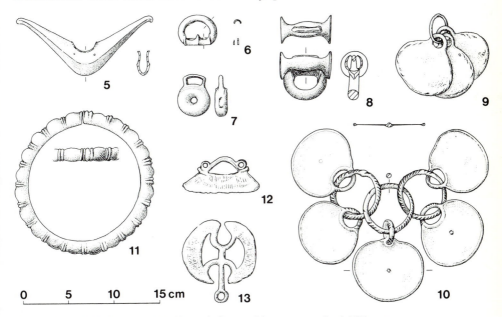

Fig. 6.43   1–4 Hallstatt and Hallstatt-influenced bronze swords: 1 Ebberston, Yorks.; 2 Cookhall, Co. Roscommon; 3 Ewart Park, Northumberland; 4 River Bann, Co. Antrim or Derry (after Burgess 1968c and Eogan 1964).

5–13. Continental bronze types in the latest phase of the British bronze age: 5 Ebberston, Yorks.: sword scabbard chape; 6–8, 10 Parc-y-meirch, Denbighs.; ? harness fittings including (10) jangle-plates; 9 Lissanode, Co. Westmeath: jangle-plates; 11 Scarborough, Yorks.: neck-rings; 12–13 Staple Howe, Yorks.; razors (after Burgess 1968c, Eogan 1964, Savory 1976c and Cunliffe 1974).

noticeable that Hallstatt swords are absent from indigenous hoards and this, taken with what he regards as strong Gündlingen influence in Ewart Park swords, convinces Burgess (1968c: 28ff.; 1974: 213ff.) that at least some Hallstatt settlers must have been involved. It is assumed that the long Hallstatt sword was in use for about a century until the introduction, once more into the Thames Valley, of the new Hallstatt D fashion for short dirks or daggers (cf. Jope 1961).

How the majority of Hallstatt C material reached Britain continues to be a matter for dispute. Theories include gift exchange, patronage of foreign smiths, or the movement of warriors; this last possibly explains such earlier phenomena as the number and size of south-eastern Carp's Tongue hoards and even the gold hoards of Ireland, buried as the result of external threat (cf. Hawkes and Clarke 1963: 240; Bradley and Ellison 1975: 113). The so-called 'Thames' variant of the Hallstatt sword, which

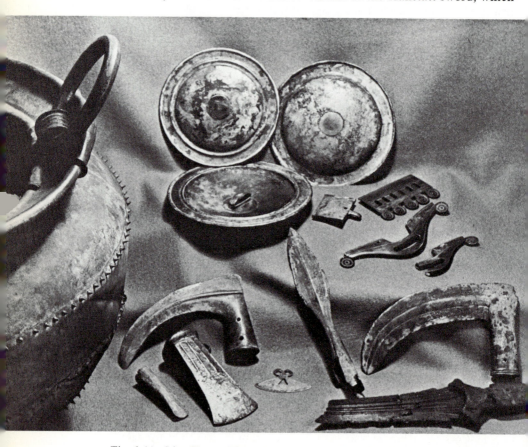

Fig. 6.44   Llyn Fawr, Glam.: late bronze age hoard with cauldron (*extreme left*), imported wing-shaped cheek-pieces, fragmentary Hallstatt C iron sword (*bottom right*), iron socketed sickle and iron spear head. Diameter of discs c.15cm (photograph A. Pacitto: courtesy S. E. Thomas).

occurs on the Continent and is usually considered an example of the continuing reciprocal trade across the Channel, has also been claimed as yet another continental introduction (Schauer 1972). But although knowledge of ironworking technology in certain native contexts may have resulted from foreign prospectors, the occurrence for example of an iron vase-headed pin from All Cannings Cross, Wiltshire, suggests an earlier beginning. The Llyn Fawr, Glamorganshire, hoard (Fox and Hyde 1939) has recently been described as 'loot seized by the local hill-men during a raid on some rich settlement in the fertile lowlands of the lower Severn basin' (Savory 1976c: 122; cf. also *idem* 1976b: 19ff.). The Llyn Fawr bronze Hallstatt C type razors, harness mounts comparable to those from the Belgian Hallstatt cemetery of Court-St-Etienne (Mariën 1958: esp. 236ff.; Britnell 1976), the unique if fragmentary iron Hallstatt C sword and iron spear (but including the clearly local but iron-socketed sickle), and bronze axes (fig. 6.44), have all been linked with other supposed evidence for Hallstatt C influence in hillforts of the Marches. These, with extensive timber-reinforced fortifications may, however, again indicate a purely native development (contrast Savory 1976a and cf. p. 290 above). Other Hallstatt C metal types which occur in Britain include chapes, which are not chronologically diagnostic. It might be remarked here that the characteristic Hallstatt C winged chape may reflect equestrian use, the wing being hooked under the foot when the sword is drawn. We have already noted the occurrence of Hallstatt razor types (cf. p. 292; Piggott C. M. 1946) which occur mainly on settlement sites. Two razors come from the south-west of Britain where Hallstatt swords are absent.[39]

In addition to this Hallstatt C material, indigenous metal types of course continued, though some distinctive forms appear right at the close of the bronze age in southern Britain. For example, there are massive socketed axes, the largest and heaviest in the whole of the late bronze age; even some of the small ones of this form, the Sompting type (Burgess 1969), have a massive look, with a heavy collar, expanded blade, and ribbed pellet decoration (fig. 6.30:4). These would appear to be related to the Armorican axes of north-western France which are also placed at the end of the late bronze age period; a radiocarbon date for the hoard of Saint-Bugan, Côtes-du-Nord, is 559 ± 130 bc (Briard 1965: 241ff.; Dunning 1959). These Breton axes frequently contain a high proportion of lead and some were made entirely of lead, which casts doubt on their utility: a use as standard ingots has been suggested. Linear faceted socketed axes, with a marked East Anglian distribution, also appear to belong to this phase.

The phase of the occurrence of Hallstatt material in the highland zone of Britain north of the border has been termed 'Adabrock' by Coles (1959–60: 42ff.), after a hoard on the Isle of Lewis. This contains fragments of a bronze Hallstatt C cross- or T-handled bowl (fig. 6.29:11) as well as razors and other tool types with Irish affinities. There is one faceted axe, matched with the probably pre-Adabrock phase hoard from Horsehope, Peebles-shire, with its small-scale cart fittings, harness rings and local axes (cf. Piggott S. 1953b). Whether brought by sporadic settlement or trade from the south, Hallstatt swords in Scotland (fig. 7.55) have a markedly riverine distribution, while there is negligible Hallstatt influence to be detected on the native bronzes, apart from possibly the grip forms of certain late Scottish swords. Finally the appearance of swan's neck sunflower pins (Coles 1958–9) makes another small group of eastern material largely complementary to the distribution of 'Covesea' types; this group is named after a hoard from Tarves in Aberdeenshire. Tarves material incorporates certain features of north German pins of the late Hallstatt period in association with late Ewart Park type swords with cast bronze pommels – possibly again a Hallstatt borrowing.

The end of the bronze age in Ireland is a much disputed period, argument hinging largely around the date of the introduction of native ironworking (cf. Champion T. C. 1971; Scott B. G. 1974a, b; Herity and Eogan 1977: 219ff.). Sompting and Breton axes in Ireland probably indicate some continuing if limited contact with southern England. Cup-headed pins (Eogan 1974b: 93ff.) are also a feature of the period (fig. 6.37:3). As we have seen, Hallstatt-type bronze swords in Ireland appear as a separate insular development and a number of winged and boat-shaped chapes are also known; local swords also are modified under the influence of the Hallstatt form (fig. 6.43:2). The finds however are isolated, as is the 'flesh-hook' from Dunaverney Bog, Co. Antrim (cf. Megaw 1970: no. 27), with its procession of aquatic birds (fig. 6.45:2), another Hallstatt C piece to be compared with the sole Scottish 'flesh-hook' from the Duke of Argyll's Inverary estates taken by Coles (1959–60: 25) as part of his 'Poldar' phase (cf. also Jockenhövel 1974).

In conclusion, it must be observed that no major culture explanation

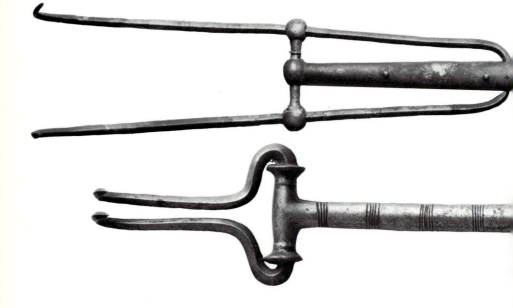

beyond the adoption of ironworking has yet been advanced for the ending of native British late bronze age industries more or less contemporary with the commencement of the Hallstatt D phase on the Continent c. 600 BC.

As the next chapter will show, it is certainly possible that society may have continued to be dominated by a warrior class of swordsmen and spearsmen, whose existence can be deduced from, for example, the weapons of the Thames Valley and the general technology of the Wilburton and successive phases (cf. Hawkes 1972: 113f.). Equally certainly there is little which can be convincingly offered comparable to the 'invasion' model which has been developed for the Low Countries by De Laet (1976), with a native substratum controlled by a Hallstatt warrior class and its new iron technology (but compare Coombs 1974). Earlier features of sudden change are equally difficult to explain, such as the apparent breakdown of the Wilburton industries of southern England and the appearance of the specialist axe industries of East Anglia, Lincolnshire and Sussex, matched by a failure by such industries to penetrate into northern Britain. The appearance of both weapons and 'horsey' gear is certainly indicative of a stratified warrior society in which the bronze industries may have been centrally controlled, but as with the Carp's Tongue hoards there seems now no clear evidence of population movement or settlement. Whatever their cultural significance, neither the Carp's Tongue complex nor the Hallstatt material seem to have greatly influenced local British technology any more than subsequent continental iron age introductions. Research into the wider aspects of later bronze age society in the British Isles has still many unsolved questions to answer.

Fig. 6.45 Later bronze age 'flesh-hooks'. 1 Little Thetford, Cambs.; length of hook 32·5 cm; 2 Dunaverney, nr Ballymoney, Co. Antrim; length 61 cm (photographs courtesy Trustees of the British Museum).

Notes

1. Apart from such sites as Eldon's Seat, Dorset (Cunliffe and Phillipson 1968), there are the late dates for the Dorset cemetery at Simons Ground ranging from 917 ± 55 bc to 71 ± 50 bc (Barrett 1976: 291ff.).

2. Hawkes' suggestion (1972: 114) that 'Britain, possibly Ireland too, could in fact have abandoned pottery, north and west of a line from the middle east coast to central Wales' from the outset of the middle bronze age seems somewhat of an over-statement.

3. For lists of radiocarbon dates see in particular Burgess (1974: 223–32); see also Preface, p. 3.

4. Rowlands (1976b: 10) notes that both stone and bronze moulds would have had a life of about 50 casting operations and cites the 50 palstaves in the Marshall Estate, Bognor, Sussex hoard.

5. Particularly useful for typology are the various sets of *Inventaria Archaeologica* of which some nine have been published on British material (GB.1–55, 1955–1968). The majority of these have dealt with later bronze age metal hoards. They include: the fourth set with hoards and grave-groups from the north-east Midlands (Great Freeman Street, Nottingham; Bagmoor, Lincs.; Welby, Leics.); the sixth set with late bronze age hoards in the British Museum (Feltwell Fen, Norfolk; Wickham Park, Surrey; Beachy Head, Sussex); the seventh set comprising mainly 'ornament horizon' hoards (Monkswood, Taunton Workhouse, and Edington Burtle, Somerset; Blackrock, Sussex) (fig. 6.3); and the ninth set devoted to the Heathery Burn Cave, Co. Durham (fig. 6.34). Of the continental sets, *The Netherlands* 2. set (NL. 11–16), 1971 (Drouwen and Bargeroosterveld, Drenthe; Voorhout, South Holland (fig. 6.6); Epe, Gelderland), *France* Fasc. I (F. 1–6), 1954 (St-Yrieix, 'Vénat', Charente), and *España* Fasc. 1–4 (E.1), 1958 (Huelva, Carp's Tongue hoard) contain comparative material of importance.

6. There are now three classifications available for the rapiers of middle and – possibly – late bronze age date (Trump 1962; 1968; Burgess 1968b; Rowlands 1976b: 64ff.), the four main types of Burgess based on blade cross-section being most frequently cited; his groups I and II belong clearly to the earlier part of the period. Coles (1963–4: 111–14) however has indicated good grounds for rejecting too detailed a typology and certain trapezoidal rapiers – the type found in the Malassis (Cher) hoard (Briard, Cordier and Gaucher 1969) – probably continue into the full British late bronze age.

7. 'Bishopsland', 'Auchterhouse' and 'Glentrool' phases in Ireland and Scotland are part of Burgess' 'Taunton' phase.

8. The Earls Barton, Northants., bell barrow and the Hove, Sussex, barrow, both with Camerton-Snowehill daggers, are dated to c. 1,250 bc; qv. p. 229. The only association with the Mold gold cape was some amber beads; it is therefore difficult totally to dismiss an early bronze age date – preferred also by J. J. Taylor (1970a) – for the find.

9. Burgess (1974: n.196 and 238) cites a palstave from Waterford made from the same mould as one from north Wales as well as an actual Group I palstave bronze mould from Ireland.

10. It seems probable that at least some of the gold of this period found in west and northern Britain came from Ireland, which had developed the use of solid bars for twisted ornaments. Some analytical work indicates that copper alloying was a key feature of the goldwork (or rather natural electrum owing to the silver present in the Wicklow Mountains ores) of the later Irish bronze age, though more particularly in the post-ornament horizon period (cf. Hall and Roberts 1962; Hawkes 1962; Megaw 1964).

11. The recent publication of a mid-Montelius II bronze collar from near Weston-super-Mare, Somerset (Lawson 1976) does not really help current arguments since it is a stray find.

12. For example, the Stogursey, Somerset, hoard – which contains not only large numbers of South Welsh socketed axes (as found in France) (fig. 6.30:3) and palstaves but includes a number of weapon types and seems to link various late bronze age regional traditions – the Broadward, Carp's Tongue and Heathery Burn groups (cf. McNeil 1973 and p. 312 below).

13. See Piggott S. (1973: 396–403) for a handy summary of the Wessex Deverel-Rimbury settlements, to which may be added Bradley and Ellison (1975: esp. 199ff.) on the development of enclosure boundaries.

14. Musson (1970) and Avery and Close-Brooks (1969) have indicated some of the problems in reconstructing bronze age house plans, the latter having re-interpreted the Shearplace Hill huts as being built on a double ring plan, a plan which was to extend into the iron age (fig. 6.14:1).

15. In view of the long life of leaf-shaped razors, which extend into the final stages of the bronze age, Piggott (1973: 390) has suggested dropping the numerical classifications in favour of a triple phaseology contemporary with, respectively, Wessex biconical urns, the Taunton-Glentrool or ornament horizon and Heathery Burn-Adabrock period.

16. Burgess (1974: n.361) supports a middle bronze age date for the comb, despite more than a hint for iron age occupation at the site (cf. Avery and Close-Brooks 1969), but on the question as to whether such combs could ever have been used for weaving see now Hodder and Hedges (1977).

17. As so frequently with French archaeology, evidence for comparable settlements and field systems on the other side of the Channel is sparse, but an extensive programme of aerial photography may remedy the situation (cf. Gaucher and Mohen 1974: 92). 'Celtic' fields in northern Germany and the Low Countries are clearly later iron age phenomena (cf. Zimmermann 1976 and Brongers 1976 for main references).

18. Death in battle seems represented by one of the inhumations found roughly buried in a pit at Todmarton, Glos. Two broken middle bronze age side-looped spear-tips were found embedded in the backbone and pelvis; the burials are dated to 977 ± 90 bc; Knight, Browne and Grinsell (1972) cite another example of death by a spear thrust evidenced by the remains of a burial found near Dorchester, Oxon., and now in the Ashmolean Museum, Oxford.

19. Despite local availability and the circumstantial evidence for Irish trading or prospecting ventures (cf. Hawkes and Clarke 1963: 230ff.), evidence for prehistoric exploitation of Cornish tin is scanty (cf. Rowlands 1976b: 6). Apart from Dean Moor, a hoard of cassiterite nodules was found in a hut at Trevisker, St Eval (ApSimon and Greenfield 1972: 312f.), and tin slag has been found associated with an early bronze age barrow at Carloggas, St Austell (Miles H. 1975: 35ff.). Early smelting of bog iron in northern Europe is, however, indicated by the discovery of an iron punch or awl on a wooden trackway at Bargeroosterveld in Drenthe dated by radiocarbon to about 1,170 bc; the trackway leads to a deposit of siderite.

20. ApSimon prefers the more correctly descriptive term 'pierced lug' noting the confusion which has arisen in connection with the early bronze age series of Armorican urns, which 'are without significant similarities' to the pottery of the south-west (ApSimon and Greenfield 1972: 364).

21. For recent summaries of the Hilversum culture see Butler (1969: 43–60), who here offers good distributional reasons for claiming the palstaves in the

Voorhout hoard as local, and De Laet (1974: 324–48); the end point of the culture at about 1,150 bc is contemporary with the last of the undisputed British imports. See also van Impe (1976) for comparison of British barrow types with those of the Kempen region of Belgium.

22. Burgess (1974: 214f.) and Barrett (1976) have some pertinent comments on the dangers of lumping together under a general 'Deverel-Rimbury' banner regional urn cemetery groups of the later bronze age.

23. It should be noted that in a review of Savory (1971a), Alcock (1972c) disputes the interpretation of the stratigraphical evidence.

24. Iron age hillforts containing later bronze age material include Ham Hill, Dorset, and South Cadbury, Somerset (Alcock 1972b: 120ff.), the already mentioned Ivinghoe Beacon, Bucks, site – another timber-framed hillfort with a scatter of Carp's Tongue bronzes (Cotton and Frere 1968) – and, from the Midlands, Beacon Hill, Leics. The last-named site has a scatter of material including a bronze mould for a plain socketed axe (Hodges 1960: pl. VI: C 'Charnwood Forest, Nottinghamshire') and a late bronze age hoard with pottery, two peg-socketed spears, a gouge and a socketed axe (*PSAL 4*, 1859: 323–4; cf. Burgess 1974: 220). The late bronze age smith's hoard with Irish gold tress- or lock-ring found within the ramparts of Portfield Camp, Lancs., is another case in point (Blundell and Longworth 1967). Traprain Law, Midlothian, also discussed in the next chapter, has indications of on-site smithing with clay moulds for a lunate spear head and, as at Jarlshof in the Shetlands, a 'late' Ewart Park sword (cf. Jobey 1976: 193).

25. Cf. Coles (1958–9); Eogan (1974b); Spratling (1974). The Scottish series – related to the period of the Covesea material – may develop independently of Ireland and Eogan regards some late pins (the cup-headed form – fig. 6.37:3) as coming direct from the Continent to Ireland; qv. also p. 338. In this context attention should be drawn to the 900 late bronze age objects found in an urn at Villethierry near Auxerre which include several pins similar to the British and Irish types (Mordant and Prampart 1976; see also n. 28).

26. In Scotland remains of an Irish/British bucket come from a crannog in Dowalton Loch, Wigtowns., and old accounts indicate the possibility of Duddingston Loch having been the site of a crannog-type settlement; cf. Coles (1959–60: 29).

27. Hawkes' view (1961) that there was an ultimately east Mediterranean influence in Irish goldworking techniques is countered by Eogan who prefers a central European source for Irish ear-rings (Herity and Eogan 1977: 176). Stephen Green informs us that the Caergwrle bowl has been recently identified as not having been made out of pottery.

28. Even if the Voorhout palstaves must now be considered as local (cf. n. 21 above), the massive hoard from Malassis, Cher, contains definite British pieces as well as objects common to both sides of the Channel in the middle bronze age (Briard, Cordier and Gaucher 1969; Burgess 1976a: 97). In a later period South Welsh axes originating in the Bristol Channel region are common in France (Burgess, Coombs and Davies 1972: esp. 232–4). Burgess (1974: 201) cites a Group II rapier from Cascina Ranza, Italy.

29. The new Villethierry, Cher, later bronze age find, clearly a finished collection ready for disposal, is another major addition to evidence of merchants' hoards (Mordant and Prampart 1976).

30. Burgess (1968c: 34; 1974: 205) summarizes the evidence for Urnfield imports. As discussed more fully on p. 331, shields claimed by Coles (1962) to be no earlier than HaB3 or Montelius V on the Continent may indeed have an early Urnfield background (cf. also Gräslund 1967; Coombs 1975b: 51ff.; May

1976: 107f.). Bronze arrowheads, less easy to date, are a form represented in the Penard hoard itself (cf. Mercer R.J. 1970b).

31. Analysis of three of the Hemigkofen swords from the Thames indicates all to have been made of non-leaded bronze (Brown and Blin-Stoyle 1959a).

32. Burgess (1968a: 36ff.; 1974: 209) sees such actual Wilburton material as is present in northern Britain and Wales as late arrivals following a period of decline and industrial unrest in the eighth century BC.

33. For axe hoards of eastern and central England, on occasion with more than 50 pieces, cf. Kennett (1975).

34. It is noticeable that British Carp's Tongue swords contain less lead than those of the Wilburton phase (Brown and Blin-Stoyle 1959a). See also Jockenhövel and Smolla (1975) for the hoard of Juvincourt-Damary, predominantly with Urnfield affinities but including Carp's Tongue and Heathery Burn-Adabrock-Dowris forms.

35. Britton (1971: 26) points out that the often-cited illustration in Childe (1940: fig. 61) purporting to be of Heathery Burn cheek-pieces in fact illustrates one of Greenwell's (1894) Swiss parallels and a bone 'toggle' from the cave.

36. The Pyotdykes, Angus, find, a 'personal' hoard, comprises two Ewart Park swords, one with remains of a wood and leather sheath, and a basal-looped spear with a decorative gold band (Coles, Coutts and Ryder 1964). The spear has affinities with the Penard phase and is yet another example of the 'survival' of old forms, perhaps in this case as a ceremonial piece.

37. The Irish horns, unlike the *lurer*, are not exclusively found in otherwise unassociated contexts; of the 120 or so examples recorded by Coles one only comes from outside Ireland: an end-blow horn from Battle, Sussex, now lost.

38. In addition to the continental evidence, the low lead content of, for example, the Brumby Common, Lincs., shield could suggest an introduction certainly at the beginning of the Wilburton phase (cf. Butler 1963: 127ff.; May 1976: 108).

39. One site is South Cadbury where Alcock (1972b: 118ff.) favours a Hallstatt refugee settlement.

7 The iron age (c. 600 BC–AD 200)

A. SOUTHERN BRITAIN AND IRELAND

Introduction

By the end of the bronze age the range of archaeological evidence has changed almost completely. The established funerary traditions disappear in the middle bronze age in southern England, and even earlier elsewhere, and in the iron age burials occur only sporadically, with the exception of a few very restricted regional traditions. The end of the bronze age also sees the end of the deposition of hoards, the other major source of bronze age evidence. For the first time in British archaeology the primary source of material is an abundance of settlement sites. And yet, despite a long tradition of excavation on these sites, which at least in the south and east regularly produce a wealth of material, it is perhaps surprising how little the opportunities provided by this new source of evidence have been realized. There are few totally or extensively excavated sites, and fewer studies of settlement distribution; only in the last few years has any progress been made in studying the economy of the period and integrating the sites into a wider picture of the landscape and its exploitation. Instead, the questions pursued have been more concerned with details of artifactual typology and chronology, although the material is less amenable to such traditional treatment than are grave groups and hoards. These problems will be more fully discussed below.

Although the idea of an iron age was an integral part of antiquarian thought throughout the nineteenth century, there was little material to substantiate the existence of such a period in Britain except for coins and some decorated metalwork found mainly in rivers.[1] It was only with the development of settlement excavation, especially by General Pitt-Rivers, that a more detailed picture of the iron age began to emerge. At first the only conceptual framework into which this material could be set was the established system of the Hallstatt and La Tène iron age cultures of continental Europe. Comparisons were sought across the Channel, and similarities explained by the theory of migration from the Continent. As the quantity of insular material grew it was eventually possible to present an independent classification. Hawkes' threefold division (1931) into iron age A, B and C represented observed differences of English iron age culture, but was still closely related to the continental scheme for both chronology and explanation. Iron age A was the earliest iron age material, ascribed to invaders from Hallstatt Europe; B was represented by groups in Yorkshire and the south-west with affinities to continental Early La Tène, while C was the term given to the regional tradition in south-eastern England comparable to the late La Tène of Western Europe. Like A, the development of B and C was ascribed to immigrant populations.

Hawkes' ABC was a necessary step in furthering iron age research, and indeed the ideas and explanations underlying it have dominated iron age thought ever since. Considerable archaeological activity was stimulated in the 1930s, especially the excavation of hillforts. As a result of such research in Sussex, Hawkes presented a modification of his scheme (1939b). Construction of the hillforts on the South Downs was envisaged as the response to an invasion from Europe, which introduced elements of continental early La Tène culture and was dated by virtue of this material to c. 250 BC. This hypothesis was adopted for other regions, especially by the advocacy of Childe (1940: 212–27), who christened the invaders Marnians, and saw them as one element in a series of migrations bringing early La Tène styles to Britain. Hallstatt invaders were equally enthusiastically accepted as the bringers of the earliest iron age culture, as were the Belgae, emigrants from Belgium mentioned by Caesar, to account for iron age C (Hawkes and Dunning 1930).

With the rapid increase in the rate of discovery it became clear that regional and chronological subdivisions of the original ABC could be discerned, and Hawkes eventually (1959) presented a revised version of his scheme. In a framework of geographical provinces and regions and chronological periods, various local groups distinguished by pottery, structures, metalwork and burials were defined and arranged. Despite the objective framework of space and time, which has in fact proved too complicated for general adoption, the regional groups were again assigned to the original ABC classification, which was still used for broad cultural divisions, and still represented the same mode of explanation in terms of immigrants.

Objections to the scheme were formulated by Hodson (1960; 1962; 1964). He argued against the restrictive nature of the geographical and chronological framework, and suggested that instead regional groups should be defined independently by their characteristic types rather than by reference to a previously established scheme of classification and explanation. He also argued specifically against the Marnian invasion, both on the grounds of the imprecise stratigraphy of the Sussex sites and because of the small quantity and varied dates of the continental-style La Tène metalwork, which together made it difficult to accept the hypothesis of a single invasion horizon. Hodson also called into doubt the Hallstatt invaders, but was far from denying altogether the hypothesis of culture change by invasion. For the Yorkshire burial tradition, termed the Arras culture (see p. 407), and the late iron age cremations of the south-east, his Aylesford culture (see p. 409), the traditional explanation was retained. Though much of the British iron age was attributed to native bronze age roots, what was in dispute was not so much the principle of invasions but the question of how much continental material there was in Britain, and how much was needed to warrant the suggestion of an invasion.

These arguments for and against Hawkes' ABC system have dominated subsequent interpretation and explanation of the British iron age. Cunliffe (1978a) embodies the ideas of Hodson and supplies some of the regional grouping that was missing in his original scheme, while D.W. Harding (1974) restates the case for Hallstatt, Early La Tène and Late La Tène immigrants as the impetus to British iron age developments. Though opposed on details of interpretation, these two accounts share some fundamental assumptions (Champion T. C. 1975). They both find it necessary to account for cases of similarity between Britain and the Continent in terms of the introduction of ideas to Britain from abroad rather than as a sign of a common cross-Channel cultural province, and they both offer explanations of such similarities simply in terms of the alternatives, trade or invasion. As will be seen, these concepts do not offer a satisfactory explanation for many developments, especially in the fields of structures, technology and ritual.

Concentration on problems of chronology and typology and on the parallels and prototypes for artifactual and structural types has meant that questions of social and economic development have received too little attention. Even for those objects actually imported from abroad or those ideas of continental inspiration, it is necessary to consider the nature of the society that received and adopted them. The alternatives, invasion or independent development, invasion or trade, are too simple to account for the complex progress of iron age society and culture, and a more sophisticated set of explanatory hypotheses must be proposed.

Another concept that has been widely used in the interpretation of the iron age is Fox's distinction between highland and lowland zones. He was one of the first to study the significant part played by environment in the formation of human culture, but few would now follow all his conclusions. 'In the Lowland of Britain new cultures of continental origin tend to be imposed on the earlier or aboriginal culture. In the Highland, on the other hand, these tend to be absorbed by the older culture' (Fox C.F.1932:31). Such ideas, not only of regional variation but also of regional variation in patterns of cultural development, now seem to place undue weight on the deterministic role of the environment, and on the explanation of culture change by immigration and invasion, fundamental to Fox's view. Environmental factors are, of course, important – for instance, in the differential availability of stone and timber for building purposes (Hamilton 1966a), or in the choice of agricultural strategy – but it will be suggested below (p. 354) that a distinction between arable farming in the lowland zone and pastoral in the highland is too extreme; it is also possible that this highland/lowland distinction was of less significance in earlier periods and that these regional variations in subsistence economy, such as they were, may have been due to the effects of over-exploitation. Even in the iron age there are other patterns of geographical variation that do not correspond to the highland/lowland division, such as the distribution of hillforts (p. 365). For all these reasons, and also because the distinction has never satisfactorily accommodated Ireland, it has not been adopted in the present assessment of the iron age.

One other interpretative framework that has been used for the iron age is documented history, for even before the Roman conquest, as the classical world's knowledge of northern Europe developed, references increased in the works of Greek and Latin writers to the Celts in general and also specifically to Britain.[2] Many are of a purely topographical nature, but others record details of the settlements, economy and society of the barbarian world; these may afford valuable evidence to supplement archaeological material, but there are also other references which describe historical events such as Caesar's two expeditions to Britain, sporadic political contacts between Britain and Rome in the century between Caesar and Claudius, and even a migration into southern Britain. It is these references, together with the inscriptions found on some coins of the late iron age, that have formed the basis for a type of history which purports to describe the political and military events of the century or more before the Roman conquest, and to trace the fluctuating fortunes of the various British tribes (p. 417). The references, though meagre, have been used as a framework to which the archaeological evidence has been fitted, often at the cost of severe distortion. Although there is a legitimate expectation that such references should be considered in an explanation of the archaeology, they cannot be the basis for that interpretation, for the archaeological data of settlements, artifacts and economies are not the same as the historical data of peoples and events, and the interpretative frameworks into which they can be synthesized are likewise very different. Hachmann (1976) has emphasized the distinction between archaeological and historical problems, and what is needed is a more sophisticated assessment of the correspondence between the two: for instance, even if the distributions of coin types cannot be taken to indicate the boundaries of the political units issuing them (Hogg 1971), the coins themselves are signs of the existence of that authority, and may be evidence, not for its geographical extent, but for its development and function. With a clear view of the limitations of the various categories of evidence, and of the various questions that they can be legitimately used to answer, there is no reason why archaeology and history should not eventually be blended into a unified picture of the late iron age.

Chronology

In the south and east most iron age sites produce a wealth of artifacts, especially pottery. This has been extensively studied with particular emphasis on chronological problems, and since it is so abundant and the finer wares at least change considerably through time, it has a valuable role to play as a basis for a relative chronology. Further to the north and west, there is no such abundance of iron age material, and before the advent of radiocarbon dating the establishment of a reliable chronology was a major problem. Many sites produced little material, and that, when datable, was mostly of the Roman period; they were consequently assigned totally to that period, and although it can now be appreciated that on many sites such datable material came from merely the final phase of a long occupation, such conclusions were impossible before the availability of a dating method independent of artifacts.

Radiocarbon dating has also brought new possibilities of providing absolute dates for the relative chronology established by artifactual sequences. Previously there had been a curious reversal of normal archaeological principles for deducing such dates. So readily accepted were the invasions suggested by Hawkes, popularized by Childe, and still widely given credence today, that they were themselves used as a basis for chronology, and instead of using associations of pottery with objects intrinsically datable in the continental system, such as brooches, the pottery styles were dated by reference to the invasions and the known chronology of associated metalwork was in consequence distorted.

The Marnian invasion of c. 250 BC, for example, was taken as the stimulus to hillfort building, and the first possible date for material of early La Tène type in Britain, although that was the very date at which it was disappearing on the Continent.[3] Similarly, the possible flight of refugees from Caesar's conquest of northern Gaul in 56 BC was taken as the origin of iron age B at Maiden Castle and more generally (Wheeler 1943: 55–7).[4] Though subsequent work showed this date to be impossible both in France and in Britain, it was for a long time accepted. In south-east England too, 75 BC was the agreed date for the beginning of iron age C, more because it was ascribed to migrants recorded by Caesar than because any of the continental parallels warranted such a date (see below, p. 416). With the dismissal of these historical dates, the whole basis of the absolute chronology collapses, but it is difficult to resist the suspicion that many dates are still derived from a pottery chronology dependent on such arguments.

A new absolute chronology could be established by the analysis of stratigraphic sequences and associations with objects datable by reference to the continental sequence, but unfortunately such associations are rare. After the Hallstatt C metalwork of the seventh century (p. 331), there is little except brooches of early La Tène style (p. 391), though few of these occur in useful associations; local imitations of early La Tène pottery styles may also be of use (p. 398). Thereafter there is nothing until the occurrence of late La Tène brooches in the first century BC, though mostly in small grave groups. The first datable material of widespread occurrence is imported pottery, especially the Gallo-Belgic wares beginning c. 10 BC and their local imitations (p. 402).

From the disappearance of later bronze age metalwork to c. 10 BC there is, therefore, a critical dearth of datable material, and radiocarbon dating is of vital importance, even though at this comparatively recent period the standard deviation is liable to be a relatively wide range. As well as revolutionizing the chronology of the areas where artifacts are rare, it will increasingly provide absolute calibration for the relative dates of the south and east. Sites such as Gussage All Saints (Wainwright and Spratling 1973; Wainwright and Switsur 1976) and Danebury (Cunliffe 1976c), where long occupation affords the opportunity of a continuous ceramic sequence, will be of particular use for this purpose.[5] Until these dated sequences are available, the chronology is inevitably vague. It is still largely supplied by pottery in the south-east, and sporadic radiocarbon dates elsewhere. In areas such as Ireland, where both artifacts and radiocarbon dates are rare, it is still difficult to see what sites should be assigned to this period.

Environment and economy

By the end of the bronze age, as has been noted above (p. 261), pollen evidence suggests a contrast between the widely deforested chalk-lands of the south and east, and the rest of the islands, where clearances had been on a smaller scale;[6] thereafter, especially after the middle of the 1st millennium BC, wide-spread clearance of the forest is demonstrated in many parts of England and Wales, though apparently not till the 1st millennium AD in the north-west and in Ireland (Turner 1970).

Turner's evidence for iron age expansion, drawn from sites in East Anglia, Yorkshire, Somerset and Wales, can now be supplemented. In Derbyshire, for example, the East Moor shows extensive clearance for pastoral use c. 400–300 BC (Hick 1972), and a similar development can be seen at the same period in the north Yorkshire moors (Atherden 1976); in both areas cereals only begin to appear some time after clearance. Rather later dates are recorded for clearances associated with arable farming in the Pennine Dales (Roberts et al. 1973), Lowland Durham (Bartley et al. 1976) and north Lincolnshire (Holland 1975). In Kent pollen from soils buried beneath hillforts suggests that they were associated with the spread of agriculture onto poorer soils away from the chalk.[7] More analyses and closer correlation with archaeological remains are needed before this pattern of expansion can be understood; it is likely to show great regional variation, both in chronology and in the use to which the cleared areas were put.

But the iron age did not see only expansion, for there are also areas, especially uplands such as Dartmoor (Simmons 1969b), where occupation virtually disappears in this period. This has often been attributed to a worsening of the climate, and climatic deterioration has even been cited as a more general explanation of many of the changes in the late bronze age and early iron age (Burgess 1974: 166–7 and 194–8). It is, however, difficult to distinguish climatic from anthropogenic causes. Change in climate has traditionally been suggested as the stimulus to observed changes in the pollen record, in peat stratigraphy and in the development of blanket bog, but it is now far from clear that climate played a significant, or even any, part in these developments. The boundary between Godwin's pollen zones VIIb and VIII, marked by a decrease in lime and increase in beech, hornbeam and birch, cannot now be seen to be synchronous throughout Britain or be attributed to a worsening climate.[8] The gross changes in the rate of peat growth used to define the transition from the sub-Boreal to the sub-Atlantic climatic periods are now appreciated as a very much more complex phenomenon,[9] and the spread of upland blanket bog was in many areas already initiated long before the iron age;[10] in both these processes, increasing weight is now given to the activities of man as a causative factor. Independent assessments of past climate, where anthropogenic causes can be ruled out, are needed before the theory can be used as a more general explanation of social and economic changes. Whatever the relative importance assigned to climate and man's over-exploitation, it is certain, however, that many areas were increasingly hostile to human occupation; it is possible, too, that in other areas where environmental data are lacking, such as the chalklands, earlier exploitation had had similar effects in reducing agricultural yields.

It would be instructive to compare this environmental data for colonization and abandonment with studies of settlement distributions, but few such surveys have been attempted, and in some areas the best evidence of iron age activity is in the form of dated pollen profiles. Small-scale field surveys in such different regions as the chalk downland at Chalton, Hampshire (Cunliffe 1973: 180) and the valley soils of Wharfedale, Yorkshire (Raistrick 1939) show a proliferation of small, closely spaced sites; in Wiltshire, iron age sites show a preference for high-quality arable and downland soils (Ellison and Harriss 1972: 924), though this is made questionable by an almost total lack of fieldwork off the chalk. There are, however, few larger-scale surveys of iron age occupation designed to show changes through time. Fox's work in East Anglia (1933) showed a discontinuity between the distributions of earlier and later iron age sites, and he attributed this to Belgic immigrants. This seems to be the most substantial foundation for a more generally held theory of late iron age expansion on to heavier soils, facilitated by possession of a heavier plough. Even Fox's survey, however, does not fully support this conclusion, for many of the soils he defined as heavy would be more usually assigned to other categories, especially the medium range of loams (Wooldridge and Linton 1933), and there is even less evidence for a heavier or improved plough in the late iron age (Manning 1964). Neither has fieldwork elsewhere substantiated the suggestion.

The evidence for the way in which iron age man exploited this landscape comes partly from the pollen record, partly from such features as field systems and land divisions, but more especially from finds from excavated sites. A distinction has been drawn on this basis between the economy of the lowland zone, with mixed farming incorporating extensive cereal production, and of the highland zone, with a greater emphasis on pastoralism, respectively Piggott's Woodbury and Stanwick types (1961).

In the lowland zone the most obvious signs of arable farming are the many field systems recognizable, especially on the chalk downs; medieval and modern farming have destroyed these fields, masking the true extent of prehistoric agriculture (Bowen and Fowler 1966). These small, approximately square so-called 'Celtic' fields (Bowen H.C. 1961) are widely distributed in southern England, especially Wessex (e.g. RCHM Dorset III: 318–46) (fig. 7.1), and have also been discovered on the Yorkshire Wolds (Challis and Harding 1975: 155). The ploughs used were probably of the simple bow-ard type (Payne 1947; Manning 1964; Bowen H.C. 1969: 18) (fig. 6.10), and the crops sown are known from carbonized

Fig. 7.1   Chiseldon, Wilts.: 'Celtic' field system (photograph: National
Monuments Record, Crown Copyright reserved).

grains and impressions on pottery (Helbaek 1952). Hulled barley replaced the naked varieties dominant in the bronze age, and emmer gave way to spelt as the commonest wheat, though bread wheat and club wheat were also grown.[11] The advantage of spelt and hulled barley was that both could be winter sown, thus allowing the labour of ploughing and harvesting to be spread. Regional variations may have existed, with a greater proportion of barley to wheat in the chalk areas than elsewhere (Dennell 1976). The subsequent processing of the crop, from harvesting through cleaning, parching and threshing to grinding, has left little trace except for the sickles and quern stones (p. 394). Pits are a frequent site find, and experiment has shown that they are ideally adapted to the storage of grain (Reynolds 1974); they vary considerably in size and shape, but cylindrical and beehive-shaped profiles are most frequent, with depth up to 2m.

The evidence for stock rearing is mainly in the form of animal bones from excavations, but, though found in abundance, there are few adequate studies. Most sites produce bones of the five major domesticates, cattle, sheep, pig, horse and dog, but in widely varying proportions.[12] The bones found on sites are indicative more of the consumption than necessarily of the stock maintained there, and of the final function of the animals as meat rather than any prior, possibly more important, use. Study of the bones can, however, show the strategy underlying the rearing of the animals. At Hawk's Hill, Surrey (Carter and Phillipson 1965), few sheep were killed in their first two years and the pattern conforms to that expected from a herd kept mainly for wool and manure; at Barley, Hertfordshire (Ewbank et al. 1964), on the other hand, the majority were killed within the first two years, the best time for meat, indicating a greater reliance on sheep for food. There is not yet sufficient information for generalization, neither have there been many similar studies of cattle, to assess the relative importance of meat against other uses such as milk, leather or traction. Evidence from Hawk's Hill and Eldon's Seat (Cunliffe and Phillipson 1968: 229) shows that the majority reached maturity, suggesting that the provision of meat was not the dominant function.

Hunting and gathering do not appear to have played a significant part in supplementing the diet. Deer bones are uncommon, and fish rare, though adequate recovery techniques have seldom been employed. Oysters and other shell-fish are more frequent, especially near the coast, though curiously they do not seem to have been generally exploited before the first century BC. Other bird and animal bones are occasionally found, but it is not clear whether they were hunted for meat, other products such as skins or feathers, or merely for sport.

Arable and pastoral were closely linked in a complex farming system. It would have been impossible to maintain crop production without manuring, achieved mainly by grazing sheep in the fields. On the other hand, it was essential to provide winter fodder for livestock; this was successfully achieved, since there is no evidence for an annual autumn slaughter (Higgs and White 1963). No detailed reconstruction of the agricultural system has been made,[13] but clear signs of the necessary organization of land-use can occasionally be seen, for example, at

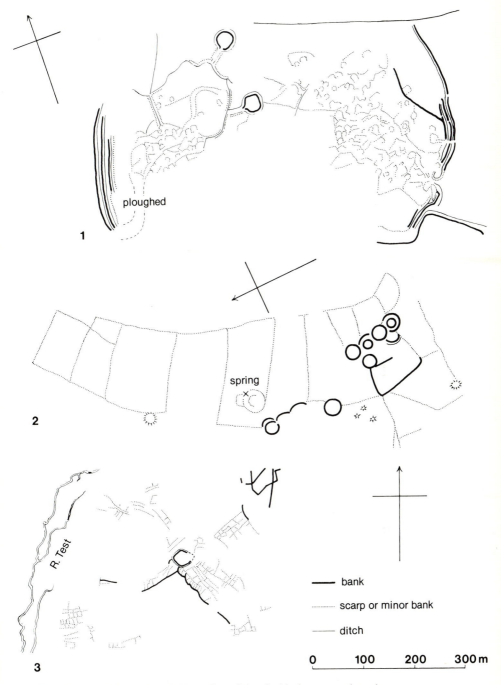

Fig. 7.2 1 Hamshill Ditches, Wilts.: plan of 'banjos' in larger earthwork system (after Bowen 1975); 2 Cush, Co. Limerick: ring-forts and field systems (after Ó Ríordáin 1940); 3 field systems around Woolbury, Hants. (after Cunliffe 1978a).

Woolbury, Hampshire (Cunliffe 1978a: 188) (fig. 7.2), where linear earthworks define areas of arable and pastoral. Great care was needed in the managing of stock, especially if winter-sown crops were grown, and a variety of enclosures have been linked with stock control. There are in Wessex a number of roughly circular enclosures with long entrance passages, termed 'banjos', and other small rectangular ditched enclosures, both frequently associated with linear earthworks (fig. 7.2), which may have had some such function (Cunliffe 1978a: 165; Perry 1966; 1969: 37), though recent excavations suggest that they should also be regarded as settlements.

In some regions fieldwork is now beginning to reveal the complexity of the iron age settlement pattern and its changing relationship to the physical environment: in the Upper Thames Valley (Lambrick 1978) a variety of site forms reflects economic specialization and the intensive use of available land resources, while in the Trent Valley (Smith C. 1977; 1978) human activity has been successfully integrated into the wider ecological system.

There is also some evidence of organization of land use on a larger scale. Cross-ridge dykes in the Chilterns (Dyer 1961), combined with natural features such as rivers, define a series of territories, each including a variety of downland and valley soils, and in Hampshire Cunliffe (1976a: fig. 1) has suggested a similar sharing of available resources in the territories of hillforts.

In the highland zone, evidence for subsistence production is much less common. Storage pits are absent, and this may be one reason why the major emphasis has been placed on pastoralism. But the role of arable farming should not be minimized. It is attested in many pollen records, and querns are regularly discovered in excavations. Field systems are also known, as at Kestor on Dartmoor (Fox A. 1954) and in Derbyshire (Posnansky 1956) and Yorkshire (Raistrick 1938). Feachem (1973), summarizing this evidence, suggests an abandonment of upland agriculture in the mid-1st millennium BC, but it is doubtful if such a conclusion could be supported by the pollen evidence, though this does suggest an increase in arable late in the iron age (p. 349). In Ireland it is possible that the field system at Cush, Co. Limerick, dates to the iron age (Ó Ríordáin 1940) (fig. 7.2).

The evidence for pastoralism in the highland zone is similarly scarce, as on many sites animal bone does not survive in the acid soil conditions. From the limited data available, it appears that the highland sites regularly show a lower proportion of sheep than the lowland ones, possibly reflecting the importance of sheep for manuring the extensive arable areas of the lowland zone.

Settlement

A wide variety of different types of settlement have so far been recognized, but the attention paid to them in survey and excavation has been far from even. The earliest work was naturally devoted to the most easily recognizable sites, and hillforts with their surviving defences were an obvious focus. The results of this early exploration formed the basis of our knowledge of the period, and these sites still play a major part in iron age studies. Research into other types of site has been affected by a number of factors. In the highland zone, where post-iron age agriculture has been less extensive, and structures were in many cases of stone, smaller enclosures and individual structures have survived, but in other areas where timber and earth were the structural materials, agricultural development has caused widespread destruction, and few sites are visible on the ground. Some sites survive as earthworks in regions of unploughed downland, especially in Wessex, and these have been regularly excavated. Elsewhere, discovery has been mainly by aerial photography (fig. 7.3), which has led to the exploration of sites with more easily identifiable features such as ditched enclosures, or by rescue work in the course of their actual destruction; in this case, the very nature of their recognition and excavation has prevented extensive examination. It is possible, therefore, that our knowledge of iron age settlement types is biased towards the hillforts and enclosures with too little emphasis given to other forms of unenclosed occupation.

Hillforts are the iron age's most obvious legacy to the landscape, but the term has been applied to a wide range of sites, of very different size, function and chronology.[14] Essentially they are sites with defences constructed of earth, timber or stone, on high ground or in other naturally defensible locations. This concentration on the surface morphology of the site, and the particular characteristic of the possession of defences has not only included in one concept sites of very different function (p. 365), but has also led to the inclusion of defended sites in other locations, such as hill-slopes (Fox A. 1952) or valleys, for example Salmonsbury (Dunning 1976), though in these cases the terminology is often simplified to 'fort'. More normally, hillforts are sited to take advantage of natural features such as cliffs or promontories, either inland or on the coast, or follow the contours of hills or plateaus. They range in size from over 50ha to less than 0·5ha.

Most excavations until recently concentrated on the defences, and a wide range of structural techniques is now known. The defences usually consist of one or more lines of fence, wall or bank, with an external ditch, and sometimes a small bank or 'counterscarp' beyond the ditch. There are a number of exceptions, however; on very steep slopes the upcast of the ditch is occasionally thrown downhill to give an external bank, and in Ireland there is an important group of forts with internal ditches (p. 365), while in north Wales and Ireland some forts have no ditches at all. Other elements of the defences are the gates, which are often elaborate, and sometimes *chevaux-de-frise* of wood or stone (Harbison 1971).

The banks that are the most prominent part of the hillfort defences conceal a variety of structures. The simplest is a timber palisade, a type which, though commonest in northern Britain (p. 451), is also found in the south, as at Hollingbury, Sussex (Curwen 1932), Blewburton, Berkshire

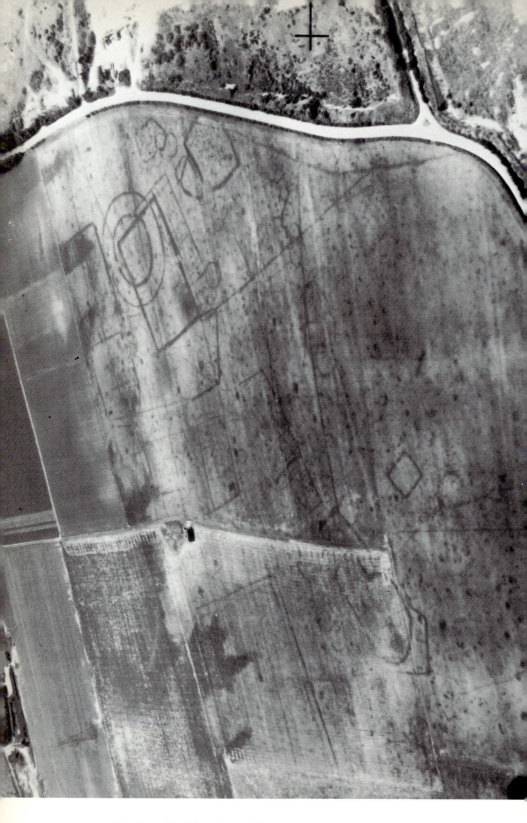

Fig. 7.3   Mucking, Grays Thurrock, Essex: crop marks of enclosures and related features on gravel (photograph: courtesy Director in Aerial Photography, University of Cambridge).

(Harding D.W. 1976b), or Castle Hill, Eddisbury, Cheshire (Varley 1952); on these sites they precede more complex structures of timber and earth or stone, though not always following the same line.[15] More common than palisades are vertically walled ramparts and dump banks.

Vertically faced ramparts were constructed in a variety of techniques, dependent in part on the availability of suitable materials (fig. 7.4). The box rampart as at Ivinghoe, Buckinghamshire (Cotton and Frere 1968) or Grimthorpe, Yorkshire (Stead 1968) is one such form, with timber walls to front and rear consisting of vertical posts set in individual post-holes and facings of turf, logs or planks to retain the earth fill. The weight of the rampart filling may well have imposed too great a force on the timber walls, for there are other designs to provide a vertical front face with less strain. At Hollingbury, Sussex (Curwen 1932), an earthen bank was piled against the rear wall, and at Poundbury, Dorset (Richardson 1940), the rear wall was dispensed with completely. At Blewburton, Berkshire (Harding D.W. 1976b), a bank was added behind the rear wall and three tiers of horizontal timbers tying front and rear walls were recovered; this internal timber-lacing must have been much more frequent, but such structural details rarely survive.

In areas where suitable stone was available, this was frequently used for the wall facing, but again a variety of techniques are found. At South Cadbury, Somerset (Alcock 1972b: 122) and Moel y Gaer, Flintshire (Guilbert 1975b), timber posts were set into a dry-stone wall, and at Crickley Hill, Gloucestershire (Dixon 1976: 163–6; 1977), vertical timbers were built into the body of the rampart but not into the front wall, while horizontal timbers like those at Blewburton linked front and back, being exposed in the front face. Similar horizontal timber-lacing is found, for example, at Leckhampton, Gloucestershire (Champion S. 1971; 1976), and in various forts in the Welsh marches (Varley 1948).[16]

Environment did not always determine the materials used. On some sites where stone was available, the earliest fortifications were of timber and earth construction, as at Dinorben (Gardner and Savory 1964: 78), Fridd Faldwyn, Montgomery (O'Neil 1942) and the Breiddin, Montgomery (Musson 1976); at all three, original box ramparts were indeed replaced by defences incorporating stone. Occasionally, too, stone was transported to the fort, as at Maiden Castle, Dorset (Wheeler 1943: 34), for use in the east entrance.

Ramparts were also built entirely of stone, especially in Wales and Ireland. At Dinorben (Gardner and Savory 1964: 85), stone ramparts replaced the box and timber-laced construction from Phase III onwards. The technique was also widely used in north Wales for the ditchless walled forts, such as Tre'r Ceiri and Garn Boduan (Hogg 1960). Structural devices to increase stability included internal walls, as at Worlebury, Somerset (Dymond 1902).

The third major style of defence is the dump rampart, sometimes called *glacis* construction, which presents a continuous slope from the top of the bank to the bottom of the ditch. It may have arisen when it was realized that this was a more efficient and less complex technique, or it may

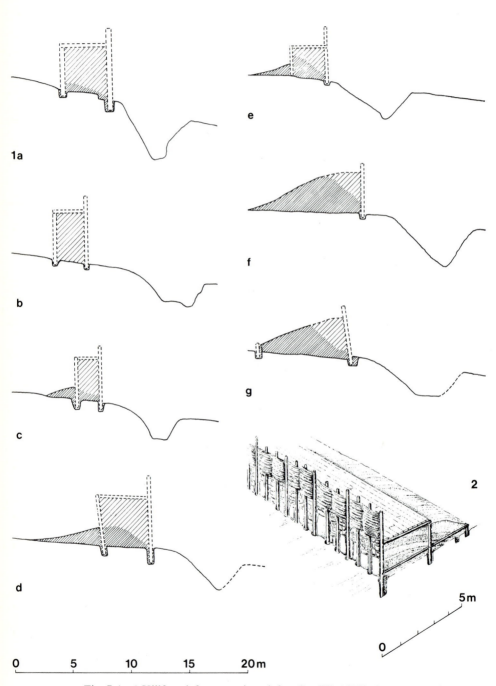

Fig. 7.4   1 Hillfort defence sections (after Cunliffe 1978); 2 reconstruction of Moel y Gaer, Flints. (after Guilbert 1975b).

possibly have been adopted as simple means of repairing a dilapidated walled rampart. This style is often found as the replacement of a walled rampart, as at Maiden Castle (Wheeler 1943) (fig. 7.5), Danebury (Cunliffe 1971a: 245) or Rainsborough (Avery *et al.* 1967: 220), though it was also used for the first fortifications of sites such as St Catharine's Hill, Hampshire (Hawkes *et al.* 1930: 13–27; Hawkes 1976: 70). The dump construction is a simple one, but it is occasionally elaborated; the sloping front is sometimes revetted with stone to prevent slumping, while palisades on the crest, as at Maiden Castle (Wheeler 1943: pl. XI), may have been more frequent than excavation so far suggests.[17]

Where the fortifications consist of more than one line of bank and ditch, the outer ramparts are usually set close to the inner; such multivallation may not be found along the whole circuit, but sometimes only at those points needing extra defence. In south-western England a series of forts have wide-set outer ramparts (Fox A. 1961), and a wide spacing is found in some Irish forts (Raftery B. 1972).[18]

The entrance was an important element in the defences, being the weakest point but also offering opportunities for architectural display. The simplest form is a gap in the bank with one gate or a pair of gates; single and double portals of this sort are seen successively in the first two phases of the Danebury entrance (Cunliffe 1971a: fig. 7). Greater defence could be provided by setting the gate at the rear of the rampart, thus controlling the approach to it, as at St Catharine's Hill (Hawkes 1976: fig. 6) (fig. 7.6:1a, b). This effect could be increased still further by inturning the ends of the ramparts; access to the gate was then through a defended corridor, as at Bredon Hill, Gloucestershire (Hencken T.C. 1938: 38–58) (fig. 7.6:3), or Torberry, Sussex (Cunliffe 1976b: fig. 6).

Other defensive devices found associated with the entrances include guard-chambers and outworks. Guard-chambers (Gardner and Savory 1964: 87–90) were set into the ends of the ramparts behind the gates, as at Rainsborough (Avery *et al.* 1967: 253–4) (fig. 7.6:2) or Leckhampton (Champion S. 1971: 12). Complex outworks were sometimes added, as at Maiden Castle (Wheeler 1943: 106–31) or Danebury (Cunliffe 1971b: 64). At Crickley (fig. 7.7), a hornwork with an outer gate formed part of the second phase of fortification (Dixon 1976: fig. 7; 1977: fig. 3).

There is in general a progression from simpler to more complex fortifications, as in the sequence of palisade, wall and dump, seen for example at Blewburton, or as in the provision of outer banks or gateway outworks, for example at Danebury. But it is now known that multivallation need not be a late feature,[19] and that features such as guard-chambers can vary widely in date,[20] and it would probably be better to regard such sequences as reflecting the development of the individual sites than as a general chronological scheme.

In recent years more attention has been paid to the large-scale excavation of hillfort interiors. Although much information about internal occupation is being gained, it is also becoming clear that on many soils even quite substantial buildings may have disappeared beyond recovery. At Moel y Gaer (Guilbert 1975a; 1976), an early palisaded settlement was

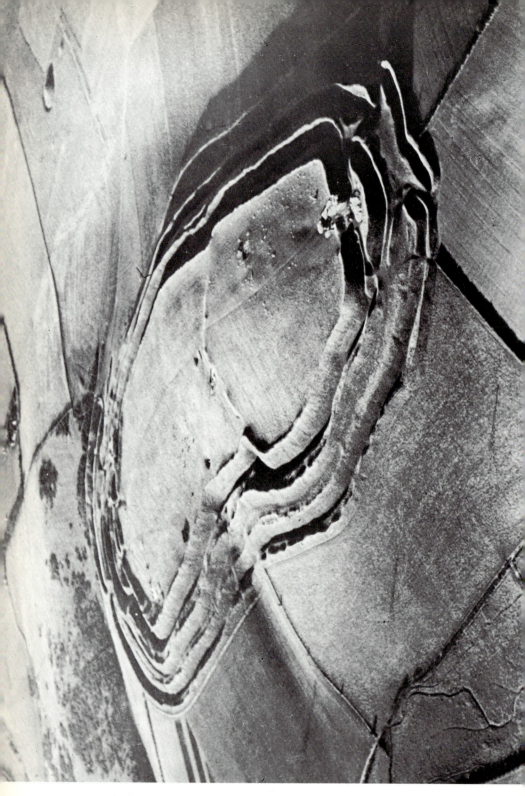

Fig. 7.5 Maiden Castle, Dorset: hillfort (photograph: Major Allen; courtesy Ashmolean Museum, University of Oxford).

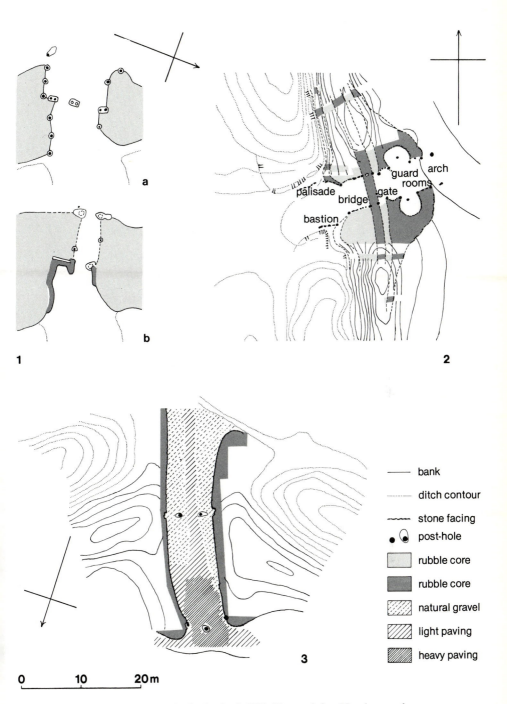

Fig. 7.6 Hillfort entrances: 1 St Catharine's Hill, Hants. (after Hawkes *et al*. 1930 and Cunliffe 1978a); 2 Rainsborough, Northants. (after Avery *et al*. 1967); 3 Bredon Hill Camp, Worcs. (after Hencken 1938).

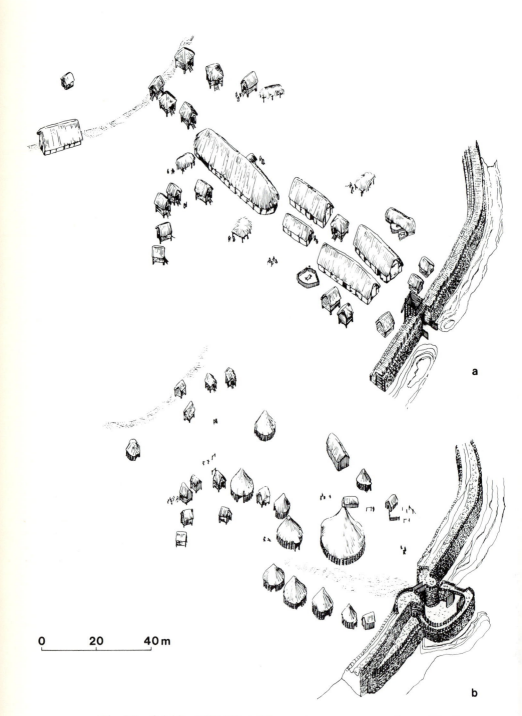

0   20   40 m

a

b

Fig. 7.7   Crickley Hill hillfort, Glos.: entrance reconstruction. a. The first
hillfort, c. 600 BC; b. The second hillfort, c. 500 BC (after Dixon and Borne 1977).

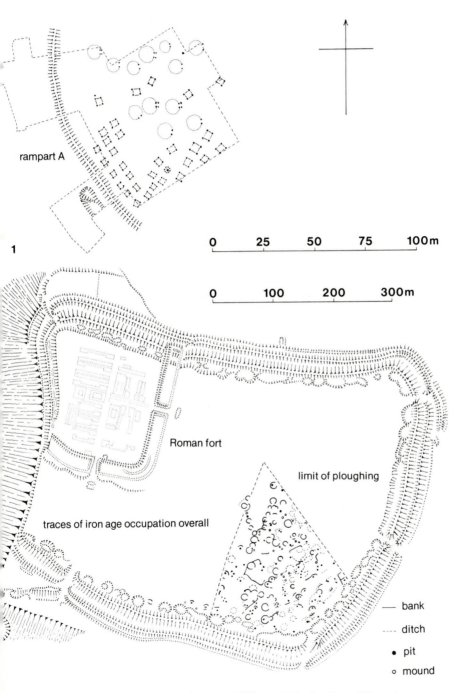

rampart A

1

| 0 | 25 | 50 | 75 | 100 m |

| 0 | 100 | 200 | 300 m |

Roman fort

limit of ploughing

traces of iron age occupation overall

—— bank

---- ditch

• pit

○ mound

Fig. 7.8 Traces of occupation in iron age hillforts: 1 Moel y Gaer, Flints. (after Guilbert 1975a); 2 Hod Hill, Dorset (after RCAHM).

replaced by a second phase with a timber and stone rampart enclosing a planned arrangement of round-houses and square four-post structures (fig. 7.8). On other sites round-houses in this stake-wall construction (p. 381) would not have survived, leaving only the deeper post-holes of the four-post structures. These have been the only structures recovered in some hillfort interiors, for example at Grimthorpe (Stead 1968), Credenhill (Stanford 1970) or one phase at Danebury, where a similar ordered pattern may be suspected. This evidence for planning exists from an early stage, for Moel y Gaer is dated to 580 ± 90 bc.

A very different picture is given by Crickley (fig. 7.7), where two phases of occupation have been examined (Dixon 1976; Dixon and Borne 1977). The first comprised rectangular houses and four-post structures aligned along a street leading to the gate; this was replaced by a single large round-house, surrounded by smaller, slighter structures. Both phases belong to the late bronze age or early iron age.

Many sites show signs of long and possibly continuous occupation, such as Dinorben, Maiden Castle, Danebury and Croft Ambrey (Stanford 1974). By the end of the iron age occupation is frequently of great density; despite the small size of the excavated areas this can be seen at Maiden Castle (Wheeler 1943: 90–100) and South Cadbury (Alcock 1972b; 79–101). At other sites traces of the final occupation survive on the surface, as at Hod Hill, Dorset (Richmond 1968: fig. 2–3) (fig. 7.8:2), Tre'r Ceiri and Garn Boduan (Hogg 1960).

The advent of radiocarbon dating has radically altered views concerning hillfort dating, and it is now clear that the fort-building tradition was well established in the late bronze age, at least in some areas (p. 288ff. above). At Grimthorpe, two successive phases of ditch fill were dated 970 ± 130 bc and 690 ± 130 bc, and at Dinorben phase I was dated 895 ± 95 bc. Slightly later dates come from Moel y Gaer (620 ± 70 bc for the palisaded site, 580 ± 90 bc for the timber and stone rampart), Almondbury (595 ± 95 bc for the first rampart), Rainsborough (540 ± 35 bc, 510 ± 70 bc, 500 ± 75 bc, 480 ± 75 bc) and Castercliff (510 ± 60 bc). Some sites have also produced late bronze age metalwork, but it is often difficult to relate internal occupation to the construction of the defences. As we have already seen, at the Breiddin (Musson 1976), occupation layers with late bronze age metalwork were associated with dates of 868 ± 64 bc and 754 ± 50 bc, which compare well with dates from the rampart of 828 ± 71 bc and 800 ± 41 bc. At Ivinghoe (Cotton and Frere 1968: 204–13), late bronze age metalwork was found in the interior but the rampart may be later,[21] and at Mam Tor, Derbyshire (Coombs 1976b), the defences certainly overlay earlier occupation.[22] Fewer indications of a late bronze age origin are available in southern England, but this may be a result of less intensive excavation and far fewer radiocarbon dates. In south-eastern England, however, it is possible that the fort-building tradition was only initiated at a significantly later date.[23]

The great increase of recent years in evidence for hillfort occupation and chronology has made possible a more informed discussion of their origin and function. These are not simple questions, for hillforts were built and occupied over a period of some thousand years, and it would be surprising if their function remained constant throughout that time; it is also possible that one site may have played different roles during a long period of occupation. The term hillfort covers an enormous variety of types of sites, and these quite clearly had different functions. Nor should it be forgotten that hillforts were not a universal phenomenon; there are large areas, especially in eastern England, which have few, if any. Clearly, whatever roles hillforts played elsewhere, they were not an essential part of iron age society.

Some regional traditions can be distinguished. In south Wales and Cornwall, the name hillfort is often given to defended sites perhaps better treated as enclosed settlements (p. 372). In Cornwall too the defended coastal promontories called cliff castles, as at The Rumps, St Minver (Brooks 1974), may also be little more than individual farmsteads. For the south-east of England, it has been suggested above that hillforts may be a comparatively late phenomenon. In fact, a landscape dominated by hillforts is seen only in southern central England, the Cotswolds, the Welsh marches, north Wales and, to a lesser extent, northern England.

In Ireland, univallate and multivallate hillforts and promontory forts have been recognized, fitting well into the general stone-building traditions found in western Scotland, Wales and Cornwall (Raftery B. 1972). Little excavation has yet taken place, but at Rathgall, Co. Wicklow (Raftery B. 1976a) (fig. 7.9), extensive late bronze age occupation was probably contemporary with the surrounding defences. There also exists a group of sites which figure prominently as royal centres in the Early Christian period, such as Downpatrick, Emain Macha (Navan Fort), Clogher, Dún Ailinne and Ráth na Riogh at Tara; all are defended, but except for Downpatrick, have internal ditches. At Downpatrick (Proudfoot 1954; 1956) late bronze age occupation was found, but its relation to the ramparts is not clear. At Emain Macha (Selkirk and Waterman 1970), an early palisaded enclosure with late bronze age metalwork, dated to 680 ± 50 bc, gave way to a more strongly defended occupation; this phase, still of a normal domestic nature, was replaced by a series of massive circular post structures similar to those at Dún Ailinne (Wailes 1976). Radiocarbon dates from Clogher suggest an equally early origin there (Raftery B. 1976b: 193). These sites may have had, at least finally, a ceremonial rather than a domestic role, but they show the antiquity of fortification in Ireland.

Clearly, then, there is no single function for the various sites called hillforts, but a number of different themes can be seen in their origin and development. Firstly, there is the tradition of hilltop settlement, but, as we have seen, this was not restricted to hillforts, for many indeed began as open settlements on hilltops. The preference for such a location had its origins at least in the bronze age, as at Mam Tor, but it is still difficult to discern the reasons for it. Secondly, the provision of fortifications;[24] this may have arisen as a response to increased aggression, in competition for available resources. Bradley (1971a; 1971b) has suggested that intensification of arable and pastoral farming may have led to the development of hillforts on the South Downs. Thirdly, the existence of an authority

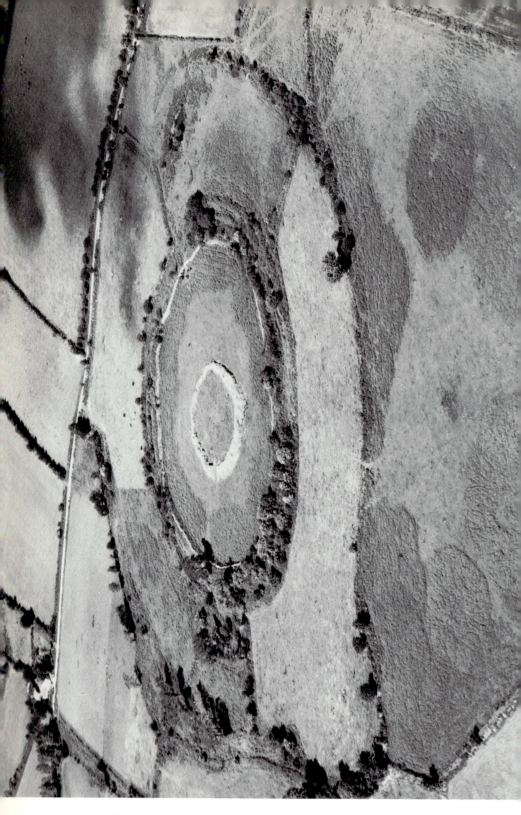

Fig. 7.9 Rathgall, Co. Wicklow: ring fort (photograph: courtesy Director in Aerial Photography, University of Cambridge).

sufficient to organize the labour necessary to construct the forts and to impose the planned layouts that are evident in some forts from an early date. Fourthly, though possibly related to the existence of such an authority, the opportunity for display; gateways in particular may have been elaborated beyond purely defensive purposes, and the combination of gate and single large round-house at Crickley suggests a certain social distinction for its occupants. The correlation between iron age defended sites and later royal centres in Ireland has been discussed above. A fifth theme is the emergence of larger units in the settlement pattern. In contrast to the predominantly dispersed settlement of the bronze age, the nucleation already visible for example at the Breiddin or Moel y Gaer may point to a new social and economic order.

During the course of the iron age, there are two further related themes of great significance. One is the constant and intense occupation of some hillforts, with frequent reconstruction of buildings and the maintenance of planned layouts through long periods. Allied to this is the abandonment of many hillforts. Cunliffe has shown (1971b) how, in Sussex and in Wiltshire (fig. 7.10), certain hillforts emerge as the dominant sites, while others are abandoned. The surviving sites may then take on a new role as economic and administrative centres. By the end of the iron age, they have many of the characteristics of towns (Cunliffe 1976a: 138–41), as Wheeler has argued for Maiden Castle (1943: 68–72) and Alcock for South Cadbury (1972b: 131–73).

Enclosures,[25] like hillforts, display a wide variety of size and development history, and indeed the dividing line between larger enclosures and smaller hillforts is difficult to draw; some of the ploughed-out enclosures of the lowland zone may well have been of precisely the same social and economic status as sites, for example in south Wales, which by virtue of their still surviving defences are often counted as hillforts.

The classic iron age enclosure of southern England is Little Woodbury, Wiltshire (fig. 7.11), where Bersu (1940) excavated about one-third of the 1·4ha area. The dense occupation, from about the fourth century BC, consisted of houses, small rectangular buildings, storage pits and other features; though the sequence was not thoroughly analysed, it seems there was only one house in use at once. The surrounding bank and ditch were a late form of the defence, for they had been preceded by two phases of palisade. A very similar enclosure of the same size has been totally excavated at Gussage All Saints (Wainwright and Spratling 1973; Wainwright and Switsur 1976) (fig. 7.12). Here all the main features of the occupation were the same as at Little Woodbury, but unfortunately most of the traces of houses had been destroyed. Three phases could be distinguished on pottery evidence, spanning the period from the fifth or fourth century bc to the first AD. In the first, a small ditch enclosed a central area of buildings surrounded by a zone of pits: in the second, the ditch was enlarged, the antenna ditches on either side of the entrance were dug, and the occupation consisted of pits grouped predominantly on the north side of the enclosure; in the third phase, the occupation was more

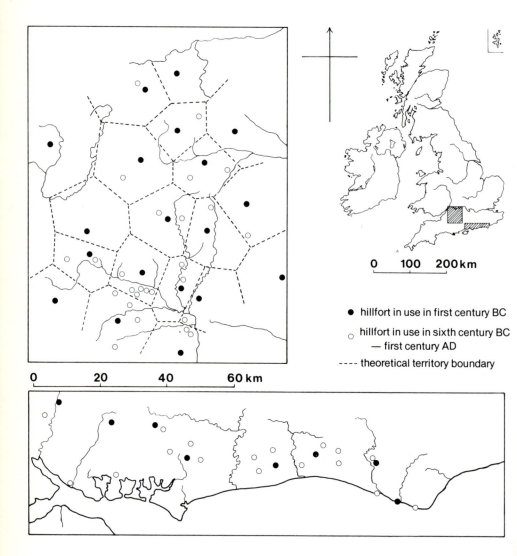

Fig. 7.10   Hillforts and defended enclosures in Sussex (*below*) and Wiltshire (*left*) (after Cunliffe 1978a).

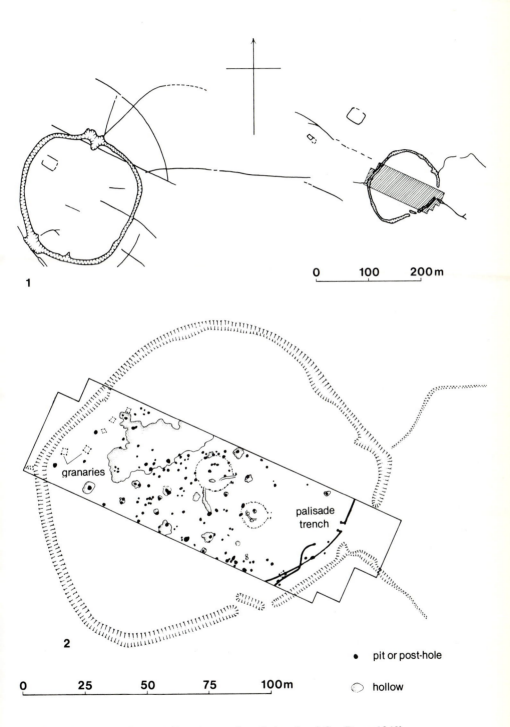

Fig. 7.11 Little Woodbury, Wilts.: 1 area plan; 2 site plan (after Bersu 1940).

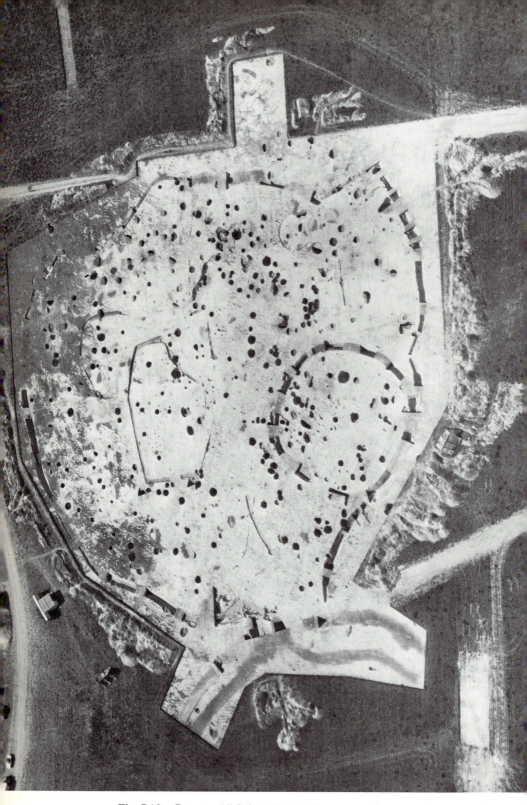

Fig. 7.12   Gussage All Saints, Dorset: iron age settlement under excavation
(photograph: Aerofilms Ltd).

dispersed, and smaller internal enclosures had been added. As well as the usual traces of domestic and agricultural remains, there was a vast quantity of debris from metalworking, especially the casting of bronze horse-gear (p. 384).

These two sites show that the enclosed settlements, like the hillforts, can have long and complex histories, both for their occupation and for their defences, and that their most prominent feature, the bank and ditch, may well be a later addition. At Bishopstone, Sussex (Bell 1977), for example, a rectangular enclosure cuts through a zone of structures and pits from the earliest phase of the site.

Little Woodbury has often been taken as the typical iron age site, at least for southern England. But though it does conform to a pattern of a mixed arable and pastoral economy, and of material culture and structural types found generally, but not universally, in the south, it could scarcely be called a typical settlement. For, apart from the wide range of unenclosed settlements (p. 374), there are many different sizes and shapes of enclosures with a corresponding variety of internal occupation; they range in size up to the 14ha of Hog Cliff Hill, Dorset (Bowen and Fowler 1966). Even in the area around Little Woodbury itself there are the larger and more massively ditched Great Woodbury, and some much smaller rectangular enclosures; though not excavated, and possibly not all contemporary, they at least reveal the variety of site that existed.

Few of these small rectangular enclosures have been excavated anywhere, but at Tallington, Lincolnshire (Simpson W. G. 1966), a site 67m by 50m contained a few pits, though all traces of a house had disappeared. At Ardleigh, Essex (Erith and Holbert 1970), the penannular ditch showed the existence of one house in an even smaller enclosure, 30m by 20m. D.W. Harding (1972: 11) has noted such rectangular enclosures as elements in larger complexes of settlement.

Other small enclosures with single houses have been excavated at Tollard Royal, Wiltshire (Wainwright 1968) and Blackthorn, Northamptonshire (Williams 1974) (fig. 7.13); both represent single farmsteads occupied for possibly quite a short time. Larger enclosures are seen at Draughton, Northamptonshire (Grimes 1961), where three circular buildings were found in a site no more than 50m in diameter, and at Colsterworth, Lincolnshire (Grimes 1961); there an enclosure of 0·5ha contained several buildings, with a central open space.

There is a group of sites in southern central England dating from towards the end of the iron age, such as Casterley Camp, Wiltshire (Cunnington and Cunnington 1913) or Worthy Down, Hampshire (Dunning et al. 1929), characterized by multiple enclosure ditches. At Owslebury, Hampshire (Collis 1968; 1970), the development of such a site has been traced. It started with a banjo enclosure of about 1ha, and in about the second century BC it was completely remodelled with ditched trackways leading to a complex of enclosures, and a small cemetery of the first centuries BC and AD.

In the north of England, many of the same features are also to be found in the enclosures, though their closest affinities are to sites further north

(p. 482). West Brandon, Co. Durham (Jobey 1962) (fig. 7.14:2), for example, not only shows the development from open site to palisade to enclosure ditch, but also represents the single house site. A larger palisaded enclosure can be seen at Staple Howe (Brewster 1963) (fig. 7.14:1), where three circular houses were found on a site occupied at the very beginning of the iron age as discussed earlier (p. 291).

In the south-western peninsula the commonest settlement type is the round (Thomas A.C. 1966). These vary in size up to about 1ha, and although the dating evidence from the few excavated examples indicates occupation in the late iron age and Roman period, as at Carloggas (Murray-Thriepland 1956), their use may well have begun earlier. At Trevisker (ApSimon and Greenfield 1972), two circular houses occupied the round, and overlay an earlier, smaller enclosure with only one house. The peculiarly Cornish courtyard house is also found in rounds, as at Goldherring (Guthrie 1969).

In south-west Wales small enclosed sites are similarly predominant. Little excavation has taken place, but Walesland Rath (Wainwright 1969) (fig. 7.15:1) may well be typical. There were signs of dense occupation, with at least six round-houses, some frequently rebuilt, and a range of timber buildings on the inside of the bank; the main entrance in the south-east had six substantial post-holes for a massive gateway. Occupation may have begun late in the iron age, and certainly continued into the Roman period.

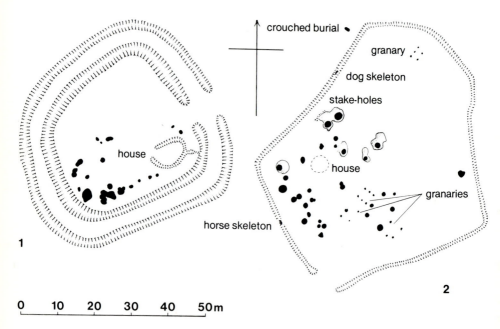

Fig. 7.13 Settlement plans: 1 Blackthorn, Northants. (after Williams 1974); 2 Tollard Royal, Wilts. (after Wainwright 1968).

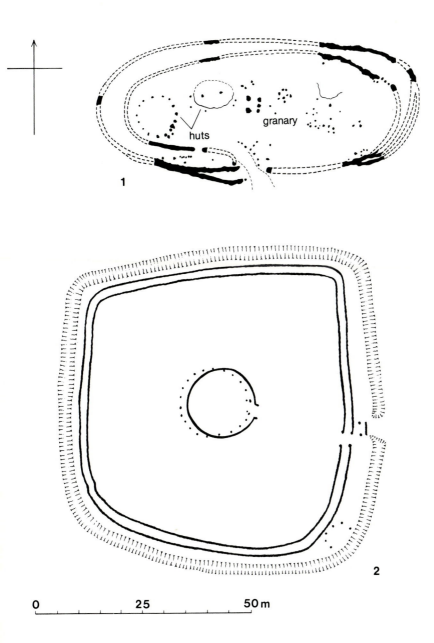

Fig. 7.14   Settlement plans: 1 Staple Howe, Yorks. (after Brewster 1963) (see also fig. 6.20); 2 West Brandon, Co. Durham (after Jobey 1962).

In Ireland ring-forts of earth or stone are the counterparts to the rounds of Cornwall and the enclosures of south Wales. Though traditionally dated to the Early Christian period, they may well prove to have a long prehistoric ancestry. Little evidence of iron age occupation has yet been found, but wider application of radiocarbon dating will solve the problem.[26]

Unenclosed settlements have received less attention, but are found in many areas. They survive best in the highland zone; on Dartmoor, for example, isolated round-houses are found in the field system at Foales Arrishes (Radford 1952), while further west in Cornwall groups of round-houses have been excavated at Bodrifty (Dudley 1956) (fig. 7.15) and of courtyard houses at Chysauster (Hencken H.O'N. 1933). Such hut groups are also known in Wales, and in northern England (Challis and Harding 1975: 138–42).

In the south and east few such sites have been extensively excavated. At Ancaster, Lincolnshire (May 1976: 133–41), huts, pits, post-holes and a short length of ditch were found, part of a more extensive occupation. At Boscombe Down West, Wiltshire (Richardson 1951), an area of more than 6ha was covered with pits and other traces of occupation, without a surrounding ditch, and at Little Waltham, Essex (Drury 1978), a large area filled with circular houses was excavated; similar extensive clusters of occupation are now known more widely in eastern England, as at Twywell, Northamptonshire (Jackson D.A. 1975). D. W. Harding (1972: 11) has drawn attention to large spreads of occupation on the Upper Thames gravels consisting of small rectangular enclosures, lengths of linear ditches and clusters of pits.

Some other locations for iron age settlements can also be noticed. Caves were occupied at various times, especially in the limestone areas of the Pennines in Yorkshire and Derbyshire, and in the Mendips. Crannogs, artificial islands, were also constructed and occupied, in southern Scotland and particularly in Ireland. At Lough Gara, Crannóg 62 shows in successive layers the transition from bronze to iron metallurgy (Raftery J. 1972). The so-called lake villages of Somerset, at Glastonbury (Bulleid and Gray 1911; 1917) and Meare (Bulleid and Gray 1948; 1953; Gray 1966), have now been re-assessed, and can be seen as small but long-lived settlements on the edge of the water (Tratman 1970; Avery 1968; Clarke D. L. 1972).

Oppida[27] is the name given to a group of the sites of the final phase of the iron age linked less by their actual form than by their nature as large nucleated settlements, with shared economic characteristics such as the use of small-denomination coinage and an abundance of imported material, especially pottery, and functions such as centres of production and distribution. They vary greatly in size, and in the type of defences, if any. The amount of excavation that has so far taken place is extremely small in proportion to the size of the sites, and many are known only from surface indications; it is therefore in many cases possible only to surmise the nature of the occupation of these sites, and there is certainly a wider

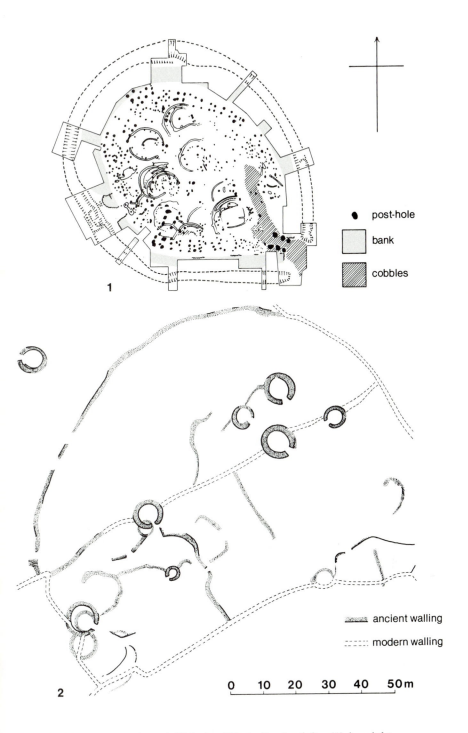

Fig. 7.15 Settlement plans: 1 Walesland Rath, Pembs. (after Wainwright 1969); 2 Bodrifty, Cornwall (after Dudley 1956).

range of functions and hierarchical organization, as well as regional variation, than can be adequately demonstrated at present.

At Colchester, excavation at the Sheepen site (Hawkes and Hull 1947) has provided plentiful evidence of occupation including some buildings, pits and ditches, enormous quantities of metalwork and pottery, including much imported ware, and the debris of a mint. The site was thought to begin about AD 10, but reconsideration of the imported amphorae suggests that this may be too late (Peacock 1971: 178). Certainly the system of dykes (fig. 7.16) which cuts off about 30km² south of the river Colne is extremely complex (Rodwell 1976: 339–59), and it is probable that an earlier nucleus existed to the south-west at the Gosbeck's Farm site.

A similar dyke system (fig. 7.16) demarcates a large tract of land around Chichester (Bradley 1971c), but the centre of iron age occupation has not yet been identified. At Bagendon, Gloucestershire (Clifford 1961) (fig. 7.17), an area of about 80ha was partly cut off by dykes; excavation showed metalworking and coin minting, and large quantities of imported pottery, probably starting near the beginning of the first century AD. A complex of dykes at Silchester, Hampshire (fig. 7.17), has not been fully explored, and none is definitely pre-Roman, but it is quite possible that some at least were contemporary with the late iron age occupation; here again large quantities of material, including much imported pottery, coins and coin-moulds were found (Boon 1969).

In addition to those defined by dyke systems, there were also sites of a similar nature with no known defences. At Canterbury and Rochester similar occupation traces have been found sporadically under the later Roman towns, and the same is true north of the Thames at Baldock (Stead 1975), Cambridge (Alexander 1975) and many of the small towns in Essex (Rodwell 1975). The nature, extent and chronology of the iron age settlements are difficult to establish, but more can be said of sites that were not immediately overlain by Roman occupation. At Braughing, Hertfordshire (Partridge 1975), extensive pre-Roman occupation spread on either side of the river Rit, possibly starting before 10 BC, but comparatively little excavation has yet taken place. More extensive work on the Prae Wood site at St Albans, Hertfordshire (Wheeler and Wheeler 1936), has shown a complex of enclosures with houses and gullies flanked by a boundary ditch, outside which were cemeteries. Occupation here probably began about the end of the first century BC. A similar site may also exist at Welwyn (Rook 1974).

Further north in the east Midlands, especially in Lincolnshire, large nucleated settlements of up to 40ha are known (May 1976: 175–91). Excavation at Old Sleaford produced quantities of pottery, much of it imported, and massive debris from coin minting. More extensive work at Dragonby (May 1970a) has shown continuous occupation from perhaps the second century BC to late Roman times. The iron age settlement consisted of a regular pattern of rectangular enclosures, with circular huts (fig. 7.18). Many of these sites were occupied into the Roman period, and such occupation may underlie the Roman towns at Lincoln and Leicester.

Comparable sites are being revealed elsewhere. At Beckford, Worces-

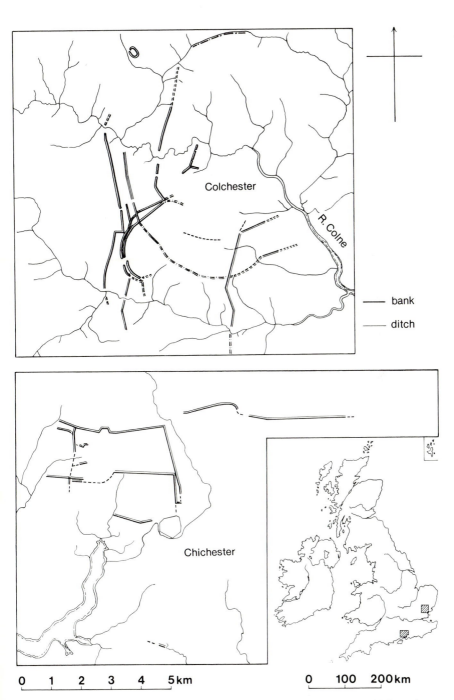

Fig. 7.16 Plans of iron age dykes at Colchester, Essex (after Rodwell 1976), and Chichester, Sussex (after Bradley 1971c).

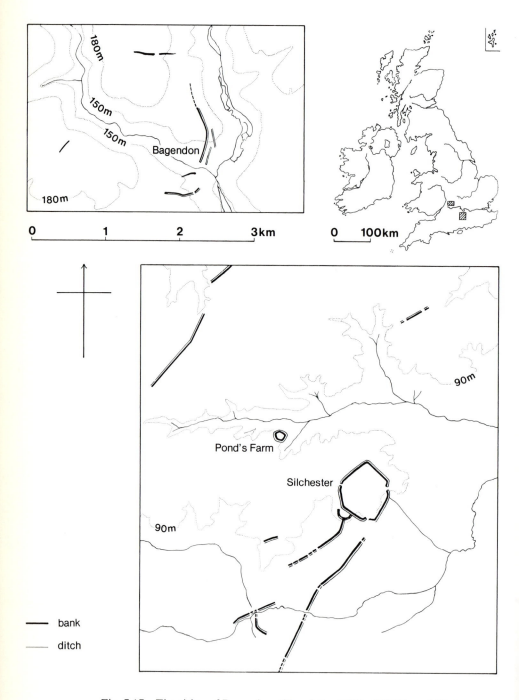

Fig. 7.17   The siting of Bagendon, Glos. (after Clifford 1961), and Silchester, Hants. (after Boon 1969).

tershire (Britnell 1974), a similar pattern of enclosures was demonstrated, and occupation spread over a large area. Sites in the Thames Valley, such as Stanton Harcourt (Benson and Miles 1974: 46), may also be of this type.

There is also a group of sites about which little is known, but which may also be comparable; they are large defended enclosures sited in the bottom or on the side of a river valley (fig. 7.19). Salmonsbury, Gloucestershire (Dunning 1976), has been partly excavated, but almost nothing is known of the occupation of Winchester (Biddle 1975: fig. 1), Loose, Kent (Kelly 1971) and Dyke Hills, Oxfordshire.

The promontory site of Hengistbury Head, Dorset (Bushe Fox 1915), yielded massive evidence of occupation in the late iron age, with metalworking debris and vast quantities of pottery imported from France and the Mediterranean. The amphorae suggest that it flourished in the first half of the first century BC (Peacock 1971: 173), and that the site's main function was as a centre of production, importation and distribution (Cunliffe 1978b).

Though comparatively little is yet known about these large nucleated centres of occupation or about their function in contemporary society and economy, it is clear that they represent a marked degree of centralization. Another regional variation could be defined in the final stages of hillfort occupation in Wessex (p. 367), where a similar process of centralization can be discerned, but there using the sites of old-established settlements.

Structures

Our knowledge of iron age structures will never be more than partial, not only because many of the materials used, such as timber, thatch and daub, are perishable, but also because it is quite possible to build even substantial structures such as framed buildings with sill-beams with no disturbance of the subsoil, or with slight traces that would not survive natural or human

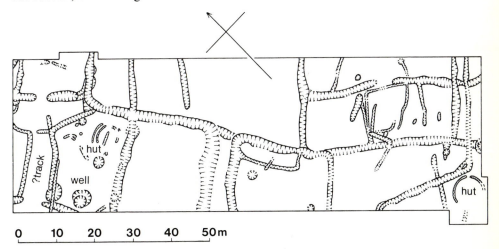

Fig. 7.18   Plan of the earlier phases of the iron age settlement at Dragonby, Lincs. (after May 1970a).

disturbance. Survival is obviously better where more permanent materials were used, or where agriculture has done less damage, but on many sites houses are totally absent or represented by no more than a cluster of post-holes, which may not even have been associated with major structural features. The evidence is therefore greatly distorted and restricted, but points to a variety of structural types, round and rectangular.

One common type is the double-ring round-house, inherited from the bronze age (Avery and Close Brooks 1969). The main weight of the rafters for the conical roof was taken on the inner ring of posts, while the outer ring marks the line of the screen wall; a porch was provided, and in many cases the entrance faces south-east. The outer line, not supporting any great weight, did not need to be substantial, and was constructed in a variety of forms, not all of which survive archaeologically. At Little Woodbury, the outer ring was marked by post-holes, but this building is unique in the presence of a central setting of four posts, and unusual in its size; with its diameter of 14m, it is comparable to other large examples from early iron age sites in Wessex, such as Pimperne, Dorset (Harding and Blake 1963), but is considerably larger than most. Elsewhere the outer

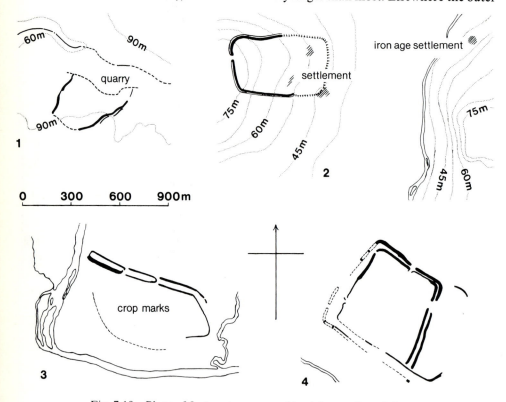

Fig. 7.19   Plans of first-century BC oppida: 1 Loose, Kent (after Kelly 1971); 2 Winchester, Hants. (after Biddle 1975); 3 Dyke Hills, Oxon. (after Cunliffe 1978a); 4 Salmonsbury, Glos. (after Dunning 1976).

ring could be defined by a ring-groove, to take closely packed upright wall-timbers; this technique is commonest in the north, as at West Brandon, Co. Durham (Jobey 1962) (fig. 7.20:1), but is also found further south, as at Twywell, Northamptonshire (Jackson D.A. 1975), and Puddle Hill, Dunstable, Bedfordshire (Matthews 1976). On some sites where stone was available, as at Maiden Castle, Dorset, House DB2 (Wheeler 1943: fig. 18), or Bodrifty, Cornwall, House E (Dudley 1956: fig. 5) (fig. 7.20:2), the wall was founded on a stone base. At many sites, however, the outer line of the original wall has disappeared; at Moel y Gaer (Guilbert 1976: fig. 4), it was recovered in part for one building, but had to be conjectured for the rest (fig. 7.20:4). At many other sites, too, the evidence for a house may be only a ring of posts, not necessarily regular. It was not strictly necessary for even the inner ring of weight-bearing posts to be set in post-holes; they could as well have been placed directly on the ground or on pad stones, and consequently be harder to recover. At Charlbury, Dorset (Whitley 1943), the outer stone base has survived, but it is not certain that an inner ring ever existed.

Certainly there was also a contemporary tradition of single-ring round-houses. One clear expression of this tradition is in the stake-wall round-houses that can be recovered under favourable conditions (Guilbert 1975a: 214–17), as at Danebury (Cunliffe 1976c), South Cadbury and Moel y Gaer (Guilbert 1975a; 1976) (fig. 7.20:5, 6). A circular wall of stakes would have been strong enough to support the weight of a roof, but, with the exception of the paired post-holes for the entrance, little may survive. Like the post-ring round-houses, they vary in size typically from 4m to 8m. These buildings had no central support, but there was also a tradition of single-ring houses with central posts, for example at Maiden Castle, House DA (Wheeler 1943: fig. 17) or Bodrifty, Hut C (Dudley 1956: fig. 4).

One form in which the evidence for a structure frequently survives is as a penannular gully, as at South Cadbury (Alcock 1972b: fig. 10) or Little Waltham (Drury 1978). These seldom have any internal features that can be sensibly fitted to a structural plan, and have been variously interpreted as drainage gulleys or as foundation trenches for the walls. They are in many cases almost complete circles, but elsewhere, as at Barley, Hertfordshire (Cra'ster 1961) or Blackthorn, Northamptonshire (Williams 1974; fig. 7.20:3), they are so irregular and incomplete that it is impossible that they were for anything other than drainage.

The contrast between round-houses in Britain and rectangular houses on the Continent has been frequently stressed, but it is now clear that on neither side of the Channel was the building tradition so consistent (Harding D.W. 1973). The best examples of post-built rectangular houses in Britain are at Crickley (Dixon 1973), where structures up to 20m in length have been excavated, marked by double lines of aisle-posts, with the line of the wall only recoverable in parts, as is so often the case with post-ring houses. But rectangular houses too could be built without earth-fast posts, and features best interpreted as the remains of such structures have been recognized at All Cannings Cross, Wiltshire (Cunnington 1923:

58), and Moel y Gaer (Guilbert 1976: 304–6). Fragmentary traces of rectangular timber buildings are also known from late iron age sites in the south-east (Rodwell 1978).

One form of structure with a very restricted regional distribution must be mentioned: that is the courtyard house of west Cornwall. This is essentially an open yard with surrounding rooms opening off it, usually with a large enclosing wall and a single entrance to the yard. Dating evidence, as at Chysauster (Hencken H.O'N. 1933), indicates a date from the first century BC onwards, but an earlier timber phase at Carn Euny (Selkirk 1974b) suggests that some sites may have a longer history. The reasons for the development of this local style are not yet understood.

Apart from houses, the most common structures are rectangular settings of post-holes, usually four, six or nine in number. They are found frequently in the earliest hillforts, often in an ordered disposition, for example at Moel y Gaer, the Breiddin or Grimthorpe, and are thereafter found regularly on iron age sites in the lowland zone. Bersu, the first to recognize them at Little Woodbury (1940: 97–8), interpreted them as granaries, and this remains their most common explanation. It is, of course, possible that they supported sheds or platforms for a wide variety of other purposes (Ellison and Drewett 1971), and Stanford (1970; 1974) prefers to see them as houses; they are, however, frequently no more than 2m square, and spaced so closely that the floor area could scarcely have been much bigger, if the post-holes do not mark the original wall lines.

Apart from such circular and rectangular structures, iron age sites frequently show short lengths of ditch or post-holes which cannot be definitely interpreted. Paired post-holes have been explained as drying racks for grain or skins (Bersu 1940: 94–6), but it is possible that some may represent the doorways of stake-wall round-houses now otherwise not surviving.

Other features found commonly on sites include pits. These are found in many sizes, and though one obvious use is grain storage (Reynolds 1974), other functions may have been served, for instance tanning, or the more irregular examples may be merely quarries for the extraction of the subsoil. On a number of chalkland sites in southern England large depressions up to 70m long in the chalk have been found, termed 'working hollows' by Bersu (1940: 64–78). It is possible that these may have had some such agricultural function as threshing, but they are mostly very irregular, and they too may be quarries rather than deliberate structures.

Technology

The processes of production have left little trace, and more often the nature of the technology and the organization of production have to be inferred from the finished objects. Occasionally, however, more informative evidence of actual manufacturing has survived, but although it tells us much about the technology involved, it is often difficult to place in its proper social and economic context.

Metalworking was an important industry, for personal ornaments as

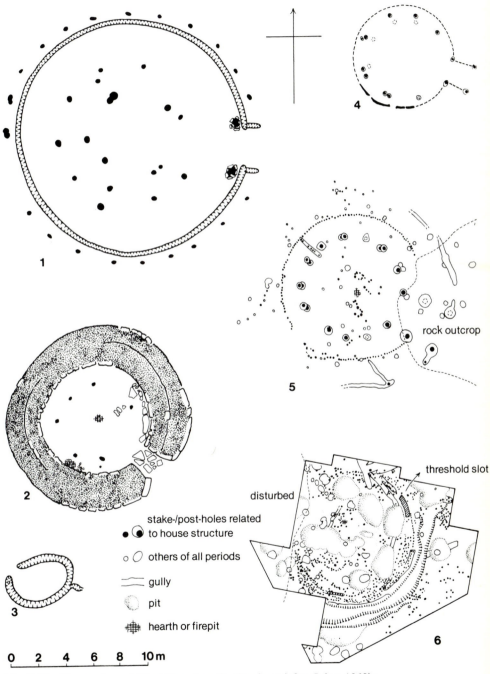

stake-/post-holes related
● ◉ to house structure

○ ◯ others of all periods

〰 gully

◌ pit

⊞ hearth or firepit

disturbed

threshold slot

rock outcrop

1   2   3   4   5   6
1   2   3   4

0   2   4   6   8   10 m

Fig. 7.20   House plans: 1 West Brandon, Co. Durham (after Jobey 1962);
2 Bodrifty, Cornwall (after Dudley 1956); 3 ditches at Blackthorn, Northants.
(after Williams 1974); 4 and 5 Moel y Gaer, Flints. (after Guilbert 1975a); 6
South Cadbury, Som. (after Alcock 1972b).

well as a wide variety of tools, weapons and other implements. Ironworking was established at least by the seventh century BC, as is shown by the presence of a local sickle of iron in a hoard with Hallstatt C bronzes at Llyn Fawr (Savory 1976b: 19–21), and the end of the bronze hoard tradition in the seventh century reflects the supplanting of bronze by iron for many purposes. Many other types, such as socketed axes (Manning and Saunders 1972), also imitated in iron forms more appropriate to bronze.

Few furnaces for iron smelting have been found, but, as at Kestor (Fox A. 1954), they were of the simple bowl furnace type. Other signs of ironworking, such as slag and cinders, have been found more widely on settlement sites (Tylecote 1962: 192–201), but little attempt has been made to distinguish the different processes of smelting and forging. Both may have been practised domestically since iron ores are widely available, but the possibility of more centralized extraction and smelting cannot be ruled out. Certainly by about the second century BC ingots appear, the so-called 'currency bars' (Allen 1967a).[28] These are found in a variety of forms, such as the sword-shaped bars commonest in Wessex but also occurring further north, the spit-shaped bars of the Somerset–Gloucester region, and the plough-shaped ones of the south-east. They demonstrate a significant advance towards the standardized measurement of commodities, and probably also the emergence of centres of iron smelting, from which these ingots were distributed. Little is yet known about which iron resources were exploited, but part of the wealth and importance of Hengistbury Head may have been derived from its ores; there is, however, little evidence of pre-Roman working of Wealden iron (Cleere 1974).[29]

While iron came to be used for tools, weapons and some ornaments, bronze was still retained for many items of an ornamental or decorative nature. Several hoards are attributable to bronzesmiths,[30] and evidence, especially crucibles, has also been recovered from a number of sites (Tylecote 1962: 131–3). Special bronzeworking areas have been suggested not only at hillforts such as Bredon Hill (Hencken T.C. 1938) and South Cadbury (Alcock 1972b: 154–6), but also at smaller sites such as Carloggas (Murray-Thriepland 1956). The best evidence has come from Gussage All Saints (Wainwright and Spratling 1973), where an enormous quantity of debris from the casting of bronze chariot and harness fittings was found; this included furnace fragments, crucibles, moulds, modelling tools and raw metal (fig. 7.21). The method used was the *cire perdue* technique, where the mould is invested round a wax model, which is then melted and poured out. The metal was a leaded bronze typical of iron age castings. The production of these objects would have necessitated a complex organization to supply the quantities of clay for furnaces, moulds and crucibles, of wax for the patterns, and of timber for fuel, as well as the bronze itself; it is scarcely conceivable that such an enterprise could have been undertaken by an itinerant smith, and a resident specialist must be supposed. His output was limited to vehicle fittings, but it is not known how wide an area was supplied from Gussage All Saints, or where the next similar producers worked. It is possible that even with smiths specializing in so restricted a range of products, their work may only have been seasonal.

The most abundant artifact on iron age sites in lowland England is pottery, but there is little evidence for its production. No kilns are known, and firing must have been in bonfires. Pottery was not wheel-thrown until the first century BC, when the introduction of the wheel was accompanied by a new level of standardization in the form and decoration of the vessels. But, though hand-made, earlier iron age pottery could be of a high technical standard, some of the finer wares being very well constructed and fired.

In the absence of manufacturing sites, some insight into the production of pottery is provided by petrological analysis. Examination of decorated pottery in the west Midlands (Peacock 1968) has isolated four different geological sources for the clay, and similar study of pottery in the south-western peninsula (Peacock 1969b) has recognized six different sources; in both cases petrological groupings do not totally coincide with classifications on the basis of form or decoration, but some degree of regional variation can be discerned. The pottery is frequently distributed some distance from the original source of its clay, and in one case vessels with gabbroic inclusions from west Cornwall are found as far away as Somerset and Hampshire. These analyses suggest that these wares at least were not made domestically, but were the output of specialists supplying a considerable area. The evidence is so far drawn only from fine decorated wares from the later part of the iron age, perhaps the third century BC at the earliest, and it would be unwise to extend the conclusions more widely; but some of the earlier fine wares, if not coarse wares, may eventually prove to have been similarly produced.

Salt was an important commodity in the iron age, and although there is evidence for its extraction in the middle bronze age, it is only in the 1st millennium that signs of the industry proliferate. Three main regions of salt production have been recognized in the south-west, in Essex and in Lincolnshire, but the debris is very varied and fragmentary, and no total reconstruction of all stages of the process has been achieved.[31] In the Isle of Purbeck (Calkin 1948) sites dating to the fifth century or earlier have produced a range of rectangular and semi-cylindrical troughs and clay supports for them; they served in the final moulding of the salt rather than primary evaporation (Farrar 1975). Further east, many salt-working sites are known around Portsmouth and Chichester harbours (Bradley 1975). In Lincolnshire (May 1976: 143–55), moulds and supports comparable to those in Dorset have been found, as well as other remains including possibly hearths and salt-pans. The most extensive evidence is along the coast of Essex, where the 'red hills' are the dumps of fire-reddened industrial waste (Reader 1909; 1910; Rodwell 1976: 298–301); clay containers, bars and supports have been found in large numbers, and occasionally more substantial structures. Some indication of the distribution of salt is seen in the finds of *briquetage* containers on inland sites (Bradley 1975: fig. 9; Rodwell 1976: fig. 42).

Glass beads are found occasionally throughout the iron age, but no traces of glass-working have been found. It has been suggested (Newton 1971) that glass was distributed in ingot or cake form from manufacturing centres, to be turned into the finished object locally. From the first century BC at least, an opaque red glass, commonly but incorrectly termed 'enamel', was used to decorate bronze objects (Hughes M.J. 1972). These glass inlays have a consistent composition, with high proportions of lead oxide and cuprous oxide; although they, too, may have been a specialist product, there is no need to believe, with Hughes, that this glass was all imported from the Mediterranean.

Several natural resources were exploited in addition to metal ores, salt and potting clay; clay was also used for sling-shots, spindle-whorls, loom-weights, industrial equipment and domestic ovens. Shale in Purbeck and jet in Yorkshire were used mainly for producing ornaments such as bracelets. Debris from shale-working has been found at Eldon's Seat, Dorset (Cunliffe and Phillipson 1968: 225), and elsewhere (e.g. Calkin 1948: 37–8); towards the end of the iron age lathe-turning was introduced (Calkin 1953). Shale products are spread widely over southern England.

Stone was utilized for a variety of purposes. Chalk and limestone were used, where locally available, for spindle-whorls and loom-weights, though not to the exclusion of clay, for example at Maiden Castle (Wheeler 1943: 294–7). Suitable outcrops were exploited for querns and whetstones; quernstones from some deposits such as the Lower Greensand of the Weald or the sandstones of western Britain are found at considerable distances from their sources.

Bone was also used for ornaments and tools. Bone rings are occasionally found, as well as dice (Clarke D. V. 1970: 217). The commonest tools are weaving combs and needles, and 'gouges': their true purpose is unknown, but they may have had a role in textile- or basket-making.

The craft which has left little trace is carpentry. Tools such as saws, chisels and files are known (fig. 7.21), but actual products have only rarely survived, particularly in the damp conditions of Glastonbury and Meare (Bulleid and Gray 1911: 310–51; 1953: 275–80), where, among other things, a lathe-turned wooden bowl was found. Other vessels such as buckets (Stead 1971a) and tankards (Corcoran 1952) were also made, and a considerable degree of competence is implied by the remains of houses and wheeled vehicles.

One other very necessary craft was weaving (Henshall 1950), and the tools for it are so frequent and widespread that production must have been a regular domestic activity (fig. 7.22). Bone combs were used for carding the wool, which was then spun; the surviving evidence of this process is the spindle-whorl of clay or stone. The cloth was woven on an upright loom, with weights to maintain the tension of the vertical threads; curiously these loom-weights are scarcely known from the north and west, though common elsewhere. The cylindrical weights of the bronze age were replaced by pyramidal ones, as for example at Staple Howe (Brewster 1963: 128) or Ivinghoe Beacon (Cotton and Frere 1968: 214–15). Later, from perhaps the fifth century, clay loom-weights were made in triangular shape, though those of stone continued to be roughly pyramidal. In

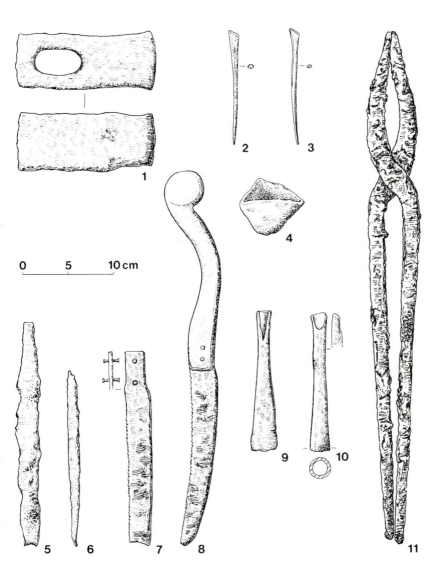

Fig. 7.21   Metalsmith's and carpenter's tools: 1 hammer, Bulbury, Dorset (after Cunliffe 1972); 2, 3 wax modelling tools, Gussage All Saints, Dorset (after Wainwright and Spratling 1973); 4 crucible, Meare, Som. (after Bulleid and Gray 1953); 5, 6 files, Glastonbury, Som. (after Bulleid and Gray 1917); 7 saw, Barley, Herts. (after Cra'ster 1961); 8 saw, Glastonbury, Som. (after Bulleid and Gray 1917); 9, 10 gouges, All Cannings Cross, Wilts. (after Cunnington 1923); 11 tongs, Garton Slack, Yorks. (after Brewster 1976).

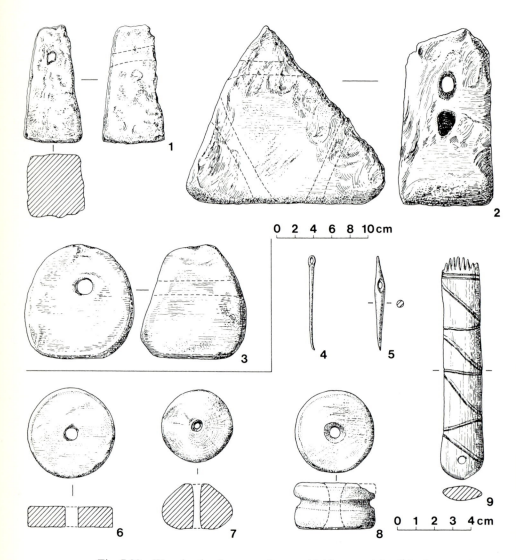

Fig. 7.22   Weaving implements: 1 pyramidal loom-weight, Ivinghoe, Bucks. (after Cotton and Frere 1968); 2 triangular loom-weight, Maiden Castle, Dorset (after Wheeler 1943); 3 bun-shaped loom-weight, Croft Ambrey, Herefords. (after Stanford 1974); 4, 5 bronze needles; 6–8 spindle whorls; 9 bone weaving-comb, Maiden Castle, Dorset (after Wheeler 1943).

Right Fig. 7.23   Personal ornaments: 1 swan's neck pin; 2 ring-headed pin, Woodeaton, Oxon. (after Harding D. W. 1974); 3 bent silver ring, Park Brow, Sussex (after Smith R. A. 1927); 4 penannular brooch, Maiden Castle, Dorset (after Wheeler 1943); 5 bronze bracelet, Arras, Yorks. (after Stead 1965).

western Britain, as at Croft Ambrey (Stanford 1974: 182), bun-shaped weights occur. The processes of finishing and dyeing have left no trace, but needles of bone and bronze occur frequently (e.g. Wheeler 1943: fig. 88, 10 and 11; fig. 105, 2–9).

Material remains

The abundance of settlement sites of the iron age has provided a wealth of material objects, supplemented by occasional hoards and river finds, and by burials where they occur. Apart from the objects associated with the various technologies described above, these finds can be grouped as personal ornament, prestige or luxury items, and domestic equipment.

Personal ornaments occur sporadically as site finds, and also in graves. At the end of the late bronze age a number of different pin types were current, and some of them were made in iron. The commonest type is the swan's neck pin (fig. 7.23:1), from which was derived the ring-headed pin (fig. 7.23:2), which was made in both bronze and iron, and was in fashion in the earlier part of the iron age (Dunning 1934); though most of the earlier types have close continental parallels, the derivative ring-headed form is purely insular. Other forms are occasionally found, such as the iron swan's neck pin with bronze disc from Fengate, Peterborough (Hawkes and Fell 1943: fig. 1; Spratling 1974).

In the course of the iron age, the pin gave way to the brooch, an innovation introduced from the Continent, as a means of fastening clothes. A number of brooches are known in Britain dating to the eighth to sixth centuries BC (Ridgeway and Smith 1907; Harden 1950; cf. also Challis and Harding 1975: 41f.), but unfortunately not one has been found in an indubitable iron age context; some are almost certainly modern

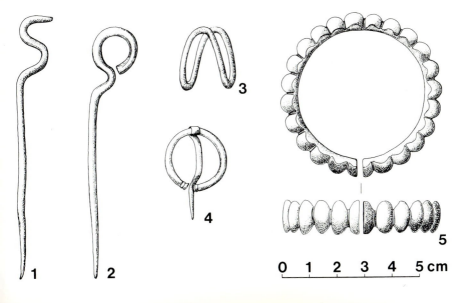

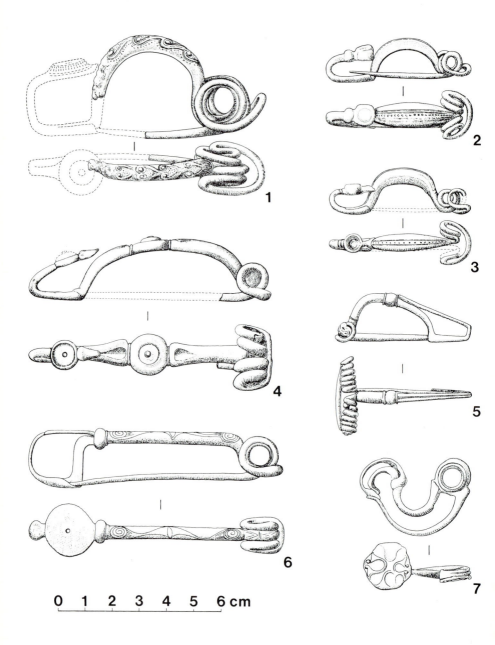

Fig. 7.24　Brooches: 1 Hunsbury, Northants. (after Fell 1936); 2 Blandford, Dorset; 3 Avebury, Wilts. (after Smith R. A. 1925); 4 Deal, Kent (after Hawkes 1940b); 5 Spettisbury, Dorset (after Gresham 1939); 6 Sawdon, Yorks. (after Watson 1947); 7 Beckley, Oxon. (after Harding D. W. 1974); 8 Aylesford, Kent (after Stead 1976a); 9 Deal, Kent (after Bushe Fox 1925); 10 Colchester, Essex (after Hawkes and Hull 1947); 11 Hod Hill, Dorset (after Brailsford 1962).

imports, but some also may be genuine. By the fifth century, however, there can be no doubt that the fashion for brooches had appeared in Britain, for brooches of early La Tène form are widespread. Some of these may be actual imports from the Continent, such as the examples from Deal (Hawkes 1940b: fig. 1) (fig. 7.24:4) or Hunsbury (Fell 1936: fig. 2a) (fig. 7.24:1), which both have very close parallels in Europe, but others are without doubt insular products. The British sequence indeed diverges from the continental, showing distinctive techniques of construction such as a hinged, not sprung, pin, or a preference for devices found only rarely on the Continent, such as a central axis to strengthen the spring, or novel styles of elaborating the brooch (Hodson 1971: 50–2); there are also obvious local groups, such as the Wessex series with incised lines and impressed dots on the bow (Cunliffe 1978a: fig. 14:8) (fig. 7.24:2–3).

The British brooch styles diverge even further later, for as well as some of the continental middle La Tène form (fig. 7.24:5), there are purely insular types. In the flat-bowed brooch (fig. 7.24:6) the bow was elongated and flattened parallel to the pin, while in the involuted brooch (fig. 7.24:7) the whole object was bent back on itself.

During the course of the first century BC[32] brooches of late La Tène type came into use. The earliest still retained a knob or boss on the bow, a survival from the fastening of the foot on middle La Tène brooches (Stead 1976b: 402–10) (fig. 7.24:8). From about 10 BC these were replaced by a range of late La Tène styles, which remained in fashion until the Roman

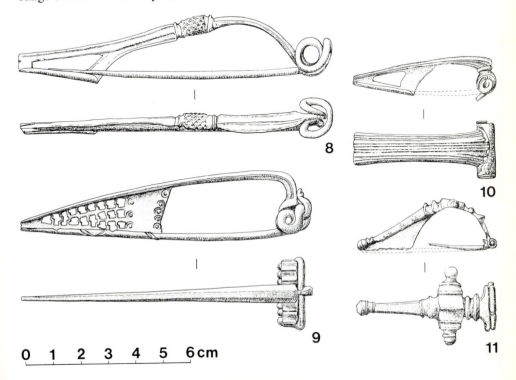

0 1 2 3 4 5 6cm

conquest and later. The Colchester brooch (fig. 7.24:9), with an external cord fastened to the head by a hook, and frequently with a pair of wings to protect the spring, was the dominant pre-conquest type. The Langton Down type (fig. 7.24:10) had a two-piece construction with a wide flat parallel-sided bow, often elaborately decorated, and a tube to protect the spring, and the Hod Hill type (fig. 7.24:11) had a bow with protruding knobs. There were also simpler types, such as the Nauheim brooch (Jope and Wilson 1957: fig. 2). Many of these forms occur in Ireland (Jope 1961–2), albeit infrequently, as well as a purely Irish type, the Navan brooch with a split bow.

Apart from these forms, penannular brooches are also found (Fowler 1960) (fig. 7.23:4). Other types of personal ornament include spiral finger-rings (Jope and Wilson 1957: fig. 3), bracelets and beads. Small blue glass beads are found throughout the iron age, and occasionally more elaborate examples occur. Bracelets are known in a variety of forms, including one comparable to those of late Hallstatt and early La Tène Europe, and more simple bands of bronze (fig. 7.23:5). A bent silver finger-ring from Park Brow, Sussex (Smith R. A. 1927) was a third century BC import from Switzerland (fig. 7.23:3).

Prestige or luxury items have been found mainly in rivers or hoards, in the burials of the final period of the iron age, and occasionally also as site finds. Many of them continue themes of display already established in the bronze age, such as weapons and armour, horse-drawn vehicles, and feasting (Coombs 1975a: 70–5).

The earliest iron age weapons, as has been discussed in the previous chapter (p. 331), are the seventh-century BC Hallstatt C bronze swords of Gündlingen type (Cowen 1967). These are part of a widespread western European sword form, of which the British and Irish weapons are distinct regional variants; there is also a type combining some features of local late bronze age swords, the so-called Thames hybrids, found in the south-east.[33] The first iron swords also appear at this time, for example in the Llyn Fawr hoard (Savory 1976b: 19–21) (fig. 6.44).

In the sixth and fifth centuries BC, the sword is replaced as the fashionable weapon by the dagger (Jope 1961). The British examples (fig. 7.25:1) are again of continental inspiration; there are a few that may have been imported, but the majority are clearly local products, showing distinctive developments of such features as the suspension loops and the scabbard chapes. The scabbards were often elaborately decorated, sometimes in a variant of early La Tène art, as seen on those from Hammersmith (fig. 7.25:2) and Minster Ditch. Swords reappear in the early La Tène period, and the British series (fig. 7.25:3–4) again closely follows that of western Europe, with regional variants of middle and late La Tène swords, as well as derived local forms (Piggott S. 1950). The scabbards are often highly ornamented, and like the bronze swords and daggers before them, they are frequently found in rivers (figs. 7.38c, 7.39b).

A similar provenance is also common for pieces of armour, such as the shields from the river Witham and from the Thames at Battersea, or the helmet from the Thames at Wandsworth (Brailsford 1975a) (fig. 7.39a).

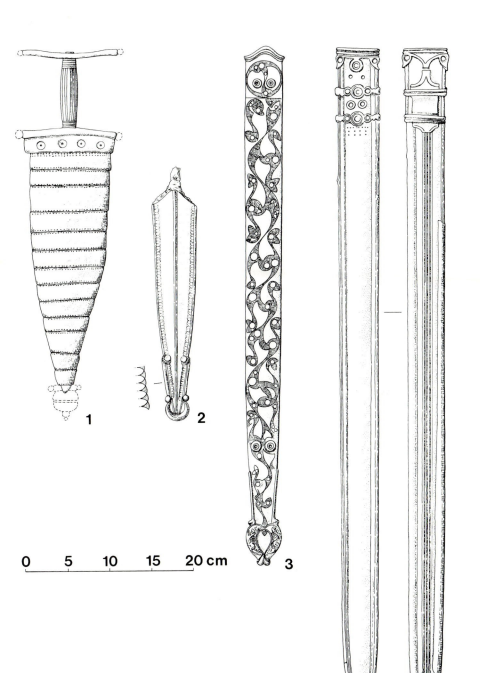

Fig. 7.25   Daggers and swords: 1 River Thames at
Mortlake, Surrey (after Jope 1961); 2 River Thames at
Hammersmith, Middx (after Schwappach 1974);
3 Bugthorpe, Yorks.; 4 River Thames at Battersea,
London (after Piggott S. 1950).

0   5   10   15   20 cm

Items associated with horses and vehicles (fig. 7.26) are comparatively frequent finds, but it is difficult to prove that much, if any, of such material dates before the first century BC; it would be odd, however, if there were a break in this tradition of horse-driving between the beginning and end of the iron age. There are vehicle and horse trappings in such Hallstatt C hoards as Llyn Fawr, but the later evidence – which in Ireland may be of second century AD date – is mainly in the form of bridle-bits, terrets and linch-pins.[34]

Feasting and drinking were important activities in iron age society. In the late Hallstatt and early La Tène periods many of the objects imported across the Alps from the Mediterranean were connected with them, and Britain received some of this influx. Though there is considerable debate concerning classical material of this date in Britain,[35] it is probably safe to accept as authentic the Italian bronze bucket from the river Wey (Smith R.A. 1908), the Attic red-figure cup from the Thames near Reading (Boon 1954), and the Etruscan beaked flagon from near Northampton (Harbison and Laing 1974: 6–8). At the end of the iron age, a similar emphasis on drinking is found in late La Tène bronze vessels (Birchall 1965: 295 and map IV), bronze bowls with animal spouts (Megaw 1963; May 1971; 1976: 171f.; Stead 1967: 23–5), the Roman silver cups in the Welwyn and Welwyn Garden City burials (Stead 1967: 20–3) (fig. 7.27:3), buckets (Stead 1971a) (fig. 7.27:1), tankards (Corcoran 1952) (fig. 7.27:2) and the amphorae in which the wine was imported (Peacock 1971). The importance of the hearth and the fire is seen in firedogs (Piggott S. 1971) (fig. 7.27:4) and cauldron-hangers (Piggott S. 1953a). All these are found in recurring associations in graves and hoards.

Other prestige objects include the massive gold torcs of the final iron age, such as those from Snettisham (Clarke R. R. 1954) and Ipswich (Owles 1969; 1971). Mirrors, though found on very rare occasions in graves of the earlier iron age (Stead 1965: 55–7; Brewster 1976: 110), are more frequent in the first centuries BC and AD; their back plates gave scope for the most intricate development of insular iron age art (Fox C. 1958: 84–105). Further discussion of this material follows (p. 421).

Domestic equipment is, not surprisingly, well represented, though internal features of iron age houses have for the most part perished; apart from the tools connected with metalworking, carpentry and textile production described above, most of the objects are associated with the preparation and consumption of food. Grain was ground on querns; at first, there were simple saddle querns, but during the iron age, possibly in the third century BC, rotary querns were introduced. Clay ovens are also known, as at Maiden Castle (Wheeler 1943: 93).

Pottery, however, is the most abundant domestic find, at least in the south and east of England. The surviving bulk of this fragile but durable material makes it hard to assess how much might have been in use at any one time, or the relative importance of pottery to leather and wood; certainly in parts of the highland zone pottery is rare or totally absent, and in Ireland the association of pottery with hillforts might suggest its limitation to one section of society. It appears to have been used for

Fig. 7.26   Horse-gear: 1 terret, Hod Hill, Dorset; 2 terret, Hagbourne Hill,
Berks.; 3 terret, Hod Hill, Dorset; 4 bit, Ulceby, Lincs.; 5 linch-pin, Llyn Cerrig
Bach, Anglesey; 6 ?pendant, Hunsbury, Northants.; 7 ?pendant, Cadbury
Castle, Som.; 8 strap-union, Arundel Park, Sussex; 9 strap-union, Hod Hill,
Dorset (after Wainwright and Spratling 1973).

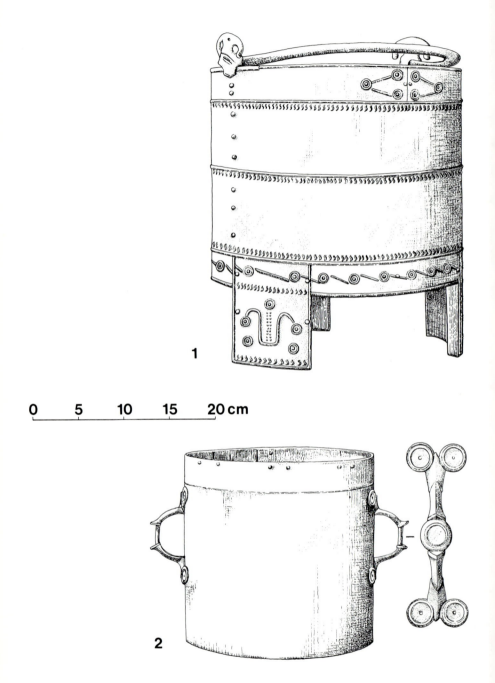

0   5   10   15   20 cm

Fig. 7.27   1 Baldock bucket (after Stead 1971a); 2 Aylesford tankard (after Evans A. J. 1890); 3 Welwyn Garden City cup (after Stead 1967); 4 Welwyn firedog (after Smith R. A. 1912).

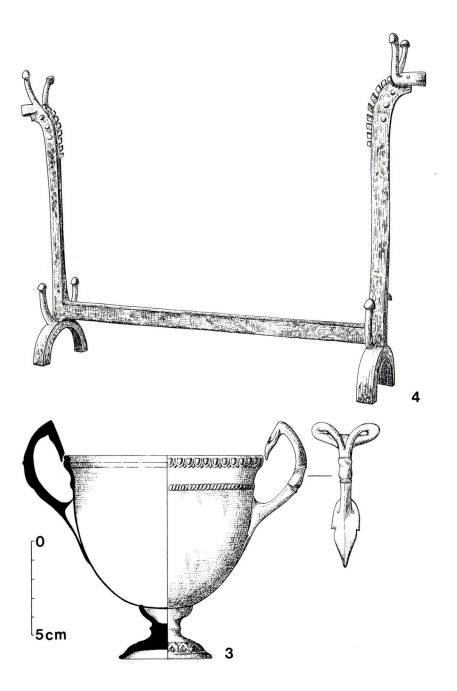

4

3

0

5cm

storage and cooking, as well as eating and drinking, though few specialized forms have been identified. Most attention has been paid to typological and chronological problems; the quantity and diversity of the pottery is so great that only a brief outline can be attempted here.[36]

The pottery of the first half of the 1st millennium BC is still little understood, but it is now becoming clear that there is a phase between the end of the Deverel-Rimbury tradition and the beginning of what is generally recognized as iron age pottery. This phase is characterized by pottery with no very prominent features of form or decoration. Only at Ram's Hill, Berkshire (Barrett 1975), has a stratigraphic sequence yet been recovered; there straight-sided jars, jars with convex profiles and hooked rims and wider squat jars with rounded shoulders were recognized (fig. 7.28:1). Comparable assemblages have been found at Ivinghoe Beacon (Cotton and Frere 1968) and at Kirtlington, Oxfordshire (Harding D.W. 1972: 84–5). The sequence at Ram's Hill, the association with late bronze age metalwork at Ivinghoe and the radiocarbon dates for a phase with similar material at South Cadbury (quoted by Barrett 1975: 103) all show that this pottery belongs early in the 1st millennium BC.

After this phase a major change is apparent in the ceramic tradition. Finer wares are found, bowl forms occur, and a variety of decorative techniques were used, including incised geometric patterns and finger-tip or finger-nail impressions. In eastern England this new style is found at Staple Howe (Brewster 1963) (fig. 7.28:2–4) and at Mucking (Jones and Jones 1975: 141 and fig. 48), with fine ware bowls alongside jars with finger-tip ornament often on applied cordons. In Wessex the bowls were frequently decorated with horizontal furrowing above the shoulder (fig. 7.28:5–6), and many had a reddish surface given by a slip containing the iron-ore haematite (Harding 1974: 148–51). The date of these innovations cannot yet be precisely determined, but it is clear that it was still in the late bronze age; the associations with bronzes at Staple Howe and Mucking are clear evidence, and other sites also may be as early (Champion T.C. 1975: 135–8).

The development of the iron age sequence is seen best in the finer wares, which are both more recognizable and more liable to change through time than the coarser wares, which have not yet received much attention. Concentration on the changes in these fine wares may, however, give an unwarranted picture of constant innovation, and it must always be remembered that they may only form a small proportion of the total range.

The next ceramic phase is marked by the influence of early La Tène pottery in the fifth and fourth centuries BC. This was noticed by Hawkes (1940a) in pottery from Worth, Kent, in profiles of some vessels and the presence of such features as the pedestal base. D.W. Harding (1974: 159–64) has drawn attention to a similar series of vessels in the Upper Thames

Fig. 7.28   Late bronze age and early iron age pottery: 1 Ram's Hill, Berks. (after Barrett 1975); 2–4 Staple Howe, Yorks. (after Brewster 1963); 5, 6 All Cannings Cross, Wilts. (after Cunnington 1923); 7 Chinnor, Oxon.; 8 Woodeaton, Oxon.; 9 Chinnor, Oxon. (after Harding D. W. 1974).

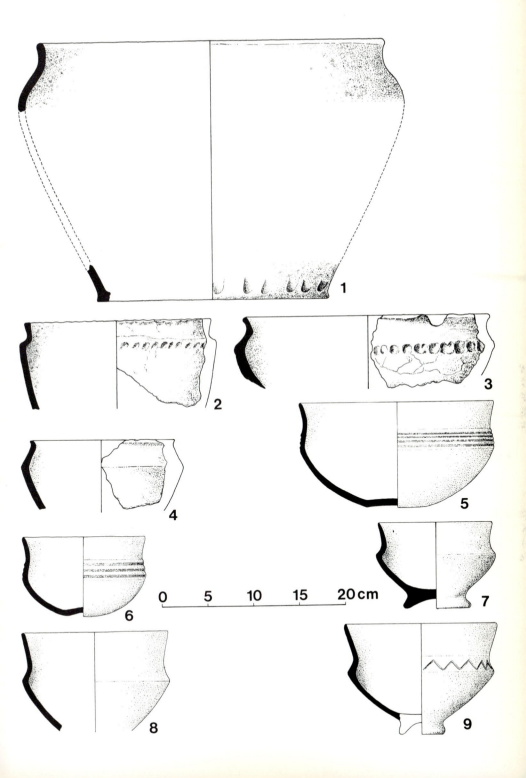

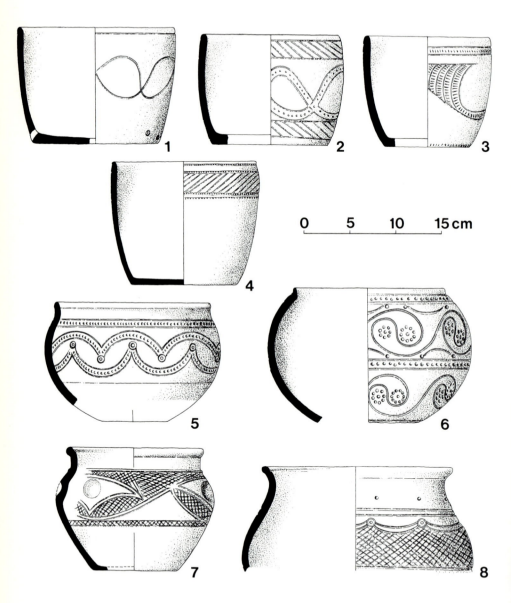

Fig. 7.29   Middle iron age decorated pottery: 1 Little Woodbury, Wilts. (after Brailsford 1948); 2, 3 Blewburton Hill, Berks. (after Harding D. W. 1974); 4 Maiden Castle, Dorset (after Wheeler 1943); 5 Frilford, Berks.; 6 Hunsbury, Northants. (after Harding D. W. 1974); 7, 8 Glastonbury, Som. (after Bulleid and Gray 1917); 9–11 Sutton Walls, Herefords. (after Kenyon 1953); 12 Cleeve Hill, Glos. (after Cunliffe 1978a); 13, 14 Ancaster Gap, Lincs. (after May 1976); 15 Crayford, Kent; 16 Langenhoe, Essex (after Ward Perkins 1938).

region, with tripartite angular profiles recalling those of some contemporary early La Tène pottery (fig. 7.28:7–9), and also to another series in Wessex (1974: 172–3 and pl. XXI), with pedestal bases copied from continental prototypes.[37] A contemporary but contrasting tradition appears in the east Midlands, where pots were decorated with a characteristic scoring (May 1976: 138).

At a later date, probably in the third century BC, the pottery begins to display a more uniform character over wider areas, and a series of regional groups can be distinguished on the basis of decorated vessels. In the south the characteristic form is the so-called saucepan-pot, a bowl with vertical sides (fig 7.29:1–4); south of the Thames from Sussex to Dorset and Wiltshire variations on this form are found with local styles of decoration (Cunliffe 1978a: 45–8 and fig. 3.6). In the south Midlands, globular bowls with curvilinear ornament, as at Cassington, Oxfordshire, Frilford, Berkshire (Harding D.W. 1972: pl. 67), and Hunsbury, Northamptonshire

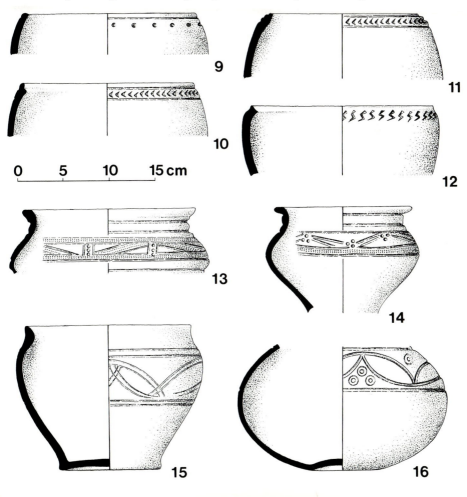

9

11

10

0   5   10   15 cm

12

13

14

15   16

(Fell 1936: 74–9 and fig. 6), are found (fig. 7.29:5–6). Other groups are less well defined; in Kent and Essex S-sided vessels with interlocking arc decoration, termed south-eastern B (Ward-Perkins 1938) (fig. 7.29:15–16), in the south-western peninsula the so-called Glastonbury wares (Peacock 1968) (fig. 7.29:7–8), and in western England the linear tooled and impressed wares (Peacock 1969a) (fig. 7.29:9–11) may all be contemporary regional equivalents. In Lincolnshire too, by the first century BC if not before, a local style of stamped and rouletted decoration had been developed (May 1976: 175, 184–6; Elsdon 1975: 26–37) (fig. 7.29: 13–14 above).

In the first century BC the wheel was introduced, and pottery styles became more standardized. In the south-east one tradition (fig. 7.30:1–4) is seen in the cemeteries of Aylesford and Swarling (Birchall 1965: 242–9) and at sites in Essex and Hertfordshire such as Colchester (Hawkes and Hull 1947) and St Albans (Wheeler and Wheeler 1936). A related group in Lincolnshire is also now known (fig. 7.31:5–8), developed out of the local hand-made styles (May 1976: 175–91). In Dorset a rather different tradition is found (Brailsford 1958; Wheeler 1943: 230–41); although sharing some forms such as a cup with a tall pedestal base, it is distinguished by highly characteristic bowl forms, large jars with countersunk handles and pottery tankards (fig. 7.31:1–4). Elsewhere in southern England other less well-defined groups of wheel-turned pottery are found, for instance at Carloggas, Cornwall (Murray-Thriepland 1956), Oare, Wiltshire (Cunnington 1909; Swan 1975), or Owslebury, Hampshire (Collis 1968: 23, 27 and pl. X).[38]

Throughout the first century BC amphorae from the Mediterranean had been reaching southern England (Peacock 1971), but from around 10 BC the quantity of imported pottery grew enormously. It included Mediterranean fine wares, at first Arretine and then the earliest south Gaulish samian, but the bulk was the products of the Gallo-Belgic industry of northern France and the Rhineland.[39] The imported cups, plates and butt-beakers were quickly copied in England (fig. 7.30:5–8), and imports and imitations form a substantial component of all large assemblages from c. 10 BC to the conquest, alongside the continuing local forms.

Burial and other ritual

Something is known to us from classical authors of iron age religion and its priestly class, the Druids (Piggott S. 1975). It was a religion whose holy places were not temples but natural locations such as rivers and woods, and it is therefore not surprising that there is little evidence of such ritual structures; there is, however, some. Several of the Romano-Celtic temples common in Roman Britain have yielded pre-Roman material (Lewis 1966; Harding D.W. 1974: 103–8), especially coins, as at Harlow, Essex (Allen 1964; 1967b; 1968b), but since these coins remained in circulation till after the conquest, their presence, though suggestive, is not conclusive. At Worth, Kent (Klein 1928), three small bronze votive shields were found with late La Tène brooches, though their relation to the Roman temple is

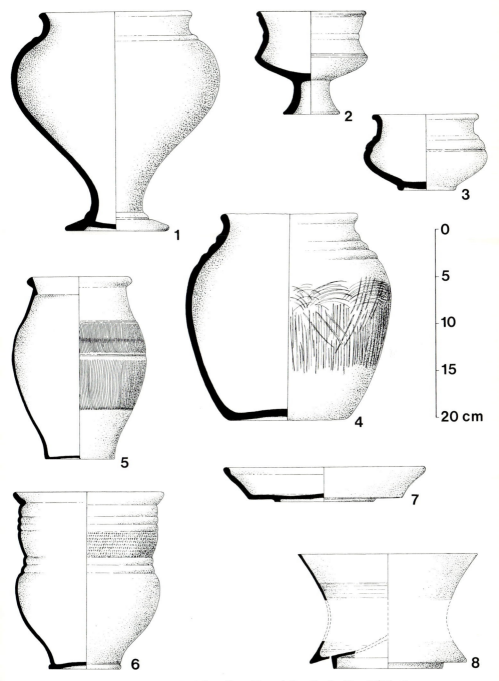

Fig. 7.30 Late iron age pottery: 1–4 Swarling, Kent (after Bushe Fox 1925); 5–8 Colchester, Essex (after Hawkes and Hull 1947).

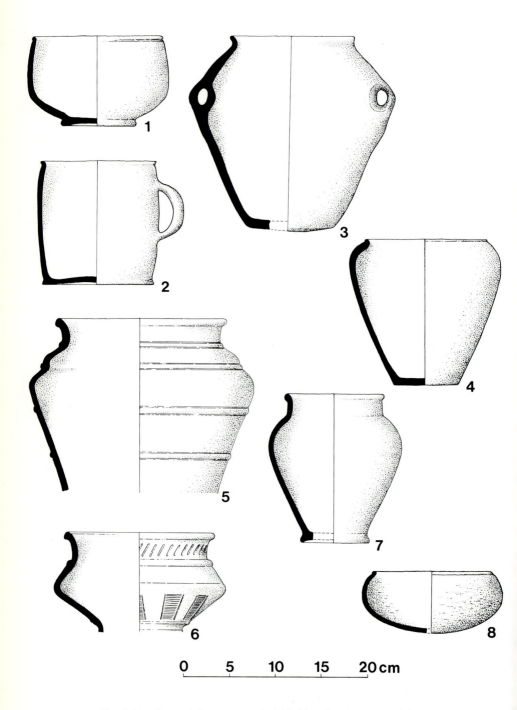

Fig. 7.31 Durotrigian pottery: 1–4 Maiden Castle, Dorset (after Wheeler 1943); Lincolnshire pottery: 5–8 Dragonby, Lincs. (after May 1976).

not clear. The possibility of a pre-Roman origin for some of these sites is most clearly seen at Frilford, Berkshire, and Brigstock, Northamptonshire (Harding D.W. 1974: 103, 108, figs. 23, 27), where penannular ditched structures, apparently of iron age date, underlie Roman temples (fig. 7.32). The most surprising temple, however, is the unique wooden post-built structure at Heathrow Airport (Grimes 1961), which displays a striking similarity to the ground-plan of the square Romano-Celtic temple with portico;[40] a similar structure has also been found at South Cadbury (Alcock 1970) (fig. 7.32).

The veneration for rivers and other watery places is well demonstrated by archaeological finds. Torbrügge's study (1972) of finds from such contexts has shown a persistent tradition of the deposition of certain types throughout north-western Europe from at least the middle bronze age. In

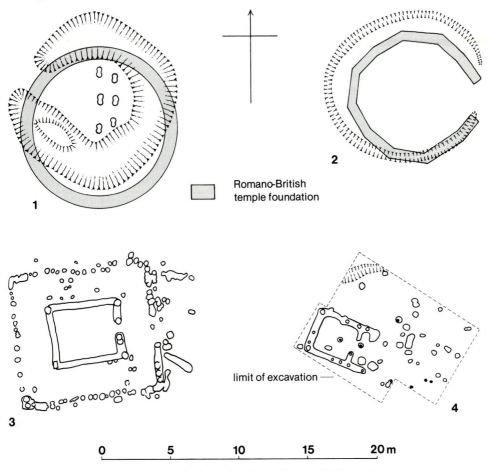

Fig. 7.32   Iron age shrine or temple plans: 1 Frilford, Berks.; 2 Brigstock, Northants. (after Piggott S. 1975); 3 Heathrow, Middx. (after Grimes 1961); 4 South Cadbury, Som. (after Alcock 1970).

Britain the bronze age rapiers have a predominantly riverine provenance, and they are followed by the late bronze age swords, Hallstatt C bronze swords, Hallstatt D and early La Tène daggers, and the successive sword types of La Tène date. Prestige armour, especially shields, has frequently come from rivers, as have imported objects such as the Reading red-figure cup and the Weybridge bronze bucket (p. 394). The Thames in particular has produced notable concentrations of iron age material at Wandsworth and Battersea, and other rivers such as the Witham in Lincolnshire (May 1976: 129–32, 165–7) have also yielded several objects. Though some of the items may have been casual losses, or the product of erosion of sites by the river, it seems unlikely that such a large body of material could have been anything but the result of a long-lasting tradition of deliberate deposition.

Hoards of ironwork are known (Manning 1972), and some may be ritual deposits. The hoard at Llyn Cerrig Bach in Anglesey (Fox C.F. 1946) had been deposited in a peat bog; it consisted of swords, shield ornaments, horse harness and vehicle fittings, a trumpet, cauldrons, gang-chains and a variety of other objects.

Ross (1968) has argued that a large group of shafts and deep pits in south-eastern England were the religious centres of the late iron age, but their interpretation is problematical. Their ritual nature is inferred only from their filling, which in many cases does not date before the Roman conquest, and their primary purpose may have been purely utilitarian, as wells. Their contents are often only what would be expected to survive in the damp context of a well shaft, but in some there are signs of a more deliberate disposition of objects. It is perhaps possible that there was some ritual connected with the filling of disused wells.

The most obvious focus for ritual activity in prehistory is in the disposal of the dead, but for much of the iron age most parts of Britain show no evidence of burials (Whimster 1977). This absence of burials is not specific to the iron age, for the established bronze age funerary traditions died out in southern and eastern England in the middle bronze age, and earlier elsewhere; a new form of burial was obviously practised by the late bronze age. What that practice was, if indeed there was one generally followed rite, is not known, for it has left no archaeologically recoverable trace. It is unlikely to have been inhumation, and may have been cremation followed by the scattering of the ashes or their interment without an urn; alternatively, the corpses may have been exposed, for fragments of human bone, found frequently on settlement sites, suggest that this was the fate of at least some of the dead. Whatever the rite, there is no implication of any disregard for the dead, only that archaeology cannot detect it.

A number of burials are known, but except in some regions they are too few to be accepted as the normal rite. Cremations under barrows are occasionally found, as on Ampleforth Moor, Yorkshire (Wainwright and Longworth 1969), where burials belonging to the early part of the iron age have been excavated. Burials are also found in pits on settlement sites; though known throughout the area where pits were dug in southern and eastern England, they can scarcely be regarded as the regular rite there.

One region which does show a persistent burial tradition is the south-western peninsula. Inhumations, usually crouched, in stone cists are known from Devon at Mount Batten (Bate 1871), from Cornwall at Harlyn Bay (Crawford 1921), Trelan Bahow (Hencken H.O'N. 1932: 115–21) and Trevone (Dudley and Jope 1965), and from the Isles of Scilly (Ashbee 1974: 120–47). Grave goods were mostly limited to personal ornaments such as pins, brooches and bracelets, but mirrors and bronze vessels were also deposited; the early La Tène brooches from Harlyn Bay have Iberian affinities. These cist burials seem already to have begun by the early iron age, as the swan's neck pin from Harlyn Bay shows, and to have persisted into the Roman period. Cists are also known elsewhere; in Wales, the decorated bronze bowl from Cerrig-y-drudion was found in a stone cist, though there is no record of a burial (Smith R.A. 1926).

In Ireland the number of burials certainly attributable to the iron age is small, but, although inhumations do occur, there is a persistent tradition of cremation (Raftery B. 1976b: 195–7; Herity and Eogan 1977: 242–5). Some of these are found under mounds, especially ring barrows. Grave goods include glass beads and La Tène brooches, for example at Loughey, Donaghadee, Co. Down (Jope and Wilson 1957). The large collection of objects from Lambay Island (Macalister 1928–9), which includes late La Tène brooches and scabbards, probably came from a cemetery, though nothing is known of its nature.

The best-known regional tradition is that of east Yorkshire, usually named after the cemetery at Arras (Stead 1965; 1971b; Challis and Harding 1975: 166–73 and fig. 100). Extensive inhumation cemeteries (fig. 7.33) have been found by excavation and aerial photography, several of them, such as Danes Graves, including hundreds of burials; many thousand such burials are now known. The graves were mostly under barrows, and surrounded by round or square ditches, both forms being found in the same cemetery; flat graves have also been recorded at some sites. The inhumations are predominantly crouched, though extended ones are also found, and many were buried in wooden coffins. Grave goods (fig. 7.34) included brooches, bracelets, pins and other ornaments as well as mirrors at Arras itself. Brooches of early La Tène form at Cowlam (Stead 1965: fig. 25, 1) and Burton Fleming (Stead 1971b: fig. 6, 3) show that this rite was established at least by the fourth century BC, and there are no finds at all to suggest that it continued after the first century BC.

Most of these cemeteries were excavated in the nineteenth century, but recent work has taken place at Burton Fleming (Stead 1971b: 24–7; Challis and Harding 1975: 168; Stead 1976b) and Garton Slack (Brewster 1976). At Burton Fleming (fig. 7.33), the burials excavated formed part of a linear cemetery arranged along a boundary ditch; they were mostly crouched inhumations, orientated north–south, with grave goods including pottery, pig bones and small ornaments, though a few were extended inhumations orientated east–west with different grave goods including iron knives and a sword. At Garton Slack the valley seems to have been turned over from agriculture and occupation to funerary purposes in the latter part of the iron age; by contrast the burials are grouped in small

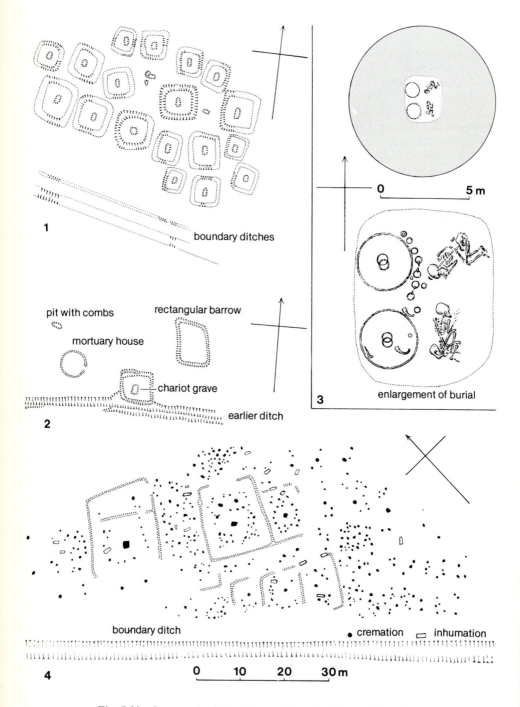

Fig. 7.33   Iron age burials: 1 Burton Fleming, Yorks. (after Stead 1971b);
2 Garton Slack, Yorks. (after Brewster 1976); 3 Danes Graves, Yorks. (after
Stead 1965); 4 Prae Wood, St Albans, Herts. (after Stead 1969).

clusters, and a variety of other ritual enclosures and mortuary houses has been found. In addition to ordinary grave goods, the site has produced many chalk figurines, always decapitated (fig. 7.34:5). These two excavations give an idea of the variation to be found in the Yorkshire tradition, but also of the place of the cemeteries in an organized landscape.

Among the Yorkshire burials are at least ten which included vehicles; again, most are old finds (Stead 1965: 5–9, 89–96), the only modern excavation being at Garton Slack (Brewster 1971; 1976: 110–13) (fig. 7.33). Here, in a square-ditched barrow which formed part of a larger complex of features, the dead man had been laid on the wheels of his dismantled chariot, with his whip, full harness and a pig's head. Similar burials are known from Arras and Danes Graves (fig. 7.33), while in two burials further north the vehicles were buried complete, with slots for the wheels at Pexton Moor. The burial of two-wheeled vehicles, together with the square-ditched barrows and some of the grave goods, clearly links the Yorkshire cemeteries to funerary traditions common in western Europe in the La Tène period, but there is no one place on the Continent where these various practices can all be matched.[41]

It is not until the first century BC that any more widespread burial rite is encountered, in the form of the Aylesford cremations, named after the cemetery in Kent where it was first recognized (Evans A. J. 1890). The cremations were buried in urns, frequently without other grave goods; where these do occur, they are seldom more than accessory vessels or

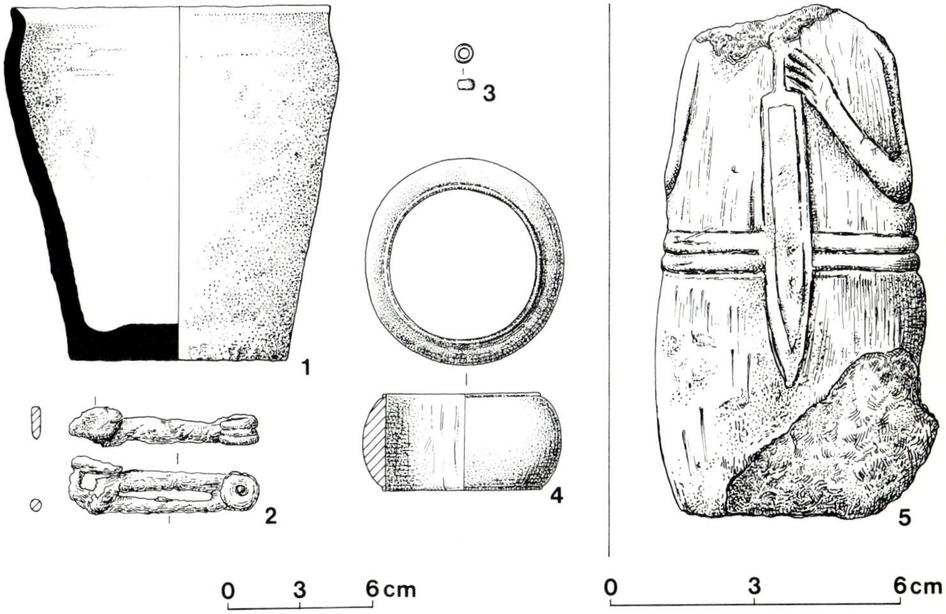

Fig. 7.34 Grave group from Burton Fleming, Yorks.: 1 pottery jar; 2 iron flatbow brooch; 3 blue glass bead; 4 shale bracelet (after Stead 1971b); 5 chalk figurine from Garton Slack, Yorks. (after Brewster 1976).

brooches. The burials are found in cemeteries whose size depends on the nature of the associated occupation; most are small, but at St Albans a cemetery of 481 burials was excavated (Stead 1969), possibly only one of several serving the settlement (fig. 7.33). Cremation, though vastly predominant, was not universal; 18 of the burials in the St Albans cemetery were inhumations, and others are known, for instance at Mucking (Jones and Jones 1975: 147). The rite was practised widely in the south-east, in Kent, Essex, Hertfordshire, Bedfordshire, and into Suffolk and Cambridgeshire; to the south-west at Owslebury, Hampshire (Collis 1968: 23–8), similar burials are found but with different pottery. The introduction of this cremation rite was attributed to the Belgae, immigrants to Britain mentioned by Caesar (Hawkes and Dunning 1930), but Birchall (1965) has shown that little, if any, of the pottery should date before the middle of the first century BC. The surest evidence for chronology is the brooches (Stead 1976a); the earliest types were current in the second half of the first century BC, but how much earlier, if at all, the rite was introduced cannot at the moment be answered.

Within this cremation tradition there is a small group of extremely rich graves, known as Welwyn burials, after two such graves found there at the beginning of this century (Stead 1967). Grave goods include Mediterranean amphorae, bronze and silver vessels for serving and drinking wine, hearth furniture such as firedogs, spits and tripod cauldron-hangers, pottery and various wooden objects and personal ornaments. The most thoroughly excavated grave, at Welwyn Garden City, also contained a board game complete with gaming pieces (fig. 7.35). The emphasis is on the recurring themes of feasting and drinking, and, in addition to the wine itself, many of the vessels, both of pottery and of metal, were imports, first of late La Tène, then of early Roman, types (fig. 7.44).

Other rich graves are also found, such as the burial under a barrow in the Lexden cemetery at Colchester, which yielded amphorae and other pottery, bronze figurines, bronze statuettes, a medallion of Augustus and other objects, including some of gold and silver (Laver 1927). There is also a series of burials containing buckets (Stead 1971a); they show no consistent use of the bucket as a cinerary vessel, and it is probably best regarded as merely one of the grave goods. Some of these bucket burials were richly furnished, for example Hurstbourne Tarrant (Hawkes and Dunning 1930: 304–9) or Aylesford Grave Y (Evans A. J. 1890: 317; Birchall 1965: 302), where brooches and other wooden vessels had been deposited with a bronze jug and ladle of late La Tène type.

The Aylesford cremations of the south-east were not the only new regional rite to be established in the first century BC, for in Dorset the practice of inhumation was adopted (Brailsford 1958: 112–13). These were usually crouched, and sometimes furnished with a pottery bowl or tankard, as in the Maiden Castle 'War Cemetery' (Wheeler 1943: 118–19); in south-east Dorset, inhumations both crouched and extended are found in stone cists (e.g. RCAHM *Dorset* II, South-east pt III: 527, 599).

Two other groups of burials also appear in the first century BC, if not rather earlier; these are not regional in distribution, but represent the

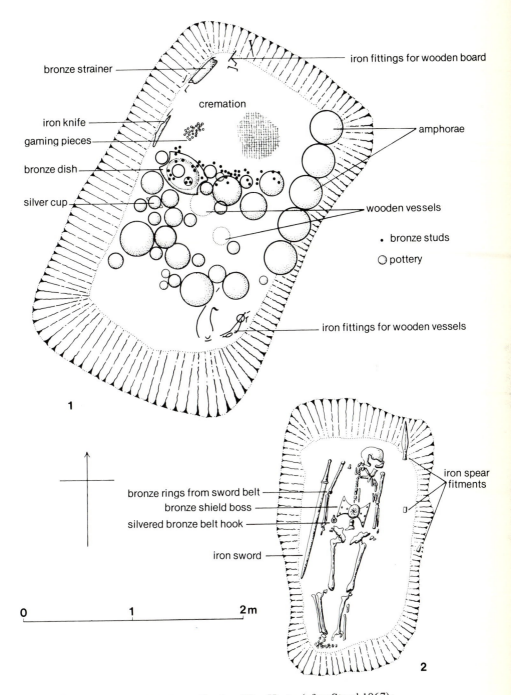

Fig. 7.35 Grave plans: 1 Welwyn Garden City, Herts. (after Stead 1967);
2 Owslebury, Hants. (after Collis 1973).

widespread adoption of standard customs, presumably for a particular rank in society. One group consists of males buried with swords, frequently also with scabbard fittings and attachment rings, and sometimes with a spear and shield (Collis 1973); these warrior burials are found from Dorset to Yorkshire. At Owslebury, Hampshire (Collis 1968: 25), such an inhumation (fig. 7.35) was the nucleus of a small cremation cemetery. The other group may be regarded as the female counterpart of these weapon-burials; characteristic grave goods are mirrors and bronze bowls, as well as small personal ornaments. At Birdlip, Gloucestershire (Green C. 1949), the mirror was found with bronze bowls, rings and a bracelet, a necklace and a silver gilt brooch, in a stone cist containing an extended female inhumation. Others are known from the south-western cemeteries of Trelan Bahow and Mount Batten, and from Colchester (Fox and Hull 1948), conforming to the local burial rites of inhumation in a cist and cremation respectively. Burials with mirrors are also found in Yorkshire, at Arras and Garton Slack.

The development of the iron age

Much emphasis has been placed in many explanations of the development of the iron age (e.g. Childe 1940) on the introduction of new types by immigrants or invaders from Europe, but the idea of a new population at the beginning of the iron age bringing knowledge of hillforts and characteristic pottery and settlements, as well as iron technology, is now hard to maintain. The first indication that such concepts needed revision came from the radiocarbon dates for early hillforts, but, as has been shown above (p. 348), it is now becoming clear that much of what has traditionally been regarded as iron age was in fact already current in the late bronze age, especially in the case of pottery and settlements. In fact, the only innovations that can clearly be assigned to the onset of the iron age are the widespread change from bronze to iron for many purposes, and metal objects of Hallstatt C type; yet even these residual novelties are sometimes attributed to immigrants (e.g. Burgess 1974: 213).

Hallstatt C innovations in bronze types were limited to swords, razors, horse-gear and a series of heavy axes (Burgess 1968a: 26–33). Much has been made of the fact that these types are seldom found in association with 'native' bronzes, suggesting possibly two separate industries serving separate populations; it is, however, at least as likely that this dissociation is a chronological feature, and that, as elsewhere in western Europe, Hallstatt C bronzes are not found with other types because by the seventh century the bronze industry, and the practice of hoard deposition, were giving way to iron (Champion T.C. 1975: 139). This theory would receive some support from the fact that the hoards with Hallstatt C bronzes at Llyn Fawr (Savory 1976b: 19–21) and Sompting (Curwen 1948) also contained iron objects. Nor do the swords themselves necessarily suggest new people. As Cowen has shown (1967: 401–9), the British examples are better regarded as regional variants than as imports, and they form part of a continuous tradition in Britain which adopted and copied current western European fashions in weapon types from bronze daggers to late

La Tène swords; the absence of such swords would be more surprising than their presence. The razors and horse-gear too are part of a longer tradition of prestige objects widespread in western Europe.

It is difficult to find any evidence that conclusively suggests the arrival of a new population at the beginning of the iron age, and it is also possible to suggest a different sort of explanation for the change to iron itself. The major feature of the late bronze age metal industry was the expansion of the quantity and range of output, the adoption of a leaded bronze alloy for ease of casting and the development of a complex industrial organization; all this points to an industry developing to meet a growing demand for products. It is possible that, if this expansion continued, it would have become advantageous, or necessary, to change to the more readily available material, iron (Champion T.C. 1975: 139–42).

This sort of explanation, in contrast to the invocation of constant immigration, stresses the relationship between Britain and the Continent, both in artifact types such as swords and in economic processes such as those that may have led to the change from bronze, and also the role of internal growth without sudden stimuli from abroad. It also removes the emphasis from the seventh century and the introduction of iron as a major turning point; the significant developments were occurring over a period in the first half of the 1st millennium. The growth argued for the metal industry can perhaps be seen also in the expansion of agriculture and the introduction of new crops (p. 352), and the appearance of a new pottery tradition, with a wider range of forms (p. 398).

This phase of development also saw the construction of the first hillforts, but it must be remembered that on present evidence the early hillforts are geographically limited, to north Wales and the Marches, northern Britain, Ireland and Scotland. Some areas, especially Wessex, though having many hillforts, have not yet produced indications of a similarly early date, while in others, as in eastern England, hillforts of any date are rare. Our knowledge of contemporary settlement in the east is still very limited, but there is not yet any evidence for the internal planning or scale of organized construction seen in the early hillforts elsewhere; even nucleated settlements the size of, for example, Moel y Gaer are so far lacking. It is possible, however, that the double-ditched enclosure at Mucking (Jones and Jones 1975: 141), called a 'mini-hillfort' by its excavator, with one central round-house, may correspond to some of the possible functions of hillforts as prestige residences.

There were clearly considerable regional variations, which we cannot yet fully appreciate, in the developments of the first half of the 1st millennium BC, but the evidence of industry, agriculture and settlement suggests a period of expansion, possibly accompanied by or in response to a growth in population. If conclusions from the hillforts can be applied more widely, it may also have been a period when larger settlement units were emerging, and when competition led to increased aggression, the need for defence and possibly also more marked social distinction. This competition, which would have been an important factor in agricultural expansion and intensification, and the introduction of new crops, may have been due to increasing population, diminishing land resources or both; it has been suggested above (p. 349) that climatic deterioration may have been of less importance in the reduction of available land than over-exploitation by earlier agriculture.

This mode of explanation, evolved as an alternative to invasions, does not rely solely on insular continuity, for, although some things, such as the double-ring round-house and cylindrical clay loom-weights, can be clearly shown to have a native bronze age ancestry, other types are equally clearly related to innovations on the Continent. This is true not only of objects such as swords and horse-gear, even of pottery too, but also of concepts such as hillforts and details of their construction. At the heart of such parallels there may lie a basic similarity between Britain and western Europe in economic and social structure and the processes that affected them. There was also, especially in such spheres as prestigious or fashionable display, a constant culture parallelism; this must have been maintained by long-lasting cross-Channel contacts. These contacts may have been of a social, economic, political or even military nature, but to describe such a system of relationships as 'invasions' is unnecessarily to restrict their scope.

The same principles can be used to assess the nature of those objects of late Hallstatt and early La Tène type in Britain, for the latter of which D.W. Harding (1974: 157–76) has again revived the explanation of Marnian invaders. The difficulties of the invasion explanation are typified by the Arras burials of east Yorkshire, for although the ditched enclosures and the vehicle burials belong to funerary practices that are widespread in western Europe, there is no one place from which the Yorkshire rites could have been derived. Furthermore, it is only the burial rites that are new, for what little is known of the contemporary settlements and pottery is entirely of native type. The apparent concentration of objects such as bracelets in Yorkshire, and relative absence elsewhere, may also be deceptive, for a similar burial context, where small ornaments might be expected to occur, is found nowhere else except in the south-west. It is therefore an innovation in burial rites that has to be explained. The similarity to west European La Tène practices is so strong that a connection cannot be denied, yet a simple immigration to Yorkshire cannot be found a continental origin, and cannot account for the lack of any other form of innovation in Yorkshire. On the other hand, it is difficult to see why the native population of Yorkshire, and nowhere else, should have adopted a form of La Tène burial practices. Both explanations are clearly beset with serious difficulties.

The objects used elsewhere to substantiate a Marnian invasion are of an almost equally restricted nature, with nothing in the fields of settlements or burials. These are of two sorts, firstly objects made in or transmitted through La Tène Europe and secondly the local imitations of continental types or styles. The imports can be divided into two classes: there are those objects that are no more than the contemporary continuation of a long-standing pattern of imports, and there are also those that represent a new departure in the range of goods to reach Britain. In the first category fall the late Hallstatt and early La Tène daggers found especially in the Thames, which are merely the sixth- and fifth-century counterparts of the imports of fashionable sword types from late Urnfield and early iron age Europe. In the second category are the vessels such as the Weybridge bucket and the Attic cup from Reading, and the very small number of personal ornaments, especially brooches. But if these types are without comparable predecessors they are not unique to Britain, but form just a small part of a wider diffusion of objects from or through the Hallstatt and La Tène regions, throughout northern and western Europe. Their occurrence in Britain is in no way remarkable, but is rather a sign of the wealth and prestige of this central European zone and its far-flung social and economic contacts.

The insular imitation of the continental types presents a similar picture, for there are both the local adaptations of the weapon types, as with all earlier and later forms, and the adoption of brooch and pottery fashions; these La Tène types were, however, widely copied in other areas of northern and north-western Europe, and Britain is but part of a larger pattern. The pottery, as too often in the study of the British iron age, has been given a great importance, but even in areas where such parallels are known they are far from being the only styles, or even the majority of the pottery. The insular reflections of the Hallstatt and La Tène world, if thus seen in their proper context, both diachronously in Britain and synchronously through northern Europe, are simply parts of much wider and more long-lasting social and economic contacts, and can easily be accounted for in terms of the well-documented patterns of connections across the North Sea and English Channel that existed throughout prehistory.

The evolution of urban society

The interior part of Britain is inhabited by tribes declared in their own tradition to be indigenous to the island, but the maritime part by people who crossed over from Belgium to invade and loot; nearly all of them are known by the names of the states from which they derived when they came to Britain; after the invasion they stayed there and began to till the fields. (Caesar, *Gallic Wars*, Bk V: 12.)

This sentence has dominated the explanation of the final century of the iron age. In the eighteenth and nineteenth centuries various antiquities in southern Britain, including even Stonehenge, were attributed to these immigrants, but then in 1890 Evans' publication of the Aylesford cremations gave the first archaeological demonstration of cross-Channel parallels, which were tentatively compared to Caesar's record. In the following years this equation of Belgic immigrants and cremation burial was widely accepted, though not universally. Caesar's reference to the maritime part, defined elsewhere as the region south of the Thames, coincided well with the historical groupings of Atrebates and Belgae, with their capitals respectively at Silchester and Winchester, known in the Roman period in an appropriate place and with appropriate names for immigrants. As the knowledge of the cremation burials grew, however, it became clear that they were centred north of the Thames in Essex and Hertfordshire, and it was open to question (Fox C.F. 1923: 118) whether the identification was still possible.

One solution to this problem was outlined by Bushe Fox (1925) and elaborated by Hawkes and Dunning (1930). The identification of the cremations with the Belgae was maintained, and the question of names was solved by relating the Catuvellauni, known in the Hertfordshire region, with the Catalauni in northern France; their migration to Britain was dated to 75 BC. The historical evidence of Belgae south of the Thames was explained by a second Belgic invasion, but this idea found little favour.[42] A Belgic immigration of c. 75 BC was thus established as a fundamental basis of iron age thinking, and the whole of late La Tène culture, such as coins, brooches and pottery, was attributed to these Belgae, to their expansion by military conquest and to cultural diffusion or 'belgicization': thus at Maiden Castle 'the arrival of Belgic elements was the result of no mere "culture creep" but came suddenly in the train of new masters' (Wheeler 1943: 59).

This widely accepted theory was called into question when Allen (1961a) dated the earliest coins not to 75 BC, but to the second century BC. This was too early for the traditional migration, and raised the question whether any of the other late iron age material could be of similar date. Birchall (1965) showed on the contrary that little, if any, of the pottery and cremations could be even as early as 50 BC. The coins themselves were thus left as the only possible pre-Caesarian indicators of immigrants, and the implications of the new chronology were boldly accepted by Hawkes (1968); he now abandoned the identification of the Belgae with the Aylesford cremations, and sought them instead in the various series of coins.

Stead (1976a) has now confirmed Birchall's dating of the earliest Aylesford burials, though on rather different grounds, and the identifica-tion of the coins with Caesar's immigrants is still the most widely accepted view of the final phase of the iron age (e.g. Cunliffe 1978a: 67–81), though modifications have been suggested.[43] Much ingenuity has been expended in maintaining the identification of the Belgae, despite the fact that neither the geography nor the chronology of the material matches the historical facts. There are also important objections to the whole method of explanation, for the concentration on the forms of the material, whether coins, pottery or burial rites, and on their typological ancestry has obscured questions of their function and of the development of new types of settlement site, new systems of industrial production and new political and economic structures. These developments transformed iron age society in southern and eastern England in the first century BC, and are not in the least explained by identifying coins with Belgic immigrants.

Underlying such explanations is the assumption that historical entities, such as a population of Belgae, can be identified with archaeological distributions, in this case not even a culture with a full range of characteristic traits, but just one type, the coinage; furthermore, that the wider extension of coin-using can be explained in terms of further migration or political expansion. It is far from clear, however, that archaeology and history should be equated in such a simple manner. Hachmann (1976) has stressed that the problem of the Belgae is one of literary history, and that correlation with archaeology is a difficult theoretical as well as practical question. In historical terms, therefore, Caesar's Belgic immigrants can be identified with the Belgae and Atrebates recorded in southern England in the Roman period, and the fact that no archaeological substantiation of them can be offered need not be considered a problem.

Concentration on the Belgae and on south-eastern England has drawn attention away from many of the significant developments of the later iron age elsewhere, and it is necessary to see all these changes in a wider context. One of the most obvious indications of change is the renewal of trade with the Continent. In the first half of the first century BC this is centred on Hengistbury Head, where Mediterranean amphorae and pottery from France have been found (Cunliffe 1978b); after mid-century, the emphasis switches to the east coast, with more amphorae and bronze vessels. After 10 BC the quantity of imported material grows rapidly, including amphorae again, Gallo-Belgic and Arretine pottery, glass and metalwork. As well as the imports themselves, there are local versions of late La Tène and early Gallo-Roman styles, in particular brooches and pottery, but also swords, buckets and other types. The Aylesford cremations can also be regarded as an imitation of the Continent, for a similar cremation rite was well established there from the third century BC, and the richly furnished Welwyn graves and bucket burials have close continental parallels.

Coinage[44] (fig. 7.36) was also derived from the Continent. The earliest coins are of types found on both sides of the Channel, forming six series termed Gallo-Belgic A-F; these in turn gave rise to a large number of purely insular types, British A-Q, which between them are distributed over southern and eastern England from Dorset to Lincolnshire.[45] As described above, discussion has concentrated mainly on these coins as indicators of migration and conquest, and in the later development of the coinage towards the end of the first century BC, when inscriptions appear, a similar mode of interpretation has been followed. The inscriptions and family relationships expressed therein, coupled with the assumption that the distribution of a coin type delimits the political boundaries of the ruler issuing it, have enabled a kind of dynastic history of the final period of the iron age to be written (Allen 1944), though analysis of the coin distributions (Hogg 1971) shows no sign of curtailment at a boundary. Coin series centred in the Essex–Hertfordshire region were of particular importance; Tasciovanus minted at St Albans, while his successor, Cunobelinus, whose inscriptions proclaim him his son, minted at both St Albans and Colchester.[46] Another family ruled in Sussex, founded by Commius, who was in turn succeeded by his three sons, Tincommius, Eppillus and Verica. The fluctuating balance between these dynasties and other rulers have been studied in detail.

Fig. 7.36   Celtic coins from the British Isles.

1. Ambiani, north-east Gaul. 'Gallo-Belgic AB1' gold coin, the earliest
continental Belgic coin type found equally in south-east Britain and Gaul. Late
second century BC. Obverse based on head of Apollo, diameter 27mm
(photograph: Nicholson Museum of Antiquities, University of Sydney).
2. Kent. Gallo-Belgic C imitation of gold stater of Ambiani. Early first century
BC. Diameter 17mm (photograph: courtesy Trustees of the British Museum).
3. Kent and Thames Valley. Speculum or tin-rich bronze coins which, like the
'potin' coins of central Gaul, are based on coins of Massalia, the obverse
showing a head of Apollo and the reverse a charging bull. Although introduced
in the first century BC the type continued in use into the Claudian period.
Diameters 17 and 14mm (photographs: courtesy Trustees of the British
Museum).

4. Catuvellauni. Gold coin of Tasciovanus, king of the major tribe centred on the Home Counties north of the Thames. Late first century BC. Obverse, diameter 17mm (photograph: Cabinet des Médailles, Bibliothèque Nationale, Paris).

5. Catuvellauni. 'Ear of barley' gold coin of Cunobelin based on Apollo wreath of early uninscribed coinage (see (1)). One of the later issues from the tribal mint at Camulodunum (Colchester). Diameter 17mm (photograph: courtesy Trustees of the British Museum).

6. Catuvellauni. Gold coin of Tasciovanus. Reverse showing Celtic rider with carnyx (see fig. 7.71). The name SEGO may indicate an as yet unidentified mint. Diameter 16·5mm (photograph: courtesy Trustees of the British Museum).

7. Coritani. Gold coin of 'South Ferriby' type struck by the tribe controlling Leicestershire and Lincolnshire. Late first century BC. Diameter 17mm (photograph: courtesy Trustees of the British Museum).

Even if the fundamental assumptions which allow such history to be inferred from the coinage are accepted, other important questions have been largely ignored. Little attention has been paid to the function of the earliest coins, nor to the fact that they were minted only in gold. Such large denominations would have been unsuitable for everyday exchange purposes, and must have functioned more as a standard means of storing and counting wealth, and making a variety of payments such as tribute or tolls (Allen 1976). They are more a sign of the existence of an authority able and needing to mint such objects, than of commercial activity.

Later in the first century BC smaller denomination coins appear, in silver, bronze and potin.[47] These show an obvious clustering on the oppida and large nucleated settlements of the period, and clearly circulated in a different way and fulfilled a different function from gold; they indicate an exchange system using small coins in existence in the major late iron age centres[48] (fig. 7.36:3).

There are also signs of internal development, to complement the evidence of continental influence. The existence of a social or political organization of sufficient complexity to need coinage is indicated by the rapid adoption and imitation of the Gallo-Belgic series. Something of this social structure can be seen in the conspicuous displays of wealth in the rich Welwyn, bucket, warrior and mirror burials, and in the proliferation of such prestige items as mirrors and horse-gear and an elaborate decorative art style. The appearance of this wealth does not imply the first emergence of an aristocratic élite, for the burials of the earlier period in which they might have been seen are lacking; but if it is not the emergence of a new hierarchy, then it is the acquisition by an established group of significant new sources of wealth to reinforce their position.

Economic growth, too, can be seen. The introduction of the potter's wheel throughout southern and eastern England coincided with a standardization of the forms of pottery produced, and brooches also appear to have been more uniform and plentiful than before. Both pottery and metal industries may have undergone a change to larger scale and more standardized production and distribution from a specialist centre. Such a development would have been approximately contemporary, in the second half of the first century, with the first minting of small coins and the emergence of market centres.

These major settlements of the late iron age have been described above (p. 374). Though sites in Essex and Hertfordshire such as Colchester, Braughing and St Albans are the richest and best known, comparable sites are known from Dorset to Lincolnshire. They are united by many shared characteristics of size, density of occupation, imports, small denomination coinage and sometimes mints. There are nonetheless significant differences. In Wessex, sites such as Maiden Castle and South Cadbury grew out of old-established hillforts, in Lincolnshire the evidence of Sleaford, Ancaster and Dragonby suggests that there the large nucleated settlements have an ancestry at least in the second century BC, but in the south-east none of the oppida has yet shown conclusive evidence for pre-Augustan occupation. Information concerning their origins is still slight, but many of them appear to have been new foundations, possibly sited to take advantage of cross-Channel or internal trade, for they have predominantly coastal or riverine, not hill-top, locations.

These differences emphasize not only the regional variation in broadly comparable developments, but also that it would be wrong to regard them as sudden changes in the first century BC. The sites themselves may have a long history, and the economic and social changes may also be the result of long-term processes. The growing complexity of production can be seen earlier in the iron age, in the central production and distribution of such commodities as salt, querns and pottery (p. 385). The 'currency bars' show a similar production of iron, and also the introduction of standard units of measure; the earliest coins can be regarded as another sign of this same standardization. A system of weights was in use in Britain, as in north-western Europe, and weights, scale-pans and balance-beams are well known (Wainwright and Spratling 1973: 119–20). By the first century BC this was also a literate society, as can be seen not just from the coin inscription, but from the papyrus imported from the Mediterranean, and given a secondary use in the minting of some potin coins (Wild 1966; Allen 1971). What was written on it is not known, but if a parallel with the Continent is accepted, it might have been official figures of population or tribute (Jacobi G. 1974).

The process of urban development was long and complex, and the details of its chronology cannot yet be fully elucidated; even less than the chronology can a totally satisfactory account of the causes of this process be given. What is clear is that by the end of the iron age there was in southern and eastern Britain a complex urban society, with a highly organized system of production and distribution, market centres where a small denomination coinage was used in exchange, and a political authority which minted coins and kept records. The reasons for the evolution of such a society must be sought in the interaction of the long process of internal growth visible in the iron age and the new opportunities offered by the expansion of the Roman empire into north-western Europe in the first century BC.

Iron age art in southern Britain and Ireland

The study of early iron age art in the British Isles is afflicted by the same problem as many other aspects of the material culture of the period – the absence of a firm chronology. The majority of fine metalwork comes from isolated find spots, in many cases giving clear evidence of the Celtic propensity for the deposition of objects in streams, rivers and lakes (cf. Torbrügge 1972) and, with the exception of the radiocarbon dates for the Gussage All Saints, Dorset, workshop (cf. p. 367; Spratling 1973; Wainwright and Switsur 1976), early iron age art in Britain is without any firmly dated contexts prior to the later part of the first century BC. Chronology, even relative, has therefore largely been a matter of guesswork.

The pioneering modern studies of the beginnings of insular Celtic art (Fox C. F. 1958: 1ff.; Jope n.d.)[49] were bound chiefly by two factors: the relationship of insular La Tène developments to a putative third century BC Marnian invasion, and what was seen as a close stylistic affinity with art of the second or 'Waldalgesheim' phase of Paul Jacobsthal's (1944) tripartite divisions, beginning in the latter part of the fourth century BC.

In contrast, more recent writers have favoured a low chronology which suggests a beginning for insular art hardly before the second century BC (cf. Megaw 1970: esp. 34ff; Duval 1977: esp. 127ff.), and the study is not aided by a general phenomenon of pre- and post-Roman Celtic art – a constant but often seemingly discontinuous rediscovery of certain basic abstract forms (cf. Jope 1972).

Imports of fine metalwork are not totally unknown but hardly assist the problem. A gold buffer-terminalled torc from Clonmacnois, Co. Offaly (Megaw 1970: no. 174), belongs to a third-century La Tène B2 Middle Rhine class. The fragments of the unique bronze hanging bowl from an apparent cist burial at Cerrig-y-drudion, Denbighshire (Megaw 1970: no. 114; Savory 1976b: 26f.) (fig. 7.37), are best compared to the designs of northern French decorated pottery of not earlier than late fourth century date, pottery which itself has a background in a class of engraved central and eastern French metalwork with designs based on classical acanthus scrolls (cf. Frey with Megaw 1976: 53ff.). This apparent link with Armorican decorated pottery (Schwappach 1969: esp. 258ff.) has given rise to suggestions that British decorated pottery – and by implication insular art as a whole – must have developed within this period. Detailed studies (Avery 1973; Elsdon 1975), however, indicate that none of this insular pottery can be dated earlier than the second century BC.

Careful re-examination of other pieces of British metalwork, originally thought to be related to or actual examples of continental 'Waldalgesheim' style, such as the bronze arm-ring from a possible chariot burial at Newnham Croft, Cambridgeshire, and a so-called chariot horn-cap from Brentford, Essex (fig. 7.40a), relate rather to motifs developed in the various sword sub-styles which evolved on the Continent around 300 BC (cf. Frey with Megaw 1976; Szabó 1977). With the exception of one probable import and two other pieces similar to Swiss products (De Navarro 1972: 330ff.), those pieces which seem closest to continental material are a fragmentary scabbard in Wisbech Museum (May 1976: 127f.) and another scabbard with bronze attachments from Standlake, Oxfordshire (Jope n.d.; Megaw 1970: no. 250[50]). A group of sword scabbards from Northern Ireland, notably three allegedly from a crannóg site at Lisnacrogher, Co. Antrim, are often considered early in the insular sequence (fig. 7.38c). But the generally symmetrical and all-over layout of design and details of execution are wholly at variance with continental material and in any case the Lisnacrogher scabbards must have been made over a number of generations (cf. Piggott S. 1950; Jope 1954; 1971: 118; and compare Frey with Megaw 1976: 55ff.). These products of a Lower Bann workshop – or group of workshops – which could well be of no earlier than second century date, on the other hand do have affinities with what Atkinson and Piggott (1955) termed the 'Torrs-Witham' group, a group which apparently had connections (or exported) across the Irish

Sea (Megaw 1970: no. 246; cf. also p. 479) (figs. 7.38–9). The southern British members of this class are mainly long rectangular bronze parade shields or shield mounts from the Thames and Lincolnshire (cf. May 1976: 128ff.), of which the shield with coral inlay and appliqué boar mount dredged from the river Witham near Lincoln is the finest piece (fig. 7.39a). Other shield fittings, including fragments from South Cadbury hillfort (Spratling 1970; Alcock 1972b),[51] may be somewhat later than the late third/early second century date most recently ascribed to the Witham finds, although it seems difficult to substantiate the argument advanced by Jope (1971; 1976) that the type was introduced to Britain from Italy. Notable in the decoration of the shields are the occasional allusions to animal and human forms, most frequently to be seen in bird-like terminals (figs. 7.38c, 7.39a–b).

Savory (cf. 1976b, d) has drawn attention in a number of studies to the existence in north Wales of another group of shields and related mounts which clearly indicate an important regional tradition and one unrecognized by C.F. Fox (1958) in his pioneering attempt to establish such geographical divisions in the iron age art of the British Isles. Again, however, chronology is a problem: for example, Savory favours at least a third century date (contemporary with the earliest estimations given for the Witham find) for the hoard from Tal-y-Llyn on Cader Idris (fig. 7.40b–c), a hoard whose deposition at least cannot have been before the first century AD in view of its association with a Roman lock-plate (cf. Spratling 1966). Frey, however, has drawn attention to a general feature of both the Welsh material and the 'Torrs-Witham' group which is certainly foreign to the continental material advanced as possible arguments for an early date: that is, the manner in which many pieces – including both the 'early' Tal-y-Llyn mounts and the generally accepted first-century BC disc from the Llyn Cerrig Bach deposit (Fox C.F. 1946; Megaw 1970: no. 254) – are based on compass-constructed designs (Frey with Megaw 1976: 60ff.). Certainly, parade shields continued to be produced up to the period of the Roman conquest, as in the case of that from the Thames at Battersea (Megaw 1970: no. 253; Brailsford 1975a).

Complex compass-based ornament is a feature of the southern series of engraved bronze mirrors, the first group of material for which associations indicate a more or less firm chronology in the century before and the years just after the Roman conquest (cf. Fox and Pollard 1973; Brailsford 1975a: 66ff.; Lowery, Savage and Wilkins 1976) (fig. 7.42a–b). It is certainly to such material rather than to continental art of the fourth century that the unique carved stone from near a rath or small fort at Turoe, Co. Galway – the only undisputed example of pre-Roman iron age sculpture from the British Isles (Duignan 1976) – must be related (fig. 7.41a–b).

One group of weapons, for example an iron spear with bronze mounts (fig. 7.42c), sword scabbards from the Thames at Henley and from a possible burial at Bugthorpe, Yorkshire, exhibits the use of the 'mirror' style inclusive of cross-hatching or 'basketry' (cf. Megaw 1970: nos. 257, 259; Rutland 1972). Contemporary with the mirrors, and now some of the best evidence in the 'Belgic' graves of southern Britain for a close cross-

Channel relationship with Gallia Belgica, are the sheet bronze decorated buckets of which Aylesford (fig. 7.44) and Marlborough are simply the most sophisticated (cf. Stead 1971a). Buckets from burials in Luxembourg, France and Germany (cf. Haffner 1974; Vidal 1976; Polenz 1977) are all more or less contemporary with the Roman conquest of Britain and may add some support to the late chronology now being advanced for other aspects of supposed Belgic settlement, such as the uninscribed series of Gallo-Belgic coinage (cf. p. 417; Scheers 1972).

Wholly insular are the Snettisham-Ipswich group of gold and electrum rings (Brailsford 1975a: 144ff.) (fig. 7.43) which, together with a bronze helmet from the Thames at Waterloo (Megaw 1970: no. 294) and the bits from the now partially lost Ulceby, Lincolnshire, hoard (cf. May 1976: 156ff.), and including a Scottish outlier (cf. p. 480), are products of craftsmen seemingly restricted to the East Anglian territory of the Iceni; the use of 'basketry' fill-in and comma-spirals with trumpet-like terminals relate them to the mirrors. Again there is a suggestion of the occasionally far-flung nature of gift-exchange in the large Snettisham tubular torc from hoard 'A' which, together with that found with a miniature gold boat and other objects in 1895 at Broighter, Co. Derry, has close parallels in northern France and Belgium (cf. Megaw 1970: nos. 173, 289).[52]

The workshop scrap from Gussage All Saints (Spratling 1973) gives evidence for the manufacture of harness mounts of a type found in hoards from Norfolk and from Seven Sisters, Glamorgan, which contain pieces of Roman military equipment (cf. Davies and Spratling 1976). Seven Sisters also seems likely to have been the product of a local workshop attached to a native homestead and has provided useful material for consideration of the mechanics of fine metalwork production in the early decades of the Roman occupation. Stylistically, links can be found once more with the southern mirrors in compass-based designs, typical Celtic ambiguity of imagery and a contrast of light and shade, achieved in the mounts by the use of enamel (fig. 7.41c); the Turoe stone may also be cited. Hoards in the south-west such as Polden Hill, Somerset (Brailsford 1975b), like finds from North Britain (cf. MacGregor M. 1976: 24ff.), indicate that whatever the nature of crafts organization in later iron age Britain, material and motifs were freely exchanged across tribal boundaries and beyond – even to the Fayum.[53] Outside the south and east of Britain other less accomplished regional products can be found, such as the heavy bronze – and brass – neck rings from the West Country (cf. Megaw 1971).

By the middle of the first century AD, however, native metalwork outside Ireland has taken on a provincial look (figs. 7.45–7). Certain of the so-called 'casket-ornaments' and disc-brooch covers of repoussé sheet bronze (cf. Megaw and Merrifield 1970; MacGregor M. 1976: 156ff.), and notably the enamelled mount from Elmswell, Yorkshire (fig. 7.47a), betray the direct influence of Roman motifs no less than do native examples of provincial Roman brooch types (fig. 7.47b), not only from their context but in their adaptation of such features as the Augustan vine-scroll. Other details of the art of this late period – duck-like terminals, trumpet finials and pointed-arched extensions – are truly native and find their counterpart in the handful of largely unassociated bronzes from Ireland (figs. 7.45, 7.46, 7.48a). Evidence for chariotry seems to survive in Ireland well into the 1st millennium AD, much longer than in the rest of the British Isles, as has been noted above (cf. p. 394). The decoration of such material is wholly insular, with the possible exception of a bridle bit, unfortunately without provenance, in the National Museum, Dublin, which exhibits one of the rare explicitly human representations in insular art (Raftery B. 1974). The scatter of bronze at such sites as the possible cemetery on Lambay Island, Co. Dublin – most recently considered as the equipment of Brigantian refugees (Rynne 1976) – includes obvious first-century AD imports from highland Britain such as the massive bracelet from Newry, Co. Down (cf. Herity and Eogan 1977: 242ff.; MacGregor M. 1976: 98ff.), a type well exemplified by the fine pair from Pitkelloney (fig. 7.46c). But such isolated finds as the Loughan Island, Co. Antrim, discs from the river Bann (fig. 7.48a), the so-called Petrie 'crowns' and the Cork horns and bronze 'offering bowls' (Jope and Wilson 1957; O'Kelly 1961; Megaw 1970: nos. 269–71), are examples of what has been termed 'the ultimate La Tène style' whose precise date is, yet again, a matter of conjecture. The tooled-down and geometrically laid-out designs and terminals of the Bann disc and the 'crowns' look forward to the art of the British Early Christian manuscripts. The trumpet terminal became also a feature of a widespread group of open-work mounts of later first century AD date which became popular throughout the Roman frontier provinces from Dura Europos to Hadrian's Wall (MacGregor M. 1976: 186–9) (fig. 7.48b). But here, as with the later native art of mainland Britain, one is strictly beyond the bounds of British prehistory.

Notes

1. For a brief history of iron age research, see Cunliffe 1978a: 1–10.
2. There is no general treatment of classical references to the barbarian world, though useful discussions will be found in Powell (1958) and Piggott (1975: 18–21 and 91–121). For the Celts generally the main source was Posidonius, now surviving only as fragments in other authors (Tierney 1960; Nash 1976). Caesar was an eye-witness of the late iron age in Gaul and Britain and though he was not primarily interested in providing an ethnographic account, many useful comments are found in his *Gallic Wars*. Strabo's *Geography* gives an account of Britain, though it is only as good as his understanding of his various sources, while other references occur in Suetonius' lives of the emperors and in Diodorus Siculus. An account of the first stages of the Roman conquest is found in Cassius Dio; Tacitus, whose version of the Claudian invasion is now lost, provides details of the later part of the conquest in the *Annals* and *Agricola*.
   As well as the classical sources, there are also the later Irish traditions, which Powell (1958) has used extensively to illuminate the iron age. K.H. Jackson (1964a) has shown that one cycle of these traditions relates to a time before the fifth century AD, but fixes its earlier limit at the second century BC, a date based on a very late assessment of the archaeological evidence for the

beginning of the iron age in Ireland; in view of the now undoubted antiquity of some of the royal centres of this period (p. 365), this tradition may have a wider application to the 1st millennium BC.

3. The horizon of 250 BC was suggested by Hawkes (1939b) from evidence in Sussex hillforts, and as an apparent historical date offered a *terminus post quem* for other areas, especially those where hillforts could not be dated because of a lack of pottery. It led to very late dates for Early La Tène material; La Tène I brooches, for example, were thought to last as late as the first century BC (e.g. Wheeler 1943: 253). It also served to depress iron age dates generally, even if the details of the invasion were disputed (Kenyon 1952). Hodson (1962) showed that the La Tène material was not all contemporary, and reasserted the normal archaeological principles of dating.

4. It was thought necessary to derive from abroad the new features of Wheeler's Wessex Iron Age B, including multivallation and decorated pottery. The similarity between certain south-western pottery, the so-called Glastonbury style (see now Peacock 1969a; Avery 1973), and decoration known from Brittany suggested that the origin lay there, and Caesar's conquest in 56 BC provided a suitable context. The idea was adopted, and other groups of decorated pottery assigned to similar Breton immigrants to other areas (Ward-Perkins 1938: 156). It served to confirm the late dating based on the Marnian invasion, and to delay into the first century AD the continental La Tène III styles datable to the first century BC. Further work by Wheeler and Richardson (1957) showed that the styles of pottery allegedly brought to Britain in 56 BC were no longer in use then in Brittany, and Allen's (1961a) discussion of the Le Catillon hoard dated the Maiden Castle coins of Iron Age C nearer to 50 BC than to AD 25, thus moving back the whole chronological sequence and making the 56 BC hypothesis untenable.

5. Cunliffe (1978a: 31–55) has attempted to provide a geographical and chronological scheme of pottery groups, though his 'style-zones' are defined by a variety of characteristics, and they are intended as much to be indications of local 'communities' as a chronological framework. The dating criteria of the various groups are not rigorously specified (Avery 1974). For an example of a regional pottery sequence, see D.W. Harding (1972: 73–130), though here, too, the details of stratigraphy or associations on which chronology must be based are not given.

6. This contrast may be exaggerated, for pollen data are rare for the chalklands, and the major evidence for earlier clearance comes specifically from buried soils beneath man-made monuments (Evans J.G. 1972b: 242–79) and is therefore not comparable to the highland zone pollen record. The limited pollen evidence available does, however, show extensive bronze age clearance in Kent, but with a massive increase in agriculture at the beginning of the iron age (Godwin 1962; Turner 1970: 99).

7. High Rocks, Tunbridge Wells (Dimbleby 1968), Squerryes Camp, Westerham (Dimbleby 1970) and Caesar's Camp, Keston (Dimbleby 1969), all show limited clearance and agriculture on less productive soils; though dating is difficult, it is certainly in the later part of the iron age.

8. The decline in lime varies from late neolithic to iron age, and is probably anthropogenic (Turner 1962). Beech and hornbeam are thermophilous species, and though their expansion is not understood, it is likely to be a result of human activity (Pennington 1974: 103–4). Birch is a species quick to respond to anthropogenic disturbance of the forest, and when its expansion is more closely documented, it may well prove to be a non-synchronous reaction to local clearance (Pennington 1974: 84).

9. The change from humified to unhumified peat, used by Blytt and Sernander to define the onset of the Sub-Atlantic and termed the *Grenzhorizont* by Weber, was shown by Granlund to be merely one of a series of such surfaces. Further work has shown the picture to be even more complicated, with many non-synchronous series of recurrence surfaces, and widely differing dates for a single horizon in one bog complex (Godwin 1966; recent research on the Continent summarized by Moore and Bellamy 1974: 154). Recurrence surfaces may represent not climate but local changes in the drainage system.

10. Recent research on upland peat stresses the role of factors other than climate, especially interference by man, either by ploughing, leading to pan formation and waterlogging, or just by forest clearance, affecting the cycle of evapotranspiration and increasing ground water supply (Moore 1973; 1975; Mitchell 1972; Merryfield and Moore 1974; Smith A.G. 1975).

11. It is possible that the proportions of the various cereals have been affected by differential survival. Grain survives when carbonized, and a principal cause of this may have been accidents in the course of parching. Since it was not necessary to parch bread wheat and club wheat, but only glume wheats, spelt and emmer, the former may be seriously under-represented.

12. Detailed bone reports are available from Glastonbury (Bulleid and Gray 1917), Stanwick (Wheeler 1954), Sutton Walls (Kenyon 1953), Hawk's Hill (Carter and Phillipson 1965), Coygan Camp (Wainwright 1967), Rainsborough (Avery *et al.* 1967), Grimthorpe (Stead 1968), Eldon's Seat (Cunliffe and Phillipson 1968), Croft Ambrey (Stanford 1974) and Abingdon (Parrington 1978). There is not yet a general discussion of iron age livestock.

13. The only attempt has been by Applebaum (1954), using the traces of fields, enclosures and settlements on Figheldean Down, Wiltshire; his conclusions need reconsideration in the light of more recent fieldwork (Bowen 1969: 22).

14. The bibliography of hillforts is large. The seminal study was Hawkes 1931; for an introduction and list of excavations, see Avery 1976; for surface evidence, Forde-Johnston 1976; for summaries of recent major sites, Harding D. W. 1976a; for Wales, Savory 1976a; for Ireland, Raftery B. 1972; 1976a.

15. Such palisades can, of course, only be recognized where they diverge from the later line, or sufficient length of the later defences is removed. They may, therefore, originally have been more common.

16. Much attention has been paid to details of timberwork in ramparts (e.g. Cotton 1954; 1957), and a greater weight than they can probably bear has been put on such distinctions as chronological and cultural indicators.

17. Wheeler and Richardson (1957: 8) have defined a Fécamp style of defence, common in northern France, and characterized by a massive rampart of dump construction and a wide, flat-bottomed ditch typically 20m wide. Since Ward-Perkins' publication of Oldbury (1944), it has been customary to ascribe this name to certain forts in southern England, but though the refortification at Oldbury approximates most nearly to the true Fécamp proportions, none of the other alleged examples, such as High Rocks, Tunbridge Wells (Money 1968), bears a close resemblance and these are better regarded as ordinary dump ramparts.

18. Such wide-spaced concentric defences may, of course, represent not two contemporary lines of defence, but two separate chronological phases, as at Yarnbury, Wiltshire (Cunnington 1933).

19. The argument that multivallation was a late feature of defences rested primarily on its late occurrence in the structural sequence of hillforts such as Maiden Castle, but at Rainsborough it has been shown that there were two

banks from the outset. Though there are still few cases of early multivallation, the simple picture has been made more complex.

20. The C14 dates quoted (p. 364) for Rainsborough should be compared with dates of 460 ± 135 bc for Croft Ambrey phase V with similar guard-chambers, 420 ± 185 bc for Midsummer Hill, where the stone guard-chambers were not built till phase II, and 535 ± 85 bc, 420 ± 70 bc and 150 ± 80 bc for Dinorben period II, which is earlier than guard-chambers there. These dates do not warrant the attribution of such structures to a single horizon.

21. The interior occupation at Ivinghoe, with its associated metalwork, was regarded by the excavators as contemporary with the defences. This necessitates the interpretation that one of the houses was not circular but a D-shaped structure against the back of the rampart (Cotton and Frere 1968: 195 and fig. 7: Structure III); it might be more natural to assume that this building underlay the rampart, which was therefore later than at least some of the occupation.

22. It should be carefully noted that the 2nd millennium C14 dates from Mam Tor refer to internal occupation and are not in any stratigraphic relationship to the defences, which are theoretically undated.

23. Dates of 430 ± 120 bc for Anstiebury, Surrey, and of 310 ± 100 bc for Holmbury, Surrey, have only an uncertain reference to the date of construction of the defences, but at Castle Hill, Tonbridge, Kent, charcoal on the old ground surface below the bank yielded dates of 315 ± 50 bc and 228 ± 61 bc. Little is known of the occupation of these south-eastern hillforts, but such a late date compares well with the material evidence, for example from Oldbury (Ward-Perkins 1944), High Rocks (Money 1968) or Caesar's Camp, Keston (Piercy Fox 1969).

24. The military role of hillforts is difficult to demonstrate archaeologically. Some show signs of burning, though no evidence that it was done in battle, and where violence had occurred, as at Maiden Castle (Wheeler 1943), Spettisbury (Gresham 1939) or Bredon Hill (Hencken T.C. 1938), it is at the time of the Roman conquest. For the role of hillforts in war, see Avery 1976: 46–51, and Rivet 1971.

25. The division of sites into hillforts, enclosures and unenclosed settlements is used here not because it is necessarily the only, or the best, classification, but because such classes have been widely used in earlier literature. It would also be possible to ignore the presence or absence of defences, and consider sites in terms of their size, from single houses to nucleated settlements, or of their economic and social function; neither of these criteria is easy to apply, however, without extensive excavation.

26. The earthen *raths* and stone *cashels* of Ireland are usually regarded as settlements of the early historic period, and it has even been suggested that they were still being constructed in considerable numbers in the medieval period. Evidence is, however, beginning to accumulate that the settlement type may have a long ancestry in prehistory (O'Kelly M.J. 1970; Raftery B. 1976b: 192). Examples certainly of iron age date are rare.

27. The Latin *oppidum* denotes no more than a defended site, but in the Mediterranean its connotations were urban. Hence Caesar applied it to defended sites of Gaul. Its modern archaeological usage varies; in France, it is used for a defended site, rather like the English 'hillfort', while in Germany it refers specifically to the large late La Tène nucleated settlements of urban character. The term is used here, however, far removed from its original denotation, in reference to sites of proto-urban nature, regardless of defences: many, in fact, may have been undefended.

28. The name 'currency bars' is perhaps misleading, for they could never have circulated like modern all-purpose currency. They had a value as a raw material, and could have been used for the storage and assessment of wealth, as well as for the distribution of ingot metal.
29. The only attempt to relate iron artifacts and ore sources, with limited success, is Haldane 1970. Otherwise, identification of ores exploited is by archaeological inference, though the range and distribution of ores of potential value to the iron age smith were so great that conclusions are not yet possible. It may be that the wealth of Hunsbury (Fell 1936) was derived from the local ironstone, and that the large settlements of Lincolnshire were exploiting local outcrops; Hengistbury Head (Bushe Fox 1915) may also have based its economy on the iron ores available on the peninsula.
30. e.g. Santon, Norfolk (Smith R.A. 1909), Polden Hills, Somerset (Brailsford 1975b), Seven Sisters, Glamorgan (Davies and Spratling 1976), Somerset, Co. Galway (Raftery J. 1960).
31. For different reconstructions of salt production, see Nenquin (1961), Riehm (1961). No area of salt-working has produced all stages of the process, and some sites, by virtue of their location on cliff-tops, would have been inappropriate for the boiling or evaporating of sea-water.
32. Brooches form the basis for the continental La Tène chronology, from which the British sequence is largely derived. The late La Tène types are dated by their occurrence in a series of historically dated sites relating to the Caesarian conquest of Gaul and the Augustan expansion into Germany (see n. 39 below), and hoards and grave groups (Collis 1975: 53–66). Types of the Augustan-Claudian period are comparatively common in Britain; those of pre-Augustan date are rare.
33. The typological sequence established by Cowen (1967), of true Gündlingen swords, developing into hybrids in south-east England, and also influencing the native sword tradition, has been challenged by Schauer (1972). He has claimed that the so-called derivative types in north-western Europe are earlier, not later, than the true Ha C Gündlingen form, and that the sequence should be reversed. If accepted, this hypothesis would stress the development of the type in regions away from central Europe, and reduce Britain's dependence on that area for all innovations.
34. Much discussion has been devoted to the typological sequence of horse-bits: for various views, see Ward-Perkins (1939); Fox C.F. (1946: 30-1); Clarke R.R. (1951); Jope (1955); Barber and Megaw (1963); Stead (1965: 41–2); Haworth (1971); Wainwright and Spratling (1973: 123); Raftery B. (1974); MacGregor M. (1976: 24–31). For terrets, see Leeds (1933: 118–26); MacGregor M. (1976: 38–48). For linch-pins, see Ward-Perkins (1940; 1941); MacGregor M. (1976: 48–50).
35. The Mediterranean imports have been studied by Harden (1950). None has been found in a reliable archaeological context, and they are therefore dismissed by some as modern importations; Harbison and Laing (1974) accept few as genuine. The question of an archaeological context is, however, misleading, for in continental Europe such imports are found regularly in graves, which are lacking in Britain. As Torbrügge (1972) has shown (p. 405), objects found in graves in central Europe regularly occur as finds in watery contexts in the north-west, to the extent that a river or bog is not only an acceptable provenance for such objects in Britain, but precisely where they should be expected. For Etruscan metalwork as a source for native design, see Champion T. C. (1977), and for the possibility of direct seaborne trade with the Mediterranean later in the iron age, see Boon (1977).

36. The bibliography of pottery is enormous, but mainly based on finds from individual sites, and concentrated on typology and chronology. Most attention has been given to the finer or more distinctive wares, and papers cited in the text reflect this. There is a mass of coarser and less distinctive material which is as yet hardly assimilated. One attempt is Kenyon 1952, though framed in terms of the late chronology then fashionable. The only modern synthesis is Cunliffe (1978a), but his concept of a style-zone is not defined or applied consistently (Collis 1977).

37. D.W. Harding (1972: 86–96) has defined an 'angular horizon' of iron age pottery, influenced by early La Tène styles in France; it is now clear that not all sharply angular vessels are of such date, for bipartite angular bowls occur in substantially earlier contexts, and the concept requires more precise definition. Harding (1974: 157–64) restricts it to the tripartite angular vessels of south-eastern England, especially the Upper Thames region. It should also be noted that early La Tène influence on British pottery is varied: as well as these angular shapes, which were also imitated elsewhere in north-western Europe, the examples in Wessex display curvilinear profiles and retain the pedestal base, and in Kent the vessels with pedestal bases at Worth may stand at the head of a development into the foot-ring bowls defined by Ward-Perkins (1944: 145).

38. Swan (1975) has argued that the Wiltshire wheel-turned wares post-date the Roman conquest, and that the earlier iron age tradition persisted till that time. Her dating evidence for this phase is, however, derived primarily from Roman military sites, post-conquest by definition, and does not therefore necessarily reflect its beginning. The overwhelming bulk of the imported pottery points clearly to a pre-conquest date for the Wiltshire pottery. The Owslebury evidence also confirms a similar innovation in Hampshire in the first century BC. There are, though, some regions of southern England, e.g. Surrey, where it is still difficult to identify pre-conquest wheel-turned pottery.

39. The Gallo-Belgic pottery industry was established to meet the demands of the Roman army in its attempted expansion into Germany under Augustus, and its development can be seen in successive historically dated military sites such as Dangstetten, Rödgen, Oberaden and Haltern (Wells 1972). The importation of these wares into Britain in the period after 15–10 BC marks the first certain link with the continental chronology since the early La Tène brooches. The forms were predominantly plates, pedestalled cups, girth-beakers and butt-beakers, in distinctive grey, black and reddish fabrics (Hawkes and Hull 1947: 202–5; Rogers and Laing 1966; Rigby 1973).

40. The date and origin of the Heathrow temple have been much discussed. Grimes originally (1961) suggested that the building had been in use throughout the occupation of the whole site, but it now seems that there is a difference between the material associated with the round-houses, which includes loom-weights and other objects datable to the late bronze age, and the pottery from the temple, which belongs to the later iron age (V.C.H. *Middlesex* I: 57). The temple need not therefore be as early as sometimes thought (e.g. Harding D.W. 1974: 108) nor compared to a Greek original, but can be given a relatively late date in the iron age and compared both to contemporary examples in late La Tène Europe and to subsequent Romano-Celtic temples in Britain, as suggested by Powell (1958: 146).

41. The Yorkshire vehicle burials are poorly furnished in comparison to those of early La Tène France, in particular in the scarcity of pottery and the total absence of weapons. The dismantling of the vehicles is unknown in the Marne region, but can be paralleled in the rather earlier four-wheeled vehicle burials

of the Hallstatt period in eastern France and Switzerland. The dominant rite of crouched inhumation in Yorkshire is virtually unknown in western Europe in the La Tène period. In view of the widespread differences in vehicle burials throughout Europe, and the distinctive nature of the Yorkshire burials, it would be better to regard it simply as a regional variant on an established iron age practice, and to ask, not where it came from, but why it is found at all in Yorkshire. These burial rites may not be totally confined in Britain to Yorkshire, for square-ditched enclosures are known in Derbyshire (May 1970b), and there are a number of other possible vehicle burials, such as Newnham Croft, Cambridgeshire (Fox C.F. 1923: 81).

42. Bushe Fox (1925: 33) suggested the identification of the Belgae in southern central England with imported Arretine and Gallo-Belgic pottery, though this was too late to be relevant. Hawkes and Dunning (1930) referred instead to the bead-rim pottery of Wessex; this idea found little favour with local archaeologists (Cunnington 1932) and despite the reply by Hawkes and Dunning (1932), the theory of the western Belgae has been largely ignored.

43. D.W. Harding (1974: 223–6) has attempted once again to reconcile the distribution of this 'Belgic' material, lying predominantly north of the Thames, with the long ignored evidence of Caesar that the Belgae settled south of that river. He has suggested that only the earliest two series of coins, Allen's Gallo-Belgic A and B, which he claims lie south of the Thames, should be identified with the immigrants; to the north of the Thames were the Catuvellauni, now no longer classed among the Belgae, who nevertheless adopted all the elements of Belgic culture, including coinage, pottery, brooches and burials, from their immigrant neighbours to the south. This argument may accord with Caesar's evidence for the location of the Belgae, but it fails to offer any substantiation for the retention of the original names, and can only be maintained at the expense of giving two different explanations for what is quite obviously a single cultural phenomenon: south of the Thames the explanation is invasion, to the north acculturation. Rodwell too (1976) regards the Catuvellauni as not being among the Belgic immigrants, placing greater emphasis on the Trinovantes, their eastern neighbours in Essex, as the people represented by the Aylesford-type burials and pottery, the distribution of which delimited their expansion. In essence his interpretation is that of Hawkes (1968): the immigrants are seen in the various series of coins, and Caesar's reference to their settlement south of the Thames is denied, but with the exchange of the Catuvellauni for the Trinovantes there is no attempt even to substantiate Caesar's reference to the names.

44. For a list of types see Mack (1974); origins of coinage, Allen (1961a); later inscribed issues, Allen (1944). The later regional series have also been studied: Coritani, Allen (1963), May (1976: 196–201); Dobunni, Allen (1961b); Durotriges, Allen (1968a); Iceni, Allen (1970); potin, Allen (1971); Cunobelinus, Allen (1975). On function, see Allen (1976), Collis (1971a; 1971b). For an introduction to Celtic coinage, see Allen (1978).

45. Allen's chronology for the earliest coins (1961a) is based on the evolution of the typological sequence, dated back from the Le Catillon hoard. It is possible that the Caesarian date given to this hoard may be too early (Krämer 1971); if so, then the British coin sequence may also have to be redated. Scheers (1972), however, emphasizing the role of coinage to finance the campaign against Caesar, has confirmed the dating of Gallo-Belgic E to the 50s.

46. The apparent eclipse of St Albans has suggested a transfer of the capital of the Catuvellauni from there to Colchester, and the conquest of the Trinovantes of Essex. Rodwell (1976), following Allen (1964; 1967b; 1968b), has doubted the

relationship of Cunobelinus to Tasciovanus as anything more than propaganda, and has stressed the Trinovantes of Essex as the dominant force throughout the later iron age.

47. Allen (1971) has suggested that the potin coins of south-eastern England were a small-value coinage minted from early in the first century BC, thus considerably anticipating the bronze and silver issues. To reconcile this dating with his theory that such small denominations were not in use before the Augustan period, Collis (1974) has suggested that the earliest potin coins had a higher value. This seems improbable, and if an earlier appearance of such a small coin is unacceptable, it is possible that Allen's chronology, based almost entirely on typological and historical considerations, may be too extended.

48. Collis (1971a; 1971b) has demonstrated a concentration of small coins on the oppida, and a different distribution for gold. This appears to hold good for bronze and potin in the south-east, and for Durotrigian, Dobunnic and Coritanian silver. Rodwell (1976) argues against a difference in function for gold and other metals, but his arguments are not entirely convincing.

49. In anticipation of publication of Jacobsthal and Jope (in press), details of individual pieces referred to in the following paragraphs will be found in such sources as Piggott and Allen (1970), Megaw (1970), Savory (1976b) and Duval (1977).

50. Although the fragmentary scabbard with incised 'latticing' from Walthamstow is probably the only example of the continental swordsmith's skill – to be taken with such other probable Swiss pieces as the La Tène IC bent finger-ring from Park Brow and a handful of brooches from the Thames (cf. Harding D.W. 1974: 157f.) – there are indications that central European decorated swords were reaching the west, thus bridging the geographical stylistic gap which has long seemed an unsurmountable problem: cf. Bonnamour and Bulard (1976).

51. It should be noted that Spratling has retracted his (1973) view that the tools and scrap found in the area of the shield fragments are part of an iron age smith's workshop.

52. That such torcs are a north-eastern French–southern Belgian late first-century BC type seems confirmed by recent finds, including one gold example from a riverside settlement at Pommeroeul, Hainaut (cf. Joffroy 1969; De Boe and Hubert 1977). On the Broighter find and in particular the gold boat see also Farrell, Penny and Jope (1975).

53. Cf. MacGregor M. (1976: 44ff.). Spratling (1973) is strongly for local-based and, following Rowlands (1971b), perhaps part-time smithing activities. Clearly, however, there is no simple model which will fit all the evidence. Different types of organization may be envisaged, for example, for the production of pottery and fine metalwork, and distribution through the fortunes of war reasonably explains the odd outlier, best known of which is the British mirror from Roman Nijmegen (cf. Megaw 1970: no. 263). In this context, it is unfortunate that Spratling's (1972) companion survey to MacGregor M. (1976) remains unpublished.

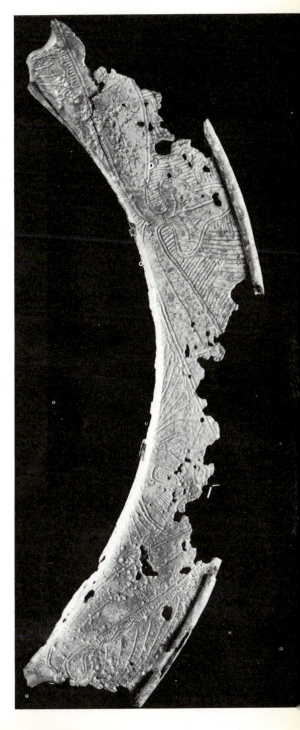

Fig. 7.37 Cerrig-y-drudion, Denbighs.:
fragment of bronze bowl rim; width of
fragment 3cm (photograph National
Museum of Wales).

a

Fig. 7.38 *a* Torrs, Melton, Kirkcudbright: detail of pony cap; length of spiral c. 3cm (photograph National Museum of Antiquities of Scotland); *b* Torrs, Melton, Kirkcudbright: detail of bronze horn; height of head c.11cm (photograph J. V. S. Megaw); *c* Lisnacrogher, Co. Antrim: bronze sword scabbard no.2; width 42mm (photograph Belzeaux-Zodiaque).

b

c

Fig. 7.39 *a* River Witham, Lincs.: shield detail; diameter of roundel 14cm (photograph courtesy Trustees of the British Museum); *b* River Witham, Lincs.: sword scabbard mount; length 13cm (photograph Phototèque l'Univers des Formes: courtesy P.-M. Duval).

b

a

a

b

c

Fig. 7.40   *a* Brentford, Middx:
'horn cap'; diameter 73mm
(photograph Museum of London);
b,c Tal-y-Llyn, Merioneth: bronze
shield mount and scheme of
decoration; diameter of engraved
area c.85mm (photograph National
Museum of Wales, drawing O.-H.
Frey).

a

Fig. 7.41 *a,b* Turoe, Co. Galway: carved pillar stone and exploded drawing; height 120cm (photograph Green Studios, Dublin, and drawing courtesy Michael Duignan); *c* Santon, Norfolk: enamelled harness mount; height 79mm (photograph University Museum of Archaeology and Anthropology, Cambridge).

c

b

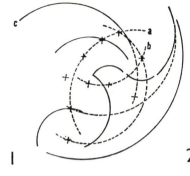

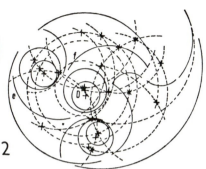

1

2

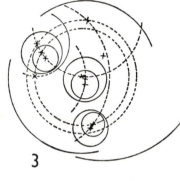

3

4

b

c

Fig. 7.42   *a* Unprovenanced:
'Mayer' mirror; height 225mm
(photograph Merseyside County
Museums); *b* Holcombe,
Devon: scheme of compass
construction of roundel on
bronze mirror (drawing courtesy
Philip Lowery and R. D. A.
Savage); *c* River Thames at
London: iron spearhead with
bronze mounts; length of mount
9cm (photograph J.V.S.
Megaw).

a

Fig. 7.43 *a* Ken Hill, Snettisham,
Norfolk: electrum torc; diameter 20cm
(photograph Phototèque l'Univers des
Formes: courtesy P.-M. Duval); *b,c*
Shaw Hill, Netherurd, Peebles.: gold
torc terminal and detail; diameter
55mm (photograph National Museum
of Antiquities of Scotland).

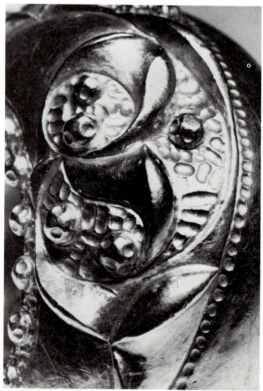

b   c

Fig. 7.44   Aylesford, Kent: grave Y: bronze-covered wooden bucket; height of head c.4cm (photograph J. V. S. Megaw).

Fig. 7.45 *a* Dowgate, City of London: bronze plaque; width 10cm (photograph Museum of London); *b* Stichill, Roxburghs.: bronze neck-ring; outer diameter 19cm (photograph Malcolm Murray); *c* Mortonhall, Midlothian: sword scabbard; width of chape 55mm (photograph National Museum of Antiquities of Scotland).

a

b

Fig. 7.46   *a* Deskford, Banff: bronze 'carnyx'
terminal; length 21·5cm (photograph National
Museum of Antiquities of Scotland; see also
fig. 7.71); *b* Norries Law, Fife: silver plaque;
width 12·6cm (photograph National Museum
of Antiquities of Scotland); *c* Pitkelloney,
Muthill, Perths.: one of pair of massive
bronze armlets with enamel insets; width
83mm (photograph Phototèque l'Univers des
Formes: courtesy P.-M. Duval).

c

a

b

Fig. 7.47   *a* Elmswell, Yorks.: bronze
casket mount with enamel inlay; width 24cm
(photograph courtesy Trustees of the British
Museum); *b* Great Chesters (*Aesica*),
Northumberland: gilt-bronze brooch; length
11·5cm (photograph Museum of Antiquities,
University of Newcastle upon Tyne).

a

Fig. 7.48　*a* Loughan Island, river Bann,
Co. Antrim: bronze disc; diameter 10·5cm
(photograph Ulster Museum); *b* South
Shields, Co. Durham: bronze triskele
mount; width 64mm (photograph Museum
of Antiquities, University of Newcastle upon
Tyne).

b

B. NORTHERN BRITAIN

Introduction

As is the case with a number of fields within European prehistory, the first distinctly modern treatment of the later prehistory of North Britain was that of Childe (1935). This synthesis drew on both nineteenth-century works (cf. Piggott S. 1966: lf.; MacKie 1970a: 8–9) and the results of new excavations, notably by Childe himself, which were just becoming available. Thereafter, several factors contributed to a fresh analysis of the nature and content of the iron age in North Britain in the early 1960s. Amongst these may be mentioned increased fieldwork on late prehistoric sites, enhanced by the availability of aerial photography, and marked in particular by the Royal Commission inventories produced in the mid-1950s, and the research undertaken for others which appeared during the following decade (RCAHM 1956; 1957; 1963; 1967). The late 1940s and early 1950s were also marked by a further series of excavations, most notably in the Border counties.

Several general tendencies are exhibited in the various contributions to the 1962 synthesis edited by Rivet (1966). Crucial is the general adoption of the Hawkesian model of Provinces and Regions, as well as the cultural and chronological inputs of this scheme. A second feature is the lengthening of the time-span of the north British iron age to harmonize with contemporary chronological thinking in southern Britain. A third aspect, and one which continues to be the subject of some debate, is the reliance on 'exotic objects', defined by D. V. Clarke (1971) to mean imports or indigenous interpretations thereof, to provide the chronological framework and, in some cases, the cultural divisions within the Scottish iron age material.

The use of radiocarbon dating to produce a chronology at least partially independent of artifactual interpretations has radically altered our comprehension of later Scottish prehistory to the extent that it has been argued that the conventional labels of 'bronze age' and 'iron age' are now difficult to apply to the material remains of the middle part of the 1st millennium BC (cf. MacKie 1971a[1]). The impact of radiocarbon dating has been to extend the chronology so that certain classes of field monument, conventionally regarded as of iron age date, now appear to have originated in the context of bronze-using cultures. Recent statements, including MacKie's (1969c) first grouping of the dates on the overlap period, have tended to stress the aspect of 'cultural continuity', reflecting the model favoured for southern Britain in the writings of Hodson. The new isotopic chronology has similarly allowed the problem of early incursions from north Germany, suggested by Piggott (1966:7) as the background for the early fortifications, to come into slightly clearer focus.

In terms of Fox's generalizing thesis, North Britain falls totally within the highland zone, a label which perhaps unduly masks the range of topography present. As the four Provinces – Atlantic, North-Eastern,

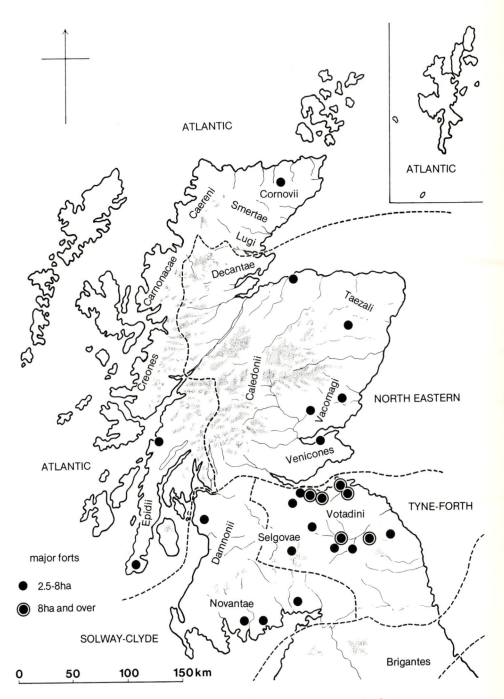

Fig. 7.49 North Britain in the iron age: boundaries of provinces, major forts and tribal names (after Piggott S. 1966; Feachem 1966).

Tyne-Forth, Solway-Clyde – first described by Piggott in 1956 and subsequently elaborated on (Piggott S. 1966) (fig. 7.49) seem to remain a useful means of orientation, they are retained here as convenient geographical labels. The characteristics of iron age settlement have long indicated a contrast between the east and west of the country (Fairhurst 1954): similarly, a distinction between north and south, reflecting a pattern noted in historical times, seems valid for much of the period under study. Maxwell has recently summarized the evidence for accepting the Forth–Clyde isthmus as a line of 'cultural cleavage', though the case is far from being an open-and-shut one (Maxwell 1975).

The Atlantic Province stretches along the indented coastline of western Scotland from Kintyre northwards and includes the upland area of Sutherland, the Caithness plateau and the Northern Isles: in this area, the pattern of inhabitable areas interspersed with inhospitable uplands, which characterizes all four Provinces to a lesser or greater extent, is at its most fragmented. Both the Lowland Provinces, Tyne-Forth and Solway-Clyde, contain areas of coastal plain of variable width, backing onto the hills and valleys of the Southern Uplands. Almost all the iron age evidence from the North-Eastern Province comes from the lower hills and valleys which skirt the Central Highlands.

The iron age inhabitants of Scotland were heirs to an increasingly uninviting physical landscape. During the first quarter of the 1st millennium BC, the climatic régime of the sub-Boreal was giving way to the sub-Atlantic, characterized by moister conditions, although temperatures may have been slightly higher than those of today. Landscape changes brought about by this deterioration were large-scale. Lowland peat-bogs became water-logged and their surfaces were colonized afresh by sphagnum and heather; upland blanket peats extended to lower altitudes. Elsewhere, leaching continued to diminish the nutrient value of those brown forest soils which had not already suffered from podsolization. Soil impoverishment and erosion are indicated by chemical evidence in inwashed material in lake sediment profiles from north-west Scotland and Aberdeenshire. The extent of man's impact in hastening these environmental changes[2] is still a moot point, but the demand for timber for construction must have made further inroads into the forest cover, as would the grazing of stock animals. Certainly, the pollen record from one hillfort indicates that its surroundings were almost devoid of woody vegetation, at least by the Roman period, and similar conditions are indicated on Tiree (Dimbleby 1960; Pilcher 1974). Seaborne contact may well have been more difficult, because of stormier conditions, than previously (Piggott 1972).

For the most part, the evidence for regional groupings within the material discussed below is of a different character from that presented in areas further south. The importance of 'exotic' finds has already been alluded to. After the demise of the local bronze industries in the fifth century BC (Coles 1959–60), the importance of local metalwork in defining regional traditions declines markedly. Generally speaking, although exceptions can be noted particularly within the Atlantic Province, much of the pottery is too insensitive to be of much value as a cultural or chronological indicator, as well as being an infrequent discovery. The general impoverishment in the artifactual record means that architectural studies are of major importance in defining group traditions. The evidence from both excavation and surface fieldwork (Feachem 1966) is critical here. On the economic front, pastoralism seems to have been of greater importance than in many of the agricultural strategies of southern Britain, and its concomitant in a country of marked altitudinal variation, transhumance, must be considered very likely. A consequent blurring of cultural distinctiveness is therefore not unexpected.

The Tyne-Forth Province

Largely through the work of Jobey and the officers of the Royal Commission, the field evidence in this area has been more thoroughly investigated than that elsewhere in Scotland in recent years. A distinctive characteristic of this area is the large number of small forts, often enclosing less than a hectare. During the course of the pre-Roman iron age, these show a sequence of structural development, the earliest use sometimes taking the form of a stockaded camp,[3] in time succeeded by a hillfort with more substantial defences, sometimes culminating in multivallation. This structural model was first shown by excavation at Hownam Rings, Roxburghshire (Piggott C. M. 1948), and more recent work suggests that considerable variations on the theme are to be expected. A few late hillforts have previously been separated from this group, on the grounds of size, and classed as oppida (Feachem 1966: fig. 13), but this term should probably be abandoned in the Scottish context for the time being (see below, p. 488). In addition, homesteads and settlements[4] enclosed by palisades, low stone walls or bank-and-ditch combinations are present, the latter varieties appearing to continue into the early centuries AD (cf. RCAHM 1967: 24–6) (fig. 7.50). A linking feature amongst the various classes of occupation sites is the presence of timber-built houses of varying degrees of structural complexity.

Unenclosed settlement, incontestably of the last millennium BC, is rare in this Province, the more so since recent excavations by Jobey at Green Knowe in the Meldon Valley of Peeblesshire have produced radiocarbon dates which suggest that this site belongs in the latter part of the 2nd millennium BC. Green Knowe, previously partially investigated by Feachem (1961), remained for long the sole excavated example of a class known as unenclosed platform settlements, which were characterized by the distribution of level aprons of material, drawn forward from quarried scoops, usually strung out along hill-slopes. Feachem's excavation showed one such level apron to have been the stance for a circular house marked by a ring of 11 post-holes, surrounded by a double ring of stake-holes for a filled-cavity wall, usually regarded as a pre-iron age feature (RCAHM 1967: 23). The distribution of unenclosed platform settlements is centred on Peeblesshire and upper Clydesdale (Feachem 1965: RCAHM 1978: fig. 7), but this is almost certainly in part a reflection of fieldwork and field survival, as such sites are easily destroyed. Early open settlement preceding

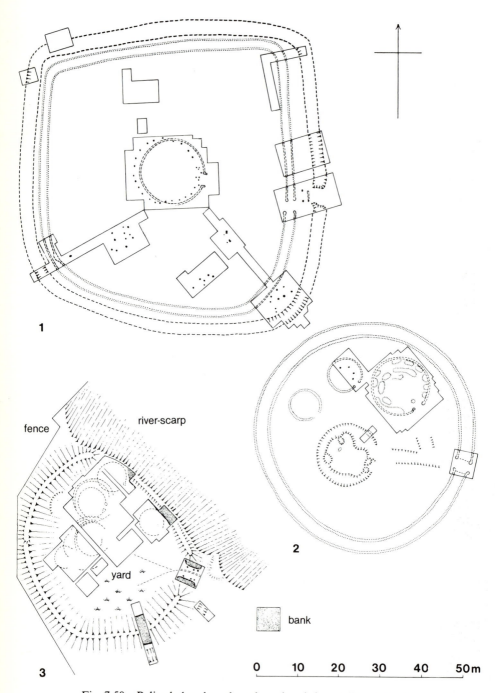

Fig. 7.50   Palisaded and earthwork-enclosed sites: 1 West Brandon, Co. Durham;
2 High Knowes A, Northumberland; 3 Boonies, Dumfries. (after Jobey 1962;
Jobey and Tait 1966; Jobey 1974b).

a palisaded phase is most clearly demonstrated at West Brandon, Co. Durham (Jobey 1962), and is inferred from the structural sequence at Harehope, Peeblesshire (Feachem 1960). A phase of open settlement may similarly begin the sequence at a ditch-enclosed settlement at Hartburn, Northumberland (Jobey 1973). The appearance of stone-built houses in this area does not seem to predate the early centuries AD, when non-defensive stone-built settlements are frequently found overlying earlier farmsteads with timber-built houses as well as more substantial fortified sites (Steer 1964: esp. 16–8; Jobey 1974a; 1977).

The classic demonstration of the complex development of the small forts of the Borders was the excavation of Hownam Rings by C. M. Piggott: we are only concerned here with the earlier defences of the site, as occupation evidence from the interior is limited to the use of the site during the Roman period (Piggott C. M. 1948; RCAHM 1956: no. 301). An area approximately 0.6ha in extent was enclosed by a single palisade, set in a bedding trench, subsequently replaced by a similar stockade. The next phase consisted of a contour fort delimited by a single dry-stone wall, approximately 3m wide, revetted on both faces. This defence was subsequently partially dismantled, and material from it used in the construction of the innermost of four ramparts, this multivallate stage of ramparts and ditches marking the last defensive construction on the site. A similar constructional sequence, though lacking the palisaded phase, was subsequently obtained from Bonchester Hill, Roxburghshire, and the limited number of small finds lent support for the short chronology then favoured (Piggott C. M. 1950).

The fact that palisaded enclosures begin early in the North British sequence has been confirmed stratigraphically by subsequent investigations (Ritchie A. 1970: 54) and supported by radiocarbon dates. The area enclosed ranges up to 1ha, and Ritchie has distinguished between sites defined by a single palisade, two closely-spaced palisades, and others marked by a pair of palisades separated by a space that could usefully have served, in the upland situations which typify the series, as a corral for livestock. Generally, the more complex systems of stockades are found associated with the larger examples of both settlements and homesteads. No North British example of the series except Broxmouth has been totally excavated, but Ritchie has argued that available evidence suggests a pattern of development in the prevalent social unit represented by them. The broad indications are that the larger social units represented by the settlements seem to precede the smaller groupings present in the homesteads, with the former being progressively replaced by hillforts, during the third quarter of the millennium (Ritchie A. 1972). Other sites show evidence of a decrease in size in successive phases, as at Horsbrugh Castle Farm, Peeblesshire (RCAHM 1967: no. 195). Apart from an iron spear-head, possibly a Hallstatt import, from Hayhope Knowe (Piggott C. M. 1949b; cf. also Ritchie A.1970: 50), most finds, including a range of coarse pottery, are little susceptible to cultural diagnosis. Ritchie sees these sites as representing the development of widespread permanent settlement in North Britain, equivalent to the rise of Deverel-Rimbury in

South Britain at an earlier date: no population change is required to account for them.[5]

The first major large-scale excavation of a hillfort in the Province indicates the complexity of the structural sequence that may be represented in some of these sites. The hillfort at Broxmouth, Dunbar, East Lothian (fig. 7.51), has been stripped by P. Hill and his continuing excavations suggest not a Hownam-like development as originally reported (*Discovery and Excavation in Scotland 1977*: 13), but a much more elaborate sequence beginning with a homestead. Thereafter, the first defence to have enclosed the low eminence on the Lothian coastal plain appears to have been bivallate. Successive defences included a palisade enclosing 0.6ha (smaller than the bivallate fort), and several univallate enclosures, which generally extended the area of the site. The interior contains a number of wooden round-houses of various types, as well as stone-built houses which appear to post-date the defences. In contrast to many North British sites, quantities of shell and bone have been preserved in various contexts and along with other material, notably worked bone, pottery, bronze and slag, these will allow a much fuller assessment of the economy than is usually possible in many upland sites where soil acidity has destroyed so much of this evidence. It is perhaps worth pointing out that this site was discovered through aerial photography and represents another instance, along with, for example, Balbridie, of how that branch of archaeology is contributing to considerable reassessment of North Britain's archaeological potential.

Apart from the series of palisaded sites, the clearest evidence of early settlement in the late bronze age/early iron age transition period comes from the important site of Traprain Law, East Lothian (Jobey 1976; Hogg 1975; Burley 1956). The putative earliest fortification on the site, represented by a line of stone, running east/west, may tentatively be claimed as a potential stockade, isolating 4ha on the summit, though it must be stressed that no excavations have taken place on this part of the site. The late bronze age material recovered from the site comes from the western flank of the hill and includes a range of local types with moulds for their production as well as a Hallstatt C element, represented by a bronze razor (Coles 1959–60:48).[6] Loosely associated with some of these bronzes was a looped socketed iron axe, of a type related to late bronze age bronze axes: as has recently been shown (Manning and Saunders 1972), the production in iron of a tool originally designed to be cast in bronze is a technical feat indicative of a high level of iron technology, and must be an indication of a developed iron industry in Britain by the seventh/sixth century BC, if the association is a valid one. MacKie has characterized the sequence represented on these south Scottish sites as the 'Hownam culture', though this term has not won general acceptance (1969c; 1970b).

The North-Eastern Province

Since Childe first defined the Abernethy complex (1935: 193–7; 236f.), its nature and content has changed on more than one occasion. The beginnings of the forts with timber-laced walls as at Castle Law,

Fig. 7.51   Broxmouth, East Lothian: multi-phase iron age site under excavation 1978 (photograph RCAHM: Crown Copyright).

Abernethy, Perthshire (fig. 7.52), are now known to predate the *murus gallicus*[7] of Caesarian Gaul, from which they were supposed to be derived (cf. Cotton 1954; Childe 1946), by several centuries. Many similarly-constructed forts exhibit signs of vitrification. Similarly, the small series of exotic metalwork believed to have marked the initial stages of colonization by invaders with a developed iron industry, direct from Gaul, has been pushed back chronologically (Fowler E. 1960; Stevenson 1966). In any case, consideration of this metalwork is now regarded as a separate issue from that of hillfort origins.

MacKie, in the wake of the newly-available radiocarbon dates, proposed a 'new' Abernethy culture (1969c). He viewed this culture as 'a solid North British counterpart to the widespread and largely-indigenous Woodbury culture'. MacKie's Abernethy culture, contemporary with his southern Hownam culture, is characterized by a range of mundane artifacts, including jet rings and armlets, crude stone lamps, saddle querns and plain bucket- and barrel-shaped urns, in addition to the defended sites (compare MacKie 1970a, b with Ritchie A. 1970). Although we still await full publication of a number of sites of considerable importance to the closer definition of the Abernethy culture, and some of its 'diagnostic' artifacts are also found on sites further south in Scotland, the different concentrations of sites recorded – for instance the clustering of oblong timber-laced forts like Tap o' Noth, Aberdeenshire, in the north-east (Feachem 1966: 66ff.) (fig. 7.53), and the comparative lack of palisades north of the Forth, perhaps due in some measure to past fieldwork and excavational policy – suggest there is some validity in retaining 'Abernethy' and 'Hownam' as descriptors for differently-focused, though by no means mutually exclusive, constructional traditions (cf. Cunliffe 1974 for a simple unitary view).

Activity in the north-east in recent years has been directed almost exclusively on the vitrified forts.[8] Re-investigation of the vitrified fort at Finavon, Angus, specifically to obtain C14 material, provided some of the first indications of the much-elongated chronology now favoured. This small fort (0.4ha) had previously been excavated by Childe (1934–5; 1956), whose report indicated that the wall, which contained vitrified material, had stood to a height of 6m. The recently dated material comes from organic material in the tumble from the wall, and from an occupation layer overlying timbers sealed below this. Both excavations combine to indicate that occupation seems to have been concentrated in the zone behind the defences, and artifacts found included two iron objects, a plain jet ring, spindle whorls (one incised), and very coarse, ill-fired pottery (Childe 1934–5: fig. 16). A fragment of a rotary quern may be taken to suggest at least slight reoccupation of the site at a later date. Childe also emptied a rock-cut cistern or well within the enclosure, a feature also recorded elsewhere in the north-east. Subsequent excavations at Craig Phadrig, Inverness-shire, and Green Cairn, Kincardineshire, have both provided early dates for vitrified ramparts (and for an additional outer rampart of rather more varied construction at the former site). Unfortunately, preliminary reports for both sites (Small and Cottam 1972;

Fig. 7.52   Castle Law, Abernethy, Perths.: inner face of timber-laced wall
which encloses the site (photograph courtesy Society of Antiquaries of Scotland).

Fig. 7.53   Tap o'Noth, Rhynie, Aberdeens.: hillfort with heavily-vitrified
defences (photograph Kenneth Walton).

Wedderburn 1973) indicate that, owing to prior disturbance, the interiors
have produced little either by way of structures or small finds.

The most instructive early site in the Province is that at Cullykhan,
Banffshire (Greig 1970; 1971; 1972). The initial occupation of the site was
marked by at least one palisade, with associated entrance, marked by the
slot for a timber gate drawn across the westernmost part of the promontory.
Subsequently, a defensive wall, with vertical timbers in its outer face, and
a substantial entrance-way, marked by paired post-holes, was erected (fig.
7.54). Contemporary evidence from the promontory itself indicates
bronze-[9] and iron-working. This industrial area had previously had
domestic usage, and was subsequently sealed by a vitrified wall. Although
undated, this final defence is arguably later than the Preist-type outer wall,
whose destruction presumably postdates c. 106 bc, a date obtained from
a timber which perhaps constituted a repair to the earlier wall. No
occupation contemporary with the vitrified wall has been located.
Amongst the finds, pottery from the earlier occupations includes rather

Fig. 7.54   Gateway of first fort at Cullykhan, Banff: reconstruction drawing
(after Greig 1972).

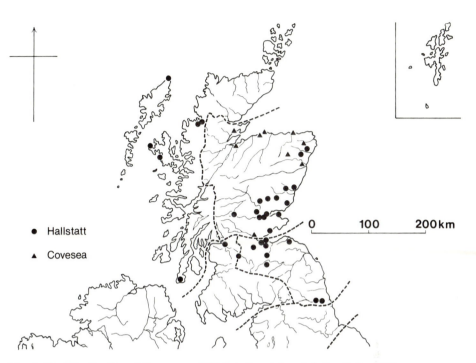

Fig. 7.55 Distribution of Covesea and Hallstatt metalwork (after Coles 1959–1960; MacKie 1970a).

finer wares alongside coarser pottery with large grits. A tanged chisel or leatherworker's knife from the industrial area is of interest. Of Roth's type II (1974), it has parallels on east coast settlements at Traprain Law and Staple Howe, and there, as in a hoard from Adabrock, Lewis (Coles 1959–1960: esp. 127; p. 337 above), its associations are with material which includes a Hallstatt C element. The type is however widely distributed in the British Isles and in France, where it occurs in the Carp's Tongue complex (cf. p. 314 above). The association of bronze and iron, noted at Cullykhan, is also found in the hoard of Balmashanner, near Forfar, Angus, where a cast bronze bowl, perhaps locally made, and armlets, belonging to Coles' Covesea phase, were discovered with a small iron ring. A further instance of external relations round the North Sea littoral is suggested by the pottery of the earliest phase of the use of another promontory on the south coast of the Moray Firth. The initial defence of the Green Castle, Portknockie, Banffshire, consists of a palisade. Associated pottery suggests parallels with Cunliffe's West Harling-Staple Howe group (*Discovery and Excavation in Scotland 1978*; Cunliffe 1978a: 36–7).

These finds raise the question of the nature of contacts between north-eastern Scotland and the Continent in the centuries prior to 500 BC, already briefly reviewed in the previous chapter (p. 322) (fig. 7.55). Coles' Covesea phase is marked by a series of bronze bracelets, best known from the eponymous cave site, and with Late Urnfield parallels on the Continent, necklets and cast bronze bowls. The distributional evidence shows a marked concentration on the north-east knuckle of Scotland. Now that the pottery which accompanied the important metalwork in the cave is envisaged as a local product,[10] there is perhaps less reason for advocating immigration on any noteworthy scale into north-east Scotland at this period. Unfortunately, none of the Covesea bronzes is associated with the defensive architecture which Piggott was the first to compare with Late Urnfield types on the Continent.[11] Coles and Taylor (1969–70) prefer to consider this metalwork as 'perhaps only a further instance of the existence of exchange patterns between prehistoric communities' and, apart from it, we have only the defensive walls to cite as a potential indicator of an 'intrusive military class' (Savory 1971b: 259) within the continuum of pre-Hallstatt traditions in eastern Scotland.

In the north-east, as in the Tyne-Forth Province, metalwork of both Hallstatt C and D types is also represented. Again a variety of mechanisms, from actual immigration, the activities of interant smiths, to social and economic means, has been proposed to account for this presence. Only one Hallstatt bronze sword of continental manufacture has been found in Scotland, the remainder falling within Cowen's class d, envisaged as a product of the highland zone of Britain (1967: esp. 445–6). The Scottish examples all lack useful contexts[12] and their distribution is exclusively eastern and/or riverine. Cowen preferred to envisage the arrival of these weapons by a range of socio-economic means, from princely exchanges to metalworking by itinerant Hallstatt smiths whose work was subsequently imitated locally, to the implantation of Hallstatt culture by invasion. This view has not been universally accepted: Burgess has argued that the distribution is suggestive of a 'classic raiding pattern' and pointed out that the class of swords, which differ from the standard type of British late bronze age sword in which Hallstatt influence is sometimes perceptible, may accordingly not be the product of local smiths (Burgess 1974: 211 ff.; cf. also p. 412 above). Continuing contact with the Continent during the sixth and fifth centuries BC is indicated by a group of swan's neck sunflower pins, which Coles considers to represent a fusion of Hallstatt and Irish-Scandinavian types.[13] Again a preponderantly eastern distribution argues for continuing direct contact with northern Europe, but need amount to no more than casual trade (Cunliffe 1974: 143–4).

The Solway-Clyde Province

In some ways, the settlement types of the Solway-Clyde Province have affinities with those of the eastern part of the Lowlands, but a pronounced difference lies in the overall number of sites present. Apart from a fairly dense distribution – mostly of very small sites – in Kirkcudbright and along the coast of Galloway, and a further concentration of sites in eastern Dumfriesshire, defended settlement is otherwise sparse (cf. Rivet 1966: map insert). Many of the settlements of Ayrshire and Renfrewshire are heavily defended in relation to their size, and can be classed as 'duns'; this type of site will be discussed in more detail in dealing with the Atlantic

Province. The extreme south-west of the country is characterized by a series of promontory forts, for which a wide chronological range has been proposed (Feachem 1966: 76).

The hillfort of Burnswark (Jobey 1971a; Hogg 1975: 148–50), Dumfriesshire, recently excavated, encompasses some 7ha. If the stockade, marked by twin rows of closely-set post-holes, which underlies the rampart follows the same circuit, it would be by far the largest such camp in north Britain. The radiocarbon dates for this, and for the subsequent defence, which consisted of a bank of earth and rubble with an outer stone revetment, might suggest that the more substantial defence was constructed only a short time after the palisaded phase.[14] Sampling of the interior has revealed the presence of superimposed round timber-built houses. Jobey has suggested that palisaded defences may directly underlie the more substantial fortifications of some of the later iron age forts in the Borders, such that early timber-built centres of considerable size may have escaped detection. Castle O'er, Dumfriesshire, is a possibility (Jobey 1971a: 81ff;. RCAHM 1920: no. 171).

Of other palisaded enclosures in the area, it may merely be noted that the association between much earlier artifacts and the palisaded enclosure of Beckton, near Lockerbie, in Annandale, is not absolutely secure (Cormack 1963). At Camp Hill, Trohoughton, Dumfriesshire, a sequence of twin palisades followed by a more heavily defended enclosure with twin stone-faced ramparts and accompanying V-shaped ditches was inferred, in the absence of stratigraphic evidence, by analogy with sites in the Tyne-Forth Province. Numerous post-holes and gullies were observed in the interior but interpretation is difficult (Simpson and Scott-Elliot 1963). MacNaughton's Fort, Kirkcudbright, with an internal area some 18 m in diameter, must represent a homestead unit, encompassed by a single palisade, which the excavators argued was contemporary with the surrounding stone-revetted rampart. One-third of the interior was excavated, and the pattern of post-holes recovered suggested either an oblong timber hut, some 10m long, with an external hearth, or that the entire area inside the palisade was roofed. Neither postulated structure has local parallels (Scott-Elliot, Simpson and Coles 1966; cf. Ritchie A. 1970). Although the radiocarbon date, centred on the early third century bc, is comparatively late, it is by no means unacceptable and can usefully be compared to that from Ingram Hill, Northumberland (Jobey 1971b).

At Craigmarloch Wood, Renfrewshire, a small univallate timber-laced fort, partially vitrified, represents the sole instance of this type of monument replacing a palisaded site in the Province and may be compared to Cullykhan (p. 456) and Fenton Hill, Northumberland, with a palisaded phase dated to 690 ± 100 bc (Clack and Gosling 1976: 24ff.; Jobey 1974a: 10). Preliminary reports indicate that the palisaded site at Craigmarloch was larger than its successor. In the partially-vitrified wall, as well as the horizontal wooden framework typical of the Scottish sites, traces of vertical timbers were also noted. Although the context of the radiocarbon date for this walled phase is not absolutely secure (*Discovery and Excavation in Scotland 1966*: 39; MacKie 1969c: 18f.; MacKie 1976), there is no overwhelming reason to reject the presence of timber-lacing at this late period in Scotland, perhaps particularly in view of its occurrence in at least five radiocarbon-dated Dark Age fortifications (Ralston, in press). In MacKie's view the earlier phase, with occupation debris (*Discovery and Excavation in Scotland 1963*: 42) including thick pottery with large grits and jet rings and armlets, belongs to his Abernethy culture, as does the vitrified fort with associated midden at Sheep Hill, Dunbartonshire, to the north of the Clyde.

Amongst other settlement varieties, artificial lake-edge settlements, constructed principally of wood, have long been recorded in the Solway-Clyde Province. They were believed on the evidence of associated finds to begin in the Roman iron age, or marginally earlier, though use of sites of this type here, as elsewhere in Scotland, was known to continue into the medieval period (cf. Munro 1882; RCAHM 1978: 27). A crannog in Milton Loch (fig. 7.56), the most recently excavated, consisted of a raft-like sub-structure, on which a circular wooden house, with internal wattlework partitions, was raised. This was surrounded by a boardwalk, constructed on a series of piles which bordered the main structure and seemingly led round to a small harbour delimited by two jetties of piled stones. Access to the land was by a wooden causeway. The excavator felt that the evidence indicated a unitary construction (Piggott C. M. 1953), so that the radiocarbon date now indicates that the site is very much older than the small bronze of the Roman period previously used to date it (Guido 1974). Other crannogs may be similarly early: Hyndford shows evidence of considerable replacement of floors prior to its abandonment in the second century AD and Stevenson (1966: 21) compared the pottery from the supposed crannog at Bishop's Loch, Old Monkland, which also produced an unlooped socketed iron axe (Manning and Saunders 1972: 201 and no. 19) with that from the iron age fort at Dunagoil, Bute, though such pottery is extremely long-lived. At the Lochlee crannog, Ayrshire, nineteenth-century excavations indicate more than one phase of use (Munro 1882: 38; Piggott C. M. 1953: 147), and here too the site may partially predate the Roman and late Celtic metalwork which suggests occupation in the first two centuries AD. MacKie (1969c) included crannogs in his revised definition of the Abernethy culture.

The Atlantic Province

Reference to any physical map will clearly indicate the difficulties involved in settlement and communication in this last North British Province to be discussed (Kirk 1957). Nowhere else in North Britain is the role of the sea liable to have been so critical: a 'sea-change into something rich and strange' with which the word 'broch' may be regarded as synonymous – has always been liable to throw links with the better-known areas to the south into high relief.

The map of iron age monuments in North Britain (Rivet 1966), which shows marked concentrations of monuments in several areas within the Province, disguises the fact that many of these sites, in terms of area, are exceedingly small, enclosing only a fraction of a hectare. This characteristic

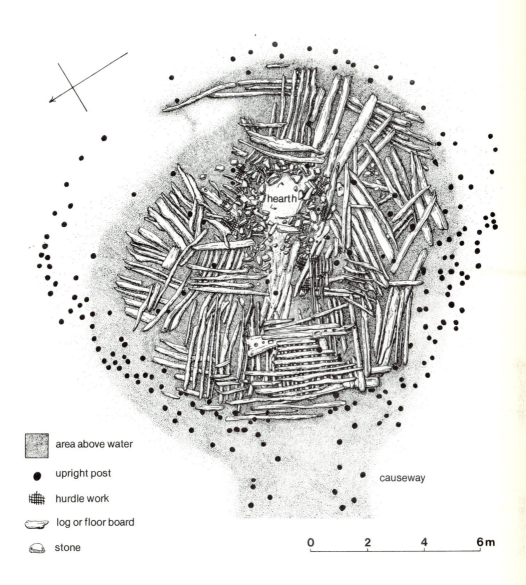

area above water

upright post

hurdle work

log or floor board

stone

hearth

causeway

0   2   4   6 m

Fig. 7.56   Milton Loch crannog 1 (after Piggott C. M. 1953).

smallness, taken in conjunction with the massiveness – both relative and absolute – of their stone-built defences, led Childe (1935: esp. 197–208, 237–49) to link duns,[15] small forts and brochs together in a 'castle complex'. However, he envisaged that subsequent research might lead to the attribution of these diverse monuments to distinct, though allied, waves of colonization. Both architectural similarities with Cornish cliff-castles, and the finds from the Atlantic sites, suggested the arrival of a 'conquering minority' from south-western England.

Most subsequent work has been concerned with the elaboration of the structural sequence of monuments within the Province, and with the assessment of the role played by incomers (cf. Hamilton 1956; 1966b; 1968a, b; MacKie 1965a, b; 1969a; 1971b; 1974; 1975a). The cultural significance and economic meaning of the large quantities of less immediately diagnostic material (fig. 7.57) – the whalebone artifacts from brochs, to which D. V. Clarke (1971: 33) has recently drawn attention, are a case in point – have been much less fully studied (but see MacGregor A.G. 1974). It should be emphasized that, despite the fact that brochs in particular have attracted the attention of Scottish antiquarians for well over a century, statigraphically-recorded excavations, adequately published, are few in number.

Recently, new dating evidence has added one class of site to the beginning of the occupation record. The burnt mounds of Orkney have been shown to date to the end of the 2nd millennium and to have continued in use, as a class, well into the succeeding millennium. They have been convincingly interpreted as cooking-places, especially adapted to the preparation of foods in a largely treeless environment, utilizing peat as a fuel (Hedges 1974; 1975; Huxtable et al. 1976) (fig. 7.58).

Permanent settlement in the northern islands is best discussed on the basis of the classic settlement sequence, established by Hamilton, at Jarlshof and Clickhimin, both on Shetland (cf. Hamilton 1968b; Fairhurst 1971b; MacKie 1969b). The sequence at Jarlshof began with late bronze age and iron age villages followed by a broch and subsequent re-utilization of the site through to Viking and later times. The settlement evidence here begins with a late bronze age village (briefly described on p. 292), whose structures hark back to earlier Shetland traditions, as Piggott noted (1966: 7; Hamilton 1956: 18 prefers a Mediterranean origin) (fig. 7.59). After a hiatus, during which Village I was partially sand-covered, a second village consisting of round-houses with which souterrains were associated, was established on the site. The duration of this hiatus is uncertain but this second village, initially interpreted as late bronze age, has since been re-assigned on the basis of the ceramic evidence to the initial phase of the iron age (Piggott S. 1966: 8; Stevenson 1966: 19). The structures were envisaged to mark a further modification of the autochthonous traditions, and Dwelling VI, architecturally the least complex, had an attached souterrain, as did the more elaborate Dwelling IV (compare Thomas A.C. 1972: 75ff.). In terms of material culture, the main distinctions between Villages I and II are to be seen in changing pottery types, in the replacement of bronze by iron technology, and in the consequent decline of the slate, quartz and bone industries (Hamilton 1956: 30ff.). The site was unfortified prior to the construction of the broch.

Contrastingly, Clickhimin exhibits pre-broch fortification. Here, too, the site begins with a farmstead sequence whose use spanned the transition from the bronze age to the iron age. No metal remains were in fact recovered from these phases. Thereafter, at a date sometime between the fifth and second century BC (MacKie 1969b; 1975b: 275–81), the first fortification, consisting of a massive stone ring-wall, took place on the promontory site; new internal features were limited to timber buildings

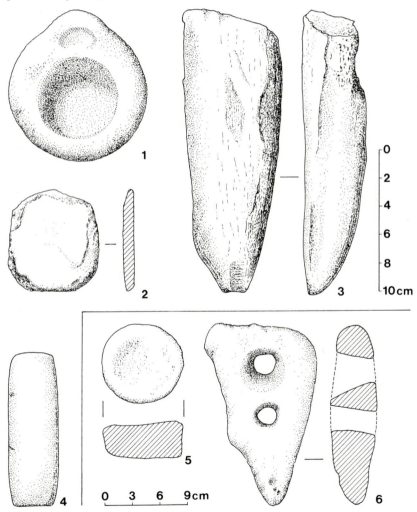

Fig. 7.57   Stone and cetacean bone objects from brochs: 1 stone lamp, Clickhimin; 2 stone disc, Clickhimin; 3 tip of stone bar share, Burrian; 4 hone, Clickhimin; 5 bone rubber, Burrian; 6 block of bone with two perforations, Burrian (after Hamilton 1968b; MacGregor A. G. 1974).

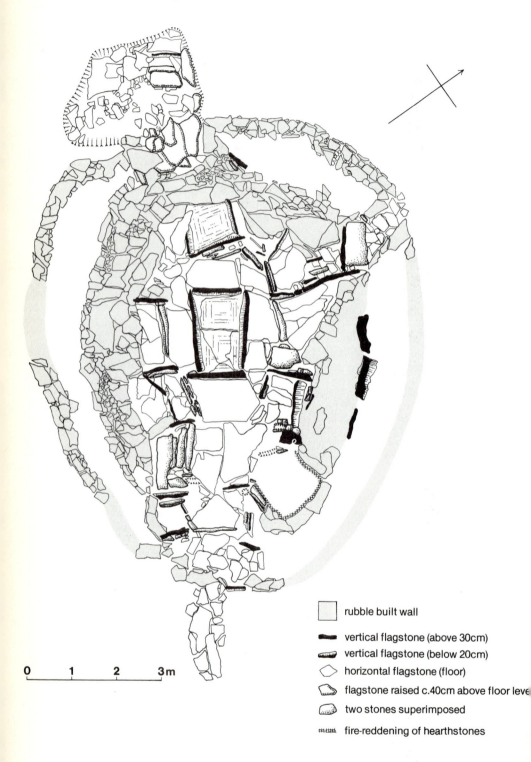

rubble built wall

vertical flagstone (above 30cm)

vertical flagstone (below 20cm)

horizontal flagstone (floor)

flagstone raised c.40cm above floor leve

two stones superimposed

fire-reddening of hearthstones

0   1   2   3m

Fig. 7.58   Liddle Farm 1, Orkney: house in burnt mound (after Hedges 1975).

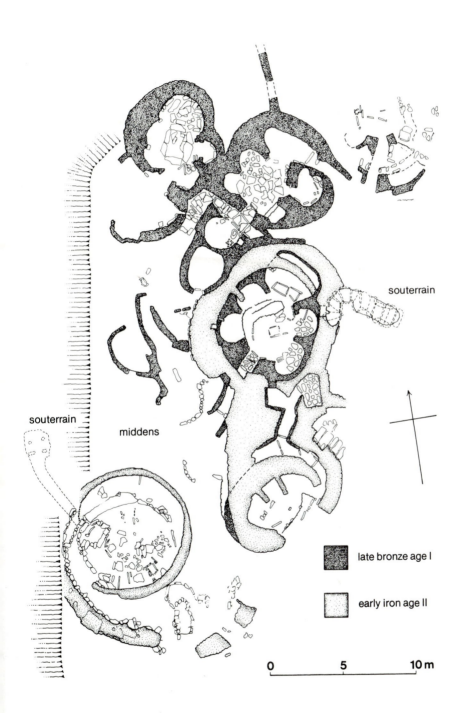

souterrain

souterrain   middens

late bronze age I

early iron age II

0   5   10 m

Fig. 7.59   Jarlshof, Shetland: early unfortified villages (after Hamilton 1956).

ranged against the inner face of the defensive wall. The elaborate elevation proposed by the excavator for these timber structures must be regarded as conjectural, since, in the absence of the necessary architectural refinements (notably a scarcement ledge), the hypothetical reconstruction depends very largely on literary accounts in the early Irish tales (Hamilton 1968a; 1968b: esp.63ff.). The elaborate blockhouse, with architectural sophistication partly matched in the Hebridean area and more generally amongst the brochs, is the major surviving element of the later pre-broch fortification. It stands behind the entrance to the earlier ring-work, and is envisaged by MacKie originally to have been linked to a galleried defensive wall, largely robbed for the construction of the broch in the succeeding century (MacKie 1975b: 277ff.). Again, the triple-storeyed timber range on stone footings envisaged to have been constructed against

Fig. 7.60   Dun Lagaidh, Loggie, Ross and Cromarty: the multi-period site sits on this isolated ridge beside Loch Broom (photograph E. W. MacKie).

the blockhouse must be regarded as conjectural, in the absence of much supporting evidence in the publication.[16] In the remainder of the Province, the earliest fortified sites have affinities with the timber-laced forts of the North-Eastern Province, and can either be ascribed to the adoption of the new mode by the native population, or viewed as the physical manifestation of the westward percolation of immigrants of ultimately German origin. Dun Lagaidh, in Wester Ross (fig. 7.60), produced radiocarbon dates suggesting a date for its construction not far removed from that of Finavon: finds from this small fort were limited to a fragment of bronze, and, less certainly, one or two iron objects (MacKie 1968). The fort at Dunagoil, on Bute, vitrified and characteristically elongated in form, may have similarly early beginnings, though at least intermittent occupation of the site continued into the first century AD (Marshall 1915; Mann 1915; 1925; Stevenson 1966). Amongst other forts exhibiting indications of vitrification, Duntroon, overlooking Loch Crinan, produced saddle querns, suggesting comparatively early occupation.

Small-scale timber-laced sites are in fact plentiful in Argyll and south Inverness-shire, and certainly exhibit a structural sequence which at least suggests replacement of the timber-laced forts by solid-walled duns; some 40 per cent of known vitrified sites lie in the southern region of the Atlantic Province and adjacent coastlines (Maxwell 1975). The clearest sequence – univallate, elongated stone-walled fort followed by oval timber-laced dun and finally a solid-walled dun – is illustrated by Dun Skeig, Kintyre (RCAHM 1971: 18 and no. 165; cf. RCAHM 1975: no. 136). The chronological span of duns shows every indication of being a lengthy one and, in the absence of isotopic dates, except for Langwell, Ross, we are forced to fall back on the exotic La Tène IC brooch from the timber-laced and heavily vitrified dun at Rahoy in Morvern to postulate a fourth-century beginning for the class (cf. Childe and Thorneycroft 1937–8a). Otherwise, in this part of Scotland, available dating evidence suggests use of this type of site from the first century AD through to the medieval period (RCAHM 1971: 18f.; RCAHM 1975: 18ff.; Maxwell 1975: 39f.) (fig. 7.61). Duns are located on a wide range of uneven kinds of terrain, from coastal stacks to inland ridges, and the constructional elaborations present in them, such as an outward batter to the wall-face and the presence of intra-mural galleries, are partly responses to the physical difficulties of the task being undertaken. Other architectural details are shared with the brochs: these include guard-cells, entrance passages with door-checks and bar-holes (for wooden fitments), and intramural staircases.

Amongst other types of site, at least potentially of comparatively early date, the series of crannogs, particularly in Loch Awe, deserves mention (RCAHM 1975: 20). In the southern part of the Atlantic Province brochs are scarcely represented, but further north they are found in similar numbers to duns: in the far north, and particularly in the Northern Isles, brochs greatly outnumber duns (cf. Maxwell 1975: 40).

The broch, as 'the only really advanced architectural creation ... invented entirely within Britain' in later prehistoric times (MacKie 1975a: 72) (fig. 7.62), has tended to be shrouded in a cloud of mystery, which can

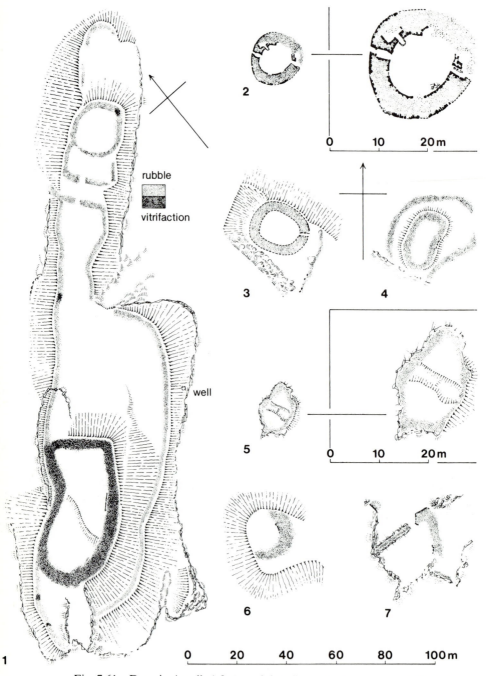

rubble

vitrifaction

well

Fig. 7.61   Duns in Argyll: 1 forts and dun, Dun MacSniachan; 2 Killdalloig; 3 The Bastard; 4 Eascairt; 5 Eilean Arach Mhoir; 6 Dun a Bhuic; 7 Fiart, Lismore (after RCAHM 1971; 1975).

be largely dispelled by envisaging it, along with the other monument types of Childe's 'castle complex', as 'an aberrant development from the hillfort tradition' in the difficult terrain of Atlantic Scotland.[17] The essential features of broch architecture are dry-stone construction, general circularity in plan, the great height – initially up to 14m – of the defences, and the massiveness of the wall-base relative to the size of the enclosed area. The height of the defences is achieved by constructing two walls, bonded together by horizontal courses of flat stone lintels, leaving a series of hollow galleries within the wall. These galleries, whose function seems to be essentially constructional (brochs are also provided with stone staircases), with the result of diminishing the load bearing down on the wall-footings, were the fundamental prerequisite of broch construction.

The origin of the type has been ascribed by MacKie to a small group of structures referred to as semi-brochs, which share with brochs the utilization of superimposed intra-mural galleries, but which are not circular, depending on natural features, such as precipices, for a sector of the defensive circuit (MacKie 1971b: 41 ff.; 1965a: fig. 1 for semi-brochs). Few in number, they are an essentially western phenomenon within the Province. The two excavated examples, Dun Ardtreck on Skye, and Dun an Ruidh Ruaidh ('Rhiroy') in Ross, have produced radiocarbon dates which are not inconsistent with the interpretation placed upon them as progenitors of the broch series (MacKie 1968).

The development of brochs during the last century BC and the following century has been charted by MacKie (1971b): the general picture presented is one of increasing sophistication from west to north, marked

Fig. 7.62   Dun Telve, Glenelg, Inverness.: view of broch from east; maximum surviving height 10·1m (photograph Nicholas Hawley).

by a structural improvement to the wall design by the elimination of the gallery at basal level seen for example at Dun Telve, Inverness-shire (figs. 7.62–3), as well as a series of refinements to details such as the design of the entrance, including the provision of double doors in some northern examples, particularly in Caithness. Part of this elaboration can be attributed to the greater need for artificial fortification in the north, where natural locations of a defensive character are less frequent than in the west. By this token, the celebrated broch of Mousa on Shetland, with a massive solid wall-base and relatively small internal court, may be envisaged as amongst the last of the series. Supplementary defences, consisting of ramparts and ditches, are recorded both in the north, as at Burrian and Gurness, Orkney, and, less frequently, in the west (RCAHM 1928: esp. xxxviii; Graham 1947).

The function of the brochs is, because of the lack of many modern excavations, difficult to discuss in general. The best evidence comes from the early ground-galleried broch of Dun Mor Vaul on Tiree where MacKie has argued for the initial use of the fortification as a sporadically-occupied refuge for a sizeable community: later, the defences were partially demolished and the court converted into a single dwelling (MacKie 1974; 1975a). Apart from the general accomplishment of the architecture, two pieces of evidence may be combined to suggest that the diffusion of the brochs, of which there are over 500 known examples in the Atlantic Province, may have been due to the movement of specialized craftsmen in the manner of those known to have existed in later Ireland (Graham 1951). Individually unconvincing, perhaps, is the evidence of preferential diet present in one context contemporary with the construction of Dun Mor Vaul (MacKie 1975a; 80f.), but much more impressive is the recent discovery of the utilization of a standard unit of measurement and the geometrical accuracy of the layout of some 30 brochs analysed (MacKie 1975a: 85ff.).

Here, discussion of the structural development of the brochs has been separated from the evidence of material culture, because the assessment of the artifactual record has provoked a certain amount of controversy. Some general points need to be made: first is Alcock's general acceptance of the idea of an Irish Sea Province (Alcock 1972a), of which Atlantic Scotland may be envisaged as a northerly prolongation. The indications are that contacts on this westerly route were both small-scale and sporadic: the contacts suggested by *chevaux-de-frise* may serve as an indication of this (Harbison 1971). Actual folk movement, at least by the first century AD, may be implied by similarities in tribal names (see fig. 7.49) between widely-dispersed parts of Britain, as recorded by the geographer Ptolemy: as an example, 'Cornavii' occurs in the Cheshire area, and also in the extreme north of the Scottish mainland (Richmond 1958b: 131–55; Alcock 1972a: esp. fig 21). Second, most of the material from the brochs has been little used in the definitions proposed and reliance has been placed on a quantitatively minute fraction of exotic material; resulting in a controversy essentially between those who favour continuity and/or diffusion and those who prefer migration (cf. Clarke D.V. 1970; 1971; MacKie 1971b; 1974).

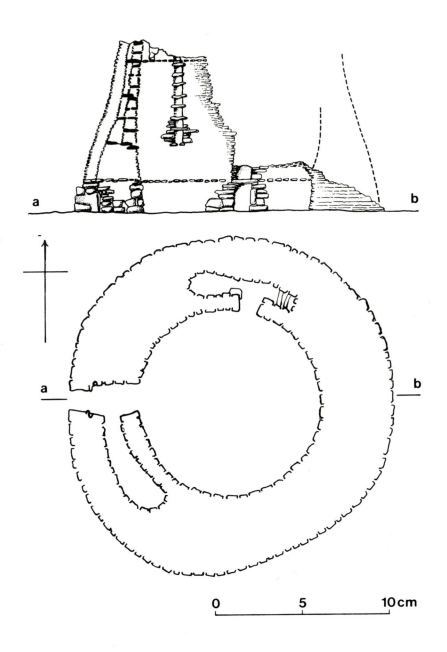

Fig. 7.63   Elevation and plan, Dun Telve, Inverness. (after MacKie 1975a).

Third, there is considerable ceramic evidence from the broch sites, and also from earlier sites in the west, for instance at Balevullin (MacKie 1963) and from the pre-broch occupation at Dun Mor Vaul, and also from the excavated sites on Shetland.

D. V. Clarke has stressed the importance of the fuller exploitation of the broch artifactual record, and has pointed the way to the utilization of ethnographic data to fill out the economic and cultural significance of some frequently-occurring finds (cf. Hamilton 1968b; 113ff. Clarke D. V. 1971; MacGregor A.G. 1974)). This however substantially remains a task for the future.

Amongst the pottery (fig. 7.64) MacKie distinguishes two broad groups, best exemplified on Tiree. The antecedents of 'native pottery' are held to be for the most part local, though incorporating some decorative elements for which an English earliest pre-Roman iron age or indeed continental Urnfield origin might be claimed. This Vaul ware is extremely long-lived, and continues in use alongside everted rim ware, which appears at this site prior to the construction of the broch. Its decorated sub-type, Clettraval ware, has generalized parallels with the pottery of the Wessex area though certain elements foreign to this, and seemingly of French origin, are

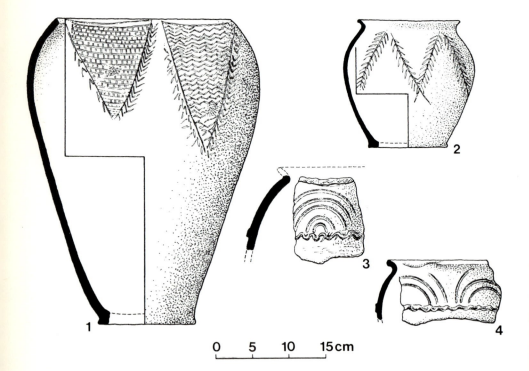

Fig. 7.64   Pottery from Dun Mor Vaul, Tiree. 1 urn of Vaul ware; 2 vase of Vaul ware; 3 sherd of Clettraval style of everted rim ware; 4 sherd of Clettraval style of everted rim ware, later degenerate example (after MacKie 1974).

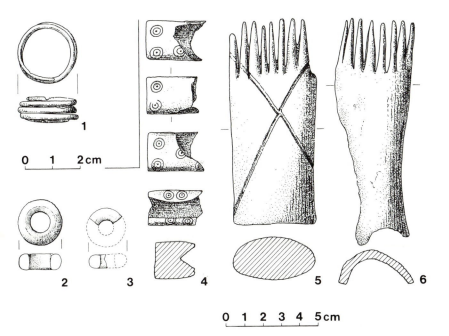

Fig. 7.65   Exotic material, primarily from the Atlantic Province, c. last century
BC. 1 bronze spiral ring, Hyndford crannog (after Clarke D. V. 1971); 2, 3
annular yellow glass beads, Dun Mor Vaul (after MacKie 1974); 4 bone dice,
Dun Mor Vaul (after Clarke D. V. 1970); 5, 6 long-handled weaving combs,
Burrian (after MacGregor A. G. 1974).

incorporated. The amalgamation of these diffuse elements (not including
Vaul ware) apparently occurred in the Hebrides prior to the broch-
building period – there is everted rim ware from pre-broch contexts at
Clickhimin – yet MacKie considers that the Vaul and everted rim wares
represent two distinct human populations which continued to live side by
side, on terms of varying amicability, for the duration of the occupation of
the Vaul site. Given that everted rim pottery already represents a local
hybridization, functional differences, for example, would seem to account
for the continuation of two pottery traditions equally well (MacKie 1974:
esp. App. B).

   More contentious has been the explication of the presence of a range of
artifacts, which MacKie attributes to the presence of incomers from the
Wessex area during the earlier iron age. These include spiral finger rings,
long-handled weaving combs, vertically-handled disc querns, triangular
crucibles, bone dice, and small yellow glass rings (fig. 7.65). We may note
with Clarke the fairly wide chronological range possible for a number of
those artifacts, and record that some at least could be derived from
Yorkshire. However, in our present state of knowledge, it is difficult
convincingly to repudiate MacKie's hypothesis of migrants arriving from
the Wessex-Somerset area within the first century BC, perhaps stimulated

by the arrival of Belgic settlers in their homeland c. 75 BC. Less convincing, however, is MacKie's assertion about the role of these migrants in the development of broch architecture, for which the evidence may best be described as tenuous. Although certain 'exotic' elements predate the early broch at Vaul, one must beware of the *post hoc ergo propter hoc* fallacy, which is difficult to eliminate in many archaeological contexts. The architectural development of the brochs stems from local prototypes, as MacKie has argued, and the only structural component that he views as a southern innovation is the presence of double guard-chambers (MacKie 1971b: 60ff.). Both Rainsborough's stone-lined guard-rooms, destroyed in the fifth century bc, and Welsh parallels have been cited, but the general tendency in recent years has been to push back the date of these examples, although further radiocarbon dates would help to clarify the picture (cf. Cunliffe 1978a: 262ff.). This chronological disparity, coupled with architectural differences between the corbelled series of guard chambers of Atlantic Scotland and those of the south, the pre-existing tradition of dry-stone corbelled cells in the north, and the presence of what might be termed a proto-guard-chamber at Dun Ardtreck, as well as the isolated mural cells of the semi-broch-influenced blockhouse at Clickhimin, combine to suggest that independent invention of the guard-chamber idea within Atlantic Scotland is an attractive alternative hypothesis.

As well as the fortified settlements noted above, a common occurrence in parts of the region is the hut-circle, marked by a low circular bank of stones. These occur, both isolated and in groups, frequently on sloping hill-sides. The limited excavation on this class of monuments that has as yet been undertaken suggests utilization at various stages in the iron age (Fairhurst 1971a; Fairhurst and Taylor 1971), though a much wider date range cannot be ruled out. Culturally diagnostic material, such as pottery, is rare and the indications are that such settlements housed communities in whose economy agriculture featured. In the Atlantic Province, they are concentrated in eastern Sutherland, being much less frequent in Caithness or in the west generally. Similar sites are also located further south, notably in the North-Eastern Province: discussion of their economies will be dealt with below.

Burials and religion

Recent statements on burial and its attendant rituals in the North British iron age have tended to stress the aspect of continuity from earlier, bronze age practices (MacKie 1971b: 56f.; Tait and Jobey 1971; Challis and Harding 1975: 174ff.). Much of the evidence was recovered during the nineteenth century, and is not susceptible to close dating; it would also seem to be premature to attempt any cultural divisions within this range of material. It might be inferred from the available evidence that a trend towards formal burial may be recognized in the late pre-Roman iron age, but, overall, evidence for burial is still largely elusive.

In so far as a normal rite can be recognized, this would seem to consist of inhumation in cists. These can range from short cists, structurally indistinguishable from those of the bronze age, to much larger examples

Fig. 7.66   Moredun, Edinburgh: cist burial as excavated in 1903 (photograph courtesy of Society of Antiquaries of Scotland).

containing multiple interments. Cairns are sometimes recorded. Available evidence suggests that formal cemeteries of long cists are not pre-Roman and they certainly continue into the Early Christian period (Henshall 1956). Although some examples are located near souterrains, as at West Grange of Conon, Angus, no direct chronological association can be demonstrated (Wainwright F.T. 1963: 177–80) but elsewhere, as MacKie (1971b) has suggested, some individual instances of long cist burial may be of pre-Roman iron age date.[18] The four graves of this character excavated by Piggott which mark the final use of the ritual and burial site at Cairnpapple, West Lothian, are presumptively pre-Christian, and have been used tentatively to suggest that this earlier monument may be the *medio nemeton* or middle sanctuary, located by a classical source in the Scottish Lowlands (Piggott S. 1948; Ross 1967).

Among the short cist burials, a few have metalwork associations which allow fairly close dating. At Moredun, Midlothian, a short cist (fig. 7.66)

containing two crouched inhumations included a possible 'dolphin'-type
descendant of a late La Tène fibula, along with an iron penannular brooch
of Fowler type Aa: MacGregor considers the fibula unlikely to predate AD
50 (1976: 118 f.). Other examples, for instance at Kingoldrum and Airlie
in Angus, contain Roman glass of third- to fourth-century date (Robertson
1970: esp. Table VII). An early example of the series would be marked by
the pottery found with inhumed bone at Sundaywells, Aberdeenshire
(Stevenson 1966: 19f.).

Multiple inhumations are also recorded. At Lochend, Dunbar (Longworth 1966), a long cist (fig. 7.67) served as a true burial vault, in which
were found skeletal remains of 20 adults and a child, mostly incomplete,[19]
and representing successive depositions in the grave. Both accompanying
brooches were of iron, one example being of Fowler's long-lived type A2:
the only other find was a small iron stud, with traces of red enamel. At
Beadnell 2, Northumberland (Tait and Jobey 1971), fragmentary remains
of 18 individuals came from a later extension to a standard bronze age
short cist beneath a disturbed round cairn. Dating evidence is provided by
a penannular brooch of Fowler's type A3 (I–IIIAD) from one of the latest
burials, thus providing a *terminus ante quem* for the earlier burials. As at
Lochend, the size of the cist seems to preclude the possibility of a single
mass burial. Although inhumation seems to be the general rite, occasional
instances of cremation are recorded, as at Glenluce, Wigtownshire, where
late second century AD samian pottery provides a date. At Alnham,
Northumberland, one of four cairns excavated in a cairnfield near the
palisaded settlements of High Knowes A and B, produced evidence of *in
situ* cremation within a kerbed area, surrounded by a ditch, and
subsequently covered by a cairn. The accompanying bronze pin, although

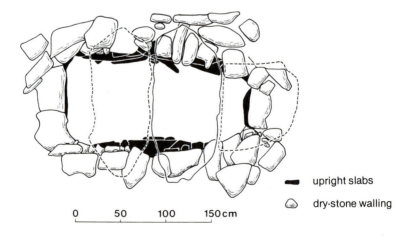

■ upright slabs

◌ dry-stone walling

0   50   100   150 cm

Fig. 7.67   Massive cist, Lochend, East Lothian (after Longworth 1966).

comparable to Irish examples, has been considered by Jobey possibly to be of Yorkshire origin and first century BC date. The other cairns examined contained bronze age material (Jobey and Tait 1966).

In view of the general lack of accompanying finds, it seems most likely that advances in sub-dividing the rather diffuse assemblage of burials in the iron age will require the use of carbon dating on suspected cases. The date from skeletal material below one element of a complex kerb cairn at Lundin Links, Fife, where long cists were also recorded, may be taken as an indication of the possibilities, as may the dates for the old land surface at Claggan 2, Argyll (Ritchie et al. 1975).

However, it is clear that many burials must have been carried out in such a fashion as to be archaeologically undetectable. Fragments of skeletons found on settlement sites indicate that physical disposal of the dead may have been perfunctory, even if the rituals involved were complex. Another possibility is disposal in rivers and other watery places: in support of this suggestion one may cite the frequent association of fine metalwork, including the bronze Hallstatt swords and much of the Celtic artwork, with water. Religious traditions involving warriors and wetness are also suggested by the recovery of pinewood figures and a boat from Holderness, recently discussed by Challis and Harding (1975: 175f.), who suggest that this find may date to the late iron age.

In terms of structures or objects for which a cult use can be upheld, comparatively little evidence can be adduced. From Ballachulish, Argyll, comes a wooden female figure (Piggott and Allen 1970: no. 82) (fig. 7.68), widely paralleled in the Celtic world, and dated to the first century BC or earlier. This was excavated within a wickerwork hut, which represents one of the few architectural survivals that can be related to Celtic religion in northern Britain. More problematical is the question of shafts, pits and wells: many of these latter two categories had purely utilitarian functions, though shafts have a widespread distribution in Europe and are on occasion clearly associated with ritual practices (cf. Ross 1968; Piggott S. 1968: 80 ff.). Amongst the Scottish evidence, the group of over 100 pits of varying dimensions excavated within the Roman fort and its south annexe (and also outside it) at Newstead, Roxburghshire, provides the largest group of examples, although the interpretation of these is not straightforward (Ross and Feachem 1976). Ross attributes the North British pits to the presence of Belgic elements either serving in the Roman army or coming as settlers shortly before the Roman encroachment (Ross 1968: 279), and whilst Manning (1972) is prepared to envisage that some of the pits may be votive, he considers that many are filled with surplus and damaged equipment buried prior to the abandonment of the fort, and subsequent retreat through hostile territory. The finds include a wide range of military equipment, both undamaged and fragmentary, as well as human and animal remains, both complete and partial. The pits fall into two main groups, respectively Flavian (first century) and Antonine (second century) in date. However, the possibility that some of the pits may predate the appearance of the Roman army cannot be wholly discounted, and it is possible that the site may have begun as a cult centre related to the

Fig. 7.68   Wooden figurine from
Ballachulish, Argyll (after Ross 1967).

0   15   30 cm

neighbouring major fort of the Selgovae on Eildon Hill North (Ross 1968: 276; Ross and Feachem 1976: 234).[20]

Dalladies Site 2, Kincardineshire, consists of an enigmatic complex of post-holes, pits and ditches stretching for some 400m by 30m on a gravel terrace. Normal domestic debris is absent on the site, although two structures might be considered as conventional wooden huts. A recurrent feature is that the ditches show signs of having been rapidly filled with dark soil, which contained an admixture of charcoal and calcined bone. Cattle and horse skulls were also recovered. Datable finds are limited to a few fragments of Roman material, and the site has been described as religious and related to the funereal, since both cremation and the disposal of cremated remains took place there (Watkins 1974).

The sole sculptured stone from Scotland which seems, on stylistic grounds, to antedate the Roman occupation is a granite tricephalos, apparently from Sutherland, for which a date ranging between the third century BC and the first century AD has recently been proposed (Piggott and Allen 1970: no. 72; Megaw 1970: no. 286; Ross 1967). The head has typical Celtic features, such as a drooping moustache, and a hollow in the top suggests a small portable shrine. Although the cult of the head was widespread in the Celtic world, and the triple element is strong in later Welsh and Irish tradition, such tricephaloi are in fact rare in Britain. Both Ross and Megaw suggest that the head may have arrived in Britain during the incursions from Gaul in the last century BC. It may not have reached northern Scotland until much later.

Iron age art in North Britain

Much of the decorated metalwork found in North Britain, recently re-examined by M. MacGregor (1976), does not predate the first appearance of the Roman military in northern England, and the occupation of Scotland from AD 78. The sheer quantity of metalwork produced thereafter would, as MacGregor has remarked, indicate that 'some disturbing and momentous event had taken place' even if we were totally unaware of the Roman presence. As elsewhere in the British Isles, many of the finds are strays, though deposition in watery surroundings is a not infrequent occurrence. Comparatively few objects are associated with settlement sites. Elements of this fine metalwork were utilized by Piggott (1966: esp. 10), in the absence of other evidence, tentatively to indicate some groupings, for instance Solway-Clyde First B, within the family of Scottish iron age cultures. He was clearly aware of the shortcomings of this approach.

The earliest find is the Torrs pony cap and horns, previously described as a chamfrein, from the base of a bog in Kirkcudbright (Atkinson and Piggott 1955) (fig. 7.38a–b). Although the decoration shows affinities with continental Waldalgesheim and Plastic styles, Piggott has subsequently remarked on the archaistic character of the Torrs-Witham group of insular material, a view supported by other writers (cf. Frey with Megaw 1976) and as a result it is quite feasible to consider a second century BC date for Torrs. The main decoration of the cap is repoussé, contrasting with the incised decoration of the horns. MacGregor's conclusion, however, is that the same craftsmen may have been responsible for the sword-style decoration on the horns and for similar work on antique patching of the cap (cf. MacGregor M. 1976: 146f.). Differences in technique suggested to Megaw (1970: no. 244–5) that the horns and cap need not have been made at the same place or time. Piggott's original thesis advocating manufacture in the Solway-Clyde Province should be replaced by one which sees the cap as an heirloom, reaching Scotland some time after its manufacture in the Midlands, or east central England (Stevenson 1966: 24). Divorced from the cap (cf. Stevenson 1966: 39), the function of the horns is uncertain, if roundly aristocratic. In view of the one-sided character of their decoration, mountings for a helmet may perhaps be preferred to drinking-horn mounts.

Other Lowland Scottish finds from the last century BC include the small hoard of gold alloy from Shaw Hill, Peeblesshire, which comprised three penannular twisted torcs and about 40 bullet-shaped electrum coins from the Paris region – one of the few native coin finds from north Britain (Stevenson 1966: 23f.) – as well as a gold torc terminal with close parallels to East Anglian finds such as Snettisham (fig. 7.43b–c) (cf. Feachem 1958; Megaw 1970: nos. 290, 292), a scabbard, from the English stretch of the Tweed at Carham, and two sword chapes. These last belong to Piggott's Bugthorpe type (Group III), a small group distributed between the Trent and the Forth, and are closely related to Group II, which have analogies in continental Middle La Tène products (Piggott S. 1950: esp. 12–16; Challis and Harding 1975: 71). The Bargany House, Ayrshire, scabbard may be an import from Ulster in the last century BC, though local manufacture is also feasible (MacGregor M. 1976: 79).

In the first century AD the situation is complicated by the Roman advance. Refugees, including displaced metalworkers, from areas to the south are to be expected. In addition, we know from Tacitus' account (*de Vita Iulii Agricolae*: 29) that Agricola had auxiliary troops from Britain with him before the battle of Mons Graupius. Influences from both Belgic and non-Belgic areas have been discerned.

MacGregor has tentatively identified four schools supplying northern demand, differentiated by product-range and artistic repertoire. The two main canons of southern influence are reflected, though an admixture of these is present in many northern finds.

Amongst the material which has been attributed to a southern Brigantian School is the Meyrick Collection bronze helmet, with repoussé ornament suggesting north English manufacture, but with a wide neckguard exhibiting Roman influence (Megaw 1970: no. 300; MacGregor M. 1976: 89f.).[21] Other related finds include the Balmaclellan mirror (MacGregor M. 1976: 142f.) and the Stichill collar (fig. 7.45b) (Megaw 1970: no. 298), both from the Scottish Lowlands.[22]

Some types of object are either products of this school, or of a second, which makes greater use of polychromy, an element of decorative metalwork associated with the borderlands of the Iceni and the Belgic tribes in south-east Britain. Such shared products would include swords of Piggott's Brigantian type (Group IV), whose Scottish distribution extends northwards to Perthshire (MacGregor M. 1976: 92), and a group of beaded torcs (MacGregor M. 1976: 15). The Mortonhall bronze sheath typifies the later development of the Celtic scabbard in North Britain: its narrowness suggests that it could not have contained a fighting weapon (fig. 7.45c) (Piggott S. 1950: fig. 9; Ritchie and Ritchie 1972: fig. 34). Note that the suspension loop occupies a central position on the decorative front plate, in contrast to Group III products, where it is located on the back, and from which group the Brigantian swords are derived. The type starts in approximately AD 50, and survives into the second century.

The hoard of horse-trappings from Middlebie, Dumfriesshire (fig. 7.69) has been colourfully viewed as largely local work produced for an Icenian who had fled northwards in the wake of the failure of the Boudiccan uprising. Certain elements, such as an elaborate cruciform strap junction

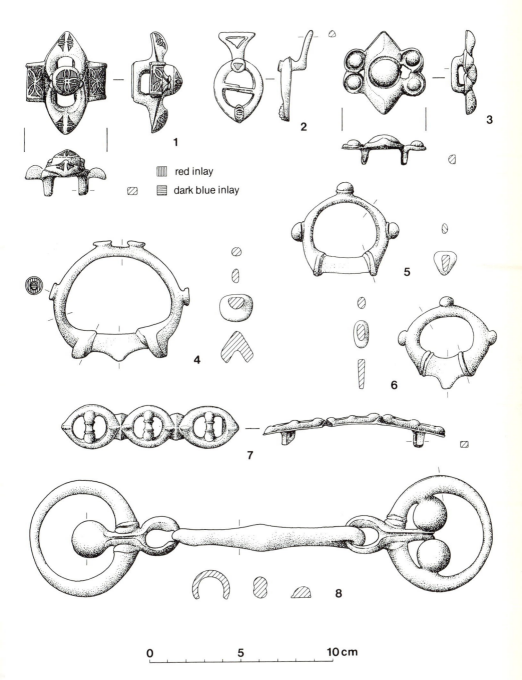

red inlay

dark blue inlay

Fig. 7.69   Horse trappings from Middlebie, Dumfries.: 1 cruciform strap junction; 2 button-and-loop fastener; 3 cruciform strap junction; 4 platform terret; 5 and 6 knobbed terrets; 7 elongated strap junction; 8 bridle bit of derivative three-link type (after MacGregor M. 1976).

and the largest terret, may be viewed as East Anglian imports. Other elements seem to be Lowland Scots products, adopted from the South, and characterized by a decoration both more restricted and stereotyped in range. Examples of this Lowland Scots school would include platform-decorated and knobbed terrets of first/second century AD date (MacGregor M. 1976: 68–9).

In contrast to the groups discussed above, only one school is focused to the north of the Forth–Clyde line. The distribution of massive terrets reveals a concentration in the north-east of Scotland (MacGregor M. 1976; Kilbride-Jones 1935), with examples found to the south of that area usually being ascribed to post-Agricolan irruptions of the northern barbarians, most notably towards the end of the second century. This distribution (fig. 7.70) is totally at variance with those of other types of horse-trapping mapped by MacGregor, and is one shared by two types of armlet – massive armlets and spiral snake types – though neither of these is found in any numbers in Scotland south of the Forth–Clyde line (MacGregor M. 1976; Stevenson 1966:fig. 5). The find of a bronze boar's head at Deskford, Banffshire, was convincingly demonstrated to be the terminal for a war trumpet or carnyx by Piggott (1959) (figs 7.46a, 7.71). Originally fitted with a movable wooden tongue and eyes in the now empty sockets, stylistic parallels with Brigantian work of mid-first-century date such as the Melsonby hoard suggest that the piece may have been the work of a refugee craftsman, possibly c.AD 70, from northern England (cf. Megaw 1970: no. 272).

The cast bronze snake armlet from the Culbin Sands (Megaw 1970: no. 302) is one of a small group of 'Caledonian' pieces which continue a long-lived tradition of animal-headed jewellery in the Celtic world. The immediate ancestor of these examples would seem to be the Belgic snake-armlet from Snailwell, though many of the decorative elements can be paralleled more immediately in the Trent-Forth area (MacGregor M. 1976: 103–6). The range in size and variation in quality – a feature also noted in the massive armlets (fig. 7.46c; cf. Simpson M. 1968) – of the snake armlets suggest 'immigrant bronze-smiths and local imitators' (Stevenson 1966: 32), with production extending from the later first century into the third century AD.

This distinctively north-east group is matched in other products. Stevenson (1956; 1966: fig. 3; 1976) noted that the area stood apart from Scotland south of the Forth with regard to glass bangles of first/second century AD types. A similar distribution, though with greater penetration of the Atlantic Province, may be noted for handled stone cups (Steer 1956: esp. 243ff. and fig. 7).

Although the place of manufacture of many of the objects discussed here is open to a measure of doubt, the assemblage of horse gear, weaponry and jewellery along with other types, such as beaten bronze vessels (fig. 7.72), must be taken as testimony to the penetration of people archaeologically classifiable as Celtic, though in what numbers it is hard to say. Some of the objects are manifestly high-status goods. This, and the likely existence of specialist groups of craftsmen, are further indicators of

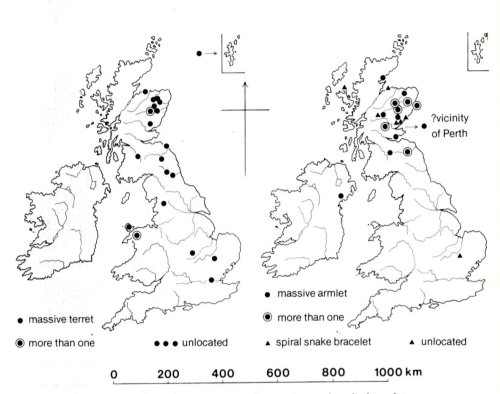

massive terret
● more than one   ●●● unlocated

massive armlet
◉ more than one   ▲ spiral snake bracelet   ▲ unlocated

0   200   400   600   800   1000 km

Fig. 7.70   Distribution of massive terrets, massive armlets and snake bracelets (after MacGregor M. 1976).

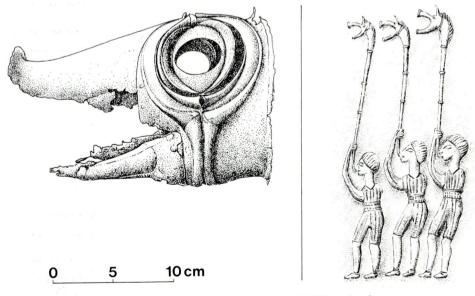

0   5   10 cm

Fig. 7.71   Deskford carnyx, Banff (after MacGregor M. 1976) (see also fig. 7.46a); (inset: carnyx on silver cauldron from Gundestrup, Denmark).

the presence of developed hierarchical societies in North Britain in the later pre-Roman period.

Economy and society

Two decades ago in a classic essay, Piggott (1958) drew attention to one aspect of the pre-Roman iron age cultures of Britain that had received inadequate treatment: that of the production of foodstuffs. On the available evidence, Piggott was able to suggest that Childe's (1946) view of 'indirectly intensified agriculture and an increased reliance on cereal food', generalized from southern English investigations, was inapplicable to North Britain. Regional differences existed and were marked by the presence or absence of more or less regularly-patterned spreads of small rectangular fields and of pits for corn storage, of the types first discussed by Bersu at Little Woodbury. Literary evidence,[23] as well as the distribution of certain objects, in particular rotary querns, helped to fill out the picture. With further support from Wheeler's (1954) investigation of Stanwick, Yorkshire, where a prime function seems to have been as a cattle (and possibly horse) corral, Piggott in 1958 proposed an antithesis between the single-farmstead-and-cereal-cultivation (though also stock-raising) Woodbury type of economy, typical of the south, and a Stanwick type 'based on pastoralism and with a probable element of limited nomadism' to the west and north of the Jurassic ridge.

The Stanwick type of economy seemed generally applicable to Scotland, even within the Roman period. Stone-built farmsteads, like Tamshiel Rig,

Fig. 7.72   Elvanfoot, Lanarks.: bronze cauldron; first century BC–second century AD; maximum diameter 458mm (photograph Hunterian Museum, University of Glasgow).

Roxburghshire (RCAHM 1956: 426–7), associated with a sizeable (13 ha) field system, were uncommon and most of the evidence suggested 'Celtic cow-boys and shepherds, footloose and unpredictable, moving with their animals over rough pasture and moorland' (Piggott S. 1958). Such an economic picture suggests a fragmented social pattern, so that small-scale population movements from southern Britain could radically affect local groups. In a recent discussion of the evidence from the Trent-Tyne area, Challis and Harding have remarked on the over-generalization presented in Piggott's analysis and have collected evidence which suggests that in certain climatically- and topographically-favoured areas there was a move towards mixed and generally more intensive agriculture during the course of the iron age (Challis and Harding 1975: Ch. 10). Evidence collected in Scotland since the mid-1950s suggests that a similar model of pastoralism and mixed agriculture dictated by geographical considerations may better describe the situation, though the chronological picture, in the absence of sufficient isotopic dates, is often obscure (cf. Dennell 1976; p. 350f. above).

Many upland areas are studded with the remains of field systems and cairnfields. In the classic study of the latter, Graham (1957) noted the association of some groups of small cairns with other features, notably rickles of stones, which may be indications of small plots, and stone-built hut circles: clearance of land in agricultural use was suggested as their *raison d'être*, though some may contain burials (Jobey and Tait 1966). Dating evidence for groups of small cairns is presently slight and an extended chronology, beginning as early as the neolithic, may be envisaged (RCAHM 1978: 8–10). The number of cairns in a group can vary from a handful to several hundreds: the irregularity of their spacing on a site suggests cultivation using hand-tools rather than by the plough, though two ard beams of iron age date are known from south-west Scotland. Feachem (1973) has recently considered the evidence of field systems and has proposed a sequential development, based largely on the criteria of typology and association with other types of site. His conclusions are essentially speculative, and it is difficult to accept the idea of a break in arable farming in north Scotland during the second half of the 1st millennium BC on the slender evidence available. Field plots occur with a range of settlement types in use during the last millennium BC of which amongst the earliest on current thinking are the unenclosed platform settlements, including examples in north Scotland, as at Loch Laide, Inverness-shire. Other examples indicate sequential use of the same area as at Stanshiel Rig, Dumfriesshire, where part of the system of 26.3 ha is marked by a set of longer, less irregular banks, details of which suggested Roman influence to Feachem (fig. 7.73)

The most illuminating example of a hut circle settlement associated with a plot system is at Kilphedir in eastern Sutherland (Fairhurst and Taylor 1971), where excavations have been carried out recently on a very common, if unevenly distributed and infrequently studied, class of monument (fig. 7.74). Fairhurst suggests, on the archaeological evidence and the available radiocarbon dates, that two phases of occupation are represented on the site. The second phase, dating to the end of the millennium, is marked by the architectural elaboration of one of the huts of the earlier settlement, which dates to around the middle of the last millennium bc, and predates the onset of sub-Atlantic conditions locally. Pollen and phosphate evidence suggest that a cultivation phase associated with the settlement appears to be very short-lived, though more intensive than that at a comparable site, Dalnaglar in Perthshire (Stewart 1962). If all the examples of the house-type in the Kilphedir area had been occupied contemporaneously, Fairhurst estimates that the settlement density would have been higher than at the time of the Sutherland Clearances, when pressure on local resources was substantial. He concludes by suggesting that this earlier settlement plan 'could have been produced by a small semi-nomadic population occupying the upland for no great length of time' (Fairhurst 1971a: 7). There was no direct evidence of stock-raising. The small area of arable (c. 2ha) would have been inadequate to support the population of several huts; Fairhurst suggests hunting retained some

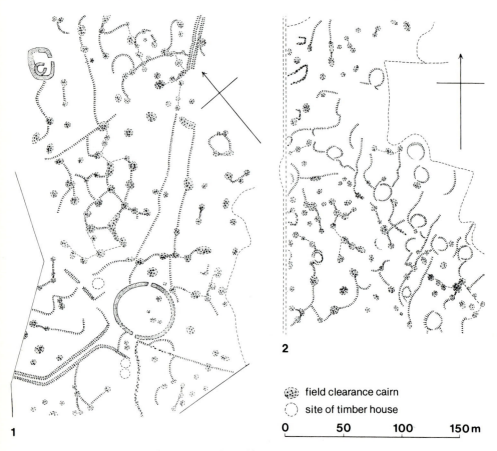

field clearance cairn
site of timber house

0   50   100   150 m

Fig. 7.73   Field systems: 1 Stanshiel Rig, Dumfries.; 2 Loch Laide, Inverness. (after Feachem 1973).

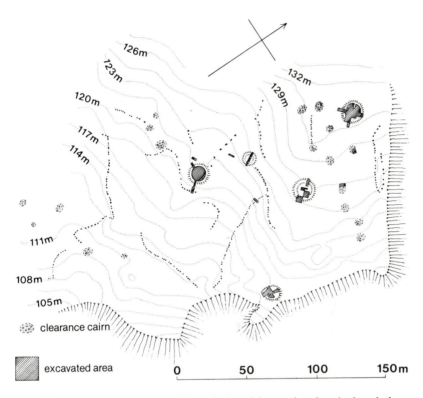

Fig. 7.74   Kilphedir, Sutherland: hut circles with associated agricultural plots (after Fairhurst and Taylor 1971).

considerable importance. The reoccupation of one hut-circle may correlate with a change in cultivation methods: socially it may represent the replacement of a small loosely-associated population by a single family.

Small (1975) has produced a generalized model for the settlement system of the small-scale societies envisaged in the iron age of the northern part of the country. The high altitude of many of the Scottish forts suggests to him that permanent occupation is unlikely: some support can be drawn from his failure to find evidence of domestic structures within Craig Phadrig, though the site had suffered from the attention of earlier antiquarians. He envisages the hut circles, normally located at the break of slope, on a valley side or at the junction of upland and coastal plain, to be in the prime location, in economic terms, for the exploration of a range of environmental niches (Small 1975: esp. fig. 2). As such they would have formed the basic unit of settlement in iron age northern Scotland: alluring as Small's hypothesis is, confirmation will depend on the development of suitable excavation strategies, as he is clearly aware. Because of the lack of evidence dating to the later part of the preceding millennium it is also difficult to estimate to what extent the agricultural pattern of the iron age may represent a continuity from earlier practices: it would be unwise to generalize from the apparent continuity of use of burnt mounds and their association with the better agricultural land in Orkney to the Scottish scene generally (Hedges 1975).

The small size of the ancillary building at the homestead of West Plean, Stirlingshire, tentatively interpreted as a byre, prompted Steer to remark that 'the lack of stabling for more than one or two beasts suggests that the main occupation was corn growing rather than cattle raising, but in the absence of any traces of a contemporary field system the methods and the extent of cultivation are alike obscure' (Steer 1956: 249). Although more field systems are known in Scotland south of the Highland Line since this statement was made, the relative importance of cereals in the agricultural economy remains uncertain. Of considerable interest too has been the discovery from the air of sizable enclosures associated with forts in Tweeddale and the Lothians, as at Kaeheughs fort in the Garleton Hills. Although material culture from the sites is generally sparse, both saddle and rotary querns are known, the latter now being thought to have arrived in Scotland prior to Roman military settlement (MacKie 1972).

Unfortunately, the material culture from the forts is often uninformative with regard to the role of these sites in the agricultural economy. Much of the ironwork from Traprain Law suggests agricultural use, but its dating is insecure and, like the fragments of rotary quern, from the lowest level of the excavation, may not predate the Roman Conquest by long. Much remains to be done before it will be possible to talk, other than speculatively, of the role of the larger fortified settlements with regard to settlement units in their environs (Maxwell 1970; Jobey 1976).

Although some of the larger forts have been classified as oppida, there is little evidence that any possessed the urban features represented on some of the immense late La Tène sites on the Continent (cf. Collis 1975). The only possibilities would seem to be Traprain Law and the site attributed to the Selgovae on Eildon Hill North, Roxburghshire (fig. 7.75). Despite the fact that a considerable part of the outermost and final enclosure at the latter site has been afforested, 296 house platforms have been identified: assuming that up to 200 further houses have been destroyed, and that all these structures were inhabited contemporaneously, Feachem (1966: 77–9) has postulated a population of 2–3,000 within the 16ha enceinte. Only a minute fraction of the site has been excavated. Such sites do not seem on our present knowledge qualitatively very different from major hillforts in southern Britain, such as Maiden Castle, Dorset. Accordingly, we would prefer to abandon the use of the term 'oppidum', with its overtones of socio-economic complexity, in the Scottish context, as Avery has suggested (1976: 41).

Coinage was not in use in the pre-Roman iron age. Certain objects may have been traded some distance, but the preponderant impression is of production to satisfy essentially local needs: the range of crafts undertaken can perhaps best be illustrated from the broch sites, such as Burrian, Vaul and Clickhimin. The only site which seems to have an area devoted to a single industry – metalworking – is Cullykhan (p. 456f.) in its earlier

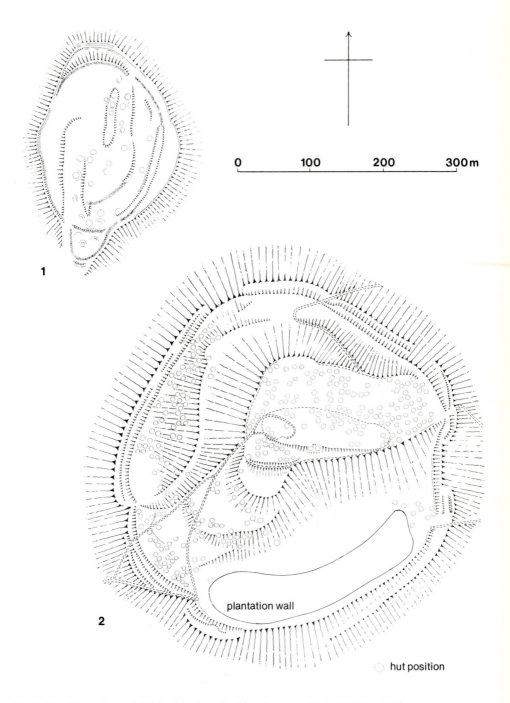

0   100   200   300m

plantation wall

hut position

Fig. 7.75   Major forts: 1 White Meldon, Peebles. (approx. 3ha); 2 Eildon Hill
North, Roxburghs. (approx. 16ha) (after RCAHM 1967; 1956).

period, and even this is comparatively small-scale: but this may be nothing more than a reflection of the limited scale of excavation of fort interiors.

The smallness of settlement units, particularly the forts, suggests that pre-Roman iron age society in Scotland was more fragmented than in southern England and on the Continent. During the last millennium BC, Celtic speakers had certainly augmented the local population, and many, though not all, of the tribal names are Celtic.[24] Some of these names are very similar to tribal names further south in Britain, and a direct link may be suggested for instance between the Damnonii of Upper Clydesdale and Ayrshire and the Dumnonii of south-western England. But to what extent the Celtic-speakers dominated the aboriginal population is open to a measure of doubt. Of interest here is the emergence from the third century AD of the Picts as a power-group in the north-east of the country: as K.H. Jackson has noted, the dominance of a Celtic-speaking ruling element amongst the Picts of the Dark Ages was not sufficient to eliminate the presence of a non-Celtic language unintelligible to us, nor to change the essentially non-Celtic pattern of accession to the throne (Jackson K.H. 1964a). It is in the southern half of the country that the presence of aristocratic weaponry and art-work more strongly betokens the presence of a Celtic-speaking warrior-nobility, whose appearance in North Britain must have been associated with the arrival of an unquantifiable number of their followers. The role of some of these incomers in the Atlantic West has been discussed above: in the south of the country, their appearance may have had some impact on the settlement record. For example, the beginnings of multivallate defences in the late stages of the pre-Roman iron age may correlate with the arrival of settlers, displaced northwards by the Claudian Invasion or by the earlier folk-movements of the Belgae (Piggott S. 1966: 10; RCAHM 1967: 32), though this defensive change might be controlled by purely military factors, such as the advent of sling-warfare.

The institutions of Celtic society in Scotland prior to the Agricolan campaigns of the later part of the first century are little illuminated by the classical authors. However, there is no reason to suspect that the pattern of a stratified and heroic society, like that portrayed in the early Irish tales, would be very far from the mark (Jackson K.H. 1964b). The emergence of Calgacus and his ability to organize a comparatively cohesive military force need indicate little more than the ability of a number of small-scale societies to band together, in the short term, in the face of military oppression. Calgacus, a nobleman, was a war-leader, the northern equivalent of Vercingetorix in Gaul, and sundry others around whom opposition to the Roman military machine must have formed in High Barbarian societies. There are no indications of any long-term political cohesion within Scotland: the institution of kingship, known amongst the Brigantes, is not recorded by the classical authors amongst the northern tribes, but, by analogy with other Celtic territories – as exemplified by Agricola's receiving an Irish king while on his Scottish campaigns (Tacitus de Vita Iulii Agricolae: 24) – both kingship, and the attendant system of clientship, almost certainly existed.

In conclusion, we may safely say that the life-style of the northern tribes c. AD 200 as portrayed by Cassius Dio seems wildly exaggerated: he records them as 'possessing neither walled places nor towns nor cultivated lands, but living by pastoral pursuits and by hunting and on certain kinds of berries . . . they live in tents, naked and shoeless' (cf. Steer 1958: 92–4). Pastoralism and hunting may well have retained a dominant role in the economy, but the settlement record and the accompanying societies were more complex than his record implies, even if they were but a pale equivalent of the continental late La Tène culture of the last century BC.

The later pre-Roman iron age in North Britain

The Claudian invasion across the English Channel in 43 AD seems to have had very little direct impact in North Britain until more than a generation had passed. It may have triggered off afresh the displacement of some aristocrats and their followers northwards, perhaps more particularly after the extension of Roman military activity into north England around 70 AD. But, with the exception of the metalwork discussed by Stevenson (1966: esp. fig. 2), Piggott (1966) and MacGregor (1976), it is difficult to assess the scale and impact of new arrivals in the Scottish archaeological record at this time: indeed other mechanisms might have been devised to account for the presence of much of this material in Scotland, were not the historical and archaeological records of Roman aggression comparatively fulsome.

There would now seem to be no reason to envisage any Roman advance into Scotland before the Agricolan campaigns of the 80s AD (Hartley 1972). It was this date that Piggott, in his adaptation of the Hawkesian scheme to Scotland, chose as the termination for Period 3 of the Scottish iron age. However, the character of the Roman occupation of north Britain, essentially military and intermittent (cf. Breeze and Dobson 1976), meant that the impact on many aspects of the native societies was much less clearly marked than in southern Britain, if indeed any indication can be perceived at all. Many traits of iron age culture continued through, and survived later than, the Roman Occupation of Scotland. To allow for this late survival, Piggott added a Period 4 to the iron age scheme. The terminal date for this period is uncertain, but to it should belong, for example, such Belgic influences as are detectable in Lowland Scotland (compare Piggott S. 1966; Stevenson 1966; Ross 1968; Manning 1972). These later manifestations of the Scottish iron age lie outwith our period of study, but it should be noted that the period 3/4 boundary is very difficult to detect, particularly in northern Scotland, where Roman military successes were never consolidated.

One anomalous event dating to the Claudian period is the apparent submission of the Orkney Islands to the Roman Empire, at that time confined to Lowland England. If this event did in fact occur, it would suggest that some of these northern inhabitants were aware of the diplomatic etiquette required, and consequently that they must previously have lived cheek-by-jowl with the expanding Roman territories. First drawn to the attention of archaeologists by Childe (1946: 129; cf. also Cunliffe 1974: 117–18), this event is recorded only in classical authors of the fourth and fifth centuries: the evidence has recently been reviewed by Maxwell (1975: 31–5), who would prefer to discount the reference as a textual error, made all the more unlikely by the absence of supporting archaeological data.

Tacitus' record of the Agricolan advance may be read to suggest that campaigning was more arduous in north Scotland than in the Lowlands, both because of the nature of the country and because of the resistance offered. However, a season's campaigning was lost after the rapid seizure of southern Scotland, in order to consolidate the hold on territory up to the Forth–Clyde line. The disposition of the tribes within Scotland (fig. 7.49), as indicated by Ptolemy's map, indicates that groupings were more extensive in the south of the country. These tribal groups, the Votadini, Selgovae, Damnonii and Novantae, perhaps exhibited some centralizing tendencies not displayed in the Highlands. The major fortified sites such as Eildon Hill North, Birrenswark, Traprain Law and perhaps Walls Hill, Renfrewshire (Newall 1960), suggest the topmost tier of a settlement hierarchy very different, at the other extreme, from the numerous small fortifications of the Atlantic West.

Amongst the developments in hillfort design which may be attributed to this period is the appearance of multivallation (Cunliffe 1974: 233) (fig. 7.76). In certain cases this development is marked by additional defences being constructed at already-fortified sites, as at Hownam Rings (Piggott C. M. 1948), but other sites seem to have received their initial defences at this stage, such as Barmekin of Echt, Aberdeenshire (St Joseph 1974: pl. vii). The siting of the Chesters, Drem, East Lothian, diminishes the defences of its multivallate enclosure, and suggests the appearance of a novelty (RCAHM 1924: no. 13).

Some of these schemes are unfinished, as at Dunnideer Hill, Aberdeenshire (Feachem 1966: fig. 6), and have been considered as refurbishings of forts, incomplete at the time of the Agricolan advance into north-east Scotland, where most of the more elaborate examples are situated. Only an adequate programme of excavation supported by radiocarbon dating may demonstrate whether this apparent bunching of incomplete multivallate works is a reality (cf. Feachem 1971).

Amongst the lightly-enclosed and open sites a modicum of change may be observed. Ritchie has postulated that only the smaller palisaded sites seem to be a feature of the last centuries BC (cf. p. 451f. above). In the north, further excavation will be required to verify whether the pattern suggested by Kilphedir is a suitable basis for generalization, but there seems little reason to doubt that this type of settlement continued in use into the 1st millennium AD. Some of the smaller sites in the south of Scotland and Northumberland yield evidence of successive rebuildings, which argues for a prolonged – though not necessarily continuous – period of use. At least 12 phases, perhaps beginning as early as the sixth century BC, are represented by the internal buildings at Hartburn, and seven at Boonies, Dumfriesshire. Both these sites continued in use in Romano-

Fig. 7.76 Chesters, Drem, East Lothian: view of west end of small multivallate fort (photograph Ian Ralston).

British times: indeed the latter is only doubtfully a pre-Agricolan foundation (Jobey 1973; 1974b).

The overall impression, borne out by the continuing poor quality of the pottery and lack of many small finds, is one of cultural continuity for most of the country throughout the pre-Roman iron age. It may however be considered that the cultural archaism exhibited in the north relative to developments in southern Britain is more apparent than real.

The concentration of resources over the last 25 years on the smaller sites has been in many ways commendable. However, it is certainly possible that archaeologists in the north have over-indulged in the recognition of what might be considered the northern variant of Hodson's (1964) 'Woodbury culture', characterized by Piggott (1974) as the 'isolation of the lower-class element in a highly-stratified, hierarchical society, to the exclusion of the rest'. Only by large-scale excavations of the interior of at least one of the major hillforts, coupled with an investigation of its agricultural (? and economic) hinterland, may archaeology perhaps fill out the role of the upper echelons of society, still all too meagrely depicted by the occasional literary reference and item of aristocratic metalwork. As elsewhere in the British Isles the period when British prehistory merges into history is paradoxically still very much the Dark Age of archaeology.

Notes

1. Indeed this had already been seen to be the case, in particular in the dating of the earlier settlement sites in the Border area: cf. Feachem (1959).
2. We are grateful to K. J. Edwards, Queen's University, Belfast, for help in compiling this section and for unpublished information on Dinnet, Aberdeenshire; cf. Durno (1956); Durno and Romans (1969); Vasari and Vasari (1968); Evans, Limbrey and Cleere (1975). For early dates for the climatic deterioration, see Burgess (1974: 166–7 and 293, nn. 5–8): in Scotland: Moss of Achnacree and Cultoon (radiocarbon appendix).
3. The term 'stockaded camp' is used here following Challis and Harding (1975: 101) to distinguish hilltop palisaded enclosures, where defence seems to be of some importance, from others less defensively sited.
4. The classification used by the Royal Commission on the Ancient and Historical Monuments of Scotland and adopted by Ritchie (1970) and other workers is thus: 'homestead', site containing up to three houses; 'settlement', containing more than three houses; 'enclosure', occupation absent or unknown.
5. In contrast to the situation of Staple Howe, Yorkshire, exotic metalwork is rarely recorded from the North British palisade series (but cf. Hayhope Knowe, p. 451 above). Hallstatt material is known from the Tyne-Forth Province: cf. fig. 7.55 above; cf. also p. 458 above. Small-scale incursions, represented archaeologically by trappings associated with wheeled transport, may be indicated (Piggott 1953b; Cunliffe 1978a: 144).
6. The razor is T 27 in Burley's (1956) catalogue. The main series of excavations at this crucial site, in the first quarter of the century, executed by a series of arbitrary levels, has left a cloud of interpretative difficulty that cannot be wholly dispersed.
7. The classic variety of this, with transversal and longitudinal timbers nailed at their intersections, remains firmly late in the continental sequence: Collis and Ralston (1976). Burghead, the first Scottish fort to produce nails from the core of its defences, did not do so on its most recent re-examination. Available radiocarbon dates suggest that it is a later work: Small (1969). The Primary Dun at Dundurn, Perthshire, similarly carbon-dated to the mid-1st millennium ad, also has nailed timberwork in the defences (Alcock 1978).
8. The view taken here is that vitrification results from the destruction by fire of stone walls containing substantial amounts of timber, and is not a constructional technique to strengthen the defences. It thus follows that vitrification is not of cultural significance in its own right (cf. MacKie 1969d; Nisbet 1974; 1975; Challis and Harding 1975: 110). Arguments that vitrification was a deliberate process and is a cultural tradition have been put forward by Brothwell et al. (1974), but fail to account for the wide range of dates now available for vitrified structures, e.g. the vitrified wall at Mote of Mark, Kirkcudbright (Laing 1975: esp. 100). Further analytical work (Youngblood et al. 1978) indicates that the fire which produced the vitrification took place in reducing conditions at temperatures in excess of 900° Centigrade, and concludes that 'it is unreasonable to assume that melting could result from setting fire to a simple *murus gallicus*'. Their postulated 'vitrified fort' type wall seems to imply some kind of internal timber

framework, compact construction, and a probable cover of peat, moss or similar substances to reduce the rate of combustion. They are unable to conclude whether the process is constructional or not. Maybe it is time to repeat Childe and Thorneycroft's experiment under more controlled conditions (1937–8b), but we remain unconvinced that the Scottish sites are anything other than burnt examples of timber-laced ramparts. For a new discussion of the Abernethy culture and its relations with vitrified forts see MacKie (1976).

9. Sheep Hill, Dunbartonshire, also has indications of bronze-working; MacKie (1976).

10. Since Benton's (1930–1) first expression of the theory that flat-rimmed pottery was a distinct entity, this too was considered to be an exotic element in the assemblage. Coles (1959–60: 43–4) attempted a tighter definition of a Covesea group within the flat-rimmed ware tradition, in connection with his delineation of the Covesea metalwork. Subsequent investigation has indicated the wide chronological spread of this pottery in Scotland and recent re-assessment suggests that the division of this pottery into regional groups is 'highly suspect'; cf. Coles and Taylor (1969–70).

11. Cf. Piggott S. (1966: esp. 10); for a view of the Welsh evidence see Savory (1971a, b): at Dinorben, a bronze crook-headed pin, paralleled in iron from the timber-laced fort at Abernethy, Perthshire, predates the construction of two timber-laced defences, of which the earlier is in Cunliffe's 'Ivinghoe Beacon style' (1974: 229) and the latter more closely akin to the Scottish series, with French Urnfield parallels. Savory looks to these Urnfield groups as inspirations for the early British forts, and cites timber-laced forts as far west as the Atlantic coasts of France, but as commented elsewhere in the present volume a wholly native evolution is by no means discounted (cf. pp. 335ff.).

12. Cowen (1967: 396 n. 3) is sceptical about the possible association of the two swords from Leuchland Farm, Brechin, Angus, with a hoard of late bronze age material from the same parish.

13. Cf. Coles (1958–9); Spratling (1974) has recently argued for a later terminal date for the series.

14. At Huckhoe, Northumberland, the indications are that the stone-built defensive wall followed the destruction of the twin palisade (another palisade is present further out) without an appreciable chronological gap: Jobey (1968b).

15. The definition of this term has varied over the years; that utilized by the Royal Commission, now more generally adopted, characterizes this class of monument as follows: 'a comparatively small defensive structure with a disproportionately thick dry-stone wall, usually but not always, subcircular or oval in plan, and enclosing an area not exceeding 375 sq m'. The inner and outer facings of the wall are frequently of massive proportions. Architectural details exhibit some similarities with the brochs. The enclosed area indicates a homestead, rather than a settlement unit (RCAHM 1975: 18). Some 500 examples of the type are known, mostly in Argyll, Bute, Renfrewshire and Ayrshire: Maxwell (1969).

16. The 'guard-cells', paralleled on Shetland at Loch of Huxter and Ness of Burgi, cannot be entered at ground level at Clickhimin, and therefore seem unlikely to have fulfilled the same function (RCAHM 1946: nos. 1316 and 1154). A single scarcement ledge survives at the Clickhimin blockhouse, and behind it there was a cobbled floor; no post-holes were recovered in association with this.

17. MacKie (1974: 97). The structural development and geographical origin of the brochs presented here follows the argument developed by MacKie in several papers published since 1965. An alternative view sees the brochs originating in the far north in the areas of their greatest surviving concentration: the leading proponent of this view in recent years has been Hamilton. Problems with this latter approach include the lack of a suitable prototype, and are dealt with by MacKie. However, the search for a geographically discrete origin for the brochs may prove futile. It should be noted that hillforts are present on the northern mainland, though in small numbers and show certain local features, notably in the treatment of the entrances, e.g. Garrywhin, Caithness (Hogg 1975: 216 and fig. 73). They are, however, essentially undated.

18. Cf. Craigie, Stannergate, Dundee, with iron type A2 penannular fibula (MacKie 1971b), but this was also associated with a projecting ring-headed pin for which a later date has usually been suggested (Stevenson 1966), though MacKie (1974: 128–30) has ring-pin stamped sherds from an early context at Dun Mor Vaul. The complexities of the dating of this type are discussed by Clarke (1971: 28–32), with distribution map. In any case, the type survived into the early centuries AD, the latest examples being cast (Stevenson 1955).

19. Evidence of articulation suggests that this was not a case of partial inhumation, particularly since most of the missing bones were those most prone to decay and fragmentation. But note that four skulls are missing, and a fifth is represented solely by the lower jaw; cf. Brothwell and Powers (1966).

20. The placing of Roman fortifications on areas with iron age occupation has been noticed elsewhere, e.g. at Cardean, Angus, a native settlement may have been cleared away before the construction of the fort by a Roman army unit (*Discovery and Excavation in Scotland 1973*: 6).

21. Piggott (Piggott and Allen 1970: no. 12) suggests, on the basis of the figure 'II' incised on the helmet, that it was Roman loot. Fox (1958) contrastingly views the piece as the property of an auxiliary, 'a Celtic noble in Roman service'. Either view is possible since its northern provenance is by no means assured.

22. The Balmaclellan mirror has been described as 'a mongrel product of one or more craftsmen, well aware of decorative developments in the South' (MacGregor M. 1976: 142–3). A date much before AD 70/80 is precluded by the form of the mirror handle, which is related to those of Roman paterae. The mirror, and two decorated pieces of bronze, of slightly earlier date, seem to have formed a votive deposit. The Stichill collar, probably found with two massive armlets, resembles a south British class in outline, but has decoration similar to Balmaclellan, and probably dates to the late first century AD or later; cf. also Megaw (1971).

23. Cf. Piggott S. (1958: 16–17) – comments from Caesar, Strabo and Dio. To some extent the Roman commissariat's problems in a country of varying cereal-producing capabilities, may be balanced by the kinds of scandal, mentioned by Tacitus, in the corn supply when Agricola arrived in Britain (Tacitus, *de Vita Iulii Agricolae*: 19). But the Irish tales are eloquent of the high value of livestock, especially cattle (Jackson 1964a).

24. The standard view would envisage any of the presumably small-scale contacts marked by the appearance of Urnfield or Hallstatt objects in Scotland as the first episode when a Celtic language might have appeared in Scotland (Powell 1962). An alternative view would place this even very much earlier, with the appearance of the beaker phenomenon, cf. Dillon and Chadwick (1967). If this latter view is preferred, it becomes necessary to reconcile the apparent considerable penetration of north-east Scotland by the beaker complex with the survival of a non-Celtic language and institutions in Pictish culture.

Appendix   Radiocarbon dates for later North British prehistory

The following list contains a fairly full selection of radiocarbon measurements post-dating 1,000 bc for North Britain. A major exclusion is the series of 20 dates correlating with a floating tree-ring chronology from Cullykhan, Banffshire (Campbell *et al.* 1978). The most important result of this work was to imply that the error on a single radiocarbon date is considerably greater than at present accepted on the basis of analytical precision alone. All dates are bc unless otherwise stated.

	bc (calculated on the 5,568 half-life)	lab. nos.
Atlantic Province		
Moss of Achnacree, Argyll (Ritchie *et al.* 1974)		
beginning of peat growth	980 ± 80	N-1468
Cultoon, Islay (MacKie 1975c)		
early in formation of peat cover over stone circle	765 ± 40	SRR-500
Claggan kerb cairns, Argyll (Ritchie *et al.* 1975)		
charcoal accompanying cremation, cairn 3	1058 ± 40	SRR-285
charcoal accompanying cremation, cairn 1	975 ± 50	SRR-284
old land surface underlying cairn 2	586 ± 80	SRR-599
old land surface underlying cairn 2	462 ± 55	SRR-593
Liddle Farm, Orkney (Huxtable *et al.* 1976)		
peat overlying a constructional stone	958 ± 45	SRR-525
organic material at bottom of large stone cooking trough	876 ± 75	SRR-701
Quanterness, Orkney (Renfrew *et al.* 1976)		
primary occupation of round-house	620 ± 85	Q-1465
primary occupation of round-house	490 ± 85	Q-1464
subsequent to secondary phase of round-house	180 ± 60	Q-1463
Skaill, Orkney (*Radiocarbon 16*, 1974, and *18*, 1976)		
earliest occupation level	1060 ± 140	Birm-594
hearth	150 ± 100	Birm-397
as per Birm-397	170 ± 100	Birm-413
penultimate occupation level	ad 190 ± 110	Birm-593
underlying latest occupation level	ad 450 ± 120	Birm-592

	bc (calculated on the 5,568 half-life)	lab. nos.
Atlantic Province (cont.)		
Kilphedir, Sutherland (hut circle settlement)		
charcoal from hut 3	420 ± 40	GU-299
charcoal from roof poles, second phase of hut	150 ± 80	L-1061
charcoal from roof poles, second phase of hut 5	ad 42 ± 60	GU-10
charcoal from roof poles, second phase of hut 5	114 ± 55	GU-11
charcoal from roof poles, second phase of hut 5	ad 28 ± 60	GU-67
charcoal from roof poles, second phase of hut 5	150 ± 50	SRR-3
second phase of hut 5	275 ± 60	GU-514
second phase of hut 5	95 ± 95	GU-515
Dun Lagaidh, Lochbroom, Ross and Cromarty		
carbonized branch under wall of vitrified fort	490 ± 80	GX-1121
burnt grain associated with burning of timber fort	460 ± 100	GaK-2492
charred planks on dun floor	ad 840 ± 90	GaK-1947
Dun Mor Vaul, Tiree (MacKie 1974: 229–30)		
charred grain related to burning of initial wooden hut	445 ± 90	GaK-1098
roots in old ground surface below primary midden	400 ± 110	GaK-1092
animal bones from midden under outer wall	280 ± 100	GaK-1225
charcoal from primary floor in broch wall gallery	ad 60 ± 90	GaK-1097
charcoal from rubble in broch mural gallery	ad 160 ± 90	GaK-1099
Langwell, Ross and Cromarty (vitrified dun) (5730 half-life)		
charcoal from post-hole at entrance to guardchamber	230 ± 90	GaK-4860
charcoal from foundation course, inner face of wall	350 ± 90	GaK-4862
charcoal from fallen roof timber	310 ± 100	GaK-4861
charcoal from fallen roof timber	150 ± 140	GX-3274
Dun An Ruigh Ruaidh, Ross and Cromarty (prototype broch = 'semi-broch')		
start of secondary occupation	10 ± 100	GaK-2496

	bc (calculated on the 5,568 half-life)	lab. nos.
Atlantic Province (cont.)		
carbonized wood from primary post-hole 'very early'	580 ± 80	GaK-2493
late occupation inside gallery	ad 790 ± 80	GaK-2494
Dun Ardtreck, Skye (semi-broch) charcoal from rubble foundation	55 ± 105	GX-1120
North-Eastern Province		
Sands of Forvie, Aberdeens. (*Radiocarbon 17*, 1975)		
oak fragments, post-hole of Hut E	652 ± 115	Q-761
Finavon, Angus		
substantial timbers next to (but not in) defensive wall	590 ± 70	GaK-1224
charcoal from low in fallen rubble from wall	410 ± 80	GaK-1222
occupation layer of fort	320 ± 90	GaK-1223
Cullykhan, Troup Head, Banff		
outer wood of large trunk in post-hole of massive entrance to fort (phase 1)	397 ± 59	BM-639
charcoal from top of first stratified occupation level (phase 1)	387 ± 65	BM-446
charcoal from surface of cobbled area outside fort	106 ± 51	BM-443
charcoal from wooden object in occupation level producing Roman pot of 250/350 AD	ad 317 ± 40	BM-445
Green Cairn, Kincardine		
material from stake hole forming part of a structure	390 ± 95	N-1376
timber related to destruction of wall	540 ± 95	N-1375
twigs in destruction level	180 ± 100	N-1318
Craig Phadrig, Inverness		
peat and turf from outer rampart courses	370 ± 105	N-1124
carbonized horizontal wall beam	330 ± 100	N-1122
outer defence: charred timber	300 ± 100	N-1120
charcoal below rampart	180 ± 110	GX-2441
wood from sterile horizon, above lower occupation layer	80 ± 100	N-1118
Dark Age (E-ware and hanging bowl escutcheon) occupation	ad 410 ± 85	N-1119
charcoal under buried wall	270 ± 100	N-1123

North-Eastern Province (cont.)	bc (calculated on the 5,568 half-life)	lab. nos.
Lundin Links, Fife (unpublished J. C. Greig)		
skeletal material, below complex kerb cairn	390 ± 100	GX-1998
Leckie, Stirlings. (broch and dun)		
carbonized grain	ad 45 ± 120	GX-2779
bone from destruction level	ad 110 ± 150	GX-2780
Burghead, Morays. (Pictish promontory fort)		
charred oak from wall	ad 390 ± 110	N-327
charred oak	ad 390 ± 115	N-329
charred oak	ad 610 ± 105	N-328

Solway-Clyde Province

Craigmarloch Wood, Renfrews.		
charcoal from palisaded enclosure	590 ± 40	GaK-995
core of later vitrified fort wall	35 ± 40	GaK-996
Burnswark, Dumfries.		
charcoal from Phase I palisade	500 ± 100	GaK-2203b
charcoal from gateway timber of ? hillfort	525 ± 90	I-5314
Milton Loch I, Kirkcudbright (crannog)		
structural pile	490 ± 100	K-2027
ard head beneath foundation	400 ± 100	K-1394
MacNaughton's Fort, Kirkcudbright		
charcoal in palisade trench enclosing wooden round-house	280 ± 100	GaK-808
Loch Lotus, Kirkcudbright (Close–Brooks 1974–5)	101 ± 80	SRR-403
dug-out canoe		
Lochmaben, Dumfries.		
ard beam (found in peat) of alder	80 ± 100	K-1867
Boonies, Dumfries. (Jobey 1974b)		
timber remains sealed below enclosing bank	ad 108 ± 47	SRR-300
Mote of Mark, Kirkcudbright		
timber of presumed main gateway of the defence	ad 459 ± 42	SRR-321

	bc (calculated on the 5,568 half-life)	lab. nos.
Tyne-Forth Province		
Kaimes, Midlothian (5,730 half life)		
wood from wall of hut-circle	1191	GaK-1970
twigs from core of rampart 2	365	GaK-1971
Huckhoe, Northumberland		
charcoal from palisade trench	510 ± 40	GaK-1388
Fenton Hill, Northumberland		
palisaded enclosure	690 ± 100	?
Brough Law, Northumberland		
charcoal below rampart of hillfort	245 ± 90	I-5315
Ingram Hill, Northumberland		
phase 2	220 ± 90	I-5316
Belling Law, Northumberland (Jobey 1977)		
wall timbers of house 1	160 ± 80	HAR-1394
timber structure probably associated with later stone-built houses	ad 280 ± 70	HAR-1393
Hartburn, Northumberland (Jobey 1973)	35 ± 175	I-6300
bottom silts in inner ditch		
sunken hearth apparently associated with destruction of dry-stone house	ad 65 ± 90	I-6301

Abbreviations

Note Places of publication are given only for works published outside the United Kingdom. In abbreviating less frequently cited periodical titles, the commonly accepted usage of *Soc.* for society, *Trans.* for Transactions, *Arch.* for Archaeological, *Archaeol.* for Archaeology, etc., has been followed. Other abbreviations are listed below.

Ant. J.	*Antiquaries Journal*
Arch. Ael.	*Archaeologia Aeliana*
Arch. Atl.	*Archaeologia Atlantica*
Arch. Camb.	*Archaeologia Cambrensis*
Arch. Cant.	*Archaeologia Cantiana*
Arch. J.	*Archaeological Journal*
BAR	British Archaeological Reports
BMQ	*British Museum Quarterly*
B. Num. J.	*British Numismatic Journal*
CA	*Current Archaeology*
CBA Res. Rep.	Council for British Archaeology Research Reports
EcHR	*Economic History Review*
Hist. J.	*Historical Journal*
IARF	*Irish Archaeological Research Forum*
JAS	*Journal of Archaeological Science*
JHA	*Journal for the History of Astronomy*
JRSAI	*Journal of the Royal Society of Antiquaries of Ireland*
PCAS	*Proceedings of the Cambridge Antiquarian Society*
PDNHAS	*Proceedings of the Dorset Natural History and Archaeological Society*
PPS	*Proceedings of the Prehistoric Society*
PRIA	*Proceedings of the Royal Irish Academy*
PRSL	*Proceedings of the Royal Society of London*
PSAL	*Proceedings of the Society of Antiquaries of London*
PSAS	*Proceedings of the Society of Antiquaries of Scotland*
RCAHM	*Royal Commission on the Ancient and Historical Monuments of Scotland*
SAF	*Scottish Archaeological Forum*
SAC	*Sussex Archaeological Collections*
SyAC	*Surrey Archaeological Collections*
TBGAS	*Transactions of the Bristol and Gloucestershire Archaeological Society*
TDGNHAS	*Transactions of the Dumfries and Galloway Natural History and Antiquarian Society*
UJA	*Ulster Journal of Archaeology*
WAM	*Wiltshire Archaeological and Natural History Magazine*
YAJ	*Yorkshire Archaeological Journal*

Bibliography

Abercromby, J.,1912. *A Study of the Bronze Age Pottery of Great Britain and Ireland*, 2 vols.

Addyman, P.V., 1965. 'Coney Island Lough Neagh,' *UJA 28*:78–101.

Alcock, L. 1970. 'Excavations at South Cadbury Castle, 1969'. *Ant. J. 50*: 14–25.

Alcock, L., 1972a. 'The Irish Sea zone in the pre-Roman iron age', in Thomas, A. C. (ed.), *The Iron Age in the Irish Sea Province*. CBA Res. Rep. 9:99–112.

Alcock, L., 1972b. *By South Cadbury is that Camelot . . . Excavations at Cadbury Castle 1966–70.*

Alcock, L., 1972c. Review of Savory 1971a, *Antiquity 46*:330–1.

Alcock, L., 1978. *Excavations at Dundurn, St Fillans, Perthshire, 1976–77: An interim report.*

Alexander, J., 1975. 'The development of urban communities: the evidence from Cambridge and Great Chesterford', in Rodwell, W. and Rowley, T. (eds.), *The Small Towns of Roman Britain*, BAR 15: 103–10.

Allen, D.F., 1944. 'The Belgic dynasties of Britain and their coins', *Archaeologia 90*:1–46.

Allen, D.F., 1961a. 'The origins of coinage in Britain: a re-appraisal', in Frere, S.S. (ed.), *Problems of the Iron Age in Southern Britain*: 97–308.

Allen, D.F., 1961b. 'A study of the Dobunnic coinage', in Clifford 1961: 75–149.

Allen, D.F., 1963. *The Coins of the Coritani (Sylloge of Coins of the British Isles 3).*

Allen, D.F., 1964. 'Celtic coins from the Romano-British temple at Harlow, Essex', *B. Num. J. 33*:1–6.

Allen, D.F., 1967a. 'Iron currency bars in Britain', *PPS 33*:307–35.

Allen, D.F., 1967b. 'Celtic coins from the Romano-British temple at Harlow, Essex', *B. Num. J. 36*:1–7.

Allen, D.F., 1968a. 'The chronology of Durotrigian coinage', in Richmond 1968: 45–55.

Allen, D.F., 1968b. 'Celtic coins from the Romano-British temple at Harlow, Essex', *B. Num. J. 37*:1–6.

Allen, D.F., 1970. 'The coins of the Iceni', *Britannia 1*:1–33.

Allen, D.F., 1971. 'British potin coins: a review', in Hill and Jesson 1971: 127–54.

Allen, D.F., 1975. 'Cunobelin's gold', *Britannia 6*:1–19.

Allen, D.F., 1976. 'Wealth, money and coinage in a Celtic society', in Megaw 1976b: 199–208.

Allen, D.F., 1978. *An Introduction to Celtic Coins.*

Allen, I.M., Britton, D. and Coghlan, M.H., 1970. 'Metallurgical reports on British and Irish bronze age implements and weapons in the Pitt Rivers Museum', *Pitt Rivers Mus. Occ. Papers on Technology 10.*

Allen, J., Golson, J. and Jones, R. (eds.), 1977. *Sunda and Sahul: Prehistoric Studies in Southeast Asia, Melanesia and Australia.*

Annable, F.K., 1958. 'Excavation and field-work in Wiltshire: 1957', *WAM 57*: 2–17.

Annable, F.K. and Simpson, D.D.A., 1964. *Guide Catalogue of the Neolithic and Bronze Age Collections in Devizes Museum.*

Applebaum, S., 1954. 'The agriculture of the British early iron age, as exemplified at Figheldean Down, Wilts.', *PPS 20*:103–14.

ApSimon, A.M., 1954. 'Dagger graves in the Wessex bronze age', *10th Ann. Rep. Univ. London Inst. Arch.*: 37–62.

ApSimon, A.M., 1957–8. 'Cornish bronze age pottery', *Procs. W. Cornwall Field Club 2.2*:36–46.

ApSimon, A.M., 1959. 'Food vessels', *Bull. Inst. Arch. Univ. London 1*:24–36.

ApSimon, A.M., 1969. 'The earlier bronze age in the north of Ireland', *UJA 32*:28–72.

ApSimon, A.M., 1972. 'Biconical urns outside Wessex', in Lynch, F. and Burgess, C.B. (eds.), *Prehistoric Man in Wales and the West: Essays in honour of Lily F.Chitty*: 141–60.

ApSimon, A.M., 1976a. 'A view of the early prehistory of Wales', in Boon, G.C. and Lewis, J.M. (eds.), *Welsh Antiquity: Essays mainly on prehistoric topics presented to H. N. Savory*: 37–54.

ApSimon, A.M., 1976b. 'Ballynagilly and the beginning and end of the Irish neolithic', in De Laet, S. J. (ed.), *Acculturation and Continuity in Atlantic Europe*, Diss. Archaeol. Gandenses 21: 15–30 (Bruges).

ApSimon, A.M. and Greenfield, E., 1972. 'The excavation of the bronze age and iron age settlement at Trevisker Round, St. Eval, Cornwall', *PPS 38*:302–81.

Ashbee, P., 1957. 'Stake and post circles in British round barrows', *Arch. J. 114*: 1–9.

Ashbee, P. 1960. *The Bronze Age Round Barrow in Britain*.

Ashbee, P., 1963. 'The Wilsford shaft', *Antiquity 37*:118–19.

Ashbee, P., 1966a. 'The Fussell's Lodge long barrow excavations 1957', *Archaeologia 100*:1–80.

Ashbee, P., 1966b. 'The dating of the Wilsford shaft', *Antiquity 40*:227–8.

Ashbee, P., 1970. *The Earthen Long Barrow in Britain*.

Ashbee, P., 1974. *Ancient Scilly: from the first farmers to the Early Christians*.

Ashbee, P., 1978. *The Ancient British: A social-archaeological narrative*.

Aspinall, A. and Warren, S., 1973. *The problem of faience beads*. Lecture delivered at a conference held in Newcastle, January 1973.

Atherden, M.A., 1976. 'Late quaternary vegetational history of the North York Moors. III. Fen Bogs, *J. Biogeography 3*:115–24.

Atkinson, R.J.C., 1951. 'The excavations at Dorchester, Oxfordshire, 1946–51', *Arch. Newsletter 4*:56–9.

Atkinson, R.J.C., 1955. 'The Dorset Cursus', *Antiquity 29*:4–9.

Atkinson, R.J.C., 1957. 'Worms and weathering', *Antiquity 31*:219–33.

Atkinson, R.J.C., 1960a. *Stonehenge* (rev. edn).

Atkinson, R.J.C., 1960b. *A statistical consideration of the Wessex Culture*. Lecture delivered to the CBA Bronze Age Conference, London 1960.

Atkinson, R.J.C., 1961. 'Neolithic engineering', *Antiquity 35*:292–9.

Atkinson, R.J.C., 1962. 'Fishermen and farmers', in Piggott S. 1962a: 1–38.

Atkinson, R.J.C., 1965. 'Wayland's Smithy', *Antiquity 39*:126–33.

Atkinson, R.J.C., 1967. 'Further radiocarbon dates for Stonehenge', *Antiquity 41*:63–4.

Atkinson, R.J.C., 1968. 'Old mortality: some aspects of burial and population in neolithic Britain', in Coles and Simpson 1968:83–94.

Atkinson, R.J.C., 1972. 'Burial and population in the British bronze age', in Lynch, F. and Burgess, C.B. (eds.), *Prehistoric Man in Wales and the West: Essays in honour of Lily F. Chitty*: 107–16.

Atkinson, R.J.C. and Piggott, S., 1955. 'The Torrs Chamfrein', *Archaeologia 96*:197–235.

Atkinson, R.J.C., Piggott, C.M. and Sandars, N.K., 1949. *Excavations at Dorchester, Oxon.*

Avery, M., 1968. 'Excavations at Meare East, 1966', *Procs. Somerset Arch. and Nat. Hist. Soc. 112*:21–39.

Avery, M., 1973. 'British La Tène decorated pottery: an outline', *Études Celtiques 13.2*:522–51.

Avery, M., 1974. Review of Cunliffe 1974, *IARF 1*:59–64.

Avery, M., 1976. 'Hillforts of the British Isles: a student's introduction', in Harding D.W. 1976a: 1–58.

Avery, M. and Close-Brooks, J., 1969. 'Shearplace Hill, Sydling St Nicholas, Dorset, House A: a suggested re-interpretation', *PPS 35*:345–51.

Avery, M., Sutton, J.G.E. and Banks, J.W., 1967. 'Rainsborough, Northants, England: excavations 1961–5', *PPS 33*:207–306.

Barber, J. and Megaw, J.V.S., 1963. 'A decorated iron age bridle-bit in the London Museum', *PPS 29*:206–13.

Barrett, J.C., 1973. 'Four bronze age cremation cemeteries from Middlesex', *Trans. London Middx. Arch. Soc. 24*:111–34.

Barrett, J.C., 1975. 'The later pottery: types, affinities, chronology and significance', in Bradley and Ellison 1975.

Barrett, J.C., 1976. 'Deverel-Rimbury: problems of chronology and interpretation', in Burgess, C.B. and Miket, R. (eds.), *Settlement and Economy in the third and second millennia B.C.*, BAR 33:289–307.

Bartley, D.D., Chambers, C. and Hart-Jones, B., 1976. 'The vegetational history of parts of south and east Durham', *New Phytologist 77*:437–68.

Bate, C.S., 1871. 'On the discovery of a Romano-British cemetery near Plymouth', *Archaeologia 40*:501–10.

Bateman, T., 1861. *Ten Years' Digging in Celtic and Saxon Grave Hills.*

Beck, H.C. and Stone, J.F.S., 1935. 'Faience beads of the British bronze age', *Archaeologia 85*:203–52.

Becker, C.J., 1948. 'Mosefunde lerkar fra yngre stenalder: studier over tragtbaegerkulturen i Denmark', *Aarbøger f.n. Oldk. og Hist.* (1947).

Bell, M., 1976. 'Bishopstone', *CA 5*:166–71.

Bell, M., 1977. 'Excavations at Bishopstone', *SAC 115*: 1–299.

Bender, B., 1975. *Farming in Prehistory.*

Benson, D. and Miles, D., 1974. *The Upper Thames Valley: An archaeological survey of the river gravels.*

Benton, S., 1930–1. 'The excavation of the Sculptor's Cave, Covesea, Morayshire', *PSAS 65*:177–216.

Bersu, G., 1940. 'Excavations at Little Woodbury, Wiltshire', *PPS 6*:30–111.

Biddle, M., 1975. 'Excavations at Winchester 1971: tenth and final interim report: Part I', *Ant. J. 55*:96–126.

Binchy, E., 1967. 'Irish razors and razor-knives', in Rynne, E. (ed.), *North Munster Studies*: 43–60 (Limerick).

Birchall, A., 1965. 'The Aylesford-Swarling culture: the problem of the Belgae reconsidered', *PPS 31*:241–367.

Blundell, J.D. and Longworth, I.H., 1967. 'A bronze age hoard from Portfield Farm, Whalley, Lancashire', *BMQ 32*:1–2, 8–14.

Bohmers, A., 1956. 'Statistics and graphs in the study of flint assemblages', *Palaeohistoria 5*:1–38.

Bohmers, A., 1963. 'A statistical analysis of flint artifacts', in Higgs, E. and Brothwell, D. (eds.), *Science in Archaeology*: 469–81.

Bonnamour, L. and Bulard, A., 1976. 'Une epée celtique à fourreau décoré découverte à Montbellet (Saône-et-Loire)', *Gallia 34*:279–84.

Boon, G.C., 1954. 'A Greek vase from the Thames', *J. Hellenic Stud. 74*:178.

Boon, G.C., 1969. 'Belgic and Roman Silchester: the excavations of 1954–8 with an excursus on the early history of Calleva', *Archaeologia 102*:1–82.

Boon, G.C., 1977. 'A Greco-Roman anchor-stock from North Wales', *Ant. J. 57*:10–30.

Bordaz, J., 1970. *Tools of the Old and New Stone Age.*

Bowen, D.Q., 1970. 'The palaeoenvironment of the "Red Lady" of Paviland', *Antiquity 44*:174, 134–6.

Bowen, H.C., 1961. *Ancient Fields.*

Bowen, H.C., 1969. 'The Celtic background', in Rivet, A.L.F. (ed.), *The Roman Villa in Britain*: 1–48.

Bowen, H.C., 1975. 'A view of the Wessex landscape', in Fowler 1975: 44–56.

Bowen, H.C. and Fowler, P.J., 1966. 'Romano-British rural settlements in Dorset and Wiltshire', in Thomas, A.C. (ed.), *Rural Settlement in Roman Britain.*

Bowen, H.C. and Fowler, P.J. (eds.), 1978. *Early Land Allotment in the British Isles: A survey of recent work*, BAR 48.

Bowler, J.M., 1976. 'Recent developments in reconstructing late quaternary environments in Australia', in Kirk, R.L. and Thorne, A.G. (eds.), *The Origin of the Australians*: 55–77.

Bradley, R.J., 1970. 'The excavation of a Beaker settlement at Belle Tout, East Sussex, England', *PPS 36*:312–79.

Bradley, R.J., 1971a. 'Stock raising and the origins of the hillfort on the South Downs', *Ant. J. 51*:8–29.

Bradley, R.J., 1971b. 'Economic change in the growth of early hillforts', in Hill and Jesson 1971: 71–83.

Bradley, R.J., 1971c. 'A field survey of the Chichester entrenchments', in Cunliffe, B.W., *Excavations at Fishbourne Vol. I*:17–36.

Bradley, R.J., 1975. 'Salt and settlement in the Hampshire-Sussex borderland', in de Brisay, K.W. and Evans, K.A. (eds.), *Salt: the study of an ancient industry*: 20–5.

Bradley, R.J., 1978. *The Prehistoric Settlement of Britain.*

Bradley, R.J. and Ellison, A., 1975. *Rams Hill: A bronze age defended enclosure and its landscape*, BAR 19.

Brailsford, J.W., 1948. 'Excavations at Little Woodbury, part II', *PPS 14:* 1–23.

Brailsford, J.W., 1958. 'Early Iron Age "C" in Wessex', *PPS 24*:101–19.

Brailsford, J.W., 1962. *Hod Hill I: Antiquities from Hod Hill in the Durden Collection.*

Brailsford, J.W., 1975a. *Early Celtic Masterpieces from Britain in the British Museum.*

Brailsford, J.W., 1975b. 'The Polden Hill hoard, Somerset', *PPS 41*:222–34.

Branigan, K., 1970. 'Wessex and Mycenae: some evidence reviewed', *WAM 65*:89–107.

Brea, L.B., 1957. *Sicily.*

Breeze, D.J. and Dobson, B., 1976. *Hadrian's Wall.*

Brewis, W.P., 1922–3. 'The bronze sword in Great Britain', *Archaeologia 73*: 253–65.

Brewster, T.C.M., 1963. *The Excavation of Staple Howe.*

Brewster, T.C.M., 1971. 'The Garton Slack chariot burial, East Yorkshire', *Antiquity 45*:289–92.

Brewster, T.C.M., 1976. 'Garton Slack', *CA 5*:104–16.

Briard, J., 1961. 'Dépôts de l'age du bronze de Bretagne', *Travaux du Laboratoire d'Anthropologie Préhist. de Rennes.*

Briard, J., 1965. 'Les dépôts Bretons et l'age du bronze Atlantique', *Travaux du Laboratoire d'Anthropologie Préhist. de Rennes.*

Briard, J., 1970. 'Un tumulus du bronze ancien, Kernonen en Plouvorn (Finistère)', *L'Anthropologie 74*:5–55.

Briard, J., 1973. 'Bronze age cultures: 1800–600 B.C.', in Piggott, S., Daniel, G.E. and McBurney, C.D.M. (eds.), *France before the Romans*: 131–56.

Briard, J., 1978. 'Das Silbergefäss von Saint-Adrien, Côtes-du-Nord', *Arch. Korrespondenzblatt 8:* 13–20.

Briard, J., Cordier, G. and Gaucher, G., 1969. 'Un dépôt de la fin du bronze moyen à Malassis, commune de Chéry (Cher)', *Gallia Préhist. 12*:37–73.

Briggs, C.S., 1973. 'Double axe doubts', *Antiquity 47*:318–20.

Briscoe, G. and Furness, A., 1955. 'A hoard of bronze age weapons from Eriswell, near Mildenhall', *Ant. J. 35*:218–19.

Britnell, W.J., 1974. 'Beckford', *CA 4*:293–7.

Britnell, W.J., 1976. 'Antler cheek-pieces of the British late bronze age', *Ant. J. 66*:24–34.

Britton, D., 1960. 'The Isleham hoard, Cambridge', *Antiquity 34*:279–82.

Britton, D., 1963. 'Traditions of metalworking in the later neolithic and early bronze age of Britain: Part I', *PPS 29*:258–325.

Britton, D., 1971. 'The Heathery Burn Cave revisited', in Sieveking, G. de G. (ed.), *Prehistoric and Roman Studies (BMQ 35)*: 20–38.

Brongers, J.A., 1976. *Air Photography and Celtic Field Research in the Netherlands*, Nederlandse Oudheden 6, 2 vols.

Brooks, R.T., 1974. 'The excavation of The Rumps Cliff Castle, St. Minver, Cornwall', *Cornish Archaeol. 13*:5–51.

Brothwell, D.R., 1960. 'The bronze age people of Yorkshire: A general survey', *The Advancement of Science 64*:311–22.

Brothwell, D.R., 1972. 'Palaeodemography and earlier British populations', *World Archaeol. 4.1*:75–87.

Brothwell, D.R., 1977. 'Human population history from Afro-Asia to the New World and its possible relationship to economic change', in Megaw 1977: 15–23.

Brothwell, D.R., Bishop, A.C. and Woolley, A.R., 1974. 'Vitrified forts in Scotland: a problem in interpretation and primitive technology', *JAS 1*:101–7.

Brothwell, D.R. and Krzanowski, W., 1974. 'Evidence of biological differences between British populations from neolithic to medieval times, as revealed by eleven commonly available cranial vault measurements', *JAS 1*:249–60.

Brothwell, D.R. and Powers, R., 1966. 'The iron age people of Dunbar', *PSAS 98*:184–98.

Brown (Smith), M.A. and Blin-Stoyle, A.E., 1959a. 'A sample analysis of British middle and late bronze age material, using optical spectrometry', *PPS 25*:198–208.

Brown (Smith), M.A. and Blin-Stoyle, A.E., 1959b. 'Spectrographic analysis of British middle and late bronze age finds', *Archaeometry 2* (Suppl.).

Bruce, J.R. and Megaw, B.R.S., 1947. 'A new neolithic culture in the Isle of Man', *PPS 12*:139–69.

Buckland, W., 1823. *Reliquiae Diluvianae: or observations on organic remains attesting to the action of a universal deluge.*

Buckley, F., 1921. *A Mesolithic Industry from Marsden, Yorks.*

Buckley, F., 1924. *A Microlithic Industry of the Pennine Chain.*

Bulleid, A. and Gray, H.St.G., 1911. *The Glastonbury Lake Village Vol. I.*

Bulleid, A. and Gray, H.St.G., 1917. *The Glastonbury Lake Village Vol. II.*

Bulleid, A. and Gray, H.St.G., 1948. *The Meare Lake Village Vol. I.*

Bulleid, A. and Gray, H.St.G., 1953. *The Meare Lake Village Vol. II.*

Burgess, C.B., 1968a. *Bronze Age Metalwork in northern England: c.1000–700 B.C.*

Burgess, C.B., 1968b 'Bronze age dirks and rapiers as illustrated by examples from Durham and Northumberland', *Trans. Archit. and Arch. Soc. Durham and Northumberland, n.s.1*:3–26.

Burgess, C.B., 1968c. 'The later bronze age in the British Isles and north-western France', *Arch. J. 125*:1–45.

Burgess, C.B., 1969. 'Some decorated axes in Canon Greenwell's collection', *YAJ 42*:267–72.

Burgess, C.B., 1974. 'The bronze age', in Renfrew 1974: 165–232, 291–329.

Burgess, C.B., 1976a. 'Burials with metalwork of the later bronze age in Wales and beyond', in Boon, G.C. and Lewis, J.M. (eds.), *Welsh Antiquity: Essays mainly on prehistoric topics presented to H.N. Savory*: 81–104.

Burgess, C.B., 1976b. 'Appendix II: The Gwithian mould and the forerunners of South Welsh axes', in Megaw 1976b: 69–79.

Burgess, C.B., 1976c. 'An early bronze age settlement at Kilellan Farm, Islay, Argyll', in Burgess, C.B. and Miket, R. (eds.), *Settlement and Economy in the third and second millennia B.C.*, BAR 33:181–208.

Burgess, C.B., 1976d. 'Meldon Bridge: a neolithic defended promontory complex near Peebles', in Burgess, C.B. and Miket, R. (eds.), *Settlement and Economy in the third and second millennia B.C.*, BAR 33:151–80.

Burgess, C.B., Coombs, D. and Davies, D.G., 1972. 'The Broadward complex and barbed spearheads', in Lynch, F. and Burgess, C.B. (eds.), *Prehistoric Man in Wales and the West: Essays in honour of Lily F. Chitty*: 211–83.

Burgess, C.B. and Cowen, J.D., 1972. 'The Ebnal hoard and early bronze age metalworking traditions', in Lynch, F. and Burgess C.B. (eds.), *Prehistoric Man in Wales and the West: Essays in honour of Lily F. Chitty*: 167–81.

Burgess, C.B. and Shennan, S., 1976. 'The beaker phenomenon: some suggestions', in Burgess, C.B. and Miket, R. (eds.), *Settlement and Economy in the third and second millennia B.C.*, BAR 33:309–26.

Burl, H.A.W., 1969. 'Henges: internal features and regional groups', *Arch. J. 126*:1–28.

Burl, H.A.W., 1969–70. 'The recumbent stone circles of north-east Scotland', *PSAS 102*:56–81.

Burl, H.A.W., 1971. 'Two "Scottish" stone circles in Northumberland', *Arch. Ael. 4th ser. 49*:37–51.

Burl, H.A.W., 1976a. *The Stone Circles of the British Isles.*

Burl, H.A.W., 1976b. 'Intimations of numeracy in the neolithic and bronze age societies of the British Isles', *Arch. J. 133*:9–32.

Burleigh, R., 1975. 'Calibration of C-14 dates: some remaining uncertainties and limitations', in Watkins T. 1975: 5–8.

Burleigh, R., Evans, J.G. and Simpson, D.D.A., 1973. 'Radiocarbon dates for Northton, Outer Hebrides', *Antiquity 47*:61–4.

Burley, E., 1956. 'A catalogue and survey of the metalwork from Traprain Law', *PSAS 89*:118–226.

Burstow, G.P. and Holleyman, G.A., 1957. 'Late bronze age settlement on Itford Hill', *PPS 23:* 167–212.

Bushe Fox, J.P., 1915. *Excavations at Hengistbury Head, Hampshire, 1911–12.*

Bushe Fox, J.P., 1925. *Excavations of the Late Celtic Urnfield at Swarling, Kent.*

Butler, J.J., 1963. 'Bronze age connections across the North Sea', *Palaeohistoria 9.*

Butler, J.J., 1969. *Nederland in de Bronstijd* (Bussum).

Butler, J.J. and Smith, I.F., 1956. 'Razors, urns and the British middle bronze age', *12th Ann Rep. Univ. of London Inst. Arch.*: 20–52.

Butler, J.J. and van der Waals, J.D., 1964. 'Metal analysis, SAM I, and European prehistory', *Helinium 4*:3–39.

Butler, J.J. and van der Waals, J.D., 1966. 'Bell beakers and early metal-working in the Netherlands', *Palaeohistoria 12*:41–139.

Calder, C.S.T., 1949–50. 'Report on the excavation of a neolithic temple at Stanydale . . . Shetland', *PSAS 84*:185–205.

Calder, C.S.T., 1955–6. 'Stone age house sites in Shetland', *PSAS 84*:340–97.

Calkin, J.B., 1948. 'The Isle of Purbeck in the iron age', *PDNHAS 70*:29–59.

Calkin, J.B., 1953. 'Kimmeridge coal-money', *PDNHAS 75*:45–71.

Calkin, J.B., 1962. 'The Bournemouth area in the middle and late bronze age, with the "Deverel-Rimbury" problem reconsidered', *Arch. J. 119*:1–65.

Campbell, J.A., Baxter, M.S. and Harkness, D.D., 1978. 'Radiocarbon measurements on a floating tree-ring chronology from north-east Scotland', *Archaeometry 20:* 33–8.

Campbell, J.B., 1971. 'The upper palaeolithic of Britain', D. Phil. thesis, University of Oxford.

Campbell, J.B., 1977. *The Upper Palaeolithic of Britain: A study of man and nature in the late ice age*, 2 vols.

Campbell, J.B. and Sampson, C.G., 1971. 'A new analysis of Kent's Cavern, Devonshire, England', Univ. Oregon Anthrop. Papers 3.

Campbell, M., Scott, J.G. and Piggott, S., 1960–1. 'The Badden cist slab', *PSAS, 94*:46–61.

Carter, P.L. and Phillipson, D., 1965. 'Appendix I: Faunal report', in Hastings, F.A., 'Excavation of an iron age farmstead at Hawk's Hill, Leatherhead', *SyAC 62*:1–43.

Case, H.J., 1961. 'Irish neolithic pottery: distribution and sequence', *PPS 27*:174–233.

Case, H.J., 1963. 'Foreign connections in the Irish neolithic', *UJA 26*:3–18.

Case, H.J., 1966. 'Were the beaker people the first metallurgists in Ireland?', *Palaeohistoria, 12*:141–77.

Case, H.J., 1969a. 'Neolithic explanations', *Antiquity 43*:176–86.

Case, H.J., 1969b. 'Settlement patterns in the north Irish neolithic', *UJA 32*:3–27.

Case, H.J., 1977. 'The beaker culture in Britain and Ireland', in Mercer, R. J. (ed.), *Beakers in Britain and Europe*, BAR suppl. ser. 26:71–101.

Caulfield, S., 1974. 'Agriculture and settlement in ancient Mayo', in Blake, I. (ed.), *Archaeology in Ireland Today: Irish Times*, 23 April 1974: 3.

Challis, A.J. and Harding, D.W., 1975. *Later Prehistory from the Trent to the Tyne*, BAR 20, 2 vols.

Champion, S., 1971. 'Excavations at Leckhampton Hill, 1969–70. Interim report', *TBGAS 90*:5–21.

Champion, S., 1976. 'Leckhampton Hill, Gloucestershire, 1925 and 1970', in Harding D.W. 1976a: 177–90.

Champion, T.C., 1971. 'The end of the Irish bronze age', *N. Munster Ant. J. 14*:17–24.

Champion, T.C., 1975. 'Britain in the European iron age', *Arch. Atl. 1*:127–45.

Champion, T.C., 1976. 'The earlier iron age in the region of the lower Thames: insular and external factors', D. Phil. thesis, University of Oxford.

Champion, T.C., 1977. 'Some decorated iron age pottery from Chinnor', *Ant. J. 57*:91–3.

Childe, V.G., 1931. *Skara Brae*.

Childe, V.G., 1933–4. 'Final report on the excavation of the stone circle at Old Keig, Aberdeenshire', *PSAS, 68*:372–93.

Childe, V.G., 1934–5. 'Excavation of the vitrified fort at Finavon, Angus', *PSAS 69*:49–80.

Childe, V.G., 1935. *The Prehistory of Scotland*.

Childe, V.G., 1935–6. 'Supplementary excavations of the vitrified fort at Finavon', *PSAS 70*:347–52.

Childe, V.G., 1938–9. 'A stone age settlement at the Braes of Rinyo, Orkney', *PSAS 73*:6–31.

Childe, V.G., 1939. 'The Orient and Europe', *American J. Archaeol. 43*:10.

Childe, V.G., 1940. *Prehistoric Communities of the British Isles*.

Childe, V.G., 1946. *Scotland before the Scots*.

Childe, V. G., 1958. *The Prehistory of European Society*.

Childe, V.G. and Thorneycroft, W., 1937–8a. 'The vitrified fort at Rahoy, Morvern', *PSAS 72*:23–43.

Childe, V.G. and Thorneycroft, W., 1937–8b. 'The experimental production of phenomena distinctive of vitrified forts', *PSAS 72:* 44–55.

Christie, P.M., 1960. 'Crig-a-mennis: a bronze age barrow at Liskey, Perranzabuloe, Cornwall', *PPS 26:* 76–97.

Christie, P.M., 1967. 'A barrow cemetery of the second millennium B.C. in Wiltshire, England', *PPS 33*:336–66.

Christison, D., 1898. *Early Fortifications in Scotland*.

Churchill, D. and Wymer, J.J., 1965. 'The kitchen midden site at Westward Ho!, Devon, England: ecology, age and relation to changes in land and sea level', *PPS 31*:74–84.

Clack, P.A.G. and Gosling, P.F., 1976. *Archaeology in the North*.

Clark, J.G.D., 1932a. *The Mesolithic Age in Britain*.

Clark, J.G.D., 1932b. 'The date of the plano–convex flint knife in England and Wales', *Ant. J. 12*:158–62.

Clark, J.G.D., 1936. 'Report on a late bronze age site in Mildenhall Fen, West Suffolk', *Ant. J. 16*:29–50.

Clark, J.G.D., 1938. 'A neolithic house at Haldon, Devon', *PPS 4*:222–3.

Clark, J.G.D., 1952. *Prehistoric Europe: The economic basis*.

Clark, J.G.D., 1954. *Excavations at Star Carr*.

Clark, J.G.D., 1955. 'A microlithic industry from the Cambridgeshire Fenland and other industries of Sauveterrian affinities from Britain', *PPS 21*:3–20.

Clark, J.G.D., 1955–6. 'Notes on the Obanian', *PSAS 89*:103–6.

Clark, J.G.D., 1963. 'Neolithic bows from Somerset, England, and the prehistory of archery in north-western Europe', *PPS 29*:50–98.

Clark, J.G.D., 1965. 'Traffic in stone axe blades', *EcHR 18*:1–28.

Clark, J.G.D., 1966. 'The invasion hypothesis in British archaeology', *Antiquity 40*:172–89.

Clark, J.G.D., 1972. *Star Carr: a case study in bioarchaeology*, Addison-Wesley Modular Publications, Module 10.

Clark, J.G.D., 1975. *The Earlier Stone Age Settlement of Scandinavia*.

Clark, J.G.D. and Godwin, H., 1940. 'A late bronze age find near Stuntney, Isle of Ely', *Ant. J. 20*:52–71.

Clark, J.G.D. and Rankine, W.F., 1939. 'Excavations at Farnham, Surrey, 1937–8, the Horsham culture and the question of mesolithic dwellings', *PPS 5*:61–108.

Clark, J.G.D. and Thompson, M.W., 1953. 'The groove and splinter technique of working antler in the upper palaeolithic and mesolithic', *PPS 24*:148–60.

Clark, R.M., 1975. 'A calibration curve for radiocarbon dates', *Antiquity 49*: 251–66.

Clarke, D.L., 1962. 'Matrix analysis and archaeology with particular reference to British beaker pottery', *PPS 28*:371–82.

Clarke, D.L., 1970. *Beaker Pottery of Great Britain and Ireland.*

Clarke, D.L., 1972. 'A provisional model of an iron age society and its settlement system', in Clarke, D.L. (ed.), *Models in Archaeology*: 801–9.

Clarke, D.L., 1976. 'Mesolithic Europe: the economic basis', in Sieveking, G. de G., Longworth, I.H. and Wilson, K.E. (eds.), *Problems in Economic and Social Archaeology*: 449–82.

Clarke, D.V., 1970. 'Bone dice and the Scottish iron age', *PPS 36*:214–32.

Clarke, D.V., 1971. 'Small finds of the Atlantic Province: problems of approach', *SAF 3*:22–54.

Clarke, D.V., 1976. *The Neolithic Village at Skara Brae: 1972–3 Excavations.*

Clarke, R.R., 1951. 'A hoard of metalwork of the early iron age from Ringstead, Norfolk', *PPS 17*:214–25.

Clarke, R.R., 1954. 'The early iron age treasure from Snettisham, Norfolk', *PPS 20*:27–86.

Cleere, H., 1974. 'The Roman iron industry of the Weald and its connexions with the *Classis Britannica*', *Arch. J. 131*:171–99.

Clifford, E.M., 1961. *Bagendon: A Belgic Oppidum.*

Close-Brooks, J., 1974–5. 'An iron age date for the Loch Lotus canoe', *PSAS 106*:199.

Coffey, G., 1912. 'Some recent prehistoric finds acquired by the Academy', *PRIA 30C*:83–93.

Coghlan, H.H. and Raftery, J., 1961. 'Irish prehistoric casting moulds', *Sibrium 6*: 223–44.

Coles, J.M., 1958–9. 'Scottish swan's-neck sunflower pins', *PSAS 92*:1–9.

Coles, J.M., 1959–60. 'Scottish late bronze age metalwork: typology distributions and chronology', *PSAS 93*:16–34.

Coles, J.M., 1961. 'CBA conference on the British bronze age, 1960', *Antiquity 35*:63–6.

Coles, J.M., 1962. 'European bronze age shields', *PPS 28*:156–90.

Coles, J.M., 1963a. 'New aspects of the mesolithic settlement of S.W. Scotland', *TDGNHAS 41*:67–98.

Coles, J.M., 1963b. 'Irish bronze age horns and their relation with northern Europe', *PPS 29*:326–56.

Coles, J.M., 1968–9. 'Scottish early bronze age metalwork', *PSAS 101*:1–110.

Coles, J.M., 1965. 'The archaeological evidence for a "Bull cult" in late bronze age Europe', *Antiquity 39*:217–19.

Coles, J.M., 1967. 'Some Irish horns of the late bronze age', *JRSAI 97*:113–17.

Coles, J.M., 1968. 'A neolithic god-dolly from Somerset, England', *Antiquity 42*:275–7.

Coles, J.M., 1968–9. 'Scottish early bronze age metalwork', *PSAS 101*:1–110.

Coles, J.M., 1971a. 'The early settlement of Scotland: excavations at Morton, Fife', *PPS 37.2*:284–366.

Coles, J.M., 1971b. 'Dowris and the late bronze age of Ireland: a footnote', *JRSAI 101*:164–5.

Coles, J.M., 1972. 'Late bronze age activity in the Somerset Levels', *Ant. J. 52*:269–75.

Coles, J.M., 1975. *Archaeology by Experiment.*

Coles, J.M., Coutts, H. and Ryder, M.L., 1964. 'A late bronze age find from Pyotdykes, Angus, Scotland', *PPS 30*:186–98.

Coles, J.M., Hibbert, F.A. and Clements, C.F., 1970. 'Prehistoric roads and tracks in Somerset, England: 2. Neolithic', *PPS 36*:125–51.

Coles, J.M., Hibbert, F.A. and Orme, B.J., 1973. 'Prehistoric roads and tracks in Somerset, England: 3. The Sweet track', *PPS 39*:256–93.

Coles, J.M. and Livens, R.G., 1958. 'A bronze sword from Douglas, Lanarkshire', *PSAS 91*:182–6.

Coles, J.M. and Orme, B.J., 1976. 'The Meare trackway: excavation of a bronze age structure in the Somerset Levels', *PPS 42*:298–318.

Coles, J.M., Orme, B.J., Hibbert, F.A., and Jones, R.A., 1975. 'Tinney's Ground, 1974', *Somerset Levels Papers 1*:42–53.

Coles, J.M. and Simpson, D.D.A. 1965. 'The excavation of a neolithic round barrow at Pitnacree, Perthshire', *PPS 31*:34–56.

Coles, J.M. and Simpson, D.D.A. (eds.), 1968. *Studies in Ancient Europe.*

Coles, J.M. and Taylor, J.J., 1969–70. 'The excavation of a midden in the Culbin Sands, Morayshire', *PSAS 102*:86–100.

Coles, J.M. and Taylor, J.J., 1971. 'The Wessex culture: a minimal view', *Antiquity, 45*:6–14.

Collins, A.E.P. and Seaby, W.A., 1960. 'Structures and small finds discovered at Lough Eskragh, Co. Tyrone', *UJA 23*:25–37.

Collins, A.E.P. and Waterman, D., 1955. *Millin Bay, a late neolithic cairn in Co. Down.*

Collis, J.R., 1968. 'Excavations at Owslebury, Hants', *Ant. J. 48*:18–31.

Collis, J.R., 1970. 'Excavations at Owslebury, Hants: a second interim report', *Ant. J. 50*:246–61.

Collis, J.R., 1971a. 'Functional and theoretical interpretations of British coinage', *World Archaeol. 3*:71–84.

Collis, J.R., 1971b. 'Markets and money ', in Hill and Jesson 1971: 97–104.

Collis, J.R., 1973. 'Burials with weapons in iron age Britain', *Germania 51*:121–33.

Collis, J.R., 1974. 'A functionalist approach to pre-Roman coinage', in Casey, J. and Reece, R. (eds.), *Coins and the Archaeologist*, BAR 4:1–11.

Collis, J.R., 1975. *Defended Sites of the late La Tène in Central and Western Europe*, BAR Suppl. Ser. 2.

Collis, J.R., 1977. 'The proper study of mankind is pots', in Collis, J.R. (ed.), *The Iron Age in Britain: A review.*

Collis, J.R. and Ralston, I.B.M., 1976. 'Late La Tène defences', *Germania 54*: 135–46.

Connah, G., 1965. 'Excavations at Knap Hill, Alton Priors', *WAM 60*:1–23.

Coombs, D.G., 1972. 'Late bronze age metalwork in south-east England', Ph. D. thesis, University of Cambridge.

Coombs, D.G., 1974. 'Ein spätbronzezeitlicher Depotfund von Snettisham (Norfolk)', *Arch. Korrespondenzblatt 4*:31–5.

Coombs, D.G., 1975a. 'Bronze age weapon hoards in Britain', *Arch. Atl. 1.1*:49–81.

Coombs, D.G., 1975b. 'The Dover Harbour find – a bronze age wreck?', *Arch. Atl. 1.2*:193–5.

Coombs, D.G., 1976a. 'Calais Wold round barrow, Humberside', *Antiquity 50*:130–1.

Coombs, D.G., 1976b. 'Excavations at Mam Tor, Derbyshire 1965–1969', in Harding D.W. 1976a: 147–52.

Coope, G.R. and Brophy, J.A., 1972. 'Late-glacial environmental changes indicated by a coleopteran succession from north Wales', *Boreas 1*: 97–142.

Corcoran, J.X.W.P., 1952. 'Tankards and tankard handles of the British early iron age', *PPS 18*:85–102.

Corcoran, J.X.W.P., 1961. 'The Caergwrle bowl: a contribution to the study of the bronze age', in Bersu, G. (ed.), *Ber. V. Inter. Kongr. f. Vor- u. Frühgeschichte Hamburg 1958* (Berlin): 200–3.

Corcoran, J.X.W.P., 1969. 'The Cotswold Severn group', in Powell, T.G.E. (ed.), *Megalithic Enquiries in the West of Britain*: 13–72.

Corcoran, J.X.W.P., 1970. 'Excavation of two chambered cairns at Mid Gleniron Farm, Glenluce, Wigtownshire', *TDGNHAS 46*:29–90.

Corcoran, J.X.W.P., 1972. 'Multi-period construction and the origins of the chambered long cairn in Western Britain and Ireland', in Lynch, C. and Burgess, C., *Prehistoric Man in Wales and the West: Essays in honour of Lily F. Chitty*: 31–64.

Cormack, W.F., 1963. 'Prehistoric site at Beckton, Lockerbie', *TDGNHAS 41*:111–15.

Cornwall, I.W., 1953. 'Soil science and archaeology with illustrations from some British bronze age monuments', *PPS 19*:129–47.

Cotton, M.A., 1954. 'British camps with timber laced ramparts', *Arch. J. 111*: 26–105.

Cotton, M.A., 1957. '*Muri gallici*', in Wheeler and Richardson 1957: 159–216.

Cotton, M.A. and Frere, S.S., 1968. 'Ivinghoe Beacon, excavations 1963–1965', *Records of Bucks. 18(3)*:187–260.

Couchman, C.R., 1975. 'The bronze age cemetery at Ardleigh, Essex – a further consideration', *Essex Archaeol. Hist. 7*: 14–32.

Cowen, J.D., 1933. 'Two bronze swords from Ewart Park, Wooler', *Arch. Ael. 10*:197–8.

Cowen, J.D., 1951. 'The earliest bronze swords in Britain and their origins on the continent', *PPS 17*:195–213.

Cowen, J.D., 1952. 'Bronze swords in Northern Europe: a reconsideration of Sprockhoff's *Griffzungenschwerter*', *PPS 18*:129–47.

Cowen, J.D., 1956. 'Les origines des épées de bronze du type à langue de carpe', *Actes de la IV Session Congr. Intern. de Ciencas Prehist. y Protohis.: Madrid 1954* (Zaragoza): 639–42.

Cowen, J.D., 1967. 'The Hallstatt sword of bronze: on the Continent and in Britain', *PPS 33*:377–454.

Cra'ster, M.D., 1961. 'The Aldwick iron age settlement, Barley, Hertfordshire', *PCAS 54*:22–46.

Craw, H.J., 1928–9. 'On a jet necklace from a cist at Poltalloch, Argyll', *PSAS 63*:154–89.

Crawford, O.G.S., 1921. 'The ancient settlement at Harlyn Bay', *Ant. J. 1*:283–299.

Crawford, O.G.S. and Wheeler, R.E.M., 1920–1. 'The Llynfawr and other hoards of the bronze age', *Archaeologia 71*:133–40.

Crittall, E. (ed.), 1973. *A History of Wiltshire*, I pt. 2. The Victoria History of the Counties of England.

Cunliffe, B.W., 1970. 'A bronze age settlement at Chalton, Hampshire (site 78)', *Ant. J. 50*:1–13.

Cunliffe, B.W., 1971a. 'Danebury, Hampshire: first interim report on the excavations, 1969–70', *Ant. J. 51*:240–52.

Cunliffe, B.W., 1971b. 'Aspects of hillforts and their cultural environments', in Hill and Jesson 1971:53–69.

Cunliffe, B.W., 1972. 'The late iron age metalwork from Bulbury, Dorset', *Ant. J.* 52: 293–308.

Cunliffe, B.W., 1973. 'Chalton, Hants: the evolution of a landscape', *Ant. J.* 53:173–90.

Cunliffe, B.W., 1974. *Iron Age Communities in Britain: An account of England, Scotland and Wales from the seventh century* BC *until the Roman conquest* (2nd edn 1978).

Cunliffe, B.W., 1976a. 'The origins of urbanisation in Britain', in Cunliffe, B.W. and Rowley, T. (eds.), *Oppida in Barbarian Europe*, BAR Suppl. Ser. 11:135–61.

Cunliffe, B.W., 1976b. *Iron Age Sites in Central Southern England*. CBA Res. Rep. 16.

Cunliffe, B.W., 1976c. 'Danebury, Hampshire: second interim report on the excavations 1971–5', *Ant. J.* 56.2:198–216.

Cunliffe, B.W., 1978a. *Iron Age Communities in Britain* (rev. edn).

Cunliffe, B.W., 1978b. *Hengistbury Head*.

Cunliffe, B.W. and Phillipson, D.W., 1968. 'Excavation at Eldon's Seat, Encombe, Dorset, England', *PPS 34*:191–237.

Cunnington, M.E., 1933. 'Excavations at Yarnbury Castle Camp, 1932', *WAM 36*:125–39.

Cunnington, M.E., 1923. *The Early Iron Age Inhabited Site at All Cannings Cross*.

Cunnington, M.E., 1931. 'The "Sanctuary" on Overton Hill, near Avebury', *WAM 45*:300–35.

Cunnington, M.E., 1932. 'Was there a second Belgic invasion (represented by bead-rim pottery)?', *Ant. J. 12*:27–34.

Cunnington, M.E., 1933. 'Excavations at Yarnbury Castle Camp, 1932', *WAM 46*:198–213.

Cunnington, M.E. and Cunnington, B.H., 1913. 'Casterley Camp excavations', *WAM 38*:52–105.

Curle, A.O., 1936. 'Account of an excavation of an iron smeltery and of an associated dwelling and tumuli at Wiltrow in the parish of Dunrossness, Shetland', *PSAS 70*:153–69.

Curwen, E.C., 1932. 'Excavations at Hollingbury Camp, Sussex', *Ant. J. 12*:1–16.

Curwen, E.C., 1934a. 'Excavations in Whitehawk neolithic camp, Brighton', *Ant. J. 14*:99–133.

Curwen, E.C., 1934b. 'A late bronze age farm and a neolithic pit dwelling on New Barn Down, Clapham, near Worthing', *SAC 75*:137–70.

Curwen, E.C., 1936. 'Excavations in Whitehawk neolithic camp, Brighton', *SAC 77*:60–92.

Curwen, E.C., 1948. 'A bronze cauldron from Sompting, Sussex', *Ant. J. 28*:157–63.

Curwen, E.C. and Holleyman, G.A., 1935. 'Late bronze age lynchet settlements on Plumpton Plain, Sussex', *PPS 1*:16–38.

Dacre, M., 1968. 'Kimpton', *CA 11*:284–6.

Daniel, G.E., 1967. 'Northmen and Southmen', *Antiquity 41*:313–17.

Davey, P.J., 1971. 'The distribution of later bronze age metalwork from Lincolnshire', *PPS 37*:96–111.

Davey, P.J., 1973. 'Bronze age metalwork from Lincolnshire', *Archaeologia 104*:51–127.

Davey, P.J. and Knowles, G.C., 1972. 'The Appleby hoard', *Arch. J. 128*:51–127.

Davies, D.G., 1967. 'The Guilsfield hoard: a reconsideration', *Ant. J. 47*:95–108.

Davies, J.L. and Spratling, M.G., 1976. 'The Seven Sisters hoard: a centenary study', in Boon, G.C. and Lewis, J.M. (eds.), *Welsh Antiquity: Essays mainly on prehistoric topics presented to H.N. Savory*: 121–47.

Deady, J. and Doran, E., 1972. 'Prehistoric copper mines: Mount Gabriel Co. Cork', *J. Cork. Hist. Arch. Soc. 77*:25–7.

De Boe, G. and Hubert, F., 1977. 'Une installation portuaire d'époque romaine à Pommeroeul', *Arch. Belgica 192*.

De Laet, S.J., 1974. *Prehistorische Kulturen in het zuiden der Lage Landen* (Wetteren).

De Laet, S.J., 1976. 'Native and Celt in the iron age of the Low Countries', in Megaw 1976b: 191–8.

De Laet, S.J. and Glasbergen, W., 1959. *De Voorgeschiedenis der Lage Landen* (Groningen).

De Navarro, J.M., 1972. *The Finds from the Site of La Tène I: Scabbards and the swords found in them*.

Denford, G.T., 1975. 'Economy and location of bronze age "arable" settlements on Dartmoor', *Bull. Inst. Arch. Univ. London 12*:175–96.

Dennell, R.W., 1976. 'Prehistoric crop cultivation in southern England: a reconsideration', *Ant. J. 56*:11–23.

De Valera, R.,1960. 'The court cairns of Ireland', *PRIA 60*:9–140.

De Valera, R. and Ó Nualláin, S., 1961. *Survey of the Megalithic Tombs of Ireland*, vol. I (Dublin).

Dillon, M. and Chadwick, N., 1967. *The Celtic Realms*.

Dimbleby, G.W., 1960. 'Iron-age land use on Bonchester Hill', *PSAS 93*:237–8.

Dimbleby, G.W., 1962. *The Development of British Heathlands and their Soils*, Oxford Forestry Memoir, No. 23.

Dimbleby, G.W., 1968. 'Pollen analysis', in Money 1968: 193–7.

Dimbleby, G.W., 1969. 'Report on pollen analysis', in Piercy Fox 1969: 196–9.

Dimbleby, G.W., 1970. 'Pollen analysis', in Piercy Fox, N., 'Excavation of the iron age camp at Squerryes, Westerham', *Arch. Cant. 85*:29–33.

Dimbleby, G.W., 1977. *Ecology and Archaeology*.

Dixon, P.W. [n.d.]. *Crickley Hill: fifth report 1973*.

Dixon, P.W., 1972. 'Crickley Hill 1969–71', *Antiquity 46*: 49–52.

Dixon, P.W., 1973. 'Longhouse and roundhouse at Crickley Hill', *Antiquity 47*:56–59.

Dixon, P.W., 1976. 'Crickley Hill, 1969–1972', in Harding D.W. 1976a: 161–75.

Dixon, P.W. and Borne, P., 1977. *Crickley Hill and Gloucestershire Prehistory*.

Drewett, P.C., 1975. 'The excavation of an oval burial mound of the third millennium B.C. at Alfriston, East Sussex, 1974', *PPS 41*:119–52.

Drewett, P.C., 1978. 'Field systems and land allotment in Sussex, 3rd millennium BC to 4th century AD', in Bowen and Fowler 1978: 67–80.

Drury, P.J., 1974. 'Little Waltham', *CA 4*:10–13.

Drury, P.J., 1978. 'Little Waltham and pre-Belgic iron age settlement in Essex', in Cunliffe, B.W. and Rowley, T.R. (eds.), *Lowland Iron Age Communities in Europe*, BAR Suppl. Ser. 48.

Dudley, D., 1956. 'An excavation at Bodrifty, Mulfa Hill, near Penzance, Cornwall', *Arch. J. 113*:1–32.

Dudley, D. and Jope, E.M., 1965. 'An iron age cist-burial with two brooches from Trerone, north Cornwall', *Cornish Archaeol. 4*:18–23.

Duignan, M., 1976. 'The Turoe stone: its place in insular La Tène art', in Duval, P.-M. and Hawkes, C.F.C. (eds.), *Celtic Art in Ancient Europe: Five protohistoric centuries*: 201–17.

Dunning, G.C., 1934. 'The swan's neck and ring-headed pins of the early iron age in Britain', *Arch. J. 91*:269–95.

Dunning, G.C., 1936. 'Note on two urns of overhanging-rim type found abroad', *Ant. J. 16*:160–4.

Dunning, G.C., 1959. 'The distribution of socketed axes of Breton type', *UJA 22*:53–5.

Dunning, G.C., 1976. 'Salmonsbury, Bourton-on-the-Water, Gloucestershire', in Harding D.W. 1976a: 75–118.

Dunning, G.C., Hooley, W., and Tildesley, M.L., 1929. 'Excavation of an early iron age village on Worthy Down, Winchester', *Procs. Hants Field Club 10*: 178–92.

Durno, S.E., 1956. 'Pollen analysis on peat deposits in Scotland', *Scot. Geog. Mag. 72*:177–87.

Durno, S.E. and Romans, J.C.C., 1969. 'Evidence for variations in the altitudinal zonation of climate in Scotland and Northern England since the boreal period', *Scot. Geog. Mag. 85*:31–3.

Duval, P.-M., 1977. *Les Celtes* (Paris).

Dyer, J.F., 1961. 'Dray's Ditches, Bedfordshire, and early iron age territorial boundaries in the eastern Chilterns', *Ant. J. 42*:44–62.

Dymond, C.W., 1902. *Worlebury, an Ancient Stronghold in the County of Somerset.*

Edwardson, A.R., 1965. 'A spirally decorated object from Garboldisham', *Antiquity 39*:145.

Elgee, F., 1930. *Early Man in North-East Yorkshire.*

Elgee, H.W. and Elgee, F., 1949. 'An early bronze age burial in a boat-shaped wooden coffin from N.E. Yorks', *PPS 15*:87–106.

Ellison, A. and Drewett, P.C., 1971. 'Pits and post-holes in the British early iron age: some alternative explanations', *PPS 37*:183–94.

Ellison, A. and Harriss, J., 1972. 'Settlement and land use in the prehistory and early history of southern England: a study based on locational models', in Clarke, D.L. (ed.), *Models in Archaeology*: 911–62.

Elsdon, S.M., 1975. *Stamp and Roulette Decorated Pottery of the La Tène Period in Eastern England: A study in geometric designs*, BAR 10.

Eogan, G., 1964. 'The later bronze age in Ireland in the light of recent research', *PPS 30*:268–351.

Eogan, G., 1965. *Catalogue of Irish Bronze Swords* (Dublin).

Eogan, G., 1967. 'The associated finds of gold bar torcs', *JRSAI 97*:129–75.

Eogan, G., 1972. '"Sleeve-fasteners" of the late bronze age', in Lynch, F. and Burgess, C.B. (eds.), *Prehistoric Man in Wales and the West: Essays in honour of Lily F. Chitty*:189–209.

Eogan, G., 1973. 'A decade of excavations at Knowth, Co. Meath', *Irish Universities Rev. 3*:66–79.

Eogan, G., 1974a. 'Regionale Gruppierungen in der Spätbronzezeit Irlands', *Arch. Korrespondenzblatt 4*:319–27.

Eogan, G., 1974b. 'Pins of the Irish late bronze age', *JRSAI 104*:74–119.

Erith, F.H. and Holbert, P.R., 1970. 'The Iron Age "A" farmstead at Vinces Farm, Ardleigh', *Colchester Arch. Group Q. Bull. 13.1*:1–26.

Erith, F.H. and Longworth, I.H., 1960. 'A bronze age urnfield on Vinces Farm, Ardleigh, Essex', *PPS 26*:178–92.

Evans, A.J., 1890. 'On a late-Celtic urn-field at Aylesford, Kent', *Archaeologia 52*:315–88.

Evans, E.E., 1930. 'The sword bearers', *Antiquity 4*:157–72.

Evans, E.E., 1938. 'Doey's Cairn, Dunloy', *UJA 1*:7–19.

Evans, E.E. and Megaw, B.R.S., 1937. 'The multiple cist cairn at Mount Stewart, Co. Down', *PPS 3*:29–42.

Evans, Sir John, 1881. *The Ancient Bronze Implements, Weapons, and Ornaments of Great Britain and Ireland.*

Evans, J.G., 1971a. 'Notes on the environment of the earliest farming communities in Britain', in Simpson, D.D.A. (ed.), *Economy and Settlement in Neolithic and Early Bronze Age Britain and Europe*: 11–26.

Evans, J.G., 1971b. 'Habitat change on the calcareous soils of Britain: the impact of neolithic man', in Simpson, D.D.A. (ed.), *Economy and Settlement in Neolithic and Early Bronze Age Britain and Europe*: 27–74.

Evans, J.G., 1972a. 'Ice-wedge casts at Broome Heath, Norfolk', in Wainwright, G.J., 'The excavation of a neolithic settlement on Broome Heath, Ditchingham, Norfolk, England', *PPS 38*:77–86.

Evans, J.G., 1972b. *Land Snails in Archaeology.*

Evans, J.G., 1975. *The Environment of Early Man in the British Isles.*

Evans, J.G., Limbrey, S. and Cleere, H. (eds.), 1975. *The Effects of Man on the Landscape: the Highland Zone*, CBA Res. Rep. 11.

Evans, J.G. and Valentine, K.W.G., 1974. 'Ecological changes induced by prehistoric man at Pitstone, Buckinghamshire', *JAS 1*:343–51.

Evens, E.D., Smith, I.F. and Wallis, F.S., 1972. 'The petrological identification of stone implements from south-west England', *PPS 38*:235–75.

Ewbank, J.M., Phillipson, D.W. and Whitehouse, R.D., 1964. 'Sheep in the iron age: a method of study', *PPS 30*:423–6.

Eyre, S.R., 1968. *Vegetation and Soils: A world picture.*

Fairhurst, H., 1954. 'The geography of Scotland in prehistoric times', *Trans. Glasgow Arch. Soc. 13*:1–16.

Fairhurst, H., 1971a. 'Kilphedir and hut circle sites in northern Scotland', *SAF 3*:1–10.

Fairhurst, H., 1971b. Review of Hamilton J.R.C. 1968b, *Glasgow Arch. J. 2*:120–121.

Fairhurst, H. and Taylor, D.B., 1971. 'A hut circle settlement at Kilphedir, Sutherland', *PSAS 103*:65–9.

Farrar, R.A.H., 1975. 'Prehistoric and Roman saltworks in Dorset' in de Brisay, K.W. and Evans, K.A. (eds.), *Salt: The study of an ancient industry*: 14–20.

Farrell, A.W. and Penny, S. with Jope, E.M., 1975. 'The Broighter boat: a reassessment', *IARF 2.2*:15–28.

Feachem, R.W., 1958. 'The "Cairnmuir" hoard from Netherurd, Peeblesshire', *PSAS 91*:112–16.

Feachem, R.W., 1959. 'Glenachan Rig Homestead, Cardon, Peeblesshire', *PSAS 92*:15–24.

Feachem, R.W., 1960. 'The palisaded settlements at Harehope, Peeblesshire', *PSAS 93*:174–91.

Feachem, R.W., 1961. 'Unenclosed platform settlements', *PSAS 94*:79–85.

Feachem, R.W., 1965. *The North Britons.*

Feachem, R.W., 1966. 'The hill-forts of northern Britain', in Rivet 1966: 59–87.

Feachem, R.W., 1971. 'Unfinished hill-forts', in Hill and Jesson 1971: 19–39.

Feachem, R.W., 1973. 'Ancient agriculture in the highland zone of Britain', *PPS 39*:332–53.

Fell, C.I., 1936. 'The Hunsbury hill-fort, Northants.', *Arch. J. 93*:57–100.

Fell, C.I. and Coles, J.M., 1965. 'Reconsideration of the Ambleside hoard and the burial at Butts Beck Quarry, Dalton in Furness', *Trans. Cumberland and Westmorland Ant. Arch. Soc. 65*:38–52.

Field, N.H., Mathews, C.L. and Smith, I.F., 1964. 'New neolithic sites in Dorset with a note on the distribution of neolithic storage pits in Britain', *PPS 30*:352–381.

Flanagan, L.N.W., 1961. 'Wessex and Ireland in the early and middle bronze ages', *Ber. V Inter. Kongr. f. Vor- und Frühgeschichte Hamburg 1958* (Berlin): 284–91.

Flanagan, L.N.W., 1976. 'The composition of Irish bronze age cemeteries', *IARF 3.2*:7–20.

Fleming, A., 1969. 'The myth of the mother goddess', *World Archaeol. 1*:247–61.

Fleming, A., 1971a. 'Bronze age agriculture on the marginal lands of north-east Yorkshire', *Agric. Hist. Rev. 19*:1–24.

Fleming, A., 1971b. 'Territorial patterns in bronze age Wessex', *PPS 37*:138–66.

Fleming, A., 1972. 'Vision and design: approaches to ceremonial monument typology', *Man 7*: 57–72.

Fleming, A., 1973. 'Tombs for the living', *Man 8.2*:177–93.

Fleming, A., 1976. 'The Dartmoor reaves', *CA 5*:250–2.

Fleming, A., 1978. 'The Dartmoor reaves', in Bowen and Fowler 1978: 17–41.

Fleming, A., Collis, J. with Jones, R.L., 1973. 'A late prehistoric reave system near Cholwich Town, Dartmoor', *Devon Arch. Soc. 31*:1–21.

Forde-Johnston, J.L., 1976. *Hillforts of the Iron Age in England and Wales: A survey of the surface evidence*.

Fowler, E., 1960. 'The origins and development of the penannular brooch in Europe', *PPS 26*:149–77.

Fowler, P.J., 1971. 'Early prehistoric agriculture in western Europe: some archaeological evidence', in Simpson, D.D.A. (ed.), *Economy and Settlement in Neolithic and Early Bronze Age Britain and Europe*: 153–82.

Fowler, P.J. (ed.), 1975. *Recent Work in Rural Archaeology*.

Fowler, P.J. and Evans, J.G., 1967. 'Plough-marks, lynchets and early fields', *Antiquity 41*:289–301.

Fox, A., 1952. 'Hill-slope and related earthworks in south-west England and south Wales', *Arch. J. 109*:1–22.

Fox, A., 1954. 'Celtic fields and farms on Dartmoor, in the light of recent excavations at Kestor', *PPS 20*:87–102.

Fox, A., 1957. 'Excavations on Dean Moor, in the Avon Valley, 1954–1956', *Trans. Devon. Assoc. 89*:18–77.

Fox, A., 1961. 'Southwestern hillforts', in Frere, S.S. (ed.), *Problems of the Iron Age in Southern Britain*: 35–60.

Fox, A., 1973. *South West England 3,500 B.C.–A.D. 600* (rev. edn).

Fox, A. and Britton, D., 1969. 'A continental palstave from the ancient field system on Horridge Common settlement, Dartmoor, England', *PPS 35*:223–5.

Fox, A. and Pollard, S.H., 1973. 'A decorated bronze mirror from an iron age settlement at Holcombe, Devon', *Ant. J. 53*:16–41.

Fox, C.F., 1923. *The Archaeology of the Cambridge Region*.

Fox, C.F., 1928. 'A bronze age refuse pit at Swanwick, Hants.', *Ant. J. 8*:331–6.

Fox, C.F., 1932. *The Personality of Britain*.

Fox, C.F., 1933. 'The distribution of man in East Anglia, c.2300 BC – 50 AD. A contribution to the prehistory of the region', *Procs. Prehist. Soc. East Anglia 7.2*:149–64.

Fox, C.F., 1939. 'The socketed bronze sickles of the British Isles', *PPS 5*:223–78.

Fox, C.F., 1946. *A Find of the Early Iron Age from Llyn Cerrig Bach, Anglesey.*

Fox, C.F., 1958. *Pattern and Purpose: Early Celtic art in Britain.*

Fox, C.F. and Hull, M.R., 1948. 'The incised ornament on the Celtic mirror from Colchester, Essex', *Ant. J. 28*:123–37.

Fox, C.F. and Hyde, H.A., 1939. 'A second cauldron and an iron sword from the Llyn Fawr hoard', *Ant. J. 19*:369–404.

Frey, O.-H. with Megaw, J.V.S., 1976. 'Palmette and circle; early Celtic art in Britain and its continental background', *PPS 42*:47–65.

Froom, F.R., 1976 *Wawcott III: a stratified mesolithic succession*, BAR 27.

Gardner, W. and Savory, H.N., 1964. *Dinorben: A hillfort occupied in early iron age and Roman times*.

Garrod, D.A.E., 1926. *The Upper Palaeolithic Age in Britain*.

Gaucher, G. and Mohen, J.P., 1974. 'L'age du bronze dans le nord de la France', *Bull. special de la Soc. de Préhist. du Nord 9* (Amiens).

Geikie, J., 1880. 'Discovery of an ancient canoe in the old alluvium of the Tay at Perth', *Scottish Naturalist 5*:1–7.

Gelling, P.S., 1970. 'The South Barrule hill-fort reconsidered', *J. Manx Mus. 7*: 86, 145–7.

Gelling, P.S., 1972. 'The hill-fort on South Barrule, and its position in the Manx iron age', in Lynch, F. and Burgess, C.B. (eds.), *Prehistoric Man in Wales and the West: Essays in honour of Lily F. Chitty*: 285–92.

Gerloff, S., 1975. 'The early bronze age dagger in Great Britain and a reconsideration of the Wessex culture', *Prähist. Bronzefunde 6*:2 (Munich).

Giot, P.R., 1971. 'The impact of radiocarbon dating on the establishment of the prehistoric chronology of Brittany', *PPS 37*:208–17.

Giot, P.R., with L'Helgouach, J. and Briard, J., 1960. *Brittany*.

Gjessing, G., 1953. 'The circumpolar stone age', *Antiquity 27*:131–6.

Glasbergen, W., 1954. 'Barrow excavations in the Eight Beatitudes. II. The implications', *Palaeohistoria 3*:1–204.

Glasbergen, W., 1957. *De urn van Toterfout en de reformatie van de Britse Bronstijd* (Groningen and Djakarta).

Glob, P.V., 1951. *Ard og plov i Nordens Oldtid*, Jysk Arkaeologisk Selskab Skr. 1.

Glob, P.V., 1974. *The Mound People*.

Godwin, H., 1962. 'Vegetational history of the Kentish chalk down as seen at Wingham and Frogholt', *Veröff. geobot. Inst. Zürich 37*:83–99.

Godwin, H., 1966. 'Introductory address', in Sawyer, J.S. (ed.), *World Climate from 8000 to 0 B.C.*: 3–14.

Godwin, H., 1975. *The History of the British Flora: A factual basis for phytogeography*.

Gogan, L.S., 1931. 'The Ballycotton gold collar or "gorget"', *J. Cork Hist. Arch. Soc. 36*: 87–100.

Graham, A., 1947. 'Some observations on the brochs', *PSAS 81*:48–99.

Graham, A., 1951. 'Archaeological gleanings from dark age records', *PSAS 85*:64–91.

Graham, A., 1957. 'Cairnfields in Scotland', *PSAS 90*:7–23.

Gräslund, B., 1967. 'The Herzsprung shield type and its origins', *Acta Arch. 38*:59–71.

Gray, H.St G., 1966. *The Meare Lake Village, Vol. III*.

Green, C., 1949. 'The Birdlip early iron age burials: a review', *PPS 15*:188–90.

Green, M.J., 1973. 'A late bronze age socketed axe mould from Worthing', *SAC 3*: 87–92.

Greenhill, B., 1976. *Archaeology of the Boat: A new introductory study*.

Greenwell, W., 1890. 'Recent researches in barrows . . . ' *Archaeologia 52*:1–72.

Greenwell, W., 1894. 'Antiquities of the bronze age found in the Heathery Burn Cave, near Stanhope, County Durham', *Archaeologia 54*:87–114.

Greig, J.C., 1970. 'Excavations at Castle Point, Troup, Banffshire', *Aberdeen Univ. Rev. 43*:274–83.

Greig, J.C., 1971. 'Excavations at Cullykhan, Castle Point, Troup, Banffshire', *SAF 3*:15–21.

Greig, J.C., 1972. 'Cullykhan', *CA 3*:227–31.

Gresham, C.A., 1939. 'Spettisbury Rings, Dorset', *Arch. J. 96*:114–31.

Gresswell, R.K., 1958. *The Physical Geography of Glaciers and Glaciation*.

Grimes, W.F., 1961. 'Draughton, Heathrow and Colsterworth', in Frere, S.S. (ed.), *Problems of the Iron Age in Southern Britain*: 21–3.

Grinsell, L.V., 1953. *The Ancient Burial Mounds of England*.

Grinsell, L.V., 1959. *Dorset Barrows*.

Grinsell, L.V., 1974. 'Disc barrows', *PPS 40*:79–112.

Guido, C.M., 1974. 'A Scottish crannog re-dated', *Antiquity 48*:54–5.

Guilbert, G.C., 1975a. 'Planned hill-fort interiors', *PPS 41*:203–21.

Guilbert, G.C., 1975b. 'Moel y Gaer, 1973: an area excavation on the defences', *Antiquity 49*:109–17.

Guilbert, G.C., 1976. 'Moel y Gaer (Rhosesmor) 1972–1973: An area excavation in the interior', in Harding D.W. 1976a: 303–17.

Guthrie, A., 1969. 'Excavation of a settlement at Goldherring, Sancreed, 1958–61', *Cornish Archaeol. 8*:5–39.

Hachmann, R., 1976. 'The problem of the Belgae seen from the continent', *Bull. Inst. Arch. Univ. London 13*:117–37.

Haffner, A.,1974. 'Zum End der Latènezeit im Mittelrheingebiet . . . ', *Arch. Korrespondenzblatt 4*:59–72.

Haldane, J.W., 1970. 'A study of the chemical composition of pre-Roman ironwork from Somerset', *Bull. Hist. Metall. Group 4*:53–66.

Hall, E.T. and Roberts, G., 1962. 'Analysis of the Moulsford torc', *Archaeometry 5*:28–31.

Hallam, J.S., Edwards, B.J.N., Barnes, B. and Stuart, A.J., 1973. 'A Late Glacial elk with associated barbed points from High Furlong, Lancashire', *PPS 39*:100–28.

Hamilton, J.R.C., 1956. *Excavations at Jarlshof, Shetland*.

Hamilton, J.R.C., 1966a. 'The origin and development of iron age forts in western Britain', *Actes du VII CISPP* (Prague) 2 [1971]: 846–9.

Hamilton, J.R.C., 1966b. 'Brochs and broch builders', in Rivet 1966:111–30.

Hamilton, J.R.C., 1968a. 'Iron age forts and epic literature', *Antiquity 42*:103–8.

Hamilton, J.R.C., 1968b. *Excavations at Clickhimin, Shetland*, Ministry of Public Buildings and Works, Arch. Rep. no. 6.

Harbison, P., 1968. 'Catalogue of Irish early bronze age associated finds containing copper or bronze', *PRIA 67*:35–91.

Harbison, P., 1969a. 'The daggers and halberds of the early bronze age in Ireland', *Prähist. Bronzefunde 6.1* (Munich).

Harbison, P., 1969b. 'The axes of the early bronze age in Ireland', *Prähist. Bronzefunde 9.1* (Munich).

Harbison, P., 1971. 'Wooden and stone *chevaux-de-frise* in central and western Europe', *PPS 37*:195–225.

Harbison, P. and Laing, L.R., 1974. *Some Iron Age Mediterranean Imports in England*, BAR 5.

Hardaker, R., 1974. *A Corpus of Early Bronze Age Dagger Pommels from Great Britain and Ireland*, BAR 3.

Harden, D.B.,1950. 'Italic and Etruscan finds in Britain', *Atti del 1° Congresso Internazionale di Preistoria e Protostoria Mediterranea*: 315–24.

Harding, D.W., 1972. *The Iron Age of the Upper Thames Basin.*

Harding, D.W., 1973. 'Round and rectangular: iron age houses, British and foreign', in Hawkes, C.F.C. and Hawkes, S.C. (eds.), *Archaeology into History I: Greeks, Celts and Romans*: 43–62.

Harding, D.W., 1974. *The Iron Age in Lowland Britain.*

Harding, D.W. (ed.), 1976a. *Hillforts: Later prehistoric earthworks in Britain and Ireland.*

Harding, D.W., 1976b. 'Blewburton Hill, Berkshire: re-excavation and reappraisal', in Harding D.W. 1976a: 133–46.

Harding, D.W. and Blake, I.M., 1963. 'An early iron age settlement in Dorset', *Antiquity 37*:63–4.

Harding, J.M., 1964. 'Interim report on the excavation of a late bronze age homestead in Weston Wood, Albury, Surrey', *SAC 61*:29–38.

Harrison, R.J., 1974. 'Origins of the bell beaker cultures', *Antiquity 48*:99–109.

Harrison, R.J., 1977. *The Bell Beaker Cultures of Spain and Portugal,* American School Prehist. Res. Bull. 35 (Cambridge, Mass.).

Hartley, B.R., 1972. 'The Roman Occupation of Scotland: the evidence of samian ware', *Britannia 3*:1–55.

Hartnett, P.J., 1971. 'The excavation of two tumuli at Fourknocks (Sites II and III), Co. Meath', *PRIA 71*:35–89.

Hawkes, C.F.C., 1931. 'Hillforts', *Antiquity 5*:60–97.

Hawkes, C.F.C., 1932. 'The Towednack gold hoard', *Man 32*:177–86.

Hawkes, C.F.C., 1935. 'The pottery from the sites on Plumpton Plain', *PPS 1*:39–59.

Hawkes, C.F.C., 1939a. 'The excavations at Quarley Hill, 1938', *Procs. Hants. Field Club 14*:136–94.

Hawkes, C.F.C., 1939b. 'The Caburn pottery and its implications', *SAC 80*:217–62.

Hawkes, C.F.C., 1940a. 'The Marnian pottery and La Tène I brooch from Worth, Kent', *Ant. J. 20*:115–21.

Hawkes, C.F.C., 1940b. 'La Tène I brooches from Deal, Preston Candover and East Dean', *Ant. J. 20*:276–9.

Hawkes, C.F.C., 1942. 'The Deverel urn and the Picardy pin: a phase of bronze age settlement in Kent', *PPS 8*:26–47.

Hawkes, C.F.C., 1948. 'From bronze age to iron age: middle Europe, Italy and the North and West', *PPS 14*:196–218.

Hawkes, C.F.C., 1959. 'The ABC of the British iron age', *Antiquity 33*:170–82.

Hawkes, C.F.C., 1960. 'A scheme for the British bronze age', *CBA Conference on the British Bronze Age*, London (cyclostyled).

Hawkes, C.F.C., 1961. 'Gold ear-rings of the bronze age, East and West', *Folklore 72*:438–74.

Hawkes, C.F.C., 1962. 'Archaeological significance of the Moulsford torc analysis', *Archaeometry 5*:33–7.

Hawkes, C.F.C., 1968. 'New thoughts on the Belgae', *Antiquity 42*:6–16.

Hawkes, C.F.C., 1971. 'The Sintra gold collar', in Sieveking, G. de G. (ed.), *Prehistoric and Roman Studies (BMQ 35)*: 38–50.

Hawkes, C.F.C., 1972. 'Europe and England: fact and fog', *Helinium 12*:105–16.

Hawkes, C.F.C., 1976. 'St Catharine's Hill, Winchester: The report of 1930 reassessed', in Harding D.W. 1976a: 59–74.

Hawkes, C.F.C. and Clarke, R.R., 1963. 'Gahlstorf and Caister-on-Sea: two finds of late bronze age Irish gold', in Foster, I.Ll. and Alcock, L. (eds.), *Culture and Environment: Essays in honour of Sir Cyril Fox*: 193–250.

Hawkes, C.F.C. and Dunning, G.C., 1930. 'The Belgae of Gaul and Britain', *Arch. J. 87*:150–335.

Hawkes, C.F.C. and Dunning, G.C., 1932. 'The second Belgic invasion: a reply to Mrs B.H. Cunnington', *Ant. J. 12*:411–30.

Hawkes, C.F.C. and Fell, C.I., 1943. 'The early iron age settlement at Fengate, Peterborough', *Arch. J. 100*:188–223.

Hawkes, C.F.C. and Hull, M.R., 1947. *Camulodunum*.

Hawkes, C.F.C., Myres, J.N.L. and Stevens, C.G., 1930. 'St Catharine's Hill, Winchester', *Procs. Hants. Field Club 11.*

Hawkes, C.F.C. and Smith, M.A., 1957. 'On some buckets and cauldrons of the bronze and early iron ages', *Ant. J. 37*:131–98.

Haworth, R.G., 1971. 'The horse harness of the Irish early iron age', *UJA 34*:26–49.

Hedges, J.W., 1974. 'The burnt mound at Liddle Farm, Orkney', *CA 4*:251–3.

Hedges, J.W., 1975. 'Excavation of two Orcadian burnt mounds at Liddle and Beaquoy', *PSAS 106*:39–98.

Helbaek, H., 1952. 'Early crops in southern England', *PPS 18*:194–233.

Hemp, W.J., 1930. 'The chambered cairn of Bryn Celli Ddu', *Archaeologia 70*:179–214.

Hencken, H.O'N., 1932. *The Archaeology of Cornwall and Scilly.*

Hencken, H.O'N., 1933. 'An excavation by H.M. Office of Works at Chysauster, Cornwall, 1931', *Archaeologia 83*:237–84.

Hencken, H.O'N., 1942. 'Ballinderry Crannog no. 21', *PRIA 47c*: 1–76.

Hencken, H.O'N., 1950. 'Herzsprung shields and Greek trade', *American J. Archaeol. 54*:295–309.

Hencken, T.C., 1938. 'The excavation of the iron age camp on Bredon Hill, Gloucestershire, 1935–37', *Arch. J. 95*:1–111.

Henshall, A.S., 1950. 'Textiles and weaving appliances in prehistoric Britain', *PPS 16*:130–62.

Henshall, A.S., 1956. 'A long cist cemetery at Parkburn Sand Pit, Lasswade, Midlothian', *PSAS 89*:252–83.

Henshall, A.S., 1963. *The Chambered Tombs of Scotland, I.*

Henshall, A.S., 1970. 'The long cairns of eastern Scotland', *SAF 2*: 29–49.

Henshall, A.S., 1972. *The Chambered Tombs of Scotland, II.*

Herity, M., 1971. 'Prehistoric fields in Ireland', *Irish Universities Review 1*:258–65.

Herity, M., 1974. *Irish Passage Graves* (Dublin).

Herity, M. and Eogan, G., 1977. *Ireland in Prehistory.*

Hick, S.P., 1972. 'The impact of man on the East Moor of Derbyshire from mesolithic times', *Arch. J. 129*:1–21.

Higgs, E.S., 1959. 'Excavations at a mesolithic site at Downton, nr. Salisbury, Wilts.', *PPS 25*:209–32.

Higgs, E.S. and White, J.P., 1963. 'Autumn killing', *Antiquity 37*:282–9.

Hill, D. and Jesson, M. (eds.), 1971. *The Iron Age and its Hill-forts,* Univ. of Southampton Monograph Ser.

Hodder, I. and Hedges, J.W., 1977. '"Weaving combs": – their typology and distribution with some introductory remarks on data and function', in Collis J.R. (ed.), *The Iron Age in Britain: A review*: 17–28.

Hodder, I. and Orton, C., 1976. *Spatial Analysis in Archaeology.*

Hodges, H.W.M., 1954. 'Studies in the late bronze age in Ireland: 1, Stone and clay moulds, and wooden models for bronze implements', *UJA 17*:62–80.

Hodges, H.W.M., 1955. 'The excavation of a group of cooking places at Ballycroghan, Co. Down', *UJA 18*:18–28.

Hodges, H.W.M., 1957. 'Studies in the late bronze age in Ireland: 3. The hoards of bronze implements', *UJA 20*:51–63.

Hodges, H.W.M., 1960. 'The bronze age moulds of the British Isles. Pt 2: England and Wales – moulds of stone and bronze', *Sibrium 5*:153–62.

Hodges, H.W.M., 1964. *Artefacts.*

Hodson, F.R., 1960. 'Reflections on the "ABC of the British Iron Age"', *Antiquity 34*:318–19.

Hodson, F.R., 1962. 'Some pottery from Eastbourne, the "Marnians", and the pre-Roman iron age in southern England', *PPS 28*:140–55.

Hodson, F.R., 1964. 'Cultural grouping within the British pre-Roman iron age', *PPS 30*:99–110.

Hodson, F.R., 1971. 'Three iron age brooches from Hammersmith', in Sieveking, G. de G. (ed.), *Prehistoric and Roman Studies (BMQ 35)*: 50–6.

Hogg, A.H.A., 1960. 'Garn Boduan and Tre'r Ceiri: excavations at two Caernarvonshire hillforts', *Arch. J. 117*:1–39.

Hogg, A.H.A., 1971. 'Some applications of surface fieldwork', in Hill and Jesson 1971: 105–25.

Hogg, A.H.A., 1975. *Hill-Forts of Britain.*

Holden, E.W., 1972. 'A bronze age cemetery-barrow on Itford Hill, Beddingham, Sussex', *SAC 110*:70–117.

Holland, S., 1975. 'Pollen analytical investigations at Crosby Warren, Lincolnshire, in the vicinity of the iron age and Romano-British settlement of Dragonby', *JAS 2*:353–63.

Holleyman, G.A., 1937. 'Harrow Hill excavations 1936', *SAC 78*:230–51.

Houlder, C., 1961. 'The excavation of a neolithic stone implement factory on Mynydd Rhiw in Caernarvonshire', *PPS 27*:108–43.

Houlder, C., 1968. 'The henge monuments at Llandegai', *Antiquity 42*:216–21.

Houlder, C., 1976. 'Stone axes and henge monuments', in Boon, G. C. and Lewis, J.M. (eds.), *Welsh Antiquity: Essays mainly on prehistoric topics presented to H.N. Savory*: 55–62.

Hoyle, F., 1977. *On Stonehenge.*

Hughes, I., 1977. 'New Guinea stone axe trade', *Terra Australis* (ANU, Canberra), *3*.

Hughes, M.J., 1972. 'A technical study of opaque red glass of the iron age in Britain', *PPS 38*:98–107.

Huxtable, J., Aitken, M.J., Hedges, J.W. and Renfrew, A.C., 1976. 'Dating a settlement pattern by thermo-luminescence', *Archaeometry 18*:5–17.

Iversen, J., 1941. 'Landnam i Danmarks Stenalder', *Danm. geol. Unders.* II Rk. Nr. *66*:1–68.

Jackson, D.A., 1975. 'An iron age site at Twywell, Northants.', *Northants. Archaeol. 10*:31–93.

Jackson, J.S., 1968. 'Bronze age copper mines on Mt Gabriel, West County Cork, Ireland', *Archaeologia Austriaca 43*:92–114.

Jackson, K.H., 1964a. *The Oldest Irish Tradition: A window on the iron age.*

Jackson, K.H., 1964b. 'The Celtic aftermath in the Islands', in Raftery J. 1964:73–83.

Jacobi, G., 1974. 'Zum Schriftgebrauch in der keltischen Oppida nördlich der Alpen', *Hamburger Beitr. zur Archäol. 4*:171–81.

Jacobi, R.M., 1973. 'Aspects of the '"Mesolithic Age"' in Great Britain', in Kozłowski 1973: 237–65.

Jacobi, R.M., 1976. 'Britain inside and outside Mesolithic Europe', *PPS* 42: 67–84.

Jacobsthal, P., 1944. *Early Celtic Art* (reprinted with corrections 1969).

Jacobsthal, P. and Jope, E.M., (in press) *Early Celtic Art in the British Isles*.

Jessup, R., 1970. *South East England*.

Jobey, G., 1962. 'An iron age homestead at West Brandon, Durham', *Arch. Ael.* 4th ser., *40*:1–34.

Jobey, G., 1968a. 'Excavations of cairns at Chatton Sandyford, Northumberland', *Arch. Ael.*, 4th ser. *46*:5–50.

Jobey, G., 1968b. 'A radiocarbon date for the palisaded settlement at Huckhoe', *Arch. Ael.*, 4th ser.,*46*:293–5.

Jobey, G., 1971a. 'Early settlements in Eastern Dumfriesshire', *TDGNHAS* *48*:78–105.

Jobey, G., 1971b. 'Excavations at Brough Law and Ingram Hill', *Arch. Ael.*, 4th ser., *49*:71–93.

Jobey, G., 1973. 'A native settlement at Hartburn and the Devil's Causeway, Northumberland, 1971', *Arch. Ael.* 5th ser., *1*:11–53.

Jobey, G., 1974a. *A Field Guide to Prehistoric Northumberland*, Northern History Booklets, no. 46.

Jobey, G., 1974b. 'Excavation at Boonies, Westerkirk, and the nature of Romano-British settlement in eastern Dumfries-shire', *PSAS 105*:119–40.

Jobey, G., 1974c. 'Notes on some population problems between the two Roman Walls', *Arch. Ael.*, 5th ser. *2*: 17–26.

Jobey, G., 1976. 'Traprain Law: a summary', in Harding D.W. 1976b: 191–204.

Jobey, G., 1977. 'Iron age and later farmsteads on Belling Law, Northumberland', *Arch. Ael.*, 5th ser. *5*: 1–38.

Jobey, G. and Tait, J., 1966. 'Excavations on palisaded settlements and cairnfields at Alnham, Northumberland', *Arch. Ael.*, 4th ser., *44*:5–48.

Jockenhövel, A., 1972. 'Westeuropäische Bronzen aus der späten Urnenfelderzeit in Südwestdeutschland', *Arch. Korrespondenzblatt 2.2*:103–9.

Jockenhövel, A., 1974. 'Fleischhaken von den Britischen Inseln', *Arch. Korrespondenzblatt 4.4*:329–38.

Jockenhövel, A. and Smolla, G., 1975. 'Le depôt de Juvincourt-Damary (Aisne)', *Gallia Préhist. 18*:289–313.

Joffroy, F., 1969. 'Le torque de Mailly-le-Camp (Aube)', *Monuments et Mémoires Fondation Piot 56*:45–59.

Johns, B.S., 1971. 'The Red Lady of Paviland: a comment', *Antiquity 45*: 141–4.

Jones, M., 1978. 'The plant remains', in Parrington 1978: 93–110.

Jones, M.U. and Jones, W.T., 1975. 'The crop-mark sites at Mucking, Essex, England', in Bruce-Mitford, R. (ed.), *Recent Archaeological Excavations in Europe*: 133–87.

Jones, R.M., 1976. 'Tasmania: aquatic machines and off-shore islands', in Sieveking, G. de G., Longworth, I.H. and Wilson, K.E. (eds.), *Problems in Economic and Social Archaeology*: 235–63.

Jones, R.M., 1978. '"Can't finish him up"; hunters in the Australian tropical savanna', unpublished paper prepared for Burg Wartenstein symposium No. 79 *Human Ecology in Savanna Environments*, Wenner-Gren Foundation for Anthropological Research.

Jope, E.M., 1952. 'The porcellanite axes of Ireland', *UJA 15*:31–55.

Jope, E.M., 1954. 'An iron age decorated sword-scabbard from the River Bann at Toome', *UJA 17*:81–91.

Jope, E.M., 1955. 'Chariotry and paired-draught in Ireland during the early iron age: the evidence of some horse bridle-bits', *UJA 18*:37–44.

Jope, E.M., n.d. [1958]. 'The beginnings of La Tène ornamental style in the British Isles', in Frere, S.S. (ed.), *Problems of the Iron Age in Southern Britain*, Inst. Arch. Univ. London Occ. Papers 11:69–83.

Jope, E.M., 1961. 'Daggers of the early iron age in Britain', *PPS 27*:307–43.

Jope, E.M., 1961 – 2. 'Iron age brooches in Ireland: a summary', *UJA 24/5*:25–38.

Jope, E.M., 1971. 'The Witham shield', in Sieveking, G. de G. (ed.), *Prehistoric and Roman Studies (BMQ 35)*: 61–9.

Jope, E.M., 1972. 'The transmission of new ideas: archaeological evidence for implant and dispersal', *World Archaeol. 4*:368–73.

Jope, E.M., 1976. 'The Wandsworth mask shield and its European sources of inspiration', in Duval, P.-M. and Hawkes, C.F.C. (eds.), *Celtic Art in Europe: Five protohistoric centuries*: 167–84.

Jope, E.M. and Wilson, B.C.S., 1957. 'A burial group of the first century A.D. near Donaghadee, County Down', *UJA 20*:73–95.

Kavanagh, R.M., 1973. 'The encrusted urn in Ireland', *PRIA 73*:507–617.

Keef, P.A., Wymer, J.J. and Dimbleby, G.W., 1965. 'A mesolithic site on Iping Common, Sussex, England', *PPS 31*:85–92.

Kellaway, G.A., 1971. 'Glaciation and the stones of Stonehenge', *Nature 233*:30–5.

Kelly, D.B., 1971. 'Quarry Wood Camp, Loose: a Belgic oppidum', *Arch. Cant. 86*:55–84.

Kennett, D.H., 1975. 'The Wymington hoard and other hoards and finds of the late bronze age from the south midlands', *Beds.Arch.J. 10*:5–18.

Kenyon, K.M., 1952. 'A survey of the evidence concerning the chronology and origins of iron age A in southern and midland Britain', *8th Ann. Rep. Univ. London Inst. Arch.*: 29–78.

Kenyon, K.M., 1953. 'Excavations at Sutton Walls, Herefordshire 1948–51', *Arch. J. 110*:1–87.

Kilbride-Jones, H.E., 1935. 'An Aberdeenshire iron age miscellany', *PSAS 69*:448–54.

Kilbride-Jones, H.E., 1939. 'The excavation of a composite tumulus at Drimnagh, Co. Dublin', *JRSAI 69*:190–220.

Kirk, W., 1957. 'The primary agricultural settlement of Scotland', *Scottish Geog. Mag. 73*:65–90.

Kitson Clark, M., 1938. 'The Yorkshire vase food vessel', *Arch. J. 94*:43–63.

Klein, W.G., 1928. 'Roman temple at Worth, Kent', *Ant. J. 8*:76–86.

Knight, R.W., Browne, C. and Grinsell, L.V., 1972. 'Prehistoric skeletons from Todmarton', *TBGAS 91*:14–17.

Kozłowski, S.K. (ed.), 1973. *The Mesolithic in Europe* (Warsaw).

Kozłowski, S.K., 1976. 'Studies on the European mesolithic: (II) rectangles, rhomboids and trapezoids in northwestern Europe', *Helinium 16*:43–54.

Krämer, W., 1971. 'Silbernefibelpaare aus dem letzten vorchristlichen Jahrhundert', *Germania 49*:111-32.

Laing, L.R., 1975. 'The mote of Mark and the origins of Celtic interlace', *Antiquity 49*:98–108.

Lambrick, G., 1978. 'Iron age settlements in the upper Thames valley', in Cunliffe, B.W. and Rowley, T.R. (eds.), *Lowland Iron Age Communities in Europe*, BAR Suppl. Ser. 48.

Langmaid, N.G., 1971. 'Norton Fitzwarren', *CA 28*:116–20.

Langmaid, N.G., 1976. *Bronze Age Metalwork in England and Wales*.

Lanting, J.N. and van der Waals, J.D., 1972. 'British beakers as seen from the Continent', *Helinium 12*:20–46.

Lanting, J.N., Mook, W.G. and van der Waals, J.D., 1973. 'C-14 chronology and the beaker problem', *Helinium 13*:38–58.

Laver, P.G., 1927. 'The excavation of a tumulus at Lexden, Colchester', *Archaeologia 76*:205–40.

Lawson, A.J., 1976. 'An imported bronze collar from Somerset', *Somerset Arch. and Nat. Hist. 120*:109–10.

Leeds, E.T., 1930. 'A bronze cauldron from the River Cherwell, Oxfordshire', *Archaeologia 80*:1–36.

Leeds, E.T., 1933. *Celtic Ornament*.

Legge, A.J., 1977. 'The origins of agriculture in the Near East', in Megaw 1977: 51–68.

Lewis, M.J.T., 1966. *Temples in Roman Britain*.

Limbrey, S., 1975. *Soil Science and Archaeology*.

Liversage, G.D., 1968. 'Excavations at Dalkey Island, Co. Dublin, 1956–59', *PRIA 66*:53–233.

Longworth, I.H., 1960. *See* Erith, F.H. and Longworth, I.H., 1960.

Longworth, I.H., 1961. 'The origins and development of the primary series of collared urns in England and Wales', *PPS 27*:263–306.

Longworth, I.H., 1965. *Yorkshire*.

Longworth, I.H., 1966. 'A massive cist with multiple burials of iron age date at Lochend, Dunbar', *PSAS 98*:173–83.

Longworth, I.H., 1966–7. 'Contracted mouth accessory cups', *BMQ 31*:111–22.

Lowery, P.R., Savage, R.D.A. and Wilkins, R.L., 1976. 'A technical study of the designs on the British mirror series', *Archaeologia 105*:100–26.

Lynch, F., 1970. *Prehistoric Anglesey*.

Lynch, F., 1972. 'Portal dolmens in the Nevern Valley, Pembrokeshire', in Lynch, F. and Burgess, C.B. (eds.), *Prehistoric Man in Wales and the West: Essays in honour of Lily F. Chitty*: 67–84.

Macalister, R.A.S., 1928–9. 'On some antiquities discovered upon Lambay', *PRIA 38C*:240–6.

McArdle, T.D., 1969. 'Personal armament in middle and late bronze age France', Ph.D. thesis, University of Edinburgh.

McBurney, C., 1959. 'Report on the first season's fieldwork on British upper palaeolithic cave deposits', *PPS 25*:260–9.

McGrail, S., 1975. 'The Brigg raft re-excavated', *Lincoln Hist. and Archaeol. 10*:5–13.

McGrail, S. and Switsur, R., 1975. 'Early British boats and their chronology', *Internat. J. Nautical Arch. 4*:191–200.

MacGregor, A.G., 1974. 'The Broch of Burrian, North Ronaldsay, Orkney', *PSAS 105*:63–118.

MacGregor, M., 1976. *Early Celtic Art in North Britain*, 2 vols.

McInnes, I.J., 1969. 'A Scottish neolithic pottery sequence', *SAF 1*:19–30.

McInnes, I.J., 1971. 'Settlement in late neolithic Britain', in Simpson, D.D.A. (ed.), *Economy and Settlement in Neolithic and Early Bronze Age Britain and Europe*: 113–30.

McKerrell, H., 1972. 'On the origins of British faience beads and some aspects of the Wessex–Mycenae relationship', *PPS 38*:286–301.

McKerrell, H., 1975. 'Correction procedures for C-14 dates', in Watkins T. 1975: 47–100.

MacKie, E.W., 1963. 'A dwelling site of the earlier iron age at Balevullin, Tiree', *PSAS 96*:155–83.

MacKie, E.W., 1965a. 'Brochs and the Hebridean iron age', *Antiquity 39*:266–78.

MacKie, E.W., 1965b. 'The origins and development of the broch and wheelhouse building cultures of the Scottish iron age', *PPS 31*:93–146.

MacKie, E.W., 1968. *Excavations on Loch Broom, Ross and Cromarty: second interim report.*

MacKie, E.W., 1969a. 'The historical context of the origin of the brochs', *SAF 1*:53–9.

MacKie, E.W., 1969b. Review of Hamilton J.R.C. 1968a, *PPS 35*:386–8.

MacKie, E.W., 1969c. 'Radiocarbon dates and the Scottish iron age', *Antiquity 43*:15–26.

MacKie, E.W., 1969d. 'Timber-laced and vitrified walls in iron age forts: causes of vitrification', *Glasgow Arch. J. 1*:69–71.

MacKie, E.W., 1970a. 'The Scottish iron age', *Scottish Hist. Rev. 49*:1–32.

MacKie, E.W., 1970b. 'The Hownam culture: a rejoinder to Ritchie', *SAF 2*:68–72.

MacKie, E.W., 1971a. 'Some aspects of the transition from the bronze- to the iron-using period in Scotland', *SAF 3*:55–72.

MacKie, E.W., 1971b. 'English migrants and Scottish brochs', *Glasgow Arch. J. 2*:39–71.

MacKie, E.W., 1972. 'Some new quernstones from brochs and duns', *PSAS 104*:137–46.

MacKie, E.W., 1974. *Dun Mor Vaul: An iron age broch on Tiree.*

MacKie, E.W., 1975a. 'The brochs of Scotland', in Fowler P.J. 1975: 72–92.

MacKie, E.W., 1975b. *Scotland: An archaeological guide.*

MacKie, E.W., 1975c. *Excavations at the Cultoon Stone Circle, Islay, in 1974: First interim report.*

MacKie, E.W., 1976. 'The vitrified forts of Scotland', in Harding D.W. 1976a: 205–35.

McNeil, R., 1973. 'A report on the bronze age hoard from Wick Park, Stogursey, Somerset', *Procs. Somerset Arch. and Nat. Hist. Soc. 117*:47–64.

Mace, A., 1959. 'The excavation of a late upper palaeolithic open-air site on Hengistbury Head, Christchurch, Hants.', *PPS 25*:233–59.

Mack, R.P., 1974. *The Coinage of Ancient Britain* (3rd edn).

Manby, T.G., 1963. 'The excavation of the Willerby Wold long barrow', *PPS 29*:173–205.

Manby, T.G., 1966a. 'A Creswellian site at Brigham, East Yorks.', *Ant. J. 46*:211–28.

Manby, T.G., 1966b. 'The Bodwrdin mould, Anglesey', *PPS 32*:349.

Manby, T.G., 1970. 'Long barrows of northern England; structural and dating evidence', *SAF 2*:1–28.

Manby, T.G., 1971. 'The Kilham long barrow excavations', *Antiquity 45*:50–3.

Manby, T.G., 1975. 'Neolithic occupation sites on the Yorkshire Wolds', *YAJ 47*:23–60.

Manby, T.G., 1976. 'The excavation of the Kilham long barrow, East Riding of Yorkshire', *PPS 42*:111–60.

Mann, L.M., 1915. 'Report on the relics discovered during excavations in 1913 at [the] cave at Dunagoil, Bute and in 1914 at the fort of Dunagoil, Bute', *Trans. Bute Nat. Hist. Soc. 8*:61–86.

Mann, L.M., 1925. 'Note on the results of the exploration of the fort at Dunagoil', *Trans. Bute Nat. Hist. Soc. 9*:56–60.

Manning, W.H., 1964. 'The plough in Roman Britain', *J. Roman Stud. 54*:54–65.

Manning, W.H., 1972. 'Iron-work hoards in iron age and Roman Britain', *Britannia* 3:224–50.

Manning, W.H. and Saunders, C., 1972. 'A socketed iron axe from Maids Moreton, Buckinghamshire, with a note on the type', *Ant. J.* 52:276–92.

Mariën, M.E., 1958. *Trouvailles du champ d'urnes et des tombelles hallstattiennes de Court-Saint-Etienne*, Monogr. d'Arch. Nat. 1 (Brussels).

Mariette, M., 1961. 'Une urne de l'age du bronze à Hardelot (Pas-de-Calais)', *Helinium* 1:229–32.

Marinatos, S.N. and Hirmer, M., 1960. *Crete and Mycenae*.

Marshall, J.N., 1915. 'Preliminary note on some excavations at Dunagoil fort and cave', *Trans. Bute Nat. Hist. Soc.* 8:42–9.

Mason, E.J., 1968. 'Ogof-yr-esgyrn, Dan-yr-ogof caves, Brecknock: excavations, 1938–50', *Arch. Camb.* 117:18–71.

Masters, L., 1973. 'The Lochhill Long Cairn', *Antiquity* 47:96–100.

Matthews, C.L., 1976. *Occupation Sites on a Chiltern ridge: Part I, Neolithic, Bronze Age and Early Iron Age*, BAR 29.

Maxwell, G.S., 1969. 'Duns and forts – a note on some iron age monuments of the Atlantic Province', *SAF* 1:41–52.

Maxwell, G.S., 1970. 'Early rectilinear sites in the Lothians', *SAF* 2:85–90.

Maxwell, G.S., 1975. 'Casus Belli: native pressures and Roman policy', *SAF* 7:31–49.

May, J., 1970a. 'Dragonby – an interim report on excavations of an iron age and Romano-British site near Scunthorpe, Lincolnshire', *Ant. J.* 50:222–45.

May, J., 1970b., 'An iron age square enclosure at Aston-upon-Trent, Derbyshire: a report on excavations in 1967', *Derbyshire Arch. J.* 90: 10–21.

May, J., 1971. 'An iron age spout from Kirmington, Lincolnshire', *Ant. J.* 51:253–9.

May, J., 1976. *Prehistoric Lincolnshire*, History of Lincolnshire I.

Meehan, B., 1977. 'Man does not live by calories alone: the role of shellfish in a coastal cuisine', in Allen, Golson and Jones 1977: 493–531.

Megaw, B.R.S. and Hardy, E.M., 1938. 'British decorated axes and their distribution', *PPS* 4:272–307.

Megaw, J.V.S., 1963. 'A British bronze bowl of the Belgic iron age from Poland', *Ant. J.* 43:27–37.

Megaw, J.V.S., 1964. 'An Irish gold neck-ring in the Nicholson Museum, Sydney', *J. Cork Hist. and Arch. Soc.* 69:94–100.

Megaw, J.V.S., 1968. 'Problems and non-problems in palaeo-organology: a musical miscellany', in Coles and Simpson 1968: 333–58.

Megaw, J.V.S., 1970. *Art of the European Iron Age: A study of the elusive image*.

Megaw, J.V.S., 1971. 'A group of later iron age collars or neck-rings from western Europe', in Sieveking, G. de G. (ed.), *Prehistoric and Roman Studies (BMQ 35)*: 145–55.

Megaw, J.V.S., 1973. *Archaeology from Down Under, a Personal View*.

Megaw, J.V.S., 1976a. 'Gwithian, Cornwall: some notes on the evidence for neolithic and bronze age settlement', in Burgess, C.B. and Miket, R. (eds.), *Settlement and Economy in the third and second millennia BC*, BAR 33:51–79.

Megaw, J.V.S. (ed.), 1976b. *To Illustrate the Monuments: Essays on archaeology presented to Stuart Piggott*.

Megaw, J.V.S. (ed.), 1977. *Hunters, Gatherers and First Farmers beyond Europe*.

Megaw, J.V.S. and Merrifield, R., 1970. 'The Dowgate plaque', *Arch. J.* 126:154–9.

Megaw, J.V.S., Thomas, A.C. and Wailes, B.W., 1960–1. 'The bronze age settlement at Gwithian, Cornwall: preliminary report on the evidence for early agriculture', *Procs. W. Cornwall Field Club* 2.5:200–15.

Mellars, P.A., 1969. 'Radiocarbon dates for a new Creswellian site', *Antiquity* *43*:308–10.

Mellars, P.A., 1974. 'The palaeolithic and mesolithic', in Renfrew 1974: 41–99.

Mellars, P.A., 1976a. 'The appearance of 'Narrow-Blade' microlithic industries in Great Britain: the radiocarbon evidence', in Kozłowski, S.K. (ed.), *Les Civilisations du 8e au 5e millénaire avant notre ère en Europe* (Nice, International Union of Prehistoric and Protohistoric Sciences): 166–74.

Mellars, P.A., 1976b. 'Settlement patterns and industrial variability in the British mesolithic', in G. de G. Sieveking, I.H. Longworth and K.E. Wilson (eds.), *Problems in Economic and Social Archaeology*: 375–400.

Mellars, P.A., 1976c. 'Fire, ecology, animal populations and man; a study of some ecological relationships in prehistory', *PPS 42*:15–46.

Mellars, P.A. and Payne, S., 1971. 'Excavations of two mesolithic shell middens on Oronsay', *Nature 231*:397–8.

Mercer, J., 1971. 'A regression-time stone-workers' camp, 33 ft O.D., Lussa River, Isle of Jura', *PSAS 103*:1–32.

Mercer, R.J., 1970a. 'The excavation of a bronze age hut-circle settlement, Stannon Down, St Breward', *Cornish Archaeol. 9*:17–46.

Mercer, R.J., 1970b. 'Metal arrowheads in the European bronze and early iron ages', *PPS 36*:171–213.

Mercer, R.J., 1975. 'Settlement, farming and environment in South West England to c.1000 BC', in Fowler P.J. 1975: 27–43.

Merryfield, D.L. and Moore, P.D., 1974. 'Prehistoric human activity and blanket peat initiation on Exmoor', *Nature 250*:436–41.

Miles, H., 1975. 'Barrows on the St Austell granite, Cornwall', *Cornish Archaeol. 14*:5–81.

Miles, W.A., 1826. *A Description of the Deverel Barrow opened A.D. 1825* [*sic*].

Mitchell, G.F., 1956. 'Post-Boreal pollen diagrams from Irish raised bogs', *PRIA B57*:105–281.

Mitchell, G.F., 1971. 'The Larnian culture: a minimal view', *PPS 37.2*:274–83.

Mitchell, G.F., 1972. 'Soil deterioration associated with prehistoric agriculture in Ireland', *Procs. Int. Geol. Congress 24th Symposium: I. Earth Sciences and the Quality of Life*: 59–68.

Mitchell, G.F., 1976. *The Irish Landscape*.

Molleson, T., 1976. 'Remains of Pleistocene man in Paviland and Pontnewydd caves, Wales', *British Cave Res. Ass. Trans. 3*:112–16.

Money, J.H., 1968. 'Excavations in the iron age hillfort at High Rocks, near Tunbridge Wells, 1957–61', *SAC 106*:158–205.

Moor, J.W., 1963. 'Excavations at Beacon Hill, Flamborough Head, East Yorkshire', *YAJ 41*:191–202.

Moore, P.D., 1973. 'The influence of prehistoric cultures upon initiation and spread of blanket bog in upland Wales', *Nature 241*:350–53.

Moore, P.D., 1975. 'Origin of blanket mires', *Nature 256*:267–9.

Moore, P.D. and Bellamy, D.J., 1974. *Peatlands*.

Mordant, Cl. and D., and Prampart, J-Y.,1976. 'Le dépôt de bronze de Villethierry (Yonne)', *Gallia Préhist.*, suppl. 9.

Morgan, F. de M., 1959. 'The excavation of the long barrow at Nutbane, Hants.', *PPS 25*:15–51.

Morrison, A., 1968. 'Cinerary urns and pygmy vessels in south-west Scotland', *TDGNHAS 45*:80–140.

Mortimer, J.R., 1905. *Forty Years' Researches in the British and Saxon Burial Mounds of East Yorkshire*.

Mulvaney, D.J., 1975. *The Prehistory of Australia* (2nd edn) (Ringwood, Victoria).
Munro, R., 1882. *Ancient Scottish Lake Dwellings or Crannogs.*
Murray-Thriepland, L., 1956. 'An excavation at St Mawgan-in-Pyder, North Cornwall', *Arch. J. 113*:33–83.
Musson, C.R., 1970. 'Round houses', *CA 2*: 267–75.
Musson, C.R., 1976. 'Excavations at the Breiddin 1969–1973', in Harding D.W. 1976a: 293–302.
Mylonas, G.E., 1957. *Ancient Mycenae.*

Nash, D., 1976. 'Reconstructing Poseidonius' Celtic ethnography: some considerations', *Britannia 7*:111–26.
Nenquin, J., 1961. *Salt: A study in economic prehistory.* Diss. Archaeol. Gandenses 7 (Bruges).
Newall, F., 1960. *Excavations at Walls Hill, Renfrewshire.*
Newall, F., 1965. *Excavation of Prehistoric and Medieval Homesteads at Knapps, Renfrewshire.*
Newton, R.G., 1971. 'A preliminary examination of a suggestion that pieces of strongly coloured glass were articles of trade in the iron age in Britain', *Archaeometry 13*:11–16.
Newton, R.G. and Renfrew, C., 1970. 'British faience beads reconsidered', *Antiquity 44*:199–206.
Nisbet, H.C., 1974. 'A geological approach to vitrified forts: Part I', *Science and Archaeol. 12*: 3–12.
Nisbet, H.C., 1975. 'A geological approach to vitrified forts: Part II', *Science and Archaeol. 15*:3–16.

Oakley, K.P., 1968a. 'The date of the "Red Lady" of Paviland', *Antiquity 42*:168, 306–7.
Oakley, K.P., 1968b. *Flint Implements: A handbook* (3rd edn).
O'Connor, B., 1975a. 'Six prehistoric phalerae in the London Museum and a discussion of other phalerae from the British Isles', *Ant. J. 55*:215–26.
O'Connor, B., 1975b. 'Two groups of prehistoric pottery from Kettleburgh', *Procs. Suffolk Inst. Arch. 33*:231–40.
O'Kelly, C., 1967. *Illustrated Guide to New Grange.*
O'Kelly, M.J., 1954. 'Excavations and experiments in ancient Irish cooking-places', *JRSAI 84*:105–55.
O'Kelly, M.J., 1961. 'The Cork horns, the Petrie crown and the Bann disc', *J. Cork Hist. Arch. Soc. 66:1–17.*
O'Kelly, M.J., 1970. 'Problems of Irish ring-forts', in Moore, D. (ed.), *The Irish Sea Province in Archaeology and History*: 50–4.
O'Kelly, M.J., 1973. 'Current excavations at Newgrange, Ireland', in Daniel, G.E. and Kjaerum, P. (eds.), *Megalithic Graves and Ritual*, Jutland Arch. Soc., Publ. 11: 137–46.
O'Neil, B.H.St J., 1942. 'Excavations at Ffridd Faldwyn Camp, Montgomeryshire, 1937–39', *Arch. Camb. 97*:1–57.
Ó Nualláin, S., 1972. 'A neolithic house at Ballyglass, near Ballycastle, Co. Mayo', *JRSAI 102*:1–11.
Ó Ríordáin, S.P., 1937. 'The halberd in bronze age Europe', *Archaeologia 86*:195.
Ó Ríordáin, S.P., 1940. 'Excavations at Cush, Co. Limerick', *PRIA 45C*:83–181.
Ó Ríordáin, S.P., 1954. 'Lough Gur excavations: neolithic and bronze age houses on Knockadoon', *PRIA 56C*:297–459.
Ó Ríordáin, S.P. and Daniel, G.E., 1964. *New Grange.*

Owles, E.J., 1969. 'The Ipswich gold torcs', *Antiquity 43*:208–11.
Owles, E.J., 1971. 'The sixth Ipswich torc', *Antiquity 45*:294–6.

Palmer, R., 1976. 'Interrupted ditch systems in Britain: the use of aerial photography for comparative studies', *PPS 42:* 161–86.
Palmer, S., 1970. 'The stone age industries of the Isle of Portland, Dorset, and the utilization of Portland Chert as artifactual material in southern England', *PPS 36*:82–115.
Palmer, S., 1976. 'The mesolithic habitation site at Culver Well, Portland, Dorset: interim note', *PPS 42*:324–7.
Parrington, M., 1978. *The Excavation of an Iron Age Settlement, Bronze Age Ring Ditches and Roman Features at Ashville Trading Estate, Abingdon (Oxfordshire) 1974–76,* Oxfordshire Arch. Unit. Rep. 1, CBA Res. Rep. 28.
Partridge, C.R., 1975. 'Braughing', in Rodwell, W. and Rowley, T. (eds.), *The Small Towns of Roman Britain,* BAR 15:139–57.
Patay, P., 1968. 'Urnenfelderzeitliche Bronzeschilde im Karpatenbecken', *Germania 46*:241–8.
Patrick, J., 1974. 'Midwinter sunrise at New Grange', *Nature 249:* 517–19.
Payne, F.G., 1947. 'The plough in early Britain', *Arch. J. 104*:82–111.
Peacock, D.P.S., 1968. 'A petrological study of certain iron age pottery from western England', *PPS 34*:414–27.
Peacock, D.P.S., 1969a. 'A contribution to the study of Glastonbury ware from south-western Britain', *Ant. J. 49*:41–61.
Peacock, D.P.S., 1969b. 'Neolithic pottery production in Cornwall', *Antiquity 43:* 145–9.
Peacock, D.P.S., 1971. 'Roman amphorae in pre-Roman Britain', in Hill and Jesson 1971: 161–88.
Pearce, S.M., 1970–1. 'A late bronze age hoard from Glentanar, Aberdeenshire', *PSAS 103*:57–64.
Pearson, G.W., Pilcher, J.R., Baillie, M.G. and Hillam, J., 1977. 'Absolute radiocarbon dating using a low altitude European tree-ring calibration', *Nature 270*:25–8.
Pennington, W., 1970. 'Vegetation history in the north-west of England: a regional synthesis', in Walker, D. and West, R.G. (eds.), *Studies in the Vegetational History of the British Isles*: 41–79.
Pennington, W., 1974. *The History of British Vegetation* (2nd edn).
Perkins, D. and Daly, P., 1968. 'A hunters' village in neolithic Turkey', *Sci. American 219*:97–106.
Peroni, R.B., 1970. 'Die Schwerter in Italien', *Prähist. Bronzefunde 4.1* (Munich).
Perry, B.T., 1966. 'Some recent discoveries in Hampshire', in Thomas, A.C. (ed.), *Rural Settlement in Roman Britain*: 39–41.
Perry, B.T., 1969. 'Iron age enclosures and settlements on the Hampshire chalklands', *Arch. J. 126:* 29–43.
Petersen, F., 1972. 'Traditions of multiple burial in later neolithic and early bronze age England', *Arch. J. 129*:22–55.
Phillips, C.W., 1936. 'The excavation of the Giants' Hills long barrow, Skendleby, Lincs.', *Archaeologia 85*:37–106.
Piercy Fox, N., 1969. 'Caesar's Camp, Keston', *Arch. Cant. 84*:185–200.
Piggott, C.M., 1938. 'A middle bronze age barrow and Deverel-Rimbury urnfield at Latch Farm, Christchurch, Hampshire', *PPS 4*:169–87.
Piggott, C.M., 1942. 'Five late bronze age enclosures in north Wiltshire', *PPS 8*:48–61.

Piggott, C.M., 1946. 'The late bronze age razors of the British Isles', *PPS 12*:121–141.

Piggott, C.M., 1948. 'The excavations at Hownam Rings, Roxburghshire', *PSAS 82*:193–225.

Piggott, C.M., 1949a. 'A late bronze age hoard from Blackrock and its significance', *PPS 15*:107–21.

Piggott, C.M., 1949b. 'The iron age settlement at Hayhope Knowe, Roxburghshire', *PSAS 83*:45–67.

Piggott, C.M., 1950. 'The excavation at Bonchester Hill', *PSAS 84*:113–37.

Piggott, C.M., 1953. 'Milton Loch Crannog I: a native house of the 2nd century AD in Kirkcudbrightshire', *PSAS 87*:134–52.

Piggott, C.M. and Piggott, S., 1940. 'Excavations at Rams Hill, Uffington, Berkshire', *Ant. J. 20*:465–80.

Piggott, S., 1937a. 'The excavation of a long barrow in Holdenhurst parish, near Christchurch', *PPS 3*:1–14.

Piggott, S., 1937b. 'The long barrow in Brittany', *Antiquity 11*:441–55.

Piggott, S., 1938. 'The early bronze age in Wessex', *PPS 4*:52–106.

Piggott, S., 1940. 'Timber circles: a re-examination', *Arch. J. 96*:193–222.

Piggott, S., 1948. 'The excavations at Cairnpapple Hill, West Lothian, 1947–8', *PSAS 82*:68–123.

Piggott, S., 1949. *British Prehistory*.

Piggott, S., 1950. 'Swords and scabbards of the British early iron age', *PPS 16*:1–28.

Piggott, S., 1951. 'Stonehenge reviewed', in Grimes, W.F. (ed.), *Aspects of Archaeology in Britain and Beyond*.

Piggott, S., 1953a. 'Three metal-work hoards of the Roman period from southern Scotland', *PSAS 87*:1–50.

Piggott, S., 1953b. 'A late bronze age hoard from Peebles-shire', *PSAS 87*:175–86.

Piggott S., 1954. *Neolithic Cultures of the British Isles*.

Piggott, S., 1954–6. 'Excavations in passage graves and ring cairns of the Clava group', *PSAS 88*:173–207.

Piggott, S., 1955. 'Windmill Hill: East or West?', *PPS 21*:96–101.

Piggott, S., 1958. 'Native economies and the Roman occupation of North Britain', in Richmond I.A. 1958a:1–27.

Piggott, S., 1959. 'The carnyx in early iron age Britain', *Ant. J. 39*:19–32.

Piggott, S., 1961. 'The British neolithic cultures in their continental setting', in Böhm, J. and De Laet, S.J. (eds.), *L'Europe à la Fin de l'Age de la Pierre* (Prague): 557–74.

Piggott, S., 1962a (ed.). *The Prehistoric Peoples of Scotland*.

Piggott, S., 1962b. *The West Kennet Long Barrow*.

Piggott, S., 1962c. 'From Salisbury Plain to South Siberia', *WAM 58*:93–7.

Piggott, S., 1963a. 'Abercromby and after: the beaker cultures of Britain re-examined', in Alcock, L. and Foster, L. (eds.), *Culture and Environment*.

Piggott, S., 1963b. 'The bronze age pit at Swanwick, Hants.: a postscript', *Ant. J. 43*:286–7.

Piggott, S., 1965. *Ancient Europe*.

Piggott, S., 1966. 'A scheme for the Scottish iron age', in Rivet 1966: 1–15.

Piggott, S., 1971. 'Firedogs in iron age Britain and beyond' in Boardman, J., Brown, M.A., and Powell, T.G.E. (eds.), *The European Community in Later Prehistory*: 243–70.

Piggott, S., 1971–2. 'Excavation of the Dalladies long barrow, Fettercairn, Kincardineshire', *PSAS 104*:23–47.

Piggott, S., 1972. 'A note on climatic deterioration in the first millennium BC in Britain', *SAF 4*:109–13.

Piggott, S., 1973. 'The final phase of bronze technology, c.1500–c.500 BC', in Crittall, E. (ed.), *Wiltshire I.2,* Victoria History of the Counties of England: 376–407.

Piggott, S., 1974. 'Innovation and tradition in British prehistory', *Trans. Archit. Arch. Soc. Durham and Northumberland,* n.s. *3*:1–12.

Piggott, S., 1975. *The Druids* (rev. edn.).

Piggott, S. and Allen, D.F., 1970. *Early Celtic Art: an exhibition organized by the Arts Council of Great Britain . . .*

Piggott, S. and Daniel, G.E., 1951. *A Picture Book of Ancient British Art.*

Piggott, S. and Piggott, C.M., 1952. 'Excavations at Castle Law, Glencorse and Craig's Quarry, Dirleton', *PSAS 86*:191–6.

Piggott, S. and Powell, T.G.E., 1948–9. 'The excavation of three chambered tombs in Galloway', *PSAS 88*:103–61.

Piggott, S. and Simpson, D.D.A., 1971. 'Excavation of a stone circle at Croftmoraig, Perthshire, Scotland', *PPS 37*:1–15.

Pilcher, J., 1974. 'Botanical report on Dun Mor Vaul', in MacKie 1974:204–9.

Pilcher, R.R. and Bailey, M.G.L., 1978. 'Implications of a European radiocarbon calibration', *Antiquity 52*:217–22.

Pitt-Rivers, A.H.L.-F., 1898. *Excavations in Cranborne Chase, nr. Rushmore,* vol. IV.

Polenz, H., 1977. 'Ein Eimer vom Aylesford-Typus aus Geisenheim im Rheingau', *Nassauische Annalen 88*:9–34.

Posnansky, M., 1956. 'Note on the presence of prehistoric field systems in Derbyshire', *Derbyshire Arch. J. 76*:71.

Powell, T.G.E., 1950. 'A late bronze age hoard from Welby, Leicestershire', *Arch. J. 105*:127–40.

Powell, T.G.E., 1953. 'The gold ornament from Mold, Flintshire, north Wales', *PPS 19*:161–79.

Powell, T.G.E., 1958. *The Celts.*

Powell, T.G.E., 1962. 'The coming of the Celts', in Piggott S. 1962a: 105–24.

Powell, T.G.E., 1971. 'The introduction of horse-riding into temperate Europe: a contributory note', *PPS 37*:1–14.

Powell, T.G.E., 1973. 'The excavation of the megalithic chambered cairn at Dyffryn Ardudwy, Merioneth, Wales', *Archaeologia 104*:1–49.

Proudfoot, V.B., 1954. 'Excavations at the Cathedral Hill, Downpatrick, Co. Down 1953', *UJA 17*:97–102.

Proudfoot, V.B., 1955. *The Downpatrick Gold Find,* Arch. Res. Pub. (N. Ireland) 3.

Proudfoot, V.B., 1956. 'Excavations at the Cathedral Hill, Downpatrick, Co. Down, 1954', *UJA 19*:57–72.

Proudfoot, V.B., 1957. 'A second gold find from Downpatrick', *UJA 20*:70–2.

Proudfoot, E., 1963. 'Report on the excavation of a bell barrow in the parish of Edmonsham, Dorset, England', *PPS 29*:395–425.

Pryor, F., 1974. *Excavations at Fengate, Peterborough. The First Report.* Royal Ontario Mus. Arch. Monograph 3.

Pryor, F., 1976. 'Fen-edge land management in the bronze age: an interim report on excavations at Fengate, Peterborough 1971–5', in Burgess, C.B. and Miket, R. (eds.), *Settlement and Economy in the third and second millennia B.C.,* BAR 33:29–49.

Radford, C.A.R., 1952. 'Prehistoric settlements on Dartmoor and the Cornish Moors', *PPS 18*:55–84.

Radley, J. and Mellars, P., 1964. 'A mesolithic structure at Deepcar, Yorks. and the affinities of its associated flint industries', *PPS 30*:1–24.

Raftery, B., 1972. 'Irish hill-forts', in Thomas, A.C. (ed.), *The Iron Age in the Irish Sea Province*, CBA Res. Rep. 9:37–58.

Raftery, B., 1974. 'A decorated iron age horse-bit from Ireland', *PRIA 74C*:1–10.

Raftery, B., 1975. 'A late bronze age bar toggle from Ireland', *Arch. Atl. 1.1*:83–9.

Raftery, B., 1976a. 'Rathgall and Irish hillfort problems', in Harding D.W. 1976a: 339–57.

Raftery, B., 1976b. 'Dowris, Hallstatt and La Tène in Ireland: problems of the transition from bronze to iron', in De Laet, S.J. (ed.), *Acculturation and Continuity in Atlantic Europe*, Diss. Archaeol. Gandenses 21:189–97 (Bruges).

Raftery, J., 1942. 'Knocknalappa crannog, Co. Kildare', *N. Munster Ant. J. 3*:53–72.

Raftery, J., 1960. 'A hoard of the early iron age', *JRSAI 90*:2–5.

Raftery, J. (ed.), 1964. *The Celts* (Dublin).

Raftery, J., 1972. 'Iron age and Irish Sea: problems for research', in Thomas, A.C. (ed.), *The Iron Age in the Irish Sea Province*, CBA Res. Rep. 9:1–10.

Rahtz, P.A. and ApSimon, A.M., 1962. 'Excavations at Shearplace Hill, Sydling St Nicholas, Dorset', *PPS 28*:289–328.

Raistrick, A., 1938. 'Prehistoric cultivations at Grassington, West Yorkshire', *YAJ 33*:166–74.

Raistrick, A., 1939. 'Iron age settlements in West Yorkshire', *YAJ 34*:115–50.

Ralph, E.K., Michael, H.N. and Han, M.C., 1973. 'Radiocarbon dates and reality', *MASCA Newsletter 9.1*:1–20.

Ralston, I.B.M., (in press). 'Green Castle, Portnockie, and the promontory forts of north-east Scotland', *SAF 10*.

Rankine, W.F., 1961. 'The mesolithic age in Dorset', *PDNHAS 83*:91–9.

Rankine, W.F. and Dimbleby, G.W., 1960. 'Further excavations at a mesolithic site at Oakhanger, Selbourne, Hants.', *PPS 26*:246–62.

Reader, F.W., 1909. 'Report of the Red Hills exploration committee 1906–7', *PSAL 22*:164–207.

Reader, F.W., 1910. 'Report of the Red Hills exploration committee, 1908–9', *PSAL 23*:66–88.

Reinbacher, F., 1956. 'Eine vorgeschichtlicher Hirschmaske aus Berlin-Biesdorf', *Ausgrabungen und Funde 1*:147–51.

Renfrew, A.C., 1968. 'Wessex without Mycenae', *Annual of the British School at Athens 63*:278–85.

Renfrew, A.C. (ed.), 1973a. *The Explanation of Culture Change: Models in prehistory*.

Renfrew, A.C., 1973b. *Social archaeology: An inaugural lecture*.

Renfrew, A.C., 1973c. 'Social organization in neolithic Wessex', in Renfrew 1973a: 539–58.

Renfrew, A.C. (ed.), 1974. *British Prehistory: A new outline*.

Renfrew, A.C., 1976. *Before Civilization: The radiocarbon revolution and prehistoric Europe* (1973; rev. edn 1976).

Renfrew, A.C., Harkness D.D. and Switsur, R., 1976. 'Quanterness, radiocarbon and the Orkney cairns', *Antiquity 50*:194–204.

Reynolds, P.J., 1974. 'Experimental iron age storage pits', *PPS 40*:118–131.

Richardson, K.M., 1940. 'Excavations at Poundbury, Dorchester, Dorset, 1939', *Ant. J. 20*:429–48.

Richardson, K.M., 1951. 'The excavation of an iron age village on Boscombe Down West', *WAM 54*:123–68.

Richmond, I.A. (ed.), 1958a. *Roman and Native in North Britain.*

Richmond, I.A., 1958b. 'Ancient geographical sources for Britain north of Cheviot', in Richmond I.A. 1958a: 131–55.

Richmond, I.A., 1968. *Hod Hill II: excavations carried out between 1951 and 1958.*

Ridgeway, W. and Smith, R.A., 1907. 'Paper on early Italian brooches in Britain', *PSAL 21*:97–117.

Riehm, K., 1961. 'Prehistoric salt-boiling', *Antiquity 35*:181–91.

Rigby, V., 1973. 'Potters' stamps on Terra Nigra and Terra Rubra found in Britain', in Detsicas, A. (ed.), *Current Research in Romano-British Coarse Pottery*, CBA Res. Rep. 10: 7–24.

Riley, D.N., 1957. 'Neolithic and bronze age pottery from Risby Warren and other occupation sites in North Lincolnshire', *PPS 23*:40–56.

Ritchie, A., 1970. 'Palisaded sites in north Britain: their context and affinities', *SAF 2*:48–67.

Ritchie, A., 1972. 'Inferences from settlements in Britain in the first millennium BC', in Ucko *et al.* 1972:541–5.

Ritchie, A., Ritchie, J.N.G., Whittington, G. and Soulsby, J., 1974. 'A prehistoric field-boundary from the Black Crofts, North Connel, Argyll', *Glasgow Arch. J. 3*:66–70.

Ritchie, J.N.G. and Ritchie, A., 1972. *Edinburgh and South-East Scotland.*

Ritchie, J.N.G. and Shepherd, I.A.G., 1973. 'Beaker pottery and associated artefacts in south-west Scotland', *TDGNHAS 50*:18–36.

Ritchie, J.N.G., Thornber, I., Lynch, F. and Marshall, D.N., 1975. 'Small cairns in Argyll: some recent work', *PSAS 106*:15–38.

Ritchie, P.R., 1968. 'The stone implement trade in 3rd millennium Scotland', in Coles and Simpson 1968: 117–36.

Rivet, A.L.F. (ed.), 1966. *The Iron Age in Northern Britain.*

Rivet, A.L.F., 1971. 'Hillforts in action', in Hill and Jesson 1971: 189–202.

Roberts, B.K., Turner, J. and Ward, P.F., 1973. 'Recent forest history and land use in Weardale, Northern England', in Birks, H.J.B. and West, R.G. (eds.), *Quaternary Plant Ecology*: 207–21.

Robertson, A., 1970. 'Roman finds from non-Roman sites in Scotland', *Britannia 1*:198–225.

Robertson-Mackay, R., 1962. 'The excavation of the causewayed camp at Staines', *Arch. News Letter 7*:131–4.

Rodwell, W.J., 1975. 'Trinovantian towns in their setting: a case study', in Rodwell, W.J. and Rowley, T. (eds.), *The Small Towns of Roman Britain*, BAR 15:85–101.

Rodwell, W.J., 1976. 'Coinage, oppida, and the rise of Belgic power in south-eastern Britain', in Cunliffe, B.W. and Rowley, T. (eds.), *Oppida in Barbarian Europe*, BAR Suppl. Ser. 11:181–366.

Rodwell, W.J., 1978. 'Buildings and settlements in south-east Britain in the late iron age', in Cunliffe, B.W. and Rowley, T. (eds.), *Lowland Iron Age Communities in Europe,* BAR Suppl. Ser. 48.

Roe, F.E.S., 1966. 'The battle-axe series in Britain', *PPS 32*:199–245.

Roe, F.E.S., 1968. 'Stone mace-heads and the latest neolithic cultures of the British Isles', in Coles and Simpson 1968: 145–72.

Rogers, G. and Laing, L.R., 1966. *Gallo-Roman Pottery from Southampton, and the Distribution of Terra Nigra in Great Britain,* Southampton City Mus. Pub. 6.

Rook, A.G., 1974. 'Welch's Farm', *Herts. Arch. Rev. 9*:170–4.

Ross, A., 1967. *Pagan Celtic Britain.*

Ross, A., 1968. 'Shafts, pits, wells – sanctuaries of the Belgic Britons?', in Coles and Simpson 1968:255–85.

Ross, A. and Feachem, R.W., 1976. 'Ritual rubbish? The Newstead Pits', in Megaw 1976b: 229–37.

Roth, H., 1974. 'Ein Ledermesser der atlantischen Bronzezeit aus Mittelfranken', *Arch. Korrespondenzblatt 4*:37–47.

Rowlands, M.J., 1971a. 'A group of incised decorated armrings and their significance for the middle bronze age of Southern Britain', in Sieveking, G. de G. (ed.), *Prehistoric and Roman Studies (BMQ 35)*: 183–99.

Rowlands, M.J., 1971b. 'The archaeological interpretation of prehistoric metal-working', *World Archaeol. 3*:210–24.

Rowlands, M.J., 1976a. 'Appendix I: The bronze pin fragments from Gwithian, Layer 3', in Megaw 1976b: 67–8.

Rowlands, M.J., 1976b. *The Production and Distribution of Metalwork in the Middle Bronze Age in Southern Britain*, BAR 31, 2 vols.

RCAHM, 1920. *Dumfriesshire.*

RCAHM, 1924. *County of East Lothian.*

RCAHM, 1928. *Outer Hebrides.*

RCAHM, 1946. *Orkney and Shetland.*

RCAHM, 1956. *County of Roxburgh*, 2 vols.

RCAHM, 1957. *County of Selkirk*, 2 vols.

RCAHM, 1963. *Stirlingshire*, 2 vols.

RCAHM, 1967. *Peeblesshire*, 2 vols.

RCAHM, 1971. *Argyll I: Kintyre.*

RCAHM, 1975. *Argyll II: Lorn.*

RCAHM, 1978. *Lanarkshire: An inventory of the prehistoric and Roman monuments.*

Rust, A., 1956. *Die jungpälaolithischen Zeltlagen von Ahrensburg* (Neumünster).

Rutland, R.A., 1972. 'An iron age sword and scabbard from the Thames at Henley, Oxon', *Ant. J. 52*:345–6.

Rutter, J.G., 1959. 'The iron age pits on Castle Hill', *Scarborough and District Arch. Soc. 1*:32–44.

Rynne, E., 1972. 'Late bronze age rattle-pendants from Ireland', *PPS 28*:383–5.

Rynne, E., 1976. 'The La Tène and Roman finds from Lambay, County Dublin: a reassessment', *PRIA 76C*:231–44.

St Joseph, J.K., 1974. 'Aerial photography: recent results 33', *Antiquity 48*:52–4.

Sandars, N.K., 1959. 'Amber spacer-beads again', *Antiquity 33*:292–5.

Sangmeister, E., 1963. 'La civilisation du vase campaniforme', *Actes du Premier Colloque Atlantique 1961* (Brest).

Savory, H.N., 1948. 'The sword-bearers', *PPS 14*:155–76.

Savory, H.N., 1955. 'A corpus of Welsh bronze age pottery: I, Beakers', *Bull. Board Celtic Stud. 16*:215–41.

Savory, H.N., 1958. 'The late bronze age in Wales: some new discoveries and interpretations', *Arch. Camb. 107*:3–63.

Savory, H.N., 1965a. 'The bronze age', in Foster, I.Ll. and Daniel, G.E. (eds.), *Prehistoric and Early Wales*: 71–107.

Savory, H.N., 1965b. 'The Guilsfield hoard', *Bull. Board Celtic Stud. 20.2*:179–96.

Savory, H.N., 1968. *Spain and Portugal.*

Savory, H.N., 1971a. *Excavations at Dinorben, 1965–9.*

Savory, H.N., 1971b. 'A Welsh bronze age hillfort', *Antiquity 45*:251–61.

Savory, H.N., 1972. 'Copper age cists and cist-cairns in Wales: with special reference to Newton, Swansea and other multiple cist cairns', in Lynch, F. and Burgess, C.B. (eds.), *Prehistoric Man in Wales and the West: Essays in honour of Lily F. Chitty*: 117–140.

Savory, H.N., 1976a. 'Welsh hillforts: a reappraisal of recent research', in Harding D.W. 1976a: 237–91.

Savory, H.N., 1976b. *Guide Catalogue of the Early Iron Age Collections* (National Museum of Wales).

Savory, H.N., 1976c. 'Some Welsh late bronze age hoards – old and new', *Arch. Atl. 1.2*:111–25.

Savory, H.N., 1976d. 'The La Tène shield in Wales', in Duval, P.-M. and Hawkes, C.F.C. (eds.), *Celtic Art in Europe: Five protohistoric centuries*: 185–99.

Schauer, P., 1972. 'Zur Herkunft der bronzenen Hallstatt-Schwerter', *Arch. Korrespondenzblatt 2*:261–70.

Scheers, S., 1972. 'Coinage and currency of the Belgic tribes during the Gallic war', *B. Num. J. 41*:1–6.

Schuldt, E., 1961. *Hohen Viecheln: ein mittelsteinzeitlicher Wohnplatz in Mecklenburgh*, Deutsche Akademie der Wissenschaften Schriften der Section für Vor- und Frühgeschichte, 10 (Berlin).

Schwabedissen, H., 1954. *Die Federmesser-Gruppen des nordwesteuropäischen Flachlandes zur Ausbreitung des Spät-Magdalenien* (Neumünster).

Schwappach, F., 1969. 'Die stempelverzierte Keramik der frühen Latènekultur von Armorica', in Frey, O.-H. (ed.), *Marburger Beiträge zur Archäologie der Kelten, Fundber. aus Hessen*, Beiheft 1:213–87.

Schwappach, F., 1974. 'Ostkeltisches und westkeltisches Ornament auf einem älterlatènezeitlichen Gürtelhaken von Mühlacker, Kreis Vaihingen', *Fundberichte aus Baden-Württemberg 1*:337–72.

Scott, B.G., 1974a. 'Some notes on the transition from bronze to iron in Ireland', *IARF 1.1*:9–24.

Scott, B.G., 1974b. 'Reply to the papers by R.B. Warner', *IARF 1.2*:48–50.

Scott, J.G., 1969. 'The Clyde cairns of Scotland', *Megalithic Enquiries in the West of Britain*:175–222.

Scott, J.G., 1970. 'A note on neolithic settlement in the Clyde region', *PPS 36*:116–24.

Scott, W.L., 1947–8. 'The chamber tomb of Unival, North Uist', *PSAS 82*:1–49.

Scott, W.L., 1951. 'The colonization of Scotland in the second millennium BC', *PPS 17*:16–82.

Scott-Elliot, J., Simpson, D.D.A. and Coles, J.M., 1966. 'Excavations at McNaughton's Fort, Kirkcudbright', *TDGNHAS 43*:73–9.

Seagrief, S.C., 1959. 'Pollen diagrams from southern England: Wareham, Dorset and Nursling, Hampshire', *New Phytologist 58*:316–25.

Seddon, B., 1967. 'Prehistoric climate and agriculture: a review of recent paleoecological investigations', in Taylor, J.A. (ed.), *Weather and Agriculture*: 173–85.

Selkirk, A., 1971. 'Ascott-under-Wychwood', *CA 3*:7–10.

Selkirk, A., 1972a. 'The Earls Barton barrow', *CA 3.9*:238–40.

Selkirk, A., 1972b. 'The Wessex Culture', *CA 3.9*:241–4.

Selkirk, A., 1974a. 'Carn Brea', *CA 4*:360–5.

Selkirk, A., 1974b. 'Carn Euny', *CA 4*:262–8.

Selkirk, A., 1975. 'Hambledon Hill', *CA 5*:16–18.

Selkirk, A., 1977a. 'Stone axes: the second revolution', *CA 5*:294–302.

Selkirk, A., 1977b. 'Causewayed camps', *CA 5*:335–40.

Selkirk, A. and Waterman, D., 1970. 'Navan Fort', *CA 22*:304–8.

Shee, E., 1973. 'Techniques of Irish passage grave art', in Daniel, G.E. and Kjaerum, P. (eds.), *Megalithic Graves and Ritual*, Jutland Arch. Soc. 11:163–72.

Shepherd, I.A.G., 1976. 'Preliminary results from the beaker settlement at Rosinish, Benbecula', in Burgess, C.B. and Miket, R. (eds.), *Settlement and Economy in the third and second millennia BC*, BAR 33:209–20.

Shotton, F.W., 1959. 'New petrological groups based on axes from the West Midlands', *PPS 25*:135–43.

Sieveking, G. de G. *et al.*, 1973. 'A new survey of Grimes Graves, Norfolk', *PPS 39*:182–218.

Simmons, I.G., 1969a. 'Evidence for vegetation changes, associated with mesolithic man in Britain', in Ucko, P.J. and Dimbleby, G.W. (eds.), *The Domestication and Exploitation of Plants and Animals*: 110–19.

Simmons, I.G., 1969b. 'Environment and early man on Dartmoor', *PPS 35*:203–19.

Simmons, I.G. and Dimbleby, G.W., 1974. 'The possible role of ivy (*Hedera helix L.*) in the mesolithic economy of Western Europe', *JAS 1*:291–6.

Simmons, I.G. and Proudfoot, V.B., 1969. 'Environment and early man on Dartmoor, Devon, England', *PPS 35*:203–9.

Simpson, D.D.A., 1965. 'Food vessels in south-west Scotland', *TDGNHAS 42*:26–50.

Simpson, D.D.A., 1968a. Food vessels: associations and chronology', in Coles and Simpson 1968:197–212.

Simpson, D.D.A., 1968b. 'Timber mortuary houses and earthen long barrows', *Antiquity 43*:142.

Simpson, D.D.A., 1971. 'Beaker houses and settlements', in Simpson, D.D.A. (ed.), *Economy and Settlement in Neolithic and Early Bronze Age Britain and Europe*: 131–52.

Simpson, D.D.A., 1976. 'The later neolithic and beaker settlement site at Northton, Isle of Harris', in Burgess, C.B. and Miket, R. (eds.), *Settlement and Economy in the third and second millennia B.C.*, BAR 33:221–31.

Simpson, D.D.A. and Scott-Elliot, J., 1963. 'Excavations at Camp Hill, Trohoughton, Dumfries, *TDGNHAS 41*:125–34.

Simpson, D.D.A. and Thawley, J.T., 1973. 'Single grave art in Britain', *SAF 4*:81–104.

Simpson, M., 1968. 'Massive armlets in the north British iron age', in Coles and Simpson 1968: 233–54.

Simpson, W.G., 1966. 'Romano-British settlement on the Welland gravels', in Thomas, A.C. (ed.), *Rural Settlement in Roman Britain*, CBA Res. Rep. 7: 15–25.

Small, A., 1969. 'Burghead', *SAF 1*:61–8.

Small, A., 1975. 'The hill-forts of the Inverness area', *Inverness Field Club Centenary Volume*: 78–89.

Small, A. and Cottam, M.B., 1972. *Craig Phadrig*, Univ. of Dundee, Dept. of Geography, Occ. Papers 1.

Smith, A.G., 1970a. 'Late- and post-glacial vegetational and climatic history of Ireland: a review', in Stephens, N. and Glasscock, R.E. (eds.), *Irish Geographical Studies*: 65–88.

Smith, A.G., 1970b. 'The influence of mesolithic and neolithic man on British vegetation', in Walker, D. and West, R.G. (eds.), *Studies in the Vegetational History of the British Isles*: 81–96.

Smith, A.G., 1975. 'Neolithic and bronze age landscape changes in Northern Ireland', in Evans J.G. *et al.* 1975: 64–73.

Smith, C., 1977. 'The valleys of the Thame and middle Trent – their populations and ecology during the late first millennium BC', in Collis, J.R. (ed.), *The Iron Age in Britain: A review*.

Smith, C., 1978. 'The landscape and natural history of iron age settlement on the Trent gravels', in Cunliffe, B.W. and Rowley, T.R. (eds.), *Lowland Iron Age Communities in Europe*, BAR S48.

Smith, I.F., 1955. 'Late beaker pottery from the Lyonesse surface and the date of the transgression', *11th Ann. Rep. Univ. London Inst. Arch.*: 29–42.

Smith, I.F., 1961. 'An essay towards the reformation of the British bronze age', *Helinium 1*:94–118.

Smith, I.F., 1965. *Windmill Hill and Avebury: Excavations by Alexander Keiller.*

Smith, I.F., 1966. 'Windmill Hill and its implications', *Palaeohistoria 12*:469–81.

Smith, I.F., 1971. 'Causewayed enclosures', in Simpson, D.D.A., *Economy and Settlement in Neolithic and Early Bronze Age Britain and Europe*: 89–112.

Smith, I.F., 1974. 'The neolithic', in Renfrew 1974: 128–36.

Smith, I.F. and Evans, J.G., 1968. 'Excavation of two long barrows in north Wiltshire', *Antiquity 42*:138–42.

Smith, I.F. and Simpson, D.D.A., 1966. 'Excavation of a round barrow on Overton Hill, N. Wilts', *PPS 32*:122–55.

Smith (Brown), M.A., 1959. 'Some Somerset hoards and their place in the bronze age of southern Britain', *PPS 25*:144–87.

Smith, R.A., 1908. 'The Weybridge bucket and prehistoric trade with Italy', *SAC 21*:165–9.

Smith, R.A., 1909. 'A hoard of metal found at Santon Downham, Suffolk', *PCAS 13*:146–63.

Smith, R.A., 1912. 'On late Celtic antiquities discovered at Welwyn, Herts.', *Archaeologia 63*:1–30.

Smith, R.A., 1925. *A British Museum Guide to the Antiquities of the Early Iron Age of Central and Western Europe* (2nd edn.).

Smith, R.A., 1926. 'Two early British bronze bowls', *Ant. J. 6*:276–83.

Smith, R.A., 1927. 'Park Brow, the finds and foreign parallels', *Archaeologia 76*:14–29.

Smith, R.A., 1928. 'Pre-Roman remains at Scarborough', *Archaeologia 77*:179–200.

Snodgrass, A., 1975. 'An outsider's view of C-14 calibration', in Watkins T.F. 1975: 39–46.

Sollas, W.J., 1913. 'Paviland Cave: An Aurignacian station in Wales', *J. Roy. Anthrop. Inst. 43*:337–64.

Spencer, P.J., 1975. 'Habitat change in coastal sand-dune areas: the molluscan evidence', in Evans J.G. *et al.* 1975: 96–103.

Spratling, M.G., 1966. 'The date of the Tal-y-Llyn hoard', *Antiquity 40*:229–30.

Spratling, M.G., 1970. 'The smiths of South Cadbury', *CA 18*:188–91.

Spratling, M.G., 1972. 'Southern British decorated bronzes of the late pre-Roman iron age', Ph. D. thesis, University of London.

Spratling, M.G., 1973. 'The iron age settlement of Gussage All Saints: Part II The bronze foundry', *Antiquity 47*:117–30.

Spratling, M.G., 1974. 'The dating of the iron age swan's neck sunflower pin from Fengate, Peterborough, Cambridgeshire', *Ant. J. 54*:268–9.

Spriggs, M. (ed.), 1977. *Archaeology and Anthropology: Areas of mutual interest,* BAR Suppl. Ser. 19.

Stanford, S.C., 1970. 'Credenhill Camp – an iron age hillfort capital', *Arch. J. 127*:82–129.

Stanford, S.C., 1972. 'Welsh border hill-forts', in Thomas, A.C. (ed.), *The Iron Age in the Irish Sea Province*, CBA Res. Rep. 9:25–36.

Stanford, S.C., 1974. *Croft Ambrey.*

Stead, I.M., 1965. *The La Tène Cultures of Eastern Yorkshire.*

Stead, I.M., 1967. 'A La Tène III burial at Welwyn Garden City', *Archaeologia 101*:1–62.

Stead, I.M., 1968. 'An iron age hill-fort at Grimthorpe, Yorkshire, England', *PPS 34*:148–90.

Stead, I.M., 1969. 'Verulamium 1966–8', *Antiquity 43*:45–52.

Stead, I.M., 1971a. 'The reconstruction of iron age buckets from Aylesford and Baldock', in Sieveking, G. de G. (ed.), *Prehistoric and Roman Studies (BMQ 35)*:250–82.

Stead, I.M., 1971b. 'Yorkshire before the Romans: some recent discoveries', in Butler, R.M. (ed.), *Soldier and Civilian in Roman Yorkshire*: 21–43.

Stead, I.M., 1975. 'Baldock', in Rodwell, W.J. and Rowley, R.T. (eds.), *The Small Towns of Roman Britain*, BAR 15:125–30.

Stead, I.M., 1976a. 'The earliest burials of the Aylesford culture', in Sieveking, G. de G., Longworth, I.H. and Wilson, K.E. (eds.), *Problems in Economic and Social Archaeology*: 401–16.

Stead, I.M., 1976b. 'La Tène burials between Burton Fleming and Rudston, north Humberside', *Ant. J. 56*:217–26.

Steer, K.A., 1956. 'An early iron age homestead at West Plean, Stirlingshire', *PSAS 89*:227–49.

Steer, K.A., 1958. 'Roman and native in North Britain: the Severan reorganisation', in Richmond 1958a: 91–111.

Steer, K.A., 1964. 'John Horsley and the Antonine wall', *Arch. Ael.*, 4th ser. *42*:1–39.

Stevens, S., Philp, B., and Williams, W., 1976. 'Major discovery of bronze age implements at Dover', *Kent Arch. Rev. 43*:67–73.

Stevenson, R.B.K., 1955. 'Pins and the chronology of brochs', *PPS 21*:282–94.

Stevenson, R.B.K., 1956. 'Native bangles and Roman glass', *PSAS 88*:208–21.

Stevenson, R.B.K., 1966. 'Metal-work and some other objects in Scotland and their cultural affinities', in Rivet 1966: 17–44.

Stevenson, R.B.K., 1976. 'Romano-British glass bangles', *Glasgow Arch. J. 4*:44–54.

Stewart, M.E.C., 1962. 'The excavation of two circular enclosures at Dalnaglar, Perthshire', *PSAS 95*:134–58.

Stone, J.F.S., 1933a. 'A middle bronze age urnfield on Easton Down, Winterslow', *WAM 46*:218–24.

Stone, J.F.S., 1933b. 'Excavation at Easton Down, Winterslow, 1931–1932', *WAM 46*:225–42.

Stone, J.F.S., 1936. 'An enclosure on Boscombe Down East', *WAM 47*:466–89.

Stone, J.F.S., 1938. 'An early bronze age grave in Fargo Plantation', *WAM 48*:357–70.

Stone, J.F.S., 1941. 'The Deverel-Rimbury settlement on Thorny Down, Winterbourne Gunner, south Wiltshire', *PPS 7*:114–33.

Stone, J.F.S., 1949. 'Some grooved ware pottery from the Woodhenge area', *PPS 15*:122–7.

Stone, J.F.S., 1958. *Wessex*.

Stone, J.F.S. and Thomas, L.C., 1956. 'The use and distribution of faience in the ancient Near East and Europe', *PPS 22*:37–84.

Stoves, J.L., 1948. 'Report on the hair from the barrows at Winterslow', *WAM 52*:126.

Stuart, A.J., 1976. 'The nature of the lesions on the elk skeleton from High Furlong near Blackpool, Lancashire', *PPS 42*:323–4.

Suess, H.E., 1965. 'Secular variations in the cosmic-ray-produced carbon-14 in the atmosphere', *Geophysical Research 70*:5937–52.

Suess, H.E. and Clark, R.M., 1976. 'A calibration curve for radiocarbon dates', *Antiquity 50*:61–3.

Swan, V.G., 1975. 'Oare reconsidered and the origins of Savernake ware in Wiltshire', *Britannia 6*: 37–61.

Szabó, M., 1977. 'The origins of the Hungarian sword style', *Antiquity 51*:211–20.

Tait, J. and Jobey, G., 1971. 'Romano-British burials at Beadnell, Northumberland', *Arch. Ael.*, 4th ser. *49*:53–69.

Taylor, J.J., 1970a . 'Lunulae reconsidered', *PPS 36*:38–81.

Taylor, J.J., 1970b. 'The recent discovery of gold pins in the Ridgeway gold pommel', *Ant. J. 50*:216–21.

Thom, A., 1967. *Megalithic Sites in Britain*.

Thom, A., 1971. *Megalithic Lunar Observations*.

Thom, A., 1975. 'Stonehenge as a possible lunar observatory', *JHA 6*:19–30.

Thom, A., A.S. and A.S., 1974. 'Stonehenge', *JHA 5*:71–90.

Thomas, A.C., 1959–60. 'Post-Roman rectangular house plans in the south-west', *Procs. W. Cornwall Field Club 2.4*:150–62.

Thomas, A.C., 1964. 'Note on the Tredarvah hoard', *Cornish Archaeol. 3*:85.

Thomas, A.C., 1966. 'The character and origins of Roman Dumnonia' in Thomas, A.C. (ed.), *Rural Settlement in Roman Britain*, CBA Res. Rep. 7:74–98.

Thomas, A.C., 1969. 'The bronze age in the south-west', *Archaeol. Rev. 4*:3–13.

Thomas, A.C., 1970. 'Bronze age spade marks at Gwithian, Cornwall', in Gailey, A. and Fenton, A. (eds.), *The Spade in Atlantic and Northern Europe*: 10–17.

Thomas, A.C., 1972. 'Souterrains in the sea province: a note', in Thomas, A.C. (ed.), *The Iron Age in the Irish Sea Province*, CBA Res. Rep. 9:75–8.

Thomas, A.C., 1978. '2. Types and distributions of pre-Norman fields in Cornwall and Scilly', in Bowen and Fowler 1978:7–15.

Thomas, N. de L'E.W., 1964. 'The neolithic causewayed camp at Robin Hood's Ball, Shrewton', *WAM 59*:1–27.

Thomas, N. de L'E.W., 1966. 'Notes on some early bronze age objects in Devizes Museum', *WAM 61*:1–8.

Thomas, N.de L'E.W. and Thomas, A.C., 1955. 'Excavations at Snail Down, Everleigh, 1953, 1955', *WAM 56*:127–48.

Thrane, H., 1965. 'Dänische Funde fremde Bronzegefässe der jungeren Bronzezeit (Period IV)', *Acta Arch. 36*:157–248.

Tierney, J.J., 1960. 'The Celtic ethnography of Posidonius', *PRIA 60C*:189–275.

Torbrügge, W., 1972. 'Vor- und frügeschichtliche Flussfunde', *51–52. Ber. Rom.-Ger. Komm. 1970–71*:1–146.

Tratman, E.K., 1970. 'The Glastonbury Lake Village: a reconsideration', *Procs. Bristol Univ. Spelaeol. Soc. 12*:143–67.

Trump, B.A.V., 1962. 'The origin and development of British middle bronze age rapiers', *PPS 28*:80–102.

Trump, B.A.V., 1968. 'Fenland rapiers', in Coles and Simpson 1968:213–251.

Turner, J., 1962. 'The *Tilia* decline: an anthropogenic interpretation', *New Phytologist 61*:328–41.

Turner, J., 1970. 'Post-neolithic disturbance of British vegetation', in Walker, D. and West, R.G. (eds.), *Studies in the Vegetational History of the British Isles*: 97–116.

Tylecote, R.F., 1962. *Metallurgy in Archaeology*.

Tylecote, R.F., 1976. *A History of Metallurgy*.

Ucko, P.J., Tringham, R. and Dimbleby, G.W. (eds.), 1972. *Man, Settlement and Urbanism*.

Uenze, O., 1938. *Die Frühbronzezeitlichen triangulären Vollgriffdolche*, Vorges-chichtliche Forschungen, II (Berlin).

Van der Waals, J.D., 1964. 'Neolithic disc wheels in the Netherlands', *Palaeohistoria 10*:103–46.

Van der Waals, J.D. and Glasbergen, W., 1955. 'Beaker types and their distribution in the Netherlands', *Palaeohistoria 4*:5–46.

Van Impe, L., 1976. 'Ringwalheuvels in de Kempense Bronstijd: typologie en datierung', *Arch. Belgica*: 190.

Van Wijngaarden-Bakker, L.H., 1974. 'The animal remains from the beaker settlement at Newgrange, Co. Meath: first report', *PRIA 74C*:313–83.

Varley, W.J., 1948. 'The hillforts of the Welsh marches', *Arch. J. 105*:41–66.

Varley, W.J., 1952. 'Excavations of the Castle Ditch, Eddisbury, 1935–38', *Trans. Hist. Soc. Lancs. and Cheshire 102*:1–68.

Varley, W.J., 1976. 'A summary of the excavations at Castle Hill, Almondbury, 1939–1972', in Harding D.W. 1976a: 119–31.

Vasari, Y. and Vasari, A., 1968. 'Late- and post-glacial macrophytic vegetation in the lochs of northern Scotland', *Acta bot. fenn. 45*:45–116.

Vatcher, F. de M., 1961. 'The excavation of the long mortuary enclosure on Normanton Down, Wilts.', *PPS 27*:160–73.

Vatcher, F. de M., 1965. 'East Heslerton long barrow, Yorkshire: the eastern half', *Antiquity 39*:49–52.

Vatcher, F. de M., 1969. 'Two incised chalk plaques near Stonehenge Bottom', *Antiquity 43*:310–11.

Vatcher, F. de M. and Vatcher, L., 1976. *The Avebury Monuments*.

Vidal, M., 1976. 'Le seau de bois orné de Vieille-Toulouse (Haute-Garonne)', *Gallia 34*:167–200.

Vogt, E., 1953. 'Die Herkunft der Michelsberger Kultur', *Acta Archaeologica 24*:174–85.

Von Merhart, G., 1952. 'Studien über einige Gatungen von Bronzgefässen', *Festschr. des Röm.-Germ. Zentralmus., Mainz 2*:1–71.

Waddell J., 1970. 'Irish bronze age cists: a survey', *JRSAI 100*:91–139.

Waddell, J., 1976. 'Cultural interaction in the insular early bronze age: some ceramic evidence', in De Laet, S.J. (ed.), *Acculturation and Continuity in Atlantic Europe*, Diss. Archaeol. Gandenses 21:284–95 (Bruges).

Wailes, B., 1976. 'Dún Ailinne: An interim report', in Harding D.W. 1976a: 319–38.

Wainwright, F.T., 1963. *The Souterrains of Southern Pictland*.

Wainwright, G.J., 1960. 'Three microlithic industries from southwest England and their affinities', *PPS 26*:193–201.

Wainwright, G.J., 1967. *Coygan Camp.*

Wainwright, G.J., 1968. 'The excavation of a Durotrigian farmstead near Tollard Royal in Cranborne Chase, southern England', *PPS 34*:102–47.

Wainwright, G.J., 1969. 'Walesland Rath', *CA 12*:4–7.

Wainwright, G.J., 1971. 'The excavation of a late neolithic enclosure at Marden, Wiltshire', *Ant. J. 101*:177–239.

Wainwright, G.J. and Longworth, I.H., 1969. 'The excavation of a group of round barrows on Ampleforth Moor, Yorkshire', *YAJ 42*:283–94.

Wainwright, G.J. and Longworth, I.H., 1971. *Durrington Walls: Excavations 1966–68.*

Wainwright, G.J. and Spratling, M., 1973. 'The iron age settlement of Gussage All Saints', *Antiquity 47*:109–130.

Wainwright, G.J. and Switsur, V.R., 1976. 'Gussage All Saints – a chronology', *Antiquity 50*:32–9.

Walker, I.C., 1968. 'Easterton of Roseisle: a forgotten site in Moray', in Coles and Simpson 1968: 95–116.

Ward-Perkins, J.B., 1938. 'An early iron age site at Crayford, Kent', *PPS 4*: 151–68.

Ward-Perkins, J.B., 1939. 'Iron age metal horses' bits in the British Isles', *PPS 5*:173–92.

Ward-Perkins, J.B., 1940. 'Two early linch pins from Kings Langley, Herts., and from Tiddington, Stratford on Avon', *Ant. J. 20*:358–67.

Ward-Perkins, J.B., 1941. 'An iron age linch-pin of Yorkshire type from Cornwall', *Ant. J. 21*:64–7.

Ward-Perkins, J.B., 1944. 'Excavations on the iron age hillfort of Oldbury, near Ightham, Kent', *Archaeologia 90*:127–76.

Warner, R.B., 1976. 'Further notes for users of radiocarbon dates, including a method for the analysis of a stratified sequence', *IARF 3.2*:25–44.

Waterman, D., 1970. 'Navan Fort', *CA 22*:308–11.

Waterston, D., 1940–1. 'A toggle and an ivory buckle recently discovered at Brackmont Mill, near Leuchars', *PSAS 85*:205–7.

Watkins, T.F. (ed.), 1975. *Radiocarbon, Calibration and Prehistory.*

Watkins, T.F., 1974. 'Dalladies 2: archaeological excavations at an iron age site in south Kincardineshire', *Deeside Field*, 3rd ser. *1*:47–55.

Watkins, T.F., 1976. 'Wessex without Cyprus: "Cypriot Daggers" in Europe', in Megaw 1976b:136–43.

Watson, W., 1947. 'Two brooches of the early iron age from Sawdon, North Riding, Yorkshire', *Ant. J. 27*:178–82.

Wedderburn, L.M.M., 1973. *Excavations at Greencairn*, Dundee Museum and Art Gallery Occ. Papers in Archaeol. 1.

Wegner, G., 1976. 'Die Vorgeschichtlichen Flussfunde aus dem Main und aus dem Rhein bei Mainz', *Materialhefte z. Bayer. Vorg.*, Reihe A:30.

Wells, C., 1972. *The German Policy of Augustus.*

West, R.G., 1968. *Pleistocene Geology and Biology with Especial Reference to the British Isles.*

Wheeler, R.E.M., 1929. 'Old England, Brentford', *Antiquity 3*:20–32.

Wheeler, R.E.M., 1943. *Maiden Castle, Dorset.*

Wheeler, R.E.M., 1954. *The Stanwick Fortifications.*

Wheeler, R.E.M. and Richardson, K.M., 1957. *Hill-forts of Northern France.*

Wheeler, R.E.M. and Wheeler, T.V., 1936. *Verulamium: A Belgic and two Roman cities.*

Whimster, R., 1977. 'Iron age burial in southern Britain', *PPS 43*:317–27.

Whitley, M., 1943. 'Excavations at Chalbury Camp, Dorset, 1939', *Ant. J. 23*:98–121.

Whittle, A.W.R., 1977. *The Earlier Neolithic of S. England and its Continental Background*, BAR Suppl. Ser. 35.

Wild, J.P., 1966. 'Papyrus in pre-Roman Britain?', *Antiquity 40*:139–42.

Williams, J.H. (ed.), 1974. *Two Iron Age Sites in Northampton*, Northampton Dev. Corporation Arch. Monographs 1.

Wilson, D.R., 1975. 'Causewayed camps and interrupted ditch systems', *Antiquity 49*:178–86.

Woodman, P.C., 1973–4. 'Settlement patterns of the Irish mesolithic', *UJA 36–37*:1–16.

Woodman, P.C., 1977. 'Mount Sandel', *CA 59*:372–6.

Woodman, P.C. (in press). 'The chronology and economy of the Irish mesolithic: some working hypotheses', in Mellars, P.A. (ed.), *The Early Postglacial Settlement of Northern Europe: An ecological perspective.*

Woodman, P.C. [in press]. *The Mesolithic in Ireland: Hunter-gatherers in an insular environment*, BAR 58.

Wooldridge, S.W. and Linton, D.L., 1933. 'The loam-terrains of south-east England and their relation to its early history', *Antiquity 7*:297–310.

Worsfold, F.A., 1943. 'A report on the late bronze age site excavated at Minnis Bay, Birchington, Kent, 1938–1940', *PPS 9*:28–47.

Wright, E.V., 1976. *The North Ferriby Boats: A guide book*, National Maritime Museum, Maritime Monographs and Rep. 23.

Wright, E.V. and C.W., 1947. 'Prehistoric boats from North Ferriby, East Yorkshire', *PPS 13*:114–38.

Wymer, J.J., 1962. 'Excavations at the Maglemosean site of Thatcham, Berkshire, England', *PPS 28*:329–61.

Youngblood, E., Fredriksson, B.J., Kraut, F. and Fredriksson, K., 1978. 'Celtic vitrified forts; implications of a chemical-petrological study of glasses and source rocks', *J.A.S. 5*:99–115.

Zimmermann, W.H., 1976. 'Eisenzeitliche Ackerfluren im Elbe-Weser-Dreieck', in *Führer zu Vor- und Frühgeschichtlichen Denkmälern 30*:23–32.

Subject index

Index of places